Auto Mechanics

Second Edition

Jay Webster
California State University, Long Beach

GLENCOE PUBLISHING COMPANY
Mission Hills, California

Cover photo:
Three-cylinder engine used in the Chevrolet Sprint, built by Suzuki. This small, lightweight automobile engine is unique today, but may be common in the future if cars keep getting smaller.
(CHEVROLET DIVISION, GENERAL MOTORS CORPORATION)

Glencoe Publishing Company
15319 Chatsworth Street
Mission Hills, California 91345

Printed in the United States of America
Library of Congress Catalog Card Number: 84-80118
ISBN 0-02-829900-0

   2 3 4 5 6 7 8 9 10   91 90 89 88 87

Preface

The *Auto Mechanics* program is designed to meet the training needs of the automotive student of today. The purpose of the text and its supplementary materials is to help the automotive instructor present basic principles that are valuable in the instruction of students with various levels of training. The text can be used to train entry-level vocational apprentices, to retain and upgrade skills of practicing mechanics, to prepare students for certification under the National Institute for Automotive Excellence (ASE), and to provide the foundation for general and consumer automotive education courses. Moreover, the text complies with the training standards established by the Motor Vehicle Manufacturers Association (MVMA).

This comprehensive program provides students with a foundation of the basics in automotive mechanics—with special emphasis on theory and hands-on training. Students are introduced to new developments in auto mechanics through in-depth text discussions of turbocharging, electronic fuel injection, synthetic oils, the maintenance-free battery, MacPherson strut suspension systems, and modern engine rebuilding techniques.

Organization

Auto Mechanics is organized in ten parts. Part 1 introduces the reader to the automobile and to the world of work, with particular emphasis placed on the importance of shop safety. Part 2 focuses on the automobile engine components and service. The theory and servicing of the lubrication, cooling, and fuel systems are covered in Part 3. Part 4 explains the operation and servicing of automobile electrical systems and Part 5 details the function and servicing of the automotive power train. Part 6 describes the operation and servicing of the various components of the automobile chassis: the suspension system, steering and wheel alignment, the brake system, and the tires and wheels. The nature and servicing of heating and air conditioning systems are discussed in Part 7. Part 8 shows how emission control systems work, and how to service them. In Part 9, the latest electronic control systems are covered, including fuel injection and computerized engine control systems. Part 10 covers the future, with some hints about what the carmakers may do to surprise us in the next few years.

Features

Special effort has been made to make *Auto Mechanics* an effective learning tool. Illustrations provide direct visual correlation to the text material, and the text itself employs a practical, easy-to-follow approach. Topics are developed from the simple to the complex, following techniques that have been tested in both the classroom and the shop.

Particular attention was given to monitoring the reading level of the text. Professional Resources Associates, Inc., computer-analyzed the manuscript for reading difficulty. As a result of the analysis, difficult nontechnical terms, unnecessary technical terms, and complex sentence structure were adjusted. A special technical vocabulary development program was then devised. This program consists of (1) defining necessary technical vocabulary at first point of use, (2) redefining the vocabulary at the end of each chapter in the section entitled "New Terms," and (3) reinforcing of these terms in the section entitled "Chapter Review."

Other measures have been taken to develop student understanding of the text materials: Each chapter begins with a chapter preview and a list of student learning objectives, and each chapter concludes with a series of end-of-chapter activities that include discussion topics and activities in addition to the vocabulary and chapter review sections mentioned above.

Auto Mechanics is supported by an instructor's manual and key that contains an outline of each chapter, specific teaching suggestions, and the keys to end-of-chapter activities. To aid the instructor in the visual presentation of specific topics, a series of transparency/duplicating masters is also provided in the manual. These masters may be photocopied and then converted into transparencies for use on an overhead projector, duplicated for class handouts, or duplicated for class assignments.

Acknowledgments

The author wishes to express his appreciation to colleagues and students in the department of industrial education, California State University, Long Beach, for their help in field testing the instructional materials in this text.

Jay Webster

Contents

The Automobile and the World of Work

PART 1

The Automobile

CHAPTER PREVIEW

The modern automobile is made up of many different systems with hundreds of components and thousands of parts. Each component and system, however, has a purpose which can be understood. Each operates according to very basic rules or principles. Anyone who is willing to study can soon become an expert in the operation and repair of the modern automobile. This first chapter will divide the automobile into its biggest pieces: the framework, the engine, the power train, and the chassis.

OBJECTIVES

After studying this chapter, you should be able to do the following:

1. Describe the function of each of the four basic components of the automobile.
2. Recognize the common frame designs used in automobiles.
3. Describe the function of each of the five systems necessary to make the engine work.
4. Recognize the various power transmission arrangements used in power trains.
5. Name the components that make up the chassis of an automobile.

1.1 BODY

The automobile body is what the driver and passengers ride in. The body on the first automobiles was little more than a platform with seats attached. It gradually developed into a closed compartment complete with roof and windows. Since the shape of the exterior is the first thing people notice about an automobile, body styling or design has always been important (Fig. 1-1). Besides shielding people from the weather and creating a desirable image, the auto body protects driver and passengers in a crash. Body design now takes into account much that has been learned about safe construction through crash testing.

When the car is moving, the air in front of the car creates a tremendous drag on the vehicle. The automotive body is now carefully designed and tested to achieve the smallest possible drag. It is now possible to design and produce a body with little drag or one that is very aerodynamic. The less drag created by the body the less engine power that is required to move the car down the road. This results in a significant fuel savings.

The modern automobile body is constructed of sheet steel formed to the required shape in giant punch presses. Most of the body components are welded together to form a tight, rattle-free unit. Body styles can be grouped by size and type.

1.2 Body Measurements

Automobiles are measured in two ways. Tread width is the distance between the front or rear wheels (Fig. 1-2). The wider the tread, the better the vehicle hugs the road in high-speed driving and in high winds. Another way automobiles are measured is by their wheelbase. Wheelbase is the distance between the center of the front wheel and the center of the rear wheel (Fig. 1-3).

Fig. 1-1 Designed for automobile body performance.

Fig. 1-2 Tread measurement.

Fig. 1-3 Wheelbase measurement.

1.3   Classes of Automobiles

Automobiles are classed according to the size of their wheelbase. The smallest automobiles, called sub-compacts or minicars, have a wheelbase ranging from 94 to 102 inches (2,388 to 2,591 mm) (Fig. 1-4). The next larger automobile, called a compact (Fig. 1-5), has a wheelbase between 102 and 112 inches (2,591 to 2,845 mm). An intermediate-size automobile (Fig. 1-6), has a wheelbase of 112 to 119 inches (2,845 to 3,023 mm). A full-size automobile has a wheelbase of 119 inches (3,023 mm) or more (Fig. 1-7).

Automobiles may also be classed on the basis of their body style, regardless of size (Fig. 1-8):

2-door sedan	station wagon
4-door sedan	truck
convertible	van
hardtop	hatchback

Most automotive body parts are formed from sheet steel. Giant presses are used to form sheet steel to the required shape over steel dies. The steel body panels are welded together in a holding device called a fixture to form the main body structure. The completed body structure is then sprayed or dipped in a rust preventative solution prior to further assembly. The completed body is then moved on to the automobile assembly line to complete the assembly process.

One of the more important ways of saving fuel is to lower the weight of the automobile. Reducing the weight of the automobile body has been achieved by using thinner sheet steel and using lighter materials. Aluminum has been used from time to time to

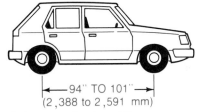

Fig. 1-4 Subcompact automobile.

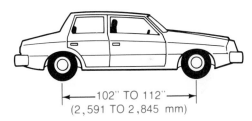

Fig. 1-5 Compact automobile.

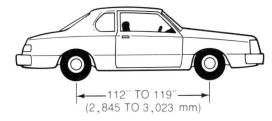

Fig. 1-6 Intermediate-size automobile.

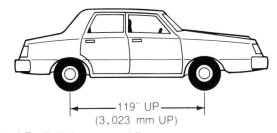

Fig. 1-7 Full-size automobile.

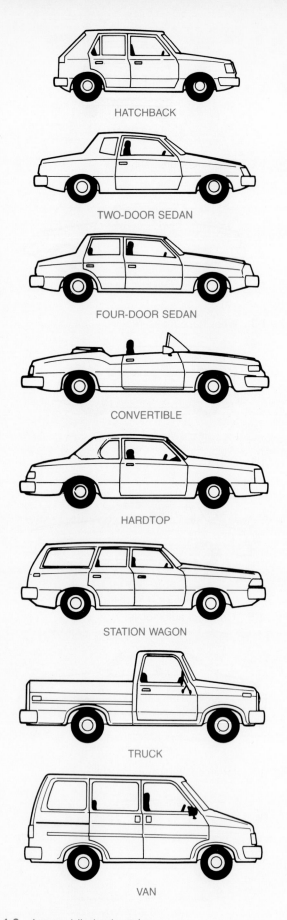

HATCHBACK

TWO-DOOR SEDAN

FOUR-DOOR SEDAN

CONVERTIBLE

HARDTOP

STATION WAGON

TRUCK

VAN

Fig. 1-8 Automobile body styles.

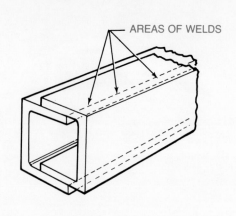

AREAS OF WELDS

Fig. 1-9 Cross section of a frame member.

make body parts and even complete bodies. Aluminum is much lighter than steel and the resulting body is much lighter than a steel body. Aluminum is more expensive to form and more difficult to repair than steel so that its use is confined mostly to very expensive high-performance vehicles.

Another light material used in body part construction is plastic. Plastic parts are relatively inexpensive to manufacture. Many body trim parts and some large parts such as hoods are currently being manufactured from plastic. Many custom and several production vehicles have the entire body manufactured from fiberglass. Fiberglass is a light, easy-to-form material but is difficult to repair.

1.4 FRAMEWORK

The framework is the foundation of the automobile. It serves as a platform to which the other automobile components are attached. The frame is constructed from square or box-shaped steel members (Fig. 1-9) heavy enough to support this tremendous weight.

The frame is usually made up of a number of members welded together. One popular design (Fig. 1-10) uses two large rails running beneath the sides of the automobile and a number of connecting pieces called cross members. This design is often called a ladder frame arrangement because it resembles a stepladder. The ladder frame has one serious disadvantage. The force of a crash on the corner of the frame could push it out of square. An expensive frame straightening would then be needed.

The X-member frame (Fig. 1-11) resulted from attempts to strengthen the ladder frame. It uses two

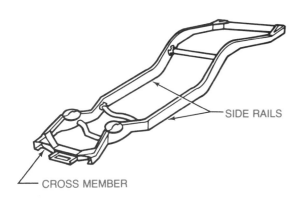

Fig. 1-10 Typical ladder frame.

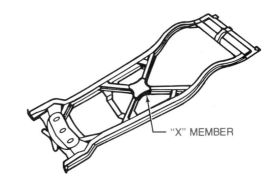

Fig. 1-11 Typical X-member frame.

large members that cross under the center of the vehicle. These members are welded to the side rails and cross members.

Many automobiles use a very thick sheet metal instead of a regular frame. In such vehicles, the body is welded directly to the floor pan, and the other components are attached to the body floor-pan assembly. This unitized body (Fig. 1-12) or monocoque design reduces vehicle weight, lowers production costs, and allows a lower floor. The reduction of weight is important because the lighter the car can be made the more efficient it will be and the less fuel it will use.

Unitized construction suffers from one clear disadvantage. On an automobile with a frame, road noise caused by the wheels and running gear can be kept from the passenger compartment by placing rubber biscuits between the frame and body. With unitized construction, the noise telegraphs from the road directly into the passenger compartment.

A variation of the unitized construction is the bolt-on sub-frame or cradle. This configuration is found in several models and is particularly noticeable in some front-wheel drive vehicles. A strong, heavy sub-frame is utilized to support the engine, accessories, power train, and running gear. This frame may have strong, sturdy cross members and will extend backward under the floor pan. Back of the cowl, the remaining structure follows the conventional unitized or integral design. The front sub-frame is bolted to the unitized body section as shown in Figure 1-12.

Platform construction is another design similar to unitized construction. This design consists of a reinforced, fairly flat section that forms the entire lower portion of the car. Volkswagen and similar types of cars utilize this construction technique. The lower sec-

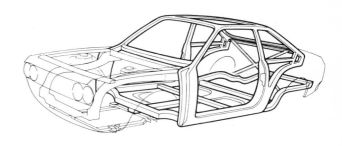

Unitized body. (Lancia)

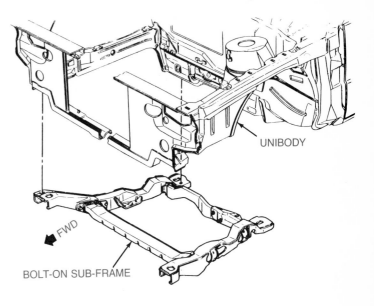

Fig. 1-12 A bolt-on sub-frame is bolted to the unitized body. (Chevrolet Motor Division, GMC)

The Automobile 5

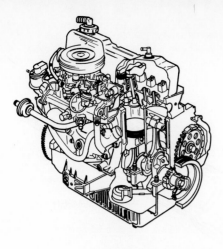 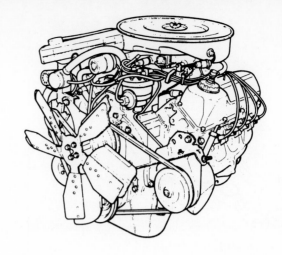

Fig. 1–13 The automobile engine. (Ford Motor Company)

tion, which includes the floor pans, is a bolt-on assembly which is joined to the body. Therefore, this section depends on the rest of the body for rigidity. This section serves as a support member for the engine, running gear, and body structure.

1.5   ENGINE

The engine (Fig. 1-13), provides power to drive the automobile. In most automobile engines, the explosive power of a mixture of air and gasoline drives down pistons. The pistons turn a crankshaft to which they are attached. The rotating force of the crankshaft makes the automobile's wheels turn.

An increasing number of cars are equipped with a diesel engine. The diesel engine uses the power of diesel fuel injected into cylinders in which air has been compressed to a very high temperature. Like the gasoline engine, the power is used to drive down pistons and turn a crankshaft.

A few automobiles are powered by another kind of engine, known as the rotary valve, rotating combustion, or Wankel, after its inventor, Felix Wankel. The rotary valve engine also draws in a mixture of air and fuel which is then compressed and burned. A rotor revolving in an elliptical chamber is connected to a shaft which finally drives the rear wheels.

In most American automobiles, the engine is mounted to the frame front of the automobile (Fig. 1-14). A front-mounted engine is easily accessible and easily cooled. European designers have often used rear-engine placement (Fig. 1-15). If the engine is in the rear, the front of the automobile can be made

more streamlined for better fuel economy. The hood can be lower, improving visibility for the driver. Finally, the weight of the engine over the rear wheels can help provide traction.

While front or rear placement is most common, it is also possible to put the engine in the middle of the automobile (Fig. 1-16). The earliest automobiles, in fact, used mid-engine placement. When something went wrong, the driver had to get out and lift up the seat to work on the engine. Mid-engine installation is now being used again in some European automobiles. Placing the heavy engine in the middle of the automobile provides the best possible weight distribution so handling is improved. However, there is still the problem of inaccessibility. Having the engine in the middle makes it hard to get to and work on.

A number of systems are necessary to make an engine work. A lubrication system is needed to reduce friction and prevent engine wear. A cooling system is required to keep the engine's temperature within safe limits. The engine must be provided with the correct amounts of air and fuel by a fuel system. The mixture of air and fuel must be ignited inside the cylinder at just the right time by an ignition system. Finally, an electrical system is required to operate the cranking motor that starts the engine and to provide electrical energy to power engine accessories.

1.6   Lubrication System

The lubrication system performs a number of important functions. It circulates oil between moving parts to prevent the metal-to-metal contact that results in wear. Parts that are oiled can move more easily, with less friction; and the less friction within an

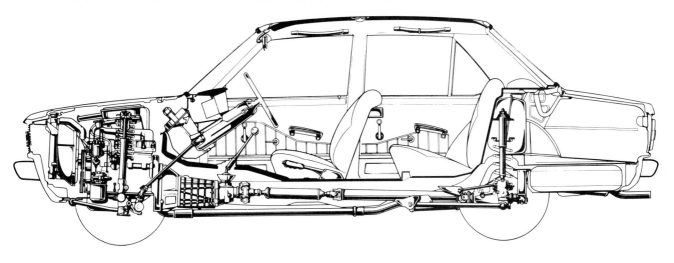

Fig. 1-14 Automobile with engine in the front. (Fiat)

engine, the more power it can develop. Circulating oil helps cool the engine by carrying heat away from hot engine components. Oil also cleans or flushes dirt and deposits off of engine parts. Finally, oil circulated on the cylinder walls helps the rings to seal and thus improves the engine's compression.

1.7　Cooling System

The burning of the air-fuel mixture that occurs during the power stroke of an engine develops tremendous heat. The cooling system keeps the engine operating at an efficient temperature whatever the driving conditions. The system is designed to prevent both overheating and overcooling.

Fig. 1-15 Automobile with rear-mounted engine. (Porsche)

1.8　Fuel System

The fuel system has three functions: (1) to store enough fuel for several hundred miles of vehicle operation, (2) to deliver the fuel to the engine, and (3) to mix the fuel with the right amount of air for efficient burning in the cylinder.

1.9　Ignition System

The purpose of the ignition system is to provide a high voltage spark in each of the engine's cylinders at the right time so that the air-fuel mixture will burn. The system must take the 12 volts of electricity available at the battery or alternator and boost it to the 30,000 or 40,000 volts required for ignition. The high voltage must be distributed to each cylinder just as it is ready for a power stroke.

Fig. 1-16 Mid-engine placement in a racing car. (BMW)

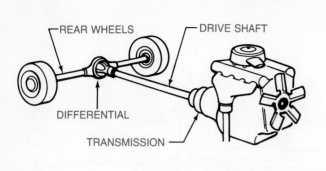

Fig. 1–17 Rear-wheel drive power train.

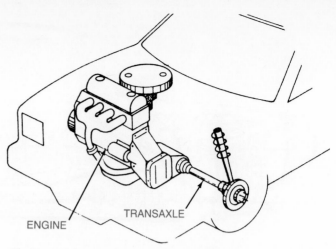

Fig. 1–18 Front-wheel drive power train.

1.10   Electrical System

The engine's electrical system provides energy to operate a starting motor and to power all the accessories. The main components of the electrical system are: a battery, an alternator, and a starting motor.

1.11   POWER TRAIN

The power of turning force developed by the engine must be applied to the drive wheels to make the car go. The system of parts which transmits the power to the wheels is called the power train. From the engine, the turning force goes into the transmission, a system of gears that makes it easier for the engine to move the car. From the transmission, the power flows into the differential assembly. There may be a drive shaft between the transmission and differential, or the two units may be directly attached to each other. The differential assembly splits the power so that half of it goes to each driving wheel. Included in the differential assembly is another set of gears to make it easier for the engine to move the car. From the differential assembly, axles take the power to each drive wheel.

One common power train system connects a front-mounted engine and a rear-wheel drive (Fig. 1-17). Rear-wheel drive is slowly disappearing on modern cars in favor of the lighter, more efficient front-wheel drive.

On automobiles that have front-wheel drive, the engine, transmission, and differential assembly are all connected together and mounted in the front of the vehicle (Fig. 1-18). The transmission and differential

are combined together in a unit called a transaxle. The drive shaft is eliminated. Front-wheel drive improves road holding on curves and eliminates the hump in the passenger compartment caused by running the drive shaft under the vehicle.

On an automobile with a rear-mounted engine, the engine, transmission, and axle assembly are all connected together in the rear. Usually this system uses rear-wheel drive. One other power train arrangement is the four-wheel drive. On a four-wheel drive vehicle, the engine's power is directed to a driving axle at both the rear and front of the vehicle. When the four-wheel drive is engaged, all of the wheels are driven by the engine. With all four wheels driving there is great traction. The vehicle can climb steep hills and go over deep sand or snow. The extra components required for four-wheel drive, however, make it expensive. It is most useful for off-the-road use or for heavy snow and mud.

1.12   CHASSIS

The parts of the automobile under the body are referred to as the chassis (Fig. 1-19). In addition to major components—the framework, engine, and power train—several other systems are mounted to the chassis assembly. The automobile wheels are connected to the frame by a system of springs, shock absorbers, and linkages. These components make up the automobile's suspension system. The suspension system absorbs shock as the vehicle goes over rough roads and permits easy handling during cornering. Another important chassis system, the steering system, allows the driver to guide the automobile with

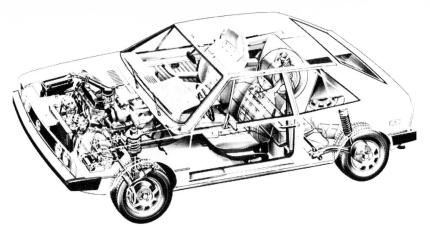

Fig. 1-19 Chassis, including all parts under the automobile body. (Fiat)

ease. The steering wheel is connected to a gearbox that increases turning force exerted by the driver. Linkages connected to the gearbox allow the front wheels of the vehicle to be turned by the driver. The last major chassis component, the brake system, stops the automobile. When the driver pushes on the brake pedal, hydraulic fluid is forced out of a master cylinder to each of the four wheels. The hydraulic pressure works a drum or disc brake assembly to stop the automobile's wheels (Fig. 1-20).

NEW TERMS

Body That part of the automobile, usually formed from sheet metal, used to house and protect the driver and passengers.

Chassis The major components—such as framework, engine and power train—under the automobile body.

Cooling system An engine system that maintains the proper engine temperature.

Electrical system An engine system that provides electrical current for starting and powering all accessories.

Engine One of the four major components of the automobile. It converts the explosive power of fuel and air into rotating power to drive the automobile. Also called a powerplant or motor.

Four-wheel drive A drive system in which all four wheels of the automobile are driven by the engine.

Framework A metal platform under the automobile to which the other automobile components are attached.

Front-wheel drive A drive system in which the front wheels of the automobile are driven by the engine.

Fuel system An engine system that provides the engine with the proper mixture of air and fuel to be burned.

Ignition system An engine system that provides the high-voltage spark necessary to ignite the air-fuel mixture in the engine.

Lubrication system An engine system that circulates oil between moving engine parts to prevent wear, reduce friction, clean, and seal.

Power train One of the four major components of the automobile. The power train delivers power developed by the engine to the driving wheels.

Rear-wheel drive A drive system in which the rear wheels of the automobile are driven by the engine.

Rotary engine An engine in which the power is developed by a rotating rotor instead of pistons.

Transaxle The combination of a transmission and differential into one unit.

Tread The width of an automobile measured between the front or rear wheels.

Unitized body A body constructed without a frame. A heavy floor takes the place of the framework.

Wheelbase The length of an automobile measured from the center of the front wheel to the center of the rear wheel.

CHAPTER REVIEW

1. Describe the function of each of the four major components of the automobile.
2. What is the purpose of the cooling system?
3. What is the purpose of the lubrication system?

Fig. 1-20 The suspension steering and brake systems

4. What is the purpose of the fuel system?
5. What is the purpose of the ignition system?
6. What is the purpose of the electrical system?
7. List two advantages of a front-wheel-drive arrangement.
8. What is a unitized body?
9. Describe a ladder frame and a X-member frame.
10. What is the difference between a compact and a subcompact automobile?

DISCUSSION TOPICS AND ACTIVITIES

1. If you designed your own automobile, where would you place the major components? Why?
2. Find and identify the major components on a real automobile.
3. A number of plastic see-through automobile chassis models are available. Build one of these models to learn how the automobile is constructed.

Working in the Automotive Service Industry

CHAPTER PREVIEW

Nearly one out of six workers in the United States has a job in an automotive-related industry. The industry may be divided into three general areas. Production or manufacturing turns raw materials such as steel, iron, plastic, glass, and vinyl into a finished automobile. Selling it is the job of the second major area, sales. The last major part of the automotive industry is service, including maintenance and repair. There are, of course, many job opportunities in all three areas of the automotive industry. In this book, we are most interested in those having to do with automotive service.

OBJECTIVES

After studying this chapter, you should be able to do the following:

1. Describe the several types of automotive service businesses.
2. Name the kinds of services that are performed at various automotive service businesses.
3. List at least ten different service jobs in the automotive industry.
4. Describe what workers do in several types of automotive service jobs.
5. Describe in detail one of the automotive service jobs you find most interesting.

2.1 WHERE AUTOMOTIVE SERVICE WORKERS WORK

Many different types of businesses service and repair automobiles. There are job opportunities in each of these businesses. We will begin by looking at some places that employ automotive service workers.

2.2 Service Station

The corner service station (Fig. 2-1) is probably the most familiar automotive service business. The owner or manager normally rents the service station from an oil company and sells that oil company's gasoline and oil.

Many service stations also repair and service automobiles. They may have one or several service bays and employ any number of mechanics. Some stations do only light maintenance: oil changes, lubrication, or installation of tires, batteries, and other accessories. Other stations do heavier types of repair, such as tune-up, brake service, front-end alignment, and even engine rebuilding.

2.3 Automotive Dealership

The goal of the automobile dealer (Fig. 2-2) is to sell new automobiles. In a dealership, a number of service people prepare the new automobiles for sale by checking and adjusting them and adding any accessories that have been ordered. Since the warranty on most new automobiles specifies that they be serviced and inspected at an authorized dealership, the dealer has a large service area and a number of mechanics to perform these tasks.

Most dealerships have a used automobile lot. This operation will normally employ several service people who clean and service the used vehicles to prepare them for sale.

A dealership often has a parts department. An important job of any dealership is the sale of parts.

Fig. 2-1 Service station.

Fig. 2-2 Automotive dealership.

Several employees may be needed to handle ordering and sales for the dealer's parts department.

2.4 Independent Garage

Every town has several independent garages with names like ''Bill's Automotive'' or ''Stan's Auto Repair.'' There are two different kinds of independent garages. The first kind is a general repair operation, which is typically owned by a mechanic turned businessperson. The general repair shop will work on any of hundreds of different makes and models of automobiles to fix any of thousands of different parts, from engines to rear axles.

The second kind of independent garage is called a specialized shop (Fig. 2-3). Such a garage may specialize in one kind of repair—automatic transmission rebuilding, engine rebuilding, tune-up, brakes—or work on one kind of vehicle—Volkswagen or Fords. A specialized shop is typically run by a businessperson who employs several mechanics. Many have grown into nationwide chains.

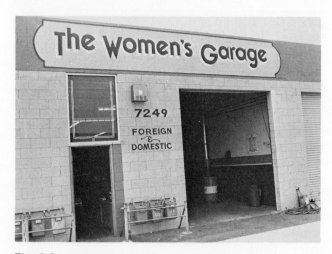

Fig. 2-3 Independent garage.

2.5 Diagnostic Centers

Diagnostic centers, or diagnostic lanes, used to be common in every large city (Fig. 2-4). They were equipped with the latest automotive testing equipment. Many were even computerized, and would check everything from wheel alignment to engine power in a few minutes. At the end of the test, the computer printed out a form that either passed or failed the parts or systems that were tested. Some of the diagnostic centers did repairs, and some were strictly for testing. Very few of the diagnostic centers are in existence today, but some of the com-

Fig. 2-4 Diagnostic center.

Fig. 2-5 Automobile steam cleaner.

Fig. 2-6 Lubrication specialist.

puterized equipment they popularized is in daily use at many dealerships and independent garages.

2.6   While-You-Wait Shops

The newest type of automotive repair shop is the quick service or while-you-wait shop. They usually specialize in tune-up or lubrication. Some are designed to do both. They are recognized by being part of a chain, all having the same name and color scheme on the building, and are usually backed up by considerable national advertising. There are so many of these shops that they are in constant need of new mechanics. However, the experience gained by the new mechanic will be limited to the narrow area of specialization.

2.7   Fleet Garages

Many large business organizations maintain a fleet of vehicles. They must also employ people to maintain and service the vehicles. A fleet garage provides job opportunities for mechanics, parts specialists, lubrication specialists, and automobile washers.

2.8   Parts Suppliers

The repair and service of an automobile usually involves replacement of some parts. The parts supplier who stocks and sells replacement parts may be an independent dealer or part of a large chain or association. Many department stores are now adding an automotive parts and accessory section.

Automobile parts suppliers employ personnel to inventory, order, and sell parts. In addition, many suppliers operate automotive machine shops which do component rebuilding. To perform these services, they hire specialty mechanics.

2.9   KINDS OF AUTOMOTIVE SERVICE JOBS

There are not only many kinds of businesses that employ automotive service workers but also many different kinds of service jobs. Let us look at the most common service jobs and see what they involve.

2.10   Automobile Detailer

The automobile detailer prepares automobiles for sale or delivery to a customer. This job involves washing and waxing the outside of the automobile as well as cleaning and vacuuming the inside. An automobile cleaner may also be called upon to steam clean (Fig. 2-5) and paint engine compartments.

2.11   Lubrication Specialist

The job of the lubrication specialist is to lubricate chassis components; drain and replace engine oil; and check fluid and oil levels in the transmission, differential, power steering, and brake system (Fig. 2-6). The lubrication specialist must know exactly where lubrication is required and what kinds of lubricants to use. Most such services also requre the lubrication specialist to make a thorough inspection of other parts such as the battery, radiator, radiator hoses, fan belts, exhaust system, tires, and brakes.

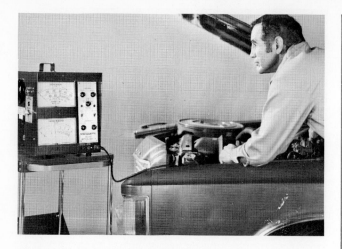

Fig. 2-7 Tune-up specialist. (Marquette)

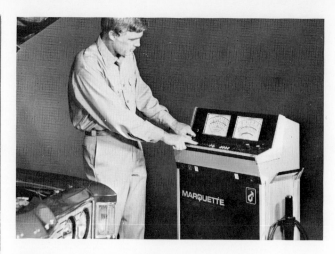

Fig. 2-8 Electrical specialist. (Marquette)

2.12   Line Mechanic—Light Repair

A line mechanic may service any part of the automobile. Light repair usually refers to minor types of service such as installation of accessories, pre-delivery inspection of new automobiles, and replacement of parts such as fan belts and radiator hoses.

2.13   Line Mechanic—Heavy Repair

A line mechanic who does heavy repair may also work on many different vehicle components. This job involves measuring, disassembling, machining, re-assembling, and adjusting complicated components such as engines, transmissions, and differentials. In addition, this mechanic will also be required to do tune-ups, brake jobs, and wheel alignments. Such a mechanic has the very difficult task of learning about many different components and systems and keeping up to date on industry changes in these components and systems.

2.14   Specialist Mechanic

As the automobile has become more complex, it has become difficult for the mechanic to keep up with all the changes. As a result, many mechanics now work in only one area of service. The specialist mechanic usually has advanced training and a great deal of experience in a certain service area. Some of the more common specialist fields are tune-up, electrical, body and fender, transmissions, front end, brake, air conditioning, and parts.

The tune-up specialist services the automobile for peak performance and efficiency. This job usually involves replacing ignition parts and overhauling carburetors. The tune-up specialist uses complicated diagnostic and measuring tools and instruments such as oscilloscopes, dynamometers, air-fuel measuring devices and exhaust emission measuring devices (Fig. 2-7).

Testing and repairing electrical components (Fig. 2-8) such as batteries, starter motors, alternators, regulators, and accessory systems is the job of the electrical specialist. This job requires a thorough knowledge of electricity as well as electrical test equipment, for the automobile's electrical system is very complex.

The body and fender specialist (Fig. 2-9) repairs damage to the automobile body. This job requires a great deal of skill in cutting, welding, metal bumping, filing, priming, and painting.

Testing, diagnosing, overhauling, and adjusting automatic and standard transmissions is the job of the transmission specialist (Fig. 2-10). This job requires considerable training and experience because of the variety of transmissions.

The front end specialist (Fig. 2-11) is an expert in the repair of steering and suspension systems. The job includes wheel balancing, front-end alignment, and replacement of suspension and steering components such as shock absorbers, springs, and tie-rod ends.

Brake system repair is a very common service. Many mechanics specialize in this area. The brake specialist is an expert at diagnosing and repairing drum and disc brake systems. The work involves drum and disc machining, brake shoe or disc pad replacement, and hydraulic system service.

An air conditioning specialist has special training in checking, adjusting and repairing auto air condi-

Fig. 2-9 Body and fender specialist. (DeVilbis Company)

Fig. 2-10 Transmission specialist. (AAMCO Transmissions, Inc.)

tioning systems, which have become increasingly common in the United States.

In order to repair an automobile correctly, a mechanic must have the correct replacement parts. The ordering, cataloging, storing, and selling of these parts is the responsibility of the parts specialist (Fig. 2-12). This worker must have a thorough knowledge of parts and their interchangeability as well as special training in reading catalogs and in inventory control.

2.15 Supervisory Jobs

Hard-working and experienced mechanics may advance into a supervisory position as shop manager, service writer, or service manager. The shop manager is in charge of a number of mechanics in a service department. The manager must schedule the work and make sure it is done correctly. The service writer greets customers and discusses their automobile problems. The service writer then prepares the cost estimates and billings required to get the needed service performed. The service manager is responsible for all the different service departments in a large garage or dealership.

2.16 WORKING IN THE AUTOMOTIVE SERVICE INDUSTRY

Anyone interested enough in automobiles to like working on them and studying about them should consider working in the automotive service industry. Working conditions for mechanics have improved greatly over the years. Mechanics no longer labor in cold, dark garages with dirt floors. Modern service centers are well lighted and roomy. The use of power equipment has greatly reduced the amount of physical

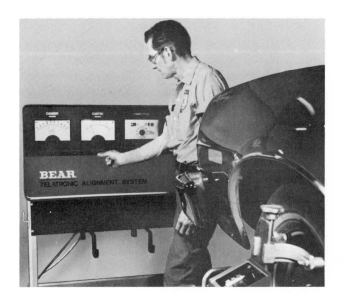

Fig. 2-11 Front-end specialist. (Bear Manufacturing Company)

Fig. 2-12 Parts specialist. (Balilamp, Inc.)

Fig. 2-13 Mechanics in Miami, Florida, take first recertification tests at Dade County Community College.

Fig. 2-14 Student working at auto service certification.

labor the mechanic must do. Most service personnel work 40 hours per week. Overtime pay is generally given for work beyond the basic 40-hour week.

The salary paid to mechanics varies considerably according to the type of work, the employer, business conditions, and the availability of mechanics. In general, mechanics are well paid. In many service centers mechanics are paid a percentage of the labor charges to the customer. Under this system the harder and faster the mechanic works the more money he or she can make.

Many mechanics belong to a union. Several unions enrolling mechanics extend benefits such as health insurance, life insurance, and retirement plans to members. Employers may also provide these benefits.

Employment opportunities in automotive services depend upon the number of vehicles that need repairs. But each year more automobiles are manufactured, and each year more complex equipment is added to them. A student considering an occupation in this field should therefore have a good chance of finding a job.

2.17 TRAINING FOR AN AUTOMOTIVE SERVICE OCCUPATION

Workers spend a very large percentage of their lives on the job. A great deal of careful thought should therefore be given to choosing an occupation. For those who enjoy working on automobiles, an automotive occupation can provide the opportunity for satisfaction (Fig. 2-13).

Before beginning any kind of training program a student should seek the advice of parents, teachers, and school counselors. If possible, try out an occupation by working summers or part time before making a firm decision (Fig. 2-14).

Once the decision is made to become an automotive service worker the next step is to get the necessary training and experience as shown in Figure 2-15. This normally means either a formal automotive training program, on-the-job apprenticeship training, or a combination of the two. There are automotive training opportunities in high schools, community colleges, trade schools, and even in the armed forces. Apprenticeships are available in the dealerships of the major automotive manufacturers as well as in independently owned repair shops.

2.18 MECHANIC CERTIFICATION

In the 1970s, an organization called the National Institute for Automotive Service Excellence (NIASE) recognized the increasing complexity of the automobile, and sought also to recognize the talents of mechanics who service them. NIASE developed a series of voluntary tests for the different automotive service areas. A mechanic working in one of the service areas or a student mechanic preparing for a career in one of the service areas may elect to sign up for a certification test.

When the test is passed, the mechanic is awarded certification and may wear the certified mechanic patch (Fig. 2-16). Certification indicates professionalism and the recognition of talent by fellow mechanics and employers. A certified mechanic takes pride in work-

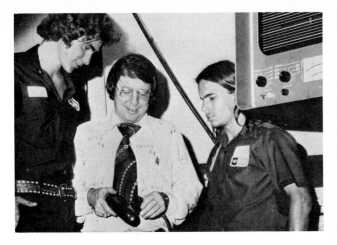

Fig. 2-15 Student mechanics learning at a training center. (Ford Motor Company)

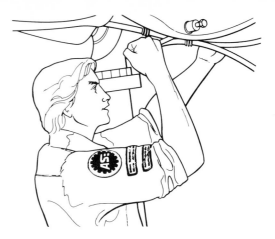

Fig. 2-16 Patch worn by a certified mechanic. (National Institute for Automotive Service Excellence)

manship. Certified mechanics are sought out by car owners to repair their vehicles. If you are planning a career in this field, you should consider certification.

NEW TERMS

Dealership A place where new automobiles are sold. Most dealerships also have a service operation.

Detailer A service worker who cleans an automobile to prepare it for sale or delivery to a customer.

Diagnostic center A service center equipped with testing equipment to analyze the automobile and determine the condition of all systems.

Fleet garage A garage which maintains a fleet of company-owned vehicles.

Independent garage An independently owned service business that may service any type of automobile.

Line mechanic A service worker who may service any part of the automobile.

Lubrication specialist A service worker who specializes in the lubrication of automotive components.

Parts supplier A business organized to stock and sell replacement parts for automobiles.

Service station A service business which is organized primarily to sell gasoline and oil but which ordinarily has a repair operation as well.

Specialist mechanic A mechanic who specializes in the repair of one component, such as brakes or transmissions.

CHAPTER REVIEW

1. Describe the service jobs performed at a service station.

2. What service activities are performed at a dealership?

3. Describe a diagnostic center.

4. What is an independent garage? How does it differ from a dealership?

5. What three things does a parts supplier do?

6. What is the worker who steams clean an engine compartment called?

7. Describe the job of lubrication specialist.

8. Describe the job of the line mechanic who does light repair. How does this differ from the mechanic who does heavy repair?

9. List and describe the duties of eight specialist mechanics.

10. Describe the working conditions for automotive service workers.

DISCUSSION TOPICS AND ACTIVITIES

1. Information on occupations can be found in the *Occupational Handbook* and the *Dictionary of Occupational Titles*. Locate these books in the library and research one of the jobs mentioned in this chapter.

2. Visit a local auto service business and report on what you see.

3. Interview a friend who works at an auto service business. List good and bad points about their job.

4. Talk to your school counselor about training requirements and opportunities in the automotive industry.

Working Safely

Each year many people are injured in accidents while they are working on an automobile. These accidents could all be prevented by greater attention to safety. Working on automobiles in the shop need not be dangerous.

The first step in preventing accidents is to think safety. If you are not sure what you are doing is safe, find out before going ahead with the job. Always be ready for an emergency. Know the layout of the shop. Know where to find the telephone, fire extinguisher, and first aid equipment.

The next step in accident prevention is to understand what the hazards are and how to protect yourself. In this chapter we will study common hazards and ways to prevent accidents.

OBJECTIVES

After studying this chapter, you should be able to do the following:

1. Demonstrate your knowledge of safety practices by working safely.
2. Recognize common hazards in the use of hand and power tools.
3. Identify the hazards of improper use of air and hydraulic equipment.
4. Describe the special hazards of automotive work connected with running engines, storage batteries, and cleaning equipment.
5. Explain how fires are prevented and extinguished.

3.1 USING HAND TOOLS

Many accidents are caused by careless use of ordinary hand tools. Greasy tools can slip out of the hand, fall into a moving part of the engine, and fly out to injure someone. Tools with sharp edges may cause cuts if not handled properly. Follow these simple rules when using hand tools:

1. Be sure your hands are free of dirt, grease, and oil when using tools.
2. Use proper type and size of hand tool.
3. Make sure that the tools you are going to use are sharp and in good condition.
4. Handle sharp-edged or pointed tools with care.
5. Make sure to point sharp edges of tools away from yourself and fellow workers.
6. Clamp small work on bench or secure in vise when using chisel or when driving screws.
7. Control chisels with one hand while the other hand supplies the power.
8. Wear a face shield or safety glasses when chipping, grinding, or cutting metal. Arrange your work so that others are protected from flying chips.
9. Pass tools to classmates with the handles first.

3.2 USING POWER TOOLS

Tools powered by electricity, hydraulic fluid, or compressed air are called power tools (Fig. 3-1). If not handled properly they may cause very serious injuries. The following rules apply to all power tools:

1. Obtain permission from your instructor before using any power tool.

Fig. 3-1   Mechanic using power tools.

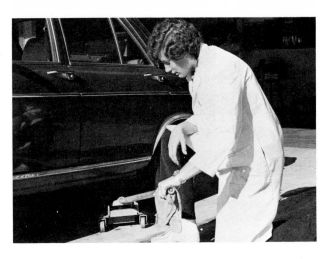

Fig. 3-2   Student using hydraulic service jack.

2. Check adjustments on machines before turning on the power. (Rotate machine one revolution by hand whenever safe to do so.)

3. Make sure that all others are clear of the power tool before turning on the power.

4. Always wear a face shield when operating a power tool.

5. Keep all machine safety guards in correct position.

6. Start your own power tool and remain with it until you have turned it off and it has come to a dead stop.

7. Stay clear of power tools being operated by others.

8. Notify the instructor when a machine does not work properly.

9. Wait for power tools to come to a dead stop before oiling, cleaning, or adjusting.

10. Be sure clothes are safe and suitable for shop work. Remove or fasten any loose clothing. Roll loose sleeves above elbows. Keep hair away from equipment in operation.

11. Observe rules concerning operators' zones.

3.3   USING COMPRESSED AIR

Compressed air has many uses in the shop. It is used to power tools, to inflate tires and to spray. Compressed air can be dangerous if not handled properly. Follow these rules to prevent accidents:

1. Check hose connections before turning on the air.

2. When turning air on or off, hold the air hose nozzle to prevent it from whipping.

3. Do not lay the hose down while there is pressure in it. It might whip about and strike someone.

4. Do not use air to dust off hair and clothing or to sweep the floor.

5. Wear safety glasses when using an air hose.

6. Never point the air nozzle at anyone or use it for practical jokes.

3.4   USING HYDRAULIC JACKS AND HOISTS

In order to work underneath an automobile it must be raised on a hoist or lifted with a hydraulic jack (Fig. 3-2). Most automobiles weigh over 3,000 pounds. If an automobile were to fall from the hoist or jack, the person working underneath would be seriously injured. Great care must therefore be taken in using jack and hoists. Follow these rules:

1. Obtain permission from your instructor before using a hoist or jack.

2. Ask your instructor to inspect blocking before the automobile is raised.

3. Make sure all persons and objects are out of the way before raising or lowering an automobile.

4. Support car with safety stands before doing work under the automobile or removing wheels.

5. Obtain permission from your instructor before getting under a raised automobile.

6. Wear face shield or safety glasses when working under an automobile.

3.5   USING CHAIN HOISTS OR CRANES

Engines and other heavy components must be lifted out of the automobile and moved around the shop with chain hoists or cranes. If they are not attached properly, they may fall on someone and

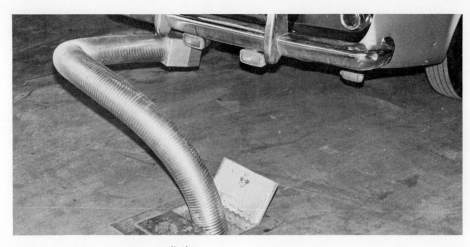

Fig. 3-3 Engine exhaust connected to shop ventilation systems.

cause a serious injury. The following rules apply to cranes and chain hoists:

1. Obtain permission from your instructor before using a crane or hoist.
2. Ask your instructor to check the way the chain is attached before raising the components.
3. Place crane or chain hoist directly over the object to be lifted.
4. Determine that chain, cable, or bolts to be used in lifting are in good condition and strong enough for the job.
5. Double check fastening of chain or cable to the object to make sure it is secure before lifting with crane or hoist. Also check the balance of the object before lifting.

3.6 RUNNING AN ENGINE IN THE SHOP

For many repair operations, the engine must be run in the shop. If the engine is still in the automobile, care must be taken to prevent the vehicle from breaking loose and running over someone (Fig. 3-3). Serious injuries may also result from the explosion of an engine operated at high speed for too long a time. Another serious hazard is carbon monoxide poisoning. Carbon monoxide is a colorless, odorless gas, which is therefore hard to detect. It is present in the engine exhaust. If an engine is operated where there is not proper ventilation, carbon monoxide may build up to dangerous levels. Follow these rules to prevent such accidents:
1. Whether engine is in a test stand or in an automobile, obtain permission from your instructor before starting it.

2. Check fuel line for possible leaks.
3. Vent exhaust to the outside of building and provide adequate ventilation whenever running an engine.
4. Keep your head and hands away from revolving fan.
5. Be sure to block the wheels of the automobile or any mobile engine test stand you may use.
6. Do not operate an engine at high rpm for long periods of time.
7. When testing an engine at high rpm, wear face and ear protection.
8. Avoid standing in front of or behind an automobile whose engine is running.
9. Be sure all the automobiles in the shop have the handbrake set firmly and if equipped with an automatic transmission the selector lever in the park position.

3.7 USING WELDING EQUIPMENT

Both oxygen-acetylene and electric arc welding equipment are often used in repairing automobiles. Careless or improper use of welders can cause burn injuries and start fires. To use oxygen-acetylene welding equipment safely:

1. Obtain permission from your instructor before using welding equipment.
2. Fasten cylinders with a chain or other suitable device so that they will not roll or fall.
3. Close cylinder valves and replace protective cover on oxygen tank before moving cylinder.
4. Keep welding equipment free of oil and grease.

Use only clean rags for wiping equipment. Oil combined with oxygen can cause an explosion.

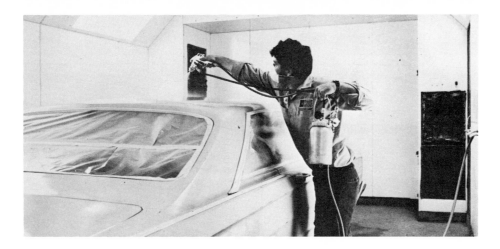

Fig. 3-4 Mechanic using paint spray equipment.

5. Inspect hoses before use.

6. Make sure that hoses are properly connected and that all connections are tight.

7. Report any leaking of cylinder hoses or connections to the instructor immediately.

8. Make sure you have good ventilation.

9. Keep all flammable material away from working area.

10. Wear welding goggles.

11. Release regulator pressure screw. Open cylinder valves gradually.

12. Open acetylene cylinder valve one and one-fourth turns or less. Keep wrench in place so that valve may be shut off quickly if necessary.

13. Keep acetylene pressure in the hose below 15 pounds per square inch.

14. Use a friction torch lighter to ignite torch. Never use an open flame.

15. Close the acetylene valve first if the torch backfires.

16. Make certain lighted torch always points away from you and other students.

17. Keep sparks and flame away from cylinders and hoses.

18. Close cylinder valve when you have finished welding.

19. Before leaving your work, either cool the section of metal that has been welded or mark the word *hot* on the metal with chalk or soapstone.

Following are safety rules to observe in using the electric arc welder:

1. Obtain permission from your instructor before using welding equipment.

2. Wear helmet with proper observation window, treated gauntlet gloves, and treated leather apron. All assistants and observers must also wear this equipment.

3. Keep sleeves and pants cuffs rolled down. Wear leather jacket.

4. Do electric welding only in a correctly constructed booth or room or behind proper screens.

5. Be sure you have good ventilation.

6. Keep all flammable material away from working area.

7. Clear floor area of all obstructions.

8. Report to your instructor at once if electrode holder, holder cable connection, cable, or cable terminals at the welding machine, ground clamp, lugs, or cable get hot.

9. Hang up electrode holder and turn off welder when work is being changed or when work has been completed.

3.8   USING PAINTING EQUIPMENT

In many shops automobiles are touched up or painted with spray equipment (Fig. 3-4). Because paint spray is extremely flammable, special precautions must be observed to prevent fire. To avoid breathing harmful paint vapors, special protective equipment must be worn when spray painting. Follow these rules to protect yourself when using painting equipment:

1. Obtain permission from your instructor before using spray painting equipment.

2. Perform spray painting only in an approved spray booth.

3. Do not apply lacquer, enamel, or synthetic materials near an open flame or sparks.

4. Be sure an exhaust fan is operating to prevent accumulation of fumes.

Fires in a service area generally fall into three classifications →	CLASS A FIRES	CLASS B FIRES	CLASS C FIRES
	Ordinary combustible materials such as wood, paper, textiles and so on. Requires ... Cooling-quenching	Flammable liquids, greases, gasoline, oils, paints and so on. Requires ... Blanketing or smothering	Electrical equipment, motors, switches and so on. Requires ... A non-conducting agent

Fig. 3-5 Fire extinguisher type A, B, or C.

5. Point the spray nozzle toward the work while spray painting. Do not point the gun toward another person.

6. Avoid splashing the eyes with lacquer thinner or other solvents.

7. Do not carry matches into a paint booth.

8. Do not use an electric drill in the paint booth. The motor brushes may arc, causing the vapor to explode.

9. Always wear a respirator or breathing filter mask when painting.

3.9   USING CLEANING EQUIPMENT

Almost every repair operation involves cleaning parts. Most shops have several ways of cleaning parts —steam cleaner, cold tank, hot tank, and solvent tank. The greatest hazard arising from the use of cleaning equipment is that harmful chemicals may get on the skin or in the eyes. There is also the danger of burns in using the hot tank and steam cleaner. To avoid such dangers, follow these rules:

1. Obtain permission from your instructor before using any cleaning equipment.

2. Never use gasoline to clean parts.

3. When operating the steam cleaner, use a face shield and gloves to protect from burns and splash.

4. Wear rubber gloves and a face shield when placing parts in a hot or cold cleaning tank and when removing them.

5. Wear overalls or shop coat when cleaning parts to prevent chemical splash on the skin.

3.10   WORKING AROUND STORAGE BATTERIES

Servicing or working around the automotive storage battery requires some special precautions. The battery gives off a gas during charging that can explode. Many explosions have occurred because a mechanic allowed a spark or a flame too close to the battery. The acid in a battery is another danger. It must not be allowed to come in contact with the skin or eyes. Follow these precautions when working with batteries:

1. Obtain permission from your instructor before servicing or charging a storage battery.

2. Use proper instruments for testing a storage battery.

3. Avoid overfilling a battery, especially if it is to be charged.

4. Use water and baking soda (a neutralizer) to clean off the top of a battery.

5. Remove and transport a battery with a battery lifter.

6. Handle battery or acid with care. Wash immediately any part of your body or clothing that comes in contact with acid.

7. Wash hands immediately after handling a battery.

8. Wear face shield when using a charger.

9. Provide good ventilation when using a charger.

10. Remove cell covers before charging a battery (unless the covers' instructions say otherwise).

11. Keep open flames and sparks away from a battery.

12. Turn off charger before disconnecting leads (wires) from charger to battery.

13. Replace cell covers before moving battery.

3.11   FIRES AND FIRE PREVENTION

The many types of flammable materials used in the automotive shop pose fire dangers. Every worker in the shop must understand the precautions of fire

| Here's how to operate the portable fire extinguisher | Soda-acid: Direct stream at base of flame | Pump tank: Place foot on footrest and direct stream at base of flames | Carbon dioxide: Direct discharge as close to fire as possible. First at edge of flames and gradually forward and upward | Foam: Don't play stream into the burning liquid. Allow foam to fall lightly on fire |

prevention and be able to fight a fire in an emergency. Fires are classified and controlled according to the types of materials involved in the fire. Class A fires involve combustibles such as paper, wood, or cloth. Class B fires involve flammable liquids such as gasoline, oil, paints, or solvents. Class C fires are electrical, involving switches, motors, and transformers. Fires involving metals such as magnesium or powdered steel are class D fires.

To have a fire, three elements must be present— oxygen, fuel, and heat. To extinguish a fire, all that is necessary is to remove one of these elements. Fire extinguishers are designed to remove oxygen or heat to extinguish the fire. Different types of extinguishers are approved for different kinds of fire. A class A fire can be extinguished with water. Flammable liquids in a class B fire are extinguished with a foam or carbon dioxide (CO_2) fire extinguisher. Electrical class C fires are best extinguished, after the power is shut off, with a CO_2 dry chemical unit. Most automotive shops are equipped with a type B or C fire extinguisher, since both of these will work also on type A or B fires (Fig. 3-5). To prevent a fire when using or storing flammable liquids:

1. Store flammable liquids·in a fireproof room or cabinet.
2. Bring into the shop only enough flammable liquid for immediate use. Keep only in a safety container approved by the Underwriters' Laboratory. Label container with name of contents.
3. Use only approved cleaning solutions.
4. Place rags containing oil, gasoline, paint, solvents, and other combustibles in designated (approved) metal containers (Fig. 3-6).
5. Keep the tops of oil drums and the area surrounding them free of combustible materials.

6. Dispose of unwanted flammable liquids and combustible materials daily.

3.12 ASBESTOS BRAKE DUST

Many types of brake friction material contain asbestos fibers. Asbestos dust can be very dangerous if you breathe it. To avoid getting asbestos dust in your lungs, follow these rules:

1. Do not blow the dust of brake parts with the air hose. This can cause the dust to circulate throughout the shop.
2. Use only approved brake-washing solvents to clean off brake parts.
3. Wear a suitable respirator when working with parts that use asbestos friction material.
4. Make sure all brake shoe arcing equipment has a functional asbestos collection system before you use it.

NEW TERMS

Compressed air Air under pressure, used to fill tires, to power tools, and to spray paint.
Electric arc welding equipment Welding equipment that uses an electrical arc to fuse metal together.
Fire prevention Stopping fires from happening by observing safe practices.
Hand tools Tools that are guided and operated by hand.
Hydraulic hoist An automobile lifting device that uses hydraulic power.

Fig. 3-6 Safety storage container for oily rags.

Hydraulic jack A hydraulic device used to lift or jack up an automobile.

Oxygen-acetylene welding equipment Welding equipment that combines two gases into mixture that burns hot enough to melt metal.

Power tools Tools powered by electricity, compressed air, or hydraulic fluid.

Storage battery A device that uses chemicals to store electrical energy.

CHAPTER REVIEW

1. How can an accident be caused by a hand tool?
2. List five rules for using hand tools safely.
3. List five rules for using power tools safely.
4. What is the purpose of a hydraulic jack or hoist?
5. What are the main hazards in using cranes or chain hoists?
6. What is carbon monoxide? Where does it come from?
7. List five safety rules to follow when running an engine in the shop.
8. What two serious hazards can result from using welding equipment?
9. List five safety rules for using oxygen-acetylene welding equipment.
10. List five safety rules for using electric arc welding equipment.
11. What are the main hazards when using painting equipment?
12. List five safety rules to follow when using cleaning equipment.
13. How can an automotive storage battery be dangerous?
14. What three elements must be present for a fire to occur?
15. List five ways to prevent a fire when using or storing flammable liquids.

DISCUSSION TOPICS AND ACTIVITIES

1. Examine your home garage for any of the hazards discussed in the chapter. Correct any hazards you find.
2. Visit a local garage and report on the hazards you find there.

Using Hand Tools

Every automobile repair job requires the use of a number of tools. These tools may be divided into groups: hand tools, power tools, metal-working tools, and measuring tools. Hand tools are those which are powered by hand. Every mechanic should have a wide variety of hand tools. In this chapter we will study the most common hand tools. Knowing the name of each tool, what it does, and what tool works best for each job is basic to any repair job.

OBJECTIVES

After studying this chapter you should be able to do the following:

1. Identify the common hand tools used in automotive repair jobs.
2. Explain the proper use of common automotive hand tools.
3. Describe how to care for automotive hand tools.
4. Demonstrate the safe use of common hand tools.
5. List the common hand tools necessary for starting a tool kit.

4.1   WRENCHES

Many automotive components are fastened together with bolts and nuts. Wrenches are tools designed to tighten or loosen bolts and nuts. Since there are many different sizes of bolts and nuts, wrenches must also be made in different sizes.

The size of a wrench is determined by the size of the nut or bolt head it fits on. The wrench shown in

Figure 4-1 has 10 mm stamped on it. This means that the opening of the wrench measures 10 millimetres across the flats and that it will fit on a bolt head or nut that measures 10 millimetres across the flats.

Wrench sizes are given either in metric system or English system units (see Chapter 7 on measurements). Metric wrench sizes are given in millimetres—11 mm, 12 mm. Sizes for English system wrenches are given in fractions of an inch—5/16, 3/8, 7/16, 1/2, 9/16. Until recently, American automobiles used only English system measurements, while foreign automobiles used metric measurements. Recently, American automakers, like other American industries, have been changing to the metric system.

4.2   Open-End Wrench

Open-end wrenches have an opening at the end which is placed on the bolt or nut. The opening is usually at an angle of 15 degrees to the handle. This makes turning in a tight space easier. Open-end wrenches are made in many different sizes and shapes (Fig. 4-2). Most open-end wrenches have two open ends of different sizes. On wrenches (b) and (d) in Figure 4-2, the opening on one end is set at 90 degrees to the handle rather than 15 degrees. Wrench (e) has one end specially fitted for fuel and brake tube fittings. It is called a tubing wrench.

4.3   Box-End Wrenches

Box-end wrenches (Fig. 4-3) are designed to fit around a bolt or nut. They cannot be used in as tight a space as an open-end wrench. But they allow the mechanic to apply more force with less chance of the

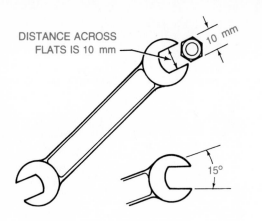

Fig. 4-1   The size of a wrench.

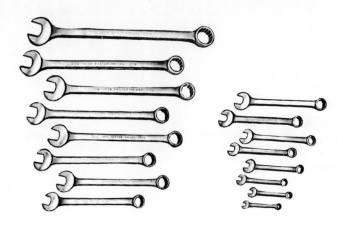

Fig. 4-4   Set of combination wrenches. (Proto)

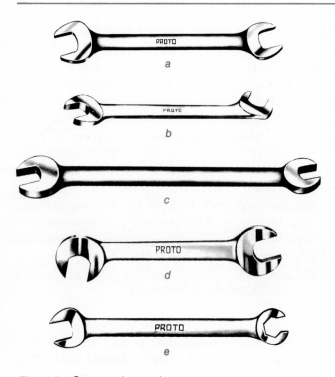

Fig. 4-2   Open-end wrenches. (Proto)

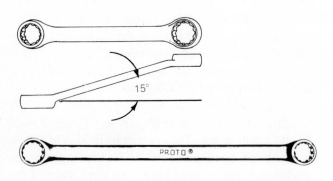

Fig. 4-3   Box-end wrench. (Proto)

wrench slipping off the nut or bolt. Like other wrenches, they come in many sizes. The handles of most are offset 15 degrees in relation to the head to give turning room in a tight space.

4.4   Combination Wrenches

Combination wrenches have one box end and one open end (Fig. 4-4). The open-end side is used where space is limited. The box-end side is used for final tightening or to begin loosening. Combination wrenches are usually the same size at both ends.

4.5   Socket Wrenches

Socket wrenches (Fig. 4-5) are like box wrenches in that they go all the way around the bolt or nut. But socket wrenches can be removed from the handle. Sockets are made in all the English and metric sizes. Sockets of many different sizes can be used with one handle.

Sockets are attached to a handle by a square hole at one end. These drive holes are also made in different sizes. For small bolts and nuts, such as automotive trim parts, socket sets with a 1/4-inch square drive are useful. For general purpose work, a 3/8 drive set is popular. Heavier work requires a 1/2-inch drive socket set. Even larger drives, 3/4-inch and 1-inch sizes are made for very large nuts and bolts.

Besides different opening sizes and drive sizes, sockets have different numbers of points and different lengths (Figs. 4-6 and 4-7). The socket shown in Figure 4-7 (a) has six points or corners to hold the nut or bolt. Figure 4-7 (b) has eight points and Figure 4-7 (c) twelve points. The fewer the points the more strength

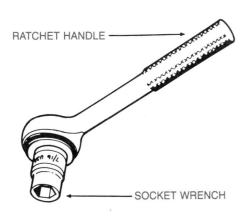

Fig. 4-5 Socket wrench and ratchet handle. (Proto)

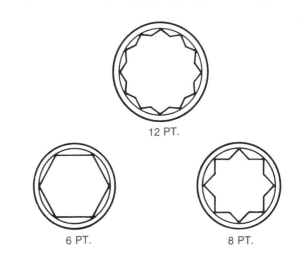

Fig. 4-6 Sockets with different numbers of points. (Proto)

the socket has but the harder it is to slip over a bolt or nut.

Figure 4-7 (d) is an example of a long or deep socket. It is useful for driving nuts on long bolts and studs or working in a deep hole. A special type of the deep socket is shown in Figure 4-7 (e). This is a spark plug socket. The cutaway view shows that this socket has a rubber part inside to protect the spark plug when it is loosened or tightened. Another type of socket is shown in Figure 4-7 (f). This is called a universal socket because of the hinge or universal joint in the middle that allows it to be used at an angle. This socket is very useful in a small space.

4.6 Socket Handles And Attachments

A large number of handles and attachments are available to drive socket wrenches. All the tools shown in Figure 4-8 have a 1/2-inch drive. They can be used only with sockets that have a 1/2-inch hole.

Figure 4-8 (a) and (b) shows two designs of ratchets. A socket wrench is attached to the square drive on the ratchet handle. The socket is then placed over a bolt or nut. The bolt or nut is tightened or loosened by rotating the socket handle. A free-wheeling or ratchet mechanism inside the ratchet allows it to drive the nut in one direction and to move freely in the other direction without driving the nut. This permits fast work in a small space because the socket does not have to be removed from the nut each time it is turned. A lever on the ratchet handle allows the mechanic to choose which direction the ratchet will drive and which direction it will turn free.

The socket drive shown in Figure 4-8 (c) is called a speeder or speed handle. The combination of a swivel handle and crank allows very quick driving of

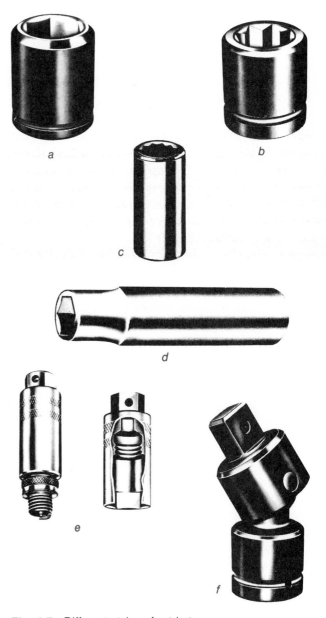

Fig. 4-7 Different styles of sockets. (Proto)

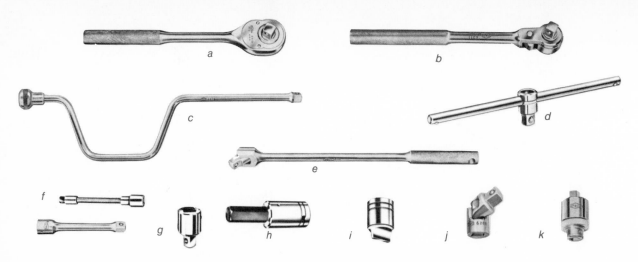

Fig. 4-8   Socket handles and attachments. (Proto)

a socket. It is used when a large number of bolts or nuts must be removed or replaced. The driver in Figure 4-8 (d), a sliding T-handle, will slide to any position along the handle. Figure 4-8 (e) has a hinge handle or breaker bar. Its drive end has a hinge that will permit driving at different angles. Its long handle lets the mechanic use a good deal of force to loosen a tight bolt or nut.

The attachments shown in Figure 4-8 (f) are called extensions. Extensions come in different lengths. One end of the extension is connected to a handle or driver and the other to a socket wrench. The extension allows the socket to be used in an area where an ordinary handle would not have enough room to turn.

Figure 4-8 (g) is an adaptor, used to connect sockets and attachments of different sizes. The attachments shown in Figure 4-8 (h) and (i) are Allen head and screwdriver sockets. The universal joint attachment shown in Figure 4-8 (j) permits a socket to be driven at an angle where space is limited. The rachetor shown in Figure 4-8 (k) has a mechanism similar to that in a ratchet handle. This allows any type of handle to be changed to a ratcheting tool.

4.7   Torque Wrench

When some automotive parts are reassembled after repair, the bolts and nuts must be tightened exactly the correct amount. A special socket handle called a torque wrench is used for this purpose. A torque wrench measures the resistance to turning of a bolt or nut. This resistance is called torque.

There are many types of torque wrenches. One popular type (Fig. 4-9) uses a beam and pointer assembly. During tightening, the beam on the wrench bends as the resistance to turning increases. The torque is shown on a scale near the handle. Another type of torque wrench, shown in Figure 4-10, has a ratchet drive head. Its adjustable handle and scale allows the mechanic to adjust the wrench to a certain torque setting. A clicking signal tells the mechanic that the bolt or nut is tightened to that torque.

Several different torque measurement systems are in use. Specifications may require that a bolt or nut be tightened to so many inch-grams, inch-ounces, inch-pounds, foot-pounds, or Newton-metres. The mechanic must either use a torque wrench scaled to the measurement given or use a torque conversion chart.

4.8   Adjustable Wrench

The wrench shown in Figure 4-11 adjusts to fit bolts and nuts of different sizes. There are adjustable wrenches from about 4 inches to about 20 inches long. The longer the wrench the larger the opening will adjust. For example, a 6-inch adjustable opens 3/4 inch wide while the 12-inch opens 1-5/16 inches.

The right and the wrong way to use an adjustable end wrench are shown in Figure 4-12. For tightening, the wrench must be placed on the bolt or nut so that stress falls on the stationary jaw. If the wrench is used incorrectly, the adjustable jaw can be damaged.

4.9   Allen Wrenches

Some automotive components are fastened with hollow head Allen screws. These screws require special Allen wrenches (Fig. 4-13). Allen wrenches

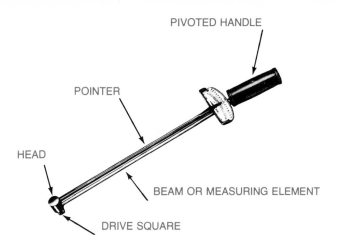

Fig. 4-9   Beam torque wrench.   (P.A. Sturtevant Company)

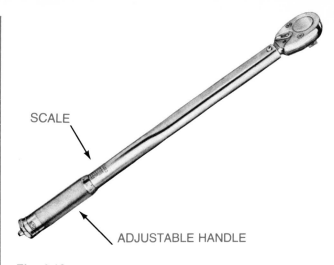

Fig. 4-10   Signal torque wrench.   (Proto)

are available in sets (Fig. 4-14) according to the size of the Allen screw in which they fit. They are made in English system sizes, 3/32 and 1/8, or in metric sizes, 4 mm, 5 mm, and 6 mm.

4.10   Special Purpose Wrenches

Many automotive repairs can be made with regular open-end, box-end, combination, and socket wrenches. Some jobs, however, require special wrenches. Three types of special purpose wrenches are shown in Figure 4-15. The box-end wrenches with special curved handles shown in Figure 4-15 (a) and (b) are called distributor wrenches. They are used to loosen and tighten distributor hold-down bolts. Figure 4-15 (c) is called a starter wrench. Its special curved handle makes it useful in removing the bolts that hold on the starting motor.

Sometimes more force is required to tighten or loosen a bolt or nut than can be applied by hand. The striking wrench (Fig. 4-16) is a special purpose wrench whose handle is designed to be hit with a hammer.

4.11   SCREWDRIVER

Many automotive components are held together with screws. A screwdriver (Fig. 4-17) is a tool used to turn or drive a screw. It should never be used as a pry bar. Some screwdriver handles are still made of wood, but nowadays they are usually plastic. Shanks are made in different lengths and shapes, some round, others square. As we will see below, screwdrivers have different types of blades to drive different types of screws.

Fig. 4-11   Adjustable wrench.   (Proto)

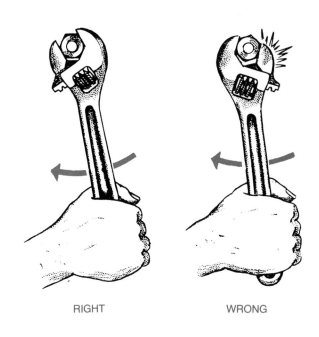

RIGHT   WRONG

Fig. 4-12   Put the stress on the stationary jaw.
(General Motors Corporation)

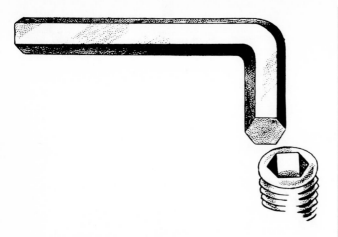

Fig. 4-13 Allen wrench and Allen head screw.
(General Motors Corporation)

Fig. 4-16 Striking wrench. (Proto)

Fig. 4-14 Allen wrench set. (Proto)

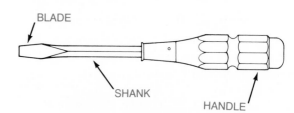

BLADE

SHANK

HANDLE

Fig. 4-17 Parts of a screwdriver.

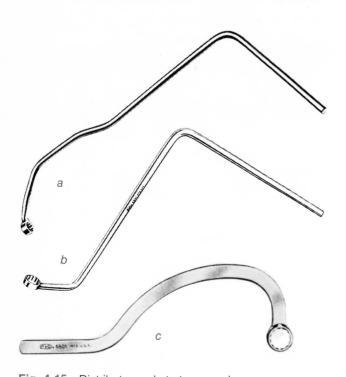

a

b

c

Fig. 4-15 Distributor and starter wrenches. (Proto)

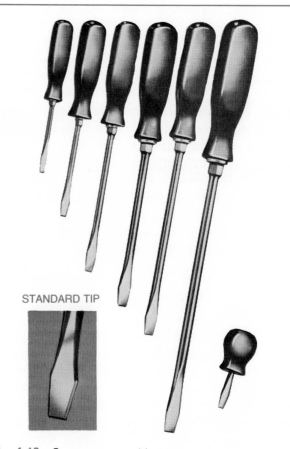

STANDARD TIP

Fig. 4-18 Common screwdriver set. (Snap-On Tools Corporation)

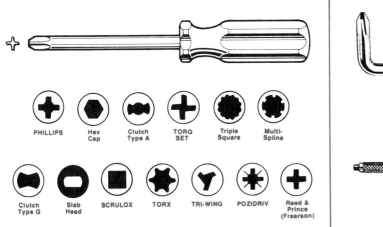

Fig. 4-19 Phillips screwdriver and other screw types. (Snap-on Tools Corporation)

Screw type labels shown in Fig. 4-19:
PHILLIPS, Hex Cap, Clutch Type A, TORQ SET, Triple Square, Multi-Spline, Clutch Type G, Slab Head, SCRULOX, TORX, TRI-WING, POZIDRIV, Reed & Prince (Frearson)

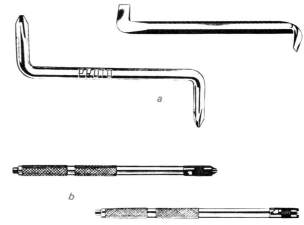

Fig. 4-20 Offset and screw-holding screwdrivers. (Proto)

4.12 Common Screwdrivers

What are called common screwdrivers (Fig. 4-18) are used to drive screws with a straight slot in the top. The stated length of these screwdrivers is sometimes the length of the shank alone and sometimes the screwdriver's overall length. The larger the screwdriver the larger its blade. Care must be taken to use a screwdriver whose blade fits the slot in the screw snugly. If the fit is loose, the head of the screw may be damaged.

4.13 Phillips and Similar Screwdrivers

The Phillips head screw is driven by a Phillips screwdriver (Fig. 4-19). The blades are sized on a numbering system from 0 to 6, 0 being the smallest and 6 the largest.

There are many variations on the Phillips head screw. A number of other screws with recessed heads are also shown in Figure 4-19. Each of these screws requires a different type of screwdriver.

4.14 Special Purpose Screwdrivers

The two tools shown in Figure 4-20 (a), called offset screwdrivers, are designed for working in a tight space. The blades at opposite ends are at right angles to each other. A screw may be turned part way with one blade and then turned some more with the other blade. Common and Phillips blade offset screwdrivers come in many sizes.

The three screw-holding screwdrivers shown in Figure 4-20 (b) have a locking mechanism at the blade that will hold a screw on the screwdriver until it can be moved into position and started. A regular screwdriver is then used to drive the screw. Both Common and Phillips blade screw-holding screwdrivers are made in many lengths.

The nut driver shown in Figure 4-21 is part screwdriver and part wrench. Its handle and shank are the same as a screwdriver's, but in place of a blade it has a small wrench. Nut drivers in small wrench sizes are useful for driving small nuts in tight places.

4.15 PLIERS

Pliers are made for gripping things that wrenches or screwdrivers do not fit. In addition, some pliers are made for cutting things like wire or cotter keys.

4.16 Slip-joint Pliers

The pliers shown in Figure 4-22 have a slip joint where the two jaws are attached. The slip joint can be set for either of two jaw openings, one for holding small objects and one for holding larger objects. These pliers are used for pulling out pins, bending wire, and removing cotter keys. They come in many different sizes and are grouped by their overall length.

4.17 Channel-lock Pliers

Channel-lock pliers (Fig. 4-23) are used to grip large objects. They get their name from the channels that allow the jaws to be set at many different openings. These pliers are made in a number of sizes and are grouped by their overall length.

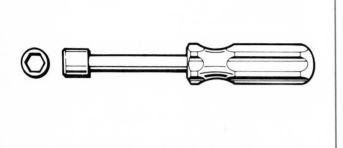

Fig. 4-21 Nut driver.

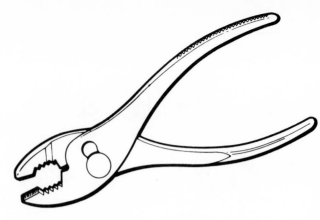

Fig. 4-22 Slip-joint pliers.

4.18 Diagonal Cutting Pliers

Diagonal cutting pliers (Fig. 4-24) are used to cut electrical wire and cotter keys. Their jaws have hardened cutting edges. Like other pliers, they are made in many different sizes and are grouped by their overall length.

4.19 Needle-nose Pliers

Needle-nose pliers (Fig. 4-25) have very long, thin jaws. They are used where there is not enough room for other types of pliers. Some needle-nose pliers have curved or bent jaws for reaching around things.

4.20 Special Purpose Pliers

Many types of special purpose pliers (Fig. 4-26) are designed for certain repair jobs. The pliers shown in Figure 4-26 (a), (b), and (c) replace brake shoe springs.

Figure 4-26 (d) and (e) are battery pliers. The jaws on these pliers are made to grip terminal nuts on battery connections. The tool shown in Figure 4-26 (f) is used to remove hubcaps and grease caps. The round pad on the one jaw is used as a hammer to replace grease caps.

Many automotive components, especially transmission assemblies, are held together with lock rings or snap rings. The snap-ring or lock-ring pliers designed to remove and replace lock rings are shown in Figure 4-26 (g) and (h).

The special purpose pliers shown in Figure 4-27 (a) and (b) are called vise-grip pliers. They lock on to

a small component and allow it to be held securely during grinding or buffing. The pliers shown in Figure 4-27 (c) are designed for removal and installation of the spring tension hose clamps used on radiator and heater hoses. A groove cut in their jaws grips the hose clamp.

4.21 HAMMERS

Many repair jobs require the use of a hammer. The ball peen hammer shown in Figure 4-28 is used to drive punches and chisels. The ball peen hammer should never be used to hammer on an automotive part. Its hardened head could easily dent or otherwise damage the part. Ball peen hammers of different sizes are listed according to the weight of their head. Small ones weigh as little as 4 ounces, and big ones weigh over 2 pounds.

Be careful not to damage an automotive part which must be hammered. A number of hammers have heads softer than automotive parts. The common soft face hammers shown in Figure 4-29 are made of (a) brass, (b) rubber, (c) plastic, and (d) rubber-covered steel. The mechanic must choose the correct soft face hammer for a particular job.

4.22 PUNCHES

Some automotive components are held together with pins. Pins are removed with a punch and hammer. Two different kinds of punches may be needed to remove a pin (Fig. 4-30). A starting punch is used to break the pin loose. Then a pin punch smaller than the hole is used to drive the pin out.

The common types of punches are shown in

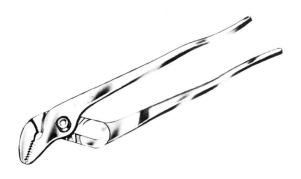

Fig. 4-23 Channel-lock pliers. (Proto)

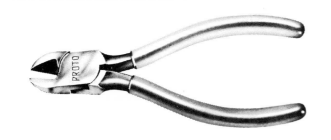

Fig. 4-24 Diagonal cutting pliers. (Proto)

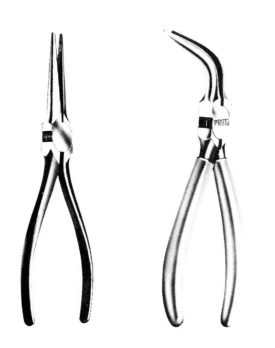

Fig. 4-25 Needle-nose pliers. (Proto)

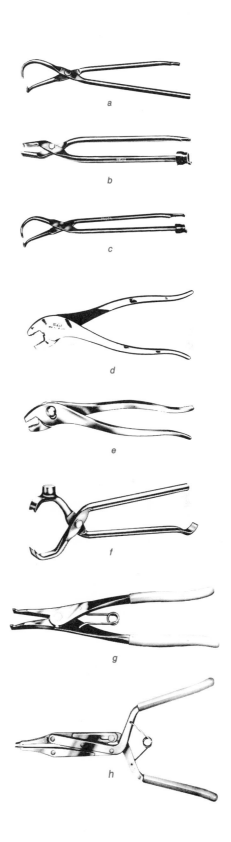

a

b

c

d

e

f

g

h

Fig. 4-26 Special purpose pliers. (Proto)

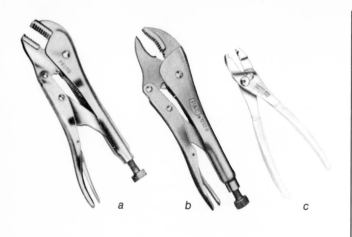

Fig. 4-27   Vise-grip and hose clamp pliers.   (Proto)

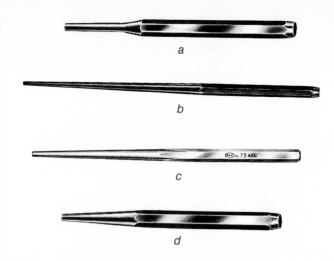

Fig. 4-31   Types of punches.   (Proto)

Fig. 4-28   Ball peen hammer.   (Proto)

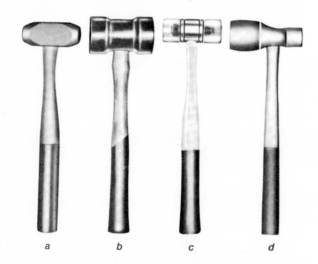

Fig. 4-29   Soft face hammers.   (Proto)

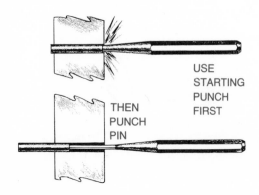

Fig. 4-30   Pin removed with a starting and then a pin punch.

Figure 4-31. Figure 4-31 (a) is a pin punch used with starting punches such as (c) and (d). The long, tapered point on the punch shown in Figure 4-31 (b) is used to align two parts with a hole in them. It is called an aligning punch. Each type of punch is available in many different diameters and lengths.

4.23   BUILDING A TOOL SET

On most jobs, mechanics must own and care for their own tools. The tools a mechanic buys should last a lifetime. Consider buying only tools made from the best materials with the best workmanship for which replacement parts are easily available. A mechanic rarely buys all the necessary tools at one time. Most mechanics begin with a basic tool set and add to it as necessary. A basic tool set like the one shown in Figure 4-32 or 4-33 should provide a good start.

NEW TERMS

Adjustable wrench   A wrench that adjusts to fit bolts of different sizes.
Allen wrench   A wrench used to tighten or loosen Allen or hollow head screws.
Box-end wrench   A wrench designed to fit all the way around a bolt or nut.
Channel-lock pliers   Pliers with channels cut so that the jaws may be adjusted to open wide or narrow.
Combination wrench   A wrench with one box end and one open end.
Diagonal cutting pliers   Pliers with cutting edges on the jaw for cutting cotter keys.
Hammer   A tool used to drive or pound on an object. Hammers for automobile use may have a hard or a soft head.

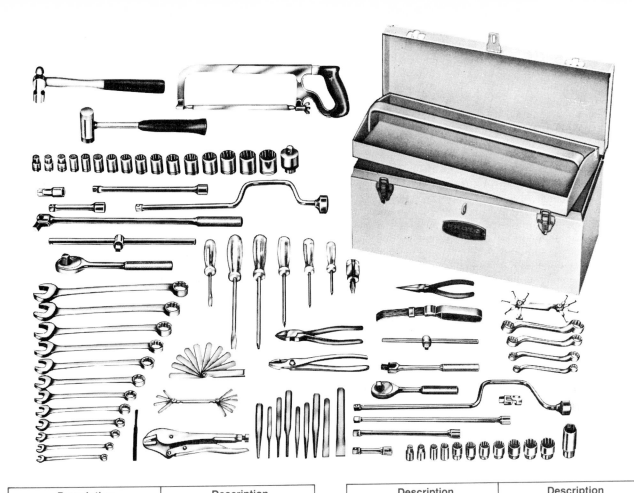

Description	Description	Description	Description
Standard Gauge Set	Comb. Wrench, 11/16"	3/8" Dr. Extension, 3"	1/2" Dr. Ratchetor
Ignition Gauge Set	Comb. Wrench, 3/4"	3/8" Dr. Extension, 8"	1/2" Dr. Ratchet
Spark Plug Gauge Set	Comb. Wrench, 13/16"	3/8" Dr. Extension, 12"	1/2" Dr. Extension, 2-1/2"
Center Punch	Comb. Wrench, 7/8"	3/8" Dr. Hinge Handle	1/2" Dr. Extension, 5"
Rivet Punch, 1/8"	Comb. Wrench, 15/16"	3/8" Dr. Universal Joint	1/2" Dr. Extension, 10"
Rivet Punch, 3/16"	Comb. Wrench, 1"	3/8" Dr. Speed Handle	1/2" Dr. Hinge Handle
Rivet Punch, 1/4"	Ball Pein, 12 Oz.	3/8" Dr. Sliding T Handle	1/2" Dr. Speed Handle
Starting Punch, 1/8"	Plastic Tip Hammer	1/2" Dr. Skt., 12 Pt., 7/16"	1/2" Dr. Sliding T Hdle.
Starting Punch, 3/16"	Ignition Point File	1/2" Dr. Skt., 12 Pt., 1/2"	Box Wrench, 3/8" × 7/16"
Starting Punch, 1/4"	Carbon Scraper	1/2" Dr. Skt., 12 Pt., 9/16"	Box Wrench, 1/2" × 9/16"
Cold Chisel, 1/2" Cut	3/8" Dr. Plug Skt., 13/16"	1/2" Dr. Skt., 12 Pt., 19/32"	Box Wrench, 5/8" × 11/16"
Cold Chisel, 3/4" Cut	3/8" Dr. Skt., 6 Pt., 5/16"	1/2" Dr. Skt., 12 Pt., 5/8"	Box Wrench, 3/4" × 13/16"
Diagonal Cutting Pliers	3/8" Dr. Skt., 12 Pt., 3/8"	1/2" Dr. Skt., 12 Pt., 11/16"	Screwdriver, Std. Tip (3)
Chain Nose Pliers	3/8" Dr. Skt., 12 Pt., 7/16"	1/2" Dr. Skt., 12 Pt., 3/4"	Screwdriver, Phillips (4)
Slip Joint Pliers	3/8" Dr. Skt., 12 Pt., 1/2"	1/2" Dr. Skt., 12 Pt., 25/32"	
Lever Wrench Pliers	3/8" Dr. Skt., 12 Pt., 9/16"	1/2" Dr. Skt., 12 Pt., 13/16"	
Hacksaw	3/8" Dr. Skt., 12 Pt., 19/32"	1/2" Dr. Skt., 12 Pt., 7/8"	
Comb. Wrench, 5/16"	3/8" Dr. Skt., 12 Pt., 5/8"	1/2" Dr. Skt., 12 Pt., 15/16"	
Comb. Wrench, 3/8"	3/8" Dr. Skt., 12 Pt., 11/16"	1/2" Dr. Skt., 12 Pt., 1"	
Comb. Wrench, 7/16"	3/8" Dr. Skt., 12 Pt., 3/4"	1/2" Dr. Skt., 12 Pt., 1-1/16"	
Comb. Wrench, 1/2"	3/8" Dr. Skt., 12 Pt., 13/16"	1/2" Dr. Skt., 12 Pt., 1-1/8"	
Comb. Wrench, 9/16"	3/8" Dr. Skt., 12 Pt., 7/8"	1/2" Dr. Skt., 12 Pt., 1-3/16"	
Comb. Wrench, 5/8"	3/8" Dr. Ratchet	1/2" Dr. Skt., 12 Pt., 1-1/4"	

Fig. 4-32 Basic tool set. Includes 89 of the most needed tools for everyday service and repair requirements. An ideal basic set for the starting mechanic. (Proto)

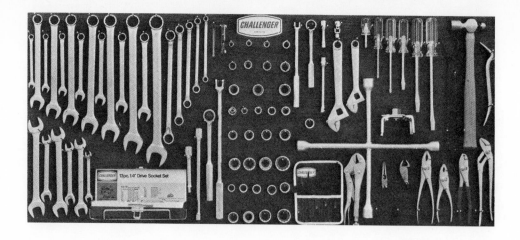

Fig. 4-33 109 piece mechanic's tool panel (Proto)

Open-end wrench A wrench with an opening at the end which can slip onto the bolt or nut.

Pliers A tool designed to grip objects that wrenches or screwdrivers will not fit.

Phillips screwdriver A screwdriver with a point on the blade or tip used for driving Phillips head screws.

Punch A tool to remove or install pins which is driven by a hammer.

Socket handles and attachments Tools used to drive socket wrenches.

Socket wrench A wrench that fits all the way around a bolt or nut which can be detached from a handle.

Torque wrench A wrench designed to tighten bolts or nuts to a certain tightness or torque.

CHAPTER REVIEW

1. What are wrenches used for?
2. In what two ways are wrench sizes specified?
3. Describe a combination wrench.
4. How does a socket wrench differ from other types of wrenches?

5. What is a socket point?
6. Describe a universal socket wrench.
7. What is a ratchet handle and how does it work?
8. List and describe three different types of socket handles and attachments.
9. What is a torque wrench and why is it used?
10. Describe an adjustable wrench and explain how to use it properly.
11. Describe an Allen wrench.
12. List three uses for slip joint pliers.
13. Describe the differences between channel-lock, diagonal cutting, and needle-nose pliers.
14. What are soft face hammers used for?
15. Explain what punches are used for.

DISCUSSION TOPICS AND ACTIVITIES

1. Study the tools in your school auto shop. How many can you identify?
2. Use a tool catalog to list the tools you would like to have. Total the cost of your tools.
3. Design and build a panel for tools you have at home.

Using Power Tools and Equipment

CHAPTER PREVIEW

Power tools and equipment make the mechanic's job easier and faster. A power tool is operated by electricity, air, or hydraulic power. In this chapter we will present the power tools and equipment used most often for general repair jobs. In later chapters we will present specialized equipment used in some repair operations.

OBJECTIVES

After studying this chapter, you should be able to do the following:

1. List and describe the uses of common electrical power tools.
2. Identify and describe the uses of common compressed air power tools.
3. List and describe the use of common hydraulic power tools.

5.1 POWER TOOLS OPERATED BY ELECTRICITY

Most specialized automotive equipment, such as oscilloscopes, boring bars, and wheel balancers, operates on electrical power. The following are common electrical power tools familiar to most mechanics.

5.2 Electric Wrench

An electric wrench (Fig. 5-1) has an electric motor operated by a trigger on the handle. Special heavy duty sockets are attached to a socket drive at the front of the wrench. Holding down the trigger spins the drive and socket. A reversing switch allows the mechanic to loosen as well as tighten bolts and nuts. The main advantage of the electric wrench is speed. Its motor drives a socket much faster than it can be drive by hand. Electric wrenches are especially useful for disassembling parts that are held together with many bolts and nuts, such as engines and transmissions.

5.3 Electric Drill

An electric motor operated by a trigger on the handle drives a chuck at the front of the electric drill (Fig. 5-2). If the chuck of an electric drill opens a maximum of 1/2 inch, it is called a 1/2 drill. The common drill sizes are 1/4 inch, 3/8 inch, and 1/2 inch. This power tool is used not only to drill holes, but also to drive engine cylinder hones, deglazers, and brake hones.

5.4 Grinder

Most automotive shops have a grinder (Fig. 5-3). An electric motor in the unit drives one or two shafts to which a grinding wheel or wire wheel may be attached. Grinding wheels remove metal to sharpen tools such as drills and chisels. They are also useful in making metal parts. A wire wheel mounted on a grinder is used to clean components, for instance, to remove carbon from engine valves.

5.5 Electric Sander and Polisher

The electric sander and polisher (Fig. 5-4) has an electric motor controlled by a trigger that drives a

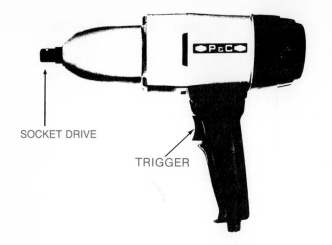

Fig. 5-1   Electric wrench. (Proto)

SOCKET DRIVE

TRIGGER

Fig. 5-5   Trouble light. (Rota-Reel)

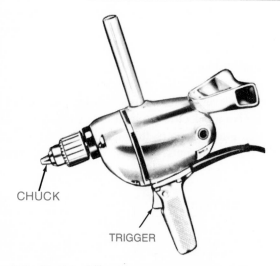

CHUCK

TRIGGER

Fig. 5-2   Electric drill. (Snap-On Tools Corporation)

MOTOR

GRINDING WHEEL   WIRE WHEEL

Fig. 5-3   Grinder. (Snap-On Tools Corporation)

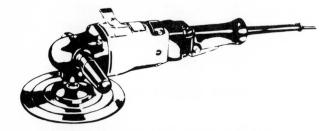

Fig. 5-4   Electric sander and polisher. (Snap-On Tools Corporation)

round rubber pad. An abrasive disk for sanding or a cloth pad for polishing may be mounted to the rubber pad. A sanding disk is used to remove metal during body work. The polishing pad is used in waxing or polishing the finish of an automobile.

5.6   Trouble Light

The trouble light (Fig. 5-5) is a light bulb mounted in a hand-held socket. The bulb is caged to prevent breakage. Some trouble lights use a reel to automatically wind up the cord. Its purpose is to light up areas where it is difficult to see.

5.7   POWER TOOLS OPERATED BY COMPRESSED AIR

Most automotive shops have an air compressor operated by an electric motor. It draws in air, compresses it, and stores it in a tank. Air lines connected to the tank send the air to various parts of the shop. In addition to inflating tires and blowing off parts during cleaning, compressed air may be used to power what are called pneumatic tools.

5.8   Air Impact Wrench

An air-operated wrench (Fig. 5-6) is connected to an air line. Pulling the trigger causes the air to rotate a socket attached to the drive on the wrench. A reversing switch allows the mechanic to loosen as well as tighten. Many air wrenches are designed with an impact feature. An impact wrench not only drives the socket but also vibrates or impacts it in and out. The force of the impact helps to loosen a bolt or nut that is difficult to remove.

Fig. 5-6 Air-operated impact wrench.

Fig. 5-7 Air-operated floor jack. (Hein-Werner)

5.9   Air Operated Jacks

A jack is a tool for raising the front or rear of an automobile. The jack shown in Figure 5-7 has a large cylinder filled with compressed air, which raises a part of the jack placed under the automobile. Jack stands (Fig. 5-8) should always be placed under the vehicle raised by a jack. Never trust a jack alone to support an automobile.

5.10   Automobile Lifts

An automobile lift is used to raise the entire automobile so that a mechanic can work underneath. Some are electrical, but most use compressed air as their power source. The lift mechanism is below the shop floor level so that a vehicle may roll over it. When the mechanic operates the controls, the lift rises and raises the vehicle.

There are several styles of lifts. The one shown in Figure 5-9 has a single post that rises. The single-post lift is simple to operate and may be adjusted for any size vehicle quickly by swinging the four large pads under the automobile frame. The large center post, however, makes working on the middle of the vehicle difficult. To work on the center of the vehicle a twin-post lift must be used. Its two posts lift the vehicle either on its ends (Fig. 5-10) or sides (Fig. 5-11).

5.11   TOOLS OPERATED BY HYDRAULIC POWER

Fluid pumped by a piston is a source of power. This power, called hydraulic force, is used in automotive equipment.

Fig. 5-8 Jack stands. (Hein-Werner)

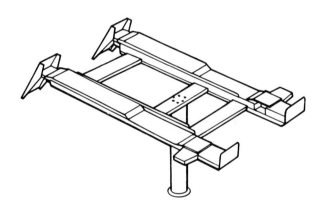

Fig. 5-9 Single-post lift. (Lincoln St. Division of McNeil Corporation)

Fig. 5-10 Twin-post lift. (Lincoln St. Division of McNeil Corporation)

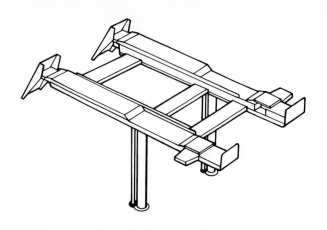

Fig. 5-11 Twin-post lift. (Lincoln St. Division of McNeil Corporation)

Fig. 5-14 Mobile floor crane. (Owatonna Tool Company)

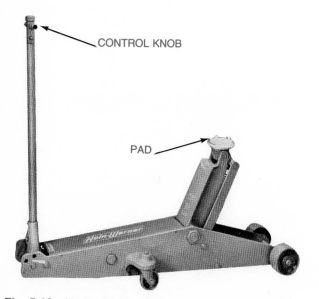

Fig. 5-12 Hydraulic floor jack. (Hein-Werner)

Fig. 5-13 Bumper end lift. (Hein-Werner)

5.12   Hydraulic Floor Jack

The floor jack (Fig. 5-12) is used to raise the automobile. The handle on the jack pumps hydraulic fluid to lift the jack pad and raise the automobile. A control knob on the handle releases the fluid to lower the vehicle. Another style of jack, called a bumper end lift (Fig. 5-13), has rubber pads that are positioned under the bumper to raise the automobile. *Caution:* Do not use a bumper end lift on cars that have energy absorbing bumpers. This type of jack could damage the energy absorbing units on the bumper. Jack stands are always used with either a floor jack or a bumper end lift.

5.13   Mobile Floor Crane

A tool capable of lifting very heavy loads is required to remove an engine from an automobile. The mobile floor crane (Fig. 5-14) is designed to lift an engine in or out of a vehicle. It is mounted on wheels so that it can be rolled into place. A lift chain or cable is attached to the engine. A mechanic pumps a hydraulic cylinder to raise the crane and engine out of the vehicle. The crane and engine may then be rolled anywhere in the shop. A control knob allows the operator to slowly lower the engine to the floor.

5.14   Hydraulic Press

A hydraulic press (Fig. 5-15) is a table to which a hydraulic cylinder is mounted. Pumping a handle attached to the cylinder causes a ram to lower with several tons of force. This force is used to press bearings on and off shafts or in and out of housings, or to straighten bent components. A lever or knob

Fig. 5-15 Hydraulic press.
(Owatonna Tool Company)

Fig. 5-16 Portable steam cleaner.
(Clayton Manufacturing Company)

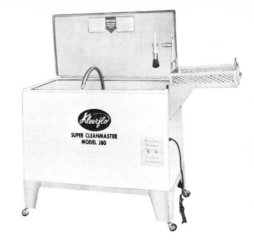

Fig. 5-17 Solvent cleaner.
(Kleer-Flow Company)

releases the hydraulic pressure to remove the component.

5.15 CLEANING EQUIPMENT

Cleaning is an important part of almost every repair job. Parts must be cleaned so that the mechanic can find problems and measure for wear. Several types of cleaning equipment are commonly found in the shop.

5.16 Steam Cleaner

A steam cleaner (Fig. 5-16) generates steam to force a soap solution over a part to be cleaned. Portable or stationary cleaners generate steam by burning natural gas or kerosene. They are normally used in an outside cleaning area. The combination of steam and soap does a good job of cleaning away grease and sludge. Many repair jobs begin by steam cleaning the outside of a component before it is disassembled.

5.17 Solvent Cleaner

Small components and parts are best cleaned with cleaning solvent, which thins and washes away grease, oil, and sludge. In a cleaner like the one in Figure 5-17, an electric motor pumps solvent through a hose that may be used to flush off parts. The solvent is circulated through a filter to remove impurities.

5.18 Cold Tank Cleaner

A cold tank cleaner (Fig. 5-18) contains a solution in which the parts are soaked for a period of time. Since no heat is used, it is referred to as a cold tank. Cold tank solutions are made to clean non-ferrous metal parts, such as aluminum and brass. They are often used on carburetors or aluminum engine parts. The solution in the tank is strong enough to remove carbon and paint. A face shield and rubber gloves must be worn when putting parts in or taking them out of the tank.

5.19 Hot Tank Cleaner

In a hot tank cleaner (Fig. 5-19) the cleaning solution is heated, usually by natural gas. The hot tank is used to soak large ferrous metal parts such as engine blocks and cylinder heads. Most hot tank solutions are so strong that they would dissolve non-ferrous metals such as aluminum along with paint and carbon oil and sludge. A face shield and gloves must be worn when using the hot tank.

5.20 Glass Bead Blaster

After cleaning in a hot or cold tank many shops further clean parts with a glass bead blaster (Fig. 5-20). The blaster uses compressed air to drive small glass beads against the part. The glass beads knock off any foreign particles of carbon or paint.

NEW TERMS

Air impact wrench A wrench powered by compressed air.
Cold tank cleaner A tank with a cold solution for cleaning nonferrous metal parts such as aluminum.
Electric drill A drill powered by electricity.

Fig. 5-18 Cold tank cleaner.
(Kleer-Flow Company)

Fig. 5-19 Hot tank cleaner.
(Kleer-Flow Company)

Fig. 5-20 Glass bead blaster.
(Inland Manufacturing Company)

Electric sander and polisher An electrically powered tool used to sand or polish an automobile body.

Electric wrench A wrench powered by electricity.

Floor jack A piece of equipment powered by air or hydraulic fluid used to raise an automobile.

Glass bead blaster Cleaning equipment in which compressed air drives small glass beads against the part to be cleaned.

Hot tank cleaner A cleaning tank in which a hot solution cleans ferrous metal parts such as cast iron or steel.

Hydraulic press A hydraulically operated table used to press parts together or apart.

Power tool Any tool powered by electricity, compressed air, or hydraulic fluid.

Solvent cleaner A tank in which cleaning solvent is used to wash off oil and grease from automotive parts.

Steam cleaner Automotive cleaning equipment that uses a combination of steam and soap to clean parts.

Trouble light An electric light with a protective hood used to light dark areas of the automobile.

CHAPTER REVIEW

1. Why have power tools been developed?
2. List the three ways to power a power tool.
3. Describe the uses of an electric wrench.
4. What are the three common sizes of electric drills?

5. Explain what a grinder is used for.
6. Describe an air impact wrench and explain its purpose.
7. What does the impact part of an air impact wrench do?
8. Why must a mechanic never trust a jack alone to support an automobile?
9. Describe the difference between a single and a twin post lift.
10. How is a bumper end lift used?
11. Explain the purpose of a mobile floor crane.
12. List two uses for a hydraulic press.
13. What type of cleaning equipment is used to clean the outside of a component before it is disassembled?
14. Small components are best cleaned in what type of cleaning equipment?
15. If a part is made from aluminum should it be cleaned in a hot tank or cold tank? Why?

DISCUSSION TOPICS AND ACTIVITIES

1. Look at all the power tools in your school shop. List the way each tool is powered—by electricity, air, or hydraulic fluid.
2. Visit a local automotive garage. How many power tools do you see the mechanics using?
3. Use a tool catalog to make a list of the power tools you would like to own. How much do they cost?

Using Metalworking Tools

CHAPTER PREVIEW

Many repair jobs require the use of metal-working tools, to cut or shape metal. Files, hacksaws, chisels, drills, reamers, taps, and dies are metal-working tools.

OBJECTIVES

After studying this chapter, you should be able to do the following:

1. Define the term *metal-working tool.*
2. Identify and describe the use of metal-shaping tools.
3. Describe and explain the use of hole-cutting tools such as twist drills and reamers.
4. Identify and explain the use of thread-cutting tools such as taps and dies.
5. Explain the function of screw extractors.

6.1　FILES

A file (Fig. 6-1) is a hardened steel tool used to remove metal for polishing, smoothing, or shaping. Rows of cutting teeth are formed on the face of the file. Files are made in different lengths, measured from the tip to the heel. A pointed end, the tang, is shaped to fit into the handle. A handle must always be attached when filing to protect the mechanic from the sharp tang. The handle is set tightly on the file by striking the handle on a workbench, as shown in Figure 6-2.

Files with cutting edges that run in only one direction are called single-cut files. Files made with cutting edges that cross at an angle are referred to as double-cut files (Fig. 6-3).

A file's cutting edges may be spaced close together or wide apart. The wider they are spaced the faster the file will remove metal. A file whose cutting edges are closer together will remove less metal and can be used to smooth or polish a metal surface. Files are classified as coarse, bastard, second-cut, and smooth (Fig. 6-4). Files are also available in different shapes—flat, half-round, round, triangular, and square.

When using a file, grip the handle with one hand. Push down on the file face with the other hand. Since a file is designed to cut in only one direction, raise the file on the return stroke. Dragging it backwards dulls the cutting edges. Mount small parts in a vise for filing. When the teeth on the file become clogged with metal filings, remove them by tapping the file handle or brushing the teeth with a file card.

6.2　HACKSAWS

There are several styles of hacksaws designed to cut metal. Mechanics use a hacksaw to cut exhaust pipes and other metal parts that are made during a repair job. The hacksaw may have a rigid frame like those shown in Figure 6-5 (a), (b), and (c), or it may have an adjustable frame like that shown in (d), which can take hacksaw blades of different lengths. The hacksaw shown in (e), called a low-clearance hacksaw, is made to work in tight places.

The hacksaw blade installed in the frame is the part that does the cutting. Hacksaw blades are made in different lengths and with different numbers of teeth (Fig. 6-6). The number of teeth on a blade is given in teeth per inch (T.P.I.). The fewer and larger the teeth, the faster the saw will cut. For cutting soft, wide materials, a blade with 14 teeth per inch is correct. Harder materials require a blade with 18 teeth per inch. For cutting pipe and tubing or metal of an

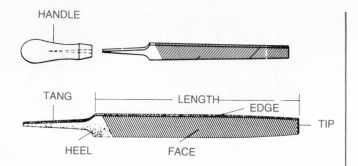

Fig. 6-1 Parts of a file. (General Motors Corporation)

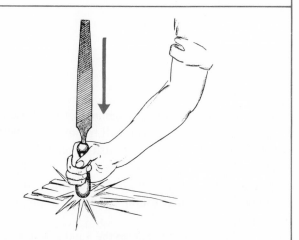

Fig. 6-2 Tightening a file and handle.
(General Motors Corporation)

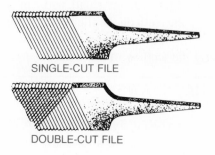

SINGLE-CUT FILE

DOUBLE-CUT FILE

Fig. 6-3 Two types of file cuts. (General Motors Corporation)

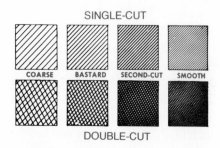

SINGLE-CUT

COARSE BASTARD SECOND-CUT SMOOTH

DOUBLE-CUT

Fig. 6-4 Files classified by cutting edges.
(General Motors Corporation)

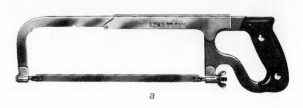

a

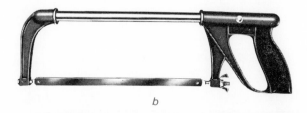

b

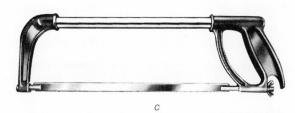

c

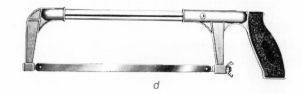

d

e

Fig. 6-5 Styles of hacksaws. (Proto)

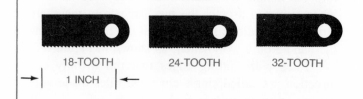

18-TOOTH   24-TOOTH   32-TOOTH

1 INCH

Fig. 6-6 Hacksaw blades have different numbers of teeth. (Proto)

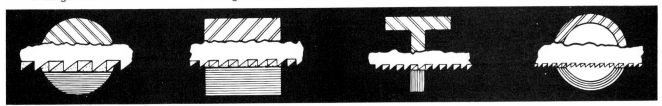

A. Mild Materials In Large Sections	B. Harder Materials In Large Sections	C. Unusual Work Shapes	D. Pipes, Tubing, Conduit
Choose coarse tooth blade to provide plenty of chip clearance, faster cutting.	Choose blade with finer teeth than in A to distribute cutting load over more teeth while still maintaining good chip clearing action.	Choose blade to always keep two or more teeth in contact with narrowest section. Coarse tooth blades straddle work, strip out teeth.	Choose blade with finest teeth per inch to keep two or more teeth in contact with wall. Keep inside of work free of chip accumulation.
Hand Blades— 14 Teeth Per Inch **Power Blades—** 4 to 6 Teeth Per Inch	**Hand Blades—** 18 Teeth Per Inch **Power Blades—** 6 to 10 Teeth Per Inch	**Hand Blades—** 24 Teeth Per Inch **Power Blades—** 10 to 14 Teeth Per Inch	**Hand Blades—** 32 Teeth Per Inch **Power Blades—** 14 Teeth Per Inch

Fig. 6-7 Rules for selecting hacksaw blades.
(L.S. Starrett Company)

unusual shape, use a blade that will keep two or more teeth in contact with the wall, one with 24 or 32 teeth per inch. The general rules for hacksaw blade selection are given in Figure 6-7.

Place the blade in the frame so that the teeth point forward. Mount the part to be cut tightly in a vise. Hold the saw with both hands, as in Figure 6-8, and push forward and down to cut. Release the pressure to back the saw up for the next stroke. Take about one stroke per second.

6.3   CHISELS

A chisel is a bar of hardened steel with a cutting edge ground on one end. It is used with a hammer to cut or shape metal. The chisel shown in Figure 6-9 (a) is a cape chisel; (b) is a cold chisel; (c) is a diamond point; (d) is a rivet shear; (e) is a rivet header; and (f) is a round nose.

Always choose large enough chisel with the correct shape for the job. Hold the chisel tightly when striking it with a hammer so that it will not jump away. Wear a face shield or goggles. After heavy use, the striking end of the chisel will curl over or mushroom. It is dangerous to use a chisel in this condition because pieces may break away and the hammer could easily slip off. The end of the chisel should be dressed off with a grinder from time to time, as shown in Figure 6-10.

6.4   TWIST DRILLS

Twist drills mounted or chucked in an electric drill are used to drill a hole. There are three parts to a twist drill (Fig. 6-11). The end of the drill is called a

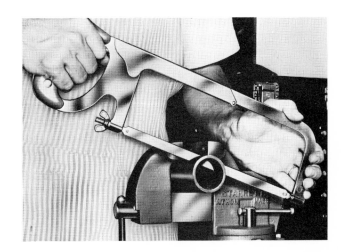

Fig. 6-8 Using a hacksaw. (L.S. Starrett Company)

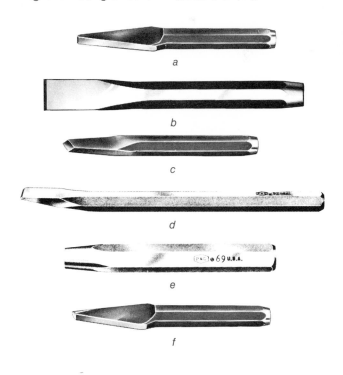

Fig. 6-9 Types of chisels. (Proto)

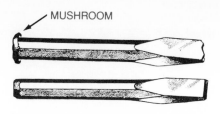

Fig. 6-10 Chisel before and after dressing.
(General Motors Corporation)

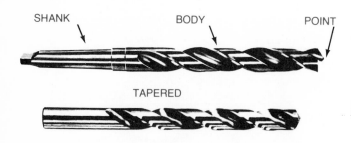

Fig. 6-11 Tapered and straight shank twist drills.
(Beloit Tool of California, Inc.)

Fig. 6-12 Drill set or index. (Beloit Tool of California, Inc.)

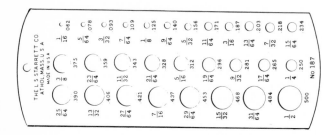

Fig. 6-13 Drill gauge. (L.S. Starrett Company)

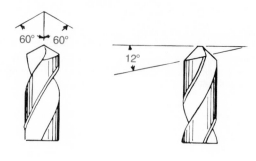

Fig. 6-14 Drill sharpening angles.

point; the spiral portion the body; and the part that fits in the electric drill motor is the shank. The tapered shank drill fits in a special tapered chuck in a drill press or lathe. The straight shank drill is commonly used in portable drill motors.

Twist drills are made in four different size groups: (1) fractional sizes from 1/64 inch to 1/2 inch and larger in steps of 1/64 inch, (2) letter sizes from A to Z, (3) number sizes 1 to 80, and (4) millimetre sizes. Drill sets or indexes (Fig. 6-12) are sold in each size group. Drill size charts are available that list each drill and give decimal and metric equivalent sizes.

The size of a twist drill is stamped on the shank, but after a lot of use, the stamp may be difficult to read. A drill may be measured with a micrometer (explained in the chapter on measuring instruments) or with a drill gauge. A drill gauge (Fig. 6-13) is a metal plate with holes identified by size. The drill to be measured is placed in the holes until it is found which size hole best matches the drill.

A twist drill must be sharp to do a good job of cutting. The point of the drill is sharpened with a grinding wheel, usually in a special fixture. The grinder fixture makes sure the point is ground to the proper angles (Fig. 6-14). Drill point angles may be checked with a special drill point gauge (Fig. 6-15).

To use a twist drill, insert and tighten the drill in the electric drill chuck. Mark the center of the hole to be drilled in the metal with a center punch (Fig. 6-16). A center punch has a sharp point which will make a mark in the metal when hit with a hammer. The center punch mark provides a place for the drill to get started and prevents it from wandering all over the metal (Fig. 6-17). Small pieces of metal to be drilled must always be clamped tightly in a vise. Always wear a face shield or goggles when drilling.

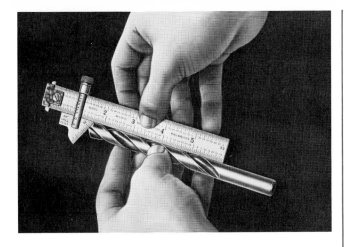

Fig. 6-15 Drill point gauge. (L.S. Starrett Company)

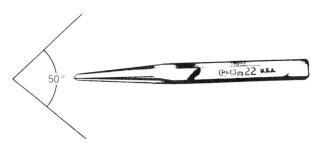

Fig. 6-16 Center punch used to mark the center of a hole. (Proto)

6.5 REAMERS

When a very precise hole is necessary for a precision fit, a reamer is used. A reamer is a tool with cutting edges designed to remove a small amount of metal from a drilled hole. Many automotive parts have bushings that must be finished to size with a reamer.

There are machine-driven reamers, but most automotive jobs require a hand-driven reamer (Fig. 6-18). Like drills, reamers are made in many different sizes. The size is stamped on the shank. Reamers are also made that adjust to many different sizes.

A reamer should be turned with a wrench or with a tap wrench in a clockwise direction. Turning a reamer backwards will quickly dull its cutting edges.

6.6 TAPS

A tap (Fig. 6-19) is a cutting tool used to make or repair internal threads. Damaged internal threads must be repaired before an automotive part can be re-assembled. The diameter and thread pattern are marked on the shank of the tap.

If a new threaded hole is needed, a drill is used to make the hole. A tap drill chart tells the correct hole size for any tap. Mount the tap in a tap wrench (Fig. 6-20) and insert it in the hole. Taking care to start the tap square, turn it clockwise into the hole to make threads.

6.7 DIES

Dies (Fig. 6-21) are used to cut external threads. The size and thread pattern are stamped on each die. A die stock is used to hold and turn the die during

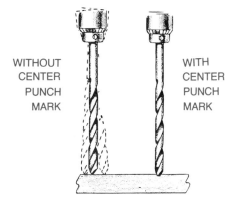

WITHOUT CENTER PUNCH MARK

WITH CENTER PUNCH MARK

Fig. 6-17 Center punch mark prevents drill from wandering. (General Motors Corporation)

Fig. 6-18 Hand reamer. (Beloit Tool of California, Inc.)

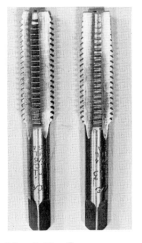

Fig. 6-19 Tap.
(Beloit Tool of California, Inc.)

Fig. 6-20 Tap wrench.
(Proto Tool Company)

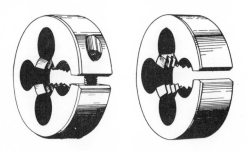

Fig. 6-21 Dies.

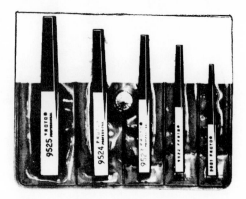

Fig. 6-24 Set of screw extractors. (Proto)

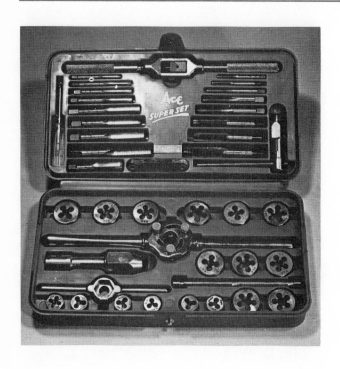

Fig. 6-22 Tap and die set. (Beloit Tool of California, Inc.)

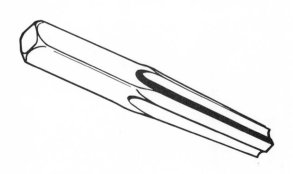

Fig. 6-23 Screw extractor. (Proto)

threading. Start the die squarely on the part and turn it clockwise to cut threads and move the die along the part.

The commonly used sizes of taps and dies are sold in sets (Fig. 6-22) which may also include a tap wrench and die stock.

6.8 SCREW EXTRACTORS

Occasionally a bolt or stud may break off in an automotive part. If a part of the bolt or stud sticks up above the surface, a pair of pliers or vise grips may be used to turn it out. When a bolt or stud breaks off even or below the surface, a screw extractor (Fig. 6-23) must be used to remove it.

Screw extractors are available in sets, often with drills of the same size (Fig. 6-24). To use a screw extractor (Fig. 6-25), drill a hole of the proper size down into the broken bolt or stud. Then drive a screw extractor into the hole. A wrench or tap wrench will turn out the screw extractor and the broken stud or bolt attached to it.

NEW TERMS

Chisel A bar of hardened steel with a cutting edge ground on one end. It is driven with a hammer to cut metal.

Die A tool used to cut external threads.

File A hardened steel tool with rows of cutting edges used to remove metal for polishing, smoothing, or shaping.

Hacksaw A saw for cutting metal.

Metal-working tools Tools used to cut or shape metal.

 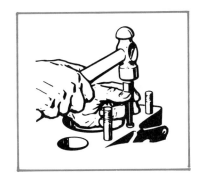 

Fig. 6-25 Using a screw extractor. (Proto)

Reamer   A tool with cutting edges used to remove a small amount of metal from a drilled hole.

Screw extractor   A tool used to remove broken bolts or studs from automotive parts.

Tap   A tool used to cut internal threads.

Twist drill   A hardened cutting tool made to cut or drill a hole.

CHAPTER REVIEW

1. What are three uses for a file?
2. Describe the difference between a single- and a double-cut file.
3. Describe one automotive repair job in which a hacksaw would be used.
4. How should a blade be installed in a hacksaw?
5. List four different types of chisels.
6. Why should the mushroomed end of a chisel always be dressed off before it is used?
7. What are two types of shanks used on twist drills?
8. List four different size classifications for drills.

9. If the size of a drill cannot be read on the drill, how can its size be determined?
10. What is the purpose of a center punch?
11. Describe a use for a reamer on an automotive repair job.
12. Explain the purpose of a tap.
13. How does a die differ from a tap?
14. If a bolt is broken off and part of it sticks above the surface, how can it be removed?
15. Explain the purpose of a screw extractor.

DISCUSSION TOPICS AND ACTIVITIES

1. Examine the tools in your school automotive shop. How many of them are used to cut or shape metal?
2. Which of the metal-working tools discussed in the chapter would be most important in a basic tool kit? Why?
3. What other kinds of metal-working tools have you used or seen used in other shops?

Using Measuring Systems and Tools

CHAPTER PREVIEW

Automotive mass production is based upon inter-changeability of parts. This means that everything must fit together just right. Therefore, precision—making and assembling each automotive part to exactly the right size—is extremely important.

Precision is also an important part of service. The mechanic is furnished with specifications, tolerances, and clearances which must be followed for the vehicle to work properly. To use these specifications, a mechanic must be able to measure precisely. The purpose of this chapter is to explain the two measuring systems the mechanic must use and to present the precision measuring tools used in automotive service.

OBJECTIVES

After studying this chapter, you should be able to do the following:

1. Explain the English measuring system and use the English measuring system units.
2. Explain the metric system of measurement and use the metric measuring system units.
3. Be able to convert between English and metric system units.
4. Identify and describe the use of common measuring tools.
5. Be able to read the measuring scales on precision measuring tools.

7.1 ANCIENT MEASURING SYSTEMS

Ancient man used measuring units based on parts of the body and his natural surroundings. The earliest recorded unit of length was the cubit, the distance from the fingertips to the elbow. Other early units of length were the digit (the width of the finger), the palm (the width of four fingers), the span (the width of three palms), and the fathom (the distance between the outstretched arms). Stones and seeds of grain were used as units of weight. One early unit of weight was the shekel, a stone, used to measure the weight of money. The karat, also a stone, was used by the Egyptians to measure the weight of precious minerals.

When the people of the ancient Eastern civilizations crossed the Mediterranean Sea to the European countries, they brought with them their system of units and measures. Europeans adopted these measuring systems and added to them. The Greeks, according to legend, developed the foot, based on the length of the foot of Hercules. The Romans divided the foot into twelve equal parts called *unciae*, from which the words *inch* and *ounce* come.

7.2 THE ENGLISH SYSTEM OF MEASUREMENT

The English system of measurement is one of two main measuring systems used in the world today. It is still the most common system used in the United States.

7.3 Origin of the English System

The English system units of length were based on body measurements (Fig. 7-1). An inch was the width of a man's thumb. A foot was the length of a man's foot. A yard was the distance from the tip of a finger to the tip of the nose with the arm extended to the side. A fathom was the distance between the tips of a

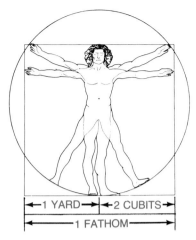

Fig. 7-1 Units of measurement based on the human body. (Go Power Systems)

Units of Length Measurement		
12	inches	= 1 foot
3	feet	= 1 yard
5½	yards	= 1 rod
40	rods	= 1 furlong
8	furlongs	= 1 mile
4	inches	= 1 hand
9	inches	= 1 span

Units of Weight Measurement		
16	drams	= 1 ounce
16	ounces	= 1 pound
14	pounds	= 1 stone
8	stones	= 1 hundredweight (cwt) (112 pounds)
20	cwt	= 1 long ton (2240 pounds)
2000	pounds	= 1 short ton

Fig. 7-2 English System Measurement Units.

man's outstretched arms. A cubit was the distance from the tip of the middle finger to the elbow.

The problem with such a system is that the units will differ because people's measurements differ. In time, the English system units were standardized. A standard is a unit of length or weight that is the same everywhere.

7.4 English System Units

The English system may be divided into units of length measurement and units of weight or mass measurement (Fig. 7-2). Units of weight or mass are not very important to automotive service. Most of the specifications the automotive mechanic uses involve measurements of length.

Automotive specifications are often written in parts of an inch. The inch may be divided in two. Each part is divided again in two, and so on. The parts are fractions of an inch, as shown below:

1 in.	(one inch)
1/2 in.	(one-half inch)
1/4 in.	(one-quarter inch)
1/8 in.	(one-eighth inch)
1/16 in.	(one-sixteenth inch)
1/32 in.	(one-thirty-second of an inch)
1/64 in.	(one-sixty-fourth of an inch)

A typical ruler is divided into such units, the smallest of which is 1/64 of an inch. Automotive work requires measurements much smaller than 1/64 of an inch. For such measurements, the decimal system is used. With this system the inch is divided by ten, each part is again divided by ten, and so on, as shown in the right column:

1.0 in.	(one inch)
0.1 in.	(one-tenth inch)
0.01 in.	(one-hundredth inch)
0.001 in.	(one-thousandth inch)
0.0001 in.	(one-ten-thousandth inch)

Many automotive components must be measured in thousandths of an inch. Some specifications even require measurements in ten-thousandths of an inch. By comparison, a human hair is about three-thousandths of an inch (0.003) thick.

7.5 THE METRIC SYSTEM OF MEASUREMENT

Up to 1790, each country and area used its own measuring system, making trade very difficult. In 1790, the French government authorized a committee of the Academy of Sciences to develop a standardized system of weights and measures.

Instead of choosing a random unit, the committee looked for a natural standard that would be unchanging and measurable to everyone. The meridian, the distance from the North Pole to the earth's equator, was chosen as the standard for length. The basic unit of length was called a metre from the Greek word *metron,* meaning measure. The metre is one ten-millionth part of the distance from the North Pole to the equator. The standard metric unit for weight or mass is the gram, the mass of one cubic centimetre of water.

The committee also decided that different sizes of units would be related by a multiple of ten. This means that 10 metres equals a unit called the decametre, 10 decametres equals 1 hectometre, and so on (Fig. 7-3). This system is much simpler than the

Number of Metres	Prefix	Symbol
1 000 000 000 000	terametre	Tm
1 000 000 000	gigametre	Gm
1 000 000	megametre	Mm
1 000	kilometre	km
100	hectometre	hm
10	decametre	dam
1	metre	
0.1	decimetre	dm
0.01	centimetre	cm
0.001	millimetre	mm
0.000 001	micrometre	um
0.000 000 001	nanometre	nm
0.000 000 000 001	picometre	pm
0.000 000 000 000 001	femtometre	fm
0.000 000 000 000 000 001	attometre	am

Fig. 7-3   Metric System units, prefixes, and symbols.

To Find		Multiply	×	Conversion Factors
millimetres	=	inches	×	25.40
centimetres	=	inches	×	2.540
centimetres	=	feet	×	32.81
metres	=	feet	×	0.3281
kilometre	=	feet	×	0.0003281
kilometre	=	miles	×	1.609
inches	=	millimetres	×	0.03937
inches	=	centimetres	×	0.3937
feet	=	centimetres	×	30.48
feet	=	metres	×	0.3048
feet	=	kilometres	×	3048.
yards	=	metres	×	1.094
miles	=	kilometres	×	0.6214

Fig. 7-4   Converting from one system to another.

English system in which 12 inches equals 1 foot but 3 feet equals 1 yard and 5-1/2 yards equals 1 rod.

The advantages of the French metric system over the English system led to its widespread use by other countries. Today it is the system used by most of the countries in the world. The United States is one of the last countries to adopt the metric system. Since the changeover from the English system will take a long time, a mechanic must be familiar with both systems.

7.6   Metric System of Units

It is not practical to measure very small and very large things with the same units. In the metric system, larger and smaller units are defined in relation to the basic metre. Their names are formed by adding one of the prefixes shown in Figure 7-3 to the word *metre*. For example, a human hair may be measured in millimetres, the length of a soccer field in metres, and the distance from the earth to the sun in gigametres.

The symbol for the metre is m. To this symbol can be added the prefix symbol. For example, 1 000 metres may be written 1 000 m or, since a kilometre is equal to 1 000 metres, it may be written 1 kilometre or simply 1 km. Similarly, one-thousandth of a metre may be written 1 millimetre or simply 1 mm.

7.7   CONVERTING BETWEEN ENGLISH AND METRIC SYSTEM UNITS

Since both the English and the metric system are in use in this country, it is frequently necessary to convert units from one system to another. A mechanic with specification written in millimetres may have tools that measure in thousandths of an inch. A conversion chart lists units of one system in one column and their equivalent from the other system in another column. An English–metric conversion chart is located in the appendix to this book.

Conversion or changeover from one system to the other may also be done through multiplying by a number called a conversion factor (Fig. 7-4). A specification of 10 mm (ten millimetres) in inches is shown in the conversion factor as follows:

Example: Multiply the number of millimetres by the conversion factor, 0.03937
$$10 \times 0.03937 = 0.3937$$
Ten mm is equal to 0.3937 of an inch

In order to change 5 miles into kilometres:

Example: Multiply the number of miles by the conversion factor, 1.609
$$5 \times 1.609 = 8.045$$
Five miles is equal to 8.045 kilometres.

7.8   USING MEASURING TOOLS

An automobile mechanic uses a number of measuring tools or instruments.

7.9   The Rule

The rule or ruler is a flat length of wood, paper, plastic, or metal divided or graduated into a number of spaces. Rules using the English system of measure are usually 6 or 12 inches long. Most rules divide the inch into 1/8, 1/16, or 1/32 divisions. Precision machinist rules have 1/64-inch divisions. This is the smallest division of an inch readable with the unaided eye.

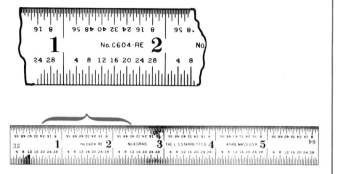

Fig. 7-5 English system rule. (L.S. Starrett Company)

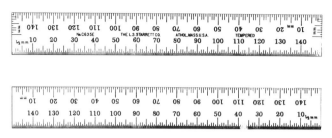

Fig 7-6 Metric system rule. (L.S. Starrett Company)

The rule shown in Figure 7-5 is 6 inches long. On one side the rule is divided into 1/32nds of an inch and on the other side 1/64ths of an inch. Place one end of the rule at one end of the length to be measured. Next, determine which of the rule marks most nearly lines up with the other end of the length to be measured.

The rule shown in Figure 7-6 is divided into units of the metric system. Metric rules are commonly subdivided into centimetres and millimetres. Some metric rules are further divided into .5-millimetre spaces. Reading the metric rule is easier than the English rule because it does not use fractions.

The metric rule in Figure 7-7 is 100 millimetres long. Every 10th mark is equal to 1 centimetre. Alongside the metric rule in Figure 7-7 is a cotter pin 20 millimetres or 2 centimetres long (10 millimetres equals 1 centimetre).

7.10 Outside Micrometer

Outside micrometers (Fig. 7-8), called mikes, provide the most precise measurements required for general automotive service work. Micrometers are made in different sizes and shapes and for a number of special purposes in metric and English system units.

A micrometer consists of a frame, anvil, spindle, sleeve, and thimble. The measuring surfaces are at the ends of the stationary anvil and the movable spindle. The spindle is actually an extension of a precision-ground screw which threads into the sleeve. Since the other end of the screw is attached to the thimble, turning the thimble moves the spindle toward or away from the anvil.

The item to be measured is placed between the anvil and spindle faces. The spindle is rotated by

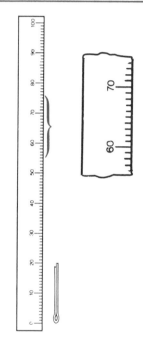

Fig. 7-7 Measuring with a metric rule.

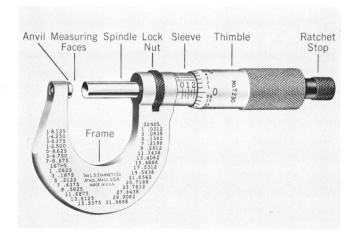

Fig. 7-8 Outside micrometer. (L.S. Starrett Company)

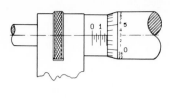

Fig. 7-9 English system micrometer measuring 0.178 inch. (L.S. Starrett Company)

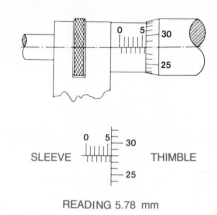

READING 5.78 mm

Fig. 7-10 Metric system micrometer measuring 5.78 mm. (L.S. Starrett Company)

means of the thimble until the anvil and spindle both contact the item to be measured. The measurement is read from the graduations on the sleeve and thimble.

7.11 Reading an English System Micrometer

The spindle screw is ground to extremely accurate specifications. The lead of the screw on an English system micrometer is exactly 0.025 (twenty-five-thousandths) inch, which means that one revolution of the screw moves the spindle 0.025 inch toward or away from the anvil. Therefore, 40 turns of the screw will move the spindle exactly 1 inch (40×0.025 =1.000).

A scale on the sleeve is divided into 40 graduations, each equal to 0.025 inch. So, starting with the spindle against the anvil, and turning the screw out, every revolution of the thimble will uncover one of the divisions on the sleeve. Every fourth division is numbered, starting with the zero mark, when the spindle is against the anvil. The next numbered division is at 0.100 inch (1/10 of an inch) from the closed position. The three unnumbered divisions between zero and one are at 0.025, 0.050, and 0.075 inch.

The bevel on the front of the thimble is also divided into equal parts. Since the thimble and spindle travel 0.025 inch per revolution, there are 25 divisions on the bevel. These divisions make it possible to read the amount of spindle travel for partial revolutions. For instance, a partial revolution from one thimble mark to the next is 1/25 of a revolution, which moves the spindle 0.001 inch.

Reading a micrometer measurement is a simple matter of addition. Add together the last visible numbered division on the sleeve, the unnumbered sleeve divisions, and the divisions on the bevel of the thimble.

To follow the explanation in the example below, look at Figure 7-9.

Example: The last visible number on sleeve 1
representing 0.100''

3 additional lines are visible, each representing
0.025'' 3 × 0.025'' = 0.075''
Line 3 on the thimble coincides with the longitudinal line on the sleeve, each line representing
0.001'' 3 × 0.001'' = 0.003''

The micrometer reading is therefore 0.178''

An easy way to remember is to think of the units as if you were making change from a ten-dollar bill. Count the figures on the sleeve as dollars, the vertical lines on the sleeve as quarters, and the divisions on the thimble as cents. Add up your change and put a decimal point instead of a dollar sign in front of the figures.

The micrometer we have been studying up to this point has a range from 0 to 1 inch. Micrometers are made in other sizes—1 to 2 inches, 2 to 3 inches, and larger to measure large components. Adapters are available for the larger micrometers to give them multiple ranges.

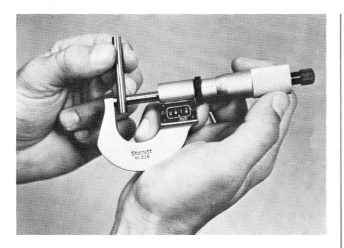

Fig. 7-11 Correct way to hold a micrometer.
(L.S. Starrett Company)

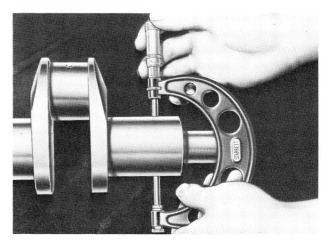

Fig. 7-12 Using a large micrometer to measure a crankshaft. (L.S. Starrett Company)

7.12   Reading a Metric System Micrometer

A metric micrometer has the same parts and works exactly the same as an English system micrometer. The pitch of the spindle screw in metric micrometers is 0.500 millimetres. One complete revolution of the thimble moves the spindle exactly 0.500 millimetres. Two complete revolutions of the thimble move the spindle exactly 1 millimetre.

The longitudinal line on the sleeve is graduated in millimetres from 1 to 25 mm, and each millimetre is subdivided in half. Therefore, it requires two revolutions of the thimble to advance the spindle a distance of 1 millimetre.

The beveled edge of the thimble is graduated in 50 divisions, every fifth line being numbered from 0 to 50. Since a complete revolution of the thimble advances the spindle 0.5 mm, each graduation on the thimble is equal to 1/50 of 0.5 mm or 0.01 mm.

Example: The 5 on the sleeve is visible,
representing   5.00 mm
One additional 0.5 mm line is
visible, representing   0.50 mm

Line 28 on the thimble coincides with
the longitudinal line on the sleeve,
each line representing 0.01 mm
$$28 \times 0.01 = 0.28 \text{ mm}$$

The micrometer reading is therefore
5.78 mm

To read a metric micrometer, add the total reading in millimetres visible on the sleeve to the reading, in hundredths, of a millimetre, indicated by the graduation on the thimble which coincides with the longitudinal line on the sleeve (Fig. 7-10).

7.13   Use and Care of the Micrometer

There are some things to keep in mind when you are taking a micrometer measurement. For instance, there is even a right way to hold the micrometer when measuring an object. The most convenient way to hold micrometers is with one hand. Insert one finger through the frame and use the thumb and forefinger to turn the spindle (Fig. 7-11). With a little practice, you will find that this gives you the best control over the position of the anvil and spindle.

It is impossible to get a correct measurement with micrometers unless the anvil and spindle are at right angles to the piece being measured. If they are cocked to one side, you will get an oversize reading. If you are measuring a diameter, make sure the spindle and anvil are centered exactly across the diameter or the reading will be undersize. Hold the micrometer loosely and gently turn the spindle down against the workpiece (Fig. 7-12). Rocking the micrometer ever so slightly as you turn the spindle down the last few thousandths will help you to tell by ''feel'' alone when the micrometer is square with the part and centered on the diameter.

Probably the most important matter in measuring with micrometers is the amount of force used to tighten the spindle down onto the part. The spindle and anvil should just contact the part lightly, so there is a slight drag when the micrometer is moved back and forth. Keep in mind that a micrometer is a precision tool, not a ''C'' clamp.

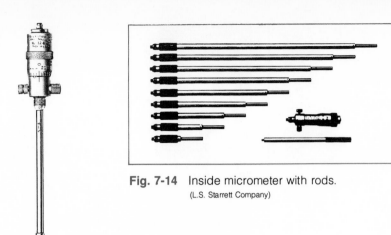

Fig. 7-14 Inside micrometer with rods.
(L.S. Starrett Company)

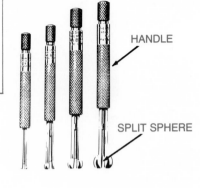

HANDLE

SPLIT SPHERE

Fig. 7-13 Inside micrometer.
(L.S. Starrett Company)

Fig. 7-15 Set of small hole gauges.
(L.S. Starrett Company)

If the spindle is cracked down too hard, the reading will not only be incorrect, but the frame may become distorted, which makes the micrometer useless. Unless you have a good feel for the correct tightness, turn the ratchet (Fig. 7-8) instead of the thimble to avoid overtightening.

To run the spindle in or out in a hurry, hold the frame in one hand and roll the thimble along the other arm or along the palm of the hand. Never hold the micrometer by the thimble and spin it like a party noisemaker. This can ruin a micrometer.

When the micrometer is not in use, it should be stored in a box in a safe place where tools will not be accidentally dropped on it. Keep a thin film of oil on it to prevent rust and corrosion. Make sure the spindle is backed off slightly from the anvil.

As with any other precision tool, a micrometer should be checked for accuracy occasionally. Use a master gauge to check the maximum and minimum limits of measurement. For instance, to check a one-inch micrometer, use the master, which is exactly one inch in diameter. Then run the spindle down gently against the anvil and check for a zero reading. Always make sure the spindle and anvil are clean before checking.

7.14 Inside Micrometer

The inside micrometer (Fig. 7-13) is especially valuable when boring and honing cylinders. It is used to measure holes. As shown in Figure 7-14, measuring rods of different lengths and spacing collars are supplied with the micrometer. Different ranges of measurement are used by assembling different rods into the micrometer head.

Inside micrometers are made with both English and metric system scales. The scale on the inside micrometer works and is read exactly like that of the outside micrometer. It takes a little more practice to get an accurate measurement with an inside micrometer. It can easily be cocked in the bore and give an incorrect reading. For accurate measurement, make sure the micrometer is at right angles to the centerline of the bore. Then move one end back and forth slightly to get the maximum reading on the scales. It is always a good idea to take two or three additional readings as a check.

7.15 Small Hole Gauge

When it is necessary to measure the inside of a hole too small for an inside micrometer, a small hole gauge is used. This tool is a split sphere. The diameter of the sphere can be changed by means of an internal wedge which is made to slide up or down by turning the handle. The gauge is placed into the hole to be measured and adjusted to fit the internal dimension. After it is removed from the hole, an outside micrometer is used to measure the diameter of the expanded sphere. Small hole gauges are available in sets (Fig. 7-15) that cover a range of 3 mm to 12 mm (0.125 to 0.500 inch).

7.16 Telescoping Gauge

The telescoping gauge consists of a spring-loaded piston which telescopes within a cylinder. It is used to measure the inside dimension of a hole. Telescoping gauges are made in sets (Fig. 7-16) to measure anything from very small to very large holes.

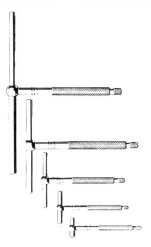

Fig. 7-16 Set of telescoping gauges.
(L.S. Starrett Company)

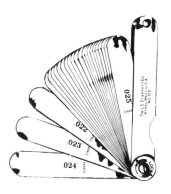

Fig. 7-17 Feeler gauge with blades marked in thousandths of an inch. (L.S. Starrett Company)

Fig. 7-18 Feeler gauge with metric blades. (L.S. Starrett Company)

The gauge is placed into the hole, permitting the spring-loaded piston to expand to the hole size. When the proper feel is obtained, the handle is turned to lock the piston in position. The exact size of the hole is then found by removing the gauge and measuring across the two contacts with an outside micrometer.

7.17 Feeler Gauge

A feeler gauge is used to measure the space between two surfaces, such as the contact points, or the gap between the two electrodes on the spark plugs. A feeler gauge is a flat blade or round wire made to a very precise thickness. The thickness is written on the gauge in thousandths of an inch (Fig. 7-17) or millimetres (Fig. 7-18). The gauge is placed in a space to be measured. If the gauge and the space are the same size, the gauge will feel tight as it is moved in and out. Feeler gauges usually come in sets.

7.18 Dial Indicator

A dial indicator is a gauge used to measure the movement or play and the contour or runout of an automotive part. The measurement is shown by a pointer on the face of the gauge. The most common type of dial indicator uses a plunger or lever connected to the pointer by a gear built into the instrument. Movement of the plunger is shown by the pointer. The dial indicator is used with a number of attachments that allow it to be mounted on an automotive part. The dial indicator assembly shown in Figure 7-19 has a magnetic base which allows it to be attached to any metal automotive part.

Dial indicators used in most automotive repair operations measure either in thousandths of an inch (0.001) or in hundredths of a millimetre (0.01 mm). The scale on the metric dial indicator face (Fig. 7-20) is divided into 100 divisions. Each division represents 1/100 of a millimetre. The pointer (Fig. 7-20) is at 32 on the scale, measuring a distance of 0.32 mm.

When mounting a dial indicator, keep the support arms as short as possible. If the arms are too long, the setup will not be rigid enough, and an inaccurate reading may result. The spring load on the indicator plunger can move the whole indicator assembly.

Mount the indicator so that the plunger is straight against the part. If the anvil is at an angle, the anvil plunger will give an incorrect reading, for the whole indicator assembly will move instead of just the anvil and plunger. Always read the dial indicator straight on. Looking at it from the side can cause a considerable error. Remember that a dial indicator is a precision instrument like a watch. It must be handled with great care.

NEW TERMS

Dial indicator A gauge used to measure movement or play and contour or runout of an automobile part.
English measuring system One of the two main measuring systems in use in the world. Most common system used in the United States.
Feeler gauge A tool used to measure the space between two surfaces.
Inside micrometer A tool used to measure the size of holes, such as an automotive engine cylinder.
Metric measuring system One of the two main

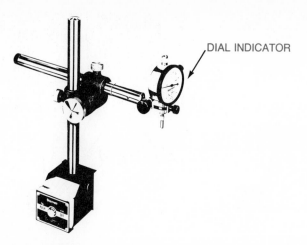

DIAL INDICATOR

Fig. 7-19 Dial indicator with magnetic base.
(L.S. Starrett Company)

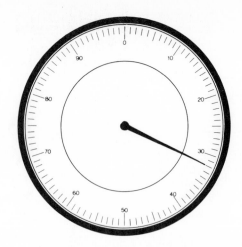

Fig. 7-20 Metric dial indicator reading of 0.32 mm.

measuring systems in use in the world, now being slowly adopted in the United States.

Metric units Standard units based upon the metre and decimal steps of the metre.

Outside micrometer A tool used to measure the outside of an object such as a crankshaft or piston.

Rule A flat length of wood, plastic or metal divided into a number of measuring units.

Small hole gauge A tool consisting of a split sphere with an internal wedge used to measure the inside of small holes such as valve guides.

Telescoping gauges A tool with a spring-loaded piston that telescopes within a cylinder, used to measure the inside of a hole.

CHAPTER REVIEW

1. What was the basic problem with a measuring system based upon the parts of the body?
2. List the divisions of an inch between 1 inch and 1/64 of an inch.
3. Write the following parts of an inch in numerals: one inch, one-tenth of an inch, one-hundredth of an inch, one-thousandth of an inch.
4. Define the term *metre*.
5. What is the advantage of the metric system over the English system.
6. List three prefix symbols used in metric units.
7. Describe an outside micrometer and explain its use.

8. List the five basic parts of an outside micrometer.
9. Describe the precautions that should be followed when using an outside micrometer.
10. Describe an inside micrometer and explain its use.
11. What are small hole gauges and how are they used?
12. Explain how a telescoping gauge is used.
13. Describe a feeler gauge and explain how it is used.
14. Describe a dial indicator and explain its use.
15. What does the term *play* mean in speaking about a dial indicator?

DISCUSSION TOPICS AND ACTIVITIES

1. Measure the following objects with an English rule and with a metric system rule. Record your results.

thickness of a penny	your height
diameter of a penny	length of your shoe
width of your thumb	your waist

2. Measure the distance you travel to school. Record the results in miles and kilometres.
3. Use an outside micrometer to measure the diameter of a hair, the diameter of a paper clip, and the thickness of a pencil lead.

Using Fasteners

CHAPTER PREVIEW

The automobile is assembled and held together with bolts, nuts, and screws. These are called fasteners because they fasten or hold automotive parts together. Every repair job involves fasteners, so the mechanic must understand their proper selection and use. In this chapter we will present the most common of these fastening devices.

OBJECTIVES

After studying this chapter, you should be able to do the following:

1. Identify and describe the use of fasteners such as screws, bolts, studs, nuts, and washers.
2. Recognize and be able to use the English thread designation system.
3. Recognize and be able to use the metric thread designation system.
4. Be able to distinguish between fasteners of different quality with the grade marking system.
5. Identify and describe the use of nonthreaded fasteners such as dowel pins, retaining rings, keys, splines, and rivets.

8.1 THREADED FASTENERS

Threaded fasteners use the wedging action of a spiral groove or thread to clamp two parts together. The common type of threaded fasteners are screws, bolts, studs, and nuts.

8.2 Screws

A screw is a fastener that fits in a threaded hole. The screw is turned or driven into the threaded hole to hold or clamp two parts together (Fig. 8-1).

Several types of screws are used in automotive assemblies. The most common type, the cap screw (Fig. 8-2), has a six-sided or hexagonal head. It is sometimes called a hex head screw. The cap screw is driven or turned with the common automotive wrenches, such as the box, open-end, combination, and socket.

Another common screw, the machine screw, is driven with a screwdriver. It may have a slotted head (Fig. 8-3) or a Phillips head (Fig. 8-4). Machine screws are often used to assemble small automotive parts.

A hollow head or Allen head screw (Fig. 8-5) is driven with an Allen wrench. This type of screw is more commonly used in aircraft assemblies than in automotive components.

Some automotive body sheet metal parts are fastened with screws that do not fit into threaded holes. These sheet metal screws (Fig. 8-6) have a wide-spaced external thread. They use the thin metal in which they are driven for the internal thread. Another type of the sheet metal screw is a self-tapping or thread-cutting screw (Fig. 8-7). This screw's hard external thread will make internal threads when it is driven into soft metal.

8.3 Bolts

A bolt is a threaded fastener used with a nut instead of a threaded hole to hold automotive parts

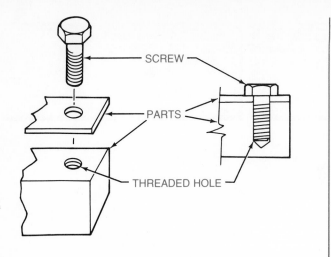

Fig. 8-1   Screw used in a threaded hole.

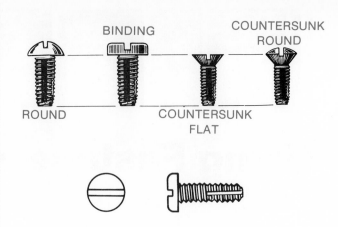

Fig. 8-7   Self-tapping screw.

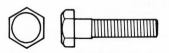

Fig. 8-2   Hex head cap screw.

Fig. 8-3   Slotted-head machine screw.

Fig. 8-4   Phillips head machine screw.

Fig. 8-5   Allen head screw.

Fig. 8-6   Sheet metal screw.

together (Fig. 8-8). Many bolts look like the hex head cap screw shown in Figure 8-2. Bolts made with a square head (Fig. 8-9) are called machine bolts. They are used to assemble parts that do not require strong fasteners or close tolerances.

Two wrenches are normally required to tighten or loosen bolts, one to drive the bolt and one to hold the nut from turning. Sometimes a bolt is used that locks itself in the component so that only one wrench is needed to turn the nut. Just below the head on a carriage bolt (Fig. 8-10) is a square shoulder that prevents the bolt from rotating once it is installed. A nut can be driven on or off the carriage bolt without turning the bolt.

8.4   Studs

A stud is a fastener with threads at both ends. One end of the stud fits into a threaded hole in a part. Another part fits over the stud, and the two parts are clamped together with a nut (Fig. 8-11). Studs are often used where the positioning of a part is important. A stud may have threads that run all along its length, as shown in Figure 8-12. More commonly, the threads are formed only on each end, as shown in Figure 8-11.

8.5   Nuts

Nuts are fasteners with an internal thread that are used with bolts and studs. Most automotive nuts are hexagonal (Fig. 8-13), but nuts used with square-head machine bolts are often square. Nuts may be driven with box-end, open-end, or socket wrenches.

Many automotive parts are subjected to extreme shaking and vibration. Ordinary nuts used on these

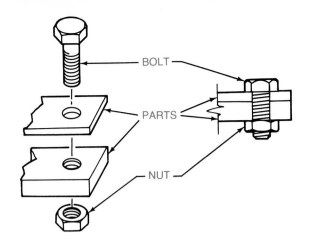

Fig. 8-8   Bolt, used with a nut to clamp two parts together.

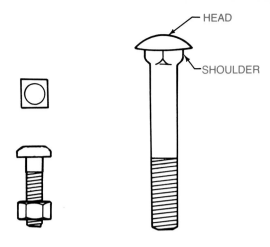

Fig. 8-9   Square-head machine bolt and nut.

Fig. 8-10   Carriage bolt.

parts easily loosen, causing the parts to fail. Where this is a problem, special nuts are used, such as a hex lock nut (Fig. 8-14). This nut has a cone-shaped end that becomes round when installed. It creates a powerful positive locking action against the bolt or stud.

To prevent a nut from working loose, a castellated or slotted nut (Fig. 8-15) and a cotter pin may also be used. After the castellated nut is tightened onto the bolt or stud, a metal cotter pin is inserted through its slots and also through a hole that has been drilled in the stud or bolt. After the cotter pin is installed, it is bent around the nut (Fig. 8-16). The cotter pin prevents the nut from working loose.

8.6   Washers

Washers are fasteners used with bolts, screws, studs, and nuts. A flat washer (Fig. 8-17) is often used between a nut and an automotive component or under the head of a screw or bolt. The washer helps spread out the clamping force over a wider area. It also prevents machined surfaces from being scratched as the bolt head or nut is tightened.

Washers used to prevent fasteners from vibrating or working loose are called lock washers. They are made with a sharp edge that will dig into a fastener or component surface. This prevents the fastener from working loose. Several types of lock washers are shown in Figure 8-18.

8.7   THREAD SIZES AND DESIGNATIONS

Several types of threads are used in threaded fasteners. Since one kind of thread cannot be used

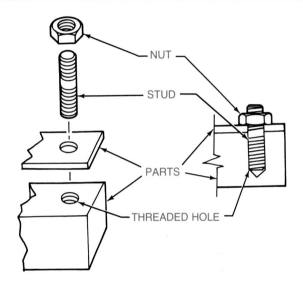

Fig. 8-11   Stud, used with nut to clamp parts together.

Fig. 8-12   Stud with threads along entire length.

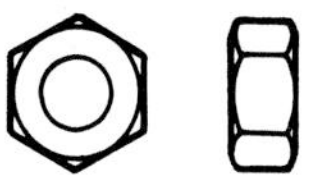

Fig. 8-13   Hex nut. 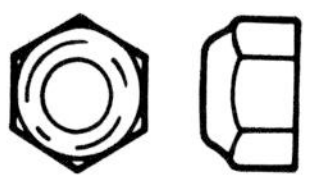   Fig. 8-14   Hex lock nut.

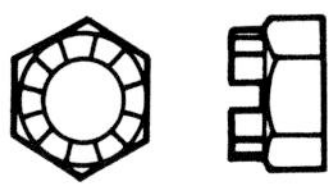

Fig. 8-15   Castellated or slotted nut.

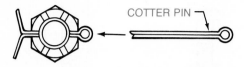

Fig. 8-16   Cotter pin used with castellated nut.

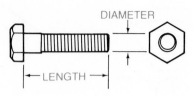

Fig. 8-20   Bolt or nut size.

Fig. 8-17   Flat washer.

SPLIT RING

INTERNAL TOOTH

EXTERNAL TOOTH

Fig. 8-18   Lock washers.

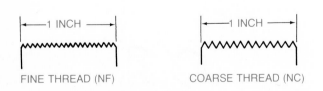

FINE THREAD (NF)   COARSE THREAD (NC)

Fig. 8-19   Unified system threads.

with another, the mechanic must understand the different thread sizes.

8.8   English System Threads

Automobiles manufactured in the United States have, until very recently, used only English system threads. This system, called the Unified System, has two types of threads: coarse and fine. They are designated by NC for national coarse and NF for national fine (Fig. 8-19). The coarse thread has fewer threads per inch than the fine thread and can be easily recognized. Trying to tighten a coarse thread cap screw into a hole with fine threads will damage the threads. Coarse threads are used in aluminum parts because they provide greater holding strength in soft materials. Fine threads are used in many harder materials, such as cast iron and steel.

English threaded fasteners are also designated by size. The many different sizes of bolts, screws, studs, and nuts are given in fractions of an inch. A typical designation is 1/2-20NF. The 1/2 represents a bolt, screw, or stud thread diameter of 1/2 inch. When applied to a nut it refers to the size of the bolt that nut fits (Fig. 8-20). The 20 refers to the number of threads in every inch of length, and the NF represents national fine threads. All 1/2-inch national fine fasteners have the same number of threads (20) per inch. A coarse thread fastener that is 1/2 inch in diameter would be designated 1/2-13NC. In this case there are only 13 threads per inch.

The length of a bolt screw or stud is also given in referring to a bolt: 1/2-13NC×1 inch long. The length of bolts and screws is measured (Fig. 8-20) from the end to the base of the head.

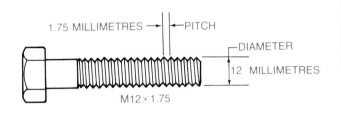

Fig. 8-21 Metric threaded bolt, M12×1.75.

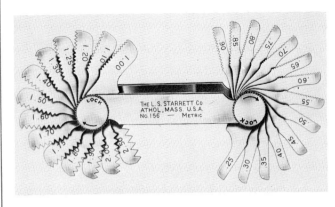

Fig. 8-22 Pitch gauge for metric threads.
(L.S. Starrett Company)

8.9 Metric System Threads

Automobiles manufactured according to the metric system have fasteners with metric threads. Metric and English system fasteners cannot be mixed. A metric nut will not fit on an English bolt. A common metric system fastener might be M12 × 1.75 (Fig. 8-21). The M indicates that the fastener has metric threads. The first number is the outside diameter of the bolt, screw, or stud or the inside diameter of a nut in millimetres. The second number, after the sign ×, is the pitch. The pitch is the distance between each of the threads measured in millimetres.

There are no abbreviations such as NC or NF to identify fine and coarse metric threads. Instead, the pitch number distinguishes between fine and coarse. For example, a fine thread metric bolt may be M8×1.0. A bolt of the same diameter with a coarser thread might be labelled M8×1.25. The larger pitch number indicates wider spacing between threads. The length of metric fasteners is measured the same as in the English system, but the measurements are given in metric units.

8.10 Using a Pitch Gauge

The fact that two different thread systems are in use, each with fine and coarse threads, is a problem for the mechanic. Metric threads cannot be used with English threads. Fine threads cannot be used with coarse threads. But some vehicles have both metric and English threaded fasteners, and all vehicles use both fine and coarse threads. It is sometimes difficult to tell one thread from another.

A thread gauge (Fig. 8-22) helps sort out fasteners. A thread gauge has a number of blades with teeth. The thread size is written on the blade. By matching the teeth on the blade with threads on a fastener, the mechanic can determine thread size. Pitch gauges are made for both metric and English threads.

8.11 Grade Markings

Bolts and screws used for different jobs require different metal strengths. A cap screw used to hold on a fender, for example, need not be as strong as one used to hold on an engine's flywheel.

Grade markings on the heads of bolts show the quality (Fig. 8-23). A Grade 1 bolt has no markings on the head and is not very strong. A bolt with three marks is called a Grade 5 bolt and is much stronger than a Grade 1. The strongest bolt for automotive use has six marks and is called a Grade 8. Metric fasteners use numbers to indicate their strength. The higher the number, the stronger the fastener. Typical metric bolt strength numbers would be 9.8 and 10.9. A mechanic must always use replacement bolts and screws of similar quality. Low-quality bolts or screws used in areas of high stress may fail.

Nuts are not always marked for quality. When marked, English nuts have dots which represent Grade markings. Metric nuts have numbers which represent strength (Fig. 8-23).

8.12 NON-THREADED FASTENERS

Non-threaded fasteners—dowel pins, retaining rings, keys, splines and rivets—are also used to hold automotive parts together.

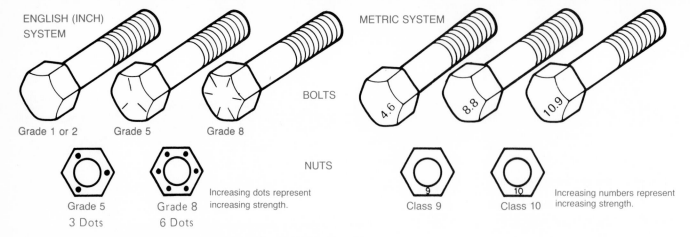

Fig. 8-23 Strength markings for English and metric bolts and nuts.

8.13   Dowel Pins

A dowel pin fits into drilled holes to position two parts that fit together. Dowel pins, sometimes called roll pins, require special pliers or a punch and hammer for removal. Dowel pins may be straight or tapered, solid or split (Fig. 8-24).

8.14   Retaining Rings

Retaining rings, sometimes called snap rings, are often used to hold transmission assemblies together. An internal ring fits in a machined groove inside a hole. The external ring fits in a machined groove on the outside of a shaft. An external ring is expanded with retaining ring pliers for installation. The spring tension from the ring holds it in the groove. An internal ring is compressed with retaining ring pliers to fit it in the groove (Fig. 8-25). Then its spring tension will hold it in position. When several gears are mounted on a shaft, a retaining ring at each end of the shaft holds the gears in place. Examples of different types of retaining rings (Fig. 8-26).

8.15   Keys

A key is a small, hardened piece of metal used with a gear or pulley to lock it to a shaft. Half of the key fits into a keyseat on the shaft; the other half fits into another slot called a keyway on the pulley or gear (Fig. 8-27).

8.16   Splines

Splines are another way to lock gears on a shaft. Splines are external teeth cut on a shaft that match up with internal teeth cut on a gear. The external and internal splines slide or mate together, allowing the shaft to turn the gear (Fig. 8-28). This fastening method is often used in transmission assemblies.

8.17   Rivets

A rivet is a soft metal pin with a head at one end that is used to hold two pieces of metal together. A hole is drilled through the two pieces of metal to be joined together. The rivet is placed in the hole through both pieces of metal. The small end of the rivet is formed into a head with a rivet set or a ball peen hammer. A rivet before and after installation is shown in Figure 8-29. A rivet is taken out by first removing the head with a drill or chisel. It may then be driven out with a punch and chisel.

NEW TERMS

Bolt   A threaded fastener used with a nut to hold automotive parts together.

Dowel pin   A round metal pin that fits into drilled holes to position two mating parts.

Grade markings   Markings on threaded fasteners used to identify their quality and strength.

Key   A small, hardened piece of metal used to lock a gear or pulley to a shaft.

Non-threaded fasteners   Fasteners that hold automotive parts together without the use of threads.

Nut   A small fastener with internal threads used with bolts and screws.

Pitch gauge   A tool used to measure the thread size of a threaded fastener.

Retaining ring   An internal or external ring used to hold automotive components together.

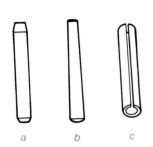

Fig. 8-24 Dowel pins: (a) straight, (b) tapered, and (c) split.

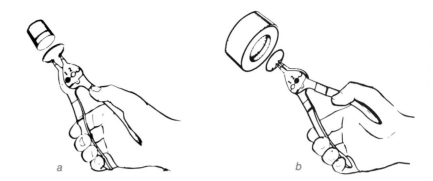

Fig. 8-25 Retaining rings: (a) external and (b) internal.

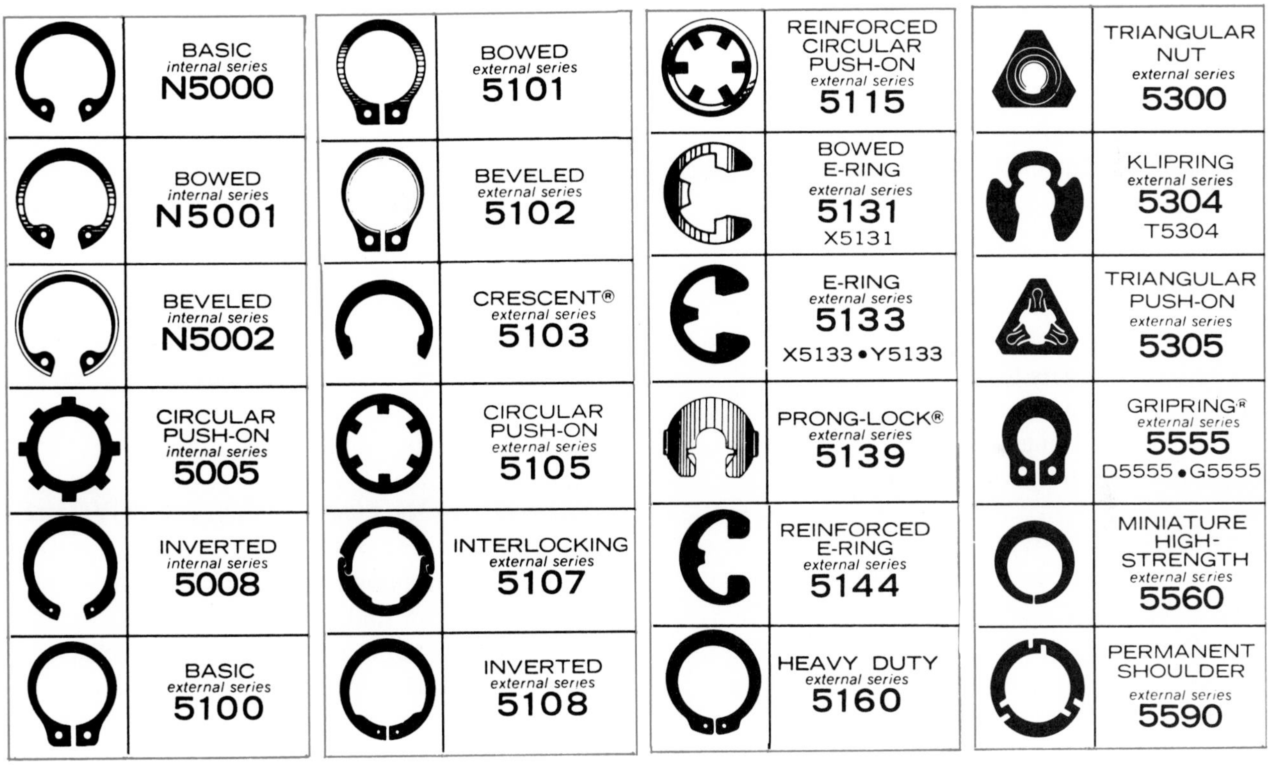

	BASIC *internal series* **N5000**		BOWED *external series* **5101**		REINFORCED CIRCULAR PUSH-ON *external series* **5115**		TRIANGULAR NUT *external series* **5300**
	BOWED *internal series* **N5001**		BEVELED *external series* **5102**		BOWED E-RING *external series* **5131** X5131		KLIPRING *external series* **5304** T5304
	BEVELED *internal series* **N5002**		CRESCENT® *external series* **5103**		E-RING *external series* **5133** X5133 • Y5133		TRIANGULAR PUSH-ON *external series* **5305**
	CIRCULAR PUSH-ON *internal series* **5005**		CIRCULAR PUSH-ON *external series* **5105**		PRONG-LOCK® *external series* **5139**		GRIPRING® *external series* **5555** D5555 • G5555
	INVERTED *internal series* **5008**		INTERLOCKING *external series* **5107**		REINFORCED E-RING *external series* **5144**		MINIATURE HIGH- STRENGTH *external series* **5560**
	BASIC *external series* **5100**		INVERTED *external series* **5108**		HEAVY DUTY *external series* **5160**		PERMANENT SHOULDER *external series* **5590**

Fig. 8-26 Types of retaining rings.

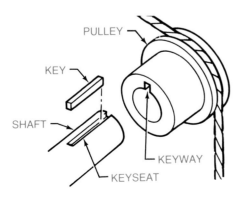

Fig. 8-27 Key used to lock pulley to a shaft.

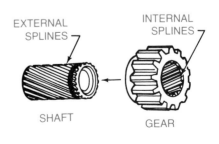

Fig. 8-28 Internal and external splines used to hold a gear on a shaft.

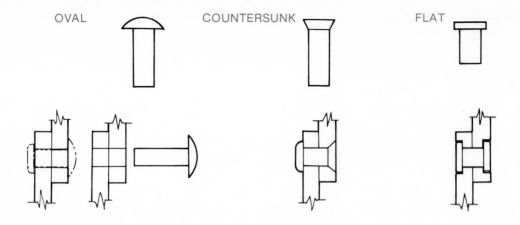

OVAL   COUNTERSUNK   FLAT

Fig. 8-29 Rivet installed in a hole to hold two pieces of metal together.

Rivet A soft metal pin with a head at one end that is used to hold two pieces of metal together.

Screw A threaded fastener that fits into a threaded hole in an automotive component.

Splines Teeth cut into a shaft or gear so that they will fit together.

Stud A fastener with threads at both ends.

Thread designation The system used to indicate the size of the threads on fasteners.

Threaded fasteners Fasteners that use threads to hold automotive parts together.

Washer A fastener used with bolts, screws, studs, and nuts to distribute the clamping force and to prevent fasteners from vibrating loose.

CHAPTER REVIEW

1. Define the term *fastener*.
2. What is a cap screw?
3. Where are sheet metal screws used?
4. Explain the difference between a bolt and a screw.
5. Explain what a stud is and where it is used.
6. Describe two methods used to prevent a nut from working loose.
7. How is a castellated nut and cotter pin used?
8. List the two thread designation systems.
9. Write a thread designation for a bolt with coarse threads that is one inch long and half an inch in diameter.
10. In a thread designated M8 $\times$ 1.0, what does the *M* refer to? The *8*? The *x*? The *1.0*?
11. What is a pitch gauge and how is it used?
12. What is a grade marking on a threaded fastener?
13. What is a dowel pin and how is it used?
14. Describe how splines are used to hold parts together.
15. What is a rivet and how is it used?

DISCUSSION TOPICS AND ACTIVITIES

1. Examine an automobile and list all the different fasteners you can find.
2. Design and build a storage tray for the fasteners you have in your home garage.
3. If you were working on an automobile that has both English and metric fasteners, how would you organize your work to prevent mixing them up? If they became mixed up, how would you sort them out?

CHAPTER 9

Using Service Manuals

CHAPTER PREVIEW

Today's automobiles are made of many parts forming complicated systems that require careful assembly and adjustment. The repair of these automobiles would be impossible without up-to-date service manuals. Service manuals are books that list step-by-step repair procedures and specifications. Specifications, sometimes called ''specs,'' are measurements and dimensions the automobile manufacturer recommends for the various parts. The mechanic must be able to read and understand service manuals. In fact, the service manual may be considered one of the mechanic's most important tools. In this chapter we will present the types and use of the most common service manuals.

OBJECTIVES

After studying this chapter, you should be able to do the following:

1. Locate correct service information for an automobile in an owner's manual.
2. Locate correct repair information for an automobile in a repair manual.
3. Locate correct service information for an automobile in a manufacturer's shop manual.
4. Identify and describe the purpose of service bulletins.
5. Explain the use and purpose of a flat rate manual.

9.1   TYPES OF SERVICE MANUALS

There are several types of service manuals: owner's manuals, repair manuals, manufacturer's shop manuals, service bulletins, and flat rate manuals.

9.2   Owner's Manual

An owner's or operator's manual is a book that comes with any new automobile. This manual usually explains how to operate the automobile's controls and accessories. In addition, many operator's manuals explain the basic services that should be performed periodically.

9.3   Repair Manual

Repair manuals (Fig. 9-1) are published for mechanics and other people who repair automobiles. They give specifications and step-by-step procedures for common repair jobs. Some cover several different years and makes of automobiles. Others give information on one particular model. The writing is technical, meant for people who understand names of automotive parts and have considerable experience in repair. The step-by-step procedures are difficult for someone without very much experience to follow. An owner with only one automobile to service will probably be happier with a manual covering only that model. A mechanic who services many different years, makes, and models will need several repair manuals.

9.4   Manufacturer's Shop Manual

Manufacturer's shop manuals (Fig. 9-2) are written by the automotive manufacturer for the mechanics in their dealerships. A shop manual covers one model of vehicle in great detail, sometimes in a number of volumes. These manuals are the source publishers use when they write repair manuals. Shop

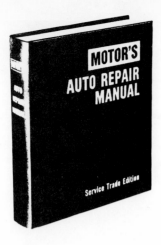

Fig. 9-1 Automotive Service Manual. (Motor's)

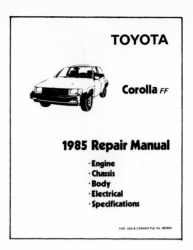

Fig. 9-2 Manufacturer's Shop Manual.

manuals are written for mechanics with a lot of experience. The writing may be difficult for the beginner to understand. The step-by-step repair procedures are even more detailed than those found in a repair manual, and the procedures may involve the use of special factory tools found only in a dealership. Shop manuals are available from the manufacturers for most newer automobiles at a price lower than that of a repair manual. Many shops have a library of shop manuals for the automobiles most commonly serviced.

9.5   Service Bulletins

Automobile repair procedures and specifications change not only each model year, but sometimes during the model year. A manufacturer that makes a service change or discovers a service problem lets dealership mechanics know about it through a service bulletin. The service bulletin is often a one- or two-page description of a particular service procedure. It is meant to be read and then placed in the shop for reference. The bulletins are often sent also to magazines and trade journals that are read by mechanics not in the dealerships. In this way, everyone in the automobile service business can read the bulletins.

9.6   Flat Rate Manuals

A flat rate manual or estimator's guide (Fig. 9-3) lists the cost of parts and labor for specific automotive repairs. A customer is charged for replacement parts and the time it takes a mechanic to perform a repair job. The mechanic or service writer, who must provide a customer with a written estimate before

starting the repair, uses a flat rate manual to estimate the job. It lists all the common repair jobs and shows the cost of parts and hours of labor needed to complete it. Flat rate manuals are revised frequently. A shop must have manuals that are up to date.

9.7   USING SERVICE MANUALS

Using service manuals involves first finding the correct type of manual—owner's, repair, shop, or flat rate—for the job. Once the proper manual is found, the mechanic must be able to locate the section covering the particular repair to be performed.

9.8   Locate the Correct Type of Manual

Most shops have a number of manufacturer's shop manuals, repair manuals, and flat rate manuals. For estimating a job, a flat rate manual or estimating guide will be required. For step-by-step repair procedures or specifications, either a manufacturer's manual or a repair manual will be necessary. The mechanic should prefer the manufacturer's service manual if it is available. This manual is always more complete and usually more accurate than the general repair manuals.

9.9   Locate the Manual that Covers the Automobile

The mechanic who knows what kinds of manuals are available and what kind to use must next find the one which matches up to the automobile. In order to do this, the mechanic must know the model and year of the vehicle being serviced, for example, a 1979 Chevrolet Camaro.

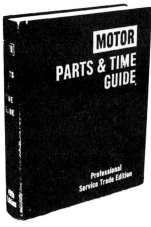

Fig. 9-3 Flat Rate Manual.

A manufacturer's service manual is written for each year and model of vehicle. The mechanic must look through the shops' collection for the manual on the 1979 Chevrolet Camaro. Many manufacturer's shop manuals consist of several volumes or separate books. If this is the case, the mechanic must decide which volume is needed. The mechanic working on brakes or suspension will need the service manual volume on Chassis. If the problem is electrical, the Electrical volume will be necessary.

When a manufacturer's service manual is not available, the mechanic must use a general repair manual. Several kinds are available, most of them similarly organized. One type covers American automobiles, one covers foreign automobiles, and another covers trucks. Most of the manuals range from five to ten model years. The latest year covered is written on the front of the manual.

To find information on the 1979 Chevrolet Camaro, the mechanic could use a general repair manual for American automobiles for the years 1973 to 1979. The automobiles covered are normally in alphabetical order: American Motors, Buick, Cadillac, Chevrolet, and so on. An index on the first page lists the vehicles in alphabetical order and gives a page or section reference. The mechanic looks at the index, finds the correct vehicle list, and then turns to that section or page number in the manual.

9.10 Locate Information About That Automobile

When the manual or section of a manual covering the 1979 Camaro is found, the next step is to find the specific information needed. The first page of

the 1979 Chevrolet service manual includes a section index (Fig. 9-4). The mechanic should look down the list of items in the index to find the right section. If the mechanic is working on an electrical tune-up, he or she will turn to section 6Y, Engine Electrical. For a brake job, the mechanic should look under Section 6, The Brake System.

General repair manuals have an index of service operations for each vehicle model. The index that covers the Camaro, Chevelle, Chevrolet, Chevy II, and Corvette is shown in Figure 9-5. Service operations are listed in alphabetical order from accessories to windshield wiper. A mechanic interested in tune-up information should look in the index to find what pages present this information and then turn to those pages in the manual.

9.11 Using the Information

The mechanic will find two types of information presented in any section: step-by-step repair techniques and specification charts. The step-by-step repair instructions explain, usually with pictures, how to disassemble or take a component apart, how to repair it, and how to reassemble and adjust it. These procedures are usually numbered. The various operations must be done in the correct order to get the job done correctly. Instructions must be read carefully and followed exactly.

Specifications are not normally included in the step-by-step instructions. They are given in charts or tables which a mechanic must know how to read. The chart in Figure 9-6 provides torque or tightening specifications for brake work on the Camaro and other models. The list on the left-hand side of the chart

SECTION INDEX	
SECTION	**NAME**
0	GENERAL INFORMATION AND LUBRICATION
1A	HEATER AND ASTRO-VENTILATION
1B	CORVETTE BODY
2	FRAME
3	FRONT SUSPENSION
4	REAR SUSPENSION AND DRIVELINE
5	BRAKES
6	ENGINE
6K	ENGINE COOLING
6M	FUEL SYSTEM
6T	EMISSION CONTROL SYSTEMS
6Y	ENGINE ELECTRICAL
7	CLUTCH AND TRANSMISSION
8	FUEL TANK AND EXHAUST SYSTEM
9	STEERING
10	WHEELS AND TIRES
11	CHASSIS SHEET METAL
12	ELECTRICAL—BODY AND CHASSIS
13	RADIATOR AND GRILLE
14	BUMPERS
15	ACCESSORIES AND AIR CONDITIONING
	SPECIFICATIONS

Fig. 9-4 Section index in 1979 Chassis Service Manual for Camaro. (Chevrolet Motor Division, GMC)

includes all the brake parts that must be tightened to specifications. The five columns to the right of this list are torque specifications for different vehicle models. The mechanic looks down the list on the left to find the item to be tightened—the caliper housing bolt, for example. To the right, the mechanic looks in the column covering the model, in this case a Camaro. To avoid error, it is best to use a ruler or piece of paper as a guide to read across the chart. Reading across the chart from caliper mounting bolt and down from Camaro the mechanic finds the specification 35 foot-pounds. The caliper mounting bolt should be tightened or torqued to 35 foot-pounds. **NOTE: To avoid error, the mechanic should always write the specification down and not rely on memory.**

A typical specification chart from a general repair manual (Fig. 9-7) lists the year and model of the vehicle in the left-hand column. The 1979 Camaro is further divided according to the type of engine (6 or 8 cylinders), displacement (250, 307, 396), horsepower rating (245, 270, etc.), and transmission (standard or automatic). The mechanic must look down the list at the left to find the vehicle being repaired. The columns at the left give different tune-up specifications. For example, the first two columns specify spark plug type and spark plug gap. The Camaro engine listed as 8-350 uses a type R45TS spark plug with a gap of 0.045.

9.12 Estimating Parts and Labor Costs on Repair Orders

Customers expect accurate estimates of what repairs will cost when they leave their cars in a repair shop. Costs may be estimated in several ways:

CAMARO • CHEVELLE • CHEVROLET CORVETTE • MALIBU MONTE CARLO • NOVA

INDEX OF SERVICE OPERATIONS

PAGE NO.

ACCESSORIES

Air Conditioning 2-25
Automatic Level Controls 2-41
Blower Motor, Replace 1-207
Heater Core, Replace 1-208
Radio, Replace 1-206
Speed Controls, Adjust 1-209

BRAKES

Disc Brake Service 1-108
Master Cylinder, Replace 1-225
Parking Brake, Adjust 1-225
Power Brake Unit, Replace 1-225
Service Brakes, Adjust 1-224

CLUTCH

Clutch Pedal, Adjust 1-218
Clutch, Replace 1-219

COOLING SYSTEM

Variable Speed Fans 2-40
Water Pump, Replace 1-218

ELECTRICAL

Alternator Service 2-64
Blower Motor, Replace 1-207
Clutch Start Switch 1-198
Dash Gauge Service 2-46
Dimmer Switch (Column) 1-199
Distributor, Replace 1-197
Distributor Service:
  Electronic 2-409
  Standard 2-399
Engine Electrical Diagnosis
  w/Diagnostic Connector 1-193
Headlight Aiming 2-45
Horn Sounder 1-199
Ignition Coils and Resistors 2-395
Ignition Lock, Replace 1-197
Ignition Switch, Replace 1-197
Ignition Timing 2-392
Instrument Cluster Removal 1-200
Light Switch, Replace 1-197
Neutral Safety Switch, Replace 1-198
Seat Belt Interlock Systems 2-104
Starter Service 2-53
Starter, Replace 1-197
Starter Switch Service 2-52
Stop Light Switch, Replace 1-198
Turn Signal Switch, Replace 1-199
Windshield Wiper Motor, Replace 1-203

ENGINE

Camshaft, Replace 1-215
Crankshaft Rear Oil Seal 1-216
Cylinder Head, Replace 1-211
Engine Identification 1-171
Engine Mounts, Replace 1-210
Engine, Replace 1-210

PAGE NO.

Main Bearings 1-216
Piston Rings 1-216
Piston and Rod, Assemble 1-216
Pistons 1-216
Push Rods 1-213
Rocker Arm Studs 1-212
Rod Bearings 1-216
Timing Case Cover, Replace 1-213
Timing Chain 1-215
Timing Gears, Replace 1-215
Valves, Adjust 1-212
Valve Arrangement 1-212
Valve Guides 1-213
Valve Lifters 1-213

ENGINE LUBRICATION

Emission Control Systems 2-435
Oil Pan, Replace 1-216
Oil Pump 1-217

FUEL SYSTEM

Carburetor Adjustments and Specs. 2-276
Emission Control Systems 2-435
Fuel Pump Pressure 1-218
Fuel Pump, Replace 1-218

PROPELLER SHAFT & U JOINTS

Propeller Shaft 1-224
Universal Joint Service 2-98

REAR AXLE & SUSPENSION

Axle Shaft, Bearing and Seal 1-223
Coil Springs, Replace 1-226
Control Arms & Bushings, Replace 1-227
Corvette Rear Wheel Alignment 1-225
Leaf Springs & Bushings, Replace 1-226
Rear Axle Description 1-222
Rear Spindle, Corvette 1-224
Shock Absorber, Replace 1-226
Stabilizer Bar, Replace 1-228
Strut Rod, Replace 1-228
Suspension Crossmember & Isolation
  Mount, Replace 1-230
Torque Control Arms & Bushings,
  Replace 1-229

SPECIFICATIONS

Alternator 1-188
Belt Tension Data 1-217
Brakes 1-186
Capacities 1-191
Carburetors 2-276
Cooling System 1-191
Crankshaft and Bearings 1-186
Distributors 1-183
Engine Tightening Torque 1-187
Fuel Pump Pressure 1-218

PAGE NO.

General Engine Specs. 1-175
Ignition Coils and Resistors 2-395
Pistons, Rings and Pins 1-186
Rear Axle 1-185
Starting Motors 1-188
Tune Up 1-177
Valve Lift Specs. 1-213
Valve Timing 1-213
Valves 1-185
Wheel Alignment 1-189

STEERING GEAR

Horn Sounder, Removal 1-199
Ignition Lock, Replace 1-197
Mechanical Gear, Replace 1-233
Power Gear, Replace 1-233
Steering Wheel, Replace 1-199

SUSPENSION, FRONT

Ball Joints, Replace
  Upper 1-232
  Lower 1-233
Ball Joints, Check for Wear 1-231
Coil Spring, Replace 1-233
Lubrication 1-231
Shock Absorber, Replace 1-233
Suspension, Description of 1-231
Toe-In, Adjust 1-231
Wheel Alignment, Adjust 1-231
Wheel Bearings, Adjust 1-231
Wheel Bearings, Replace 1-231

TRANSMISSIONS

Three Speed Manual:
  Replace 1-219
  Repairs 2-141
  Linkage, Adjust 1-220
Four Speed Manual:
  Replace 1-220
  Repairs 2-156
  Linkage, Adjust 1-221
Five Speed Manual 2-192
Automatic Units 2-203
  Linkage, 1978 1-222
Overdrive Service 2-196

TROUBLE SHOOTING 2-1

TUNE UP

Service 2-390
Specifications 1-177

WINDSHIELD WIPER

Wiper Arms, Replace 1-203
Wiper Blades, Replace 1-202
Wiper Linkage, Replace 1-204
Wiper Motor, Replace 1-203
Wiper Switch, Replace 1-204

Fig. 9-5 Index of service operations. (Motor's)

BRAKES

SECTION 5

TORQUE SPECIFICATIONS

	Chevrolet and 125" W.B. Wagons	Chevelle and 116" W.B. Wagons and Monte Carlo	Camaro	Nova	Corvette
Main Cylinder to Dash	24 ft. lbs.	24 ft. lbs.	24 ft. lbs.	24 ft. lbs.	24 ft. lbs.
Main Cylinder to Booster	24 ft. lbs.	24 ft. lbs.	24 ft. lbs.	24 ft. lbs.	24 ft. lbs.
Vacuum Cylinder to Dash	25 ft. lbs.	25 in. lbs.	25 ft. lbs.	25 ft. lbs.	22 ft. lbs.
Push Rod to Clevis		14 in. lbs.	—	14 ft. lbs.	14 ft. lbs.
Primary Brake Pipe Nut	150 in. lbs.	150 in. lbs.	150 in. lbs.	150 in. lbs.	150 in. lbs.
Secondary Brake Pipe Nut	150 in. lbs.	150 in. lbs.	150 in. lbs.	150 in. lbs.	150 in. lbs.
Brake Line to Frame Screw	100 ft. lbs.	100 ft. lbs.	100 in. lbs.	100 in. lbs.	100 in. lbs.
Brake Shoe Anchor Pin	120 ft. lbs.	120 ft. lbs.	120 ft. lbs.	120 ft. lbs.	—
Wheel Cylinder to Backing Plate	50 ft. lbs.	50 ft. lbs.	50 in. lbs.	50 in. lbs.	—
Parking Brake Equalizer	60 in. lbs.	90 in. lbs.	90 in. lbs.	90 in. lbs.	70 in. lbs.
Parking Brake Assembly Attachment	150 in. lbs.	100 in. lbs.	100 in. lbs.	100 in. lbs.	100 in. lbs.
Flex Hose to Wheel Cylinder		22 ft. lbs.	—	22 ft. lbs.	—
Tubing to Flex Hose	120 in. lbs.	120 in. lbs.	120 in. lbs.	120 in. lbs.	120 in. lbs.
Caliper Mounting Bolt	35 ft. lbs.	35 ft. lbs.	35 ft. lbs.	35 ft. lbs.	70 ft. lbs.
Caliper Housing Bolt	—	—	—	—	130 ft. lbs.
Flex Hose to Caliper	22 ft. lbs.	22 ft. lbs.	22 ft. lbs.	22 ft. lbs.	22 ft. lbs.
Support Plate to Steering Knuckle (Upper Bolt)	140 in. lbs.	140 ft. lbs.	140 in. lbs.	140 ft. lbs.	—
Support Plate/Steering Arm to Knuckle Nuts .	—	70 ft. lbs.	—	70 ft. lbs.	—
Shield to Steering Knuckle Nuts (Hold Bolt) . .		70 ft. lbs.	—	70 ft. lbs.	—
Shield to Steering Knuckle Bolt (Hold Nut) . .		95 ft. lbs.	—	95 ft. lbs.	—
Pedal Mounting Pivot Bolt (Nut).	30 ft. lbs.	—	30 ft. lbs.	—	—
Combination Valve Mounting	150 ft. lbs.	100 in. lbs.	150 in. lbs.	150 in. lbs.	—

Fig. 9-6 Service manual specification chart. (Chevrolet Motor Division)

Exc. Chevette, Monza & Vega — CHEVROLET

TUNE UP SPECIFICATIONS

The following specifications are published from the latest information available. This
data should be used only in the absence of a decal affixed in the engine compartment.

★When using a timing light, disconnect vacuum hose or tube at distributor and plug opening in hose or tube so idle speed will not be affected.

●When checking compression, lowest cylinder must be within 80 percent of highest.

▲Before removing wires from distributor cap, determine location of the No. 1 wire in cap, as distributor position may have been altered from that
shown at the end of this chart.

Year	Spark Plug		Distributor		Ignition Timing★			Carb. Adjustments					
	Type	Gap Inch	Point Gap Inch	Dwell Angle Deg.	Firing Order Fig. ▲	Timing BTDC ①	Mark Fig.	Hot Idle Speed ②		Air Fuel Ratio		Idle "CO" %	
								Std. Trans.	Auto. Trans.	Std. Trans.	Auto. Trans.	Std. Trans.	Auto. Trans.
CAMARO													
6-250⑱	R46TS	.035	—	—	H	6°	B	③	—	—	—	—	—
6-250⑲	R46TS	.035	—	—	H	8°⑳	B	—	600	—	—	—	—
8-305	R45TS	.045	—	—	I	8°⑳	B	700	500/650	—	—	—	—
8-350⑱	R45TS	.045	—	—	I	8°	B	700	—	—	—	—	—
8-350⑲	R45TS	.045	—	—	I	8°	B	—	500/650	—	—	—	—

Fig. 9-7 Specification chart from a repair manual. (Motor's)

1. Using a labor-parts guide (flat rate manual).
2. Basing costs on experience.
3. Calling parts houses or repair shops for prices.

Labor-parts guides are published yearly or quarterly so that their prices are up to date. When using a guide, be sure it is the latest edition. The guides are usually arranged by car models and car systems. For example, to find what should be charged to replace a rear brake drum on a 1984 Chevrolet, you should look in the Chevrolet section under *Brakes*. Then look through the brake section until you come to a listing for removal and replacement of a brake drum, and find the line that refers to 1984 Chevrolet, rear brake drum, replace.

Actual labor prices are usually not shown. Instead, the number of hours that the job should take is shown in hours and tenths of an hour. To determine what the total labor charge will be, multiply the shop hourly labor rate by the time shown in the labor guide.

Parts prices may be printed near the hourly labor charge, or may be listed separately. Look up the cost of the parts, and add this to the labor charge. Then add sales taxes to get the total estimate for the customer. Sales taxes are charged against the parts only, or against all or some of the labor. It depends on the law in your state. Many estimators avoid problems with the taxes by simply writing "plus tax" on their estimates. This leaves the actual calculation of the tax up to the cashier, who figures it when the customer pays the bill.

To estimate a job by experience, look at a repair order for the same or a similar car that had the same work done recently. If the shop did a brake drum replacement on a Chevrolet last week, that repair order would show exactly what the job should cost.

Experience can also help avoid losing money on a job. If you know that certain parts are going to be rusty and difficult to remove on a high-mileage car, then the estimate should allow extra time. If a job is known to be extremely difficult, then an estimate can be written on the basis of time and materials, with a maximum figure set very high to avoid losing money on the job.

To estimate a job without a labor-parts guide or experience, you must call a parts house to find out what the parts will cost. You might also call other repair shops and ask what they charge. Your customer can also help, if he will, by revealing other estimates he has received. Some customers are especially helpful if they know you do good work.

NEW TERMS

Flat rate manual   A book that lists the cost of parts and labor for automotive repairs.
Manufacturer's shop manual   A manual published by an automotive manufacturer to help the mechanic make repairs on a certain vehicle.
Owner's manual   A guide to the operation and periodic service of an automobile that comes with a new automobile.
Repair manual   A manual published for mechanics that covers many years and makes of automobiles.
Service bulletins   A description of a repair procedure not covered in a manufacturer's service manual.
Service literature   Books or manuals that provide the mechanic with step-by-step repair procedures and specifications.
Specifications   Measurements and dimensions the automobile manufacturer recommends for various parts (sometimes called specs).

CHAPTER REVIEW

1. List five different types of service literature.
2. Define the term *specifications*.
3. Describe an owner's manual and explain its purpose.
4. Describe a repair manual and explain its purpose.
5. Who publishes the manufacturer's shop manual?
6. What is the difference between a repair manual and a manufacturer's shop manual?
7. Which type of manual usually has the most detailed service information?
8. What is a service bulletin?
9. What type of manual should you use to determine the cost of a repair job?
10. List the steps to follow in locating the correct service information for an automobile in a repair manual.

DISCUSSION TOPICS AND ACTIVITIES

1. Visit a shop, school, or public library and see how many different kinds of automotive service literature you can find.
2. Locate a repair manual and a manufacturer's shop manual for your own or your family's automobile. What is the biggest difference between the two books?
3. Design and write your own owner's manual. Look up specifications, required maintenance procedures, and other useful information for your manual.

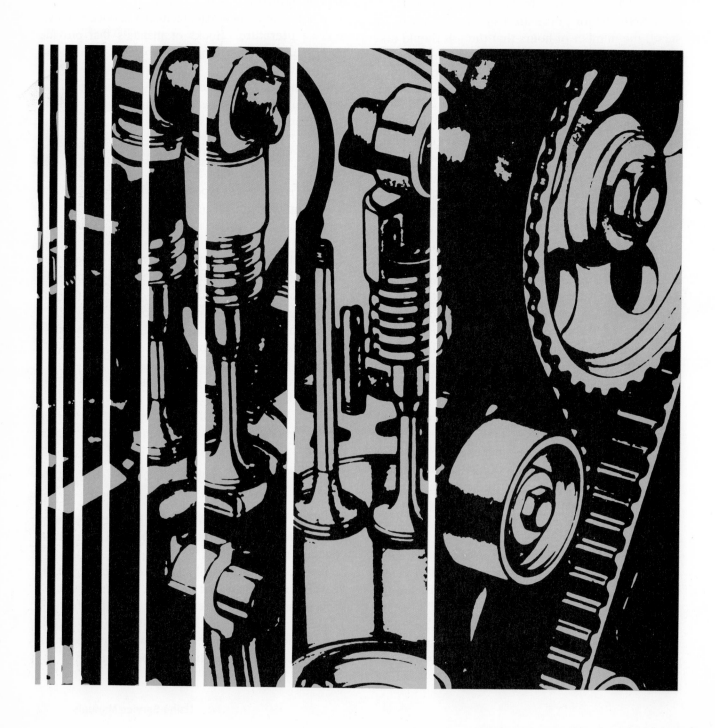

The Automobile Engine

PART 2

Fundamentals of Engine Operation

The engine is the automobile's source of power. It is a complex device with hundreds of moving parts supported by a number of complicated systems. But once some fairly simple fundamental principles are grasped, the operation of the engine can be understood.

The engine used in most automobiles may be called an internal combustion engine, a piston engine, a four-stroke-cycle engine, or a reciprocating engine. We will begin by explaining what these terms mean. At the same time, we will study the operation of the various parts and how they work to develop power.

OBJECTIVES

After studying this chapter, you should be able to do the following:

1. Define the term *engine*.
2. List and describe the operation of the basic components of an engine.
3. List in the proper order the four strokes of the four-stroke-cycle engine.
4. Explain the operation of the four-stroke-cycle engine.
5. List and describe the operation of the major components of the valve train.

10.1   WHAT IS AN ENGINE?

An engine is a machine that converts heat energy to a usable form of power. A fuel, such as gasoline, is mixed with air and burned to produce the heat.

10.2   Internal and External Combustion

The combustion or burning of the air-fuel mixture may take place either outside or inside the engine (Fig. 10-1). The steam engine is an external combustion engine. A mixture of air and fuel is burned to heat water in a container. The resulting steam is piped into the engine and used to develop power. In a steam engine, the fuel can be burned almost anywhere as long as it turns water into steam that can be led to the engine.

In an internal combustion engine, fuel is burned inside the same container where power is developed.

10.3   How the Internal Combustion Engine Works

Let us see how the ignition of fuel inside a closed container acts. We start with a hollow tube with one end closed except for a small hole. A close-fitting plug is inserted up into the open end of the tube so that only a small space is left at the top of the tube. A few drops of gasoline are squirted into this space. Next a stopper, through which a fuse has been threaded, is used to plug the hole in the top of the tube. After waiting a few moments for the gasoline to vaporize, the fuse is lit. The gasoline ignites when the spark reaches it. The resulting heat rapidly expands the air-fuel mixture, forcing the plug downward (Fig. 10-2). An explosive charge in the barrel of a cannon forces out the cannon ball the same way (Fig. 10-3).

10.4   BASIC ENGINE COMPONENTS

The power that forces a metal plug out of a tube is of no use unless it can be controlled. In order to

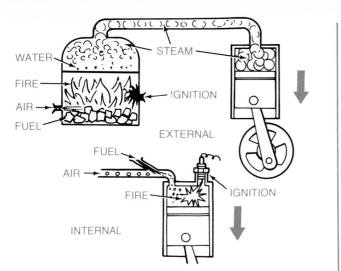

Fig. 10-1 Internal and external combustion.

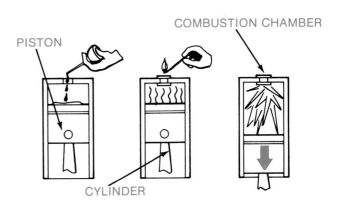

Fig. 10-2 Exploding gasoline forces the plug down.

harness the power of the exploding gasoline, some other engine parts are necessary.

10.5 Cylinder, Piston, and Combustion Chamber

The tube used for burning gasoline in Figure 10-2 is a cylinder closed at one end. In an engine, the plug that fits such a cylinder is called a piston. The space between the top of the cylinder and the top of the piston, where the burning of the air-fuel mixture takes place, is called the combustion chamber.

10.6 Connecting Rod and Crankshaft

To use the power developed by burning gasoline, the piston must be connected to some other parts. For example, a rod may be connected at one end to the bottom of the piston and at the other end to a pin located on the spoke of a wheel (Fig. 10-4).

As the expanding air-fuel mixture forces the piston downward, the rod attached to the pin on the spoke of the wheel forces the wheel to turn. In other words, heat from burning the air-fuel mixture is changed to a downward push. This, in turn, is changed to round-and-round or rotary motion (Fig. 10-5). If a shaft is inserted into the hub of the wheel, its rotary motion can be made to turn a system of wheels or gears (Fig. 10-6).

To produce a continuous rotary motion, the piston must be brought back to its starting point close to the top of the cylinder. After the piston pushes the wheel down, a balanced wheel of sufficient weight will have enough momentum to return the piston to its starting point in position for the next charge of air and fuel.

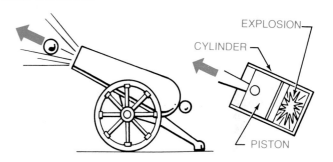

Fig. 10-3 Internal combustion in an engine and a cannon.

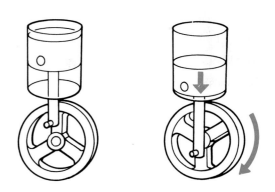

Fig. 10-4 Piston attached to a wheel.

Fig. 10-5 Downward push of piston makes wheel turn.

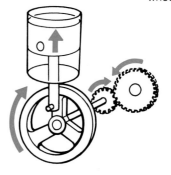

Fig. 10-6 Rotary motion is harnessed with shafts and gears.

Fundamentals of Engine Operation 77

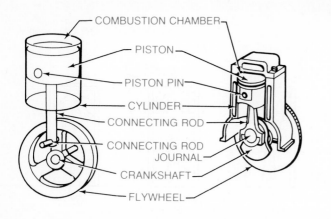

Fig. 10-7 Basic engine parts.

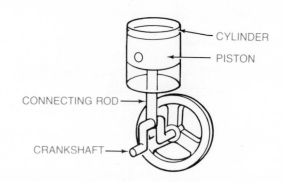

Fig. 10-8 Crankshaft receives power from the piston.

The model of these basic components is compared to an actual engine in Figure 10-7. The engine has been cut away in this view so that inside parts are visible. Note that the connecting rod between piston and the spoke of the wheel is fastened to the piston by means of a pin called a piston pin or wrist pin.

In a working engine the shaft, wheel, and spoke are combined into one part called a crankshaft (Fig. 10-8). The crankshaft's ends are mounted in lubricated bearings so it can revolve. The offset part at the middle, the crankshaft throw, rotates in a circle as the shaft turns. The lower end of the connecting rod is fastened to the crank so that it must follow the same circular path.

10.7   The Flywheel

The heavy balanced wheel which provides the momentum needed to return the piston to the top of the cylinder is called the flywheel (Fig. 10-7). It is attached to the end of the crankshaft.

10.8   THE FOUR-STROKE CYCLE

Most automobile piston engines develop power in a series of events known as the four-stroke cycle, the Otto cycle, or simply the four cycle. A cycle is one complete series of events that is repeated. When the piston moves from the top of the cylinder called top dead center, or TDC, to the bottom of the cylinder called bottom dead center, or BDC, one stroke (Fig. 10-9) has occurred. When the piston moves from the bottom of the cylinder (BDC) to the top (TDC), another stroke has occurred. A series of four strokes is a complete cycle.

10.9   Intake Stroke

Note first that two holes are provided in the top of the cylinder that can be opened or closed. One, the intake ports, lets in air and fuel. The other opening, the exhaust port, provides a passage for the exhaust gases to leave after combustion. The intake stroke begins with both the intake and exhaust ports closed. The piston is at TDC, as far up in the cylinder as the connecting rod will permit it to go.

As the piston moves down for the intake stroke, the intake port is opened, air and fuel are drawn into the cylinder because a strong vacuum is created. When the piston has traveled down to BDC, the crankshaft has turned 180° or one-half revolution. The combustion chamber is now filled with a mixture of air and fuel, and the intake port is closed (Fig. 10-10).

10.10   Compression Stroke

For the compression stroke, the piston travels up to TDC, compressing or squeezing the air-fuel mixture in the combustion chamber (Fig. 10-11). As the air-fuel mixture is compressed into a smaller space, the particles of fuel are pushed closer together, so that when the air-fuel mixture is ignited, it burns very rapidly. The pressure this burning develops depends upon the speed of combustion, providing, of course, there is no leakage. Compression, an important factor in engine power, will be explained in greater detail when we discuss horsepower.

At the end of the compression stroke, the crankshaft has turned another 180°, completing one revolution. The intake and exhaust ports remain closed.

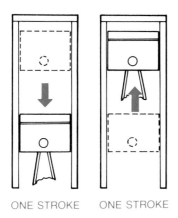

ONE STROKE   ONE STROKE

Fig. 10-9 Each stroke sends the piston from one end of the cylinder to the other.

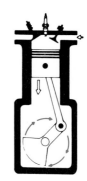

Fig. 10-10 Piston moves down on intake stroke drawing in air and fuel.

10.11   Power Stroke

As the piston reaches the top of the compression stroke, the air-fuel mixture is ignited. The rapid expansion of gases forces the piston downward for the power stroke. When the piston reaches the bottom of the power stroke, the crankshaft has turned another 180°, completing one and one-half revolutions. The intake and exhaust ports remain closed (Fig. 10-12).

10.12   Exhaust Stroke

As the piston starts up for the exhaust stroke, the exhaust port opens, and exhaust gases are forced from the cylinder through the exhaust port. When the piston reaches the top of this stroke, the exhaust port closes. The crankshaft has completed another 180° turn (Fig. 10-13).

Thus, the four-stroke-cycle engine develops power in a sequence of events: intake, compression, power, and exhaust. To complete the four strokes, the crankshaft has made two full revolutions, with power delivered during only one stroke or one-half of a crankshaft revolution. The engine has completed one cycle and is now ready to repeat.

10.13   Power Overlap

Automotive engines usually have four, six, or eight cylinders. The crankshaft is arranged so that, in a four-cylinder engine, no two cylinders perform the same stroke at the same time. One is on intake, another on power, and so on, so that there is always one piston furnishing power to turn the crankshaft. The more cylinders an engine has, the smoother the

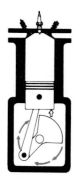

Fig. 10-11 Piston moves up on compression stroke compressing the air and fuel.

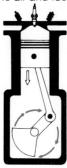

Fig. 10-12 Piston is forced down the cylinder on power stroke.

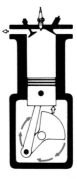

Fig. 10-13 Burned gases are pushed out on exhaust stroke.

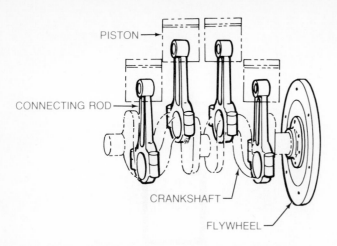

Fig. 10-14 Multiple cylinders and a heavy flywheel smooth things out.

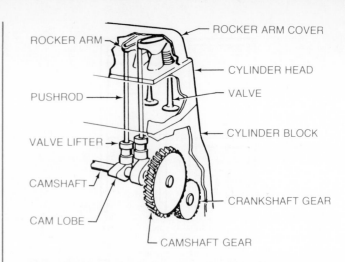

Fig. 10-15 Valve train.

engine will run. Additional cylinders mean additional power strokes so that the crankshaft receives more power impulses. With more than four cylinders there is actually an overlapping of power strokes. This makes the job of the flywheel much easier (Fig. 10-14).

10.14 Reciprocating and Rotary Motion

The piston and connecting rod move up and down in what is called a reciprocating motion. For this reason, the four-stroke-cycle engine is sometimes described as a reciprocating engine. The crankshaft in the engine turns round and round in what is called rotary motion.

10.15 THE VALVE TRAIN

In the four-stroke cycle, air and fuel enter the cylinder, are trapped and burned there, and are expelled as exhaust gases. This requires two passages or ports, which are opened and shut by means of a mechanism above the pistons called the valve train (Fig. 10-15).

The heart of the valve train is the camshaft, driven by the crankshaft. As the camshaft turns, bumps called cam lobes which are attached to the shaft push up valve lifters. Each lifter is attached through a pushrod which runs alongside the cylinder to a rocker arm assembly above the piston. As the valve lifter rises, the rocker arm pushes on the end of a valve and opens it (Fig. 10-15 and 10-16).

Further rotation of the camshaft then allows the lifter and push rod to move down, and the valve spring closes the valve (Fig. 10-17). Both valves

remain closed during the compression and power stroke. As the piston moves up on the exhaust stroke, the exhaust valve is opened to allow the burned gases to escape.

The small crankshaft gear mounted on the front end of the crankshaft drives the large camshaft gear mounted on the camshaft. The valves open and close once every complete cycle, or every two revolutions of the crankshaft because the camshaft gear contains twice as many teeth as the crankshaft sprocket. This causes the camshaft to make one revolution for every two revolutions of the crankshaft.

If the camshaft is properly timed with the crankshaft, the exhaust valve opens when the piston starts up on the exhaust stroke and closes when the piston arrives at the top of this stroke. The intake valve opens when the piston starts down on the intake stroke and closes when the piston reaches the bottom of this stroke. Both intake and exhaust valves remain closed during the compression and power strokes.

NEW TERMS

Combustion chamber Part of the engine in which the burning of air and fuel takes place.

Compression stroke One of the strokes of the four-stroke-cycle engine in which the air-fuel mixture is compressed.

Connecting rod An engine part that connects the piston to the crankshaft.

Crankshaft An offset shaft to which the pistons and connecting rods are attached.

Cylinder A tube in which an engine's piston rides.

Engine A machine that converts heat energy into a usable form of energy.

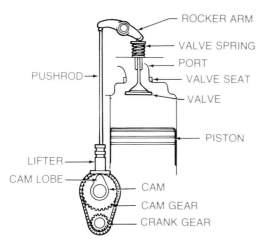

Fig. 10-16 An open valve.

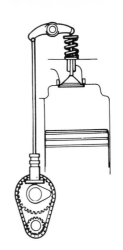

Fig. 10-17 A closed valve.

Exhaust stroke One of the four strokes of a four-stroke-cycle engine during which the exhaust gases are pushed out.

Four-stroke-cycle engine An engine that develops power through four strokes of a piston.

Flywheel A heavy wheel used to smooth out the power strokes.

Intake stroke One of the four strokes of the four-stroke-cycle engine in which air and fuel enter the engine.

Internal combustion engine An engine in which the burning of the fuel takes place inside the engine.

Piston Round metal part attached to the connecting rod which slides up and down in the cylinder.

Power overlap The timing of power strokes of different cylinders in an engine for smooth operation.

Power stroke One of the strokes of the four-stroke-cycle engine in which power is delivered to the crankshaft.

Reciprocating engine An engine in which pistons go up and down.

Reciprocating motion Up-and-down motion.

Rotary motion Round-and-round motion.

Valve train An assembly of engine parts that open and close the passageways for the intake of air and fuel as wel as for the exhaust of burned gases.

CHAPTER REVIEW

1. What is the purpose of the combustion chamber?
2. What is the purpose of the cylinder?
3. What is a piston?
4. What is the purpose of the crankshaft?
5. Why is a flywheel necessary in an engine?
6. Explain what takes place on the intake stroke.
7. Explain what takes place on the compression stroke.
8. Explain what takes place on the power stroke.
9. Explain what takes place on the exhaust stroke.
10. What is the purpose of the valve train?
11. What does the camshaft do?
12. How are the engine's valves opened?

DISCUSSION TOPICS AND ACTIVITIES

1. Examine a shop cutaway engine. Try to name the basic parts. Rotate the engine through each of the four strokes.
2. Sketch a basic engine and label as many parts as you can.
3. Sketch each of the strokes of a four-stroke-cycle engine. Explain what is happening in each stroke.

Types of Automotive Engines

CHAPTER PREVIEW

Automotive engines may be divided into categories in a number of ways. They may be classified according to some mechanical or operational feature, such as cylinder or valve arrangement. They may also be grouped according to their intended use: automotive, marine, truck, or motorcycle. In this chapter we will present a variety of engines and explain how they may be classified.

OBJECTIVES

After studying this chapter, you should be able to do the following:

1. Distinguish between types of engines classified by number and arrangement of cylinders.
2. Describe the valve arrangements used on different types of engines.
3. Understand the difference between the two- and four-stroke-cycle engines.
4. Recognize different types of engines on the basis of combustion chamber shape and ignition type.
5. Identify different types of engines on the basis of cooling system design and the way the engine is used.

11.1 Engines Classified by Number of Cylinders

Engines may have almost any number of cylinders. One-, two-, three-, four-, five-, six-, eight-, twelve-, even sixteen-cylinder automotive engines have been manufactured. Early in automotive history, the four-cylinder engine was popular. As automobiles became larger, more cylinders were required, and six- and eight-cylinder engines became the standard for American manufacturers. The energy shortage of the early 1970s, however, encouraged a return to smaller automobiles and the four-cylinder engine.

11.2 ENGINES CLASSIFIED BY CYLINDER ARRANGEMENT

Engines may be classified by the way their cylinders are arranged. An engine cylinder may be arranged in a line, in a V shape, or opposing each other. These three types of cylinder arrangements are described in the following sections.

11.3 In-line Arrangement

The in-line arrangement (Fig. 11-1) means that the cylinders are placed in a row. They may be placed straight up and down or slanted in order to lower the engine's height (Fig. 11-2). While the in-line arrangement works quite well with four cylinders (Fig. 11-3), it works less well with six and especially with eight. The more cylinders in-line, the longer the engine must be. The long engine requires a long engine compartment, which takes valuable space from the passenger area. A long line of cylinders also makes even distribution of the air-fuel mixture difficult.

11.4 V Arrangement

When the cylinder block is cast in the shape of a V (Figs. 11-4 and 11-5) there are two rows of cylinders. Pistons from both rows or banks are connected

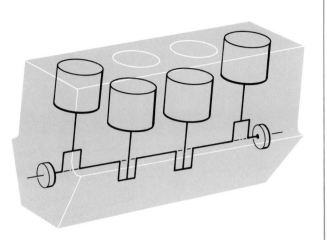

Fig. 11-1 In-line cylinder arrangement.

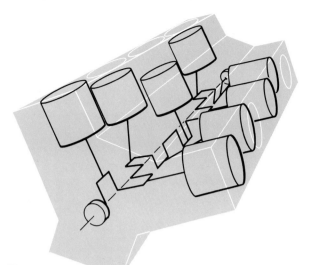

Fig. 11-4 V-cylinder arrangement.

Fig. 11-2 Cutaway view of a slanted six-cylinder in-line engine. (Chrysler Corporation)

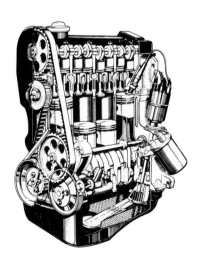

Fig. 11-3 Sectional view of a four-cylinder engine. (Chrysler Corporation)

to one crankshaft in the bottom of the V. Any even number of cylinders is possible in the V design. Motorcycles commonly use a V-2. American automobiles are most often V-8s, but V-12s and V-16s have also been made. The compact automobile boom led to the development of the V-6. The V design offers the advantages of a shorter, more rigid engine and a better distribution of air and fuel.

11.5   Opposed Cylinder Arrangement

When the engine must fit in a small compartment at the rear of the car, an opposed or flat design is often used. Two rows of cylinders are opposite each other on a flat plane. Two rows of pistons are connected to a single crankshaft located between them (Figs. 11-6 and 11-7).

11.6   ENGINES CLASSIFIED BY VALVE ARRANGEMENT

Engines may be classified by the way their valves are arranged. There are two common valve arrangements. One is described as a flathead or L-head. The other is called an overhead or I-head. Both of these types of valve arrangements are described in the following sections.

11.7   L-head

The earliest engines used an L-head valve arrangement. In this arrangement, commonly called a flathead (Fig. 11-8), the whole valve-operating mechanism was located in the cylinder block, so the cylinder head for the engine could be made very flat.

Fig. 11-5 Sectional view of a V-shaped engine. (Chrysler Corporation)

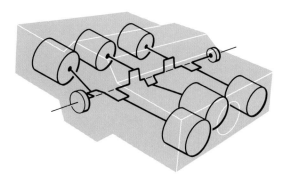

Fig. 11-6   Flat or opposed cylinder arrangement.

Fig. 11-7   Sectional view of opposed cylinder engine.

The intake and exhaust valves were located beside the piston. The camshaft operated a set of valve lifters which pushed directly on the valves to open them. The flathead was a very rugged design, but it suffered from one problem. The valves had to be opened up high for good breathing. This meant that the combustion chamber area above the piston had to be large. For high compression, however, this area should be as small as possible. The flathead design could not permit both good breathing and high compression.

11.8   I-head

The flathead was replaced by the I-head or overhead valve arrangement (Figs. 11-9 and 11-10). In this layout, the valves are located over the piston in the cylinder head. The camshaft and lifters are still placed in the block.

The overhead design requires more parts, but it makes possible a more efficient engine. Compression ratios can be made higher. Equally important, air and fuel are routed into the engine and burned gases are routed out through passageways in the cylinder head. These passageways reach the cylinders more directly than in the flathead, so the engine can breathe better.

11.9   Overhead Camshaft

The overhead camshaft engine (Figs. 11-11 and 11-12) is a type of overhead design. The overhead cam, sometimes abbreviated OHC, eliminates the pushrods and rocker arm assembly by placing the camshaft on top of the cylinder head directly above the valves. The camshaft operates a set of lifters or rocker arms which directly contact the valves. This

design, first used in racing engines, is fast becoming the standard for production automobiles. It eliminates the weight of the pushrods and allows improved breathing because the valves can be placed into the cylinder at a much more flexible angle. A number of engines use two separate camshafts above the pistons. These engines are called double overhead camshaft (DOHC) engines.

11.10   ENGINES CLASSIFIED
BY CYCLING

In the previous chapter, the principles of the four-stroke cycle used in most automotive engines were presented. A few automotive engines and many small engines used in motorcycles and chain saws develop power in two strokes.

The two-cycle engine does in two strokes what is done by the four-cycle engine in four strokes. This means that filling of the crankcase with air-fuel mixture, compression of the mixture in the combustion chamber and ignition must occur on the upward stroke. Exhaust of the burned gases and intake of the fresh air-fuel mixture occur on the upward stroke. Exhaust of the burned gases and intake of the fresh air-fuel mixture occur on the downward stroke. Figure 11-13 shows how this is done through the use of three openings or ports.

The upward stroke of the piston creates a vacuum in the crankcase which pulls in the air-fuel mixture from the carburetor. At the same time, the piston seals off the inlet and exhaust ports and compresses the fuel charge in the combustion chamber. Near the top of the upward stroke, the spark fires

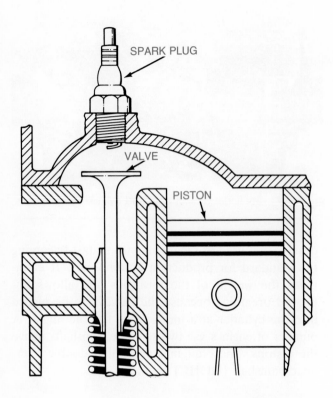

Fig. 11-8 L-head engine with valves alongside pistons.

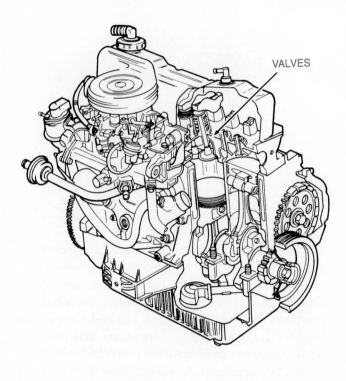

Fig. 11-10 Cutaway view of an in-line four-cylinder engine with overhead valves. (Ford Motor Company)

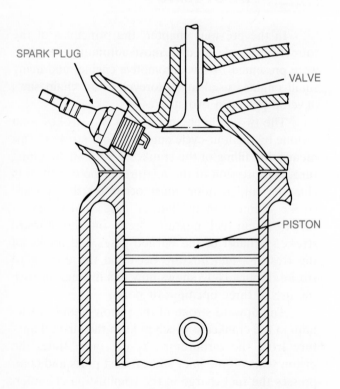

Fig. 11-9 I-head design with valves above pistons.

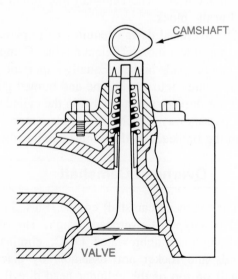

Fig. 11-11 Overhead camshaft engine with cam above valve.

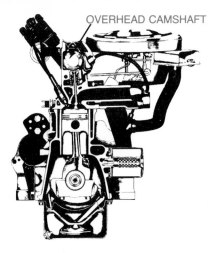

Fig. 11-12 Cross section of engine with overhead camshaft. (Chevrolet Motor Division)

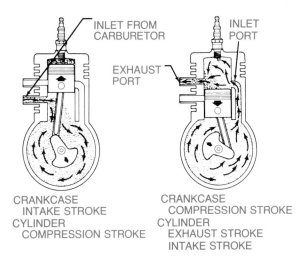

Fig. 11-13 Two-stroke-cycle operation. (McCulloch Corporation)

the fuel charge. Moving down, the piston seals off the entrance to the crankcase from the carburetor and begins to build up pressure in the crankcase. As the piston continues downward, the exhaust port is uncovered and the burned gases are allowed to escape from the combustion chamber. Near the bottom of the downward stroke, the inlet port is uncovered by the piston and the compressed air-fuel mixture in the crankcase rushes into the combustion chamber. To prevent the new fuel charge from escaping through the exhaust port, most small engine manufacturers take advantage of swirl turbulence. That is, they shape the top of the piston to develop a spinning motion in the inflowing air-fuel mixture. This clears the combustion chamber of almost all burned gases while limiting the escape of the fresh air-fuel mixture.

While many small two-cycle gasoline engines use the piston to control the flow of air and fuel, some manufacturers use several other simple devices to control the opening from the carburetor to the crankcase. Among these simple devices are the reed and the rotary valves.

11.11 ENGINES CLASSIFIED BY COMBUSTION CHAMBER SHAPE

Engines may be classified by the shape of their combustion chamber. Overhead valve engines may have either a hemispherical, wedge-shaped combustion chamber, or a precombustion chamber. The hemispherical, wedge-shaped, and precombustion combustion chambers are explained in the following sections.

11.12 Hemispherical

In a hemispherical combustion chamber (Fig. 11-14) the valves are placed on a slant at either side of the chamber. The spark plug is at the center of the chamber. The design of this "hemi" engine allows very efficient burning of the air-fuel mixture at high speeds. It is very popular, therefore, in high-performance engines.

11.13 Wedge and Precombustion

The wedge combustion chamber (Fig. 11-15, left) is designed to provide smooth burning of the air-fuel mixture. The piston squeezes the air-fuel mixture out of the squish area, causing it to swirl, with complete and smooth burning. The wedge is a common design.

The precombustion chamber is common in diesel engines and is also used in some gasoline engines (Fig. 11-15, right). This design uses a second, smaller chamber connected to the main chamber. On a diesel engine power stroke, fuel is injected into the precombustion chamber. Gasoline engines use a second intake valve. Combustion is started in the prechamber and spreads into the main chamber. The fuel spreads over the main chamber by its own energy.

11.14 ENGINES CLASSIFIED BY IGNITION TYPE

Engines may be classified by how the air-fuel mixture is ignited in the combustion chamber. There

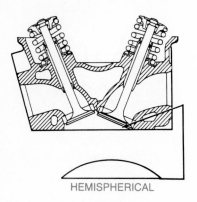

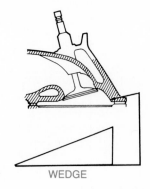

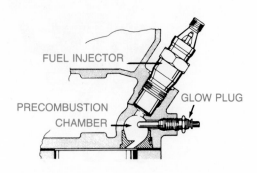

Fig. 11-14 Hemispherical combustion chamber. (Chrysler Corporation)

Fig. 11-15 Wedge and precombustion combustion chambers. (Chrysler Corporation; Volkswagen of America)

are two basic methods of ignition. One method uses an electrical spark; the other uses heat. These engines are described as spark ignition or heat ignition. The two systems are described in the following sections.

11.15 Spark Ignition

Most automotive engines use gasoline as the fuel and ignite the air-fuel mixture in the combustion chamber with an electrical spark at the spark plug. The development and control of this electrical spark is the job of the ignition system.

11.16 Heat Ignition (Diesel Engine)

Another automotive engine used in automobiles as well as in large trucks and heavy equipment, uses the heat of high compression to ignite the air-fuel mixture. This engine is called the diesel after its inventor, Dr. Rudolph Diesel.

Diesel engines can operate on either the two-stroke or the four-stroke cycle. In the two-stroke engine used in heavy equipment (Fig. 11-16), an air pump called a supercharger blows air into the cylinder. Fuel is injected at the top of the compression stroke through a fuel injector and ignites upon contact with the compressed air. The rapid expansion of the burning fuel drives the piston down against the crankshaft for the power stroke. Near the end of the power stroke, the exhaust valve opens to permit exhaust gases to escape. A short time later, the air intake ports are again uncovered and fresh air is forced into the cylinder, pushing out any remaining exhaust gases and filling the cylinder for the next compression stroke.

In a four-stroke-cycle diesel engine (Figs. 11-17 and 11-18), the order of events is the same as in the four-stroke-cycle spark ignition engine.

During the intake stroke, the piston moves down rapidly, causing a vacuum in the cylinder. Air, under atmospheric pressure, rushes into the cylinder through the intake valve to fill the vacuum.

When the piston reaches the bottom of the cylinder, the intake valve closes. As the piston moves upward for the compression stroke, the air is compressed to a much greater extent than in a spark ignition engine. At highest compression, the pressure is so great that the air reaches temperatures of 800 to 1100 degrees Fahrenheit (427 to 594 degrees Celsius).

When the piston reaches the top of the cylinder, the fuel valve opens and fuel oil is sprayed under pressure into the superheated air in the combustion chamber. At this temperature, smaller particles of fuel start burning immediately. This increases pressure and temperature, causing larger and larger particles to burn. Combustion does not happen all at once in a diesel engine. It is spread out in a wave or front. This creates a gradual increase in pressure within the cylinder, driving the piston downward for the power stroke.

When the piston reaches the end of the power stroke, the exhaust valve opens and the piston moves upward for the exhaust stroke, forcing exhaust gases out.

11.17 ENGINES CLASSIFIED BY COOLING SYSTEM

The burning that occurs during the power stroke of an engine develops tremendous heat. A cooling

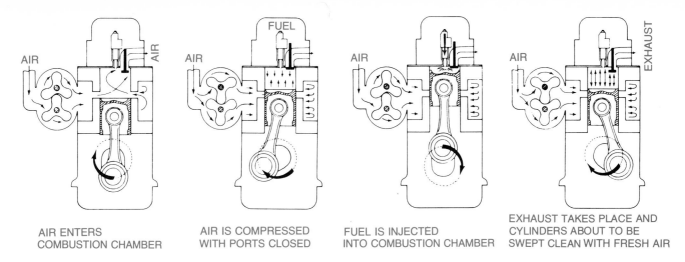

AIR ENTERS
COMBUSTION CHAMBER

AIR IS COMPRESSED
WITH PORTS CLOSED

FUEL IS INJECTED
INTO COMBUSTION CHAMBER

EXHAUST TAKES PLACE AND
CYLINDERS ABOUT TO BE
SWEPT CLEAN WITH FRESH AIR

Fig. 11-16 Two-cycle diesel operation. (Go-Power)

system is required to remove some of this heat and maintain an efficient engine operating temperature.

11.18   Air Cooling

An air cooling system circulates air around hot engine parts to carry off the heat. Cooling fins route the air so that parts that get the hottest, such as the cylinder and cylinder head, will be contacted by the greatest possible amount of cooling air.

11.19   Liquid Cooling

The liquid cooling system uses a liquid, circulated around hot engine parts, to carry off the heat. A liquid-cooled engine is made with coolant passages cast in the block and cylinder head. These passages, called water jackets, surround each cylinder in the block. They are put in the cylinder head very close to the valve area. When the engine is running, some of the heat from the burning air-fuel mixture escapes, passes through the metal of the cylinder head and cylinder wall, and enters the water jackets. The heat is then given off to the liquid coolant circulating through the water jackets.

11.20   ENGINES CLASSIFIED BY USE

Engines may also be classifed according to the type of vehicle they are intended to power: automobile, boat, truck, aircraft, or motorcycle.

11.21   Rotary Engine

In recent years another type of internal combustion engine has been used in automobiles. This

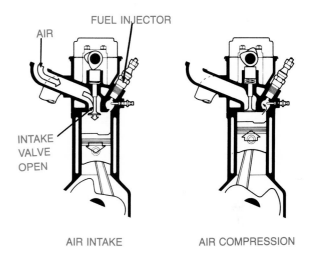

AIR INTAKE

AIR COMPRESSION

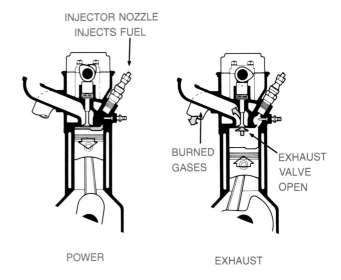

POWER

EXHAUST

Fig. 11-17 Four-cycle diesel operation. (Volkswagen of America)

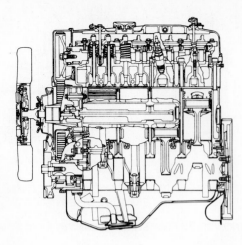

Fig. 11-18   Sectional view of diesel engine. (Chrysler Corporation)

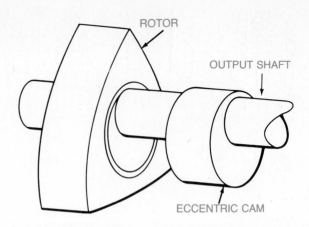

Fig. 11-19   Rotor used to develop power in rotary engine. (Go-Power Systems)

engine is known as the rotary, rotary valve, rotary combustion, or Wankel, after its inventor, Felix Wankel. The rotary engine performs the same job as a four-stroke-cycle engine. Its working parts, however, have a rotary rather than a reciprocating motion.

The rotary engine has no pistons. Instead it uses a rotor with its sides bulged out attached to an eccentric cam on an output shaft (Fig. 11-19). The rotor is placed inside an oval firing chamber with seals on each of its three points so that it can rotate in the chamber. Both ends of the firing chamber are closed and sealed. Two passageways or ports are located in the side of the chamber. One port, connected to a fuel system, allows air and fuel to enter the engine. The other, connected to the vehicle exhaust system, collects burned gases. A spark plug is screwed into the chamber.

As one face of the triangular rotor sweeps past the intake port, a partial vacuum occurs in this part of the firing chamber. Air and fuel are forced through the intake port into the firing chamber. As the rotor continues to turn, the seal crosses the intake port, sealing off the chamber. The rotor continues to turn until the air-fuel mixture is compressed into the smallest volume. The spark occurs at maximum compression. Rapidly expanding gases pushing against the rotor face force the rotor to continue turning in a clockwise direction. Power on the face of the rotor is transmitted over the eccentric to the output shaft. As the apex clears the exhaust port, the exhaust gases are swept out of the chamber. Exhaust is completed as the apex sweeps past the exhaust port. The action on each face of the rotor is shown in Figure 11-20.

The rotary engine requires the same support systems as any internal combustion engine. A fuel system provides air and fuel for combustion. An ignition system ignites the air-fuel mixture after it is compressed in the rotor housing. A lubrication system prevents wear and minimizes friction between moving parts. Finally a cooling system removes the heat caused by combustion to prevent damage.

NEW TERMS

Air cooling   A means of removing excessive heat from engine parts by circulating air around them.
Diesel engine   An engine that uses the heat of compression to burn the air-fuel mixture in the cylinders.
Flat engine   An engine with cylinders arranged on a flat plane.
Hemispherical combustion chamber   A rounded combustion chamber. Engines with this design are often called "hemi" engines.
In-line engine   An engine in which the cylinders are arranged in a straight line.
Liquid-cooled engine   An engine that is cooled by circulating a liquid around the hot parts.
Overhead   A valve arrangement in which the valves are located over the piston in the cylinder head.
Overhead camshaft   An engine design in which the camshaft is positioned on top of the cylinder head.
Precombustion chamber   A small chamber connected to the main combustion chamber used to begin the combustion process.
Spark ignition   The process by which the air-fuel mixture is ignited with an electrical spark.

American Motors Renault 1.7-liter 4-cylinder gasoline fuel-injected engine. One serpentine belt drives the alternator, power steering, and air conditioning. (American Motors Corporation)

Below
Chrysler 2.2-liter turbocharged 4-cylinder gasoline fuel-injected engine. Turbocharging and multi-point fuel injection give a 45-horsepower increase over the non-turbocharged engine. (Chrysler Corporation)

Right
Ford 5.0-liter electronic fuel injection gasoline V-8, showing one bank of cylinders and a cut-away air intake box. (Ford Motor Company)

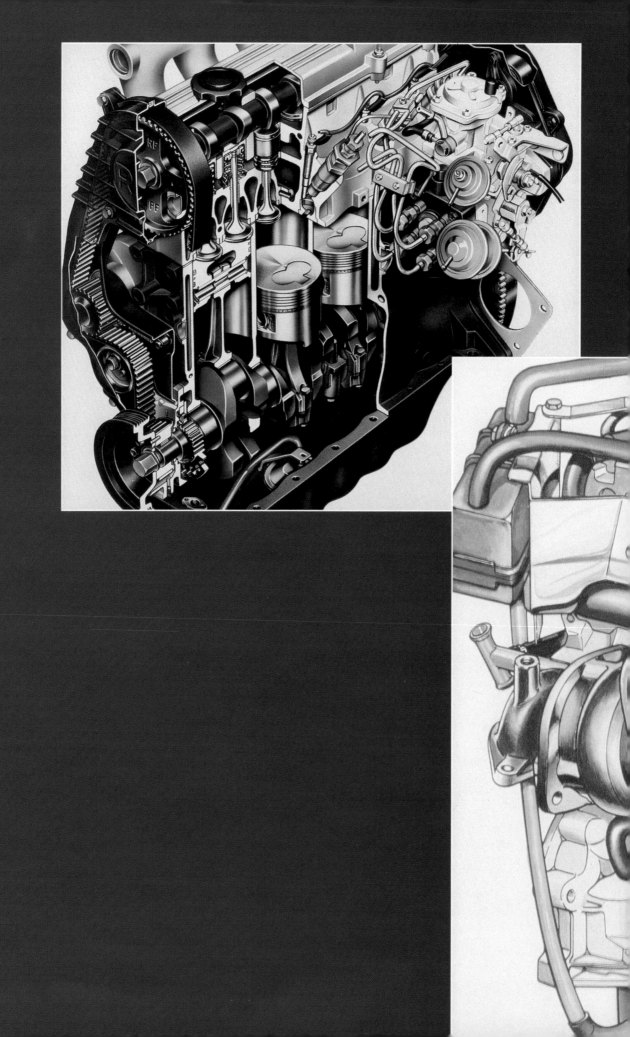

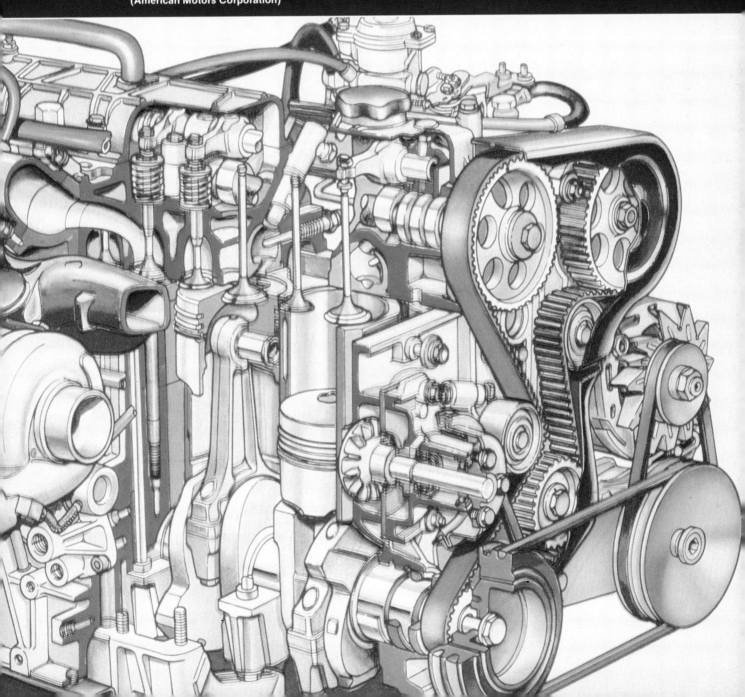

Left
Diesel 2.0-liter 4-cylinder engine used in Ford and Mercury cars. The engine is built by Mazda. (Ford Motor Company)

Below
American Motors 2.1-liter turbocharged diesel 4-cylinder engine.
(American Motors Corporation)

Chrysler LeBaron GTS powered with the turbocharged 2.2-liter gasoline fuel-injected 4-cylinder engine. (Chrysler Corporation)

Chrysler turbocharger at maximum boost pressure. The exhaust gas, shown in red, drives the turbocharger to boost the pressure of the intake fuel mixture, shown in blue. (Chrysler Corporation)

Left
Chevrolet Sprint 3-cylinder gasoline engine. It weighs less than 150 pounds, with an aluminum cylinder head and block. The cylinder liners are cast iron for durability. (Chevrolet Division, General Motors Corporation)

Below
Chevrolet Sprint engine compartment. It is a transverse engine design with front-wheel drive. (Chevrolet Division, General Motors Corporation)

Right
Chevrolet Sprint 3-door hatchback. The car was designed by Suzuki to Chevrolet specifications. It is less than 12 feet long, and has a highway mileage rating of more than 50 miles per gallon. (Chevrolet Division, General Motors Corporation)

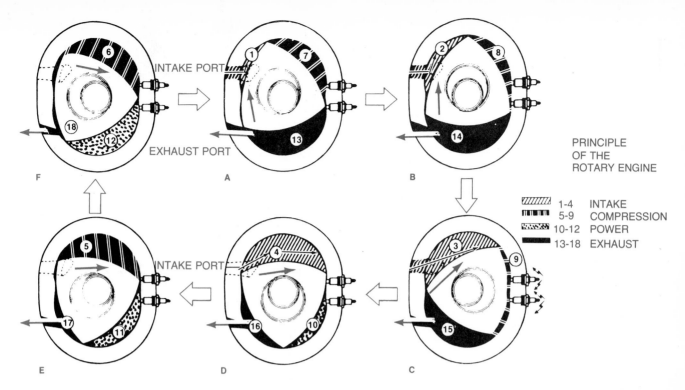

Fig. 11-20 Action on each face of rotor during one revolution. (Mazda Motors of America)

INTAKE PORT

EXHAUST PORT

INTAKE PORT

PRINCIPLE OF THE ROTARY ENGINE

/////	1-4	INTAKE
IIIIIII	5-9	COMPRESSION
:::::	10-12	POWER
■■■■	13-18	EXHAUST

Two-cycle engine An engine that develops power in two piston strokes.

V engine An engine whose cylinders are arranged in the shape of a V.

Wedge combustion chamber A combustion chamber in which the valves are located next to each other and the spark plug is mounted to one side.

CHAPTER REVIEW

1. List the eight ways of classifying engines.
2. List the three cylinder arrangements common to automotive engines.
3. Explain two disadvantages of the in-line cylinder arrangement.
4. List two advantages of the V cylinder arrangement.
5. Describe an opposed engine.
6. Describe a flathead or L-head valve arrangement.
7. Describe an overhead or I-head valve arrangement.

8. List two advantages of the overhead engine over the flathead design.
9. What is an overhead camshaft?
10. Explain how a two-stroke cycle engine works.
11. Which combustion chamber shape is most popular? Why?
12. What is the main difference between a spark ignition and a diesel engine?
13. Describe the operation of a four-stroke diesel engine.
14. What are two ways of cooling an engine?
15. List four nonautomotive uses for engines.

DISCUSSION TOPICS AND ACTIVITIES

1. How would you classify your or your family's automobile engine?
2. How many different types of engines can you identify in your school shop?
3. What do you think is the best type of engine? Why?

Piston Engine Components: Crankcase, Cylinders, Crankshaft and Bearings

CHAPTER PREVIEW

In this and the next several chapters, we will examine in some detail the major parts of an automotive piston engine. Since manufacturers use different designs in the construction of their engines, it will be necessary to present several different types of these engine components.

OBJECTIVES

After studying this chapter, you should be able to do the following:

1. Explain the purpose and identify the different designs of crankcases.
2. Describe the function and identify the different designs of cylinders and blocks.
3. Explain the purpose and identify the different designs of crankshafts.
4. Explain the purpose and requirements of engine bearings.
5. Identify the different types of gaskets and seals used in an engine.

12.1 CRANKCASE

The crankcase (Fig. 12-1), the foundation of a piston engine, houses and supports the crankshaft. Crankcases may be split or one-piece.

The split crankcase, common to air-cooled engines such as the Porsche and Volkswagen (Fig. 12-2), is made in two pieces and bolted together. During service or overhaul, the two halves are taken apart to remove the crankshaft.

The one-piece crankcase (Fig. 12-3) is more common in automotive engines. The crankshaft within a one-piece crankcase is removed and replaced by taking off bearing caps at the bottom of the crankcase housing. The one-piece crankcase is more rigid and much less expensive to make.

Both kinds of crankcase can be manufactured from either cast iron or aluminum. Aluminum is much lighter than cast iron and allows better heat dissipation. This means that engine heat passes more easily through aluminum than cast iron. On the other hand, cast iron is stronger and provides a more solid housing for the crankshaft. Crankcases of small, air-cooled engines are usually made of aluminum. Larger automotive engines generally have crankcases of cast iron.

12.2 CYLINDERS

The piston slides up and down the inside surfaces of the cylinder called the cylinder walls. Cylinders are usually cast iron made to very accurate tolerances. Some cylinders are made from aluminum. The use of aluminum makes the engine lighter and provides good heat dissipation. Aluminum, however, is very soft and tends to wear rapidly.

There are three ways to prevent rapid wear of aluminum cylinder walls. One is to put a cast iron liner, called a dry sleeve, into the aluminum cylinder. The liner, which looks like a thin piece of pipe, then becomes the surface on which the piston slides. These liners, installed when the cylinder is made, are not usually replaceable. A thin layer of chrome plate may also be applied to the aluminum cylinder. Chrome plating provides a very hard, long-wearing surface for the piston to ride on.

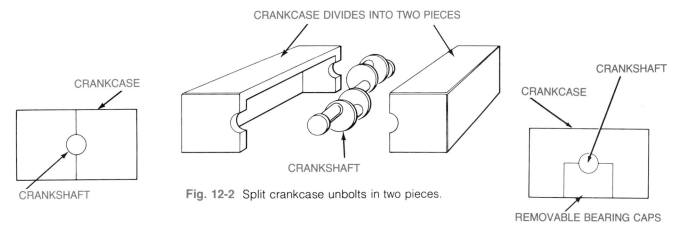

CRANKCASE DIVIDES INTO TWO PIECES

CRANKCASE

CRANKSHAFT

Fig. 12-2 Split crankcase unbolts in two pieces.

CRANKCASE

CRANKSHAFT

Fig. 12-1 Crankcase houses and supports crankshaft.

CRANKSHAFT

CRANKCASE

REMOVABLE BEARING CAPS

Fig. 12-3 One-piece crankcase.

A special type of aluminum has been used which contains a large number of silicon particles. After the cylinders are cast and machined, they are treated with a chemical that removes a thin layer of aluminum but leaves the silicon particles exposed. The pistons then ride on a layer of very slippery silicon.

The bolt-on cylinder (Fig. 12-4) is bolted to the crankcase. Another advantage of the bolt-on cylinder is easy replacement. If a cylinder is damaged it may be replaced with a new one.

Bolt-on cylinders are used on many air-cooled automotive and motorcycle engines where the circulation of air around the entire cylinder is important.

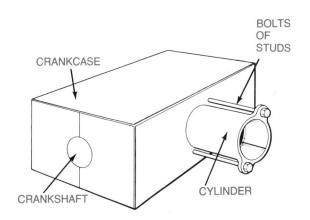

BOLTS OF STUDS

CRANKCASE

CRANKSHAFT

CYLINDER

Fig. 12-4 Bolt-on cylinder.

12.3   CYLINDER BLOCK

Most automotive engines combine the cylinders and crankcase in one large metal casting called a cylinder block. All other engine components either fit inside the block or are fastened to the outside of the block.

12.4   Making the Cylinder Block

The cylinder block is made by pouring molten metal, either cast iron or aluminum, into a sand mold. The block must have many holes and passages for oil and coolant circulation. Therefore, the mold has a complex inner core box (Fig. 12-5) around which the molten metal is poured. When the molten metal cools, it becomes solid. When the mold and inner core box are removed, a rough block has been cast. Vents and supports used in casting leave holes (Figs. 12-6 and 12-7) in the sides and top or deck of the block. The

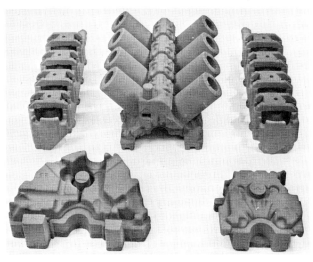

Fig. 12-5 Casting cores used in cylinder block mold.
(General Motors Corporation)

Piston Engine Components   93

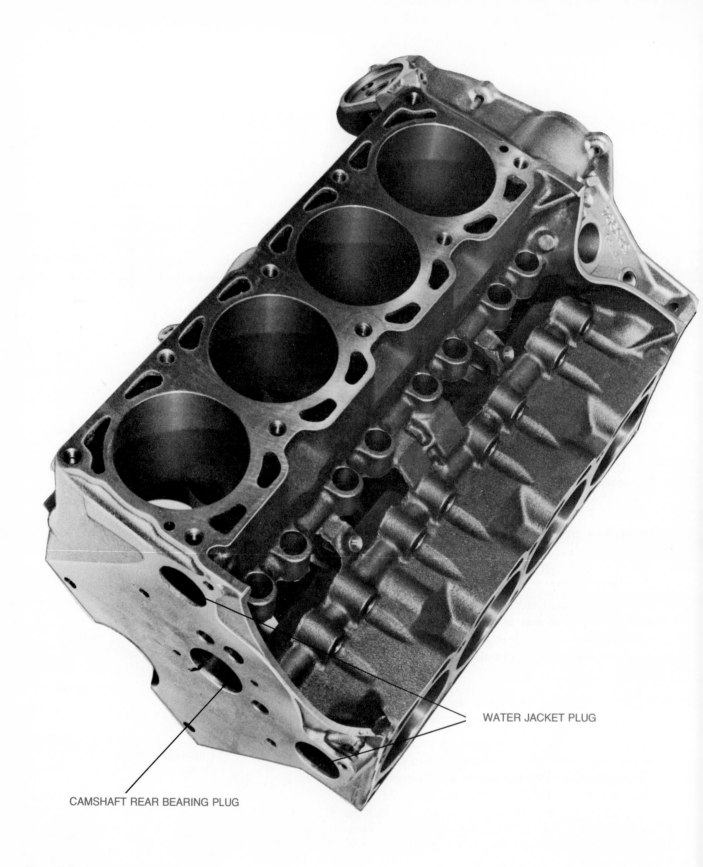

WATER JACKET PLUG

CAMSHAFT REAR BEARING PLUG

Fig. 12-6 Top view of V-8 cylinder block.
(Pontiac Motor Division, GMC)

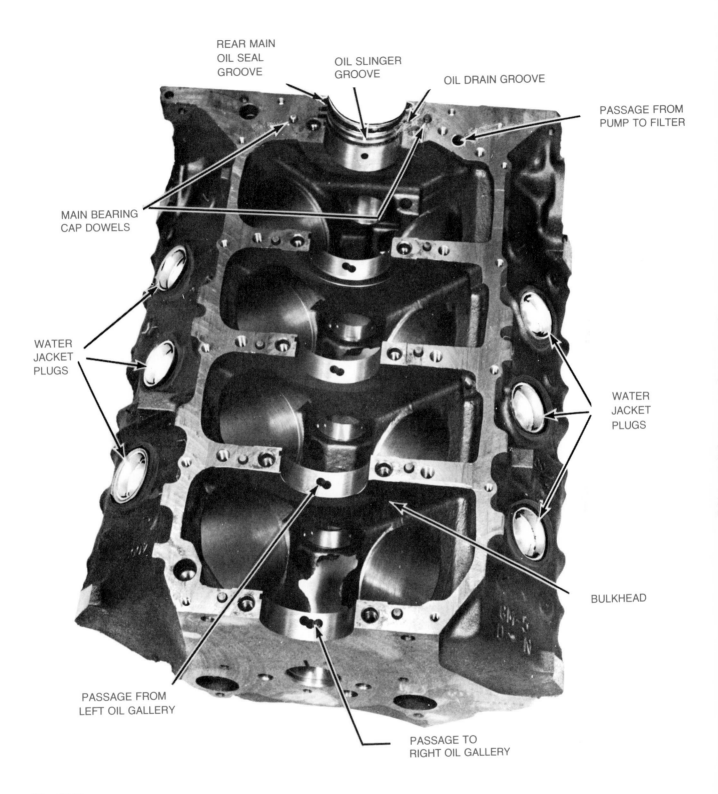

REAR MAIN
OIL SEAL
GROOVE

OIL SLINGER
GROOVE

OIL DRAIN GROOVE

PASSAGE FROM
PUMP TO FILTER

MAIN BEARING
CAP DOWELS

WATER
JACKET
PLUGS

WATER
JACKET
PLUGS

BULKHEAD

PASSAGE FROM
LEFT OIL GALLERY

PASSAGE TO
RIGHT OIL GALLERY

Fig. 12-7 Bottom view of V-8 cylinder block.
(Pontiac Motor Division, GMC)

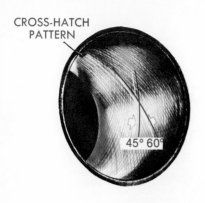

CROSS-HATCH PATTERN

45° 60°

Fig. 12-8 Cross-hatch pattern on cylinder walls.
(Chrysler Corporation)

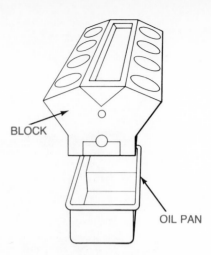

BLOCK

OIL PAN

Fig. 12-11 Oil pan attached to bottom of block.
(Ford Motor Company)

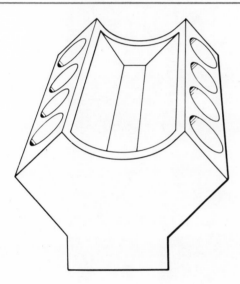

Fig. 12-9 V-shaped block.

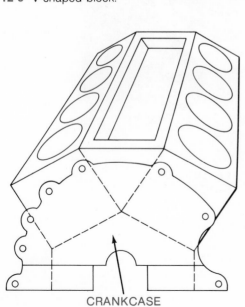

CRANKCASE

Fig. 12-10 Y-shaped block. (Ford Motor Company)

holes in the deck are closed when the cylinder heads and gaskets are mounted to the engine. The holes in the sides are closed by putting in soft metal plugs called soft plugs, water jacket plugs, or freeze plugs.

After casting, the cylinder block is thoroughly cleaned. It is then put on a machine line where the cylinders are bored and polished to very close tolerances with automatic hones. The honing leaves a cross-hatch pattern on the metal of the cylinder wall (Fig. 12-8) which helps hold lubricant for good piston ring lubrication. Surfaces where parts are to be attached are milled, and bolt or stud holes are drilled and tapped. All along the line the block is checked and inspected for any defects.

12.5 Cylinder Block Designs

The shape of the cylinder block is determined by the number and arrangement of cylinders. Cylinders are cast in a single row for an in-line block. They are normally separated from each other to allow coolant passages around each cylinder.

The cylinders are cast in two rows for a V block. The angle between the two rows is determined by the angle used in the crankshaft design (see section 12.4 following). The angle between the two rows is 90 degrees on a V-8 engine and 60 or 120 degrees on a V-6 or V-12.

There are two lower block designs for V engines. In the V design (Fig. 12-9), the cylinders and crankcase form a letter V. The Y-shaped block has more strength and rigidity. The wide flareout of the block at the rear (arrow 1 in Fig. 12-10) gives a strong attachment area for the clutch housing or bell housing, transmission, and drive line. The deep middle section and skirts of the block (arrow 2 in Fig. 12-10) extend

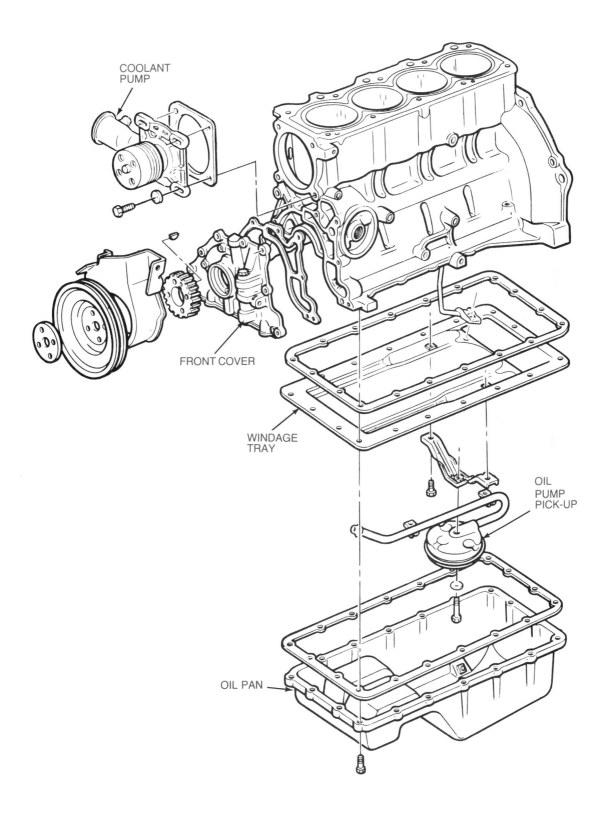

COOLANT PUMP

FRONT COVER

WINDAGE TRAY

OIL PUMP PICK-UP

OIL PAN

Fig. 12-12 Parts attached to cylinder block.

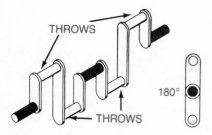

Fig. 12-13 Four-cylinder in-line crankshaft with throws spaced 180° apart.

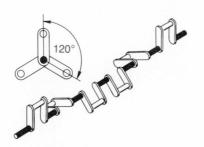

Fig. 12-14 Six-cylinder in-line crankshaft with throws spaced 120° apart.

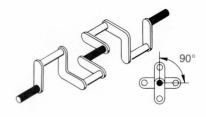

Fig. 12-15 V-8 crankshaft with throws spaced 90° apart.

well below the centerline, giving support for the crankshaft bearings nearly all the way around.

12.6 Attachments to the Cylinder Block

The oil pan (Fig. 12-11) is a stamped piece of metal bolted to the bottom of the crankcase. It houses the oil pump and acts as a reservoir for the oil and as a seal for the bottom of the cylinders. The cylinder heads are bolted to the top of the cylinder block. Figure 12-12 illustrates the relation of block and cylinder head along with other engine parts that are attached to the block.

12.7 CRANKSHAFT

The crankshaft converts the up-and-down motion of the piston to rotary motion. It also turns such accessories as the valve train, oil pump, fuel pump, water pump, alternator, distributor, and fan.

12.8 Crankshaft Manufacture

Crankshafts are manufactured in three different ways. In forging, a red-hot piece of steel is hammered into the shape of a crankshaft between two forging dies. In casting from steel alloys, molten metal is poured into a mold shaped like a crankshaft. A third manufacturing process is often used for racing engines. A round piece of high-quality steel called a billit is mounted in some machining equipment, and the crankshaft is shaped by removing metal from the billit.

12.9 Crankshaft Parts

The crankshaft in the four-cylinder in-line engine (Fig. 12-13) has four offsets, called throws. These throws, to which the connecting rods are attached, are placed directly in line with the cylinders. The throws are normally spaced 180 degrees apart. This allows a different stroke of the four-stroke cycle to occur in each cylinder at any given time. There is always one piston delivering power, one exhausting gases, one drawing in air-fuel mixture, and one compressing the air-fuel mixture.

A crankshaft for a six-cylinder in-line engine has six crank throws placed directly in line with the cylinders. As in any engine with more than four cylinders, there is some overlapping of strokes for smoother operation. The crank throws on a six-cylinder engine are spaced 120 degrees apart (Fig. 12-14).

V-8 engines have two connecting rods attached to each crank throw. The crankshaft for a V-8, therefore, has four crank throws, one for each two cylinders. The throws of a V-8 crankshaft may be arranged 180 degrees apart, as in the four-cylinder in-line engine. Most V-8 engines, however, have throws arranged 90 degrees apart (Fig. 12-15).

On every crankshaft, each of the throws has a precision ground surface called a journal where the connecting rod or rods are mounted. Crankshafts also have journals which rotate in main bearings located in the crankcase section of the block. The crankshaft in Figure 12-16 has three main bearing journals. Most V-8 crankshafts have five. In-line crankshafts may have as many as seven main bearing journals. The more main bearings the crankshaft has for support, the better.

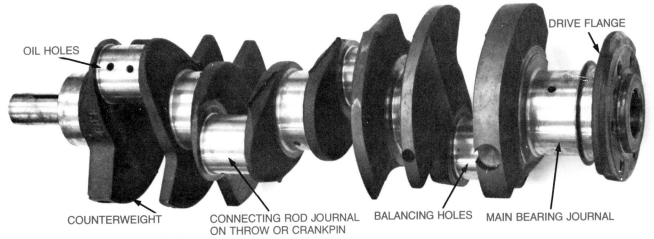

OIL HOLES

DRIVE FLANGE

COUNTERWEIGHT

CONNECTING ROD JOURNAL
ON THROW OR CRANKPIN

BALANCING HOLES

MAIN BEARING JOURNAL

Fig. 12-16 Parts of a crankshaft.

The throws of the crankshaft, with their connecting rods and piston assemblies, are very heavy. The rapid rotation of the crankshaft increases the force which this weight exerts to bend or twist the crankshaft out of shape. Heavy counterweights are attached to the crankshaft opposite the throws to balance the weight of the piston and connecting rod assembly when the crankshaft is rotating. In most engines, these weights are cast as one piece with the crankshaft. Racing engines have weights that are attached by fasteners so that they may be changed for different conditions. These are often called counterweighted crankshafts.

A crankshaft must be balanced so that it will rotate at high speeds without vibrating. After balance is measured with electronic equipment, adjustments are made by drilling in the counterweights (Fig. 12-16).

A sprocket or gear is attached to the front end of the crankshaft to drive the valve train. A drive flange is attached to connect a flywheel at the rear, where power passes to the drive train.

The complete crankshaft assembly in Figure 12-17 shows a damper and pulley arrangement mounted to the front of the crankshaft. The pulley is used to drive several V-belts that turn the engine's accessories. The damper or harmonic balancer has a heavy ring that absorbs the twisting and untwisting forces that power strokes exert on the crankshaft. The ring in the damper acts like a flywheel to hold the crankshaft at a constant speed.

12.10   BEARINGS

At the points where moving parts meet or touch, there is certain resistance, called friction. A good lubricant is needed in these areas to reduce friction, which causes heat and wear. The wear due to friction may also be reduced by making moving parts that touch or slide against each other out of different materials. Copper, tin, or lead against cast iron or steel causes less friction than steel against steel or cast iron against cast iron.

Bushings and bearings used at all major points in an engine to reduce friction (Fig. 12-18) are therefore made of material different from that of the parts they support. Bushings are used at the piston end of the connecting rod, at the oil pump, the distributor shaft, and the rocker arms. Sleeve bearings are used at the crankshaft main and connecting rod journals, at the timing gears, and to support the camshaft.

Usually, the word bushing means a full round sleeve that is small in size, pressed into place in a hole and possibly machined on the inside diameter to "fit" a shaft. The insert type bearing, on the other hand, is usually made of two halves to fit over a shaft with a cap as a part of the housing assembly. The terms bearing and bushing actually overlap each other.

12.11   Roller or Ball Bearings

Some engines use ball or roller bearings usually at the front and rear crankshaft main bearing positions. These are mainly small engines used for motorcycles. Some automotive racing engines also use roller bearings to support the crankshaft.

12.12   Connecting Rod Bearings

Two-piece insert bearings are fitted onto the big end of the connecting rods at the connecting rod

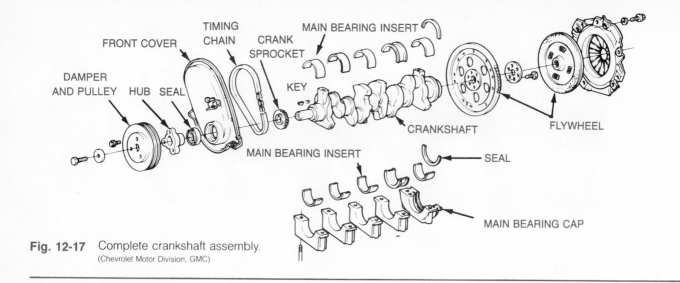

Fig. 12-17 Complete crankshaft assembly.
(Chevrolet Motor Division, GMC)

journals. Piston pin bushings are used at the small end of the connecting rods.

12.13 Main Bearings

Insert bearings used to hold the main bearing journals are called the main bearings. They are made in halves to permit them to be assembled into main bearing housings.

The crankshaft illustrated in Figure 12-17 also shows the main bearing caps and main bearing inserts. The main bearings support the crankshaft and allow it to rotate. The main bearing caps are bolted to the cylinder block (Fig. 12-20). On most designs, two large bolts fasten each cap. On high-performance engines, each cap may be retained with four bolts.

The main bearing inserts may be held in the main bearing cap in several different ways, as shown in Figure 12-21. Most bearings have what is called "spread." This means they are slightly larger than the cap or housing in which they fit and will therefore snap into place. Other bearings have a locking lip that fits into a slot in the housing. Still others are held with a dowel pin in the housing that fits into a dowel hole in the bearing.

12.14 Bearing Oil Clearance

All bearings must have oil clearance. Figure 12-22 shows a shaft supported in a housing with a bearing. The small space between the bearing and the shaft, only 0.002 to 0.003 inch (0.05 to 0.08 mm) allows oil clearance. When oil is pumped into the oil clearance area of a bearing (Fig. 12-23), the combination of the oil pressure and the rotation of the shaft

wedges a film of oil between the shaft and bearing. The shaft is lifted slightly so that it does not rest on the bearing but on an oil film. When the oil wedge is formed, there is no metal-to-metal contact.

Oil grooves (Fig. 12-24) are sometimes provided in the bearing to assist in the spreading of the oil over the entire shaft surface. Oil grooving may also allow the flow of oil to other engine bearings.

Cooling of the bearing also takes place as a result of this lubrication. The circulation of oil through the oil clearance space absorbs some of the heat of friction before it leaves the assembly. The remainder of the heat is absorbed by the parts themselves.

The oil clearance in a bearing serves one more important purpose. It allows a controlled volume of oil throwoff caused by the spinning action of the shaft. This oil thrown out of the bearing lubricates other moving parts in the engine. If the bearings have too little oil clearance, parts that depend upon this throwoff do not get enough lubrication. If the bearings have too much oil clearance, either because they were fitted that way or because of wear, too much oil is thrown off. This excessive oil is thrown by the rotating crankshaft and connecting rods over the inside of the crankcase and onto the cylinder walls. It may then seep past the pistons and piston rings into the combustion chambers and be burned.

12.15 Bearing Construction

The job of any engine bearing is to permit free and silent movement of the engine component it supports while resisting wear.

An insert bearing used on a connecting rod or main journal is made up of two pieces. Each piece has

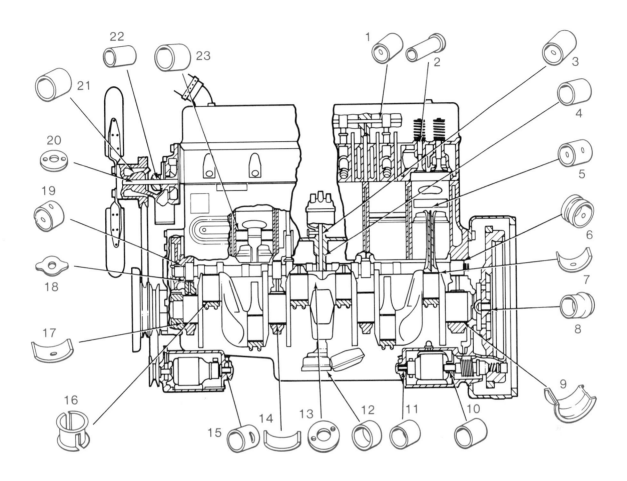

1 ROCKER-ARM BUSHING
2 VALVE-GUIDE BUSHING
3 DISTRIBUTOR BUSHING, UPPER
4 DISTRIBUTOR BUSHING, LOWER
5 PISTON-PIN BUSHING
6 CAMSHAFT BUSHING
7 CONNECTING-ROD BEARING
8 CLUTCH PILOT BUSHING
9 FLANGED MAIN BEARING
10 STARTING-MOTOR BUSHING, DRIVE END
11 STARTING-MOTOR BUSHING, COMMUTATOR END
12 OIL-PUMP BUSHING
13 DISTRIBUTOR THRUST PLATE
14 INTERMEDIATE MAIN BEARING
15 ALTERNATOR BUSHING
16 CONNECTING-ROD BEARING, FLOATING TYPE
17 FRONT MAIN BEARING
18 CAMSHAFT THRUST PLATE
19 CAMSHAFT BUSHING
20 FAN THRUST PLATE
21 WATER-PUMP BUSHING, FRONT
22 WATER-PUMP BUSHING, REAR
23 PISTON-PIN BUSHING

Fig. 12-18 Bearings and bushings used in a typical engine. (Johnson Bronze Company)

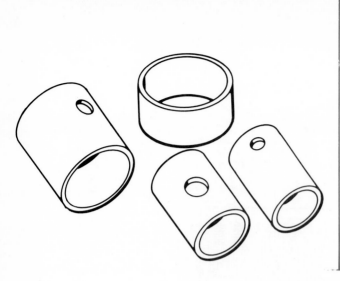

BUSHING

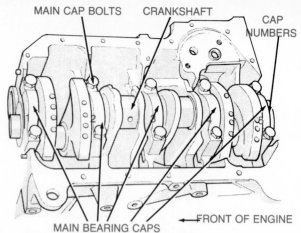

Fig. 12-20 Bottom view of four-cylinder engine showing main bearing caps. (Chrysler Corporation)

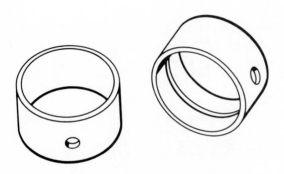

FULL ROUND SLEEVE TYPE BEARING

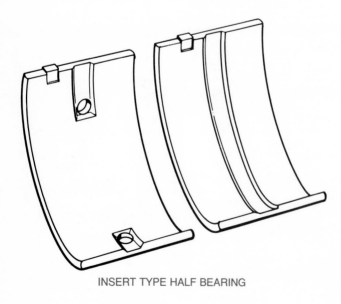

INSERT TYPE HALF BEARING

Fig. 12-19 Types of bearings. (Federal-Mogul Service)

a steel (or sometimes bronze) backing. One of any number of alloys, called bearing alloys, is molded to the backing (Fig. 12-25). The special alloy is called the bearing lining material.

No one bearing material will do every job better than any other material. The bearing engineer selects the bearing that will be best for certain applications and conditions. Many bearing materials—tin, lead, copper, cadium, aluminum, and silver—are used in various combinations or alloys.

Bearing lining material must have compatibility, fatigue strength, conformability, and embedability.

12.16 Compatibility

The first requirement for any bearing material or alloy is the ability to "get along" with a rotating shaft. Compatibility, then, is the ability of one material to slide against another under a given set of conditions.

Bronzes, for example, can be used to support a steel rotating shaft with a suitable lubricant. Steel, however, is not capable of supporting a rotating steel shaft even with a suitable lubricant. Most dissimilar materials are compatible; similar materials are not.

12.17 Fatigue Strength

Another requirement for a bearing material is its ability to turn (or allow the shaft to turn) while the bearing is under heavy pressure from the explosions against the piston which are sent along by the connecting rod. Bearing materials have different abilities to withstand these pressures without breaking down.

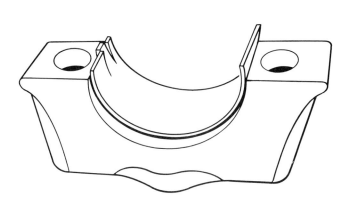

Spread allows a bearing to "snap" into place.

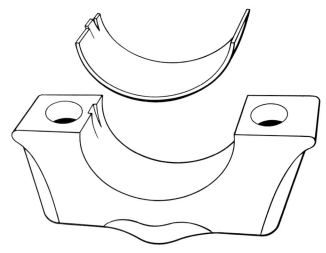

Bearing locking lip and corresponding recess in cap.

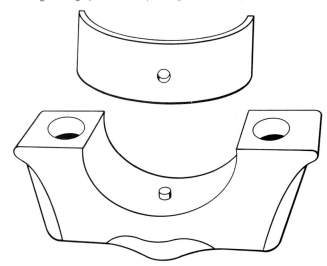

Use of a dowel to retain the bearing half.

Fig. 12-21   Holding main bearing inserts in bearing caps.
(Federal-Mogul Service)

12.18   Conformability

Crankshaft journals and crankcase or rod bores are not always true round. In order to fit tightly despite such slight irregularities, a bearing material should be soft enough so that it can change shape slightly. This reduces high areas of pressure and provides an even distribution over the entire bearing surface. This characteristic of a material is known as conformability. Conformability characteristics are not the same for all bearing lining materials.

12.19   Embedability

Dirt and other foreign material sometimes gets into the engine's oil supply. The oil pump then circulates it throughout the system.

To prevent failure of the bearings and scratching of the shaft, the bearing lining should allow hard, sharp particles to be either completely embedded into the lining or passed off. Some lining materials will "swallow up" dirt without breaking down. Others, made of stronger material, will not take in dirt. The ability of a lining material to absorb such particles is the characteristic known as embedability.

12.20   Gaskets

Gaskets are used between two automotive parts that are bolted together to form a pressure-tight seal. If the parts were fastened together without a gasket, slight irregularities on their surfaces would allow leakage. A gasket is made of soft material that, when squeezed between two parts, fills up these small irregularities.

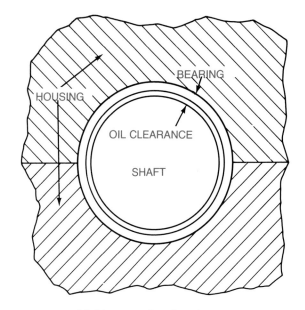

Fig. 12-22   Oil Clearance in a bearing.

Fig. 12-23 Oil pumped into oil clearance area of a bearing.

Fig. 12-24 Bearing with an oil groove. (Federal Mogul Service)

12.21 Head Gasket

The cylinder head gasket's main function is to seal in the pressures of combustion. The head gasket also seals the many lubrication and cooling passages from the block to the cylinder head and back again. Such a seal not only prevents loss of the cooling and lubricating fluids but prevents one from mixing with the other. If engine coolant were to leak into the lubrication system, the engine would overheat because of loss of coolant. Even more important, additives present in most coolants would prevent the lubricant from doing its job, and the engine would be seriously damaged.

The earliest head gaskets were simply sandwiches of asbestos and copper. These gaskets were satisfactory for engines with low combustion pressures and low operating temperatures. The soft copper was squeezed into the machining marks in the head and block, making a very tight seal between the two surfaces.

Copper gaskets were not tough enough for higher operating temperatures and higher compression pressures of later engines. The next development in head gaskets used the asbestos center layer, but substituted soft steel for the copper. This gasket was still compressible, and it was also tougher under higher heat and pressure.

During recent years, compression pressures and temperatures have increased even more. Removing the heat of combustion became a serious problem. Even the steel-asbestos-steel gaskets were no longer suitable, since the asbestos acted as an insulator between the block and head.

To improve the transfer of heat between the cylinder head and the block, it was necessary to eliminate the layer of asbestos in the head gasket. This meant using a gasket that would be all metal, but still have a certain amount of "crush" to guarantee a tight seal. A gasket was produced which consists of a single thickness of steel with raised ridges around the sealing areas. When the head bolts are tightened, these raised ridges crush to form a seal.

To provide even better sealing, the gaskets may be coated with an aluminum alloy. When the engine has been run long enough to reach operating temperature, the aluminum alloy melts into any small marks or scratches to form a tight seal. Another such coating made of a mixture of materials acts in the same way. Both coatings will not wash or burn away and will allow easy, clean removal of the gasket.

12.22 Other Gaskets

Cork gaskets are used in a number of places on automobiles, such as the oil pan and valve cover. Cork is easily formed into almost any shape and provides a tight, soft seal. Some cork gaskets have an aluminum coating which reflect heat and protects the gasket from breaking down. Paper and rubber are also common gasket materials in areas of low temperature and pressure.

12.23 SEALS

Sealing around a rotating or sliding shaft cannot be done with a gasket. This is the job of special parts called seals. Of the many different types and designs,

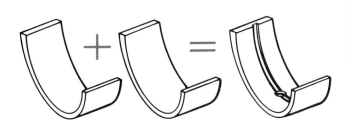

Fig. 12-25 Bearing consists of backing plus alloy lining.
(Federal-Mogul Service)

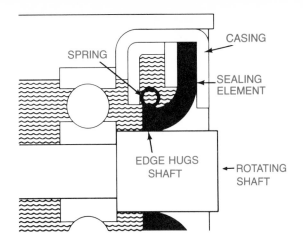

Fig. 12-26 How a lip seal seals.

the lip and the ''O'' ring seals are the most common in automotive use.

12.24 Lip Seal

The lip seal is used to seal a lubricant inside a bearing area and to keep dirt or other abrasive materials out of that area (Fig. 12-26).

Seals generally have three basic elements:

1. Casing—a metal housing for the seal assembly which also holds the seal in position once it is installed.
2. Sealing element—the rubber lip that actually contacts the shaft and holds the lubricant inside the bearing area.
3. Spring—a device that puts pressure on the sealing element to keep it in contact with the shaft.

Although most seal casings are made of metal, there are some plastic casings. Some seals appear to have no casing at all, since the metal portion is bonded inside a rubber coating.

The actual sealing job is done by a very small portion of the sealing element. The sharp edge of the lip hugs the shaft like a windshield wiper, wiping the lubricant from the shaft and preventing its escape. Despite differences in the appearance and construction of lip seals, they all work the same.

The most commonly used material in lip seals is synthetic rubber. Felt is used along with rubber to act as a dust seal, but it is too porous to be used as a lubricant seal. The synthetic rubber seals are suitable for sealing a great many liquids. They are able to withstand high temperatures and will stretch or shrink to fit tightly against a shaft whose surfaces are uneven.

12.25 ''O'' Ring Seals

An ''O'' ring is a ring-shaped seal whose cross section is circular, like an O. In fact, ring seals with cross sections of other shapes are often called ''O'' rings as well. The ''O'' rings in automotive use are made of synthetic rubber. Three types of ''O'' rings are shown in Figure 12-27.

Ring seals are used in static and dynamic situations. In a static application, there is no motion between the two members being sealed.

In a dynamic situation, there is either rotating or sliding motion. The sealing ability of an ''O'' ring is due to its elasticity. In other words, when pressure is applied, the ring shape distorts to conform to the shape of the ring groove and the other part (Fig. 12-28). Then, when the pressure is removed, the ring regains its original round cross section.

If the diameter of the ring's cross section is too small, fluid will leak past the ring, even at relatively low pressures. On the other hand, a ring that is too large will be hard to assemble, and the too-tight fit will cause high friction, so the ring will soon wear out.

NEW TERMS

Bearing A part used to reduce friction and wear between moving parts.
Block A metal box containing the crankcase and cylinders.

Fig. 12-27   Ring seals.

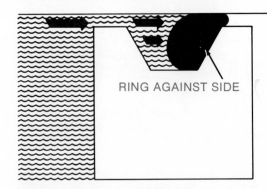

Fig. 12-28   How an "O" ring seals.

Bolt-on cylinders   Cylinders held in place with bolts or studs. Bolt-on cylinders can be removed for service.

Bushing   A sleeve that fits into a hole or bore and acts as a bearing.

Compatibility   The ability of a bearing to "get along" with a rotating shaft.

Conformability   The ability of a bearing to shape itself to minor irregularities.

Connecting rod bearing   The bearing used between the connecting rod and the crankshaft.

Crankcase   The part of the engine that supports the crankshaft.

Embedability   The ability of a bearing to absorb particles of dirt to prevent damage to the shaft.

Fatigue strength   The ability of a bearing to resist failure due to stress.

Gasket   A soft material used between two automotive parts to form a pressure seal.

Insert   A bearing made in two half-round pieces to be inserted onto an automotive component.

Journal   The part of a shaft on which a bearing is installed.

Lip seal   A seal used to keep lubricant inside a bearing area.

Main bearings   Bearings used to support the crankshaft on its main journals.

"O" ring   A ring-shaped seal.

Oil clearance   The space between a bearing and its journal provided for the flow of oil.

Seal   A device used to seal around a rotating shaft.

Throw   The offset part of the crankshaft to which the connecting rod is attached.

CHAPTER REVIEW

1. What are the two types of crankcases?
2. What are the two types of cylinder design in use?
3. List the two lower block designs used on V engines.
4. What is the purpose of the oil pan?
5. In what three ways are crankshafts made?
6. How many throws does a crankshaft for a six-cylinder engine have? How many does a V-8 have?
7. What is the purpose of counterweights on the crankshaft?
8. What is the purpose of the harmonic balancer used on the front of a crankshaft?
9. Where are the main bearings installed in an engine?
10. Explain what a bearing oil clearance is and why it is necessary.
11. List and describe four bearing requirements.
12. Describe the difference between a gasket and a seal.

DISCUSSION TOPICS AND ACTIVITIES

1. Examine the engine in your own or your family's automobile. What is the design of the crankcase? the cylinders?
2. Look in the owner's manual and try to find out how many main bearings the engine has. Why is the number of main bearings important?
3. Look at some bearings and gaskets available around the school shop. Can you identify any of the materials used and the uses?

CHAPTER 13

Piston Engine Components: Pistons, Rings, Pins and Connecting Rods

CHAPTER PREVIEW

In this chapter we will examine in detail the parts which make up the piston and connecting rod assembly. This assembly makes it possible for the power produced in the combustion chamber to turn the crankshaft.

OBJECTIVES

After studying this chapter, you should be able to do the following:

1. Identify the components of the piston and connecting rod assembly.
2. Describe the parts of the piston and explain differences in manufacture and design.
3. Explain the different types of piston rings used in an engine.
4. Describe the purpose and different designs of piston pins.
5. Describe the purpose and different designs of connecting rods.

13.1   PISTONS

The function of the piston is to transmit the force produced by burning fuel in the combustion chamber to the crankshaft through the connecting rod (Fig. 13-1). The piston must be as light as possible but strong enough to withstand the great forces exerted on it.

13.2   Piston Parts

The parts of a piston are shown in Figure 13-2. The top of the piston, which may have many different shapes, is called the head. A number of grooves called ring grooves are machined in the piston to hold the piston rings. The spaces between the ring grooves are called lands. The area of the rings and lands is the ring belt. A narrow groove that may be machined above the top ring groove to prevent heat from working its way down into the lower part of the piston is called a heat dam.

The area from below the ring belt to the bottom of the piston, known as the skirt, contacts the cylinder wall to guide the piston as it moves up and down. The two sides of the skirt are the major and minor thrust face.

A hole called the pin hole is bored through the piston for the piston pin. In most pistons the pin is supported directly on the aluminum of the piston. Some piston pins, however, rest on a bushing pressed into the pin hole. The distance between the top of the piston head and the center of the pin hole is called the compression distance.

Great force is applied to the piston pin area of the piston during the power stroke. For this reason, the underside of the piston is supported in the wrist pin area by what are called bosses. They are shown in the sectional view of a piston (Fig. 13-3).

13.3   Piston Manufacture

Pistons are cast or forged from aluminum alloys, which makes them very light. The lighter the piston, the higher the engine operating speeds. In casting,

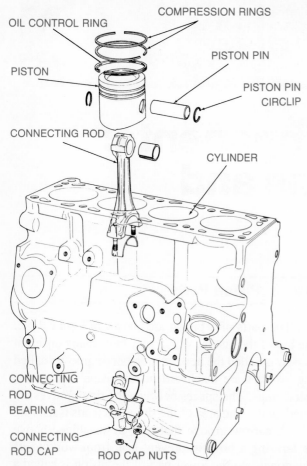

Fig. 13-1 Piston and connecting rod assembly. (Chrysler Corporation)

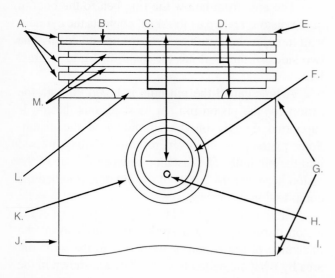

A. LAND
B. HEAT DAM
C. COMPRESSION DISTANCE
D. RING BELT
E. PISTON HEAD
F. PISTON PIN
G. SKIRT

H. PIN HOLE
I. MAJOR THRUST FACE
J. MINOR THRUST FACE
K. PISTON PIN BUSHING
L. OIL RING GROOVE
M. COMPRESSION RING GROOVE

Fig. 13-2 Parts of a piston. (Perfect Circle)

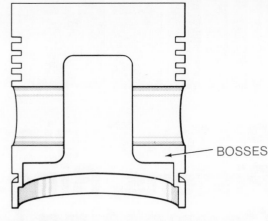

Fig. 13-3 Sectional view of a piston showing piston pin bosses. (TRW)

molten aluminum is poured into molds. Cast pistons are less expensive to produce and are strong enough for most production engines.

In forging, aluminum is hammered into shape between two dies. Forging is more expensive but provides a stronger and denser piston. A denser piston allows better heat flow through the aluminum (Fig. 13-4). Forged pistons are used in most high-performance and racing engines.

13.4 Piston Shape and Design

Piston shape has changed in two major ways over the years. The long skirts on the pistons of older engines made the pistons heavier and created more friction between the piston and the cylinder wall. Modern pistons, called slipper skirt pistons, have large portions of the skirt area cut away to lower weight and friction. This also allows more room for the counterweight on the crankshaft (Fig. 13-5).

Figure 13-5 also shows a built-up area called a balancing pad on both sides of the piston skirt. These areas are machined last to bring the piston within the specified weight tolerance.

The piston heads on early engines were flat. Higher compression pressures in the 1950s and 1960s were achieved by using pistons with domed heads which extended further into the combustion chamber. Notches were made in the domed section of the head (Fig. 13-6) to provide clearance for the intake and exhaust valves. The latest piston head (Fig. 13-7) are designed to burn the air-fuel mixture more completely and to lower emissions. They are shaped to move the air-fuel mixture past the spark plug during combustion.

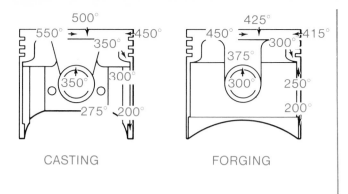

CASTING   FORGING

Fig. 13-4 Comparison of cast and forged piston temperatures under similar operating conditions. (TRW)

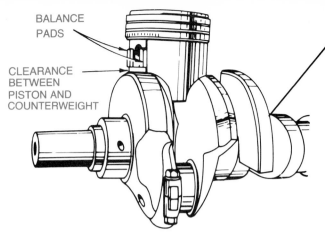

Fig. 13-5 Skirt cut away to provide clearance between piston and crankshaft counterweight. (Chevrolet Motor Division, GMC)

In high-performance engines especially, the top ring groove of a piston is subjected to great stresses. As the piston changes direction the top ring tends to rock back and forth, leading to groove wear. This groove is also subjected to very high temperatures and combustion pressures in an area that receives very little lubrication. These problems have made it necessary to build up the top ring groove area.

A ring groove may be built up by an insert of cast iron or steel cast into the head of the piston (Fig. 13-8). Forged pistons have a thin coat of hard metal spray over the area to prevent wear instead of an insert.

Another area that requires extra strength, especially in high-compression and high-performance engines, is the underside of the head. All pistons have a thick head, for this area receives the direct impact of combustion. Some have special support ribs for more support, as shown in Figure 13-9.

13.5 Piston Clearance

Since the piston must be able to move up and down the cylinder freely, it must be made slightly smaller than the cylinder. The small space between the piston skirt and the cylinder wall (Fig. 13-10) is called piston clearance. The piston clearance varies for different engines from 0.003 to 0.005 inch (0.18 to 0.13 mm).

If there is too much clearance, the piston will not be properly supported. It will make a knocking sound called piston slap as the skirt rattles against the cylinder wall. Piston slap can eventually lead to the breaking of the piston skirts.

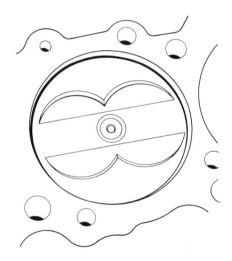

Fig. 13-6 Piston head with notches for valve clearance. (Pontiac Motor Division, GMC)

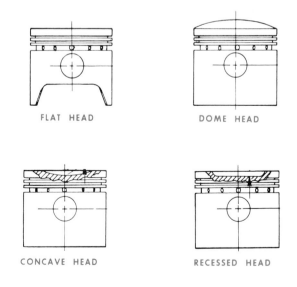

FLAT HEAD   DOME HEAD

CONCAVE HEAD   RECESSED HEAD

Fig. 13-7 Piston head shapes. (TRW)

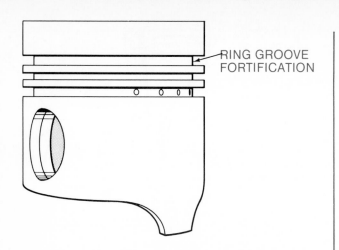

Fig. 13-8 Top ring groove must be strengthened in a high-performance piston. (TRW)

RING GROOVE FORTIFICATION

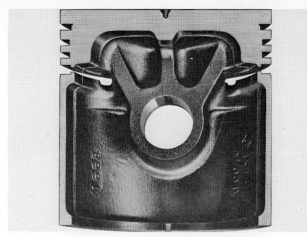

Fig. 13-9 Sectional view of piston showing support ribs and thick section under head.
(Sealed Power Corporation)

Another problem is caused when there is not enough piston clearance. As high combustion temperatures heat the piston, it expands. An aluminum piston heats and expands at a much higher rate than the cast iron cylinder walls. If the piston has very little clearance to begin with, this expansion may cause it to become wedged in the cylinder. This is called piston seize.

13.6 Piston Expansion Control

Controlling expansion as the piston heats up to keep the correct amount of clearance has always been a problem. The heat dam (see Fig. 13-2) is one way of controlling expansion. This groove or slot around the head of the piston prevents heat from moving down from the piston head to the skirt area.

Older vehicles used pistons with slots (Fig. 13-11) for expansion control. A ''T'' slot is a horizontal and vertical cut in the skirt of the piston. As the piston heats up, the slots became narrower while the overall diameter of the piston remains the same.

Another way of controlling expansion is to cast into the piston a piece of steel that tends to hold the piston from expanding (Fig. 13-12). This piece of steel may be a belt that runs around the diameter of the piston in the ring belt area. Other pistons have steel struts cast into the skirt area across the wrist pin bosses.

Most modern engines achieve expansion control by cam grinding the piston. This means that a device called a cam grinder is used to make the skirt oval rather than round. As the piston heats up, it tends to expand. The built-up area of the piston pin bosses (see

Fig. 13-3) prevents expansion across the larger diameter but allows expansion across the narrower diameter. The result is a piston that gets round, increasing the area of skirt contact with the cylinder as it heats up (Fig. 13-13). The cam ground piston provides a narrow enough clearance when cold to prevent piston slap and provides space for the piston to grow without seizing when hot.

13.7 Thrust Forces and Piston Pin Offset

The piston skirt has the job of supporting and guiding the piston as it speeds up, stops, and reverses direction for each of the four strokes of the cycle. The direction of the forces on the skirt area of the piston is different during each stroke. The piston in Figure 13-14 is on a power stroke. Notice the arrangement of the connecting rod and crankshaft. As the piston is forced down the cylinder with the rod in this direction, the piston will be thrust to the left side of the cylinder. This side of the piston skirt is called the major thrust face because it must take the load during the power stroke.

The thrust forces are on the opposite side of the piston during the intake stroke. Again, the piston is moving down, but, as shown in Figure 13-15, the connecting rod is positioned on the other side of the piston. This causes the piston to be thrust toward the other side of the cylinder wall. Since the forces pushing the piston are less during intake than power, this side of the skirt is called the minor thrust face.

The pin holes through the piston are often slightly offset to control the thrust forces on the

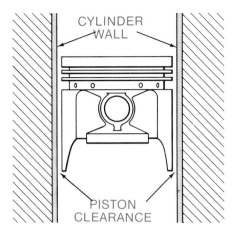

Fig. 13-10   There must be clearance between piston and cylinder wall.

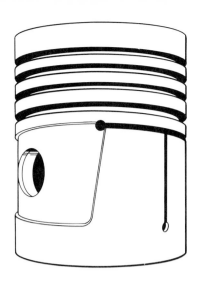

Fig. 13-11   Piston with slots for expansion control.

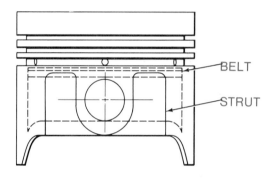

Fig. 13-12   Belt and strut used for expansion control. (TRW)

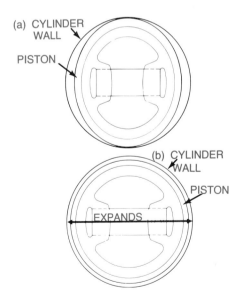

Fig. 13-13   Cam ground piston (a) cold and (b) hot.

piston (Fig. 13-16). Piston pin offset reduces piston slap caused by the crossover action that results when the connecting rod swings from one side of the piston to the other. If the pin hole were located in the center, the piston would tend to tilt during this crossover. Moving the pin toward the major thrust face causes the rod to pull the piston firmly against the cylinder wall, reducing any knocking.

13.8   PISTON RINGS

Piston rings are installed in piston grooves to provide a movable seal between the combustion chamber and the crankcase. They are made from cast iron or steel so that they always press against the cylinder walls. Their main purpose is to prevent compression pressures from leaking around the piston into the crankcase. At the same time, they keep oil in the crankcase from leaking into the combustion chamber. Piston rings also provide a means of conducting heat from the head of the piston into the cylinder wall and allow for cylinder and piston expansion and contraction.

Piston rings must provide this movable seal while operating at different speeds and accelerations. They are exposed to vacuum, high pressures, and extreme heat. They must rapidly change shape to conform to changes of shape in the cylinder wall.

In early automotive engines, what was called a compression ring with one flat side was used in all the piston grooves. At low driving speeds, these rings satisfactorily controlled the small amount of oil splashed up on the cylinder walls by the connecting rods. When driving and engine operating speeds

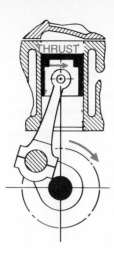

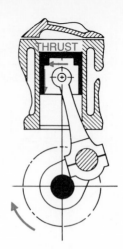

Fig. 13-14 Major thrust on piston during power stroke.

Fig. 13-15 Minor thrust on piston during intake stroke.

increased and pressure lubrication systems were introduced, connecting rod bearings, even with proper clearances, threw more oil onto the cylinder walls than these simple rings could control. The problem of excessive oil consumption had to be solved.

The solution was the development of two types of rings. Compression rings were placed in the grooves near the piston head to provide the seal for compression pressures. Oil control rings were placed in the groove or grooves below the compression rings. The oil ring wipes excessive oil off the cylinder wall and routes it back into the crankcase to prevent excessive oil consumption.

13.9   Compression Rings

The first compression rings, rectangular in cross section, formed a simple mechanical seal against the cylinder wall. Since they were larger than the cylinder diameter, they pushed out against the cylinder wall to provide a seal when compressed in the cylinder.

It was found that if a rectangular groove was cut on the lower outside or the upper inside edge of a piston ring, the internal forces of the ring would be unbalanced. When the ring was compressed to fit in the cylinder, the top of the ring face would tip away from the cylinder wall except during the power stroke. The lower outside corner of the ring would have a positive contact with the cylinder wall and the lower inside corner of the ring would form an effective blow-by seal in the ring groove. These rings, shown in Figure 13-17, are called counterbored rings.

Counterbored rings, during the power stroke, flatten against the cylinder to help in sealing. Figure 13-18 shows how compression pressures move around

the head of the piston into the area behind the ring. The pressure is sufficient to untwist the ring and push it directly on the cylinder wall. There is some leakage through the joint of the top compression ring to provide sealing pressure for the second compression ring.

Some compression rings use a tapered outer face which does a good job of wiping oil from the cylinder wall on the downstroke and slides over the oil on the upstroke (Fig. 13-19). Tapered rings, however, are not very good at sealing compression pressures. A keystone ring (Fig. 13-20), tapered on both sides, is used in diesel and aircraft engines. It was developed to overcome the problem of a ring sticking in a groove.

The latest design in compression rings is an L-shaped ring called a head land ring (Fig. 13-21) which covers the top or head land area of the piston. This ring eliminates the space between the piston head and the cylinder wall, which provided a cold area for gasoline to escape burning during combustion. Eliminating the space increases efficiency of burning and reduces undesirable exhaust emissions. A steel spring called an expander is usually used behind this ring to apply outward pressure.

13.10   Oil Control Rings

The oil control ring scrapes oil off the cylinder wall and directs it through the ring and into holes in the piston. Oil flows through the piston holes and runs back into the crankcase.

The control given by early one-piece oil rings, even when they used an expander, was not adequate for modern engine demands. As the face of a cast iron

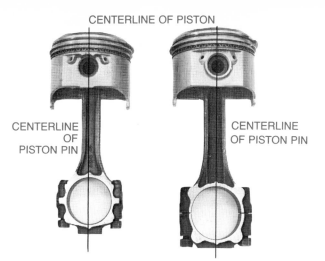

Fig. 13-16 Piston pin offset. (Pontiac Motor Division, GMC)

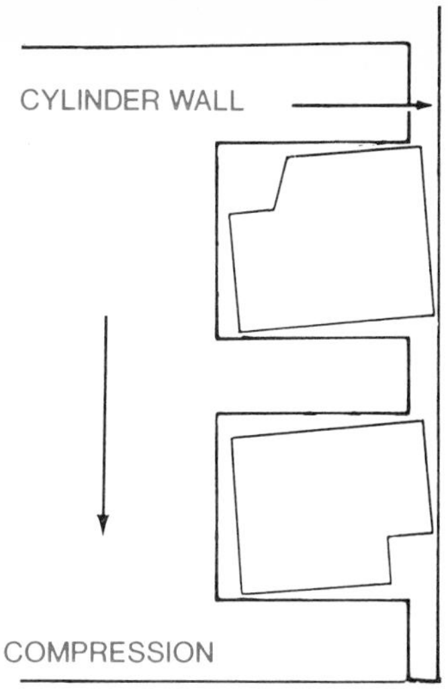

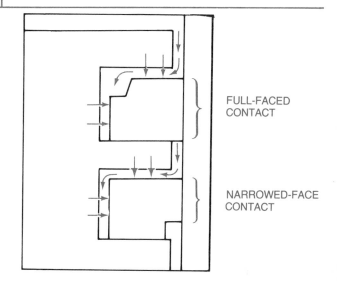

Fig. 13-17 Counterbored rings twist to seal on intake, compression, and exhaust stroke.

oil ring wears, spring tension is decreased, and the width of the face is increased. This results in a lower pressure and reduced oil control. A multiple-piece oil ring made up of a cast iron spacer and two steel rails with an expander spring (Fig. 13-22) behind them was designed to control the pressure loss due to ring face wear (Fig. 13-23).

The cast iron spacer and steel expander were later combined into one piece. The ring shown in Figure 13-24 consists of an expandable spring spacer and two rails. The spring spacer is slightly larger around than the cylinder. When assembled on the piston and in the cylinder, the spring spacer pushes the rail uniformly against the cylinder wall (Fig. 13-25).

13.11   Piston Ring End-Gap Joints

Oil control and compression rings usually come together with a joint called a butt gap. Some piston rings for automotive use have a tapered gap or seal cut gap (see Fig. 13-26). Since piston rings fit in ring grooves with some clearance they tend to rotate in the piston grooves. In a two-stroke cycle engine, the ends of the rotating ring could move into a cylinder port and cause breakage. Most two-stroke cycle pistons, therefore, have a pin in the piston groove that prevents the ring from rotating.

13.12   Piston Ring Coatings

Chromium plating has long been used to improve the service life of rings by reducing scuffing and scoring. Chromium plate is extremely hard and dense and has a high resistance to abrasive wear. Many top

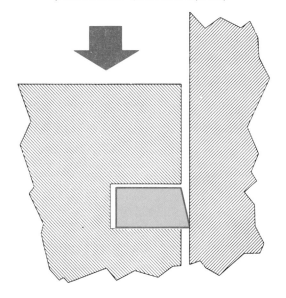

Fig. 13-18 Counterbored rings provide contact during power stroke. (Perfect Circle Corporation)

Fig. 13-19 Tapered rings scrape oil on downstroke.

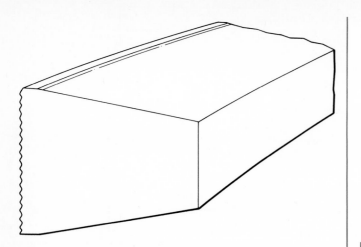

Fig. 13-20 Keystone ring. (Perfect Circle Corporation)

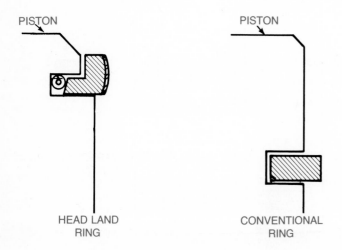

PISTON

PISTON

HEAD LAND
RING

CONVENTIONAL
RING

Fig. 13-21 Head land ring compared to conventional ring. (Sealed Power Corporation)

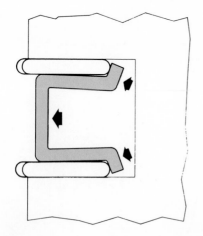

Fig. 13-22 Expander pushes rails out against cylinder wall. (Perfect Circle Corporation)

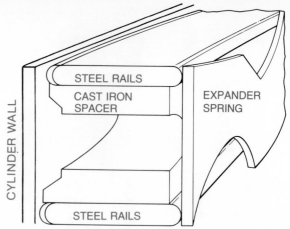

CYLINDER WALL

STEEL RAILS

CAST IRON
SPACER

EXPANDER
SPRING

STEEL RAILS

Fig. 13-23 Multiple-piece oil ring with two rails separated by spacer backed by expander. (Perfect Circle Corporation)

compression rings and oil control ring rails today still use chromium plating.

Since the 1960s, molybdenum has been sprayed on the face of the ring during manufacturing. This coating is considered better than chromium for resisting wear at high temperatures. Aluminum oxide and Teflon are also used as ring coatings. Their slick finish prevents carbon from sticking to the ring.

13.13   PISTON PIN

The piston pin, often called a wrist pin, connects the piston to the connecting rod. Since the full force of combustion pressures is transferred from the piston to the connecting rod through the piston pin, it is made from high-quality steel. To cut down on weight, it is usually tubular rather than solid.

There are several ways of attaching the pin to the piston and connecting rod. The free-floating piston pin (Fig. 13-27) is slightly smaller than the holes in the piston and the connecting rod. It is therefore free to "float" or rotate in both parts, but it is prevented from slipping along its length by two retaining rings, one on each side of the piston. The advantage of this design is that the pin could stick in either the piston or rod without locking up the assembly. The fit or clearance between pin and rod and pin and piston is one of the closest and most precise in the engine.

The pin may also be held by a press fit in the connecting rod. In this design, the piston pin is slightly larger than the hole in the connecting rod. A hydraulic press forces or presses the pin into the hole in the rod, so that it cannot move along its length or turn in relation to the rod. The holes in the piston

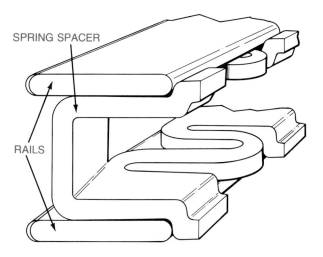

Fig. 13-24 Oil ring with spring spacer and two rails. (Perfect Circle Corporation)

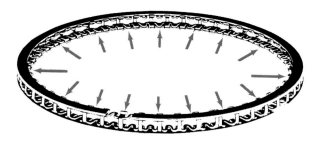

Fig. 13-25 Assembled oil ring showing direction of forces. (Perfect Circle Corporation)

provide a bearing surface which allows the rod and pin to turn with respect to the piston.

13.14 CONNECTING RODS

The connecting rod is the link between the piston and the crankshaft. Connecting rods may be either cast or forged. Most modern engines use a cast connecting rod, which is inexpensive to produce. Racing engines and motorcycles often use connecting rods forged from aluminum, which are stronger but more expensive. The connecting rod usually has an I-beam cross section to combine high strength with low weight.

The parts of a connecting rod are shown in Figure 13-28. The end of the connecting rod through which the piston pin fits is called the small end. If a free-floating pin is used, this end will be fitted with a piston pin bushing.

The other end of the connecting rod is called the big end. It is fitted with a removable cap so that it may be bolted around the crankshaft throw. Balancing pads at the small end, and sometimes at the big end as well, are formed in the final machining to remove enough metal so that rod weight meets final balancing tolerances.

Precision insert bearings are held in the connecting rod and connecting rod cap with locking grooves. In most engines, the cap is held with bolts and nuts (Fig. 13-29). The bolts must be of very high quality to withstand the high loads. Self-locking nuts are often used to prevent loosening by vibration.

The connecting rod may have holes drilled in it for oil distribution. Many connecting rods have an oil

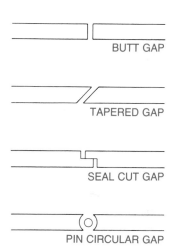

Fig. 13-26 Types of piston ring gaps.

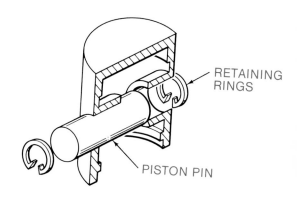

Fig. 13-27 Free-floating piston pin.

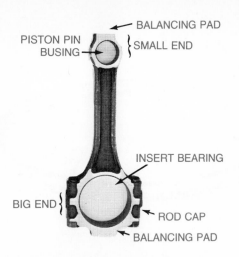

Fig. 13-28   Parts of connecting rod.

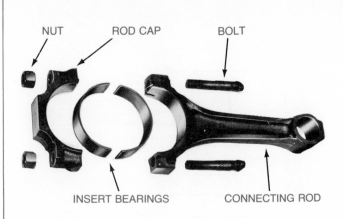

Fig. 13-29   Cap retained by bolt and nut. (Ford Motor Company)

spurt hole (Fig. 13-30) that spurts oil onto another inside engine part. A few engines have an oil passage drilled the length of the rod to provide oil under pressure to the piston pin bushing (Fig. 13-31).

Most connecting rods are symmetrical; that is, the small end and the big end are directly in line with each other. Some engines must use an offset connecting rod because of limited main bearing space. On an offset connecting rod, the big end and small end are slightly off center when viewed from the side (Fig. 13-32).

NEW TERMS

Cam ground piston   A piston ground to an oval shape that becomes round when it is heated.

Compression ring   A piston ring used to seal compression pressures in the combustion chamber.

Counterbored ring   A ring constructed so that the top of the ring tips away from the cylinder except during the power stroke.

End gap   The space between the two ends of a ring when it is installed in a cylinder.

Expander   A spring placed behind a ring to increase its tension against a cylinder wall.

Head land ring   An L-shaped ring which covers the head land area of the piston and reduces exhaust emissions.

Heat dam   A groove cut around the top of the piston to prevent heat from making its way down the skirt.

Major thrust face   The face of the piston skirt that absorbs the load during the power stroke.

Oil control ring   A piston ring used to prevent oil from getting into the combustion chamber.

Piston clearance   The space between the piston skirt and the cylinder wall.

Piston pin   Pin used to attach the piston to the connecting rod.

Piston pin offset   Locating the pin holes in the piston off center to control thrust forces on the piston.

Piston ring   An expanding sealing ring placed in a groove around the piston.

Ring groove   A groove cut in the piston to accept the piston rings.

Skirt   The lower part of the piston that is supported by the cylinder walls.

Slipper skirt   A type of skirt cut away to reduce weight and friction and to provide clearance for the crankshaft.

T slot   A T-shaped slot cut in a piston for expansion control.

Wrist pin   Another name for piston pin.

CHAPTER REVIEW

1. What are the spaces between piston ring grooves called?
2. Where is the piston skirt located?
3. What are the advantages of a forged piston?
4. What is a balancing pad for on a piston?
5. Explain piston clearance.
6. What is piston slap?
7. Describe three ways to control piston expansion.

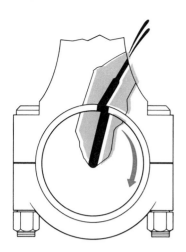

Fig. 13-30 Oil spurt hole in rod directs oil to another area. (Federal-Mogul)

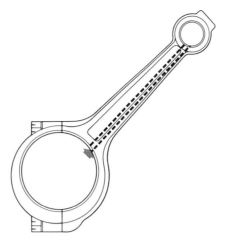

Fig. 13-31 Rod with oil passage leading to piston pin bushing. (Federal-Mogul)

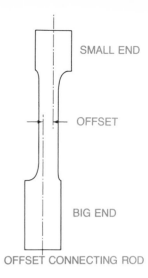

SMALL END

OFFSET

BIG END

OFFSET CONNECTING ROD

Fig. 13-32 Connecting rod offset.

8. What is the major thrust face of a piston?

9. What is piston pin offset?

10. What are compression rings used for?

11. Describe a head land piston ring.

12. What is the job of the oil control ring?

13. What is an end gap?

14. Describe two methods of keeping the piston pin in the piston.

15. How is the rod cap attached to the connecting rod?

DISCUSSION TOPICS AND ACTIVITIES

1. Examine a shop piston and connecting rod assembly. How many of the parts can you name?

2. How do pistons and rods differ in a high-performance engine from those in a standard passenger automobile engine?

3. Examine a selection of pistons found around the shop. What differences in design can you find? Which design is the best? Why?

Piston Engine Components: Cylinder Head and Valve Train

CHAPTER PREVIEW

In our discussion of engine operation in Chapter 10, we saw that the four-stroke cycle depends upon air and fuel being admitted to the cylinder, trapped there, and later expelled as burned gases. This requires two passages that are opened and shut by means of valves above the pistons. The components that perform this function are called the valve train. Part of the valve train and the passages for the intake and exhaust gases are located in the cylinder head. In this chapter we will examine these components in detail.

OBJECTIVES

After studying this chapter, you should be able to do the following:

1. Explain the operation of the cylinder head and identify its parts.
2. Describe the operation and major parts of the camshaft and camshaft drive.
3. Explain the purpose and operation of valve lifters, pushrods, and rocker arms.
4. Describe the operation and major parts of valves, valve guides, and valve seats.
5. Explain the operation of valve springs, retainers, oil seals and valve rotators.

14.1 CYLINDER HEAD

The cylinder head is a large aluminum or iron casting bolted to the top of the engine block. A head gasket between the cylinder head and the block forms a gas- and liquid-tight seal. An in-line engine has one cylinder head. A V-engine has two cylinder heads (Fig. 14-1), one for each bank of cylinders.

The combustion chamber above each piston is formed by the casting of the cylinder head. Each combustion chamber has a threaded hole for a spark and two other holes or plug ports which are opened and closed by the intake and exhaust valves.

14.2 Intake and Exhaust Ports

The intake port is connected to another casting called the intake manifold, which directs air and fuel through the intake port into the cylinder head. When the piston is on the intake stroke, the air-fuel mixture is pulled through the intake port around an open valve and into the combustion chamber (Fig. 14-2). The intake port must be free of bends and obstructions to allow a smooth, direct flow of gases into the combustion chamber. The size and shape of the port are carefully designed to meet the air-fuel needs of the engine over a wide operating range.

On the exhaust stroke, the exhaust port routes burned gases past an open exhaust valve out of the engine (Fig. 14-3). An exhaust manifold attached to the cylinder head collects the burned gases and sends them through the exhaust pipe into the muffler. The muffler quiets the exhaust and sends it through the tailpipe in the rear of the automobile (Fig. 14-4). The exhaust port must provide a smooth and direct flow of gases out of the engine so that all burned gases are removed before the next charge of air and fuel enters the combustion chamber. The size and shape of the exhaust port, like the intake port, are carefully designed to meet the needs of the engine over a wide operating range.

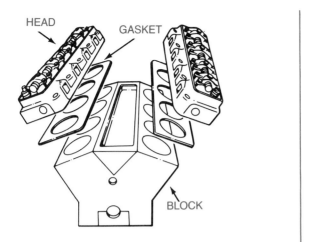

Fig. 14-1 V engine with head and gasket for each cylinder bank. (Ford Motor Co.)

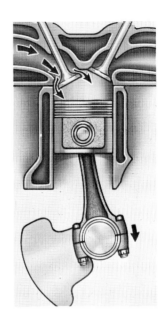

Fig. 14-2 Air and fuel routed through intake port to combustion chamber. (Chevrolet Motor Division, GMC)

14.3 Coolant and Oil in the Cylinder Head

The cylinder head provides passages for coolant and oil. Areas in the cylinder head that require cooling, such as the valve area, are next to a coolant passage. Coolant circulated through the engine block is sent through passages in the head gasket into the cylinder head. In the same way, oil from the block passes through the head gasket into the cylinder head where it lubricates the valve train. A cylinder head with oil and coolant passages identified is shown in Figure 14-5. Dowel holes in the head are used to align the head correctly with the cylinder block during installation.

14.4 THE VALVE TRAIN

The valve train (Fig. 14-6; see also Figs. 10-15 and 10-16) opens and closes the intake and exhaust ports at the correct time. The parts which make up a valve train are camshaft, valve lifter, pushrod, rocker arm assembly, and valve assembly. In the following sections we will study each of these components in detail.

14.5 Camshaft and Attachments

The camshaft (Fig. 14-7), driven by the crankshaft, has a number of bumps or cam lobes located along its length. Since there is a cam lobe for each valve, the V-8 camshaft in Figure 14-7 has sixteen cam lobes.

The camshaft has several journals which ride in bearings in the engine called cam bearings. A large

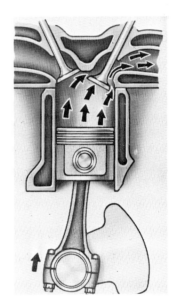

Fig. 14-3 Burned gases routed through exhaust port. (Chevrolet Motor Division, GMC)

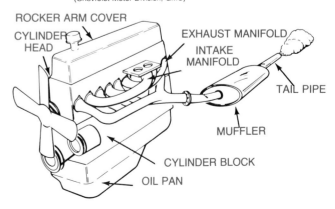

Fig. 14-4 Exhaust gases routed to rear of automobile.

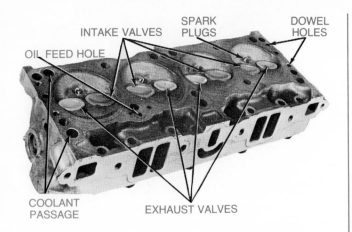

Fig. 14-5 Cylinder head with major parts and passageways. (Chrysler Corporation)

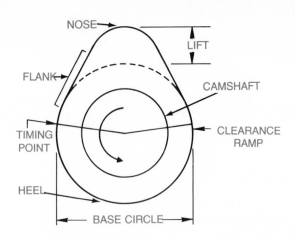

Fig. 14-8 Parts of cam lobe.

Fig. 14-6 Sectional view of valve train.
(Chevrolet Motor Division, GMC)

Fig. 14-7 Parts of camshaft. (Chrysler Corporation)

bump called an eccentric is often used on the end of the camshaft to drive the fuel pump. A gear on the camshaft drives the distributor and the oil pump.

The camshaft is usually cast and then ground to the proper shape. Each of its cams is also ground to shape to provide the correct valve action. After grinding, the surface of the cam lobe is hardened to prevent wear. A typical cam (Fig. 14-8) may be thought of as a base circle which has the center as, or is concentric with, the camshaft. A nose on the lobe sticks up past the base circle. The measurement of the nose beyond the base circle is called lift.

14.6 Lifters

Located next to each cam lobe is a lifter. When the lifter is resting on the heel of the cam the valve is closed. As the cam lobe rotates so that the timing point hits the lifter, it begins to be raised. The lifter is at its highest point when the nose of the lobe is right under it. Further rotation of the lobe allows the lifter to drop along the other flank to rest again on the heel. A clearance ramp is provided to allow a smooth movement of the lifter down the lobe.

The shape of the cam nose and flanks determines when and how long the engine's valves are opened. This duration is not measured in minutes or seconds, for it varies with engine operating speed. Instead, duration is measured by how many degrees of crankshaft rotation occur while the valve is opened. The duration is charted on a valve timing diagram.

14.7 Valve Timing and Duration

The timing diagram, Figure 14-9, shows that the intake valve begins to open 30 crankshaft degrees

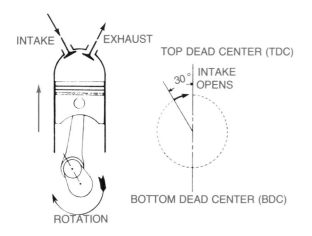

Fig. 14-9   Intake valve opens. (Iskenderian)

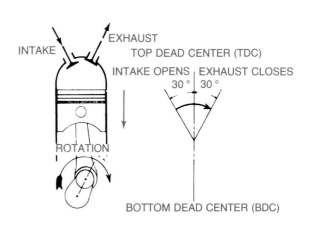

Fig. 14-10   Exhaust valve closes. (Iskenderian)

before the top of piston travel (called top dead center and abbreviated TDC). This gives the valve a head start so that at top dead center the valve will be well off its seat. The air-fuel mixture can then flow easily past the open valve.

As the piston reaches and passes top dead center, the exhaust valve is still in the process of closing. At high engine speeds, the burned gases flowing past the exhaust valve into the exhaust manifold tend to help draw in the air-fuel mixture. The short time when the intake and exhaust valves are both open is called overlap. At 30 crankshaft degrees past top dead center, the exhaust valve finally closes (Fig. 14-10).

The intake stroke continues as the piston moves downward, drawing the air-fuel mixture into the cylinder. The piston reaches the bottom of its stroke (bottom dead center or BDC) and starts to rise in the cylinder for the compression stroke. The intake valve remains open, however, for the inertia, or resistance to change, of the incoming air and fuel causes the cylinder to continue filling long after the piston changes direction. Not until 70 crankshaft degrees past bottom dead center does the intake valve close (Fig. 14-11). The intake valve total opening period or duration is 30 degrees before TDC plus 180 degrees to BDC plus 70 degrees after BDC, a total of 280 crankshaft degrees.

The piston continues upward on the compression stroke, compressing the air-fuel mixture. Just before reaching top dead center, the mixture is ignited. At top dead center, the ignited mixture is expanding for the power stroke. The piston is forced downward once again. At 70 crankshaft degrees before the piston reaches bottom dead center, the exhaust valve begins to open, well before the power stroke has actually been completed (Fig. 14-12). The hot exhaust gases

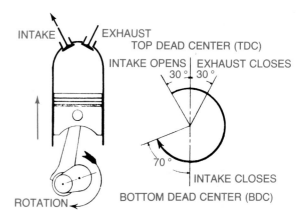

Fig. 14-11   Intake valve closes. (Iskenderian)

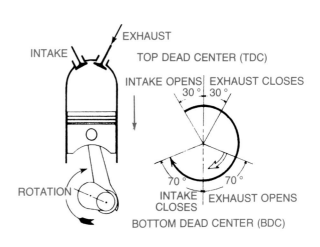

Fig. 14-12   Exhaust valve opens. (Iskenderian)

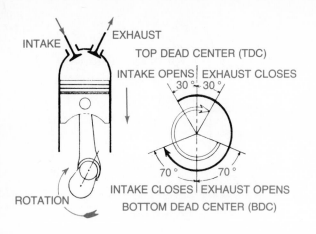

Fig. 14-13 Exhaust valve closes. (Iskenderian)

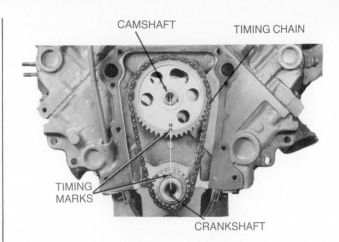

Fig. 14-16 Camshaft driven by sprockets and chain. (Chrysler Corporation)

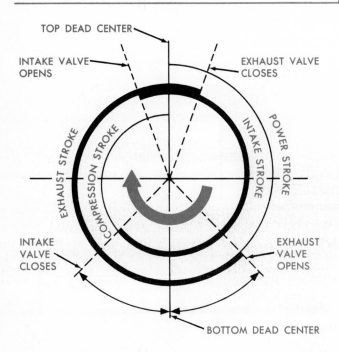

Fig. 14-14 Valve timing diagram. (Chevrolet Motor Division, GMC)

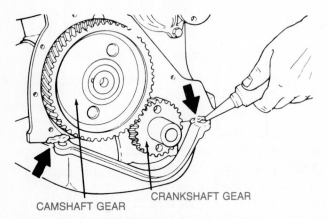

Fig. 14-15 Cam drive using two gears in mesh. (Chevrolet Motor Division, GMC)

leave the cylinder because of their own pressure. This reduces the engine's effort to push out the burned gases on the upward stroke of the piston.

The piston completes its downward travel and once again rises in the cylinder for the exhaust stroke. At 30 crankshaft degrees past top dead center, the exhaust valve closes. The total duration or opening period of the exhaust valve is 70 degrees before BDC plus 180 degrees to TDC plus 30 degrees after TDC, a total of 280 degrees (Fig. 14-13). A complete valve timing diagram illustrating the events through two revolutions or 720 degrees of crankshaft rotation is shown in Figure 14-14.

14.8 Camshaft Drives

The camshaft is driven by the crankshaft, which makes two revolutions during the four-stroke cycle. Valve action, however, is only required during two of these strokes: intake and exhaust. Therefore, the camshaft need make only one revolution during the four-stroke cycle.

Several types of cam drives are in use. Older automotive engines and many heavy truck and diesel engines use a gear on the crankshaft that meshes with and drives a gear on the camshaft (Fig. 14-15). The small gear on the crankshaft drives the larger gear on the camshaft at half speed. Timing marks on the two gears are matched up so that the camshaft is properly timed to the crankshaft. The camshaft gear is usually made of a soft material, aluminum or plastic, to reduce noise.

For another drive (Fig. 14-16), a sprocket attached to the crankshaft drives another sprocket attached to the camshaft with a timing chain. This

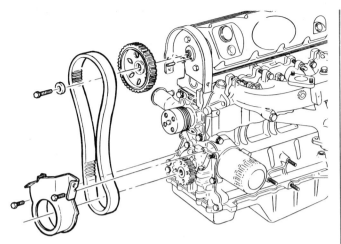

Fig. 14-17 Toothed belt to drive overhead camshaft.
(Chevrolet Motor Division, GMC)

Fig. 14-18 Solid valve lifter. (Iskenderian)

drive is very quiet. The sprockets are sized so that the camshaft is driven at half the speed of the crankshaft. Timing marks on the two sprockets are used to time the camshaft to the crankshaft.

Overhead camshafts require a more complicated drive system because of the distance between the crankshaft and cam and the possibility of two separate overhead camshafts. Overhead cams are driven with gears, chains, or toothed belts. The chain and gear drives are similar to those already described. The toothed-belt drive (Fig. 14-17) uses a rubber belt with teeth which mesh two sprockets, one on the crankshaft and one on the camshaft. The camshaft is driven at one-half crankshaft speed.

14.9 Valve Lifters

The valve lifter rides on the camshaft, rising as the cam lobe on the camshaft rotates it. Valve lifters, also called valve tappets and cam followers, are made of high-quality iron and hardened by a heat or chillplate method to prevent wear as they slide on the hardened cam lobe.

14.10 Solid Lifter Operation

There are two types of valve lifters, solid and hydraulic. The solid lifter is a one-piece unit which may have a removable seat for a pushrod. The roller tappet (Fig. 14-19) is a type of solid lifter common to racing and some diesel engines. The roller on the bottom of the tappet rides on the cam lobe with very little friction. The 1985 General Motors 2½ liter 4-cylinder engine (made by Pontiac) uses a roller

hydraulic lifter. This is the first use of a roller lifter in a high-production gasoline engine.

Some overhead camshaft engines use a small valve lifter between the camshaft and the valve. This style of lifter is often called a follower (Fig. 14-20). Most overhead camshaft engines have rocker arms mounted over the camshaft. The camshaft pushes on the rocker arm, which in turn pushes down on the valve to open it.

The valve train must allow for metal expansion due to temperature changes. This expansion could increase the length of the valve train enough to prevent a valve from closing properly. When solid lifters are used, some space is provided in the valve train for expansion. This space, called valve lash or valve clearance, is usually several thousandths of an inch or hundredths of a millimetre. Valve clearance is measured and adjusted at the rocker arm if the engine has the cam in the block, or at the cam if the engine has an overhead cam.

14.11 Hydraulic Lifter Operation

The operation of solid lifters with valve clearance results in some noise. To eliminate this noise, a hydraulic valve lifter was developed that provides for changes in valve train length. This lifter keeps all parts of the valve train in constant contact.

The hydraulic lifter assembly (Fig. 14-21) includes the cast iron body which rides in the cylinder block, boss, plunger, pushrod seat, metering valve, plunger return spring, check valve and spring, check valve retainer, and retainer ring. The operation of the hydraulic valve lifter is shown in Figure 14-22. When the lifter is riding on the low point of the

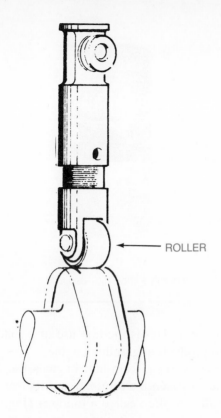

Fig. 14-19 Roller tappet. (Iskenderian)

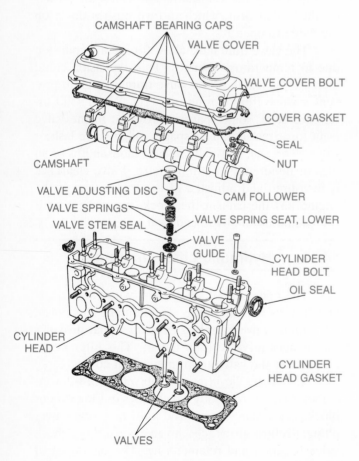

Fig. 14-20 Overhead camshaft assembly using cam followers. (Chrysler Corporation)

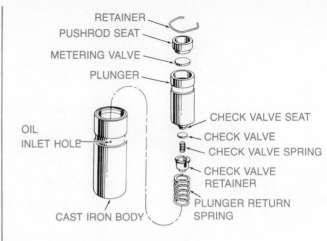

Fig. 14-21 Exploded view of a hydraulic valve lifter. (American Motors Corporation)

cam, the plunger spring keeps the plunger rod seat in contact with the pushrod. When the lifter body begins to ride up the cam lobe, the check valve cuts off the transfer of oil from the chamber below the plunger. The plunger and lifter body then rise as a unit, lifting the pushrod and opening the check valve.

As the lifter rides down the other side of the cam, the plunger follows with it until the valve closes. The lifter body continues to follow the cam to its low point, but the plunger spring keeps the plunger in contact with the pushrod. The check valve will then move off its seat and the lifter chamber will remain full.

During operation a controlled amount of oil leaks out of the lifter between the plunger body to provide continuous adjustment of the plunger position within the lifter. This leakage, called leak-down, must be kept within certain limits for correct operation.

Oil is supplied to the lifter by the cylinder block oil gallery to replace what is lost through leak-down. The groove around the outside of the lifter body matches a passage drilled from the gallery to the lifter boss. Oil enters the lifter from this groove and passes into the plunger cavity. In some engines, oil under pressure is also fed up the pushrod to lubricate the friction area between the upper end of the pushrod and the rocker arm and other upper valve train contact points.

14.12   Pushrod

Overhead valve engines, in which the camshaft is in the cylinder block, transfer the cam lobe and lifter motion up to the cylinder head area by means of pushrods. The pushrod is seated at one end in the valve lifter and at the other end in a rocker arm (Fig. 14-23).

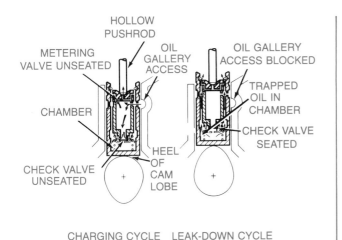

Fig. 14-22 Operation of the hydraulic valve lifter. (American Motors Corporation)

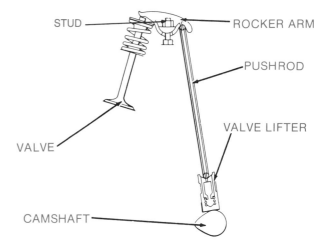

Fig. 14-23 Pushrod transfers cam movement to cylinder head. (Pontiac Motor Division, GMC)

Most pushrods are hollow to lessen weight and allow oil flow. Oil is sent under pressure through the pushrod up to the rocker arm assembly for lubrication. A male end is normally used at the pushrod end which fits into a seat in the lifter. A male or female end may be used at the rocker arm end, depending upon the rocker arm design. A very few engines use an adjustable pushrod to allow changes in valve clearance.

14.13 Rocker Arms

The rocker arm assembly is mounted to the engine's cylinder head. When the pushrod lifts one side of the rocker arm, the other side moves. One kind of rocker arm assembly (Fig. 14-25) has a stud located in the cylinder head. A stamped steel rocker arm is mounted to the stud with a ball pivot. A nut holds the rocker arm to the stud and provides a means of adjusting the clearance between the rocker arm and valve. The rocker arm is free to pivot on the ball and stud.

A variation of the stud type of mount is the pivot or fulcrum type mount shown in Figure 14-26. The rocker arm is mounted to a pedestal on the cylinder head by a pivot which fits inside the rocker arm. A bolt holds the pivot in place. The rocker arm can move up and down on the bearing surface provided by the pivot. A bridge assembly is often used to position the pivot of two side-by-side rocker arms.

Another kind of rocker arm (Fig. 14-27) uses a rocker shaft assembly. Rocker arms, which are usually cast iron, are mounted on and supported by a shaft connected to the cylinder head. Since the hole in the rocker arm is slightly larger than the diameter of the shaft, the arm is free to rock up and down. The pushrod

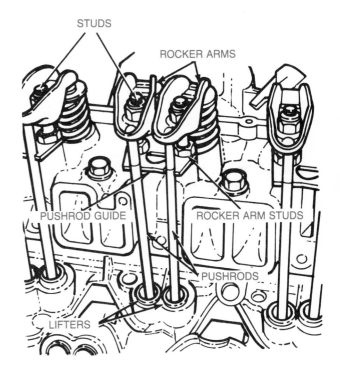

Fig. 14-25 Rocker arm assembly mounted on studs. (Chevrolet Motor Division, GMC)

end of the rocker arm may be adjustable for valve clearance (Fig. 14-27).

The rocker arm changes upward movement to downward movement. If its pivot is in the center, a given amount of upward movement will result in exactly the same amount of downward movement, a relationship or ratio of 1:1. The pivot point of many rocker arms is off center to provide a ratio of about

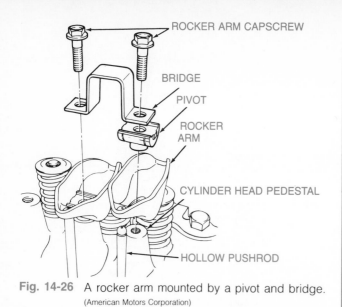

Fig. 14-26 A rocker arm mounted by a pivot and bridge. (American Motors Corporation)

Fig. 14-27 Exploded view of rocker shaft assembly. (Chrysler Corporation)

1.5:1. This means that downward motion to open the valve is 1.5 times the lift of the cam lobe.

14.14 Valve

The intake and exhaust ports are opened and closed by the intake and exhaust valves (Fig. 14-28). A valve is just a shaft called a stem with a large round head. The head of the valve has a precision ground tapered face that, when closed, seals against a seat in the cylinder head. When pushed open by the rocker arm, gases are allowed to move around the valve head into or out of the cylinder.

Valves are made from very high-quality steels because they get very hot during combustion. The intake valve is usually larger in diameter than the exhaust valve because it must control the slow-moving, low-pressure intake mixture. Exhaust valves may be smaller because the exhaust gases leave the cylinder under higher pressures. Since the exhaust valve gets even hotter than the intake valve, it is made from even higher-quality steels. Stainless and stelite steel alloys are often used.

Exhaust valves used in heavy duty engines sometimes use a hollow stem half filled with metallic sodium. The sodium turns liquid at operating temperature. The movement of the liquid sodium back and forth as the valve opens and closes moves heat from the valve head to the valve stem. The heat can then be passed through the valve guide and into the water passages in the cylinder head.

14.15 Valve Guides

The valve stem is supported and guided in the cylinder head by a valve guide. The integral valve guide (Fig. 14-29) is part of the cylinder head. Many engines use a guide that may be removed and replaced during an overhaul. Replaceable guides may be made from cast iron or a softer material such as an alloy of bronze. They are usually pressed into the cylinder head.

The clearance between the valve stem and guide must allow free movement of the valve. It must also allow a small amount of oil to work its way between the stem and guide for lubrication. If there is too much clearance, oil from the rocker arm area could work its way down the stem and into the combustion chamber. This is a real problem on the intake valve stem because the entire time the intake valve is open there is a vacuum in the cylinder. On the exhaust valve, there is a vacuum only during the period of valve overlap.

The valve guide also gets rid of heat. Coolant passages in the cylinder head are located near the valve guide area. Heat is moved out of the valve stem, into the valve guide and cylinder head, and into the coolant.

14.16 Valve Seats

The valve seat is a precision ground area at the entrance of the valve port (Fig. 14-30). It may be a part of the cylinder head or a separate unit installed in the head with a press fit. If the cylinder head is made from aluminum, the seats must be made from cast iron or steel.

The angle ground on the valve seat matches the angle ground on the valve face (Fig. 14-31), usually 45 degrees. On some engines an angle of 30 degrees is used. Some engines use an interference angle, which is a 1-degree difference in the seat and face angles.

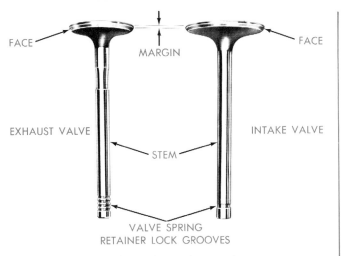

Fig. 14-28 An intake and an exhaust valve.
(Chrysler Corporation)

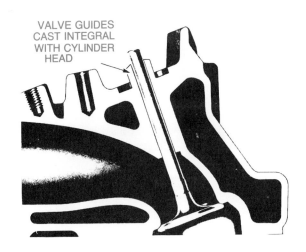

Fig. 14-29 Valve guide supports and guides the valve.
(Pontiac Motor Division, GMC)

The seat may be ground to 46 degrees and the valve to 45 degrees. Or the seat may be ground to 45 degrees and the valve to 44 degrees. This provides a hairline contact between the valve and seat for positive sealing and reduces buildup of carbon on seating surfaces.

The width of the seat is also important for good sealing. If the seat is too wide, there is a greater chance of a buildup preventing good seating. A wide seat also spreads the valve spring tension over a larger area and reduces the seal. On the other hand, too narrow a seat will reduce heat movement away from the valve head and into the coolant passages near the valve seat.

14.17   Valve Springs and Retainers

The valves are held in the closed position by valve springs. A coil spring is used on most engines. When extra sealing pressure is needed, two springs, an inner and outer, are used (Fig. 14-32).

The valve springs are held in position by a retainer (Fig. 14-33). The bottom of the spring rests on the cylinder head. The spring is compressed and a retainer is placed on top of the spring. Two split valve locks or keepers (Fig. 14-34) are inserted into grooves cut into the valve stem and fit into the retainer. This assembly locks the spring to the valve. The valve train pushes the valve open against this spring pressure when the cam lobe pushes on the valve lifter. After the lobe rotates past the lifter, the valve springs close the valve.

14.18   Oil Seals

The tip of the valve where it contacts the rocker arm must be lubricated to prevent wear. The valve

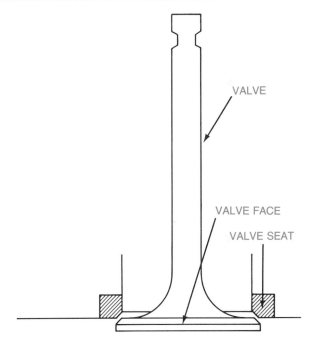

Fig. 14-30 Valve face seals against valve seat.

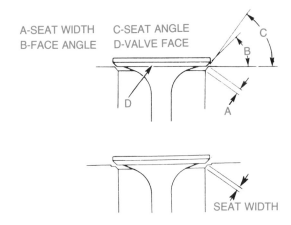

Fig. 14-31 Valve seat and face angles.
(Pontiac Motor Division, GMC)

Fig. 14-32   Inner and outer spring used to close a valve.
(Iskenderian)

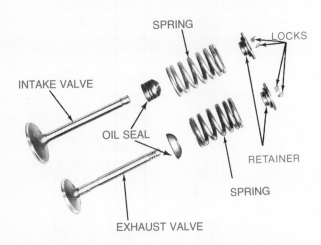

Fig. 14-33   Valve spring and retainer assembly.
(Chrysler Corporation)

Fig. 14-34   Two split valve locks used to retain valve spring on valve stem. (Iskenderian)

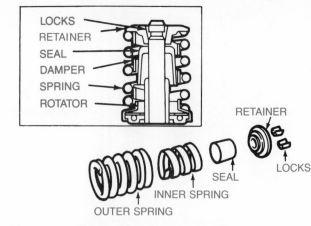

Fig. 14-35   Shield and "O" ring seal used to prevent oil from entering valve guide.
(Pontiac Motor Division, GMC)

retainer assembly has an oil seal (Fig. 14-33) to prevent too much oil from running down the valve stem. This seal is placed on top of the valve guide. Another sealing system (Fig. 14-35) uses a shield or seal called an umbrella to prevent oil from getting on the valve stem and running down toward the guide. A small "O" ring seal in a groove on the valve stem prevents oil from running past the lock and retainer cap assembly down the valve stem.

14.19   Valve Rotator

The valves should rotate on the valve seat. This prevents deposits from sticking to the seat or face. It also avoids the development of hot spots that could lead to valve burning. Some engines use a special retainer assembly that rotates the valve (Fig. 14-36). When the valve is opened, the coil spring causes the body of the rotator to turn around. Since the body is attached to the valve stem, the valve also rotates.

NEW TERMS

Camshaft   A shaft with lobes used to open the valves at the proper time.

Cylinder head   Large casting bolted to the top of the engine that contains the combustion chamber and valves.

Exhaust ports   Passages in the cylinder head used to route out burned gases from the cylinder.

Exhaust valve   Valve used to control flow of burned exhaust gases from the cylinder.

Hydraulic lifter   Valve lifter that controls valve lash or clearance hydraulically.

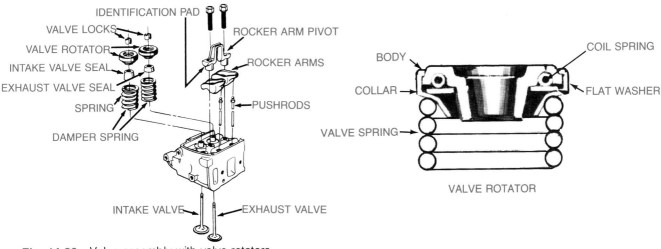

Fig. 14-36 Valve assembly with valve rotators.
(Pontiac Motor Division, GMC)

Intake ports Passages in the cylinder head that route the flow of air and fuel into the cylinder.

Intake valve Valve used to control the flow of air and fuel into the engine.

Lobe A raised section on the camshaft used to lift the valve.

Overlap The period of time when both valves in a cylinder are open.

Pushrod A rod used to transfer camshaft motion to the rocker arm.

Retainer A washer and lock assembly used to hold the valve spring in position.

Rocker arm A lever mounted on the cylinder head that pushes the valves open.

Solid lifter A valve lifter that is solid and does not use hydraulic fluid to control valve lash.

Valve A device for opening and closing a port.

Valve guide A part installed in the cylinder head to support and guide the valve.

Valve lash Space or clearance in the valve train for heat expansion.

Valve lifter A part that rides on the cam and pushes on the pushrod.

Valve rotator A device that rotates valves to prevent them from burning.

Valve seat The part of the cylinder head that the valve seals against.

Valve spring A coil spring used to close the valve.

Valve timing Opening and closing the valves at the correct time in relation to piston position.

Valve train The assembly of parts that opens and closes the ports of an engine.

CHAPTER REVIEW

1. What is the purpose of the cylinder head?
2. List the parts that make up the valve train.
3. What is the purpose of the camshaft?
4. Sketch a camshaft lobe and label the main parts.
5. Explain what the term *duration* means.
6. What is valve lash and why is it necessary?
7. Describe two types of valve lifters.
8. Between what two parts does the pushrod fit?
9. Describe the two general styles of rocker arms.
10. What is the purpose of a valve?
11. Why is the exhaust valve sometimes smaller than the intake valve?
12. What is a valve guide?
13. What is the difference between a valve seat and a valve face?
14. Explain what an interference angle is.
15. Explain how the valve spring works to close the valve.
16. What is a valve retainer?
17. Why is a valve rotator necessary?

DISCUSSION TOPICS AND ACTIVITIES

1. Examine a shop cutaway or model engine. How many of the valve train components can you identify?
2. How do you think the valve train for a racing engine would differ from that of a production engine?
3. Which type of lifters, solid or hydraulic, are used in your own or your family's automobile? How can you find out?

Piston Engine Service

CHAPTER PREVIEW

In the last several chapters we have examined the construction and operation of piston engines. In this chapter we will look at repair and service procedures for piston engines. In this and the other service chapters in this book, we will begin by explaining preventive maintenance procedures. These are very important service operations designed to prevent wear or failure of automobile parts.

Each of the service chapters in the book will also explain troubleshooting or diagnostic steps to determine what is wrong. Without a careful diagnosis, a great deal of time may be lost servicing the wrong parts.

OBJECTIVES

After studying this chapter, you should be able to do the following:

1. Describe the preventive maintenance procedures used to prevent excessive wear on engine parts.
2. Explain the troubleshooting steps to find out what is wrong with an engine.
3. Describe the steps in disassembling an engine for service.
4. Explain the main service procedures for reconditioning an engine.
5. List the steps for reassembling an engine after service.

15.1   PREVENTIVE MAINTENANCE

Preventive maintenance procedures are designed to prevent abnormal wear of engine parts. The most important are frequent oil, oil filter, and air filter changes. Also important are regular cooling system inspection and service and regular tune-ups.

15.2   Valve Clearance Problems

One important preventive maintenance job is a valve clearance or valve lash adjustment. Valve lash or valve clearance (see Chapter 14) is the space allowed for expansion in a valve train equipped with solid lifters. If the valve lash is too wide, there will be engine noise and wear on the camshaft and lifter contact faces. Pushrods may also be bent. Eventually, valve timing is affected and the engine performs poorly.

If valve lash is too small, a valve may be prevented from closing tightly on its seat and sealing the combustion chamber. The immediate result is poor engine performance. But also, a valve held off its seat gets very hot because it is not able to move heat away from the valve head into the valve seat in the cylinder head. The result is a melted valve head, called a burned valve. A burned valve cannot seal, so the engine performs poorly. If the burned valve is not repaired immediately, the valve head may separate from the stem and fall into the cylinder, resulting in cylinder wall and piston damage.

During normal engine operation, valve clearance can become larger or smaller. Wear on valve stems, rocker arms, pushrods, and lifters results in increased valve clearance. Wear at the valve face and seat area results in decreased valve clearance. In certain engines, high temperatures stretch the valves and reduce the clearance. Vibration may also affect the valve adjustment mechanism and change the clearance. For all these reasons, valve clearance must be

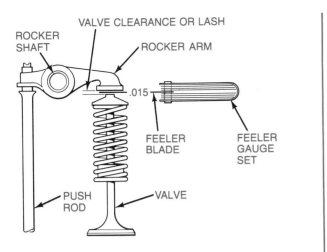

Fig. 15-1   Measuring and adjusting valve clearance.

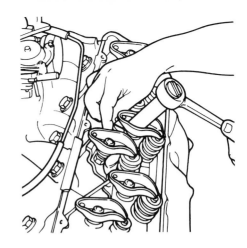

Fig. 15-2   Adjusting valve clearance on ball and stud rocker arm. (Chevrolet Motor Division, GMC)

inspected and, if necessary, adjusted at regular intervals.

15.3   Preparing for Valve Adjustment

Before the job is started, the correct service literature must be on hand. The shop or repair manual for the vehicle presents a step-by-step procedure for the valve adjustment as well as clearance specifications. Some valve trains must be adjusted when the engine is cold, since engine temperature can change the clearance. For this and other reasons, the mechanic must be careful to follow the correct procedure.

On some engines, intake and exhaust valves have different clearance specifications. This is due to higher exhaust valve temperatures and the use of different metals with different expansion rates in the two valves. If specifications differ, the exhaust valve clearance will normally be larger. The service manual will usually identify which valves are intake and exhaust.

15.4   Valve Adjustment

After the engine is at the proper temperature, the first step in most valve adjustments is to remove the rocker cover or valve cover. In an I-head engine with adjustable rocker arms, valve lash is measured by inserting a feeler gauge between the rocker arm and valve stem (Fig. 15-1). The clearance must be measured when the lifter is resting on the heel of the cam. The service manual will specify how to position the engine so that the valves are in the correct position for adjustment. A feeler gauge is selected that is the same as the clearance specification. If the feeler gauge does

not slide into the space, the adjustment screw must be turned to increase the valve clearance. If the feeler gauge fits into the space too loosely, the adjustment screw must be turned to reduce the clearance. The feeler gauge should fit with a light drag.

Ball and stud rocker arm assemblies are adjusted by turning the nut on top of the stud (Fig. 15-2). A feeler gauge is used just as shown in Figure 15-1.

Some valves can be adjusted with the engine running. The procedure is almost the same, but difficult because the valve train is moving.

Most overhead camshaft engines have adjustable lifters or adjustable rocker arms. The feeler gauge is positioned between the valve stem and rocker arm as shown in Figure 15-3. The lock nut is loosened and the clearance adjusted by rotating the rocker arm adjustment screw.

Some overhead camshaft engines use valve adjusting discs between the cam follower or lifter and the camshaft lobe (Fig. 15-4). Thicker or thinner discs are installed by pushing down the follower and compressing the valve spring with a special tool. A small magnet is used to pull out the disc. The feeler gauge is inserted between the cam and the lifter as shown in Figure 15-5. The cam shaft must be turned so the heel of the cam lobe is on the lifter.

After adjusting the valves, replace the rocker cover, using a new gasket, and torque the screws.

15.5   TROUBLESHOOTING

Normal wear takes place in an engine between crankshaft rod journals and connecting rod bearings; between main journals and main bearings; between piston rings and pistons and cylinder walls; between

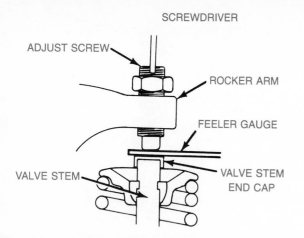

Fig. 15-3 Adjusting valve clearance on an overhead camshaft engine. (Chevrolet Motor Division, GMC)

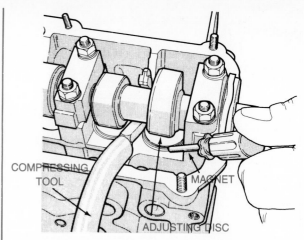

Fig. 15-4 Adjusting overhead camshaft valve clearance with adjusting discs. (Chrysler Corporation)

tappets and cam lobes; between valves and guides; and, in fact, between any moving parts. Abnormal wear and early breakdown of parts are the result of neglect: poor maintenance, too little lubrication or cooling, and many other causes.

Excessive engine wear may result in poor performance, excessive oil consumption, abnormal engine noises, and low oil pressure. Poor performance results when the combustion pressures leak around worn piston rings or worn valves and seats. When engine performance cannot be brought back by a regular tune-up and tests indicate leakage from the combustion chamber, the engine must be serviced.

15.6   Oil Leakage

Excessive oil usage may be the result of oil leakage. If an engine uses an excessive amount of oil, the outside of the engine should be examined very closely. Sometimes oil will leak around a gasket only at high engine speeds. This can happen around rocker or valve cover gaskets and at the oil pan gasket. The outside of the engine should be cleaned with a steam cleaner and then operated while looking for the leak.

Oil leaks often occur at the crankshaft rear oil seal. Many times this can be spotted only by the dripping of oil out of the vent hole in the bottom of the flywheel housing. Leaks may also occur at high engine speeds around the rear end of the oil pan, washing down this area with hot oil. Such leaks happen when the flywheel, from a fan effect, creates a vacuum around the oil seal area, sucking oil out. Replacement of the packing or lip seal stops the leak.

15.7   Excessive Oil Consumption

Excessive oil consumption results when engine oil enters and is burned in the combustion chamber. This creates a blue-white smoke from the exhaust pipe.

Oil enters the combustion chamber in two ways: past worn piston rings or around worn valve guides. The outer ring surface and the cylinder wall both wear in time, decreasing the pressure of the ring against its cylinder wall. This decreases the ring's ability to wipe oil from the worn cylinder walls. The oil gets by the piston rings and is burned in the combustion chamber.

Ring and cylinder wear can also cause loss of power, engine misfiring, smoky exhaust, and many other problems. Too much bearing clearance adds to this problem by increasing oil throwoff to the cylinder walls, making the job of the worn oil control ring even more difficult.

Oil consumption through valve guides (Fig. 15-6) can be a problem in overhead valve engines. An engine requires a large quantity of oil in the rocker arm area to reduce noise and prevent wear to rocker arms, valve stems, and guides. When valve stems, guides, and seals become worn, oil on the valve stems is drawn down into the intake ports and exhaust ports and burned. Several quarts of oil can be burned this way in a thousand miles or even a thousand kilometres of operation.

15.8   Engine Knock

Another sign of engine trouble is an abnormal sound, especially a knock. Knocking noises usually

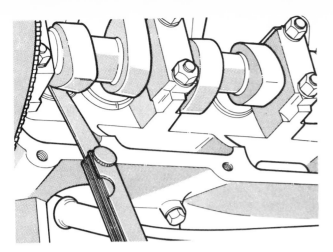

Fig. 15-5 Measuring valve clearance on an overhead camshaft with adjusting discs. (Chrysler Corporation)

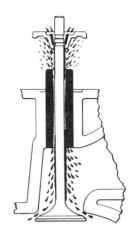

Fig. 15-6 Oil consumption around worn valve guides. (Perfect Circle)

mean the engine must be disassembled for major service. The experienced mechanic becomes expert at finding the cause of knocks by their sound and location. Engine accessories should be disconnected to make sure that the noise is inside the engine. Next, the mechanic can take the load off one cylinder at a time by disconnecting the spark plug wire. The loudness of the knocking will change when the spark plug in the cylinder with the problem is disconnected. Knocking can also result from too much clearance between any moving surfaces in the engine—main rod bearings, piston skirts, and piston pins. Knocks may also be caused by broken or fractured piston skirts and piston rings.

The experienced mechanic can also tell the trouble by the knock speed. A knock that occurs at half engine speed could be caused by a valve tappet or by the fuel pump.

Main bearing knocking, indicating too large a bearing clearance, usually occurs only when the engine is pulling. The sound becomes a heavy thump when the engine is made to pull. A lighter knock when the engine is not pulling may mean a bad connecting rod bearing.

15.9 Low Oil Pressure

A final sign of excessive engine wear is low oil pressure. Most automobiles have a warning light which goes on when the pressure is low and goes out when the pressure is above minimum level. The oil pressure warning light, however, only tells whether oil under pressure is flowing in the system. It does not show what the pressure is or if there is enough flow.

When bearing causing low oil pressure is suspected, the mechanic should attach a pressure gauge to the system. The gauge reading may be compared with the specifications for oil pressure in the service manual.

15.10 Diagnostic Tests

A mechanic who finds signs of abnormal wear should make an engine diagnosis. This includes several tests, including a compression test and a cylinder leakage test.

15.11 Compression Pressure Tests

Compression pressure tests tell the condition of piston rings, valves, and head gaskets. By comparing results of the test with manufacturer's specifications, the mechanic can tell if a cylinder is working correctly and providing its share of the engine's overall power.

A compression gauge is put in the spark plug hole of a cylinder. The compression pressure is then read while cranking the engine. This procedure is repeated for each cylinder. Readings should be taken with the engine at normal operating temperature to show the best ring and valve sealing under normal operating conditions. The carburetor throttle valves should be fully opened to allow atmospheric pressure to force a full mixture into the cylinder. All spark plugs should be removed to prevent too much engine drag during cranking. All cylinders must be tested the same number of strokes for a correct comparison. Readings should be noted on the first compression stroke as well as the last stroke to fully determine engine condition.

Fig. 15-7   Using a compression gauge.
(Chevrolet Motor Division, GMC)

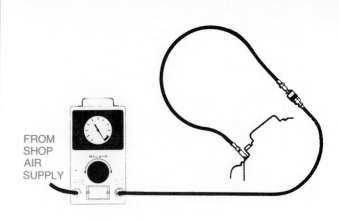

Fig. 15-8   Installing cylinder leakage gauge.
(Chevrolet Motor Division, GMC)

All cylinders should be within specifications. Differences between cylinders should not exceed 20 pounds per square inch or 1 kilogram per square centimetre.

Use the following procedure for compression pressure testing. Run the engine until normal operating temperature is reached. Stop the engine and loosen all spark plugs about one turn to break loose any accumulated carbon. Start the engine again and accelerate slightly to blow out loosened carbon from the combustion chamber. Clean the area around the spark plug with compressed air. Remove the spark plugs. Remove the air cleaner and block the throttle and choke in the wide open position. This ensures an adequate supply of air and stops fuel from the carburetor idle circuit that might wash oil off the cylinder walls and lower the reading. Disconnect the ignition primary lead to prevent shock from the plug wires. Insert the compression gauge firmly into the spark plug hole (Fig. 15-7). Crank the engine through at least four compression strokes to obtain the highest possible reading on the gauge. Check and record the compression readings.

A cylinder that is below specifications and varies more than 20 pounds per square inch or 1 kilogram per square centimetre from the highest cylinder reading is considered abnormal. An abnormal reading along with low-speed missing indicates an improperly seated valve or worn or broken piston rings. Worn piston rings are indicated by low compression on the first stroke which tends to build up on the following strokes. A further indication of worn rings is an improved reading when oil is added to the cylinder. Valve problems are indicated by a low compression reading on the first stroke which does not rapidly build up on following strokes and is not changed by the addition of oil. Leaking head gaskets give nearly the same test results as valve problems but may also be recognized by coolant in the crankcase. Head gasket leakage between two cylinders will give low readings on each of the cylinders.

15.12   Cylinder Leakage Test

The cylinder leakage test is a way of finding the smallest of cylinder leaks. Air applied to the cylinder at controlled volume and pressure measures the percentage of air leakage. It is normal for an engine to leak a small amount of air past the rings into the crankcase. However, any leak through an intake valve, an exhaust valve, head gasket, head, or block and excessive leakage past the piston rings indicates trouble.

To perform a cylinder leakage test, run the engine until normal operating temperature is reached. Clean the area around the spark plugs and remove them. Remove the crankcase oil filler cap and radiator filler cap. Set the cylinder leakage tester (Fig. 15-8) by adjusting the air supply to the right pressure at the tester input air connection. Adjust the pressure regulator on the tester to give a zero leakage reading on the gauge. Select the proper adapter and install it in the spark plug hole of cylinder number 1. Rotate the engine until the timing mark on the damper aligns with the top dead center mark. Mount a top dead center indicator on the distributor shaft or rotor and mark a reference point on an adjacent surface of the engine which aligns with the correct mark on the TDC indicator (Fig. 15-9). Connect the tester hose to the adapter and note the percentage of leakage on the tester

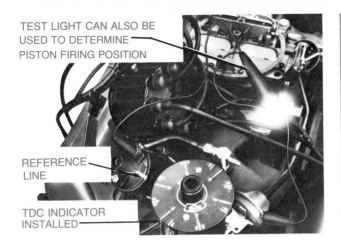

TEST LIGHT CAN ALSO BE USED TO DETERMINE PISTON FIRING POSITION

REFERENCE LINE

TDC INDICATOR INSTALLED

Fig. 15-9 Installing a top dead center indicator.
(Chevrolet Motor Dision, GMC)

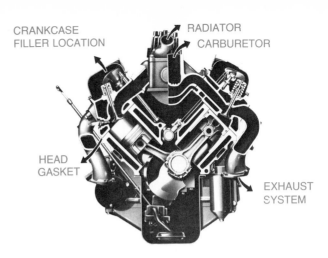

CRANKCASE FILLER LOCATION

RADIATOR

CARBURETOR

HEAD GASKET

EXHAUST SYSTEM

Fig. 15-10 Locating source of a cylinder leak.
(ChevroletMotor Division, GMC)

gauge. Listen for escaping air through the carburetor, the exhaust or tail pipe, and the crankcase filler location. Check for air bubbles in the radiator. Disconnect the tester hose from the adapter and rotate the engine until the next mark on the TDC indicator is aligned with the mark on the engine. Remove the adapter from the cylinder and install it in the next cylinder in the engine's firing order.

Continue this procedure until all cylinders have been tested. Record readings from each cylinder so that they may be analyzed to determine the condition of the engine.

Gauge readings should be about the same for all cylinders. Readings of 20 percent leakage or more indicate excessive leakage and loss in compression. Air escaping through the carburetor indicates a leaking intake valve leaking. Air escaping through the exhaust pipe indicates a leaking exhaust valve.

High leakage on cylinders next to each other can be caused by a leaking head gasket or a crack in the cylinder head. Air escaping through the radiator indicates the cylinder is leaking into the engine's water jacket. Air escaping through the crankcase filler hole indicates a crankcase leak, the result of worn piston rings. Figure 15-10 shows areas to be checked for leaks.

15.13   ENGINE SERVICE PREPARATION

Once inside engine trouble has been diagnosed, the engine must be serviced or repaired. The repair may be an engine overhaul or an engine rebuild.

The engine is disassembled, cleaned, inspected, and measured for wear. Each of the parts is recondi-

tioned. New parts are installed where necessary. The engine is then reassembled. In this section, we will examine each of these procedures.

15.14   Beginning Disassembly

The first step in most engine service operations is to steam clean the outside of the engine to make disassembly easier. If an overhaul is to be performed, the engine is normally removed from the automobile. If the engine needs only valve service, the engine is left in the vehicle. In either case, the outside accessories mounted to the engine must be removed. Engine coolant and oil are drained while the accessories are being removed.

The intake and exhaust manifolds are removed after the accessories. It is often necessary to apply a penetrating oil to the exhaust manifold bolts to loosen them. Cylinder head bolts are first loosened and then removed, working from the center of the head outward. This prevents the head from being distorted. With the head removed, the top of the pistons and cylinders can be seen.

15.15   Cylinder Ridge Removal

Before the engine can be disassembled further, the cylinder ring ridge must be removed. Most cylinder wear occurs in the top inch of ring travel. As the cylinders wear, a ridge or step forms at the top of ring travel (Fig. 15-11). When this cylinder ridge is large, piston lands may be damaged during removal of pistons from cylinders by rings catching on the ridge (see Fig. 15-12). Also, the corner of a new top compression ring will strike the rounded lower surface

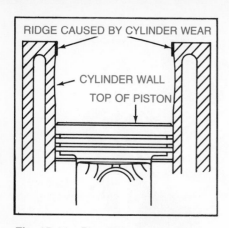

Fig. 15-11 Ring Ridge caused by cylinder wear. *(Pontiac Motor Division, GMC)*

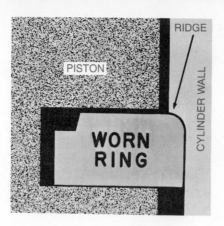

Fig. 15-12 Top ring wears to fit rounded shoulder at top of ring travel. *(Perfect Circle)*

Fig. 15-13 Square corner of new ring strikes cylinder ridge which has not been removed. *(Perfect Circle)*

of a large cylinder ridge (Fig. 15-13). This causes a clicking noise when the engine is run and may damage the top ring and bend the second land. The cylinder ridges are removed with a ridge reamer or ridge cutter (Fig. 15-14).

Follow the instructions supplied by the manufacturer of the ridge cutter. Do not cut below the ridge into the ring travel area of the cylinder. A cut deep into the cylinder wall or far down into ring travel may make reboring or replacement of the engine block necessary. Practically all worn cylinders are out of round when cold. But, regardless of the unevenness of wear at the top of ring travel, the mechanic should blend the cut made with the ridge reamer so that the area where the machined surface meets the unmachined surface is as smooth as possible. Cuttings left by the ridge removing should be carefully cleaned away before any further disassembly.

15.16   Final Disassembly

The engine may now be turned over to remove the oil pan. Wipe and inspect each connecting rod and main bearing cap for a factory marking. Not all engine manufacturers mark the position of connecting rods and main bearing caps. It is good practice to stamp unmarked connecting rods with numeral punches on both cap and rod during removal. The rods should be identified in relation to the position of the camshaft in an in-line engine, or on a specific side in a V engine.

Main bearing caps misplaced or placed in reversed position have caused many early bearing failures. Caps should be marked in numerical location, 1 for the front, 2 for the next in line, and so on. The cylinder block next to the cap position should be marked as well.

Remove the connecting rod cap bolts and rod cap from one of the rods. Push the connecting rod and piston assembly up and out of the top of the cylinder. Take care not to scratch the crankshaft journal by covering the rod cap studs with pieces of rubber hose. Repeat this procedure for each of the engine's pistons.

Before removing the crankshaft, check the condition of the timing chain. Push the timing chain outward and scribe a line on the block as shown in Figure 15-15. Then push the chain inward and scribe another line on the block. If the measurement between the two lines is bigger than specifications, the timing chain has stretched too much. A new chain must be installed when the engine is reassembled. Remove the camshaft sprocket, timing chain, and main bearing caps. Lift the crankshaft out of the engine. Keep the pushrods and lifters in order so they may be reinstalled in the same place. Pull the camshaft out the front of the block.

15.17   BLOCK AND CYLINDER WALL SERVICE

The block, especially its cylinder wall, is one of the areas of the engine subject to the most wear. In this section we will see how to determine the amount of wear in a cylinder and how a cylinder is reconditioned.

15.18   Cleaning and Measuring

Before cleaning the block, the cam bearings, soft plugs, and oil gallery plugs are removed. The cam bearings are driven out of their housings with a bearing driver and a hammer (Fig. 15-16). The soft plugs may be removed with a hammer and punch or a

Fig. 15-14 Using ridge reamer. (Perfect Circle)

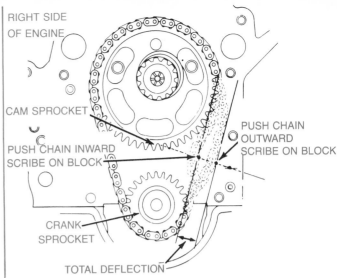

Fig. 15-15 Measuring timing chain wear. (American Motors Corporation)

special puller designed for this job. The oil gallery plugs at the rear of the block are usually pipe plugs that may be removed with a wrench. Removing the gallery plugs and soft plugs allows the inside passages in the block to be thoroughly cleaned and flushed.

The block is cleaned in a hot tank (Fig. 15-17). The empty cylinder block is lowered into a heated cleaning solution and allowed to soak for several hours. The hot tank removes grease and paint from the outside of the block and scale from the inside coolant passages. When it is removed from the hot tank, the block is steam cleaned to remove deposits loosened by the hot tank operation. Oil passageways and holes must be cleaned out with a brush.

The cleaned block must be thoroughly inspected and measured to tell what reconditioning is necessary. Each cylinder should be inspected for scoring or scratching from broken piston pin lock rings or piston rings. If there is no scoring, the cylinders may be measured for the amount of wear.

The greatest cylinder wear (Fig. 15-18) is found where the piston rings operate above the upper end of piston skirt travel. This area, called the pocket, receives the least lubrication and the most friction from the piston rings. The area of least wear is below the upper end of the piston skirt travel. The area at the very bottom of the cylinder is below ring travel and not subject to much wear.

The cylinder is measured to determine out-of-round and taper (Fig. 15-19). An inside micrometer, a telescoping gauge, or a special dial indicator on a handle called a cylinder gauge (Fig. 15-20) may be used. A measurement is made in the area of greatest wear, both in the direction the crank is installed and in a direction opposite to the crankshaft. The difference between these two measurements is out-of-round. The

Fig. 15-16 Removing cam bearings.

Fig. 15-17 Cleaning cylinder block in hot tank. (Federal-Mogul)

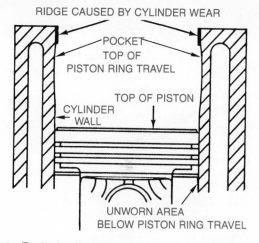

RIDGE CAUSED BY CYLINDER WEAR

POCKET

TOP OF PISTON RING TRAVEL

TOP OF PISTON

CYLINDER WALL

UNWORN AREA BELOW PISTON RING TRAVEL

Fig. 15-18 Typical cylinder wear. (Oldsmobile Motor Division, GMC)

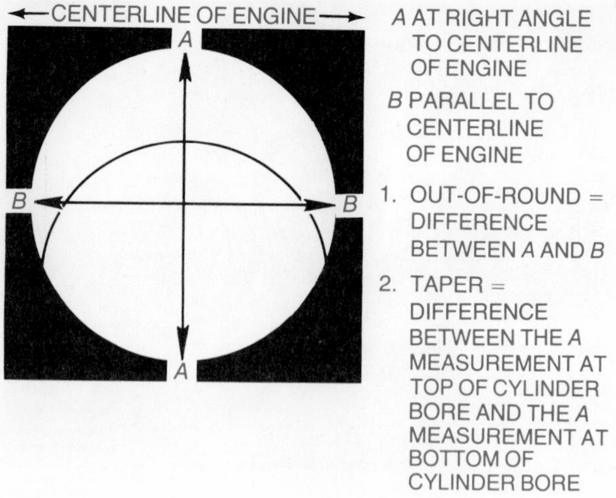

←CENTERLINE OF ENGINE→

A AT RIGHT ANGLE TO CENTERLINE OF ENGINE

B PARALLEL TO CENTERLINE OF ENGINE

1. OUT-OF-ROUND = DIFFERENCE BETWEEN *A* AND *B*

2. TAPER = DIFFERENCE BETWEEN THE *A* MEASUREMENT AT TOP OF CYLINDER BORE AND THE *A* MEASUREMENT AT BOTTOM OF CYLINDER BORE

Fig. 15-19 Cylinder out-of-round and taper measurements. (Ford Motor Company)

difference between a measurement made at the bottom of the cylinder bore and one in the area of greatest wear is called taper. The measurement at the bottom where the cylinder bore is unworn may be compared to specifications to find the size of the cylinder. This information is necessary for ordering piston rings.

15.19   Glaze Breaking

The cylinder wear measurements are compared against manufacturer's specifications to find out what reconditioning is necessary. If taper and out-of-round are within limits, all that is necessary is to deglaze the cylinder walls. The movement of the piston rings up and down in the cylinder polishes the cylinder surface with a glaze. This must be removed so that new rings will wear in or "seat" quickly and so that oil will cling to the cylinder surface and prevent ring or piston scuffing.

A set of spring-loaded abrasive stones driven by an electric drill is used to deglaze cylinders. The deglazer is pushed up and down as it rotates to put the proper cross-hatch pattern on the cylinder walls. Oil clings to the small oil grooves created by the cross-hatching. If the cross-hatch pattern is too smooth, the rings will not seat and wear in properly and quickly without scoring or scuffing. If the cross-hatch is too rough and too deep the rings will wear out fast.

After breaking the glaze, always use soap and warm water to wash the cylinders. This combination does the best job of getting the dirt and grit out of the tiny crevices that remain after honing. Soap forms around the dirt and grit, floating them out with the water. The use of kerosene would drive the particles back into the crevices where they could wear out the new rings.

15.20   Honing

If cylinder taper or out-of-round is greater than the manufacturer's wear specifications, the cylinder may be honed (Fig. 15-21). A rigid honing fixture with abrasive stones driven by an electric drill motor removes metal from the cylinder in order to straighten it. As the taper is removed, the operator strokes the entire length of the cylinder up and down to produce a cross-hatch pattern. Measurements are taken often to make sure that the smallest amount of metal possible is removed to bring the cylinder to specifications. After honing, the cylinder is cleaned the same way as after deglazing.

15.21   Knurling

Honing leaves the cylinder oversize. If the standard pistons were replaced in the cylinder, there would be too much clearance between the piston skirt and the cylinder wall. The pistons are therefore expanded or resized by knurling. Knurling increases the diameter of a piston by pressing in a pattern of hills and valleys on the two thrust faces (Fig. 15-22).

Knurled piston skirts have an irregular surface which provides greater resistance to scuffing and seizure than smooth surfaces. The valleys serve as oil pockets, improving lubrication. The irregular surface provides a series of points at which surface metal can expand sideways under heat rather than bulge and break through the protective oil film. The valleys trap

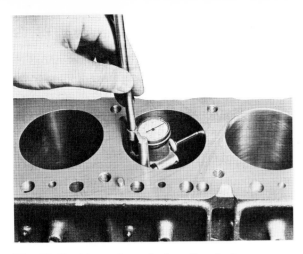

Fig. 15-20 Measuring cylinder with cylinder gauge.
(Pontiac Motor Division, GMC)

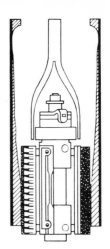

Fig. 15-21 Hone operating in bottom of cylinder to remove taper.

particles of metal or foreign substances which would otherwise break through the oil film. A knurled piston is shown in Figure 15-23.

15.22 Boring

When cylinder wear is very bad, the cylinder must be rebored. Boring involves machining the cylinder oversize with a cutter bit driven by a tool called a boring bar (Fig. 15-24). After boring, the cylinder is often polished by honing to provide the cross-hatch pattern. Since boring leaves the cylinders oversize, a set of new oversize pistons must be fitted.

The boring operation is sometimes used to machine a single cylinder oversize for the installation of a dry sleeve. This may be necessary when one of the cylinders has been damaged by a broken ring, piston, pin, or connecting rod. The sleeve is installed with a press fit. After installation it is bored to the size of the other cylinders.

15.23 Block Bearing Housings

The camshaft and main bearing housings must be measured and inspected before reassembly. Measure the camshaft bearing bores with a telescoping gauge (see chapter 7) to determine size and out-of-roundness. Inspect the main bearings to find the wear pattern for possible crankcase warpage or out-of-round housing bores. The crankcase main bearing housing bores must be round and in true alignment lengthwise or the crankshaft could be bent.

Housing bore alignment can be checked by placing a properly ground arbor as long as the crankcase into the bores (Fig. 15-25). Install the caps in the correct relation to the front of the engine. Install the bolts and tighten to specifications.

After all of the bolts have been tightened, turn the arbor with a 12-inch handle. If it will not turn, one or more of the bores may be out-of-round, or the crankcase may be warped. This condition must be corrected before continuing further.

If correction is required, the bearing housings can be bored into alignment. Main bearing housings are rebored with a tool called an align boring machine or a line boring machine (Fig. 15-26). It removes metal from the bearing housing bores to bring them into a straight line. Special main bearing inserts must be used that compensate for the metal removed from the bores during line boring.

15.24 PISTON SERVICE

The first step in piston service is to visually check each piston. Look for fractures at the ring lands, the skirts, and the pin bosses. Look for scuffed, scored, or rough surfaces. Replace pistons that show signs of too much wear or have wavy ring lands.

15.25 Examining Pistons

A careful check of the pistons and rings will often show the cause of oil consumption or engine damage. Figure 15-27 shows a burned top ring land and broken top ring caused by excessive temperature

Fig. 15-22 Knurling to expand piston. (Perfect Circle)

ARBOR

Fig. 15-25 Checking crankcase for alignment. (Federal-Mogul)

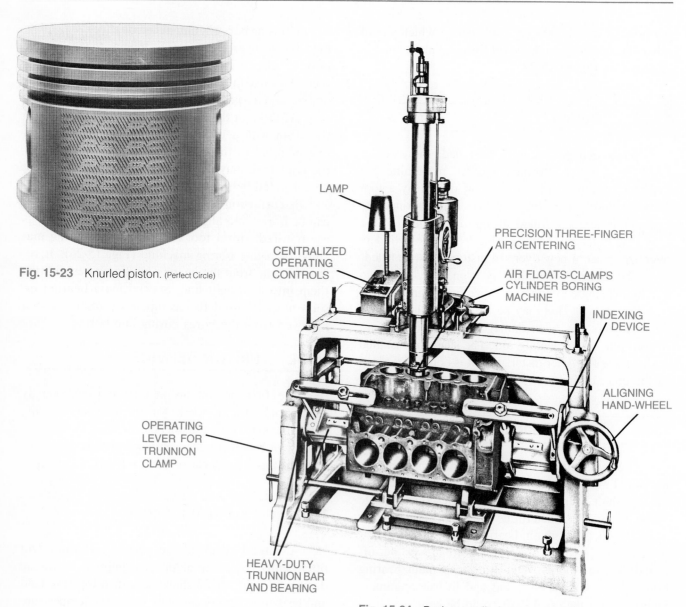

Fig. 15-23 Knurled piston. (Perfect Circle)

LAMP

CENTRALIZED
OPERATING
CONTROLS

PRECISION THREE-FINGER
AIR CENTERING

AIR FLOATS-CLAMPS
CYLINDER BORING
MACHINE

INDEXING
DEVICE

ALIGNING
HAND-WHEEL

OPERATING
LEVER FOR
TRUNNION
CLAMP

HEAVY-DUTY
TRUNNION BAR
AND BEARING

Fig. 15-24 Boring a cylinder.
(Kwik-Way/Cedar Rapids Engineering Company)

Fig. 15-26 Line boring machine. (Kwik-Way)

Fig. 15-27 Piston damaged by extreme pressure and temperature in combustion chamber. (Perfect Circle)

and pressure in the combustion chamber. Such conditions cause bad piston burning, fast top groove wear, ring breakage, scoring, piston ring sticking, and, finally, complete engine failure.

Preignition, the igniting of the air-fuel charge before the regular ignition spark, causes loss of engine power and damage to pistons (Fig. 15-28), rings, and valves. The high pressure caused by preignition sometimes drives the top ring down with sufficient force to break off the ring land below the top compression ring.

Both the piston and rings shown in Figure 15-29 are scored. When metal-to-metal contact between two rubbing surfaces raises the temperature of one of these surfaces to the melting point, scoring will result. Scuffing is a lighter form of the same damage. Scuffing and scoring are caused by overheating because of a faulty cooling system, lack of cylinder lubrication, improper combustion, incorrect or too little bearing or piston clearances, improper break-in, and coolant leakage into the cylinder.

15.26   Measuring Pistons and Ring Clearance

If the pistons pass a visual inspection, they may be measured with a micrometer. The outside diameter of the piston is measured at the centerline of the piston pin bore and at 90 degrees to the piston pin (Fig. 15-30). If the piston dimension meets the manufacturer's specifications, it may be cleaned and inspected further.

The old rings are removed from the piston with a piston ring expanding tool (Fig. 15-31). The piston may be soaked in a chemical solution or cleaned in a

Fig. 15-28 Piston with preignition damage. (Perfect Circle)

Fig. 15-29 Scored piston and piston rings. (Perfect Circle)

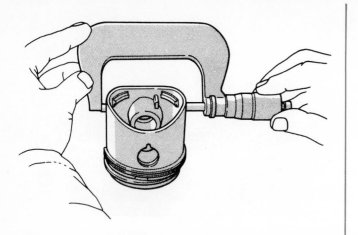

Fig. 15-30 Measuring piston with micrometer. (Chrysler Corporation)

Fig. 15-31 Using ring tool to remove or replace piston ring. (Chrysler Corporation)

bead blaster to remove carbon and other buildup. The ring grooves must be cleaned with a ring groove cleaner (Fig. 15-32). The oil drain holes and slots must be inspected and cleaned if necessary.

Check the new piston rings for side clearance (Fig. 15-33). It is not necessary to install the rings at this time. Use a feeler gauge as shown and run the ring all the way around the groove. If the clearance is over 0.006 inches (0.15 mm), use a new piston or machine the piston to accept a ring groove spacer.

The top ring is the most important ring on the piston. It acts as a compression ring to control blow-by and also as a final oil control ring. The top ring and top groove of most aluminum pistons that have been in service for a long time become worn from abrasives and high temperature in the top ring land area. This increases the top ring side clearance and causes increased blow-by and oil consumption.

If a new top compression ring is installed in a worn groove (Fig. 15-34), a proper seal cannot be formed. The worn groove forces the upper outside edge of the ring face to contact the cylinder wall, causing the oil to be wiped up into the combustion chamber instead of down into the crankcase. In addition, the continued twisting of the new top ring in the worn groove will result in ring breakage. Therefore, the top grooves should be checked and remachined or new pistons used.

If top groove clearance is too wide, machine the old pistons to accommodate a new standard width ring and a steel top groove spacer. The machining operation is done with a hand driven cutter and pilot assembly (Fig. 15-35). After the regrooving operation, install the steel spacer above the new top piston ring (Fig. 15-36).

Measure the piston skirt-to-cylinder wall clearance before installing rings on the piston or the piston on the connecting rod. Adjusting the clearance is called fitting the pistons. After boring or honing, the clearance is found by measuring the cylinder and comparing it with the piston size. It may be necessary to remove metal from the cylinder with the hone to get the clearance specified by the manufacturer.

15.27 CONNECTING ROD SERVICE

When the connecting rods have been cleaned, inspect them visually for any evidence of damage. Remove the connecting rod insert bearings, replace the rod cap in the rod, and tighten to specifications. Use a connecting rod vise to ensure the correct alignment of the rod to the cap. Inspect the connecting rod big end bore for out-of-roundness by taking several measurements around the bore with a telescoping gauge.

If the connecting rod bore is out-of-round, it must be reconditioned. A precision grinder is used to remove material from the mating surfaces of the connecting rod and cap. This makes the bore smaller but out-of-round. A honing unit is used to machine the rod bore back to specifications.

To recondition the small end of the connecting rod, press out the worn bushing and press in a new bushing (Fig. 15-37). Each new bushing must be sized to fit the wrist pin, after being pressed into the rod. A special hone or boring machine is used to make the bushing fit the wrist pin.

After both ends of the connecting rod have been serviced, check the rod for alignment (Fig. 15-38).

Fig. 15-32 Cleaning ring grooves with ring groove cleaners.

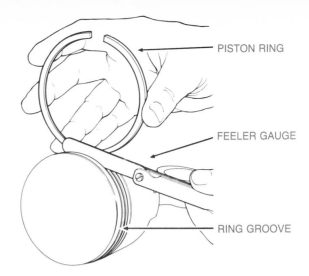

Fig. 15-33 Measuring piston pin side clearance. (American Motors Corporation)

This may be done before or after the piston is re-assembled to the rod. Correct connecting rod alignment is necessary to have the piston skirts truly square with the connecting rod bore. Misaligned connecting rods can cause engine knocks, oil pumping, and blow-by by holding the faces of the piston rings at a slight angle to the cylinder bore. A number of fixtures (Fig. 15-39) are available for checking rod and piston realignment. Corrections are usually made by twisting or bending the rod with a notched bar.

15.28 PISTON RING SERVICE

Before installing new rings, each compression ring from the ring set should be pushed down to the lower, unworn portion of a cylinder. The ring must be square in the cylinder. Pushing the ring down in the bore with the head of the piston puts the ring into the bore at the proper depth and squares it with the cylinder walls. A feeler gauge is used to measure the ring end gap (Fig. 15-40). Checking this measurement with specifications provides a double check on whether the ring set is the correct size.

All rings should have at least the minimum gap to provide for expansion between the piston ring and the cylinder. Otherwise the ring ends may butt and cause scuffing, scoring, ring breakage, or engine seizure. If end clearance is less than the required minimum, the cylinder is undersize or the wrong ring set is being used.

If the ring end gap is satisfactory, the rings may be installed on the piston. Most compression rings must be installed with their top side toward the top of the piston. Instructions provided with new piston ring sets explain which ring goes in which groove and

Fig. 15-34 New ring in worn groove. (Perfect Circle)

Fig. 15-35 Machining piston to accept top groove spacer. (Perfect Circle)

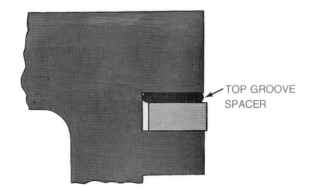

Fig. 15-36 Top groove spacer installed above ring. (Perfect Circle)

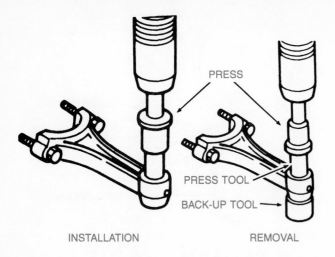

Fig. 15-37 Removing and installing piston pin bushings in the connecting rod. (Chevrolet Motor Division, GMC)

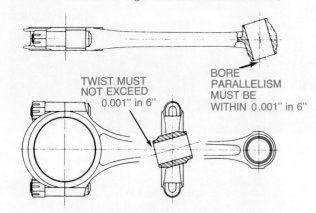

TWIST MUST NOT EXCEED 0.001" in 6"

BORE PARALLELISM MUST BE WITHIN 0.001" in 6"

Fig. 15-38 Recommended limits for connecting rod alignment. (Federal-Mogul)

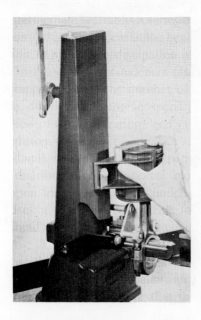

Fig. 15-39 Fixture for connecting rod alignment. (Federal-Mogul)

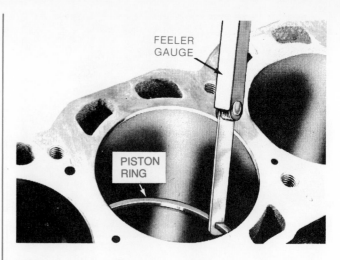

Fig. 15-40 Measuring ring end gap. (Chevrolet Motor Division, GMC)

in what direction they must be installed. When installing rings, use a good quality ring expander tool to prevent overspreading them. Do not attempt to install them by hand. They can become distorted and get small metal fractures opposite the gap that lead to ring breakage.

In most installations, ring ends may be located anywhere around the piston. Some manufacturers specify a particular spacing for the ring gaps as shown in Figure 15-41.

15.29 CRANKSHAFT SERVICE

The crankshaft should be thoroughly cleaned, inspected, and measured after it has been removed from the engine. Crankshaft journals wear out-of-round. Rod journals usually show the most wear on the underside of the throw, but main journals have no special area of wear.

A crankshaft that is out-of-round or tapered beyond specifications must be reground or replaced. If there is any scoring or ridging on the journals, the crankshaft must be reground or replaced.

To check for runout, rotate the crankshaft in V-blocks with a dial indicator on the center main bearing. Replace or straighten bent shafts.

Crankshafts are reconditioned in a precision grinder. Each of the connecting rod and main bearings is ground to a standard undersize. The bearings used with the reconditioned crankshaft must be matched to the undersize to avoid excessive oil clearance.

A crankshaft may also be rebuilt. Rebuilding is adding material to the surface of the crankshaft rod and main journals. There are several rebuilding

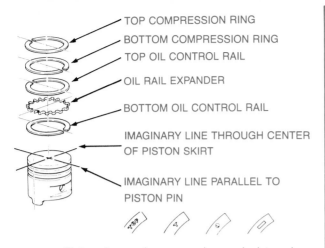

Fig. 15-41 Piston ring end gap spacing and piston ring marking. (American Motors Corporation)

TOP COMPRESSION RING
BOTTOM COMPRESSION RING
TOP OIL CONTROL RAIL
OIL RAIL EXPANDER
BOTTOM OIL CONTROL RAIL
IMAGINARY LINE THROUGH CENTER OF PISTON SKIRT
IMAGINARY LINE PARALLEL TO PISTON PIN

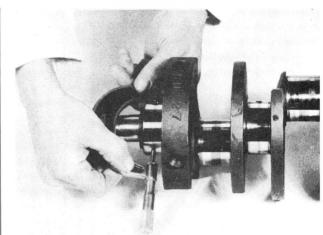

Fig. 15-42 Crankshaft journals measured with micrometer. (Chevrolet Motor Division, GMC)

methods. Chromium plating adds pure hard chromium onto rod or main journal surfaces. This makes an ideal surface for a bearing. Electro-welding is a process in which a bead of steel is deposited by an electric arc onto the crankpin or journal surface in a continuous weld. Metal spraying adds molten steel onto a journal surface to build it up.

15.30 CAMSHAFT SERVICE

After the camshaft is cleaned, an outside micrometer is used to check the height of each cam lobe (Fig. 15-45). Also, the tappet surfaces which ride on the cams should be closely inspected for surface pits. If tappets show pitting, they should be replaced. It is possible that the camshaft itself may require either reconditioning or replacing.

If required, the cam bearing journals and cam lobes can be reground to a standard undersize in a camshaft grinder. In original production, the cam surfaces are treated with a chemical which provides an oil-absorbing surface. When used with lubricating oil, it provides an oilier surface. Many engine reconditioners do the same thing after regrinding.

15.31 CYLINDER HEAD AND VALVE TRAIN SERVICE

Cylinder head and valve train servicing involves disassembly and cleaning of the components and then measuring and inspecting for wear. The valve guides, valves, valve seats, and other valve train components must be reconditioned. The procedures used to service these components are presented in the following sections.

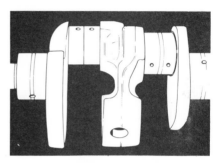

Fig. 15-43 Crankshaft journals that are worn must be reground. (Federal-Mogul)

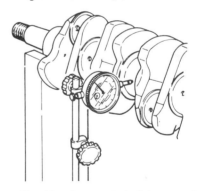

Fig. 15-44 Checking the crankshaft for runout. (Chevrolet Motor Division, GMC)

Fig. 15-45 Checking cam lobes for wear. (Federal-Mogul)

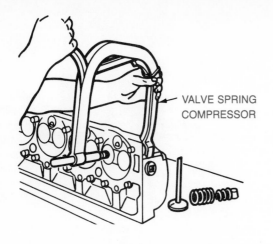

VALVE SPRING COMPRESSOR

Fig. 15-46 Valve spring compressor to remove valves from cylinder head. (Chevrolet Motor Division, GMC)

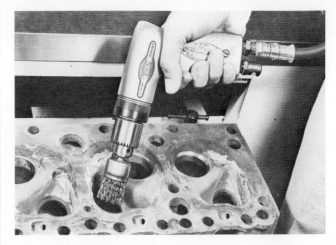

Fig. 15-47 Cleaning combustion chamber with wire brush. (Sioux)

15.32 Disassembly and Cleaning

Cylinder head and valve train service begins with disassembling the cylinder head. Remove the rocker arms first. Remove the valves by compressing the valve springs with a valve spring compressor (Fig. 15-46). When the springs are compressed, the retaining washers and locks may be removed. The valve assemblies including the rocker arms should be kept in order so that they may be reinstalled in the same position. After disassembly, clean the cylinder head in a hot tank along with the cylinder block, if it is made from cast iron. Use a cold tank if the cylinder head is made from aluminum.

Carbon not removed from the combustion chamber by the tanking may be cleaned off with a wire brush in a drill motor (Fig. 15-47). The valve guides are cleaned with a valve guide cleaner made of several flat spring tension blades that press against the guides and scrape out the carbon without scratching metal. The tool may be driven by hand or with an electric motor as shown in Figure 15-48.

15.33 Measuring and Inspecting for Wear

The cleaned parts are then measured and inspected for wear. The cylinder head is checked for flatness with a straightedge and feeler gauge (Fig. 15-49). Place the straightedge in several different directions across the cylinder head. Use a thin feeler gauge to determine if there is any space between the straightedge and the cylinder head surface. If the feeler gauge will pass under the straightedge when it is pushed firmly against the cylinder head, the cylinder head is warped. A warped cylinder head may be resurfaced by grinding with a special surface grinder.

Carbon deposits are removed from the valve by holding it against a wire wheel brush mounted on a grinder. Clean the head, face, and stem thoroughly, particularly the area from face to stem. Carbon can make a valve overheat because it will not allow the flow of heat.

Inspect the valve, valve seat, and guide for wear and damage. Even in normal use these components absorb a great deal of punishment. As a result, the valves, particularly the exhaust valves, may become pitted, burned, warped, or grooved. Then the valve begins to leak compression and hold heat. As shown in Figure 15-50, there is also wear at the stem from friction with the guide and end wear from contact with the rocker arm.

The valve seat also wears. Hot gases burn it and carbon particles which retain heat pit the valve seat. The valve guide wears against the valve stem. Between stem and guide carbon builds up which causes the valves to stick. Typical wear in these areas is shown in Figure 15-51.

The amount of wear between the valve stem and guide may be found by measuring the valve stem with a micrometer and the guide with a small hole gauge. The difference in the two measurements is the amount of clearance. Another measuring method is to mount a dial indicator to the cylinder head and rock the valve against the indicator (Fig. 15-52). The valve must be placed very close to the seat for this check.

15.34 Valve Guide Service

If the stem-to-guide clearance is more than manufacturer's specifications, several repair procedures may be used. If the guide is replaceable, install

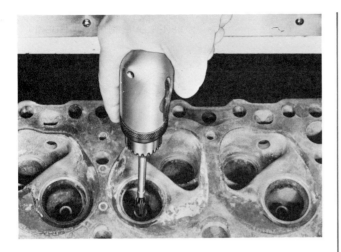

Fig. 15-48 Cleaning valve guides. (Sioux)

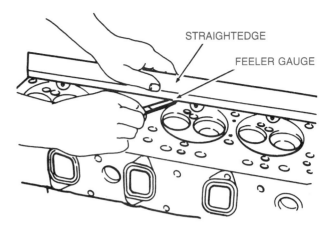

Fig. 15-49 Measuring cylinder head for flatness. (Chevrolet Motor Division, GMC)

a new one. New guides sometimes require finish reaming for proper stem-to-guide clearance.

Many cylinder heads do not have replaceable guides. If wear is within limits and the valve guides are not hardened, they can be knurled by driving a rotating cutter down the guide that displaces metal so that the inside diameter of the guide is made smaller. After knurling, the guide is finish reamed.

If guides are worn beyond knurling limits, it is often possible to ream them to a standard oversize. Then replacement valves with oversize stems are used. If oversize valves are not available or wear is excessive, the internal guide must be drilled out and a new guide pressed or threaded into place.

Another repair procedure involves the installation of a special Teflon seal at the top of the valve guide. The seal attaches to the valve guide and works like a piston ring turned inside out. The seal prevents oil from entering the valve guide. It does not interfere with the amount of oil in the rocker arm area or on the valve stem above the guide. Details of such a seal are shown in Figure 15-53.

15.35 Grinding Valves and Valve Seats

Valve faces are ground on a precision valve grinding machine (Fig. 15-54). The valve is first chucked or mounted in a chuck-head that is adjusted to the correct angle for the valve face. The valve is ground by moving the valve slowly and steadily across the wheel. Light cuts are taken by feeding the grinding wheel up to the valve just enough to make a clean, smooth face. When the valve face is ground, the grinding wheel is backed away from the valve and the valve is removed from the chuck.

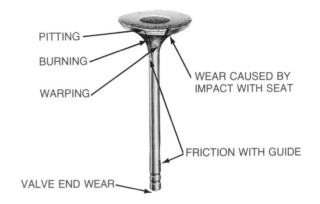

Fig. 15-50 Types of valve wear. (Sioux)

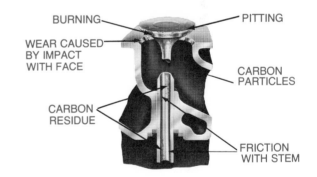

Fig. 15-51 Wear valve, valve seat, and valve guide. (Sioux)

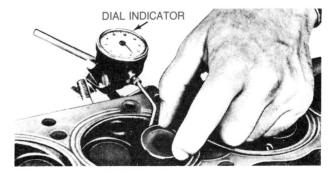

Fig. 15-52 Measuring valve guide wear. (Chrysler Corporation)

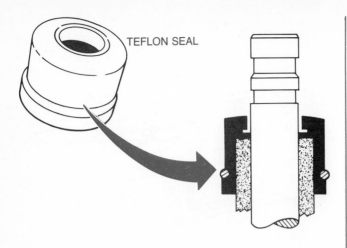

Fig. 15-53 Detail of valve guide oil seal. (Perfect Circle)

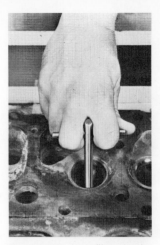

Fig. 15-56 Installing a valve seat grinding pilot. (Sioux)

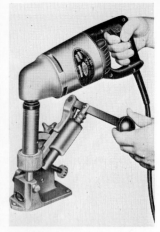

Fig. 15-57 Truing valve seat grinding stone. (Sioux)

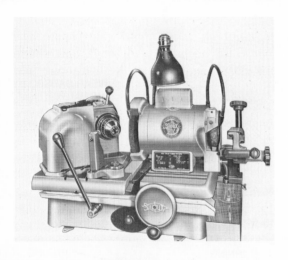

Fig. 15-54 Valve grinder. (Sioux)

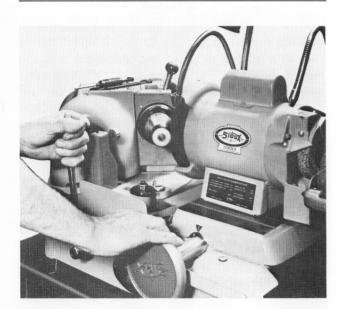

Fig. 15-55 Grinding the valve face. (Sioux)

After grinding, each valve must be inspected. Badly pitted, burned, or warped valves cannot be refaced without removing too much metal along the edge or margin. Loss of the margin gives the head of the valve a sharp edge that cannot take high temperatures. If the margin is not within the specified thickness after grinding, the valve must be replaced.

The valve seats are reconditioned by a grinding stone mounted in a holder and driven by a hand held driver. A pilot shaft of the correct diameter is inserted in the valve guide of the seat to be ground (Fig. 15-56). The pilot is used to guide and center the grinding wheel. Since the valve guide is used for centering, all valve guide service or replacement must be performed before seat grinding. A seat grinding stone is mounted to a driver and dressed to the specified angle for the valve seat in a truing unit using a diamond cutting tool (Fig. 15-57).

The grinding stone and holder are installed over the pilot (Fig. 15-58). The driver spindle is installed on the holder and the driver motor is started (Fig. 15-59). A few seconds of cutting will usually be enough to remove the pits and leave a precision ground surface. Steel seats require a roughing wheel for fast finishing; cast iron seats need only a finishing wheel. When servicing Stellite or induction hardened seats, only a small amount of metal is removed. Otherwise the grinding may go below the hardened surface. Hardened seats dull grinding wheels rapidly. The grinding wheel must be dressed frequently when servicing hardened seats.

The ground valve seat must provide the proper seat-to-face contact (Fig. 15-60). The valve face should always be larger than the valve seat. The engine manufacturer will provide specifications on

Fig. 15-58 Installing grinding wheel over pilot. (Sioux)

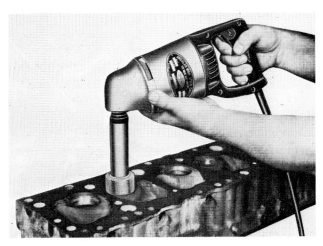

Fig. 15-59 Grinding the valve seat. (Sioux)

valve seat width. If the reconditioned seat is too wide, it must be narrowed by grinding material off the top or bottom of the seat with a special narrowing grinding stone. The valve seat shown in Figure 15-61 has been narrowed at the top for proper seat contact with a 15-degree stone.

If a valve seat is very badly pitted, grinding may not be enough for reconditioning. The valve seat may have to be replaced. Special tools are available for removing and replacing replaceable valve seats. If the valve seat is not replaceable, but part of the cylinder head, it may be machined to accept a replaceable valve seat (Fig. 15-62).

After the valve and seat have been reconditioned, they must be checked with a valve seat dial indicator (Fig. 15-63). This shows whether valve and seat are concentric, that is, whether their centers are the same point. A pilot is installed in the valve guide and the indicator is mounted to it. The indicator is rotated on the pilot with its adjustable bar in contact with the seat. Readings on the face of the indicator are compared against specifications. If the concentricity is not acceptable, the seat may require further grinding or replacement.

The tip of each valve must be inspected for wear and ground on a special wheel provided on the valve grinder if necessary. The valve is chucked on the stem and the tip is moved past the side of the wheel (Fig. 15-64). Tappets and rocker arms may also be resurfaced with attachments mounted to this side of the valve grinder.

Before reassembling the valves in the cylinder head, inspect each valve spring for squareness (Fig. 15-65) and for proper tension (Fig. 15-66). Tension is measured with a torque wrench or a tension gauge.

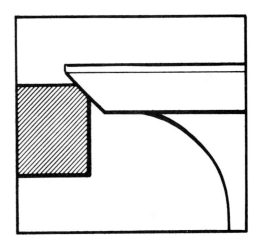

Fig. 15-60 Proper valve face-to-seat contact. (Sioux)

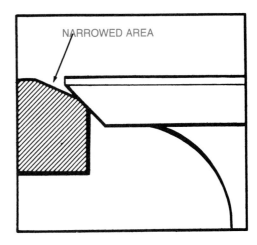

NARROWED AREA

Fig. 15-61 Narrowing the valve seat. (Sioux)

Fig. 15-62 Worn valve seats may be machined to accept a replacement. (Kwik-Way)

Fig. 15-64 Grinding material from tip of valve. (Sioux)

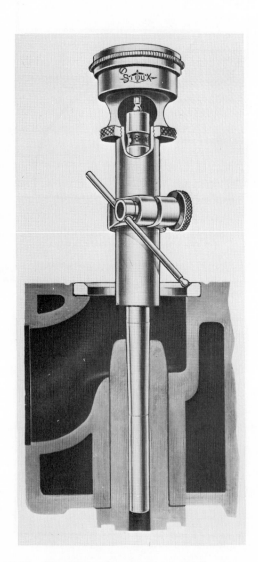

Fig. 15-63 Checking valve seat concentricity. (Sioux)

Springs below the specified tensions are either replaced or spacers called shims are used under the springs when they are reinstalled. The valve assemblies are reassembled with the valve spring compressing tool that was used for disassembly. After assembly, the assembled height of the valve spring assembly is measured and compared to specifications.

Test hydraulic valve lifters for proper operation, called leakdown rate (Fig. 15-67). The lifter is placed in a container under fluid, usually oil or kerosene. A weighted rod is mounted on the pushrod seat, and the time it takes the weighted rod to push the lifter plunger to the bottom of its bore is measured. The faster the lifter leaks down, the more wear it has. A stuck lifter would have no leakdown rate. If the leakdown rate is not to specifications, the lifter must be replaced.

15.36   REASSEMBLY

Reassembly begins by installing new camshaft bearings in the block. The same tool used for removing the old bearings is used to drive in the new ones. Be sure that the leading edge of the camshaft housing bores are hand-chamfered so that, when the bearings are installed, the sharp edges will not shave off material from the outside surfaces of the bearings. Select bearings of the proper undersize to fit the journals of the camshaft. Line up the oil holes before assembly. After assembly, check the alignment of these holes with those in the cylinder block by pushing a wire through the opening. Correct camshaft housing bore size and the correct bearings ensure that the oil clearances will be correct.

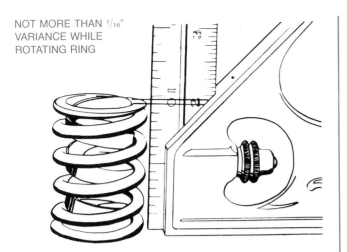

Fig. 15-65 Inspecting valve spring for squareness. (Chevrolet Motor Division, GMC)

Fig. 15-66 Checking valve spring tension. (Chevrolet Motor Division, GMC)

Before installing the crankshaft, install the upper half of the rear oil seal in the block and rear main bearing cap. Woven or rope packing is sometimes used at the crankshaft rear end. The packing should first be rolled into the groove with a suitable tool. An arbor slightly over shaft size and a mallet can further seat the packing, or a special tool can be used (Fig. 15-68). After seating in this manner, the packing can be cut off flush with the crankcase or the cap surface with a razor blade. A packing that is too free against the shaft causes leakage that is made worse by the sucking action of the rotating flywheel at high engine speeds.

Insert new main bearing inserts in each of the main bearing caps and in the cylinder block housings. Wipe the caps and housings clean and dry before installing the bearing inserts. Never oil or grease the backs of the bearings. Place the crankshaft into the block on the new main bearings and arrange the main bearings caps in the correct order and direction over the crankshaft.

The oil clearance between the crankshaft and the main bearing inserts must be measured. If the oil clearance is too small, many troubles, such as wiped bearings, worn crankshaft, excessive cylinder wear, stuck piston rings, and worn pistons, may result.

If the oil clearance is too great, the crankshaft may overheat and weld itself to the insert bearings. A specially molded, fine plastic string or Plastigauge is used to determine the oil clearance between the bearing and the shaft. A length of it is cut off, approximately 1/8 inch (3 mm) shorter than the bearing, and placed on the bearing inside surface or upon the shaft after each has been wiped free of oil.

Assemble the bearing and cap to the housing over the shaft and tighten to the recommended torque wrench reading. Do not turn the shaft. Remove the cap and bearing and measure the width of the string or Plastigauge that has been squashed in the oil clearance space (Fig. 15-69). The width of the flattened portion can be compared with the width scale provided as part of the string package to indicate clearance.

After the clearance check, oil the main bearings and torque the bolts. Then rotate the crankshaft by hand. If the job has been done properly, the shaft should turn reasonably free. Check the crankshaft end play (Fig. 15-70). Some end play is built into the thrust bearing. However, to make certain that the end play is within the specified limits, it should always be checked with a feeler gauge or a dial indicator. As a final check on the main bearing installation, recheck the cap markings. Then torque on the cap bolts to make sure the crankshaft does not bind.

The timing chain or timing gear is installed from the crankshaft to the camshaft. Align the timing marks that establish the crankshaft-to-camshaft timing (Fig. 15-71).

The piston and connecting rod assemblies may be installed in the cylinder block next. Install a new bearing insert in each of the connecting rods. Coat the piston rings and cylinder walls with oil to lubricate them during the engine cranking period until oil throwoff from the connecting rod journals is adequate.

Use a piston ring compressing tool (Fig. 15-72) to install the piston and ring into the cylinder bore. When the rings are properly compressed into their grooves, only a light tapping on the piston head with an average size hammer handle is required to push the

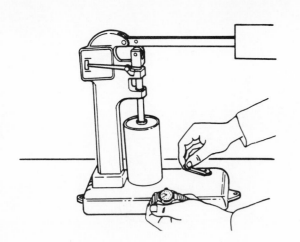

Fig. 15-67 Checking hydraulic lifter leak-down rate. (Chevrolet Motor Division, GMC)

AFTER CORRECTLY POSITIONING SEAL, ROTATE TOOL SLIGHTLY AND CUT OFF EACH END OF SEAL FLUSH WITH BLOCK

SEAL TOOL

OIL SEAL

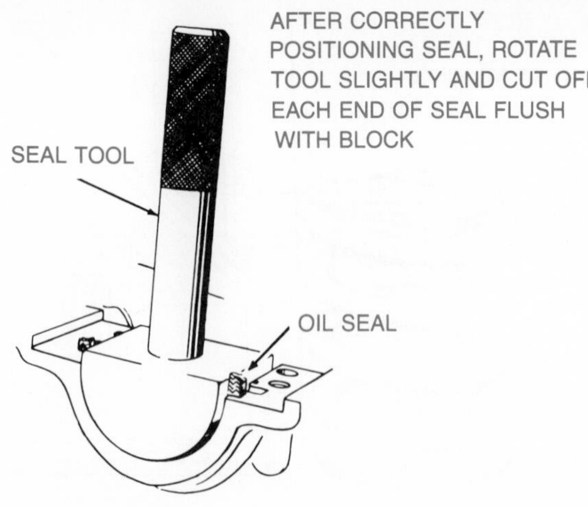

Fig. 15-68 Installing rear main upper oil seal. (Chevrolet Motor Division, GMC)

piston assembly into its bore. Take care when installing the connecting rod that the studs on the rod do not hit the crankshaft journal. The studs may be covered with rubber hose or special aluminum guides (Fig. 15-73). Install the number one piston and rod assembly into the number one cylinder, making sure the rod and piston reference marks are in correct relation to the front of the engine. With the bearing in place, seat the rod on its crankpin. The oil clearance is measured on each of the caps with plastic wire following the same procedure as that used for main bearings.

The other parts and accessories may now be installed on the engine. Torque the cylinder heads after installing a new gasket. The proper torque and tightening sequence chart (Figure 15-74 is an example) is available in the service literature. The intake manifold and oil pan bolts also often have a particular tightening sequence. Valves are adjusted following the procedure provided earlier.

Before engine startup, an engine prelubricator should be used to fill the lubrication system galleries and oil filter. This is very important to the life of engine bearings. The lag between starting the engine and getting oil to the bearings may shorten bearing life.

After the engine is prelubricated and all accessories are installed, start it up. Watch closely for oil or coolant leaks. Oil consumption in new engines or after installation of new rings is often higher than normal until the rings become seated. That period of engine operation which is required before blowby and oil consumption level off is referred to as the breakin period. Different piston ring manufacturers specify different breakin procedures.

Ring seating consists of the mating of the ring face with the cylinder wall throughout the complete stroke of the ring. This is done by wearing off the very slight irregularities of the ring face and the cylinder wall. The breakin period has been reduced as rings and cylinders have been produced with greater accuracy. Ring and engine manufacturers have not been able to duplicate the nearly perfect mating surfaces made by the engine. For this reason all new and rebuilt engines require a certain amount of running for maximum oil control.

NEW TERMS

Boring Machining away metal from a worn cylinder with a boring bar for the installation of new oversize pistons.

Camshaft grinding Refinishing the bearing journals or lobes on a camshaft with a grinder.

Compression pressure test Measuring the condition of an engine by testing the compression in the cylinders with a compression gauge.

Connecting rod alignment Checking a connecting rod in a fixture to make sure it is in alignment.

Crankshaft grinding Refinishing the connecting rod and main bearing journals on a crankshaft with a grinder.

Crankshaft rebuilding Building up a worn crankshaft journal by plating, welding, or spraying.

Cylinder leakage test Finding out the condition of an engine by measuring how fast air leaks out of the cylinders.

Engine overhaul Reconditioning parts of an engine to bring it back to factory specifications.

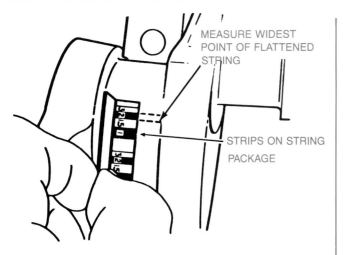

Fig. 15-69 Measuring oil clearance with plastic string. (Chevrolet Motor Division, GMC)

MEASURE WIDEST POINT OF FLATTENED STRING

STRIPS ON STRING PACKAGE

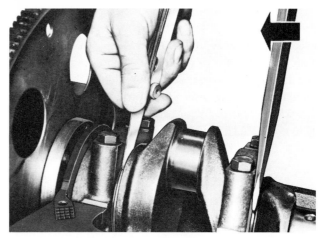

Fig. 15-70 Checking crankshaft end play. (American Motors Corporation)

Fig. 15-71 Aligning timing marks on crankshaft and camshaft.

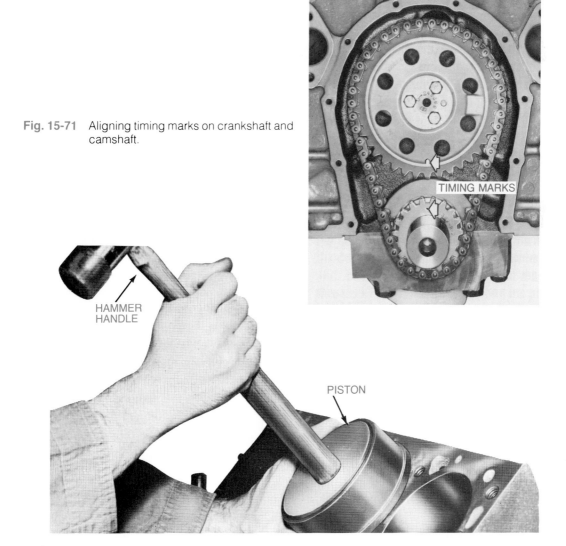

TIMING MARKS

HAMMER HANDLE

PISTON

Fig. 15-72 Piston ring compressing tool used to install piston into cylinder. (Pontiac Motor Division, GMC)

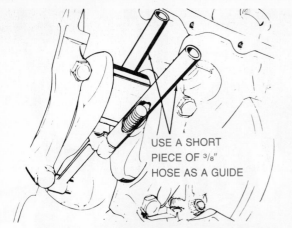

Fig. 15-73 Using guides over the connecting rod studs to prevent damage to the crankshaft. (Chevrolet Motor Division, GMC)

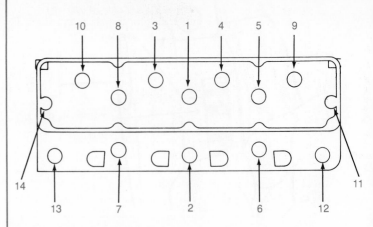

Fig. 15-74 Cylinder head tightening sequence. (American Motors Corporation)

Engine rebuild   Same as engine overhaul.

Fitting pistons   Removing metal from cylinders to get the proper piston clearance.

Glaze breaking   Roughing up the surface of a cylinder with an abrasive stone to help the rings seat.

Honing   Removing metal from a cylinder with abrasive stones to straighten it.

Margin   The outside part of the valve face that gets thinner as it is ground.

Narrowing   Removing part of the valve seat to make it narrow for better valve seating.

Knurled piston   A piston that has been made larger with a knurling tool.

Preventive maintenance   Service work done to an automobile to prevent it from breaking down.

Ring ridge   A step worn at the top of the cylinder by the piston rings.

Taper   A form of wear common to shafts and cylinders in which one end is smaller than the other.

Troubleshooting   The step-by-step procedure used to find the problem in an automobile system.

Valve lash adjustment   The setting of the valve clearance or lash to the correct specifications.

CHAPTER REVIEW

1. What is a valve lash adjustment and why is it important?

2. List some results of excessive engine wear.

3. How can oil enter the combustion chamber of a worn engine?

4. How can one find out what cylinder of an engine has a knock?

5. What is a compression pressure test and how is it done?

6. What is a cylinder leakage test and how is it done?

7. Why must the ring ridge be removed during an engine overhaul?

8. Why should rod and main bearing caps be marked before they are removed?

9. How is a cylinder measured to find out how much taper it has?

10. Explain the difference between glaze breaking and honing.

11. When is a cylinder bored?

12. How is excessive top ring groove wear on a piston corrected?

13. What does "fitting pistons" mean?

14. What could happen if new piston rings used in an engine do not have enough end gap?

15. What kind of bearings must be used with a crankshaft that has been reground?

16. What should be done to a camshaft with worn journal or lobe surfaces?

17. How is the amount of wear between a valve stem and guide determined?

18. List three ways to repair worn valve guides.

19. How are valve faces reconditioned?

20. How are valve seats reconditioned?

DISCUSSION TOPICS AND ACTIVITIES

1. Visit a shop where engines are rebuilt. Report on what you see.

2. What engine rebuilding equipment discussed in the chapter is used in your school shop? What equipment is not used in your school shop?

3. Use a flat rate manual to find out the cost of a valve job for your own or your family's automobile.

Engine Size and Performance Measurement

CHAPTER PREVIEW

Engines are described and compared by a number of measurements related to size and performance. The measurements of engine size are an engine's bore, stroke displacement, and compression ratio. These measurements determine how much power an engine can develop. The amount of power an engine actually develops is given in terms of a performance measurement, horsepower. The concept of horsepower is based upon principles such as force, work, power energy, and efficiency. Each of these principles is explained below.

OBJECTIVES

After studying this chapter, you should be able to do the following:

1. Understand the size measurements based on bore, stroke, displacement, and compression ratio.
2. Identify the elements of engine performance measurement for linear horsepower.
3. Recognize the elements of engine rotary horsepower measurement.
4. Describe the way horsepower is measured, charted, and rated.
5. Explain the different types of efficiency ratings used with engines.

16.1 ENGINE SIZE MEASUREMENTS

Engines are manufactured in different sizes to meet different requirements. Compact automobiles have a small engine. Large luxury automobiles have a large engine. Engine size comparisons are not based upon the outside dimension of an engine, but on the size of the area where power is developed.

16.2 Bore and Stroke

The bore is the diameter of the cylinder. The larger the bore, the more powerful the engine. The stroke is the distance the piston moves from the bottom of the cylinder to the top or from the top to the bottom. The size of the stroke is determined by the distance between the centerline of the crankshaft and the centerline of the connecting rod where it attaches to the crankshaft. The longer the stroke, generally speaking, the more powerful the engine. The bore and stroke are given in inches or millimetres, e.g., a bore of 3½ inches and a stroke of 4 inches or a bore of 84 mm and a stroke of 88 mm. Sometimes just the numbers are given: 3½ × 4, for example. In this case, the bore is always the first number.

16.3 Displacement

The bore and stroke are used to calculate the displacement (Fig. 16-1) of an engine, that is, the area displaced by the piston as it moves down the cylinder. The displacement is the total volume displaced by all the pistons in the engine. It is calculated for one cylinder, and that figure is multiplied by the number of cylinders to obtain the engine's total displacement.

$$\text{Displacement} = \frac{\text{Bore}^2 \; \pi \times \text{Stroke}}{4}$$

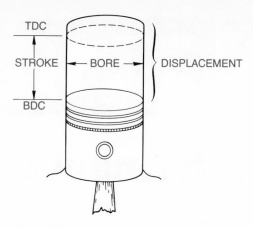

Fig. 16-1 Engine size measurements: bore, stroke, and displacement.

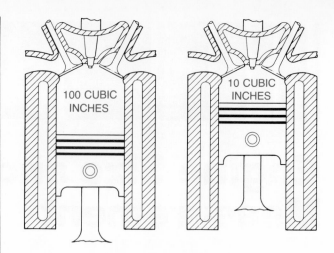

Fig. 16-2 Compression ratio of ten to one.

The bore is squared or multiplied by itself. The symbol π stands for 3.14. An engine with a bore of 3 inches and a stroke of 3 inches would have a displacement calculated as follows:

$$\text{Displacement} = \frac{3^2 \times 3.14 \times 3}{4} = 21.20 \text{ cubic inches}$$

The displacement in one cylinder is multiplied by the number of cylinders to the displacement for the entire engine. If the engine in the example above has 8 cylinders its displacement would be 21.20 × 8 or 169.6 cubic inches.

Displacement is expressed in cubic inches (CID, cubic inch displacement) or cubic centimetres (cc). A cc is much smaller than a cubic inch; a displacement of 1,131 cc equals only about 69 cubic inches. Engines using the metric system often list displacement in litres. A litre is equal to 1 000 cc. A two-litre engine has 2 000 cc. The larger the displacement, the more powerful the engine is likely to be and the more fuel it is likely to use.

16.4   Compression Ratio

Compression ratio indicates how tightly the air-fuel mixture is compressed on the compression stroke. The compression ratio is computed by first measuring the volume of a cylinder when the piston is at the bottom of its stroke. The piston is then moved to the top of its stroke and the small area above the piston, the clearance volume, is measured. For example, say the volume of the cylinder is 100 cubic inches when the piston is at the bottom of the cylinder. When the piston goes to the top, the air and fuel are squeezed

into an area only ten cubic inches in volume. This means the compression ratio is 10 to 1 (Fig. 16-2), written 10:1.

The tighter a mixture of air and fuel is squeezed, the higher the pressure buildup will be. This means that the higher the engine's compression ratio, the more powerful it is. Compression ratios on early engines were around 6, 7, or 8 to 1. Engines were eventually manufactured with compression ratios as high as 10 to 1. Because of problems related to emission control and the need to burn unleaded fuel, compression ratios have come down on most engines to around 8 to 1.

16.5   ENGINE PERFORMANCE MEASUREMENTS

Over 200 years ago, when James Watt formed a company to sell steam engines for use in the coal mines of England, the mine operators did all the lifting of coal with horses. To sell his engines, Watt developed a system for comparing the work power of his engines with the work power of the horse. It is appropriate that his name is today used for a unit of power—the watt.

The idea of horsepower is based upon a number of simple scientific principles. These principles are force, work, power, torque, energy, and efficiency. Each of these important principles and its relationship to horsepower is discussed below.

16.6   Force

In simple terms, a force is a push or pull. A person pushing against a door exerts a force on the

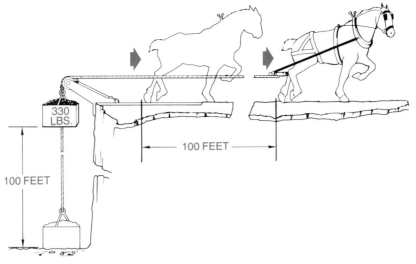

Fig. 16-3 Watt's measurement of work.

door. In scientific terms, a force is explained as an action against an object that either tends to move the object from a state of rest or one that changes the direction or speed of an object already in motion. In the English system, force is measured in pounds. To open a door, a person must push against the door with a force of so many pounds. In metric countries, a force is measured in newtons.

16.7   Work

In scientific terms, work is done when a force results in movement. If a man pushes against a door that is locked, he exerts a force. If he cannot move the door, no work is done.

James Watt measured the amount of work a horse could do by hitching a horse to a container of coal that weighed 330 lbs. He had the horse pull the container of coal 100 feet. Since the formula for work is:

Work = Distance × Force

using the example of the horse,

Work = distance (feet) × force (pounds)
Work = 100 feet × 330 pounds
Work = 33,000 foot-pounds

The horse, then, accomplished 33,000 foot-pounds of work according to the English system of measurement (Fig. 16-3). One foot-pound is equal to the force of one pound moved through a distance of one foot. In the metric system, work is measured in joules. One joule is equal to a force of one newton moved through

a distance of one metre. These ideas can be expressed as an equation:

Work = Distance × Force
foot-pounds = feet × pounds
joules = metres × newtons

16.8   Power

Power is rate or speed at which work is done. The faster work is done, the more power is involved. Consider again the example of the horse. If the horse is able to pull the container of coal one hundred feet in one minute, two horses might be able to pull the container of coal one hundred feet in one-half minute. The same amount of work is done in both cases. But the amount of power involved is different. The formula for power is

$$Power = \frac{work}{time}$$

When a single horse pulls the 330-pound weight a hundred feet in one minute, the amount of power is figured as follows:

$$Power = \frac{work\ (distance \times force)}{time\ (minutes)}$$

$$Power = \frac{100\ feet \times 330\ pounds}{1\ minute}$$

$$Power = \frac{33,000}{1}$$

Power = 33,000 foot-pounds per minute

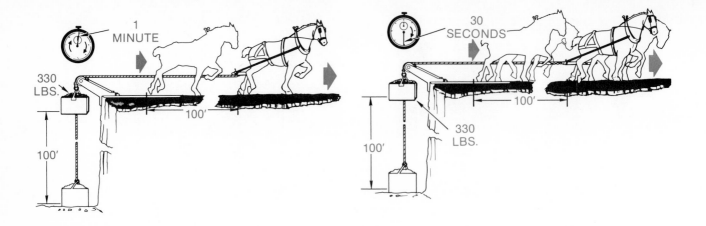

Fig. 16-4 Work and power.

When two horses pull the same weight a hundred feet in 30 seconds, or 0.5 minute, the amount of power is

$$\text{Power} = \frac{\text{work (distance} \times \text{force)}}{\text{time (minutes)}}$$

$$\text{Power} = \frac{100 \text{ feet} \times 330 \text{ pounds}}{0.5 \text{ minutes}}$$

$$\text{Power} = \frac{33,000}{0.5}$$

Power = 66,000 foot-pounds per minute

From this example (Fig. 16-4), it can be seen that the faster work is done, the more power is developed. In the English system of measurement, power is measured in foot-pounds per minute. In the metric system, the unit of power measurement is the watt. One watt is equal to one joule per second. One joule is equal to one newton moved through one metre.

16.9 Horsepower (Linear)

After watching the power produced by draft horses, Watt decided that 33,000 foot-pounds per minute was about the amount of power the average horse could produce. He was then able to write a formula for horsepower. The formula became:

$$\text{Horsepower} = \frac{\text{Distance (feet)} \times \text{Force (pounds)}}{\text{Time (minutes)} \times 33,000}$$

$$\text{Horsepower} = \frac{100 \text{ feet} \times 330 \text{ pounds}}{1 \text{ minute} \times 33,000}$$

$$\text{Horsepower} = \frac{33,000}{33,000}$$

Horsepower = 1

This idea of a horsepower proved to be very useful in comparing mechanical and animal power. The formula, however, was limited to power used for pulling a weight over a straight distance. The rotating crankshaft of an engine, however, does not develop a pulling force. Instead, as it turns, it develops a force through a circle. It was necessary to think about a rotary unit of force.

16.10 Torque

To measure power developed by an engine crankshaft, a rotary unit of force is necessary. The rotary unit of force, called torque, measures turning or twisting effort. A mechanic using a wrench to tighten a bolt applies torque to the bolt. When the bolt is so tight it no longer turns, the mechanic may still apply torque. Torque, then, is a force that produces or tends to produce rotation. If the torque results in rotation, work is done. The formula for determining torque is

$$\text{Torque} = \text{Force} \times \text{Radius}$$

The term *force* has already been explained. The radius is the distance from the point at which the force acts to the center of rotation of the shaft.

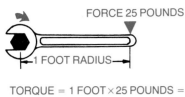

TORQUE = 1 FOOT × 25 POUNDS = 25 POUND-FEET

TORQUE = 2 FEET × 25 POUNDS = 50 POUND-FOOT

Fig. 16-5 Torque. (Go Power)

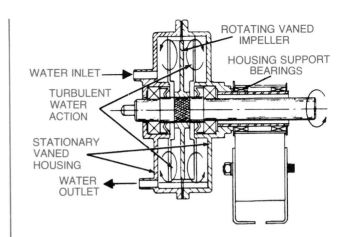

Fig. 16-6 Cross section of water brake dynamometer power absorption unit. (Go Power)

The push or pull the mechanic exerts on the wrench is a force. The distance from the center of the bolt to the part of the wrench handle where the mechanic applies the force is the radius. It is called a radius because as the wrench goes around, it traces a circle. If the wrench has a 1-foot radius and the mechanic exerts a force of 25 pounds, the torque may be calculated as follows:

Torque = Force × Radius
Torque = 25 lbs × 1 ft
Torque = 25 lb-ft

If the mechanic chooses a wrench with a 2-foot radius and exerts the same amount of force (Fig. 16-5), the torque is increased:

Torque = Force × Radius
Torque = 25 lbs × 2 ft
Torque = 50 lb-ft

In the English system, torque is always expressed in pounds-feet. There may be confusion because the units of measurement for work are expressed in foot-pounds. In both formulas pounds are multiplied by feet, but torque is always specified in pounds-feet and work in foot-pounds. In the metric system, torque is measured in newton metres. The formulas are:

	Torque = Force × Radius
English system	Torque = Pounds × Feet
Metric system	Torque = Newtons × Metres

16.11   Horsepower (Rotary)

Like linear horsepower, the rotary horsepower of an engine can be measured. Rotary horsepower measurement is based upon the formula Watt developed:

Horsepower = rpm × Torque

Torque is the turning effort developed by the engine. RPM or revolutions per minute is the element of time in the formula. Like π, 5252 is a constant number.

16.12   MEASURING HORSEPOWER

The horsepower of an engine can be found by measuring the engine's torque at any particular rpm. A dynamometer, used to measure engine torque, does not measure horsepower directly. It measures torque and rpm, the formula given in Section 16.11 is then worked out to express horsepower. Many dynamometers have the ability to do this math automatically and provide the operator with a horsepower figure.

Most dynamometers measure torque of an engine by changing the rotating torque to a stationary torque. The stationary torque is then measured with a scale, a hanging weight, load cell strain gauge, or other force measuring device at the end of a torque arm.

Most dynamometers use a hydraulic water brake to change rotating torque to a stationary torque. The water brake absorption unit (Fig. 16-6) consists of a vaned impeller that rotates in a stationary vaned housing. When the absorption unit is partly filled with water, the vaned impeller rotates and accelerates the water outward in the direction of rotation of the

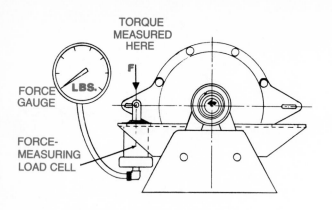

Fig. 16-7 Dynamometer absorption unit with force-measuring load cell. (Go Power)

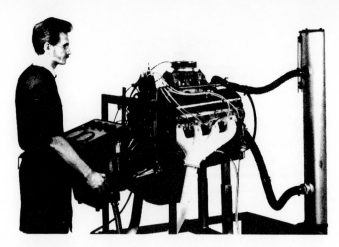

Fig. 16-8 Engine mounted on engine dynamometer. (Go Power)

impeller until the water strikes the outer edge of the housing. Here the water is deflected against the stationary housing vanes. The force of the fast-moving water striking the stationary housing tends to rotate the housing. A force-measuring load-cell (Fig. 16-7) restricts the housing from rotating and measures the torque the water exerts on the housing. The torque being measured at any rpm is controlled by changing the amount of water in the absorption unit. A water valve controls the flow of water through the absorption unit. As the water flow increases, the amount of water in the absorption unit also increases.

One type of dynamometer, the engine dynamometer, tests the engine out of a vehicle. Engine dynamometers are used to make engineering and performance studies on the engine, such as measuring and rating its horsepower (Fig. 16-8).

The other type of dynamometer, a chassis dynamometer (Fig. 16-9), is used in many service facilities for tune-up and diagnostic work. A chassis dynamometer allows the technician to duplicate road conditions and test the vehicle's ability to perform on the road. It is useful for testing brakes, drive lines, and fuel systems as well as power output and engine condition.

The dynamometer imitates road conditions by placing the rear wheels of the vehicle between two large rollers. The shaft of the forward or drive roller is attached to a power absorption unit (Fig. 16-10) that works like a hydraulic fluid coupling. It has a rotor with blades which throws fluid forward. A stator with stationary blades receives the force of the fluid flow from the rotor. The more fluid in the unit, the more power is required to revolve the rotor at any given speed.

16.13   Torque and Horsepower Curves

Torque measured on a dynamometer is recorded on a graph. Horsepower, calculated from torque and rpm, is also charted on a graph. The graph in Figure 16-11 shows horsepower figures along one side and torque in pound-feet along the other side. The bottom of the graph has engine speed in revolutions per minute. This graph allows both torque and horsepower to be compared to engine operating speed.

A horsepower and torque curve can be drawn from horsepower and torque measurements. When an operator observes a certain amount of torque on the dynamometer instruments at a particular rpm, the operator puts a mark on the graph that corresponds to the torque and rpm. When the test is complete all the marks are connected together to form a curve.

The horsepower curve in Figure 16-11 is common to most engines. The horsepower does not start at zero because an engine will not run at zero speed. Therefore, the curve is cut off at the bottom. Horsepower increases as the engine speed and load increase. The graph shows that this engine reaches its maximum horsepower of 165 at 4,000 rpm. An engine can run faster than this, but horsepower begins to decrease after reaching the maximum point.

The torque curve shows the load-carrying ability of the engine at the different speeds in pound-feet. The relationship between the torque curve and the horsepower curve shows how the engine will perform at different loads and speeds. The horsepower curve continues to climb as the engine speed increases until maximum horsepower is reached. This is also true of the torque curve, but the torque curve will reach its highest point much earlier. Notice in Figure 16-11

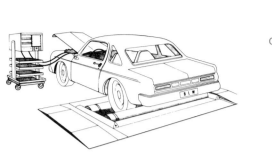

POWER METER
SPEED METER
TACHOMETER GENERATOR
VEHICLE DRIVE WHEEL
COOLING WATER SUPPLY
TORQUE BRIDGE
LOAD VALVE
COOLING WATER DISPOSAL
STRAINER
STATOR
ROTOR
FLOW CONTROL VALVE
LOAD WATER DISPOSAL
UNLOAD VALVE

Fig. 16-9   Automobile on chassis dynamometer.
(Clayton Manufacturing Company)

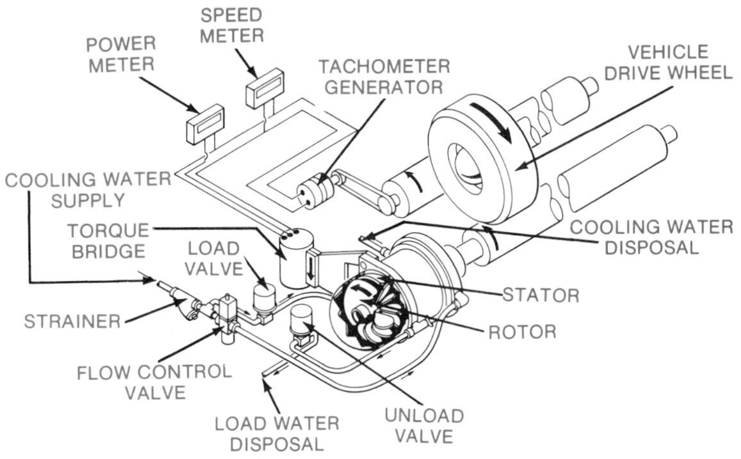

Fig. 16-10   Operation of chassis dynamometer.
(Clayton Manufacturing Company)

how the torque curve drops after it reaches its peak point (maximum) at 1,500 rpm.

The torque of most engines will change widely over the normal range of crankshaft speeds. At very low speeds—200–300 rpm—an engine develops only enough torque to keep itself running without any extra load. The net torque—the reserve beyond what is needed to keep the engine running—is practically zero.

As engine speed and load increase, torque increases to a peak. This is where the manufacturer rates the torque, very near the most efficient operating speed of the engine. At this point the cylinders are taking in the biggest and most efficient air-fuel mixture, and the exhaust gases in the cylinder are being forced out most effectively.

The torque curve drops off rapidly after its peak. At higher engine rpm there is less time for the air-fuel charge to enter the cylinder and less time for the exhaust gases to leave the cylinder. This causes a weaker push on the pistons and less torque. Other factors which contribute to the drop in torque are internal engine friction and pumping losses. Power is wasted in an engine when it is pumping in air and fuel and exhausting it.

The horsepower curve is directly affected by the torque curve, for torque is one of the elements in the horsepower formula:

$$\text{Horsepower} = \frac{(\text{Torque} \times \text{rpm})}{5252}$$

The reason that the horsepower curve does not directly correspond with the torque curve is that it is also affected by another element, time. Power, remember, is the speed or rate at which work is done. The horsepower curve is able to increase past the peak of the torque curve because the engine rpm increases beyond this point. Eventually, however, the torque drops off so much that even more rpm cannot hold the horsepower curve up.

16.14   Horsepower Ratings

There are some differences of opinion about how horsepower should be rated or specified. Widely different horsepower figures may be given for the same engine. For example, the 327-cubic-inch Chevrolet V8 may have horsepower ratings from about 200 to 375. Some of the difference is due to the various rating systems.

Horsepower measured at the flywheel of an engine is called brake horsepower, abbreviated BHP. The term comes from a device called a Prony friction brake dynamometer (Fig. 16-12). The Prony brake was a device that was wrapped around an engine flywheel to measure the amount of energy absorbed.

The brake horsepower of an engine can also be measured on a dynamometer with all accessories driven from an external power source. This results in the maximum obtainable horsepower. Horsepower measured this way is called gross horsepower.

On the other hand, the horsepower can be measured with the engine driving all the accessories, such as the standard exhaust and air cleaner, alternator, water pump, fan, and oil pump. This figure, called the net rating, is lower than the gross figure.

The horsepower of an engine is affected by barometric pressure and air temperature. Horsepower

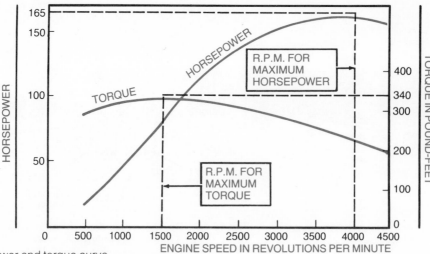

Fig. 16-11 Horsepower and torque curve.

readings taken directly from dynamometer readings, called observed horsepower, are corrected to standard atmospheric conditions, called corrected horsepower. Corrected horsepower is referred to as SAE horsepower for English system units or DIN horsepower for metric system units.

Indicated horsepower is an engineering measurement seldom used outside of the factory or laboratory. It measures the power delivered by the expanding gas to the piston inside the cylinder. It does not take into consideration the friction losses within the engine.

Horsepower measured at the rear wheels of a vehicle is called road or chassis horsepower. This figure, of course, is much lower than the engine ratings.

16.15   ENERGY

Mechanical energy is measured by the work it can do. A raised weight has stored up energy. If it is dropped, it can do work by raising another weight, compressing a spring, or pulling a rope or cable.

In an engine, the energy used to develop horsepower comes from the fuel. In a fuel such as gasoline, considerable chemical energy is stored. When the gasoline is burned with oxygen, the chemical energy is released as thermal energy.

The purpose of any engine or machine is to convert energy into useful work. How well the machine converts energy into work is a measure of its efficiency. Efficiency is the ratio of energy supplied to the work produced:

$$\text{Efficiency} = \frac{\text{work output}}{\text{energy in}} \times 100 \text{ percent}$$

No machine is 100 percent efficient. There is always loss of energy through heat and friction. In an internal combustion engine, only about 25 percent of the total energy of the fuel is converted into useful work (Fig. 16-13).

16.16   Thermal Efficiency

The internal combustion engine converts the chemical energy of gasoline into thermal energy. Thermal efficiency is a measure of the percentage of heat energy available in the fuel that is actually converted into power at the crankshaft.

16.17   Volumetric Efficiency

Volumetric efficiency is the relationship of the actual volume of a cylinder to the volume which is filled during engine operation. During high engine speeds the valves are open for such a short time that the cylinders are not completely filled. Volumetric efficiency may be calculated with an engine dynamometer and air flow equipment.

16.18   Brake-Mean-Effective Pressure

Brake-mean-effective Pressure, abbreviated BMEP, is the average effective pressure exerted on the piston during one operating cycle. Pressure used in drawing fuel into the cylinder and compressing it, plus pressure required to exhaust the burnt exhaust gases, plus pressure required to overcome internal friction are subtracted from the power delivered during the power stroke. The result is BMEP. BMEP may be calculated on a dynamometer.

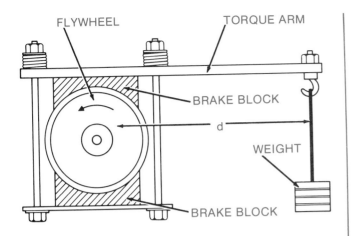

Fig. 16-12 Old Prony brake dynamometer.

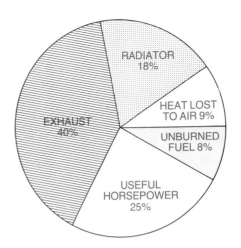

Fig. 16-13 Only about 25 percent of energy in gasoline is converted to useful horsepower. (Go Power)

16.19   Vehicle Efficiency

Even the 25 percent of the energy in gasoline converted into useful horsepower by the engine is not all used efficiently. Power available at the engine is reduced by friction in the drive train. The horsepower available at the rear wheels is much lower than the horsepower measured at the engine's flywheel. Even the power available at the rear wheels is not used completely to drive the vehicle. The friction between the automobile's tires and the road, called rolling resistance, takes power to overcome. Another friction, that of air pushing on the front of the vehicle as it moves, called air resistance, takes even more power to overcome. The result of all these factors is that only 10–15 percent of the energy in gasoline is left to propel the vehicle. In other words, the automobile is only 10–15 percent efficient.

NEW TERMS

Bore   The diameter of the cylinder.
Brake horsepower   Horsepower measured at the engine's flywheel; abbreviated BHP.
Compression ratio   The amount the air-fuel mixture is compressed during the compression stroke.
Displacement   The cylinder volume displaced by the pistons of an engine.
Horsepower   A unit used to describe the power developed by an engine. One horsepower is equal to 33,000 foot-pounds of work per minute.
Stroke   The movement of the piston in the cylinder controlled and measured by the offset of the crankshaft.
Thermal efficiency   A measure of how well an engine changes the chemical energy in gasoline to heat energy.
Torque   A turning or twisting effort or force.
Vehicle efficiency   A measure of how well the power developed by the engine is used to drive the vehicle.
Volumetric efficiency   The ratio of an engine's cylinder volume to the volume actually filled by air and fuel during engine operation.

CHAPTER REVIEW

1. Define the term *bore*.
2. Define the term *stroke*.
3. Write the formula for displacement.
4. What is compression ratio?
5. Define *force*.
6. Define *horsepower*.
7. Explain how horsepower is measured on a dynamometer.
8. What is thermal efficiency?
9. What is volumetric efficiency?
10. How much of the energy in gasoline is converted into useful power?

DISCUSSION TOPICS AND ACTIVITIES

1. Look up the horsepower and torque specifications for your own or your family's automobile engine. At what rpm is horsepower the highest? Where is torque highest?
2. What limits the horsepower and torque of an engine? How could they be increased?
3. If an engine develops 100 pounds-feet of torque at 5,000 rpm, what is its horsepower?

Automobile Engine Systems

PART 3

The Lubrication System

CHAPTER PREVIEW

The lubrication system circulates oil between moving parts to prevent the metal-to-metal contact which causes wear. Oil between moving parts allows them to move easily, with less friction. The lower the internal friction of an engine, the more power it can develop. The circulating oil also cools the engine by carrying heat away from hot engine components and cleans or flushes dirt and deposits off the engine parts. Finally, oil circulated on the cylinder walls seals the rings, improving the engine's compression.

OBJECTIVES

After studying this chapter, you should be able to do the following:

1. Understand the purpose of lubrication in an engine.
2. Define viscosity and understand what it means in relation to engine oil.
3. Be able to read and understand service ratings for oil.
4. Identify the main components of a full-pressure lubrication system.
5. Describe the operation of a full-pressure lubrication system.

17.1   LUBRICATION

The movement of any part within the engine requires support. Cylinder walls support the pistons and rings; valve guides support the valves; rocker arm shafts support the rocker arms. The rotating crankshaft and camshaft are supported by their bearings.

All points of movement between parts have a resistance known as friction. If you push a book along a table top you will notice resistance due to friction. The rougher the table and the book surface the greater the friction, because the two surfaces tend to lock together. If a weight is placed on the book, it takes even more effort to move it across the table. As the amount of pressure between two objects increases, their friction increases.

Friction between engine parts is undesirable for several reasons. First, friction takes power to overcome. The lower the friction between engine parts, the more power an engine can develop. Second, friction between two objects causes them to heat and to wear. This may be demonstrated by simply rubbing your hands together fast. Heat is caused by the friction between the skin on your hands.

The purpose of lubrication is to reduce friction on engine parts. Friction cannot be eliminated completely, but it can be reduced so that longer engine life may be expected. Suppose a slippery liquid such as oil were poured on a table top. A book pushed across the table would move with very little resistance. The friction between the book and table has been reduced. The oil forms a thin layer called a film under the book which lifts it off the table surface.

An oil film is used in lubrication to prevent friction from metal-to-metal contact. Figure 17-1 shows a shaft supported in a housing with a bearing. A small space, only 0.002–0.003 inch or 0.05–0.08 millimetre, is provided for oil clearance. Oil is directed under pressure into the oil clearance area of the bearing. The oil pressure and the rotation of the

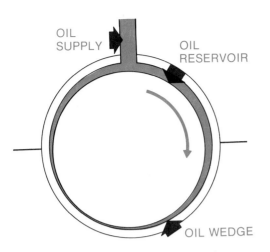

Fig. 17-1   Oil pumped in the oil clearance forms a wedge.
(Federal Mogul Service)

Fig. 17-2   Viscosity and service rating ratings on oil can.

shaft cause a film of oil to wedge between shaft and bearing. The shaft is lifted slightly so that it does not rest on the bearing but on an oil film. When the oil film wedge is formed, there is no metal-to-metal contact. Friction has been reduced as low as possible.

17.2   OIL

Oil is the most common lubricating fluid. Lubricating oil is made or refined from crude petroleum pumped from oil wells, like gasoline, kerosene, and fuel oil. Shortages of crude petroleum led researchers to look for other ways of making oil. The result is called synthetic oil.

There are four types of synthetic oils. Two belong to a class called esters, which are made by a reaction of alcohol and certain acids. The two others are synthesized hydrocarbons, in which heavy molecules similar to some found in natural petroleum are constructed atom by atom from hydrogen and carbon-containing molecules.

Synthetic oils reduce friction better than petroleum oil. This allows the engine to provide more power and better fuel mileage. Synthetic oils also operate in a wider temperature range than petroleum oil. This means that synthetic oils need not be changed as often as petroleum oil. Some manufacturers of synthetic oil advertise that their oil *never* requires changing.

Research is now being conducted to determine exactly how well synthetic oils work. In the future, the synthetic oils may be recommended for use by the automotive manufacturers. The most serious disadvantage of synthetic oils seems to be their price. They cost four or five times as much as petroleum oils.

17.3   Viscosity

One of the characteristics or properties of oil is called viscosity. Viscosity is the thickness or thinness of a fluid, also called body. A fluid with a high viscosity is said to have a heavy body. An example of a fluid with a high viscosity is the thick lubricant used in some standard transmissions and rear axles. Low viscosity fluids flow very freely. High viscosity fluids flow sluggishly. Oils used in engines must flow freely in cold conditions but have enough body during times of high temperature.

The Society of Automotive Engineers (SAE) has set up standards for oil viscosity. Thin oil receives a low viscosity number, like SAE 20, while thicker oil receives a higher number, like SAE 40 or SAE 50. The viscosity number is stamped on top of the oil can (Fig. 17-2). The owner's manual for an automobile usually specifies what viscosity should be used.

Most automobiles need SAE 30 in the summer and SAE 20 in the winter. Multiple viscosity oil, like SAE 10-40, flows freely like SAE 10 when the weather is cold, but protects like SAE 40 when it is hot. An automobile operated in different climates needs multiple viscosity oil. A viscosity rating with a *W* after it, like SAE 20W, means the oil is rated for cold temperature operation.

17.4   Viscosity Index

A fluid's viscosity changes with temperature. Pancake syrup is thick at room temperature, but it becomes thinner when heated. Its viscosity has changed from high to low. A fluid which changes a good deal with temperature changes is said to have a

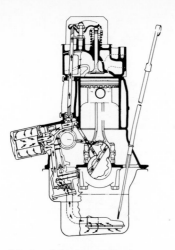

Fig. 17-3   Oil circulation in an engine. (American Motors Corporation)

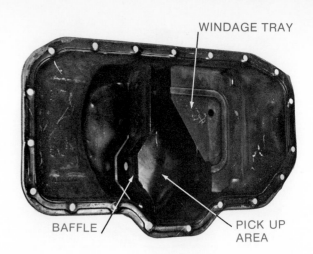

Fig. 17-4   Oil pan.

low viscosity index. A fluid which changes relatively little with a given temperature change is said to have a high viscosity index. Oils for lubricating engines must have a high viscosity index, since these engines must be protected under very hot and very cold conditions.

17.5   Service Rating

An engine oil's service rating is printed on the side of the oil can (Fig. 17-2). The service ratings, set up by the American Petroleum Institute (API), are a measure of how well the oil holds up under severe wear and tear. The categories are as follows:

SA: lowest category, not appropriate for automobiles

SB: minimum, for automobiles operated under very mild service conditions

SC: meets warranty standards for 1964–1967 automobiles

SD: meets warranty standards for 1968–1970 automobiles

SE: meets warranty standards for 1972–1980 automobiles

SF: highest current rating

The owner's manual will probably show which service classification should be used for any automobile. A higher classification can always be substituted, but never a lower one.

17.6   Oil Additives

A number of materials called additives are added to improve oils. There are oxidation inhibitors, rust preventatives, antifoamants, viscosity index improvers, detergents, and metal deactivators. After the oil has been in an engine for a period of time, many of these additives break down. This is one of the main reasons why oil must be changed frequently.

17.7   ENGINE LUBRICATION SYSTEM

The full-pressure lubricating system (Fig. 17-3) is the type almost always used in all types of automotive engines. In this system, oil under positive pump pressure is forced to parts such as the main, rod, and cam bearings.

17.8   Oil Pan

The oil pan (Fig. 17-4) stores and collects the oil. Engines usually have an oil pan that holds five or six quarts. The pan, made from steel, has baffles or sheet metal partitions to prevent oil from sloshing away from the oil pickup area during hard stops. Some high-performance engines use a shield mounted to the bottom of the crankcase to prevent air whipped by the crankshaft from churning up the oil. This device, called a windage tray, prevents air bubbles from entering the oil. It also can increase the engine's power by reducing the amount of air disturbed by the crankshaft at high speeds.

17.9   Pickup Screen

A pickup screen in the oil pan is connected by a pipe to the inlet of the oil pump. All the oil that enters

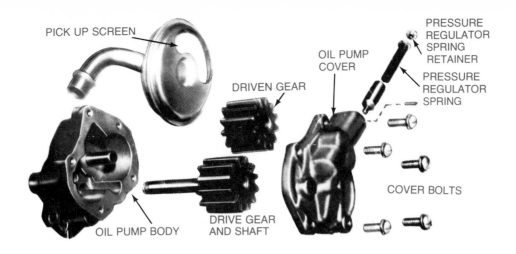

Fig. 17-5 Disassembled view of oil pump.
(Pontiac Motor Division, GMC)

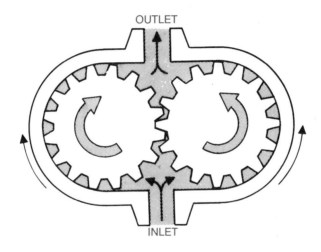

Fig. 17-6 Operation of gear-type oil pump. (Sperry Rand-Vickers)

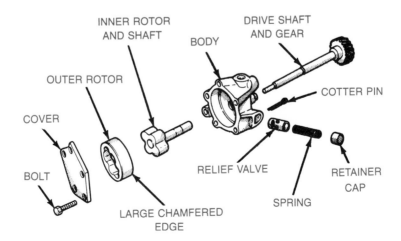

Fig. 17-7 Rotor oil pump. (Chrysler Corporation)

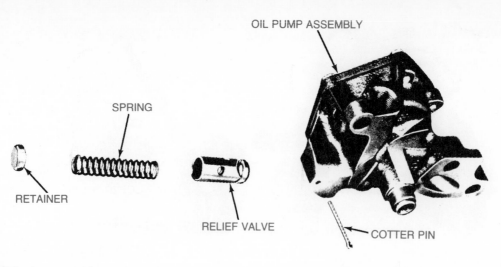

Fig. 17-8 Relief valve assembly. (Chrysler Corporation)

the pump must pass through the screen, which prevents any large particles of dirt from entering the pump.

17.10 Pump

The engine oil pump (Fig. 17-5) causes the oil to flow throughout the engine. The resistance to this flow results in a pressure buildup. One type of pump consists of two gears, in mesh with each other, in a housing at the bottom of the engine. A shaft attached to one gear extends into the engine. This end of the shaft has a drive gear that meshes with a gear on the engine camshaft. When the engine is running, the pump drive gear, in mesh with the camshaft, is turning. This causes the two gears in mesh inside the pump housing to turn. As the teeth of the two pump gears separate, a low-pressure area is momentarily created. An inlet hole positioned at this point allows oil to enter the vacuum. The oil is then carried around in the teeth of the gears and pushed out the outlet passage (Fig. 17-6).

The rotor pump (Fig. 17-7) consists of an inner rotor driven by the engine and an outer rotor driven by the inner rotor. As the rotors turn, the lobes separate, causing a partial vacuum. Oil is pulled in and carried around between the rotor lobes until it is forced through the outlet.

17.11 Relief Valve

Located near the outlet passage is a valve assembly called a relief valve to prevent too high a pressure in the system (Fig. 17-8). The unit consists of a small ball or plunger backed up by a calibrated spring. If pressure becomes too high, the ball or plunger is pushed into position to release the pressure, sending some oil back into the pan. As soon as pressure returns to normal, the relief valve spring repositions the plunger or ball.

17.12 Oil Filter

After the oil passes through the pump and relief valve, it goes to the oil filter assembly (Fig. 17-9). The function of the filter is to clean the oil before it reaches the engine parts. The oil filter assembly is threaded onto a mount on the outside of the cylinder block, where it can be changed. The filter element and canister assembly are usually made in one piece. When it is time to change the filter, the canister and filter element are changed as a unit.

Filter elements may be cotton, wool, and paper, which is the most popular. When the oil is routed through the treated paper (Fig. 17-10), the dirt and acids stick to the outside of the paper, and only the cleaned oil gets through. After the oil goes through the filter element it returns to the engine block to be circulated into the engine components.

After a long period of use, the oil filter element may become clogged with materials filtered from the oil. If oil no longer passes easily through the element, it no longer gets to engine parts. To prevent this problem, a bypass valve is located inside the filter assembly or in the block where the filter attaches. When the filter element becomes clogged, the pressure inside the canister increases and pushes open the bypass valve. The oil then goes around the filter

Fig. 17-9 Oil filter mounted outside to engine.
(Pontiac Motor Division, GMC)

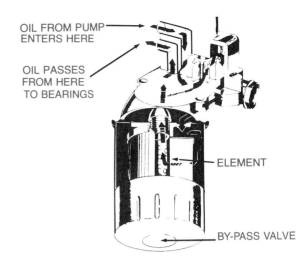

Fig. 17-10 Flow of oil through oil filter.

element, instead of through it, and directly into the engine. Oil can get to the engine parts, but it is not cleaned by the filter.

17.13 Oil Passages

When the oil leaves the filter assembly, it enters the oil passages of the block. It flows into several long channels called galleries or header lines drilled lengthwise in the cylinder block. From the main header, oil flows to oil clearance areas at main bearings. The crankshaft is drilled from the main journals to the connecting rod journals for oil flow. The connecting rods are sometimes drilled lengthwise up to the piston pin bushing so that oil may reach that area.

Oil is sent to the cam bearings, through the cylinder block from the main bearings. In a few engines the camshaft is hollow drilled; oil under pressure enters at one end and is distributed to the cam bearings through the hollow shaft.

Because of the complicated pattern of oil passageway systems, it is easy to see that foreign material from a failed bearing may restrict proper oil flow. It is important that all oil passages be carefully cleaned when bearings are replaced.

When the oil has passed through the part requiring lubrication, it falls or runs down the inside of the engine back to the oil pan. Oil which makes its way out of each of the connecting rod bearings is thrown off the crankshaft. This oil splashes up on the cylinders, lubricating them as well as the piston and ring assembly. Excess oil picked up by the oil control ring passes through oil holes in the piston. From here it is allowed to fall back to the pan.

The flow of oil is shown in Figure 17-11. The lubrication system is in Figure 17-12.

17.14 Oil Coolers

Some engines use an oil cooler to lower the temperature of the oil. The oil circulating around the hot engine components carries away much heat, which passes from the oil pan into the surrounding air. At temperatures higher than 250°F or 120°C, the oil tends to burn. Engines that are air cooled, engines with small oil capacity, and engines operated under severe conditions have trouble keeping a low enough oil temperature without a cooler.

An oil cooler (Fig. 17-13) is an aluminum or copper heat exchanger that allows fast heat dissipation. Hot oil is routed through many small passages or tubes in the cooler. Heat passes into the walls of the tubes. Air goes through spaces between the tubes and carries off the heat. The cooler is mounted in the air stream entering the engine compartment on liquid-cooled engines. It is mounted in the air circulation system on air-cooled engines.

17.15 Oil Level Indicator

If the oil level is too low, the pump will not be able to provide enough oil for lubrication. The oil level is measured with a dipstick (Fig. 17-14) inserted into the engine oil reservoir. The higher the oil level, the higher the oil will come up on the dipstick. Markings on the dipstick show whether there is enough oil.

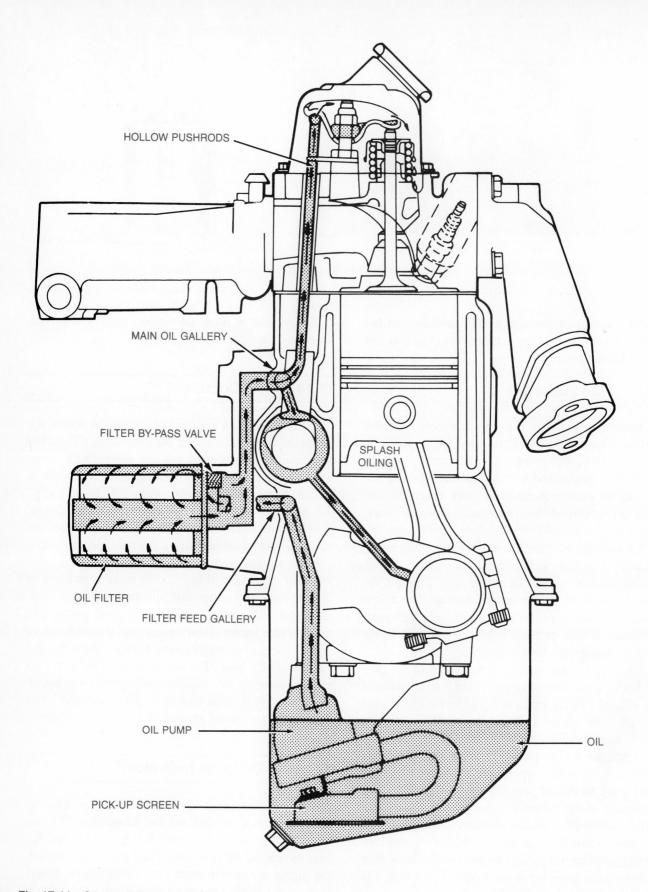

HOLLOW PUSHRODS

MAIN OIL GALLERY

FILTER BY-PASS VALVE

OIL FILTER

FILTER FEED GALLERY

SPLASH OILING

OIL PUMP

OIL

PICK-UP SCREEN

Fig. 17-11 Oil circulation in a typical engine. (Chevrolet Motor Division, GMC)

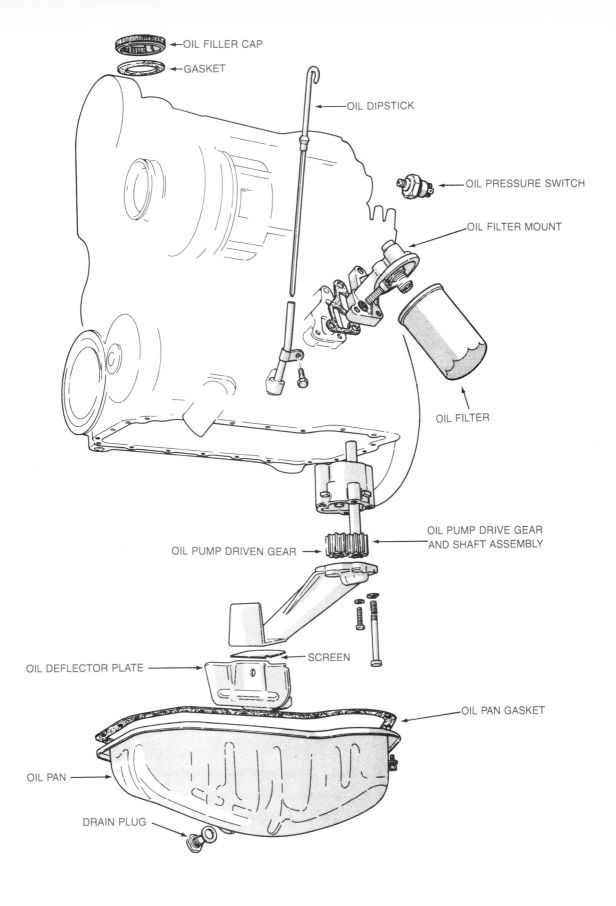

OIL FILLER CAP

GASKET

OIL DIPSTICK

OIL PRESSURE SWITCH

OIL FILTER MOUNT

OIL FILTER

OIL PUMP DRIVE GEAR AND SHAFT ASSEMBLY

OIL PUMP DRIVEN GEAR

OIL DEFLECTOR PLATE

SCREEN

OIL PAN GASKET

OIL PAN

DRAIN PLUG

Fig. 17-12 Exploded view showing the lubrication system components. (Chrysler Corporation)

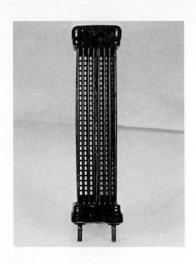

Fig. 17-13   Oil cooler.

Fig. 17-14   Dipstick used to tell oil level.

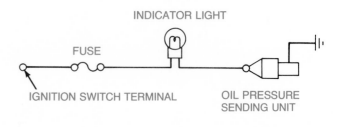

Fig. 17-15   Oil pressure warning light circuit.

17.16   Oil Pressure Warning Light

The oil pressure warning light (Fig. 17-15) warns the driver of low oil pressure. Current for the indicator light is provided from an ignition switch terminal. In order to have a complete circuit, the oil pressure sending unit must provide a path to ground. The sending unit, mounted on the engine, senses engine oil pressure. If it drops below a safe level, the sending unit provides a ground and a completed circuit lights the oil pressure indicator light. The operation of the sending unit is similar to that described below for the oil pressure gauge.

17.17   Oil Pressure Gauge

Some vehicles have a gauge to show oil pressure in pounds per square inch (Fig. 17-16). Current from an ignition switch terminal flows through a fuse and into the gauge unit. The gauge consists of a coil of resistance wire wound around a bimetal arm. The more current that flows through the coil, the more it heats and bends the bimetal arm. Bending of the bimetal arm moves the needle of the gauge.

The sending unit, mounted on the engine, is made to change the resistance in the gauge circuit as oil pressure changes. Changing the resistance will change the amount of current that flows through the bimetal arm and change the reading shown on the gauge.

A typical oil pressure sending unit (Fig. 17-17) consists of a spring-loaded diaphragm connected through a linkage to a variable resistor. Engine oil pressure directed through a pressure entrance pushes on the diaphragm. Movement of the diaphragm changes the resistance in the circuit through the variable resistor. The resistance is low when the oil pressure is high. The low resistance allows a high current flow through the bimetal arm, which then gives a high oil pressure reading.

17.18   Two-Stroke-Cycle Lubrication

Small two-stroke-cycle engines used in motorcycles and chain saws use another lubrication system. A special oil mixed with the gasoline goes into the crankcase with the fuel. The oil circulates around the components, making its way into the areas that require lubrication. In some of these engines, the gasoline and oil are mixed and then poured into the fuel tank. Other engines have two tanks—one for fuel and one for oil.

NEW TERMS

Lubrication   Reducing friction in an engine by providing oil between moving parts.
Lubrication system   A system designed to provide oil to each of the engine's parts.
Oil   Fluid used to provide lubrication.
Oil additives   Materials added to the oil to improve its lubricating ability.
Oil cooler   A heat exchanger used to cool the oil in an engine.
Oil filter   A device to filter out dirt and other foreign matter from the oil.
Oil level indicator   A dipstick inserted into the oil pan to measure the oil level.

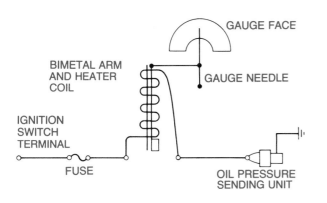

Fig. 17-16 Oil pressure gauge circuit.

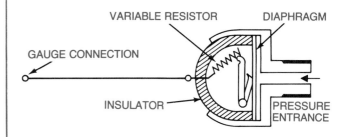

Fig. 17-17 Oil pressure sending unit.

Oil pan A metal pan covering the bottom of the engine used to store oil for lubrication.

Oil passages Holes and passages drilled in the block and in the engine parts through which oil flows.

Oil pressure gauge An instrument used to measure the amount of oil pressure in an engine.

Pickup screen A screen in the oil pan that prevents any large particles from entering the oil pump.

Pump A device used to circulate oil to the moving parts of an engine.

Relief valve A spring-loaded valve used to regulate the pressure in the lubrication system.

Service rating A system of rating how well an oil stands up under wear and tear, established by the American Petroleum Institute.

Synthetic oil Oil made from a material other than petroleum.

Viscosity The thickness or thinness of an oil.

Viscosity index The amount oil viscosity changes with changing temperature.

Warning light A light on the instrument panel that turns on to warn of low oil pressure.

CHAPTER REVIEW

1. Why is friction undesirable in an engine?
2. Describe how oil reduces friction.
3. What are the advantages of synthetic oil?

4. Define the term *viscosity*.
5. What is the difference between a viscosity rating of SAE 20 and SAE 40?
6. Explain what an oil service rating is.
7. What is an oil additive?
8. What is the purpose of the oil pan?
9. Explain how an oil pump works.
10. Why is a relief valve used in the lubrication system?
11. Trace the flow of oil from the oil pump to the engine's connecting rod bearings.
12. How does oil get on the cylinder walls to lubricate them?
13. Describe the purpose of an oil cooler.
14. Explain how a dipstick is used to find out how much oil is in an engine.
15. What is the oil pressure gauge used for?

DISCUSSION TOPICS AND ACTIVITIES

1. Inspect a variety of oil cans at an automotive parts store. How many different service ratings and viscosity ratings can you find?
2. Look up the recommended oil viscosity and service rating for your or your family's automobile.
3. Describe the oil flow path through an engine, starting at the oil pan.

CHAPTER **18**

Lubrication System Service

CHAPTER PREVIEW

If the lubrication system becomes contaminated with dirt or if it stops operating properly, the engine may be damaged in a very short time. A mechanic must be able to troubleshoot a malfunction in the system and perform preventive maninntenance to prevent a failure in the system. The troubleshooting and preventive maintenance operations are presented in this chapter along with the major service procedures for each of the components in the lubrication system.

OBJECTIVES

After studying this chapter, you should be able to do the following:

1. Explain troubleshooting procedures to find out what is wrong with the lubrication system.
2. Describe the correct method of checking oil level.
3. Explain how oil and oil filters are changed.
4. Describe how the oil pan, oil pump, relief valve, and oil passages are serviced.
5. Explain the purpose of prelubrication.

18.1   TROUBLESHOOTING

The first sign of a lubrication system problem is usually that the oil pressure warning light comes on, indicating low oil pressure in the engine.

18.2   Checking the Oil and the Gauge

The first thing the mechanic should do is make sure that the engine has the proper amount of oil. If oil level is too low, there is not enough oil flow for proper lubrication.

When there is enough oil in the engine and the warning light continues to burn, find out whether the problem is really low oil pressure or just a malfunction in the electrical warning circuit. The quickest way to do this is to install a test pressure gauge, operate the engine, and accurately measure the oil pressure. Oil pressure test gauges are available that will read pressures of 0 to 100 psi (0 to 690 kPa or so).

Remove the sending unit for the oil pressure warning light. Install an adaptor and hose for the oil pressure test gauge. Connect the oil pressure gauge to the hose and start the engine. If the gauge shows no oil pressure, stop the engine to prevent further damage. If the gauge shows there is oil pressure, operate the engine at several different speeds and note the oil pressure. Compare these readings with specifications in the manufacturer's service manual.

18.3   Oil Analysis

Another troubleshooting procedure now used in some automotive and truck fleet operations is oil analysis. A sample of oil may be removed from the oil pan and sent to an oil analysis company. Here chemists examine the oil to determine its condition and the level of contamination by dirt, water, or acid. They can also tell whether the engine is wearing normally by measuring the amount of engine metal in the oil. The more iron and steel present in the oil, the more wear is occurring in the engine. Regular oil analysis allows a fleet operator to adjust maintenance procedures to engine needs. It may also be used to predict when an engine is likely to fail.

176   AUTOMOBILE ENGINE SYSTEMS

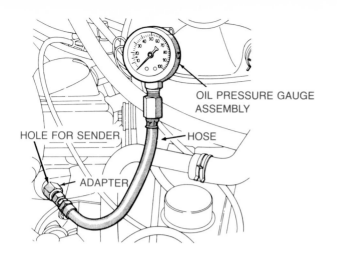

Fig. 18-1 Checking engine oil pressure with a test gauge. (Chrysler Corporation)

Fig. 18-2 Dirt has destroyed surface of these aluminum alloy bearings. (Federal-Mogul)

18.4   Checking After Engine Failure

Lubrication system troubleshooting can also be used after the engine has failed to determine the cause of failure. This is done by a close examination of the engine's bearings. In some cases, worn bearings are sent to a laboratory for expert analysis under a microscope. Usually, however, the mechanic will examine the bearings visually for two common causes of failure, dirt and not enough lubrication.

Normal engine oil and filter changes usually remove the fine dirt produced by normal engine wear. If these very fine particles, however, are permitted to build up, more and possibly larger particles are produced. The wear is no longer normal. Fine dirt particles, if they are not too numerous, will embed into the bearing lining. Large particles, however, can bottom against the steel bearing backing and damage both the bearing and the shaft (Fig. 18-2).

Insufficient lubrication means too little oil gets through the engine bearings to lubricate them. It may affect all of the bearings or only one, possibly only the mains or only the connecting rod bearings. Insufficient lubrication may be due to a dry start, too little oil clearance, low oil supply, low oil pump delivery, a malfunction in the relief valve, and oil dilution. Oil dilution is a condition in which fuel runs down the cylinder walls and gets in the oil.

A dry start is a condition in which the lubrication system has not been primed with oil before starting the engine for the first time after an overhaul. A lag occurs between the time the engine is started and the time oil is actually delivered under pressure to the bearings.

Bearing damage and seizure can also result from too small an oil clearance space between shaft and bearing. This is often shown by wear on one or two bearings in the set with little or no wear on the others.

Bearings can be affected by lack of oil or by an extremely low oil supply. This can result from extreme oil leakage at the crankshaft front or rear oil seal, around new piston rings, or at gaskets.

The oil pump is an important part of an engine that is often overlooked. It may be responsible for low oil pressure, particularly at low engine speeds. The oil pump should be serviced when the engine is overhauled.

A worn oil pressure relief valve can prevent the flow of oil. If the plunger and hole become enlarged, the plunger may cock slightly or stick open. With the plunger open, oil is bypassed to the crankcase at lower engine speeds. This lowers oil pressure to the bearings and reduces their lubrication.

Too much leakage or blow-by around the pistons and a rich combustion mixture of raw fuel can cause oil dilution in a worn engine. Oil dilution reduces the lubricating value of the oil, for the oil film thickness goes down when the oil becomes lower in viscosity. Another cause of bearing troubles is leakage of the coolant down into the crankcase, particularly if the coolant contains an antifreeze such as ethylene glycol. This substance forms a gummy material which coats the bearings and shaft, reducing oil clearance and in many cases stopping the oil flow.

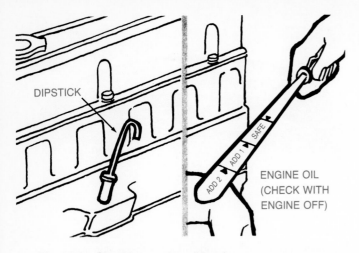

Fig. 18-3   Checking engine oil level.

Fig. 18-4   Using oil filter tool to change oil filter.
(Dodge/Chrysler Corporation)

18.5   PREVENTIVE MAINTENANCE

The lubrication system requires some periodic preventive maintenance in order to operate properly. The oil level must be checked regularly. The oil and oil filter must be changed regularly.

18.6   Checking Oil Level

The first step in checking oil level is to locate the dipstick, which is usually mounted on the side of the engine. Turn the engine off. Pull the dipstick out. Wipe it clean with a rag. Look at the marks on it. There is no standardized marking system. Some dipsticks have two lines, one marked *full* and another *add*. Many just have lines with no markings. Find out what the marks mean by looking in the owner's manual. Push the dipstick firmly back into its hole, pull it out again, and read the oil level from the marks (Fig. 18-3). Push the dipstick back into position. Make sure it is firmly seated so no water or dirt can enter the engine.

18.7   Changing Oil

Changing the engine oil regularly is the most important thing that can be done for long engine life. The more frequently oil is changed, the longer the engine can go before it needs an overhaul. Most manufacturers' oil change recommendations are based upon a time/mileage interval. For example, the interval may be 3,000 miles or three months, whichever comes first. It makes more sense to change oil on the basis of op-

erating conditions. During cold or wet weather, it should be changed more frequently, because water tends to collect in the oil and cause sludge. Short trip and stop-and-start driving are harder on oil than long trips and highway driving. Oil should be changed more frequently if the automobile is driven in areas where there is a lot of dirt and dust in the air. Most experts recommend that oil be changed more frequently than the owner's manual suggests.

Oil changes are done incorrectly at many service stations and garages. The customer drops off his car, and it is parked until the attendant gets time to change the oil. This allows the oil to cool and gives particles of dirt and water time to stick to parts of the engine. When the oil is drained, the dirt and water stay in the engine. Oil is best changed while hot, after a long drive.

Check the operator's manual to find out how many quarts of oil are required. An additional quart will be needed if the oil filter is to be changed. Set the emergency brake, put the transmission in park, and lift the automobile on a hoist, if available. Use an oil drain pan that will hold five or six quarts. Look for the engine drain plug. Do not confuse it with the drain plug for the transmission, which is located in the bottom of the transmission. When the plug is located, place the correct size open-end wrench snugly on the drain plug. Have the pan ready. Turn the drain plug counterclockwise to loosen. Pull it out quickly, allowing the oil to drain into the pan. Be careful. The oil is hot!

Allow the oil time to drain. Replace the drain plug, turning it clockwise by hand. Tighten it with the wrench. If torque specifications are available, use a torque wrench to tighten the drain plug. Remove the

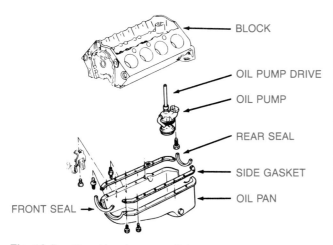

Fig. 18-5   Checking for cover flatness. (Chrysler Corporation)

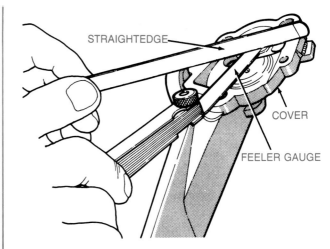

Fig. 18-6   Checking for cover flatness. (Dodge/Chrysler Corporation)

oil filter cap. Push the oil spout into an oil can and pour oil into the engine until the recommended amount has been added. Check the oil level with the dipstick. Replace the filler cap. Check the drain plug for leaks.

18.8   Changing the Oil Filter

The oil in the engine is pumped through a filter to remove particles and acids. When the filter is full, it clogs and the bypass valve is activated. The filter should be changed at least every other oil change, and preferably every oil change.

While the oil is draining, locate the filter. Most automobiles now use a throwaway cartridge. Put a pan or drain under it to catch the oil which will come out. Put the oil filter tool around the filter cartridge (Fig. 18-4). Turn it counterclockwise with the tool until it can be turned by hand. Set the filter in the pan to drain and then throw it away. With a rag, wipe the mounting surface on the engine where the filter fits. Put a light coat of grease or oil on the rubber gasket of the new filter. Open a can of oil and fill the new oil filter completely with oil. This will prevent a momentary dry start when you start the engine. Screw the filter on by turning it clockwise. Tighten it snugly by hand. Do not use the tool to tighten it.

An additional quart of oil will be required if the new filter was not filled with oil. After the oil change is completed and the required amount of oil is added, start up the engine. If the filter leaks, shut the engine off. Either the filter is not tight enough or the filter gasket is defective. Take if off, clean up the gasket area, and try again. Another filter may be used if necessary.

18.9   LUBRICATION SYSTEM SERVICE

When an engine has a major overhaul, each part in the lubrication system must be serviced. In this section we will present the typical service procedures necessary to ensure proper lubrication system operation.

18.10   Oil Pan Service

During an engine overhaul, the oil pan is removed. The pan is thoroughly cleaned, usually with a steam cleaner or in a hot tank. Inspect the threads in the oil drain plug for signs of damage. Inspect the baffles inside the pan to make sure they are tightly fastened.

The oil pan-to-crankcase surface is sealed with two side gaskets and a front and rear seal mounted to the underside of the crankcase (Fig. 18-5). Remove the old gaskets from the oil pan. After gasket surfaces are cleaned, install new gaskets and seals on the oil pan before putting it back on the engine.

18.11   Servicing the Oil Pump and Relief Valve Assembly

The oil pump and relief valve assembly is disassembled and washed in solvent. Inspect each of the parts for wear. The mating face of the oil pump cover should be smooth. If it is excessively scratched or grooved, it should be replaced. Test cover-to-rotor or gear wear by laying a straightedge across the cover surface. Use a feeler gauge (Fig. 18-6) to determine cover flatness. No feeler gauge thicker than

Fig. 18-7 Measuring outer rotor. (Dodge/Chrysler Corporation)

Fig. 18-8 Measuring thickness of inner rotor.

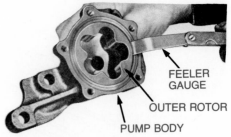

Fig. 18-9 Measuring clearance between pump body and outer rotor. (Dodge/Chrysler Corporation)

the service manual's specification should be able to slide under the straightedge.

Measure the diameter and thickness of the outer rotor with an outside micrometer (Fig. 18-7). If the dimensions are less than specified in the service manual, replace the outer rotor. Measure the inner rotor thickness with an inside micrometer (Fig. 18-8). If the dimensions are less than specifications, replace the inner rotor.

The outer rotor is assembled into the pump body. Measure the clearance between the outer rotor and the body with a feeler gauge (Fig. 18-9). If the measurement is larger than the specifications call for, replace the pump body. The inner rotor is assembled into the pump. Measure the clearance between the outer and inner rotor with a feeler gauge (Fig. 18-10). If the clearance is beyond specifications, replace the inner and outer rotors.

Place a straightedge across the pump housing over the assembled rotors and measure the clearance over the rotors with a feeler gauge (Fig. 18-11). A measurement beyond specifications means that the pump body should be replaced.

The same basic inspection and measuring procedures are used on gear type pumps. One additional measurement is made called backlash. Install a feeler gauge of the recommended thickness between the gear teeth as shown in Figure 18-12. The thicker the feeler gauge that will go between the gears the more they are worn. Replace any pump with excessive backlash.

Inspect the relief ball or plunger and bore for scratches and scoring. If there is any evidence of damage, replace the plunger or ball. Measure the length of the relief valve spring and compare against specifications. Replace springs that fail to meet

specifications. Reassemble components that pass these tests. Check the relief valve for free operation in its bore. If it moves freely, the retainer that holds the relief valve assembly in its bore may be replaced.

18.12   Oil Passages

During engine cleaning, give careful attention to the oil passages in all the components. Drilled holes in the crankshaft and rocker arms must be blown out with compressed air. The air will remove dirt, metal, and any cleaning solvent that could contaminate the new oil.

Remove the cylinder block and cylinder head oil gallery plugs during hot tanking. This allows the hot tank solution to circulate into the large oil passages. After hot tanking, flush the passages with water and then blow dry. Replace the gallery plugs during engine assembly.

18.13   Prelubrication

When the engine is reassembled and the lubrication components are in place, refill the crankcase with the proper amount of oil. To prevent a dry start, drive the oil pump with an electric drill motor. Using the electric motor to spin the oil pump, oil is pumped throughout the engine. When oil circulation reaches the rocker arm area, the system is prelubricated. If there is no oil flow, there is a problem in the system or, more probably, in the engine itself. The cause must be found before engine startup. Note: If the oil pump rotates counterclockwise, a reversing drill motor must be used.

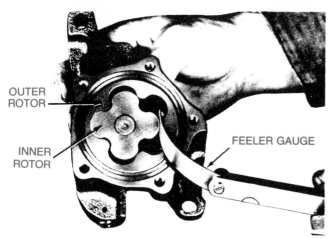

Fig. 18-10 Measuring clearance between rotors. (Dodge/Chrysler Corporation)

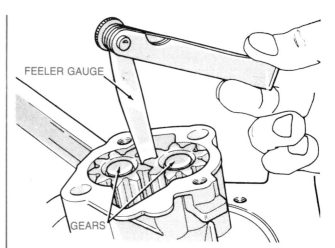

Fig. 18-12 Measuring gear oil pump backlash. (Chrysler Corporation)

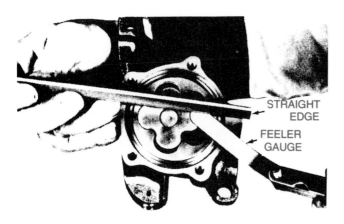

Fig. 18-11 Measuring clearance over rotors. (Dodge/Chrysler Corporation)

NEW TERMS

Filter change Removing the old oil filter and replacing it with a new one.

Insufficient lubrication A condition in which not enough oil gets to the engine parts.

Oil analysis A laboratory inspection of oil to find out its condition and the condition of the engine from which it was drained.

Oil change Removing oil from the engine and replacing with new oil.

Oil pan service Cleaning, inspecting, and installing new oil pan gaskets and seals during lubrication system service.

Pump service Cleaning and inspecting the oil pump for wear.

Test gauge An oil pressure gauge used to tell the oil pressure on an engine with a warning light.

CHAPTER REVIEW

1. What is usually the first indication of a lubrication system problem?
2. What causes low oil pressure?
3. Where can you find specifications for an engine's oil pressure?
4. Explain how to measure engine oil pressure with a test gauge.
5. Explain what an oil analysis is and why it is used.
6. What is a dry start?
7. How can a worn relief valve affect bearing lubrication?
8. Explain how the oil should be changed.
9. Explain how to change an oil filter.
10. How is the oil pan serviced?
11. Explain how an oil pump is measured for wear.
12. How is the relief valve checked for wear?
13. How are oil passages in the cylinder block cleaned?

DISCUSSION TOPICS AND ACTIVITIES

1. Look up the oil capacity and the recommended oil and filter change interval for your own automobile. Does the oil or filter need changing?
2. List the steps you would follow to find out what is wrong with a lubrication system.
3. Study some old engine bearings found around the shop. Can you find any evidence of lubrication system problems?

The Cooling System

CHAPTER PREVIEW

A cooling system is required to remove some of the heat of combustion. This keeps the engine at an efficient operating temperature. The cooling system matches engine operating temperature to changing driving conditions. It is designed to prevent both overheating and overcooling.

The effects of overheating are well known. When the temperature of the engine rises too high, coolant begins to boil and circulation of coolant stops. The oil in the lubrication system begins to break down. Bearings and other moving parts may be damaged if the overheating condition continues.

The effects of overcooling are less well known. An engine operating at too low a temperature becomes less efficient. During the power stroke, heat from the burning mixture is pushed down the piston. If too much of this heat is lost to the cooling system, power and efficiency are also lost. If the cylinder area is too cool, fuel will not be completely burned. Some of the fuel may run down the cylinder walls past the rings, washing off lubricating oil. Enough gasoline may enter the oil pan to dilute the oil. During the exhaust stroke, unburned gasoline that did not wash down the cylinder is pushed out, adding to exhaust emissions. Wherever the fuel not burned completely in the cylinder goes, power is lost and fuel economy suffers.

OBJECTIVES

After studying this chapter, you should be able to do the following:

1. Explain the purpose of the engine cooling system.
2. Describe the operation of an air cooling system.
3. Describe the operation of a liquid cooling system.
4. Identify and explain the purpose of the parts of a liquid cooling system.
5. Explain the operation of each of the parts of a liquid cooling system.

19.1   TYPES OF COOLING SYSTEMS

The heat developed by combustion may be removed in two ways: air cooling and liquid cooling. These two types of cooling systems are described in the following sections.

19.2   Air Cooling

Two cooling systems are now in use: air cooling and liquid cooling. An air cooling system uses air circulated around hot engine parts to carry off the heat. The components that get the hottest, such as the cylinder and cylinder head, have fins (Fig. 19-1) to direct the greatest amount of air into contact with the greatest amount of hot metal. The air may be directed on the engine by draft. In this case, the vehicle must be moving for air to circulate around the components. This is the usual way motorcycle (Fig. 19-2) and aircraft engines are cooled. The difficulty is that during periods when the vehicle is idling but not moving, it may overheat.

The forced air circulation system uses an air pump to draw in air and force it around the engine components (Fig. 19-3). The cylinders and cylinder heads are finned and usually covered with sheet metal shrouding to direct the air. A thermostatic control is often used to limit the intake of air when the engine is cold so as to prevent overcooling.

Fig. 19-1 Cylinder with cooling fins cast around its outside diameter.

Fig. 19-2 Movement of motorcycle creates natural air draft around cooling fins to carry away heat. (BMW)

Air cooling has certain advantages over liquid cooling. An air-cooled engine requires less metal, so it weighs less and is smaller. Another advantage of the air-cooled engine is its ease of installation. The engine may be designed with opposed cylinders and located in the rear of the vehicle. This arrangement would be very difficult to cool with liquid. Probably the greatest advantage of air cooling is that it is so simple.

19.3 Liquid Cooling

The liquid cooling system (Fig. 19-4) circulates liquid around hot engine parts to carry off the heat. Coolant passages called water jackets surround each cylinder in the block. They are also placed in the cylinder head very close to the valve area. Heat from the burning air-fuel mixture passes through the metal of the cylinder head and cylinder wall and enters the water jackets. The heat then goes into the liquid coolant circulating through the water jackets.

An advantage of the liquid cooling system is that it can take care of more heat than air cooling. A liquid-cooled engine is also less expensive to make, since the cylinders may be cast together in a block instead of made separately. An additional advantage is that liquid cooling passages reduce engine noise so that engine operation is much quieter. The rest of this chapter will study the operation of the liquid cooling system.

19.4 LIQUID COOLING SYSTEM OPERATION

The liquid cooling system is made up of a number of parts: the coolant pump, radiator, radiator hoses, radiator pressure cap, coolant recovery system, thermostat, fan, drive belts, and temperature indicator.

19.5 Coolant Pump

The coolant pump (Figs. 19-5 and 19-6) circulates the coolant through the engine and into a heat exchanger. The pump, usually located on the front of the engine, is driven by one of the engine's accessory drive belts. When the engine is running, the belt drive turns a pully that drives a shaft in the middle of the pump. The shaft is connected to a small wheel, or impeller with blades which is placed in the coolant passage. As the impeller spins, it draws coolant into its center and throws it off the blades by centrifugal force. This causes coolant to be sucked in and pushed out of the pump. The shaft that drives the pump is supported on a bearing which is sealed to prevent coolant from entering.

19.6 Radiator

The heat removed from the hot engine parts by the coolant must then be removed from the coolant. This is done by pumping the hot coolant out of the engine and into a heat exchanger, commonly referred to as the radiator (Fig. 19-7). The radiator removes heat from the coolant so that it may go back through the engine.

The radiator, mounted in front of the engine, is made up of a top tank, a bottom tank, and a center core or heat exchanger. Hot coolant is pumped out of the engine through a large hose connected to the top tank. It enters the radiator core through a large number of small distribution tubes. These tubes are

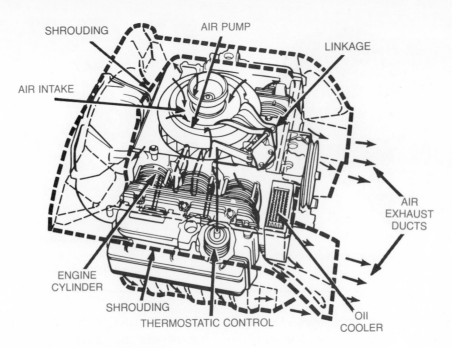

Fig. 19-3 Pump atop engine forces air around engine components. (Chevrolet Motor Division, GMC)

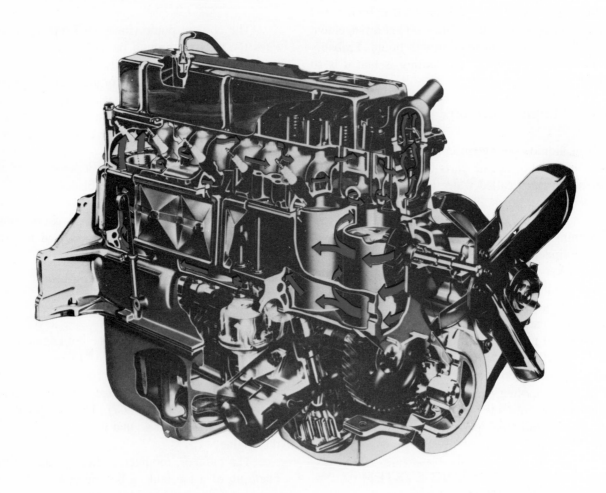

Fig. 19-4 Liquid coolant circulated through water jackets to remove heat from cylinders and heads.
(Chevrolet Motor Division, GMC)

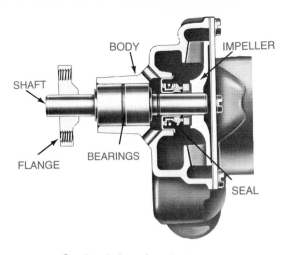

Fig. 19-5 Sectional view of coolant pump.
(Pontiac Motor Division, GMC)

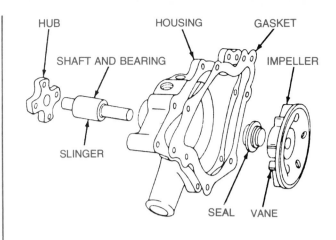

Fig. 19-6 Disassembled view of coolant pump.
(Union Carbide Corporation)

made from a metal that is a good heat conductor, usually copper or aluminum. The heat passes out of the liquid and into the wall of the tubes, which are fitted with copper or aluminum air fins. Air circulated through the core takes the heat from the fins. The cooled liquid runs into the bottom tank of the radiator. A large hose allows the coolant to be drawn from the bottom tank back into the engine to pick up more heat (Fig. 19-8).

In downflow radiators, the hot water enters the top of the radiator and flows down through the core to the bottom tank. In crossflow radiators (Fig. 19-9), hot water from the engine enters an inlet at the top of one side of the radiator. The coolant flows across the radiator core to a tank located at the other side. An outlet for the coolant is provided in the bottom of this tank. The chief advantage of the crossflow design is that it allows large cooling capacity in a limited space.

19.7   Radiator Hoses

The coolant flows from the engine to the radiator and from the radiator to the engine through rubber hoses strengthened with steel wire. The radiator is solidly mounted to the automobile chassis while the engine is attached on rubber mounts. This means that the engine rocks back and forth as it is accelerated and decelerated. But if the engine were allowed to shake the radiator, it would soon be destroyed. The use of rubber hoses prevents this from happening.

Two types of hoses are in general use. The curved hose (Fig. 19-10) is molded in the proper shape to fit on a certain engine. The straight flexible hose (Fig. 19-11), available in different lengths and diameters, will flex or bend into most required shapes.

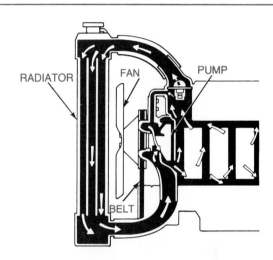

Fig. 19-7 Pump circulates coolant from engine to radiator.
(Union Carbide Corporation)

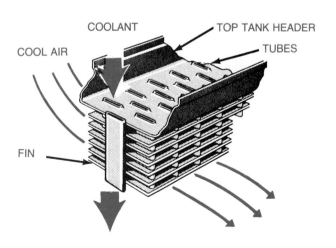

Fig. 19-8 Flow of coolant and air through radiator core.
(Union Carbide Corporation)

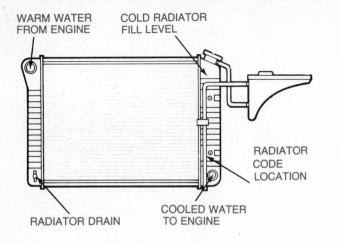

Fig. 19-9   Cross-flow radiator. (Chevrolet Motor Division, GMC)

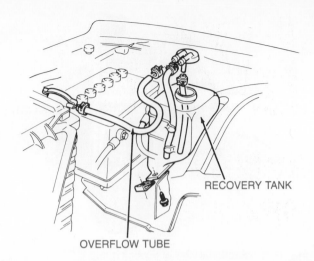

Fig. 19-14   Coolant recovery system. (Chevrolet Motor Division, GMC)

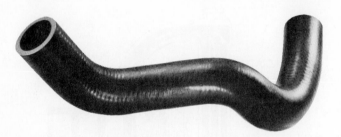

Fig. 19-10   Curved radiator hose. (Dayco Corporation)

Fig. 19-11   Flexible radiator hose. (Dayco Corporation)

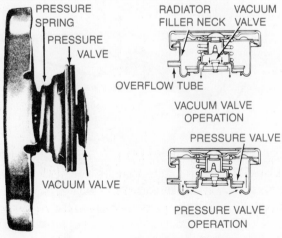

Fig. 19-12   Radiator cap.
(Plymouth/Chrysler Corporation)

Fig. 19-13   Radiator cap operation.
(American Motors Corporation)

19.8   Radiator Pressure Cap

The radiator cap (Fig. 19-12) on the top tank of the radiator can be removed to add coolant to the radiator. The radiator cap allows a slight buildup of pressure in the radiator, which raises the boiling point of the coolant. The coolant can then hold more heat.

Two spring-loaded valves in the cap (Fig. 19-13) give pressure relief. One of these valves opens up to relieve pressure before it damages the radiator and the hoses. If the pressure becomes too high, the valve is pushed up against the pressure spring, which allows pressure to escape.

The other valve in the cap is a vacuum valve. Its purpose is to prevent a vacuum buildup in the radiator as the system cools off. If a vacuum were allowed to develop, the thin walls of the distribution tubes might collapse. A vacuum in the system moves the vacuum relief valve into a position that allows air to enter.

19.9   Coolant Recovery System

The pressure relief mechanism in the radiator cap is connected to an overflow tube. On older automobiles, the tube allowed coolant to flow underneath the automobile on the ground during pressure relief. On newer vehicles, the tube is hooked to a recovery tank or coolant recovery system as shown on Figure 19-14. During pressure relief, the coolant goes through the tube and into the plastic recovery tank. When the system has cooled off, the coolant is drawn through the overflow by vacuum and re-enters the radiator.

Fig. 19-15 Different styles of thermostats.
(Plymouth/Chrysler Corporation)

19.10 Thermostat

Efficient temperature control is achieved in a liquid cooling system by regulating the flow of coolant through the system with a thermostat (Fig. 19-15). The thermostat is a temperature-controlled valve which controls the flow of water into the radiator from the engine.

In a pellet thermostat (Fig. 19-16), a wax pellet or power element in the thermostat grows when heated and shrinks when cooled. The pellet is connected through a piston to a valve. The heated pellet pushes against a rubber diaphragm which forces the valve to open. As the pellet shrinks on cooling, it allows a spring to close the valve and stop circulation of coolant through the radiator. Coolant goes through a bypass passage back into the block (Fig. 19-17).

As the engine becomes warm, the pellet gets big and the thermostat valve opens, permitting the coolant to flow through the radiator. This opening and closing of the thermostat valve permits enough coolant to enter the radiator to keep the engine within operating temperature limits (Fig. 19-18).

19.11 Fan

The radiator is usually placed in the front of the automobile, right behind the grillwork. As the vehicle is driven, air is directed through the grill and through the radiator core. As long as the vehicle is moving fast enough, there is enough air flow for cooling.

When the engine is running and the automobile is not moving, however, there is not enough natural flow of air through the radiator core. For this reason, a fan is placed between the radiator and the engine. The fan is normally mounted to the same pulley that drives the coolant pump. When the engine is running, a drive belt turns the pulley, which turns the fan. The fan pulls air through the radiator core.

There are four types of fans in use (Fig. 19-19). The cross fan or fixed blade fan has blades which are fixed in one position. This fan turns all the time the engine is running. When the vehicle is moving, however, the fan is no longer required. Yet the fixed blade fan is still being driven by the engine and using up engine horsepower.

The clutch fan and the flex fan are both designed to reduce the horsepower spent on running the fan. The clutch fan has a hydraulic clutch (Fig. 19-20) between the fan and the drive pulley which adjusts the speed of the fan to engine temperature. Fan clutches are used with many engines, especially those equipped with factory installed air conditioning units. They ensure adequate cooling at reduced engine speeds while eliminating overcooling, excessive noise, and power loss at high speeds.

A bimetallic element in the fan clutch is connected to the arm shaft so that as the temperature rises, the shaft moves the arm, exposing an opening in the pump plate (Fig. 19-21). This opening allows the silicone fluid to flow from the reservoir into the working chamber of the automatic fan clutch.

The silicone fluid is kept circulating through the fan clutch by wipers on the pump plate. The speed difference between the clutch plate and the pump plate develops high pressure areas in front of the wipers. This forces the fluid through a hole in front of each wiper back into the reservoir. But as the temperature rises, the arm uncovers more of the large opening and allows more silicone fluid to re-enter the working chamber.

The automatic fan clutch becomes fully engaged when the silicone fluid, circulating between the working chamber and the reservoir, reaches a high enough level in the working chamber to completely fill the grooves in the clutch body and clutch plate. The fluid locks the clutch body to the clutch plate, and the fan is driven by the engine. The temperature at which the automatic fan clutch engages and disengages is controlled by the setting of the bimetallic element.

The flex blade fan uses six or more flexible blades to limit power loss at high vehicle speeds. The blades

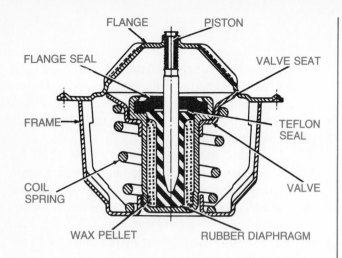

Fig. 19-16 Wax pellet thermostat. (Chevrolet Motor Division, GMC)

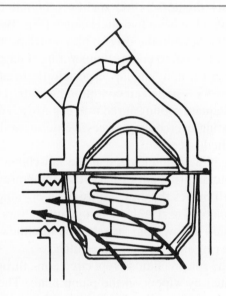

Fig. 19-17 Coolant flow into bypass when thermostat is closed. (Harrison Radiator)

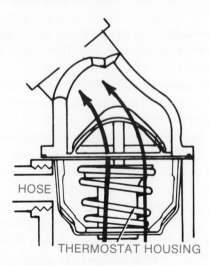

Fig. 19-18 Coolant flow through open thermostat. (Harrison Radiator)

CROSS FAN

POWER FLEX FAN

THERMO CLUTCH FAN

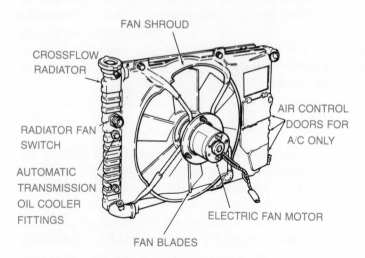

Fig. 19-19 Four types of fan. (Chrysler Corporation; Pontiac Motor Division, GMC)

Fig. 19-20 Clutch to couple and uncouple fan.
(Plymouth/Chrysler Corporation)

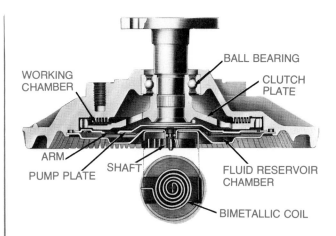

Fig. 19-21 Sectional view of fan clutch.
(Chevrolet Motor Division, GMC)

are made from very thin stainless steel, aluminum, or fiberglass. At idle speeds the curvature of the blades allows the fan to pull in a large amount of cooling air. When the vehicle reaches highway speed, the air entering the engine compartment pushes on the flexible fan blades. This force straightens the blades. With flat blades, a minimum of horsepower is required to drive the fan.

Where the amount of air moved by the fan must be increased, a sheet metal or plastic housing called a fan shroud is used. This unit, normally attached to the radiator, acts like a tunnel to direct the air flow from the fan through the radiator core.

On many front wheel drive cars, the engine is mounted transverse or sideways in the engine compartment. With this engine position, the fan can no longer be mounted on the front of the engine. In these applications, the fan is mounted to a fan shroud which is attached to the radiator. The fan is driven by an electric motor. A temperature-sensitive radiator fan switch turns the fan motor on when the engine is hot. **Safety Caution: An electric fan can switch to on even when the engine is not running. Never have your hands or tools near an electric fan.** The components of an electric fan assembly are shown in Figure 19-19.

19.12   Drive Belts

The coolant pump and the fan are driven by an accessory drive belt from the crankshaft. This V belt (Fig. 19-22) must be strong yet flexible. It is constructed from layers of fabric and rubber strengthened

with metal wire. Belt tension is adjusted by movable mountings on the units driven by the belt or by an idler pulley.

19.13   Temperature Monitoring System

If the cooling system should stop working, too much heat could seriously damage the engine. Since the cooling systems of the engine and automatic transmission are hooked together, the transmission could also be damaged. A heat sensing device is mounted into the block in a cooling system passage. The sensor is connected electrically to a temperature gauge or warning light on the instrument panel.

19.14   Coolant Temperature Warning Light

The coolant temperature warning light (Fig. 19-23) warns the driver if the coolant temperature is too high. Current, supplied by the ignition switch terminal, goes to the indicator light. A complete circuit is only available through the coolant temperature sending unit. The sending unit, mounted on the engine, senses the engine coolant temperature. Excessive temperature causes the sending unit to ground the circuit and light the warning indicator light on the instrument panel.

19.15   Coolant Temperature Gauge

Coolant temperature may be shown on the face of an instrument panel gauge (Fig. 19-24). The gauge operates in the same way as the oil pressure gauge.

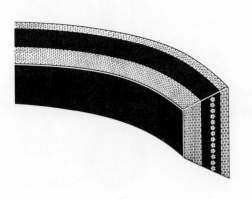

Fig. 19-22   Sectional view of V belt. (Dayco Corporation)

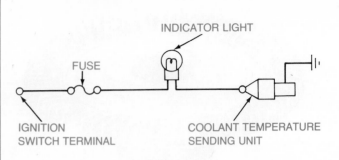

Fig. 19-23   Coolant temperature warning light circuit.

Current flows from an ignition terminal to a coil of resistance wire wound around a bimetal arm. The higher the current flow through the coil, the more heat generated to bend the bimetal arm. Linkage connected to the bimetal arm moves a needle on the temperature gauge.

The sending unit for a coolant temperature gauge (Fig. 19-25) has a bimetal spring that changes the resistance of the circuit as the coolant temperature changes. One end of the bimetal spring is connected to a variable resistance. The sending unit is mounted in a coolant passage so that the coolant circulates near the bimetal arm. Heat from the coolant passes into the bimetal arm. The more heat transferred into the bimetal arm, the more it bends. Movement of the free end of the bimetal arm changes the resistance of the circuit through a variable resistor. When the coolant is hot, the sending unit resistance is low. This allows a high current flow through the gauge resistance wire and causes a high gauge reading. When the coolant is cold, the resistance in the circuit is low, resulting in a low gauge reading.

19.16   Coolant

The coolant used in older automobiles was water. In fact, the liquid cooling system used to be called a water-cooled system. In recent years, improved coolants have been developed. Water caused the formation of rust in the water jackets, which acted as a barrier to heat transfer. Rust also tended to scale off and circulate through the system to the radiator core, where it could plug water distribution tubes. Most cooling systems now use a mixture of ethylene glycol and water as the coolant.

Ethylene glycol has long been used as an antifreeze, a solution which prevents the cooling system liquid from freezing. If the coolant freezes in the radiator and the block, expanding ice could cause severe damage. Depending upon the percentage of ethylene glycol used, the system can be protected from freezing in temperatures well below zero.

When the liquid in a cooling system boils, the coolant turns to steam. The pump is designed to move a liquid. It cannot circulate steam. Coolant circulation is therefore stopped, and the engine temperature gets dangerously high. Another advantage of ethylene glycol is that it has a boiling temperature far above that of water, which is 212°F (100°C) at sea level.

NEW TERMS

Air pump   Pump used with an air cooling system to force air around hot parts.
Coolant   Liquid used in liquid cooling system to carry away heat; usually a mixture of ethylene glycol and water.
Coolant pump   Pump used to circulate coolant around hot engine parts.
Cooling fins   Metal fins used on air-cooled engine parts to move heat away from the parts.
Cooling system   An engine system used to keep the engine's temperature within limits.
Fan   A device used to direct air over the radiator when the automobile is not moving.
Heat sensor   A part in the block used to monitor engine temperature.

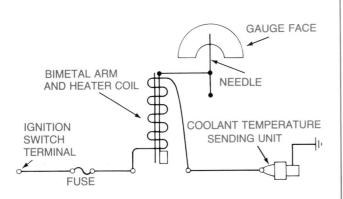

Fig. 19-24   Coolant temperature gauge circuit.

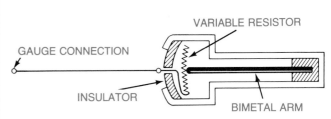

Fig. 19-25   Temperature gauge sending unit.

Pressure cap   The cap on the top of the radiator used to regulate radiator pressure and vacuum.

Radiator   A large heat exchanger located in front of the engine.

Radiator hose   Large hose used to connect the radiator to the engine cooling system.

Recovery system   A system connected to the radiator that catches overflow and sends it back into the radiator.

Temperature warning light   Light on the instrument panel used to warn the driver of too high a temperature in the engine.

Thermostat   A device in the cooling system used to control the flow of coolant.

Water jackets   Passages in the cylinder block and head for coolant flow.

CHAPTER REVIEW

1. List the effects of overheating.
2. List the effects of overcooling.
3. How is an air draft used to cool an engine?
4. Describe the forced circulation air cooling.
5. What are the advantages of air cooling?
6. What are the advantages of liquid cooling?
7. Explain the purpose and operation of the coolant pump.
8. Describe the purpose of the radiator.

9. What are the main parts of a radiator?
10. Why are radiator hoses made from flexible material?
11. Why is a slight buildup of pressure in the cooling system necessary?
12. How does the pressure cap regulate pressure?
13. Explain how the radiator cap prevents a vacuum in the radiator.
14. How does a coolant recovery system work?
15. What is the purpose of the thermostat?
16. Describe the flow of coolant when the thermostat is closed.
17. What is the purpose of the fan?
18. Why is a fan clutch used?
19. How does a flex fan work?
20. List the advantages of ethylene glycol as a coolant.

DISCUSSION TOPICS AND ACTIVITIES

1. Why are most automobiles liquid cooled while most small engines are air cooled?
2. Using the shop manual for the automobile of your choice, look up its coolant capacity, coolant type, and thermostat heat range.
3. What steps could you take to improve the operation on the cooling system on an old automobile?

Cooling System Service

The life of the engine depends upon the cooling system's ability to remove heat quickly but at a controlled rate. Each part of the system must do its job. If it does not, the engine may run too hot or too cold. The mechanic must be able to recognize and correct cooling system problems before they lead to serious engine damage.

OBJECTIVES

After studying this chapter, you should be able to do the following:

1. Identify troubleshooting steps to find out what is wrong with the cooling system.
2. Describe the preventive maintenance jobs necessary on a liquid cooling system.
3. Explain how to adjust coolant strength.
4. List the steps in replacing cooling system parts.
5. Explain the procedures for flushing and repairing a radiator.

20.1   TROUBLESHOOTING

A problem in the cooling system normally gives some warning signals. The temperature gauge or warning light may show that the engine's temperature is too high. The engine may knock or ping under a load. The radiator may vent steam from an overflow. These are signs that the engine is overheating.

On the other hand, the temperature gauge may always read too low. The engine may be hard to start or sluggish with poor fuel mileage. These are signs of overcooling.

20.2   Overheating

When an engine seems to be overheating, first check the coolant level. If the level is low, the overheating may be due to a loss of coolant. Make a visual check of the system to find any external leaks (Fig. 20-1). Check hoses, radiator clamps, coolant pump, thermostat housing, radiator drain, soft plugs in the block, heater hoses, and heater core.

Coolant may also be lost inside the engine because of faulty cylinder head gaskets or a cracked cylinder head or block. When this happens, coolant may end up in the crankcase. Pull the dipstick and check for coolant in the crankcase.

To check for exhaust leaks into the cooling system from a defective head gasket, drain the system until the coolant level is just above the top of the cylinder head. Disconnect the upper radiator hose and remove the thermostat and fan belt. Start the engine and quickly accelerate several times. At the same time, look for coolant rise or bubbles of exhaust gas. If either of these things is found, the engine will have to be disassembled for repair.

If a visual inspection fails to show the cause of coolant loss, the cooling system must be pressure tested. Put a pressure tester on the radiator filler neck (Fig. 20-2). Use the plunger to pump a specified pressure into the system. A gauge on the side of the tester shows the pressure. If the pressure drops on the gauge, there is an internal or external leak. Repeat the visual checking procedure. With the system under pressure, it is likely that the source of the leak can be seen.

If the radiator pressure cap fails to hold the specified pressure, the coolant can boil off or leak. Check the pressure cap with the same tester used to check the

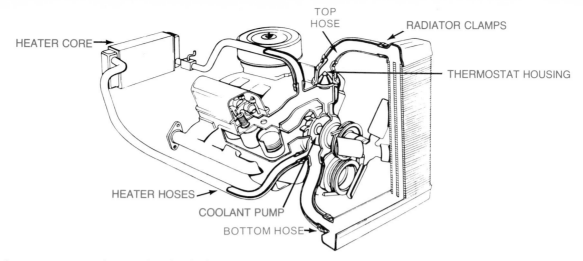

Fig. 20-1 Common sources of external coolant leakage.
(Union Carbide Corp.)

system pressure (Fig. 20-3). Place the radiator cap on the end of the tester. Pump the plunger until the specified pressure is reached on the gauge. If the cap fails to hold the pressure, replace it.

If there is no loss of coolant from the system, overheating may be due to poor coolant flow, poor air flow, or poor heat flow. Poor coolant flow may be caused by a bad fan belt. If the belt is broken or slipping, it will not drive the coolant pump fast enough to circulate coolant properly. Check coolant pump operation by running the engine while squeezing the upper radiator hose. A surge of pressure shows that coolant is being pumped. If not, the pump may require replacing.

A restriction in the radiator may slow coolant flow, resulting in overheating. Warm up the engine and then turn it off. Test for restrictions by feeling the radiator. It should be hot along the top and warm along the bottom. Cold spots in the radiator mean clogged sections. Clogged radiators require service, as explained later.

Poor coolant flow may also be due to a thermostat that fails to open or opens at too high a temperature. The thermostat must be removed from its housing for testing. Remove the bolts on the thermostat housing. The thermostat may then be lifted out (Fig. 20-4).

Check the temperature stamped on the thermostat with the specifications for the vehicle to be sure that the correct thermostat is installed. Check the operation of the thermostat by putting it inside a container of coolant. Heat the coolant, watching the temperature with a cooking thermometer (Fig. 20-5). The thermostat valve should open near its rated temperature. If it fails to open or opens far above its rated temperature, replace it.

Poor air flow across the radiator core can cause the engine to overheat. A slipping fan belt or malfunction in a fan clutch can prevent enough air from moving through the radiator core at low vehicle speeds. Radiator fins clogged with bugs, paper, or other debris from the road can also reduce air flow.

Poor heat flow may result from too much corrosion and scale buildup in the cylinder block and cylinder head water jackets. The heat developed in the cylinders and combustion chambers cannot flow properly through the barrier of corrosion and scale. This condition may be suspected if all of the other troubleshooting procedures fail to show the problem.

20.3 Overcooling

As we saw earlier, overcooling is as bad on an engine as overheating. An engine that runs too cold wastes fuel and forms sludge in the crankcase. The main cause of overcooling is a defective or missing thermostat. If the thermostat is missing or stuck open, too much coolant will flow through the radiator. Remove the thermostat housing, test the thermostat as explained earlier, and replace the thermostat if necessary.

20.4 PREVENTIVE MAINTENANCE

To avoid overheating and overcooling, the cooling system should get regular preventive maintenance. In the following sections, we will present the most common preventive maintenance tasks necessary for proper cooling system operation.

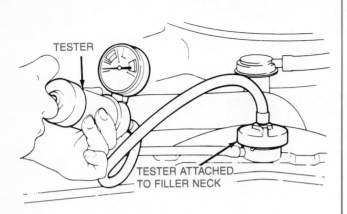

Fig. 20-2 Tester to measure cooling system pressure. (American Motors Corporation)

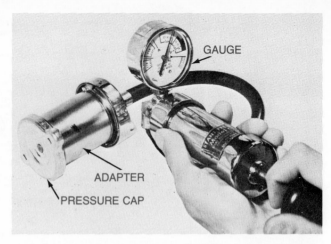

Fig. 20-3 Checking a radiator cap under pressure. (Chevrolet Motor Division, GMC)

20.5   Checking Coolant Level

The coolant level in the radiator should be checked every couple of weeks. If there is not enough coolant, the engine can overheat and be damaged. Check coolant level the engine is cold.

Vehicles with a recovery system may be inspected for proper coolant level by simply observing the level in the recovery tank. Most tanks have lines that show the proper coolant level (Fig. 20-7).

On older cars without a recovery system, or on systems which need a complete refill, you will have to do the filling through the radiator cap neck. **Safety Caution: Remember that the radiator cap keeps the coolant under pressure to raise its boiling point. If the cap is opened when the engine is hot, the coolant may overflow. Open any radiator cap with caution!**

Locate the cap on top of the radiator. Turn it counterclockwise and pull up. Look inside the radiator. The coolant level should be near the top of the radiator. If it is not, add coolant. Older automobiles use water as the coolant, but newer ones use a permanent antifreeze. Add the right coolant to the level indicated. Replace the cap by pushing it down and turning it clockwise.

20.6   Debugging the Radiator

Insects flying around in front of the automobile can get sucked into the radiator, clogging up the small air passageways. Use an air hose to blow air out through the radiator from inside the engine compartment. This will force out bugs and other debris. Clearing these passageways at least every few months will greatly improve the operation of the cooling system.

20.7   Inspecting Radiator Hoses

Radiator hoses connected to the radiator carry the coolant to and from the engine. If one of the hoses ruptures, the coolant is dumped out very quickly. Old hoses become so stiff and brittle that vibration can cause them to break. Check hoses carefully for signs of cracks. Even a small crack can soon cause trouble. Make sure to check the underside of the bottom hose. It is this hose that causes the most trouble. Replace any cracked hose.

20.8   Adjusting and Inspecting Drive Belts

Many engine accessories, including the fan and coolant pump, are operated by drive belts. If these belts break or slip, a good deal of trouble results. The belt that drives the fan also drives the coolant pump. If it breaks, coolant and air circulation stop, and the engine overheats at once.

Check the service manual for specific instructions. Most belts are adjusted by loosening the support for the alternator and moving it back and forth to tighten or loosen the belt. Find the longest span in the belt. Push on it. It should move in about half an inch. If it moves more than half an inch, the belt is too loose. If it moves less than half an inch, it is too tight. A belt tension gauge can also be used for testing belt tension (Fig. 20-6). Feel the belt all over for signs of tearing. Replace any belts that show signs of tears.

20.9   Adjusting Coolant Strength

Modern coolants are a mixture of ethylene glycol and water. A proper mix will protect against both

Fig. 20-4 Removing a thermostat for testing. (Chevrolet Motor Division, GMC)

Fig. 20-5 Testing a thermostat. (Chevrolet Motor Division, GMC)

freezing and boiling. At regular intervals, the coolant must be drained and replaced. From time to time, the coolant level must be adjusted. During cold weather operation, coolant strength is important in preventing freezing. Each of these cases requires that the percentage of ethylene glycol in the coolant be checked and adjusted as necessary.

The coolant is drained from the radiator by removing the drain plug from the bottom of the radiator (Fig. 20-8). Make sure the coolant is cold and then remove the radiator pressure cap. Removing the cap will allow air to enter the radiator and allow it to drain completely out of the drain plug hole.

The coolant can be tested with a hydrometer. The hydrometer test tells the strength of the coolant by measuring its specific gravity. A hydrometer is a glass tube with a float in it. Coolant is sucked into the glass tube with a squeeze bulb. Where the float settles in the coolant depends upon the percentage of ethylene glycol. Graduations on the float indicate the freezing point of the coolant.

If it is necessary to add ethylene glycol to the system, the engine should be operated afterwards in order to circulate and mix the coolant. Coolant strength should then be checked again to determine that enough ethylene glycol has been added to bring the solution to proper strength.

20.10 COOLING SYSTEM SERVICE

Major cooling service jobs include replacement of components such as the coolant pump and fan clutch and reverse flushing a system clogged with rust and scale.

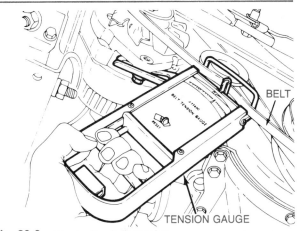

Fig. 20-6 Measuring belt tension. (American Motors Corporation)

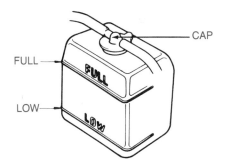

Fig. 20-7 Coolant is checked by observing the see-through reservoir. (Nissan Motor Corporation in U.S.A.)

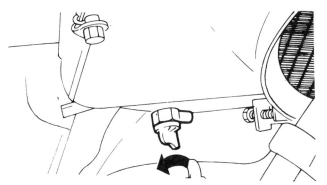

Fig. 20-8 Removing the radiator drain plug. (Chrysler Corporation)

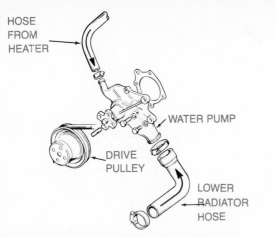

Fig. 20-9 Removing and replacing the coolant pump. (American Motors Corporation)

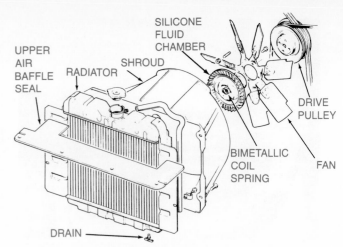

Fig. 20-10 Removing the fan and clutch assembly. (American Motors Corporation)

20.11   Coolant Pump Replacement

If the coolant pump is defective, it must be replaced, since replacement pump parts are not generally available. First, drain the radiator and break loose the fan pulley bolts. Disconnect heater hose, lower radiator hose, and bypass hose (as required) at the water pump. **Safety Caution: If you siphon coolant from the radiator, do not use your mouth to start siphoning action. The coolant solution is poisonous. Swallowing it can cause serious illness or death.** Thermostatic fan clutches must be kept in an "in-car" position when removed from the engine. Hold the assembly in the position it has on the engine to prevent silicone fluid leakage. Take off pump-to-cylinder block and power steering-to-pump bolts and remove the pump and old gasket. On in-line engines, pull the pump straight out of the block first to avoid damage to the impeller (Fig. 20-9).

Install the pump assembly on the cylinder block. Then, using a new sealer-coated pump-to-block gasket, tighten bolts to specifications. Connect the radiator hoses and add the correct coolant. Adjust the belts to specifications and start the engine. Check the cooling system carefully for leaks.

20.12   Thermostatic Fan Clutch Replacement Procedures

If troubleshooting shows that the thermostatic fan clutch is not working, it must be replaced. No repairs can be made on it. If a fan blade is bent or damaged in any way, do not attempt to repair and reuse it. Replace with a new fan assembly.

Remove the shroud attaching screws. Separate the shroud from the radiator and place it rearward on the engine. The fan attaching screws can now be removed (Fig. 20-10).

Use the correct fan spacer, if required, so the space between the fan blades and radiator is correct. Install and torque fan drive bolts. Install the shroud. Tighten the fan belt as described in Section 20-8.

20.13   Reverse Flushing

When a buildup of scale and corrosion causes poor heat flow in a cooling system, clean the system by reverse flushing. Reverse flushing forces water through the cooling system with air pressure in a direction opposite to normal coolant flow. This action causes the water to get behind corrosion deposits and force them out.

A good chemical cleaning solution should be used to loosen the rust and scale before reverse flushing the cooling system. A number of solutions are available. Manufacturer's instructions with the cleaner should always be followed.

Reverse flushing is done with a flushing gun that has a water and air hose attachment. Remove the radiator upper and lower hoses and replace the radiator cap. Attach a leadaway hose at the top of the radiator. Attach a new piece of hose to the radiator outlet connection and put the flushing gun in this hose (Fig. 20-11).

Turn on the water when the radiator is full. Turn on the air in short blasts, allowing the radiator to fill between blasts of air. Apply the air gradually, for a clogged radiator may rupture if the pressure exceeds 20 psi (138 kPa). Continue flushing until the water from the leadaway hose runs clear.

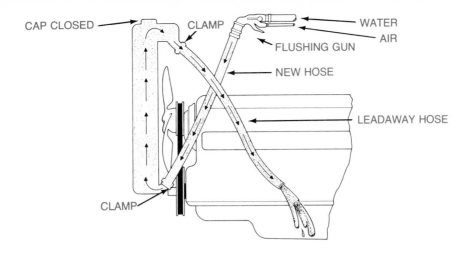

Fig. 20-11 Reverse flushing the radiator.

Reverse flush the cylinder block and cylinder by removing the thermostat, attaching a leadaway hose to the coolant pump inlet and a length of new hose to the water outlet connection at the top of the engine (Fig. 20-12). Attach the flushing gun to the new hose. Turn on the water. When the water jackets are full, turn on the air in short blasts. Continue flushing until the water from the leadaway hose is clear.

20.14   Radiator Repair

A radiator that leaks or cannot be properly cleaned by flushing requires repair. Radiator repair or rebuilding is usually done in a radiator shop. It is removed from the vehicle and soaked awhile in a vat containing a chemical solution. If it is not clear, the upper and lower tanks may be removed from the core. The core may be cleaned mechanically by rodding. In this procedure, rods are pushed through the water distribution tubes to clean them.

Leaks are repaired in the radiator tanks or water distribution tubes by first sandblasting the leaking areas and then soldering copper radiators or epoxy gluing aluminum ones. After repair, the radiator is repainted and pressure tested.

NEW TERMS

Belt tension   The tightness of a drive belt.
Coolant strength   The percentage of ethylene glycol in the coolant.
Debugging   Removing insects and other foreign material from the radiator core to improve cooling.
Hydrometer   A tool that tells the strength of the coolant by measuring the specific gravity.

Overcooling   A cooling system problem in which the engine runs below its best operating temperature.
Overheating   A cooling system problem in which the engine runs too hot.
Reverse flushing   A block and radiator cleaning method in which air and water are forced through the cooling system in a direction opposite to normal flow.
Refractometer   A tool which uses light to measure the strength of the coolant.
Rodding   A radiator cleaning procedure in which rods are passed through the water distributor tubes.

CHAPTER REVIEW

1. List two indications that an engine is overheating.
2. List two indications of overcooling.
3. Make a list of the areas to check for loss of coolant.
4. How can coolant be lost in the engine?
5. Describe how to check for exhaust leaks in the cooling system.
6. Why is cooling system pressure tested?
7. List several causes of overheating besides a loss of coolant.
8. What causes poor coolant flow in an engine?
9. How can the operating temperature of a thermostat be determined?
10. What can happen if scale builds up in the water jackets?
11. What is the main cause of overcooling?
12. Describe how coolant level should be checked.
13. How is a radiator debugged?
14. Why do radiator hoses break?

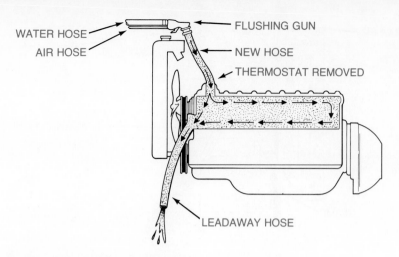

WATER HOSE
AIR HOSE
FLUSHING GUN
NEW HOSE
THERMOSTAT REMOVED
LEADAWAY HOSE

Fig. 20-12 Reverse flushing the cylinder block and cylinder head.

15. Describe how to adjust the coolant pump drive belt.

16. Describe how coolant strength can be tested with a hydrometer.

17. What is a refractometer and how is it used?

18. When should a cooling system be reverse flushed?

19. Describe how to reverse flush a radiator.

20. Describe how a radiator is rodded.

DISCUSSION TOPICS AND ACTIVITIES

1. What steps would you follow to find the reason for an engine's overheating?

2. Make a list of the effects of overcooling on an engine.

3. Visit a radiator repair shop and report on what you find.

The Fuel System

The fuel system (Fig. 21-1) has three functions: to store enough fuel for several hundred miles of vehicle operation; to deliver the fuel to the engine; and to mix the fuel with air in the proper amounts for efficient burning in the cylinder. *Note:* We will describe the operation of electronic fuel injection in Chapter 53.

OBJECTIVES

After studying this chapter, you should be able to do the following:

1. Understand the characteristics of gasoline and its combustion.
2. Explain the operation of the fuel tank, fuel pump, and fuel filters.
3. Describe the operation of carburetor types, their circuits and accessories.
4. Understand the purpose and operation of super-chargers.

21.1 GASOLINE AND COMBUSTION

This section explains the makeup of gasoline, its production and properties, and how it may most efficiently produce power in the combustion chamber.

No single chemical formula can be written to represent gasoline. Gasoline is not a single compound, but a mixture of many hydrocarbons. A hydrocarbon is a chemical compound of the elements hydrogen and carbon. There are many thousands of hydrocarbons, and every batch of gasoline has a different mix, depending on the crude oil from which it came and the refining processes through which it went. Gasoline may be defined as a mixture of the lightest or most volatile liquid hydrocarbons found in crude petroleum oil.

21.2 Normal Combustion

The proper burning of air and fuel in the combustion chamber is described as normal combustion (Fig. 21-2). The spark starts the combustion. The wall of flame spreads rapidly but evenly through the air-fuel mixture in the combustion chamber. The piston is pushed down with an even force across its top.

21.3 Detonation

Detonation, also called knock or ping, is a form of abnormal combustion in which a portion of the mixture explodes. A rapidly burning flame front raises heat and pressure on the unburned part of the air-fuel mixture so that it bursts into flame. When the two flame fronts meet (Fig. 21-3), the resulting explosion applies extreme hammering pressures on the piston and other engine parts. The extreme heat also generated can damage spark plugs and eventually pistons (Fig. 21-4).

21.4 Preignition

Another type of abnormal combustion related to detonation is called preignition. When deposits from fuel and oil build up in the combustion chamber, they cause higher pressures and reduce heat transfer to the

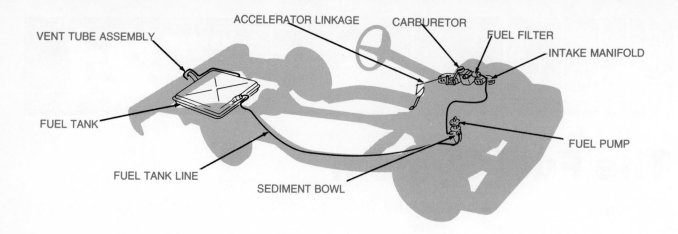

Fig. 21-1 The fuel system. (Ford Motor Company)

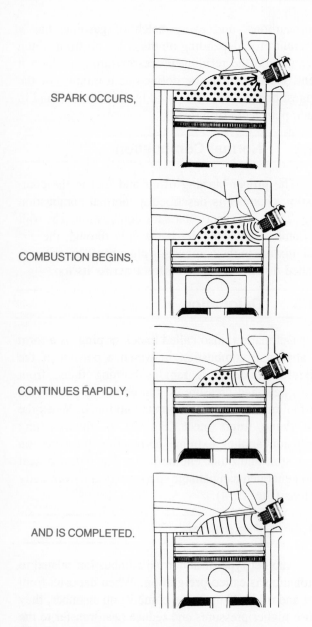

SPARK OCCURS,

COMBUSTION BEGINS,

CONTINUES RAPIDLY,

AND IS COMPLETED.

Fig. 21-2 Normal combustion. (Champion Spark Plug Company)

coolant in the jacket around the chamber. This trapped heat can raise the temperature of the unburned mixture enough so that it burns before ignition. This happens especially when the engine is operating under a heavy load or in hot weather.

Combustion chamber deposits do not expand or contract with the cast iron cylinder head. Therefore, they flake off in spots, leaving rough edges which get red hot during normal combustion. The deposit edges stay hot long enough to ignite the incoming mixture before the spark plug fires. This uncontrolled ignition causes what is called preignition knock.

Preignition can cause the engine to run after the ignition is turned off. This problem, called dieseling, is caused by the deposits igniting an air-fuel charge even though the ignition system is turned off.

21.5 Other Causes of Abnormal Combustion

High-compression engines produce more power. If we start with a compression pressure of 100 psi (690 kPa), as in a low-compression gasoline engine, the pressure after combustion is about 400 psi (2,760 kPa). A high-compression engine starts with a pressure of 200 psi (1,380 kPa), and its combustion pressure is over 800 psi (5,520 kPa). In each case, the engine has to do some work to compress the mixture. But in the high-compression engine, the power developed is much greater.

However, the greater the compression, the more likely the air-fuel mixture is to detonate from the higher pressures and temperatures in the combustion chamber. Detonation or knock can result not only from high compression and carbon deposits, but also

SPARK OCCURS, COMBUSTION BEGINS, FLAME FRONTS APPROACH, DETONATION OCCURS.

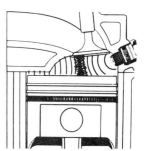

Fig. 21-3 Detonation. (Champion Spark Plug Company)

from cooling system problems, lean mixtures, and too much spark advance.

21.6 FUEL CHARACTERISTICS

Early automobiles used low-compression engines to avoid detonation. In the 1920s, two important facts about detonation were discovered. First, some kinds of gasoline hydrocarbons are more likely to self-ignite, causing detonation. Second, certain additives, such as tetraethyl lead, will reduce detonation, or increase the gasoline anti-knock qualities. Methods were found to rate the antiknock qualities of a fuel. The standard for rating fuels today, known as octane number, is based on the antiknock quality of a hydrocarbon called iso-octane.

21.7 Octane Rating and Antiknock Index

The premium gasolines required for high-compression engines are referred to as high-octane fuels. Regular gasoline is low octane. The octane number of a fuel is determined by comparing it with a mixture of iso-octane and heptane. Pure iso-octane, which has a high resistance to knock, is given an octane number of 100. Pure heptane, which detonates very easily in all but the lowest-compression engines, has an octane number of zero.

Fuels are tested in a special one-cylinder engine in laboratories. The amount of knock is measured on a knock-meter and compared with the knock of different mixtures of iso-octane and heptane. If, for example, the knock is the same as a test mixture of 90 percent iso-octane and 10 percent heptane, that fuel has a research octane rating (RON) of 90.

Under tougher lab conditions the fuel is used in an automobile engine. Here the fuel is given a motor octane number (MON) that may be up to 10 octane numbers less than the RON. But neither laboratory test shows the octane performance of gasoline under real driving conditions. The octane number found on gasoline pumps is called the antiknock index. The antiknock index—averaging of RON and MON—is a truer measure of actual road octane.

Until recently, a gasoline's antiknock value was increased by the addition of tetraethyl lead. The lead slowed down the wall of flame in the combustion chamber and reduced detonation. Fuel with tetraethyl lead was called simply "ethyl."

Recently it was found that much of this lead leaves the combustion chamber with the exhaust gases. Since lead is highly poisonous, its buildup in the air can have a bad effect on people who live near highways. Unleaded fuels were developed whose antiknock rating was achieved by a process called reforming.

Reforming converts gasolines to synthetic hydrocarbons with higher octane quality by rearranging the hydrocarbon molecules. Natural fuels contain large proportions of low-octane hydrocarbons. Heat and high pressure during reforming alter their makeup, producing higher-quality gasoline.

21.8 Performance Numbers

The performance number system was developed to rate antiknock qualities higher than 100 octane. It was also used to relate fuel quality to engine output. The performance numbering system is compared to octane numbering on the following page.

Fig. 21-4 Damage to spark plug and piston from detonation.
(Champion Spark Plug Company)

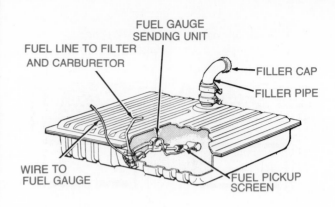

Fig. 21-5 Fuel tank components.

Performance Number	Octane Number
40	58
50	72
60	81
70	88
80	93
90	97
100	100
110	—
120	—

21.9 Volatility

A good gasoline must be a mixture of liquids with different boiling points. Some of the liquids must evaporate at low temperature so that the engine can be started easily when it is cold. Then, as the engine begins to warm up, other less volatile liquids (liquids with higher boiling points) vaporize. Too many highly volatile liquids can cause vapor lock in the fuel pump, percolation of the fuel, and considerable loss in storage from evaporation. This lowers the octane, since the more volatile liquids usually are higher in octane.

On the other hand, too many liquids with high boiling temperatures will prevent complete vaporization in the carburetor. Fuel is then wasted and the crankcase oil becomes diluted.

21.10 Sulfur Content

Sulfur, found in most crude oil, is undesirable in gasoline for several reasons. Sulfur combines with combustion products to form corrosive sulfurous acid.

It also causes wear and deposits in the engine. Some other effects are unpleasant odors and reduced octane because of sulfur's interference with the antiknock additives. Gasoline is refined to reduce the sulfur content as low as possible.

21.11 Stability

Most gasolines contain some chemically unstable hydrocarbons. These unstable compounds combine to form heavier, gummy hydrocarbons in the fuel system. The result is sticky valves and gumming up of carburetor parts unless the gum is removed.

Stability has been greatly increased in recent years by chemical treatment, by more care in selecting the crude oils from which gasoline is refined, and by gum-fighting additives.

21.12 Water

Because water vapor is always found in the air, it is impossible to keep water out of gasoline. At night when it is cool, moisture condenses out of the air on the inner surface of the fuel tank. Since water does not mix with gasoline and is heavier, it settles at the bottom of the tank.

Some of this water may enter the carburetor and fuel pump and combine with sulfur in the fuel to form corrosive acids. Fuel filters and sediment bowls prevent this. Also, keeping the tank full reduces condensation and the possibility of moisture getting beyond the tank.

21.13 De-icers

Most major oil companies use anti-icing additives in their gasoline to prevent fuel line freezeup and carburetor icing. Fuel line freezeup is usually the result of not servicing the fuel filter or sediment bowl often enough. The buildup of moisture from tank condensation freezes in cold weather and blocks fuel flow to the carburetor.

Carburetor icing is caused by moisture condensing in the carburetor and then freezing. The temperature gets low enough to condense and freeze the moisture because gasoline vaporizing in the carburetor throat soaks up heat from the metal parts. The ice interferes with the flow of air and the movement of the throttle valve.

De-icer additives are either antifreeze solvents or surface-active agents. These agents coat the ice particles to prevent them from sticking to metal surfaces.

21.14 Diesel Fuel

Diesel engines use a fuel called diesel fuel or diesel oil. These fuels are compared by their heat value. The heat value of fuel describes how much heat energy it can supply when burned. Diesel fuel has a higher heat value than gasoline.

Fuels also differ in their volatility. Volatility is how easily a fuel changes from a liquid to a vapor. When gasoline is spilled on the ground, it evaporates very rapidly; it is a highly volatile fuel. These evaporating gases may easily be ignited and can explode. Diesel fuel is much less volatile than gasoline. It evaporates more slowly. This makes diesel fuel safer. Even though the diesel fuel is less volatile, it has more energy than gasoline when it burns.

Diesel fuel also has a low viscosity index. This means it is thin when hot, but gets thick when cold. Diesel fuel, which can go through the injection system easily in warm weather, may get too thick to flow properly in cold weather. In winter, diesel fuel is supplied in several grades. The winterized diesel fuel, designated Grade D-1, is thinner or less viscous than diesel fuel for normal operating temperatures, which is designated diesel grade 2 (D-2).

Diesel fuel is injected into the cylinder in a liquid form. The fuel must be able to vaporize or change into a gas rapidly. It must be able to ignite without a flame or spark. The ability of a fuel to vaporize and ignite easily is called *ignition quality.*

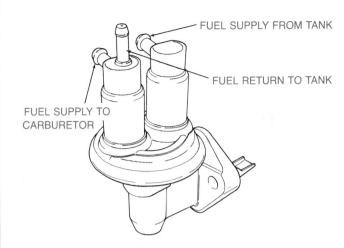

Fig. 21-6 Mechanical fuel pump. (Chrysler Corporation)

Rating the ignition quality of a diesel fuel is similar to the octane rating given to gasoline. A cetane rating scale from 100 to 0 has been established. A hydrocarbon, called cetane, with a very good ignition quality has a rating of 100. If a fuel being tested has the same ignition quality as a 70 percent cetane mixture, the fuel receives a cetane number of 70. The cetane number is posted on the service station diesel fuel pump. Diesel vehicle owner's manuals specify what cetane number fuel to use.

21.15 FUEL TANK

Fuel is stored in the fuel tank (Fig. 21-5), normally mounted to the vehicle frame. If the vehicle's engine is mounted in the front, the fuel tank is in the rear. The tank is in the front of a rear-engine automobile. Placement of the tank far from the engine improves weight distribution and lowers the chance of a fire.

Baffles in some tanks prevent the fuel from sloshing around and causing noise and shifting weight. By keeping agitation down, the baffles also keep condensed moisture from entering fuel lines. Some tanks are equipped with drains at their lowest point to remove water.

The fuel pickup has a mesh screen to block any large particles in the tank from the fuel lines. In vehicles with a float pickup, fuel is always taken from just below the surface level rather than the bottom. This reduces the possibility of taking in water, unless the tank is almost empty. A high fuel level reduces condensation of water out of the air on the inside of

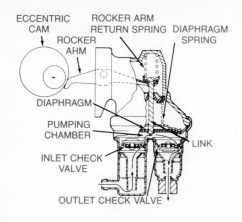

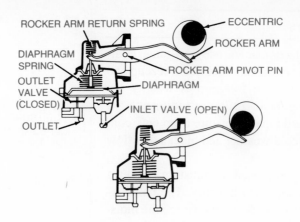

Fig. 21-7 Sectional view of fuel pump.
(American Motors Corporation)

Fig. 21-8 Operation of a mechanical fuel pump.

Fig. 21-9 Electric fuel pump.
(Volkswagen of America)

the tank. The less surface area exposed, the less condensation can take place.

The filler pipe may be welded to the tank. More often, it is a friction fit in a welded flange or it is clamped to the flange by a rubber sleeve. When the tube is installed directly in the flange, an O-ring seal prevents fuel from leaking out at the flange.

A sending unit for the fuel gauge is located in the tank. The fuel level gauge gives the driver an indication of the amount of fuel in the tank. The gauge is similar to the oil pressure and coolant temperature gauges described earlier. The sending unit is a variable resistor connected to a hinged float. A high fuel level moves the tank float up. Linkage from the float to the variable resistor allows a high current flow through the gauge circuit. The fuel gauge registers a full tank. As the fuel is used up, the float drops. Movement of the float changes the value of the variable resistance. This changes the amount of current that flows through the gauge. The needle on the gauge then points to some point below full.

21.16 FUEL LINES

Fuel lines route fuel through the fuel system. They are made of steel tubing except where movement of the line is necessary. Then flexible hoses of synthetic rubber are used. Copper tubing should never be used on a vehicle because of its poor fatigue strength characteristics. It will break sooner than steel when subjected to vibration and movement.

21.17 FUEL PUMP

The outlet on the tank is connected to the automobile's fuel line, which runs from the fuel tank

into the fuel pump in the engine compartment. The fuel pump draws fuel out of the tank and pumps it into the carburetor. The job of the fuel pump is to keep a constant supply of gasoline available at the carburetor. There are two types of pumps, mechanical and electrical.

21.18 Mechanical Fuel Pump

The mechanical fuel pump (Fig. 21-6) is mounted on the engine block. It is operated by an eccentric on the engine camshaft that moves the pump rocker arm up and down. The rocker arm spring holds the arm against the cam eccentric at all times.

The pumping element is a diaphragm that is moved by a spring and by mechanical linkage to the rocker arm. The pumping chamber of the pump illustrated in Figure 21-7 is below the diaphragm. The inlet and outlet ports and the check valves are identical, but their positions are reversed.

Intake of fuel occurs when the cam eccentric pushes down on the pump rocker arm, causing it to pivot. A link at the opposite end of the arm pulls the diaphragm up, creating a vacuum in the pumping chamber. Atmospheric pressure in the fuel tank forces fuel in past the inlet check valve. The outlet valve is held closed by a spring and by the vacuum in the chamber.

Pumping action (Fig. 21-8) takes place when the rocker arm moves downward. The diaphragm spring, compressed during intake, is now free to push down on the diaphragm. This push builds pressure in the pumping chamber. The pressure closes the inlet check valve and opens the outlet check valve. The fuel then flows to the carburetor.

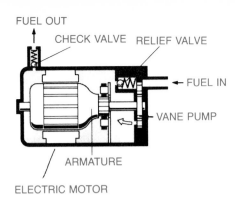
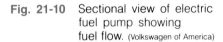

Fig. 21-10　Sectional view of electric fuel pump showing fuel flow. (Volkswagen of America)

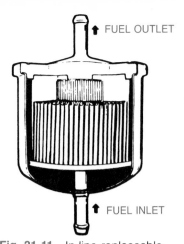

Fig. 21-11　In-line replaceable fuel filter. (American Motors Corporation)

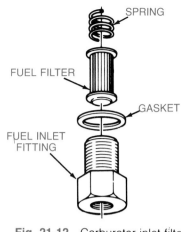

Fig. 21-12　Carburetor inlet filter. (Nissan Motor Corporation in U.S.A.)

The fuel pump can furnish more fuel than the wide open carburetor needs. Therefore, full pump capacity is never required. The pump does not operate when the float valve in the carburetor is closed.

With the carburetor float valve closed, pressure builds up in the pumping chamber. The pressure is too high for the spring to overcome, so the diaphragm stays up. The mechanical linkage between the rocker arm and diaphragm link is positive only in the down direction, so the rocker arm just moves back and forth in the diaphragm push rod slot without moving the diaphragm.

21.19　Electric Fuel Pump

An electric fuel pump (Fig. 21-9) may be mounted in any convenient location either in or out of the engine compartment. Usually it is mounted close to or inside the fuel tank. When the electric pump is mounted on the fuel tank, the armature has fuel flowing around it, and the pump is called a wet pump. There is never a combustible mixture inside the pump housing.

The electric fuel pump has two main parts: an electric motor and a vane pump. The electric motor is coupled to the vane pump (Fig. 21-10), which is the pumping part. It has a set of rollers positioned in slots in a hub. The hub is driven by the electric motor. As the hub spins, centrifugal force causes the rollers to press against the outer wall of the housing. The hub and housing are not concentric. As the hub turns, the rollers must move in and out (back and forth). As the clearance between the rollers and the wall housing increases, a vacuum is formed. Fuel is pulled into the housing through an inlet. Further rotation causes the clearance to get smaller. Fuel is

then discharged from the outlet. The electric motor of the pump is a permanent magnet type of motor. A key switch, or ignition switch, is used to activate the electric motor. An oil pressure switch is used in many applications so that if the engine stops, the fuel pump will also stop, even if the ignition switch is on. This is a safety feature in the event of a collision.

The electric fuel pump delivers several times the quantity of fuel actually required. Excess fuel is diverted at the pressure regulator and flows under low pressure back to the fuel tank. The check valve prevents an abrupt drop of pressure in the fuel line when the engine is stopped. Fuel flow through the electric fuel pump is also shown in Figure 21-10.

21.20　FILTERS

Gasoline reaching the carburetor must be clean to prevent clogging of the carburetor jets and passages. Also, keeping water from entering the carburetor prevents freezeup in the carburetor throat. Most fuel systems have at least one filter to remove impurities from the gasoline.

Fuel tank filters used on earlier automobiles are still used on some vehicles. These filters are usually made of porous bronze that separates dirt and water from the gasoline before it flows to the fuel pump inlet line. As the fuel sloshes in the tank, impurities wash back into the tank where they settle to the bottom.

A sediment bowl may be built into the fuel pump, though it can be installed anywhere before the carburetor float valve. This filter has a strainer screen and a bowl to collect impurities. Gasoline passes through the strainer into the bowl. Particles of dirt settle at the bottom of the bowl along with water.

The Fuel System　205

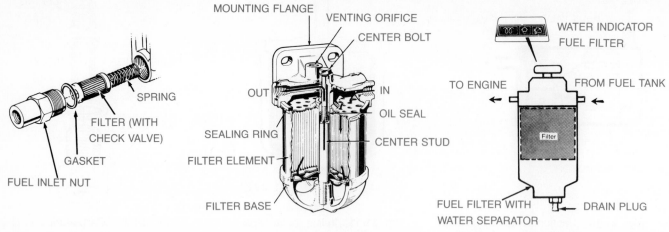

Fig. 21-13 Inlet filter with check valve. (Oldsmobile Motor Division, GMC)

Fig. 21-14 Sectional view of a diesel fuel filter. (Chrysler Corporation)

Fig. 21-15 A diesel water-fuel separator. (Chrysler Corporation)

Since gasoline floats on water, the filter outlet is above the bowl.

Sediment bowls have been largely replaced by in-line filters located between the fuel pump and carburetor. Most in-line filters consist of a throwaway plastic can with a paper filter element (Fig. 21-11). The gasoline enters one end, flows through the element to its center, and then to the outlet.

Another type of in-line fuel filter is usually mounted at the fuel inlet of the carburetor (Fig. 21-12), and such filters sometimes have a check valve to prevent fuel flow back to the pump when the engine is off (Fig. 21-13). The filter element may be paper or screen. It is held in position in the carburetor by a spring at one end and the fuel inlet nut at the other end. A gasket at the fuel inlet nut prevents fuel leakage. Fuel enters the inlet nut and flows through the filter element, where it is cleaned before it enters the carburetor.

21.21   Diesel Fuel Filtering Systems

Diesel fuel systems require very clean fuel for proper operation. Water, acids, and other foreign material must be removed from diesel fuel before it enters the injection system. The typical diesel fuel system inludes both in-tank and in-line fuel filters as well as a water-fuel separator.

A typical engine-compartment-mounted diesel fuel filter is shown in Figure 21-14. In this filter, the paper element is contained in a metal canister and the paper strips forming the element are wound around a cylindrical core in the form of a spiral. The strips are cemented together at the top and bottom so as to form a series of continuous V-shaped coils.

This provides a large filtering area. The filter unit consists of three main parts: the filter head, the element, and the base. The filter is the cross-flow type. Inlet and outlet connections are arranged on the filter head which also incorporates the mounting bracket. Fuel flows through the paper element which traps acid and other foreign material.

The water-fuel separator is usually found between the supply tank and the fuel filter. Its purpose is to separate water from fuel so the engine receives a good supply of fuel. The separator works on the principle that water, being heavier than diesel fuel, will sink to the bottom. A float valve or an insulated sensor is installed so that when the water reaches a certain level, a lamp in the instrument panel will light to notify the operator that the separator should be drained.

A water-fuel separator on the diesel engine is shown in Figure 21-15. Fuel enters the filter, which screens out impurities and separates out water. The water settles to the filter's bottom and can be drained off through the drain plug, located on the bottom. A water symbol on the instrument panel lights up when water in fuel threatens to damage the engine.

21.22   CARBURETION

The carburetor mixes fuel with air in the proper proportions to burn inside the engine. Carburetors have developed into fairly complex devices. They all have similar parts, however, and operate on the same basic principles. The three jobs of a carburetor on a gasoline engine are to meter, atomize, and distribute the fuel throughout the air flowing into the engine (Fig. 21-16). These jobs are carried out by the carburetor automatically over a wide range of

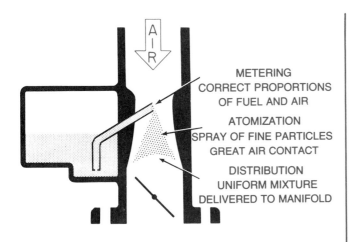

Fig. 21-16 Three functions of a carburetor.
(Chevrolet Motor Division)

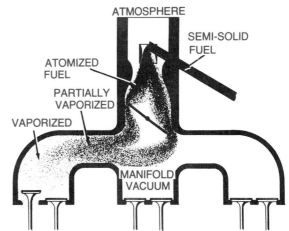

Fig. 21-17 Fuel must be atomized and vaporized to burn.
(Chevrolet Motor Division, GMC)

operating conditions, such as changing engine speeds, load, and operating temperature.

21.23 Atomization and Vaporization

Before gasoline can be used as fuel for an engine, it must be atomized. Atomization means breaking the fuel into fine particles so that it can be mixed with air to form a mixture that will burn. Gasoline in its liquid state will not burn. Only gasoline vapor will burn.

Vaporization is the changing from a liquid to a gas. This change occurs only when the liquid soaks up enough heat to boil. This is what happens in a teakettle to change water to water vapor, or steam. Heat is transferred to the water, raising its temperature until it finally reaches the boiling point. At this time, the water changes to steam.

In a carburetor (Fig. 21-17), gasoline is drawn into the incoming air stream as a spray. The spray is then atomized, or torn into tine droplets, to form a mist. The resulting air-fuel mixture is drawn into the intake manifold. At this point, the fuel mist is vaporized.

Since the pressure in the intake manifold is far less than atmosphere, the boiling point of the gasoline is lowered a great deal. At this reduced pressure, heat from the air particles surrounding each fuel drop causes the gasoline to vaporize.

21.24 Metering

A correct mixture or ratio of fuel and air is needed for efficient burning. The metering job of the carburetor is to provide the proper air-fuel ratio for all conditions.

If we analyze the amount of hydrogen and carbon in gasoline, and the amount of oxygen in the air, we would find that it takes just about 15 pounds of air to completely burn 1 pound of gasoline. This can be called a 15:1 ratio of air-fuel. With more fuel, we would have a richer mixture. With less fuel, we would have a leaner mixture.

Air-fuel ratios are based upon weight, not volume (Fig. 21-18). The reason for this is that the volume of air and fuel changes with pressure or temperature. The weight is not affected by such changes. For example, during most efficient (and economical) combustion, 9,000 gallons of air are required to burn 1 gallon of gasoline, an air-fuel ratio of 9,000:1 by volume. By using weight as the base we can make the same comparison (Fig. 21-18). A gallon of gasoline weighs about 6 pounds whereas 100 gallons of air are needed to produce 1 pound of air. Converting our volume air-fuel ratio weight, we find that 9,000 gallons of air weighs 90 pounds (100 gal equals 1 lb; therefore 9,000 divided by 100 = 90 lb) and 1 gallon of gasoline weighs 6 pounds. Ninety divided by 6 equals 15; therefore, we arrive at an air-fuel ratio of 15:1 by weight.

Most engines will operate on air-fuel ratios from 11:1 (very rich) to 17:1 (slightly lean). A mixture richer than about 11:1 is seldom used, regardless of conditions. Below are some air-fuel ratios used for different conditions. We will see why richer mixtures are needed at times as we go over the various systems in the carburetor.

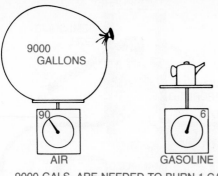

Fig. 21-18 Fuel ratios are based upon weight.
(Chevrolet Motor Division)

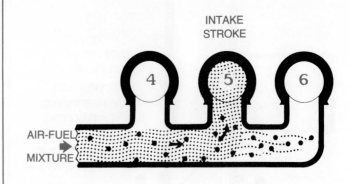

Fig. 21-19 Fuel must be properly distributed for good combustion. (Chevrolet Motor Division, GMC)

Type of Operation	Air-Fuel Ratio
Idle	11:1 to 12:1
Light load (cruising	15:1 to 17:1
Heavy load	12:1 to 13:1

21.25   Distribution

For good burning and smooth engine operation, air and fuel must not only be thoroughly and uniformly mixed. It must be delivered in equal amounts to each cylinder and evenly distributed within the combustion chamber.

Good distribution requires good vaporization. A gas mixture will travel easily around corners in the manifold and engine. Liquid particles, being relatively heavy, will continue in one direction, hitting the walls of the manifold or traveling on to another cylinder.

As an example, think of a 6-cylinder engine whose carburetor is mounted at the center of the manifold. The mixture for cylinders 4, 5, and 6 travels towards the rear of the engine. If number 5 is on the intake stroke, the mixture will be drawn sharply around the corner to number 5 (Fig. 21-19). Large drops of gasoline will not make such a sharp turn but will continue in their path to the rear of the manifold, where they will probably be drawn into number 6 on its intake stroke. As we can see, number 5 receives a leaner mixture and number 6 receives a richer mixture than originally entered the manifold.

To solve these problems, manifolds are built to reduce the sharp corners and provide as smooth a flow as possible. The carburetor assists distribution by breaking up the fuel as finely as possible and providing a uniformly vaporized mixture to the manifold.

21.26   A BASIC CARBURETOR

In order to understand how a carburetor operates, let us build a basic carburetor. We can begin with a tube or barrel (Fig. 21-20) placed to permit an airstream to enter at the top and pass through to the intake manifold and cylinders. The fuel is vaporized and mixed into this airstream in the barrel.

Manifold vacuum causes the airstream. The pistons move down on their intake strokes, creating a vacuum in the combustion chamber. Since the intake valves are open at this time, the vacuum is also felt in the intake manifold. But the air above the carburetor tube is at atmospheric pressure. The pressure difference, then, forces the air down the barrel to fill the vacuum. With the engine operating, there is a continuous stream of air through the barrel.

If the engine operated at the same speed with the same load all the time, a volatile fuel could be sprayed into this airstream at a constant rate. The fuel would vaporize and mix with the air. No other controls would be necessary. But, since the amount of mixture must be changed for different speeds and/or power outputs and since the air-fuel ratio must be changed for different operating conditions, there must be other components in the carburetor.

21.27   Throttle Valve

The throttle valve is a butterfly valve placed in the barrel near the bottom to control the volume of air flow. It is opened and closed by a mechanical linkage to the accelerator pedal. Opening the throttle valve

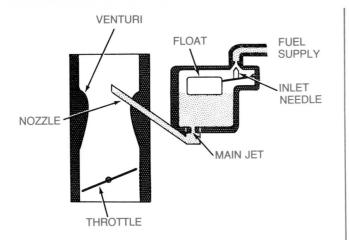

Fig. 21-20 A basic carburetor. (Chevrolet Motor Division)

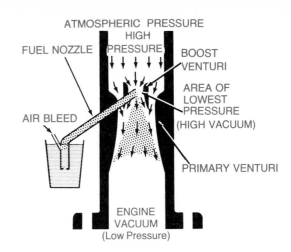

Fig. 21-21 The Venturi creates low pressure to pull fuel from the nozzle. (Chevrolet Motor Division, GMC)

lets air flow through unrestricted. Closing it restricts or blocks air flow so that less air is taken in.

The throttle valve position also has an important effect on the manifold vacuum. When the throttle valve is closed and less air enters to fill the void, the manifold vacuum stays high. When the throttle valve is open and the airstream rushes in to fill the void, the vacuum drops. The carburetor we are building now has air flow and a control for the volume of air. Next, fuel must enter the airstream in the right amount.

21.28   Float and Fuel Supply

A supply of fuel is stored in the carburetor bowl or float bowl. This bowl is connected through passages in the carburetor to the nozzle in the carburetor throat which sprays it into the airstream.

The float and needle valve control the fuel level in the float chamber. The float moves up and down with the fuel level. As fuel is used, the float drops, opening the needle valve to admit fuel from the fuel pump. Then, when the level rises to the correct point, the float closes the needle valve and blocks flow from the pump. A vent in the top of the bowl prevents pressure from changing during the slight changes in fuel level.

With the float valve maintaining a certain level of fuel in the bowl at something close to atmospheric pressure, fuel is forced out of the nozzle into the airstream. This is done by lowering the pressure at the end of the nozzle. Reducing the pressure in the barrel is done by a venturi.

21.29   Venturi

A venturi is a restricted area in the carburetor barrel. When air flows through such a restriction, its speed increases and its pressure decreases.

If the venturi is placed around the fuel nozzle (Fig. 21-21), the nozzle works as an atomizer. As the stream of air flows past the nozzle, its pressure falls. When pressure is reduced at the venturi, atmospheric pressure in the carburetor fuel bowl forces the fuel through the nozzle and into the airstream. The fuel atomizes or mists in the airstream, and vaporization is aided by the reduced pressure.

21.30   Main Jet

The main fuel supply system so far consists of the fuel supply bowl and float system, the discharge nozzle and venturi forming a fuel atomizer, and a throttle valve to control the airstream. Next, an orifice is needed to control flow from the bowl to the discharge nozzle. This flow control orifice, called the main metering jet, controls the air-fuel mixture by restricting the flow of fuel to the main discharge nozzle.

The same thing could be done by closely controlling the inside diameter of the fuel nozzle. However, since the main metering jet is removable, a jet of another size can be substituted to change the air-fuel ratio.

21.31   Air Bleed

The main metering jet gives precise control of the air-fuel ratio at moderate speed. But at very high

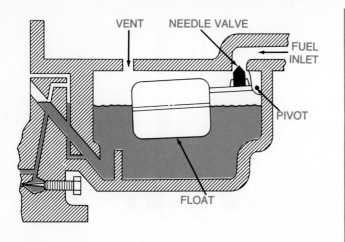

Fig. 21-22 Float circuit.

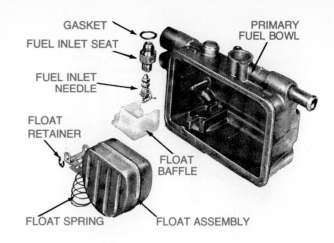

Fig. 21-23 Disassembled view of float circuit parts.

speed, with a large volume of air, the air is less dense and the fuel mixture becomes richer. This is usually offset by air bleeds. The air bleeds introduce air into the fuel nozzle. This helps the fuel to vaporize and improves its response to changes in air flow.

21.32   CARBURETOR CIRCUITS

All common automotive carburetors use a venturi and fuel nozzle to provide the engine with an air-fuel mixture. Different mixtures of air and fuel, however, are required for particular driving conditions. To provide these different mixtures, a number of different systems or circuits are required. Most carburetors have the following circuits:

1. Float circuit
2. Idle circuit
3. Low-speed circuit
4. Main metering circuit
5. High-speed circuit
6. Acceleration circuit
7. Choke circuit

21.33   Float Circuit

The float circuit is part of the basic carburetor discussed earlier. A float bowl inside the carburetor is filled by the fuel pump (Fig. 21-22). When the level of fuel is high enough for proper carburetor operation, the float pushes a small needle valve into the inlet. The needle prevents fuel from entering the carburetor. When fuel is used up and the float drops, the needle valve moves out of the inlet hole, allowing fuel to enter the carburetor. A vent in the float bowl maintains atmospheric pressure to force fuel out the main nozzle.

If the difference in pressure between the carburetor fuel bowl and the nozzle tip controls fuel discharge into the airstream, this pressure difference must depend only on air flow. However, the carburetor air cleaner resists air flow, depending on how clean it is. Thus, pressure in the carburetor air horn, the upper part of the barrel where air enters, will be less than atmospheric pressure. How much less depends on the pressure drop through the air cleaner. In a balanced carburetor, the fuel bowl is vented to the air horn, not the atmosphere. The fuel bowl is therefore always at air horn pressure. Then air flow alone affects the pressure.

A low fuel level in the bowl causes poor performance in the main metering system and could cause loss of power. High fuel level causes metering delivery too early and fuel spillage during turning, which result in an overly rich air-fuel mix. Fuel level is adjusted by bending a tab on the float arm. The correct operation of all other systems depends on the proper level of fuel in the float bowl. A disassembled view of a float circuit is shown in Figure 21-23.

21.34   Idle Circuit

When the engine is idling (Fig. 21-24), the throttle valve is nearly closed. Not enough air is drawn through the carburetor to create a vacuum in the venturi. Fuel cannot be pulled up the fuel nozzle. A system called the idle circuit is required to get enough air and fuel below the closed throttle valve. A small hole in the carburetor above the venturi admits air. The air is directed through a passage where it can siphon some fuel out of the float bowl. This mixture of air and fuel is drawn out of a small

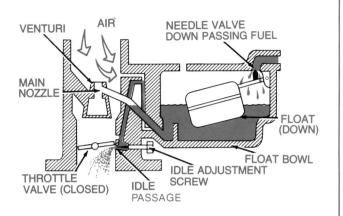

Fig. 21-24 Idle circuit.

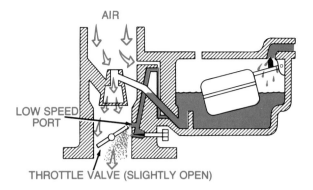

Fig. 21-25 Low-speed circuit.

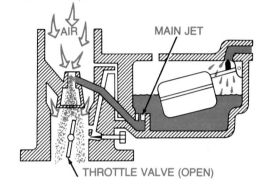

Fig. 21-26 Main metering circuit.

hole just below the throttle valve, enabling the engine to run at idle speed.

An idle adjustment screw controls the amount of air and fuel that can get through the idle discharge hole. This screw can be set to suit the individual engine. The mixture for idling is slightly richer than for cruising because there is less efficient fuel distribution in the manifold when air is in short supply. At cruising speed, greater air flow improves distribution or "breathing."

During idle, the throttle valve is held slightly open by the idle stop screw. The small amount of air which passes the throttle valve is regulated by this screw to provide the correct engine idle speed.

21.35   Low-Speed Circuit

When the automobile is operated at low speed, the throttle opens slightly. Increased air speed would make the mixture lean immediately except for the low speed port (Fig. 21-25). This opening slightly higher in the barrel provides a second discharge for fuel when the throttle begins to open. This prevents a flat spot between idle and main metering system operation. An idle restriction controls flow to the idle system. In some carburetors, this restriction is a removable orifice or idle jet.

21.36   Main Metering Circuit

As the driver pushes down on the accelerator pedal, the throttle valve opens further (Fig. 21-26) to create a strong flow of air through the carburetor. The vacuum at the venturi is strong enough to pull fuel out of the fuel nozzle. The fuel that enters the

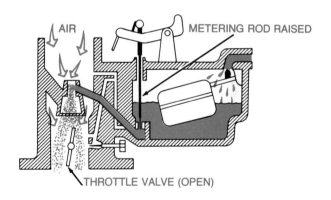

Fig. 21-27 High-speed circuit.

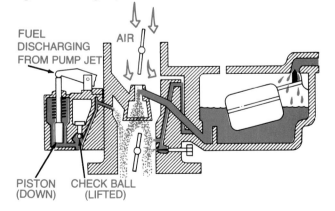

Fig. 21-28 Accelerator circuit.

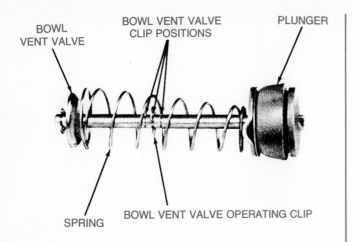

Fig. 21-29 Piston accelerator plunger. (Chrysler Corporation)

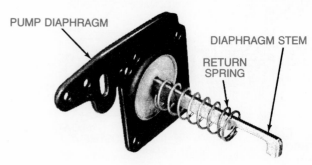

Fig. 21-30 Diaphragm accelerator plunger. (Chrysler Corporation)

nozzle is pulled out of the float bowl. To enter the nozzle, the fuel passes through the main jet. A jet with a larger or smaller hole can be installed to change the operating mixture.

21.37 High-Speed Circuit

During high-speed operation, the throttle valve is opened all the way (Fig. 21-27). Air flowing through the carburetor creates a very strong vacuum at the venturi so that more fuel passes through the nozzle. The high-speed circuit allows more fuel to enter the nozzle for high-speed operation. A rod with steps in it, called the metering rod, is connected to the accelerator pedal linkage. The metering rod is placed in the main jet to limit fuel flow during most operating conditions. During high-speed operation, the linkage pulls the rod up to allow more fuel to get through the jet and into the nozzle.

On many carburetors, a vacuum-operated diaphragm or piston known as a power valve is used instead of a metering rod. The power valve opens an additional passage for fuel to the nozzle. The power valve fuel supply system is operated by manifold vacuum on a small piston or diaphragm. This piston has a long stem that opens the power valve when vacuum drops off. At idle or cruising speeds, the high vacuum holds the piston up against spring force and the power valve remains closed.

If the driver depresses the accelerator pedal for more power, the throttle valve opens and vacuum drops off. Spring force moves the piston and stem down to open the power valve. Additional fuel flows through metering holes in the power valve. This extra

fuel discharged from the main discharge nozzle makes the mixture there richer.

21.38 Accelerator Circuit

When the driver wants to accelerate quickly to pass another automobile or start up fast, the acceleration circuit (Fig. 21-28) provides a squirt of extra fuel. It consists of a small round piston (Fig. 21-29) or diaphragm (Fig. 21-30) connected to the throttle linkage. When the driver steps down hard on the accelerator pedal, the piston is pushed down. Fuel below the piston is quickly forced out a small nozzle in the venturi area. The circuit cannot discharge fuel again until the driver lets up the accelerator pedal. The piston has to move back up into position for fuel to enter the area below it from the float bowl. A small check valve in the circuit makes sure the fuel is squirted into the nozzle and not back into the float bowl.

21.39 Choke Circuit

The last major circuit of the carburetor is the choke circuit (Fig. 21-31). The choke system delivers a great deal of fuel into the engine for cold starts. Its main part is a choke valve, placed in the air horn of the carburetor above the venturi. When the choke valve is closed, it chokes or restricts the amount of air that can go through the carburetor. As the driver cranks the engine to start it, a strong vacuum is created by the pistons. If the choke valve is closed and the throttle valve is open, this vacuum in the venturi area pulls a great deal of fuel out of the main noz-

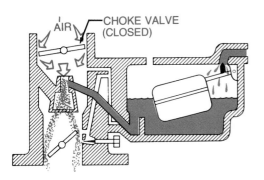

Fig. 21-31   Choke circuit.

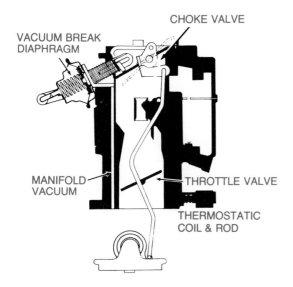

Fig. 21-32   Choke system with thermostatic spring mounted on the intake manifold. (Chevrolet Motor Division, GMC)

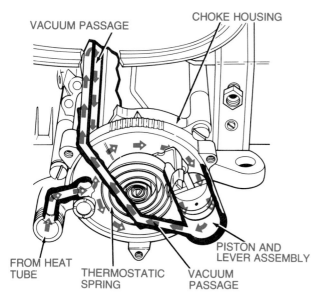

Fig. 21-33   Choke system with thermostatic spring mounted to carburetor body. (Ford Motor Company)

zle, into the intake manifold, and from there to the cylinders.

Since the choke is required only to start a cold engine, it is connected to a thermostatic device that senses temperature. The thermostatic device closes the choke valve when the engine is cold and opens it when the engine is warmed up. The device usually consists of a bimetallic spring in a housing mounted on the side of the carburetor or on the intake manifold. It is connected through linkage to the carburetor. A vacuum-operated piston or diaphragm is also used in the system. The choke operation is controlled by a combination of intake manifold vacuum, the offset choke valve, thermostatic coil, atmospheric temperature, and exhaust heat.

The remote thermostatic coil on the engine intake manifold (Fig. 21-32) is adjusted to hold the choke valve closed when starting a cold engine. Air velocity against the offset choke valve causes the valve to open slightly, against the action of the thermostatic coil. When the engine is started, manifold vacuum applied to the vacuum diaphragm unit mounted on the carburetor air horn opens the choke valve just enough so that the engine operates without loading up from a rich mixture or stalling from a lean one. The choke valve remains in this position until the engine begins to warm up. Exhaust heat, directed at the thermostatic coil through a passage in the intake manifold, causes it to relax gradually until the choke valve is fully open.

The carburetor shown in Figure 21-33 has the choke shaft hooked to a thermostatic choke mounted on the carburetor body. The automatic choke is equipped with a bimetallic thermostatic spring and a vacuum piston. The bimetallic thermostatic spring mechanism winds up when cold and unwinds when warm. When the engine is cold, the thermostatic spring, through attaching linkage, holds the choke plate in a closed position. Manifold vacuum channeled through a passage in the choke control housing, draws the choke vacuum piston downward, opening the choke plate slightly. When the engine is started, manifold vacuum acting on the piston in the choke housing and the flow of air acting on the offset choke immediately move the plate against the tension of the thermostatic spring to a partially open position to prevent stalling.

As the engine continues to operate, manifold vacuum draws heated air from the exhaust manifold heat chamber. The amount of air is controlled by restrictions in the air passages in the carburetor. The warmed air entering the choke housing heats the thermostatic spring, causing it to unwind. The tension of the thermostatic spring gradually decreases as the

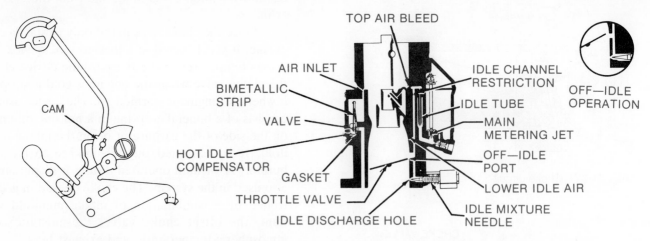

Fig. 21-34 Fast idle cam and linkage. (Chevrolet Motor Division, GMC)

Fig. 21-35 Idle system with hot idle compensator. (Pontiac Motor Division, GMC)

temperature of the air from the heat chamber rises, allowing the choke plate to open. The air is drawn into the intake manifold.

When the engine reaches its normal operating temperature, the thermostatic spring no longer pushes on the choke piston. The piston then pulls the choke plate to the full-open position. In this position, the choke piston is at its lowest point in the cylinder. Slots in the piston chamber wall allow sufficient air to bleed past the piston and into the intake manifold past the thermostatic spring housing. The spring thus remains heated and the choke remains fully open until the engine is stopped and allowed to cool.

During warmup, if the engine reaches the stall point because of a lean mixture, manifold vacuum will drop. The tension of the thermostatic spring then overcomes the lowered vacuum acting on the choke piston, and the choke plate moves toward the closed position, providing a richer mixture. The linkage between the choke lever and the throttle shaft keeps the choke plate partially open when the accelerator pedal is fully depressed. This permits unloading of a flooded engine.

21.40 CARBURETOR ACCESSORIES

Along with the basic circuits, most carburetors have some additional equipment. The most common carburetor accessories will be presented in this section.

21.41 Fast Idle Cam

The fast idle cam (Fig. 21-34) is mounted to the side of the carburetor next to the idle stop screw. The choke rod works the fast idle cam during choking.

Steps on the edge of the fast idle cam hit the idle stop screw, which permits a faster engine idle speed for smoother running when the engine is cold. As the choke plate is moved from the closed to the open position, the choke rod rotates the fast idle cam. Each step on the cam permits a power idle rpm as engine temperature rises and choking is reduced.

21.42 Antipercolation Valve

Percolation, also called fuel boiling or fuel push-over, occurs when high temperatures under the hood vaporize fuel in the carburetor. As vaporizing fuel expands, pressure buildup pushes the carburetor float open, flooding the engine. You can see the fuel bubbling or percolating in the carburetor barrel with the air cleaner off.

A spring-loaded valve mounted on top of the fuel bowl allows these vapors to vent and reduce the pressure. On older vehicles, the venting allowed the vapors to escape into the atmosphere. On newer vehicles, the vapors are trapped in a recovery system that is part of the emission control system.

21.43 Hot Idle Compensator

The hot idle compensator (Fig. 21-35) used on some carburetors is located in a chamber on the float bowl casting. It is next to the carburetor bore, on the throttle lever side of the carburetor.

The compensator consists of a thermostatically controlled valve, a bimetallic heat sensitive strip, a valve holder, and a bracket. The valve closes off an air channel which leads from a hole inside the air horn to a point below the throttle valve where it exits into the throttle body bore.

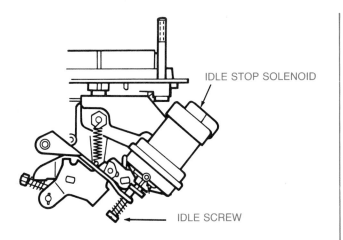

Fig. 21-36 Idle stop solenoid. (Ford Motor Company)

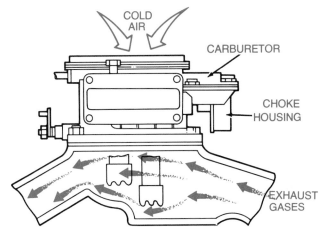

Fig. 21-37 Hot exhaust gases routed near carburetor for warmup.

Normally, the compensator valve is held closed by tension of the bimetallic strip and engine vacuum. During extreme hot engine operation, excessive fuel vapors in the carburetor can enter the engine manifold, making the mixture richer than required. This results in rough engine idling and stalling. At a specific temperature, when extra air is needed to offset the enriching effects of fuel vapors, the bimetallic strip bends and unseats the compensator valve, uncovering the air channel from the compensator valve chamber to the throttle body bore. Enough air is drawn into the engine manifold to offset the richer mixture and maintain a smooth engine idle. When the engine cools and the extra air is not needed, the bimetallic strip closes the valve and operation returns to normal.

21.44   Throttle Positioners

Modern carburetors use a variety of equipment to return the throttle at a controlled rate when the driver releases the accelerator. An electrically controlled stop solenoid (Fig. 21-36) is used on many engines. When the ignition key is on, the solenoid allows the idle stop screw to be open far enough for engine idle. When the key is off, the solenoid changes position and the idle stop screw completely closes the throttle plates to prevent dieseling when the ignition is off.

The position of the throttle, especially on deacceleration, plays an important part in emission control. As a result, more complicated throttle positioners are used on some vehicles with emission control systems. These systems will be described in Chapter 51.

21.45   Manifold Heat Control System

Cold temperature operation can be improved by the addition of a manifold heat control system. Hot exhaust gases are routed from one side of the engine through passages in the intake manifold and circulated around the base of the carburetor (Fig. 21-37). This preheats the air-fuel mixture in the carburetor so that the engine runs more smoothly when it is cold.

This system uses a bimetallic thermostatic coil that controls a valve in the exhaust manifold. When the coil is cold, it closes the valve, forcing exhaust gases into the intake manifold. As the coil heats up, it changes the position of the valve to allow normal exhaust flow through the exhaust system.

21.46   CARBURETOR TYPES

There are many different types of carburetors. They are classified according to the direction air enters the carburetor and the number of barrels.

21.47   Air Direction

The first carburetors, known as updraft carburetors, allowed air flow upward to get to the intake manifold (Fig. 21-38). Today's downdraft carburetors (Fig. 21-39) are mounted above the engine so that the air-fuel mixture moves down by gravity. This lessens the energy used to supply the mixture to the cylinders. Other reasons for the change to the downdraft design were easier starting, more efficient operation, greater power, and smaller size.

The Fuel System   215

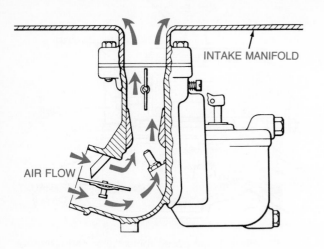

Fig. 21-38 Updraft carburetor.

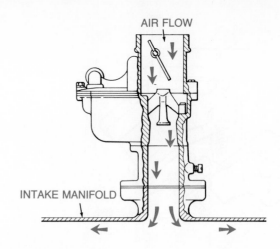

Fig. 21-39 Downdraft carburetor.

21.48 Variable Venturi Carburetors

The diameter of the venturi in most carburetors is fixed. For good running at low speed and better gas mileage, venturis are made in small sizes. To get maximum power and speed, venturis are made in large sizes. A variable venturi carburetor has a sliding valve that varies the diameter of the venturi according to the demands of the engine. If the engine is putting out maximum horsepower at high speed, the venturi will open up. When the engine is running at low speed under a light load, the venturi closes down to give better mileage.

Some imported cars have for many years used a variable venturi carburetor with a vertical sliding valve (Fig. 21-40). A chamber at the top of the carburetor contains oil and a piston to dampen the movement of the sliding valve. The only United States car manufacturer to use a variable venturi carburetor is Ford Motor Company. The Ford carburetor is a two-barrel (Fig. 21-41). It has two black sliding valves at the top. Both the import and Ford carburetors have a metering rod attached to the sliding valve. When the sliding valve opens up the venturi, it pulls the metering rod out of the jet to allow more fuel to pass.

The movement of the sliding valve is controlled by the vacuum between the throttle and the sliding valve. This vacuum operates a vacuum diaphragm or vacuum chamber and piston to move the valve. Because the vacuum is sensed above the throttle plate, the venturi size is self-regulating. The venturi size depends on the speed and load on the engine. On the Ford carburetor, a mechanical linkage holds the venturi valve open at wide-open throttle. Because of the self-regulating feature, variable venturi carburetors are considered best for smooth running and good gas mileage, not maximum horsepower.

21.49 Multiple Barrel Carburetors

Carburetors may be classified by the number of openings controlled by throttle plates that allow air and fuel into the intake manifold. Small engines use a carburetor with a single opening or barrel. Higher engine displacement requires a larger carburetor. A very large single-barrel carburetor with a very large venturi might meet the air-fuel needs at high speed but not at low speed. A better solution is a carburetor with several small venturis and barrels. The small venturis allow good low-speed operation, and several provide enough air-fuel delivery for high-speed operation.

Carburetors are made with one to four barrels (Fig. 21-42). A two-barrel carburetor is two complete carburetors with only the float system in common. A three- or four-barrel carburetor is made up of two sections. The primary section is identical in operation to a two-barrel carburetor. The secondary section operates only when full power is needed, that is, when the primary throttles are wide open. The secondary throttles usually are opened by delayed action linkage from the primary throttles. They can also be activated by air flow from the primary venturis or by vacuum diaphragms. The three- or four-barrel carburetor provides more power through better breathing at high speeds. But there is no reduction or economy at low speeds.

Fig. 21-40 Side draft sliding valve carburetor.

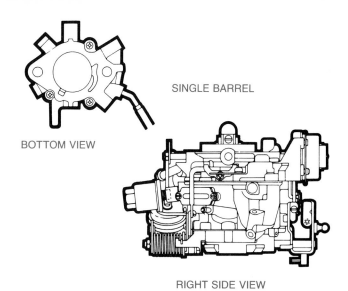

SINGLE BARREL

BOTTOM VIEW

RIGHT SIDE VIEW

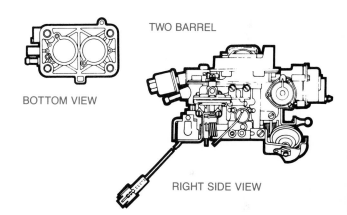

TWO BARREL

BOTTOM VIEW

RIGHT SIDE VIEW

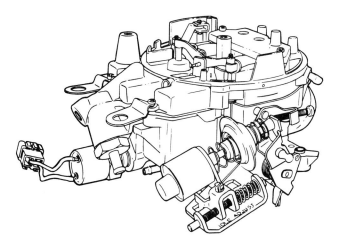

Fig. 21-41 Variable venturi carburetor. (Ford Motor Company)

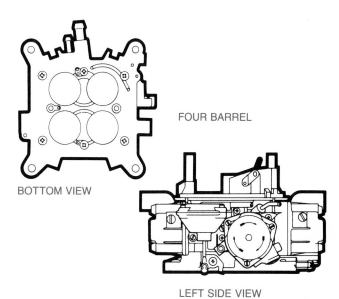

FOUR BARREL

BOTTOM VIEW

LEFT SIDE VIEW

Fig. 21-42 Carburetors classified by number of barrels. (Ford Motor Company)

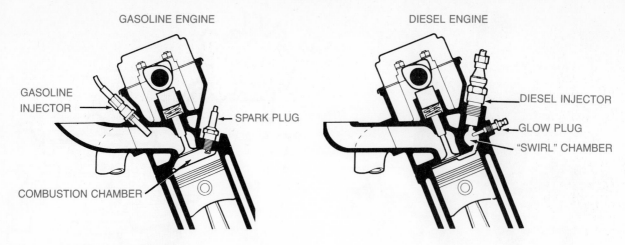

GASOLINE ENGINE

DIESEL ENGINE

GASOLINE INJECTOR

SPARK PLUG

COMBUSTION CHAMBER

DIESEL INJECTOR

GLOW PLUG

"SWIRL" CHAMBER

Fig. 21-43 Comparison of diesel and gasoline fuel injector location. (Volkswagen of America)

21.50   FUEL INJECTION

Delivery to the engine of a precise amount of air and fuel gives the greatest power and economy along with the lowest emissions. Even though carburetors have improved over the years, they are a relatively crude means of delivering fuel to the engine's cylinders.

21.51   Mechanical Fuel Injection

The need to deliver fuel directly into the cylinder of a diesel engine led to the development of fuel injection. This system used a pump that forced fuel under pressure to small plunger-like devices in each combustion chamber. At the correct time, the plunger was activated mechanically to inject fuel into the combustion chamber. Mechanically operated fuel injection is still used in diesel engines.

21.52   Continuous Flow Fuel Injection

The expense and complexity of mechanical fuel injection prevented its use in regular gasoline engines. Another type of fuel injection was developed for gasoline engines, primarily by racing engine developers. A high-pressure pump forced fuel under pressure to injector nozzles mounted in the intake manifold very near the engine's intake valves. The injectors were not activated mechanically but provided a continuous stream of fuel on demand. High fuel delivery rates were possible for high speed operation. This system was less efficient than the mechanical type but much less complicated. Since the fuel was metered continually into the manifold, the system was called continuous flow fuel injection.

21.53   Electronic Fuel Injection

In the 1970s, fuel injection technology and electronics technology joined in the development of a fuel delivery system called electronic fuel injection (E.F.I.). Electronic fuel injection was the product of efforts to lower emissions and improve fuel mileage.

This system uses fuel spray nozzles mounted in the intake manifold or cylinder head near each of the engine's intake valves. The nozzles are supplied with fuel under high pressure by a mechanical or electric fuel pump. The nozzles are controlled electronically. The electronic controls insure that the fuel injected at any given moment is precisely the amount the engine needs. Sensing devices on the engine tell the control unit the actual load condition, engine speed, and operating temperature. Electronic fuel injection is covered in detail in Chapter 53.

21.54   Diesel Fuel Systems

The power in a diesel engine is developed when fuel is injected into the compressed air in the cylinder. On the intake stroke only air is pulled into the cylinder. When the engine is ready for a power stroke, a small quantity of fuel is injected into the compressed air. The diesel fuel system serves two functions: it provides the source of fuel and it also provides the source of ignition.

The fuel injection system developed for diesel engines is different from that used on a gasoline engine. The fuel injector on a gasoline engine is mounted in the intake manifold whereas the diesel injector is mounted in a swirl chamber directly in the combustion chamber (Fig. 21-43).

Top
Ford Mustang GT powered by a 5.0-liter electronic fuel injection high-output gasoline V-8 with automatic overdrive. (Ford Motor Company)

Bottom
Ford Motor Company 4-speed automatic overdrive transmission. The fourth speed is an overdrive, which results in a lower engine speed on the highway and better gas mileage. (Ford Motor Company)

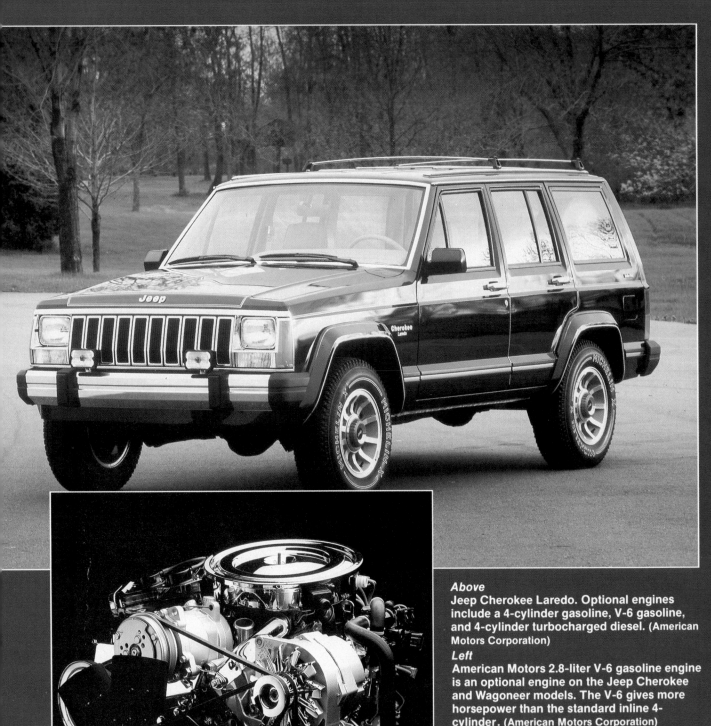

Above
Jeep Cherokee Laredo. Optional engines include a 4-cylinder gasoline, V-6 gasoline, and 4-cylinder turbocharged diesel. (American Motors Corporation)

Left
American Motors 2.8-liter V-6 gasoline engine is an optional engine on the Jeep Cherokee and Wagoneer models. The V-6 gives more horsepower than the standard inline 4-cylinder. (American Motors Corporation)

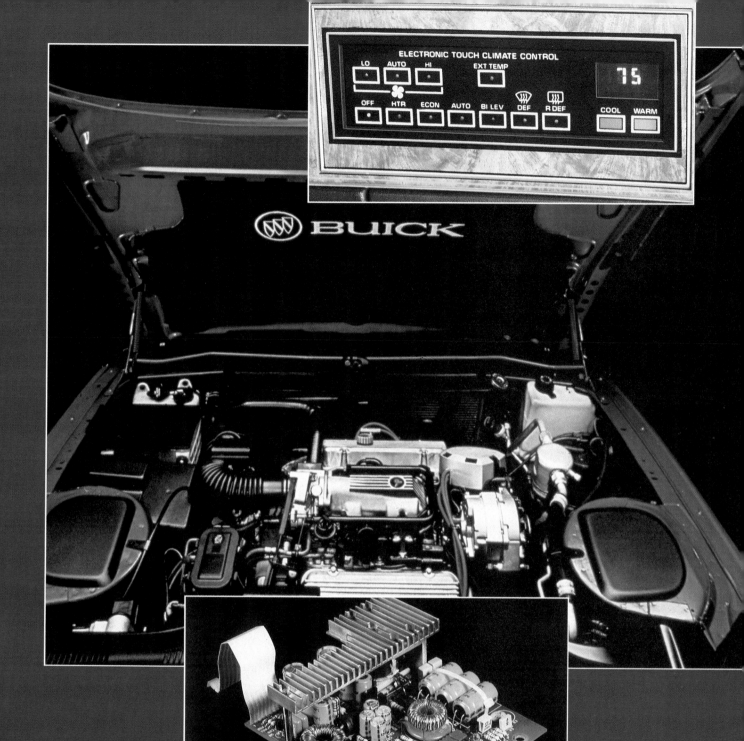

Top
Buick Electra Electronic Touch Climate Control. (Buick Division, General Motors Corporation)
Center
Under the hood of a Buick Electra. (Buick Division, General Motors Corporation)
Bottom
Electronic power supply used in Buick Electronic Touch Climate Control. (Buick Division, General Motors Corporation)

Dodge Datona Turbo Z. It is powered by a turbocharged 2.2-liter fuel-injected gasoline 4-cylinder engine. The skirts are patterned after the ground effect skirts that reduce air pressure under a race car and make it hug the ground. (Chrysler Corporation)

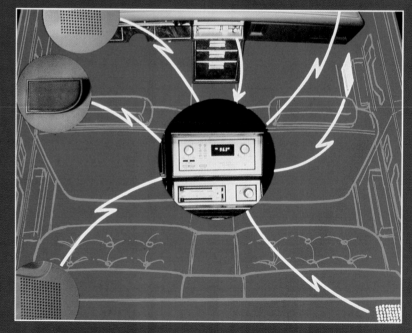

AM-FM stereo cassette sound system used in Chrysler cars. It has six speakers, instead of the usual four. (Chrysler Corporation)

Experimental Aero 2002 from Chevrolet. If the Aero 2002 body could be put on an ordinary Chevrolet Citation, the Citation would get 65 miles per gallon at highway speeds because of reduced air resistance. (Chevrolet Division, General Motors Corporation)

Ford 2.3-liter electronic fuel-injected gasoline 4-cylinder engine, with transmission. (Ford Motor Company)

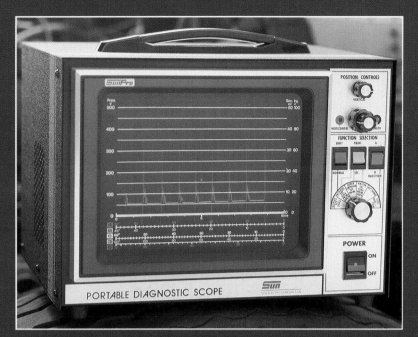

Portable diagnostic scope from Sun. It shows a pattern of the ignition on the screen just like the large garage scopes. (Sun Electric Corporation, Instrument Products Division)

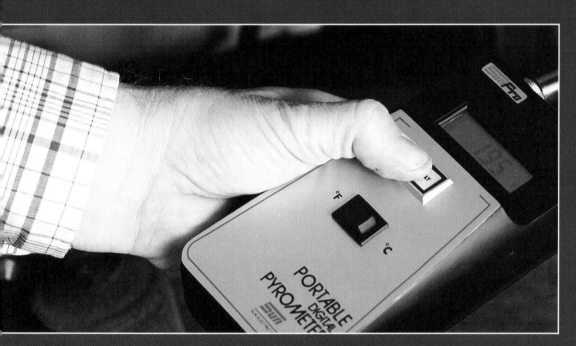

Sun portable pyrometer. A digital readout shows a complete range of temperatures, but is most useful in checking the exhaust temperature of individual cylinders to see if they are producing power. (Sun Electric Corporation, Instrument Products Division)

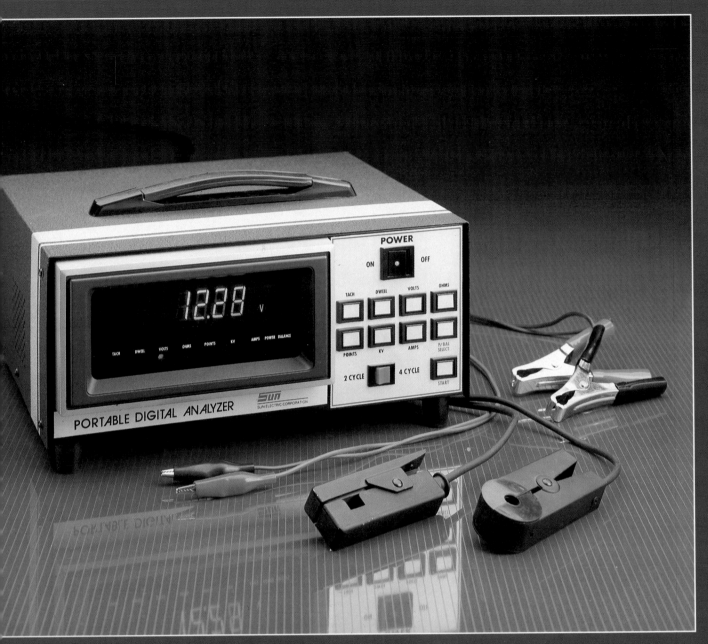

Sun portable digital analyzer. It has all the usual engine readouts, but with a unique Automatic Power Balance feature that kills individual cylinders to measure their power. (Sun Electric Corporation, Instrument Products Division)

Diesel engines use a mechanical fuel injection system because injectors must inject fuel at just the right time and also because they must overcome the high combustion-chamber pressures. A mechanical injection system forces fuel through spray nozzles by hydraulic pressure.

Four general systems of mechanical fuel injection have been developed:

1. common rail system
2. pump controlled system
3. unit injection system
4. distributor system

The common rail system consists of a high pressure pump that distributes fuel to a common rail or header to which each injector is connected by tubing.

The pump-controlled system provides a single pump for each injector. The pump is separately mounted and is driven by an accessory shaft. Connection to the injectors is made by suitable tubing.

The unit injector system combines the pump and the injector into a single unit. High-pressure fuel lines are eliminated. Operation of the unit injector is usually by means of push rods and rocker arms.

Most automotive diesel engines use a distributor system. There are several types of distributor systems. One type provides a high-pressure metering pump with a distributor which delivers fuel to the individual cylinders. Another design provides a low-pressure metering and distribution. High pressure needed for injection is provided by the injection nozzles which are cam operated.

A typical distributor-type injection system is shown in Figure 21-44. The injection pump is driven by gearing from the engine. Fuel is drawn from the tank through the filter by the injection pump. The injection pump meters and distributes fuel under pressure to the injectors in the correct firing order. Excess fuel from the pump and injectors returns to the tank via a separate line.

The main purpose of the fuel injector or nozzle is to direct and atomize the metered fuel into the combustion chamber. The combustion chamber design dictates the type of nozzle, the droplet size, and the spray required to achieve complete combustion within a given time and space. The injectors are threaded into the cylinder head and are subject to the direct heat of combustion like a gasoline engine spark plug.

A cross-sectional view of a fuel injection nozzle or injector is shown in Figure 21-45. The nozzle consists of a housing about the size of a spark plug,

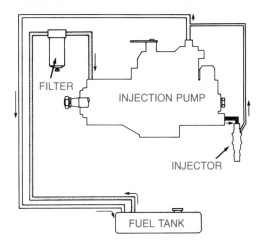

Fig. 21-44 Basic components of the distributor type mechanical fuel injection system. (Volkswagen of America)

which is threaded into the combustion chamber. Inside the housing is a needle valve which is held in position by a pressure spring. The spring works to hold the small tapered end of the needle valve in the small opening called a spray orifice at the bottom of the nozzle.

The nozzle is operated by the fuel pressure. The pressure developed by the injection pump acts on the exposed annular area of the needle valve. It is lifted from its seat as soon as the force acting on the annular area exceeds the force of the pressure spring. The fuel is then injected through the nozzle orifices into the combustion chamber.

During injection, the fuel goes through the injection pump lines to the fuel inlet passage of the injector housing, into the pressure chamber, and through spray orifice(s) into the combustion chamber. Fuel leaking past the valve stem is returned to the fuel tank by the return line. After injection of the fuel into the combustion chamber, the pressure spring forces the needle valve back on its seat. The injector nozzle is then closed and ready for the next pressure stroke.

21.55   AIR CLEANER

The engine pulls in a tremendous amount of air through the carburetor or fuel injection air horn. To filter dust and dirt out before it enters the engine, air is routed through an air cleaner. This large, round housing is located above the carburetor or fuel injection assembly (Fig. 21-46). Inside the housing is a paper or polyurethane foam filter element. Air passes through the porous filter element, but the openings are small enough to trap dirt and dust.

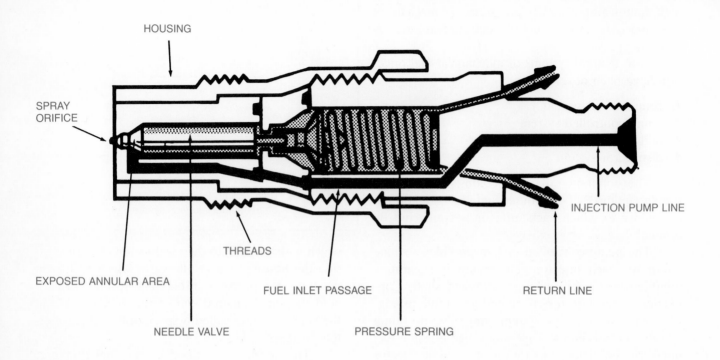

HOUSING

SPRAY
ORIFICE

EXPOSED ANNULAR AREA

THREADS

NEEDLE VALVE

FUEL INLET PASSAGE

PRESSURE SPRING

INJECTION PUMP LINE

RETURN LINE

Fig. 21-45 Parts of a diesel fuel injection nozzle. (Volkswagen of America)

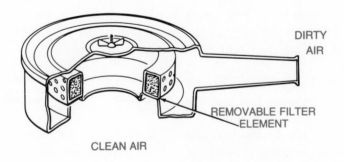

DIRTY
AIR

REMOVABLE FILTER
ELEMENT

CLEAN AIR

Fig. 21-46 Removable air filter element.

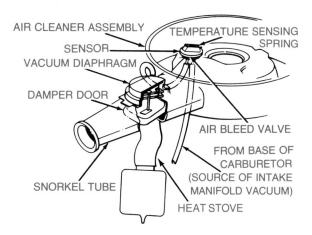

AIR CLEANER ASSEMBLY

TEMPERATURE SENSING
SPRING

SENSOR

VACUUM DIAPHRAGM

DAMPER DOOR

AIR BLEED VALVE

FROM BASE OF
CARBURETOR
(SOURCE OF INTAKE
MANIFOLD VACUUM)

SNORKEL TUBE

HEAT STOVE

Fig. 21-47 Thermostatically controlled air cleaner. (Chevrolet Motor Division, GMC)

Many newer vehicles use a thermostatically controlled air cleaner. This system improves carburetor operation and engine warmup characteristics by keeping air entering the carburetor at a temperature of at least 100° F (38° C).

The thermostatic air cleaner (Fig. 21-47) system includes a temperature sensor, a vacuum diaphragm and control damper assembly mounted in the air cleaner, vacuum control hoses, manifold heat stove, and connecting pipes. The vacuum motor, controlled by the temperature sensor, operates the air control damper assembly to regulate the flow of hot air to the carburetor. The hot air is obtained from the heat stove on the exhaust manifold when the engine is cold.

When the underhood temperature rises, the temperature sensor allows vacuum from the intake manifold to operate a vacuum diaphragm. The diaphragm closes the passage from the heat stove and opens the passage from the snorkel tube. Air is now pulled through the air cleaner in the normal way.

21.56 SUPERCHARGERS

At high engine speed, there is hardly time to fill the cylinder with enough air and fuel. One solution to this problem is to pump air and fuel into the cylinder under high pressure. The air pump used to compress air and force it into the cylinder is called a supercharger or blower (Fig. 21-48).

There are two types of superchargers: positive displacement and centrifugal. A positive displacement supercharger (Fig. 21-49) has two three-lobed impellers in mesh with each other in a housing. One of the impellers is driven by belts or gears from the front of the engine. As the lobes rotate, air is pulled

into the low-pressure area created as the lobes unmesh. The air is then pumped around the housing and into the intake manifold. Since the unit will pump the same charge on each revolution it is called a positive displacement pump.

The positive displacement supercharger is commonly used on large truck diesel engines. One disadvantage of this type of supercharger which has limited its use in passenger vehicles is that it uses crankshaft power to drive the impellers. A great deal of the engine's power goes to drive the supercharger.

The centrifugal supercharger (Fig. 21-50) accelerates the air to a high speed and forces it into the intake manifold. This is the same type of pump used in the cooling system to pump coolant. As the impeller rotates at high speed, air is pulled into the low-pressure area in the center of the impeller. The blades on the impeller force the air through the housing and into the intake manifold.

The centrifugal supercharger may be driven by belts or gears from the engine. More commonly, exhaust gases routed at a turbine wheel cause the turbine wheel to rotate at high speed. The turbine wheel turns the impeller in the supercharger. The advantage of this system, called a turbocharger (Fig. 21-51, left), is that power from burned exhaust gases is used to drive the supercharger. The amount of exhaust gas directed at the turbine is controlled by a valve called a waste gate. The waste gate can be controlled manually or automatically to increase or decrease the turbocharger pressure or "boost" into the engine.

The turbocharger works very well on either gasoline or diesel engines. More and more engines are being equipped with turbochargers. The turbocharger provides an excellent method of getting more

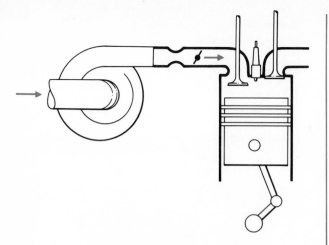

Fig. 21-48 Supercharger forces air into the cylinder under pressure.

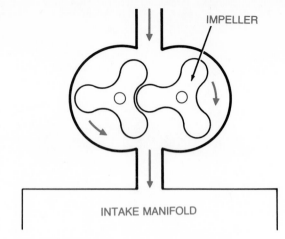

IMPELLER

INTAKE MANIFOLD

Fig. 21-49 Positive displacement supercharger.

power out of small displacement engines and at the same time maintaining good fuel mileage. A turbocharger is shown on a gasoline engine in Figure 21-51 (right).

NEW TERMS

Acceleration circuit A circuit in the carburetor that provides fuel for acceleration.

Air bleed Passages for air to enter the fuel in the carburetor.

Air cleaner A large filter assembly mounted above the carburetor to clean the air before it enters the engine.

Atomization Breaking the liquid fuel into small drops.

Carburetor Part of the fuel system that mixes air and fuel in the correct amount to burn in the engine.

Cetane number A number assigned to diesel fuel describing its ignition quality.

Choke circuit A circuit in the carburetor used for cold starts.

De-icers Chemicals added to the fuel to prevent ice from forming in the carburetor.

Detonation Abnormal combustion in which a portion of the mixture explodes during combustion.

Fast idle cam An accessory on the carburetor that allows a fast idle speed during warmup.

Float circuit A carburetor circuit that provides the correct amount of fuel for all the other circuits.

Fuel injection A fuel mixing device that injects the fuel directly into the cylinders or intake manifold.

Fuel pump A pump used to draw fuel out of the fuel tank and into the carburetor.

Fuel system The engine system that provides the engine with the correct mixture of air and fuel.

Fuel tank The tank used to store fuel on the automobile.

Gasoline A fuel made from refining crude oil.

High-speed circuit A carburetor circuit that provides fuel for high-speed operation.

Idle circuit A carburetor circuit that provides the fuel mixture for idle.

Injection pump Fuel injection component that delivers fuel to the injector nozzle.

Low-speed circuit A carburetor circuit that provides the fuel mixture for low-speed operation.

Main jet A hole through which fuel passes for the main metering operation.

Main metering circuit A carburetor circuit that provides the fuel mixture for cruising.

Mechanical fuel injection Diesel fuel injection system in which a single pump provides fuel to all cylinders in a manner similar to those used in an ignition distributor.

Mechanical injector nozzle Device mounted in the diesel engine combustion chamber and used to spray fuel for ignition.

Needle valve Valve in an injector nozzle that opens to allow fuel to spray into the combustion chamber.

Normal combustion A condition in which the combustion in the cylinder is smooth.

Octane A rating of a fuel's antiknock ability.

Performance number A numbering system used to rate fuels above 100 octane.

Preignition Abnormal combustion in which something other than the ignition system explodes the air-fuel mixture.

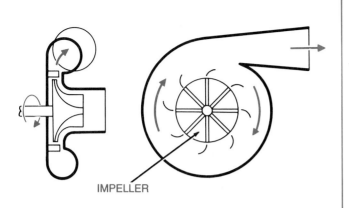

Fig. 21-50 Centrifugal supercharger.

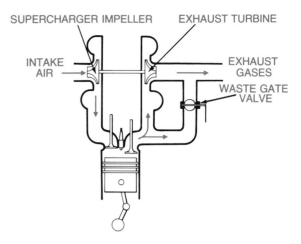

Fig. 21-51 Turbocharging system.
(Ford Motor Company)

Supercharger A pump used to force air into an engine.

Throttle valve A valve controlled by the throttle linkage that controls engine speed.

Turbocharger A supercharger driven by the exhaust gas of an engine.

Venturi A restricted area in the carburetor air horn used to develop low pressure to pull in fuel.

Vaporization Turning liquid gasoline into a gas or vapor.

Volatility The ease with which a fuel vaporizes.

CHAPTER REVIEW

1. What is detonation?
2. What is preignition?
3. Explain the octane rating of gasoline.
4. Define volatility.
5. Why is ice undesirable on a carburetor?
6. Explain the purpose of the fuel tank.
7. Explain how an electric fuel pump works.

8. What is the purpose of the fuel filter?
9. Define atomization and vaporization.
10. What is a venturi?
11. List the seven carburetor circuits.
12. Explain how the float circuit works.
13. Explain how the main metering circuit works.
14. Why is a choke circuit necessary?
15. What is the difference between fuel injection and carburetion?
16. What is the purpose of the air cleaner?
17. What are the basic parts of a turbocharger?
18. What is the purpose of a turbocharger.

DISCUSSION TOPICS AND ACTIVITIES

1. Identify and explain the operation of the main fuel system components on a shop engine.
2. Use a cutaway carburetor to trace and identify basic carburetor circuits.
3. Why do multiple carburetors make an engine more powerful? What effect does a turbocharger have on engine power? Why?

Fuel System Service

An engine that stops running or will not start even though it has ignition may have a problem with the fuel system. There may be no fuel or too much fuel.

Too much fuel in the engine means that fuel enters the cylinders as a liquid instead of a gas. Liquid gasoline will not burn. A spark plug that is wet with gasoline has difficulty producing a spark. Too little fuel makes the engine stop or fail to start. A mechanic must be able to find fuel system problems and make necessary repairs.

OBJECTIVES

After studying this chapter, you should be able to do the following:

1. List the troubleshooting steps to find out what is wrong with a fuel system.
2. Describe the maintenance on the fuel filter, air cleaner, manifold heat control valve, and choke.
3. Explain removal of a fuel pump or carburetor.
4. Describe the steps in disassembling, cleaning, and reassembling a carburetor.
5. Explain how a carburetor is adjusted.
Note: See Chapters 53 and 54 for fuel injection and computerized engine control system service.

22.1   GENERAL TROUBLESHOOTING

The first step in troubleshooting the fuel system is to check the whole system to find out whether the problem is too much or too little fuel and to eliminate any obvious problem. Too much gasoline is called flooding. Pumping the accelerator pedal too many times when trying to start it will flood the engine. When an engine is flooded, there is normally a strong odor of gasoline under the hood. Open the hood and smell. Allow a flooded engine a short time to dry out, or crank it with the accelerator pedal all the way to the floor. This allows a lot of air to get into the engine and dry it out.

An engine can also be flooded because of a problem in the carburetor. Here again, there will be a strong smell of gasoline under the hood. If the cause is a problem with the float system in the carburetor, the outside of the carburetor may be wet with gasoline. Remember, an overflowing carburetor is a serious fire hazard.

Too little fuel will cause the engine to stop or fail to start. The most frequent reason for this is driver failure to note that the fuel gauge reads empty.

The engine can get too little fuel if something is wrong with the fuel system. A few simple checks may identify the problem. If there is plenty of gasoline in the tank, no gasoline smell under the hood, and the ignition system is okay, the rest of the fuel system must be checked out. Remove the air cleaner element. Look down the carburetor and pump the accelerator pedal linkage. Each time the accelerator pedal is depressed, gasoline should squirt into the venturi from the accelerator pump jet. If no gasoline comes out, the carburetor may be dry.

Removing and inspecting the spark plugs is a good way to determine if the engine is getting the correct air fuel mixture. The spark plug firing end should be dry and colored a light tan or almost white. If you find the spark plug wet with gasoline or black soot, the fuel system is providing too rich a mixture. These spark plugs are illustrated on page 342.

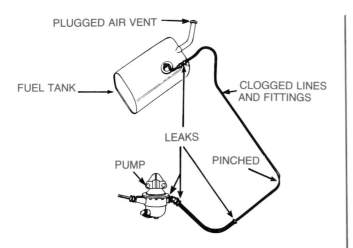

Fig. 22-1 Common problems in the suction side of the fuel system.

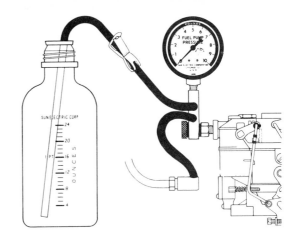

Fig. 22-2 Fuel pump tester between pump line and carburetor. (Sun)

These quick checks should allow the mechanic to identify the fuel system component that requires service. But they will only determine whether a component is operating, not how well it is operating. During a major tune-up, the fuel system is inspected and serviced to bring engine operation up to peak efficiency. These troubleshooting procedures, outlined in the following sections, are more complex and require specialized testing equipment.

22.2   Fuel Tank and Lines

During operation, the fuel pump lowers the pressure on its inlet or suction side. The fuel tank and lines are often described as the suction side of the fuel system. If the correct amount of fuel does not get to the pump from the tank, the carburetor will not have enough fuel for high-speed operation.

Common causes of failures in the suction side of the system are shown in Figure 22-1. The gasoline tank air vent must be open to allow atmospheric pressure to push on the fuel in the tank. If a plugged vent is suspected, operate the engine without the cap or with a different cap. Clogged, pinched, or leaking fuel lines can also stop the flow of fuel in the suction side. Clogged lines may be disconnected and blown clear with compressed air. Pinched lines should be replaced. Leaking lines or fittings should be tightened or replaced.

22.3   Fuel Filters

Clogged fuel filters on either side of the fuel pump result in a loss of engine power or a rough, pulsating feel, especially at high engine speeds. Most newer automobiles use an in-line throwaway paper

filter between the fuel pump and carburetor. Some use a bronze filter element mounted at the carburetor inlet. Check the bronze element by blowing on one end. The element should allow air to pass freely. Check the paper element by blowing on the fuel inlet end. If the filter does not allow air to pass freely, replace the element.

22.4   Fuel Pump

If there is poor high-speed performance, the fuel pump may be at fault. If pump pressure or volume are too low, lack of fuel to the carburetor will cause high speed miss. If pressure is too high, the carburetor will flood. The fuel pump should be checked in two ways: fuel pump volume check and fuel pump pressure check.

The pump volume and pressure may be checked with a fuel pump tester (Fig. 22-2). Remove the air cleaner and disconnect the main fuel line at the carburetor, or at the "T" or junction if there is more than one carburetor. Mount the tester to the carburetor inlet with the gauge vertical and facing the operator. Use adapters supplied with the tester. Connect the fuel line to the fitting on the fuel pump tester hose. Close the shutoff valve on the fuel discharge hose of the tester.

Start the engine and adjust the speed to approximately 500 rpm, unless specified otherwise. Insert the volume test hose into a graduated container and open the shutoff clamp. When fuel reaches the 4 ounce (120 mm) level in the container, put the end of the hose in the fuel and look for bubbles. **Safety Caution: Use care to prevent combustion from fuel spillage.** Note the time required to pump one pint of fuel. Then close the shutoff clamp. **Be sure to**

Fig. 22-3 Analyzer connected to vehicle exhaust. (Marquette)

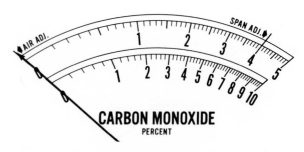

Fig. 22-4 Carbon monoxide gauge on infrared analyzer. (Marquette)

dispose of fuel in the graduated container to avoid fire hazard. With the engine still running at test speed, note the gauge pressure reading on the fuel pump tester. Compare volume and pressure test readings with the vehicle's specifications.

If pressure is too low or too high or if it changes a great deal at different speeds, the pump should be replaced. Remove the gauge and reconnect the fuel line to the carburetor. Inspect fuel lines for kinks and bends and check all connections for leaks.

22.5   Air Cleaner

A clogged air cleaner reduces the amount of air reaching the engine. The air cleaner handles the most air when the engine is running under load at full throttle high speed. At this time, air cleaner restrictions are most evident.

The air cleaner may be checked for clogs after removing the filter element. Direct a trouble light or flashlight through the element. If light passes through the element, it is probably in satisfactory condition. If there is any doubt, a new element should be installed.

22.6   Carburetor

How well the carburetor is working may be determined by analyzing the engine's exhaust. Most current exhaust analyzers use an infrared light beam to measure an exhaust sample (Fig. 22-3).

Exhaust gas is collected at the tailpipe and drawn into a water trap where the collected water is removed. The gas continues through a selector valve and a particle filter which removes solids. The gas then flows into the infrared sampling tubes in the tester. An infrared light beam is directed through the sample tubes and focused on a detector. The amount of energy that makes its way through the exhaust sample to the detector depends on the amount of carbon monoxide in the exhaust gas.

The amount of carbon monoxide (CO) in the exhaust depends on the air-fuel ratio. CO instruments read in percent—the higher the reading on the gauge (Fig. 22-4), the richer the mixture. Some automotive manufacturers specify carburetion settings in CO, and many states check it.

A second instrument found on the infrared analyzer measures unburned hydro carbons (HC) in the exhaust. This reading shows how much gasoline does not get burned in the cylinders. The readings on the gauge (Fig. 22-5) are in parts per million (ppm). High HC levels are caused by leaking exhaust valves, ignition misfires, or intake manifold leaks that make the mixture too lean to ignite.

After the tester is connected to the vehicle and calibrated, a series of tests determine whether carbon monoxide and hydrocarbon levels are within specifications. Tests are normally conducted at idle speed, cruising rpm, and during acceleration and deacceleration. The tester is often used with a chassis dynamometer so that actual road conditions can be duplicated.

High CO and HC readings at idle with rough idle and black smoke from the tailpipe indicate one of the following:

1. idle mix too rich;
2. leaking needles and seats;
3. leaky power valve;

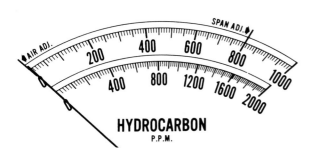

Fig. 22-5 Hydrocarbon gauge on infrared tester. (Marquette)

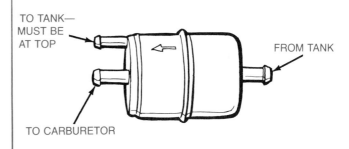

Fig. 22-6 In-line fuel filter is replaced at regular intervals. (American Motors Corporation)

4. wrong float setting;
5. faulty choke action.

Low CO readings and high HC readings during cruising operation with surging indicate a carburetion mixture that is too lean.

Normal CO readings and high HC readings at cruising speeds with black smoke indicate one of the following:

1. float not properly set;
2. cruise circuit too rich;
3. incorrect power circuit action.

Low CO readings and normal HC readings at high speed with engine detonation indicate a mixture that is too lean or a power circuit that is not operating.

The manufacturers of infrared testers normally provide a test procedure for the mechanic to follow and a diagnostic chart to help in understanding the results. This analyzer is useful for testing much more than the carburetion system. Anything that affects combustion, such as ignition and compression, will be shown in the tests. A very important use of this equipment, as we will see in a later chapter, is to find out whether exhaust emission control equipment is working properly.

22.7 PREVENTIVE MAINTENANCE

Preventive maintenance operations on the fuel system are periodic service or replacement of fuel filters, cleaning or replacement of air cleaner elements, inspection of manifold heat control valves, and inspection and adjustment of the automatic choke.

22.8 Fuel Filters

In-line fuel filters (Fig. 22-6) eventually become plugged with solids from the gasoline. Most manufacturers specify regular change intervals. Remove the two clamps, and separate the fuel lines from the filter. **Safety Caution: Use a metal container to catch any fuel spillage and prevent a fire.** Place a container under the filter to catch the fuel. Install the new filter. An arrow for fuel flow direction or the words *inlet* and *outlet* show the correct direction. Some filters have a third outlet for fuel return to the fuel tank (Fig. 22-6). Replace the clamps. Run the engine for several minutes and check for leaks.

22.9 Air Cleaners

Air cleaner elements are serviced at regular intervals to make sure that air entering the engine is cleaned properly. Automobiles operating in very dusty areas must be serviced more often.

After removing the air cleaner cover (Fig. 22-7), the paper filter may be removed. A dusty air cleaner can be cleaned by blowing compressed air through the element from the inside out (Fig. 22-8). **Safety Caution: Wear eye protection when using compressed air.** Use low pressure and hold the air nozzle at least three inches from the element to avoid rupturing the element. An extremely dirty or oil-soaked element should be replaced.

The polyurethane element should be inspected, cleaned, and oiled regularly, depending upon how dirty the air is. To service the element, remove cover wing nut, cover, and filter element. Visually check the element for tears or rips and replace if necessary.

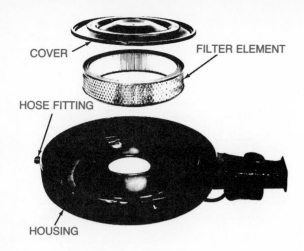

COVER

FILTER ELEMENT

HOSE FITTING

HOUSING

Fig. 22-7 Filter element is removed by lifting off the cover.
(Dodge/Chrysler Corporation)

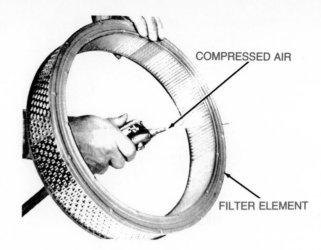

COMPRESSED AIR

FILTER ELEMENT

Fig. 22-8 Cleaning the paper filter element.
(Dodge/Chrysler Corporation)

Clean all dirt and grime from the air cleaner bottom and cover.

Remove the support screen and wash the element in kerosene or mineral spirits. Squeeze out excess solvent (Fig. 22-9). Do not use a hot degreaser, acetone, or any solvent containing acetone. Dip the element into light engine oil and squeeze out the excess oil. Do not shake, swing, or wring the element. The polyurethane material may tear.

Install the element on the screen support. Using a new gasket, replace the air cleaner body over the carburetor air horn. Place the element in the air cleaner. Take care that the lower lip of the element is properly placed in the assembly. If the filter material is folded or creased in any manner, it may cause a bad seal. Make sure in replacing the cover that the upper lip of the element is in the proper position. On units that have one, remove and clean the flame arrestor with kerosene or other suitable solvent. Replace the cover and wing nut.

22.10 Manifold Heat Control Valve

A manifold heat control valve (Fig. 22-10) stuck in the closed position will make the carburetor overheat. Poor fuel mileage and vapor lock may result. A valve stuck in the open position will not allow proper carburetor operation during warmup.

The valve must be checked from time to time to make sure it is operating properly. Check for freedom of operation by rotating the counterweight and valve shaft back and forth. To free up the valve, tap the control valve shaft back and forth with a small hammer and rotate the counterweight back and forth until the valve is free. To prevent it from sticking again, apply heat control solvent to both shaft ends.

22.11 Automatic Choke

Normally, the automatic choke should not require service between major carburetor overhauls. However, it may need readjustment for cold or hot weather operation. There may also be gum buildup on the choke valve that prevents proper valve movement.

To test the choke closing, remove the air cleaner, open the throttle to release the fast idle cam and use light finger pressure to close the choke valve. If it does not close easily and fully, choke operation is the cause of the trouble.

Some automobiles develop gum, varnish, and choke-sticking problems more quickly than others. This depends on the type of fuel used, the type of driving, and conditions of weather and temperature. Flushing the piston, cylinder, and choke shaft bearing areas with carburetor cleaner at least every six months will slow down the buildup of these deposits. This should be done as part of any winter service.

The automatic choke on carburetors with a thermostatic spring mounted to the carburetor body is adjusted by rotating the choke thermostatic spring cover. Adjust the choke when the engine is cold. Remove the air cleaner. Prod the throttle open. Loosen the screws that retain the choke thermostatic spring cover. Rotate the cover to close the choke valve. A very light finger pressure should open the valve against the thermostatic spring. Reference and index marks on the cover and carburetor (Fig. 22-11) allow the cover to be positioned according to specifications. An arrow on the cover often indicates which way to rotate for lean or rich choke operation. When the cover is in the desired position, tighten the screws.

Fig. 22-9 Cleaning a polyurethane element.
(Chevrolet Motor Division, GMC)

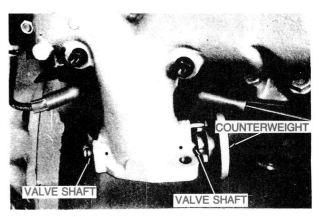

Fig. 22-10 Manifold heat control valve.
(Plymouth/Chrysler Corporation)

When the thermostatic coil is mounted on the engine's manifold, the choke is adjusted by bending the rod that links the coil to the choke valve. Remove the air cleaner. Disconnect the thermostatic coil rod from the upper choke lever and hold the choke valve completely closed. Push downward on the rod to the end of travel. With the rod in this position, the top of the rod should be even with the hole in the choke lever. If it is not, bend the rod to make it longer or shorter (Fig. 22-12). After the adjustment, warm up the engine and check that the choke valve opens fully.

22.12 FUEL SYSTEM SERVICE

Major fuel system service is necessary when troubleshooting indicates a problem in one of the fuel system components.

22.13 Removing and Replacing Fuel Pump

A fuel pump that fails to meet volume or pressure specifications must be replaced. Disconnect the outlet fuel line (tubing) between the fuel pump and the carburetor. Disconnect the inlet line between the pump and the fuel tank. **Safety Caution: When disconnecting a fuel line, catch any leaking fuel in a metal container and dispose of the fuel properly to prevent a fire.** If the pump has a vapor recovery line, disconnect it. Remove the bolts and lock washers and the pump.

When installing a new pump, you must be able to hold the pump in a position flat against the mounting surface. If there is resistance, remove the pump and crank the engine to a new position and try again. Forcing a pump into position may cause

major engine damage when the engine is started. Start the engine and check for leaks.

22.14 Removing the Carburetor

Major carburetor service must be done with the carburetor off the engine. Remove the air cleaner and gasket. Disconnect the fuel and vacuum lines from the carburetor. **Safety Caution: When disconnecting a fuel line, catch any leaking fuel in a metal container and dispose of the fuel properly to prevent a fire.** Disconnect the choke coil rod. Disconnect accelerator linkage. If the automobile has an automatic transmission, disconnect the throttle valve linkage. Remove all vacuum hoses and electrical connections. Remove nuts and/or bolts, gasket or insulator, and remove carburetor.

22.15 Carburetor Disassembly and Cleaning

Locate and follow the correct shop manual when disassembling a carburetor. An exploded view of the carburetor found in the shop service manual is a helpful aid in disassembly and reassembly. The carburetor is disassembled according to set procedure.

When disassembled, clean the major components in a cold tank filled with carburetor cleaner. **Safety Caution: Wear eye protection and rubber gloves when using the cold tank.** Rubber parts, plastic parts, diaphragms, and pump plungers should not be put in carburetor cleaner.

Blow out all passages in castings with compressed air. **Safety Caution: Always wear eye pro-**

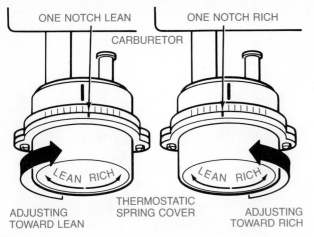

Fig. 22-11 Adjusting the choke by turning the thermostatic spring cover.

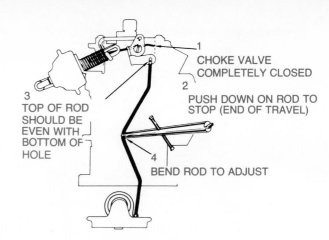

Fig. 22-12 Adjusting an automatic choke with an externally mounted thermostatic coil.
(Chevrolet Motor Division, GMC)

tection when using compressed air. Do not pass drills through jets or passages. Inspect idle mixture screws for damage. Examine the float needle and seat assembly for wear. Install a new factory-matched set if worn. Inspect upper and lower casting sealing surfaces for damage or warping. Inspect holes in levers for excessive wear or out-of-round condition. If levers or rods are worn, they should be replaced. Examine the fast idle cam for excessive wear or damage. Check the throttle and choke levers and valves for binds and other damage. Replace the filter element. Check all springs for distortion or loss in tension and replace as necessary.

22.16 Carburetor Assembly and Adjustment

The right service manual will provide step-by-step reassembly procedure for the carburetor. During reassembly, several adjustments must be made.

The carburetor float level provides the correct amount of fuel for all the operating circuits.

If an adjustment is necessary, bend the float tab (which touches the head of the fuel inlet needle) with needle-nosed pliers. Do not let the float tab contact the float needle head during this operation. This may compress the synthetic rubber tip of the needle used on some units, giving a false setting.

Other on-the-bench adjustments specified by the service manual are made as the carburetor is reassembled.

22.17 Reinstalling the Carburetor

The installation of the carburetor is the reverse of the disassembly procedure. Be sure throttle body and intake manifold sealing surfaces are clean. Connect all the hoses, fuel lines, and wires or linkage and run the engine to check for leaks.

22.18 Idle Mixture Adjustment

The idle mixture screws adjust the richness or leanness of the idle mixture. There is one mixture screw for each primary barrel. Adjustment is usually necessary only after carburetor overhaul. First, the screws are set to a specific number of turns out from the seated position. Next, set the speed screw to the correct idle rpm, using a tachometer, with the transmission in the specified gear. Then adjust the mixture screws to lean best idle, which is the leanest possible without reducing speed. Next, adjust the lean drop, so the engine speed drops by the specified amount. Finally, adjust the speed screw, if necessary. Instead of lean drop, some engines are adjusted a specified number of turns out from lean best idle, or from a specified lean drop. In all these adjustments, the mixture screws must be kept balanced at an equal number of turns out from the seated position. After the adjustment, limiter caps, if used, should be installed on the heads of the mixture screws against the rich stops.

Propane enrichment is used to check whether the lean drop was done correctly, without removing the limiter caps or exposing hidden mixture screws. Feeding propane gas into the air cleaner will speed up the engine by the same amount that it was slowed down by the lean drop adjustment (Fig. 22-13). This saves a lot of time on late model cars, because you have to remove the carburetor to expose the mixture screws.

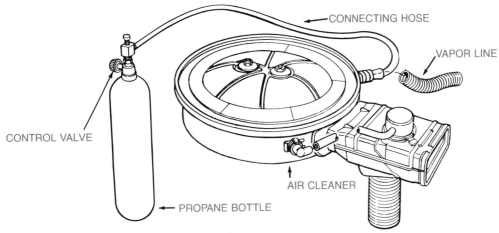

Fig. 22-13 Propane enrichment method of idle mixture adjustment. (Ford Motor Company)

22.19   Idle Speed Adjustment

Engines with an anti-dieseling solenoid have two idle speed adjustments. Make the curb idle adjustment with the solenoid. Make the "solenoid off" adjustment with the throttle screw. A solenoid might be hooked up by the factory so that it only comes on when the air conditioning is turned on. If so, adjust the curb idle with the throttle screw. The air conditioning solenoid speed must be adjusted with the air conditioning on.

22.20   Adjustment Precautions

Adjustments must be made according to factory specifications in the shop manual. Making adjustments outside manufacturer's specifications or procedures is considered tampering. It is against federal law in some situations, and may be against state law as well.

NEW TERMS

Carbon monoxide (CO) A byproduct of combustion measured to check fuel system operation.
Float gauge A tool used to measure carburetor float setting.
Flooding A condition in which liquid gasoline entering the cylinders prevents the engine from running.
Fuel pump pressure The amount of fuel pressure measured at the outlet of the fuel pump.
Fuel pump volume The amount or volume of fuel that a fuel pump can provide.
Idle mixture The amount of air and fuel that goes into the engine during idle, adjusted with an idle mixture screw or screws.

CHAPTER REVIEW

1. What is flooding?
2. Explain how to check whether the carburetor is getting fuel.
3. List the common causes of problems on the suction side of the fuel system.
4. What happens if a fuel filter is restricted?
5. List the two tests to find out whether a fuel pump is working correctly.
6. Explain how to use a fuel pump tester.
7. Describe how to check for a restricted air cleaner.
8. What is the relationship between carbon monoxide and air-fuel ratio?
9. What do hydrocarbon readings tell about engine operation?
10. How can a stuck manifold heat control valve be repaired?
11. Describe how to find out whether the automatic choke is working.
12. How is an automatic choke adjusted?
13. What carburetor parts should not be cleaned in a cold tank?
14. Explain what adjustments are made when the carburetor is reinstalled on the vehicle.

DISCUSSION TOPICS AND ACTIVITIES

1. List the steps for troubleshooting a fuel system.
2. Visit a shop where an infrared analyzer is used. Watch a vehicle being tested and report on what you see.
3. Disassemble a shop carburetor. Identify all the parts and then reassemble and adjust it.

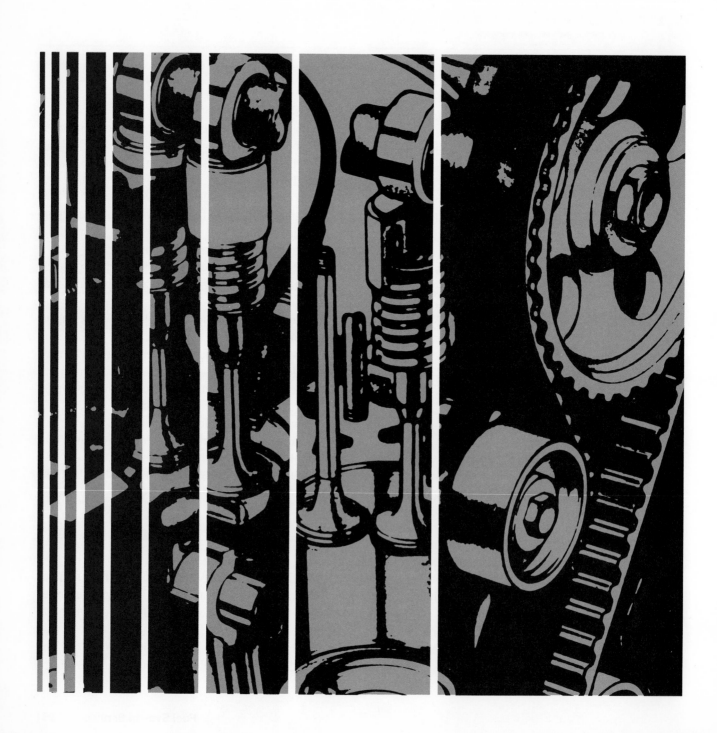

Automobile Electrical Systems

PART 4

Electrical Systems and Fundamentals

CHAPTER PREVIEW

The electrical system has two main functions. First, it must supply the electrical energy to start and operate the engine. Secondly, it must provide the power to operate the lights, instruments, and other electrical accessories.

The electrical system (Fig. 23-1) is much easier to understand and service if it is divided into smaller systems: the charging system, the starting system, the ignition system, and the lighting and accessory system. This chapter introduces each of these systems. In later chapters we will study each system in detail. This chapter will also cover the fundamentals of electricity necessary to understand electrical equipment.

OBJECTIVES

After studying this chapter, you should be able to do the following:

1. Explain the purpose of the automobile electrical system.
2. List and describe the purpose of the main circuits or systems of the electrical system.
3. Understand the fundamentals of electricity.
4. Describe the fundamentals of magnetism.
5. Describe the electronic components used on an automobile.

23.1 CHARGING SYSTEM

Electrical energy must always be available to operate the engine and power all the automobile's electrical accessories. To provide this electrical energy, there must be a source of stored energy ready for instant use and a way of generating electrical power to replace that used from the stored source. The parts that work together to provide this electrical energy are called the charging system (Fig. 23-2).

There are three basic components in the charging system: the battery, the alternator, and the regulator. The battery is a source of stored electrical energy. It provides power to all the electrical systems and accessories when the engine is not running. It also provides reserve power anytime the alternator is not able to supply all the electrical power needed.

Electrical energy drawn from the battery must be replaced or battery power will be used up. This is one of the important jobs of the alternator. The alternator, driven by a V belt off the automobile engine, changes some of the mechanical energy of the engine into electrical energy. The electrical energy is used to charge the battery and power all the electrical systems and accessories. A regulator used with the alternator protects the battery and the other electrical equipment from receiving too much electrical power.

23.2 STARTING SYSTEM

The starting system, as shown in Figure 23-3, cranks the engine fast enough to start it. The starting system has five main components. The battery is a source of power to operate a starter motor. The starter motor converts electrical energy from the battery into mechanical energy. A starter motor drive mechanism drives a small pinion gear that meshes with the engine flywheel for starting and unmeshes when

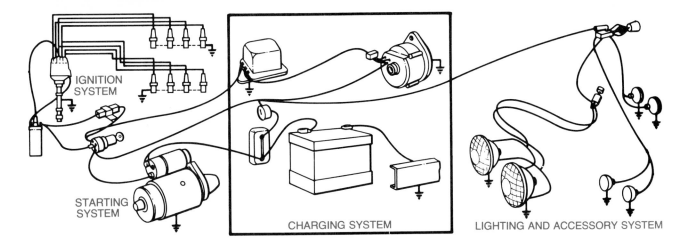

Fig. 23-1 Automotive electrical system.

the engine runs. A remote control switch called a solenoid shifts the pinion into mesh with the flywheel and closes a switch between the battery and starter motor. The driver controls the starting system with a key switch located on the steering column.

23.3 IGNITION SYSTEM

The ignition system (Fig. 23-4) provides a series of precisely timed, high-voltage sparks to ignite the compressed air-fuel mixture in the combustion chamber. The main components of the ignition system are a source of electrical power, an ignition key switch, an ignition coil, a distributor, and as many spark plugs as there are cylinders.

The power source for the ignition system is the battery or alternator. A key switch on the steering column allows the driver to control the system. The ignition coil steps up the 12 volts available from the battery or alternator to the high voltage necessary to ignite the air-fuel mixture.

The distributor has three major jobs in the ignition system. Its switching device helps the coil develop high voltage. Then the distributor distributes the high voltage to each of the cylinders. Finally, the distributor gets the high voltage to the cylinders at the correct time.

High voltage from the coil is distributed through spark plug wires to each of the engine's spark plugs. The spark plug has a space or gap for the high-voltage ignition current to jump across. When current jumps across the spark plug gap, it creates a spark that ignites the air-fuel mixture.

23.4 LIGHTING AND ACCESSORY SYSTEM

The lighting and accessory system (Fig. 23-5) is made up of many small circuits that operate the lights and accessories on a modern automobile: headlights, stop lights, turn signal indicators, instrument panel lamps, gauges, and horns. The system also includes hundreds of feet of wiring that connect these devices to a power source and many control switches that operate them.

23.5 FUNDAMENTALS OF ELECTRICITY AND MAGNETISM

In order to service automotive electrical equipment, a mechanic must understand the fundamentals of electricity and magnetism.

The electron theory is the way science today explains how electricity behaves and how to use it. In order to understand the electron theory, it is necessary to look briefly at what scientists call the composition of matter.

23.6 Matter

Everything in the universe that has weight and takes up space is matter. Even things that cannot be seen, like air, are matter. Matter may exist in three forms: solid, liquid, or gas.

23.7 Atoms

All matter is composed of particles called atoms. An atom is so small that it is not visible even under

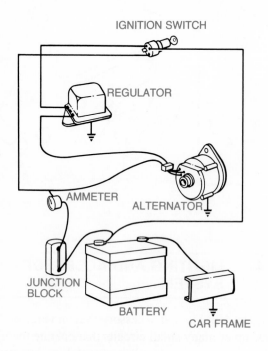

Fig. 23-2 Charging system.

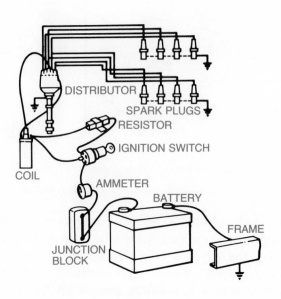

Fig. 23-4 Ignition system.

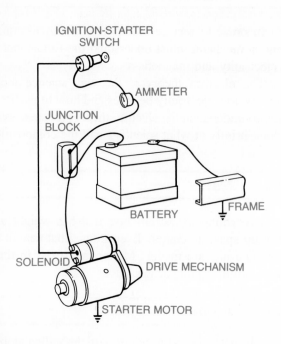

Fig. 23-3 Starting system.

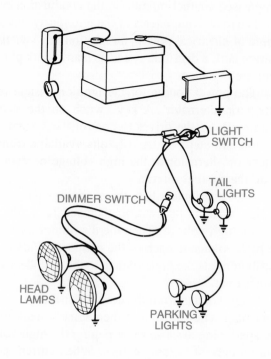

Fig. 23-5 Lighting and accessory system.

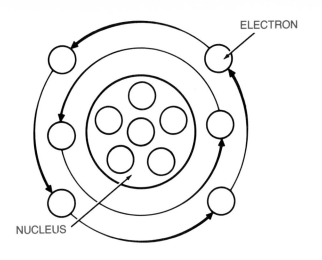

Fig. 23-6 An atom.

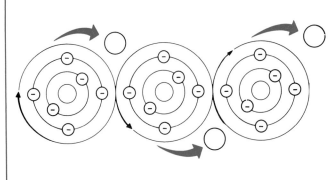

Fig. 23-7 Electricity is the movement of electrons from one atom to another.

the most powerful microscope. Atoms are made up of even smaller particles.

An atom (Fig. 23-6) is constructed somewhat like our solar system with its sun and the various planets which revolve around it. An atom has a center called a nucleus. This nucleus is the equivalent of the sun in our solar system. Other small particles called electrons circle in orbits around the nucleus as the planets circle around the sun. Electrons travel at a tremendous speed.

23.8   Positive and Negative Particles

The particles which make up the atom have positive and negative electrical charges. This means simply that the two charges are unlike each other. They are completely opposite. The symbol + is used to indicate a particle with a positive charge, and — to indicate one with a negative charge. Anyone who has experimented with a set of magnets has observed that there are two ends of the magnets that repel each other and two ends that attract each other. Electrical charges act in much the same way: two positively charged particles repel each other; two negatively charged particles repel each other. A positively charged particle and a negatively charged particle attract each other. This positive-negative attraction is what holds the atoms together.

The nucleus of an atom is made up of positively charged particles. The electrons that orbit in a fixed pattern around the nucleus are negatively charged particles. The difference between atoms of the different kinds of matter are the number of particles in the nucleus and the number and spacing of the electrons that orbit around the nucleus.

The nucleus of the atom is composed of protons with a positive charge and neutrons with a neutral charge. Electrons with a negative charge orbit the nucleus at a fixed distance. An atom may have one, two, or three rings of electrons, depending upon their number. Each of these rings has a fixed number of electrons.

23.9   Bound and Free Electrons

Electrons remain in their orbit because of the electrical attraction of the nucleus. This may be compared to the gravitational pull of the sun on the earth. The electrons that orbit closest to the nucleus are strongly attracted to it. These are called *bound* electrons. The electrons that are farther away from the pull of the nucleus can be forced out of their orbits. These are called *free* electrons. Free electrons can move from one atom to another in what is known as electron flow (Fig. 23-7).

23.10   Electricity

According to the electron theory, electricity is the movement or flow of electrons from one atom to another. A movement of electrons requires a condition of imbalance. In a normal atom, the positively charged nucleus balances the negatively charged electrons, holding them in orbit. If an atom loses electrons, it becomes positive in charge. It then attracts electrons in order to regain its balance.

The flow of electricity is made possible by causing electrons to leave their atoms and gather in a certain area, leaving behind atoms without their normal number of electrons. There are a number of

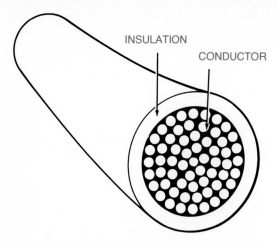

Fig. 23-8 Insulation around a conductor makes sure current doesn't "leak" out.

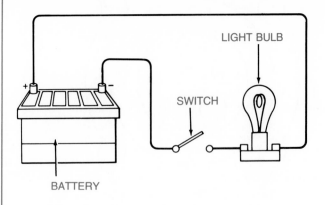

Fig. 23-9 Elements of circuit.

ways to create an imbalance to start an electron flow. The storage battery and the alternator are two devices studied in later chapters that can cause electron flow.

23.11 Direction of Electron Flow

An important rule of the electron theory is that negatively charged electrons always move toward atoms that have a positive charge. This means that the flow of electrons is from negative to positive (− to +). Before the electron theory it was thought that electricity flowed from positive to negative (+ to −). Many books and service manuals still explain the operation of electrical components as an electricity flow from positive to negative. This description of electrical flow is called the conventional current flow. Regardless of whether a system is described according to the electron theory or conventional current flow, the things that can be measured and observed are the same.

23.12 LANGUAGE OF ELECTRICITY

A mechanic must understand the meaning and relationship of a number of electrical terms in order to service electrical components. The terms described below are the foundation for all electrical troubleshooting and servicing.

23.13 Voltage (Volt)

In order to have a flow of water in a fire hose, pressure is necessary. In order to have an electron flow in an electrical system, pressure is also necessary. In electricity the force or potential that pushes electrons is called voltage. Electrical pressure is measured in volts, abbreviated E or V.

Voltage may be considered a source of potential energy that exists when there are unequal amounts of electrons in the parts of a system. The voltage of your house wiring may be 110 volts. This voltage is present even though no household appliances are turned on. The voltage "stands by" until an appliance is turned on. An automotive storage battery provides a potential of 12 volts. This potential exists even when all the electrical devices on the automobile are turned off. Voltage can exist without electron flow but electron flow cannot exist without voltage.

23.14 Current (Ampere)

Water flow in a fire hose may be measured in gallons per minute. Electron flow in an electrical system, called current, is measured in amperes, abbreviated I (A is used in the metric system). The flow of current is measured by the number of electrons passing a given point per second. One ampere is equal to 6.28 billion electrons per second.

23.15 Resistance (Ohm)

The diameter of a fire hose determines the amount of water that can flow through it in a given amount of time. A smaller hose provides more resistance to the flow of water. There is also resistance to electron flow in an electrical system. Resistance is the opposition offered by a material to the free flow of electrons. The unit of resistance is called an ohm, abbreviated R.

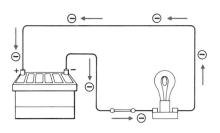

Fig. 23-10 Current can flow in a closed circuit.

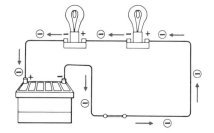

Fig. 23-11 Series circuit.

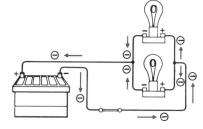

Fig. 23-12 Parallel circuit.

When current runs into resistance, electrons must work harder to get through. The rate of their flow is reduced because some of the energy is used up as heat. The heat built up by resistance is sometimes used to do work. For example, in an ordinary household toaster, current is directed through a strong resistance, producing heat to toast the bread.

23.16 Conductors

A conductor is any material that allows a good electron flow. In the automotive electrical system, copper wires are used to conduct electricity because they allow good electron flow. To be a good conductor, a material must be made of atoms that give off free electrons easily. Also, the atoms must be close enough to each other so that their free electron orbits overlap. Of all the metals, silver is the best conductor, but it is too expensive for use in automotive wiring.

23.17 Insulators

Insulators are materials whose atoms will not part with their free electrons. These materials will not conduct current. The copper wire in an automotive electrical system is covered with an insulator so that the current does not "leak" out (Fig. 23-8). Plastic and rubber are good insulators.

23.18 Circuit

A circuit is a path or network of paths that allows current flow to do some work. Any circuit, no matter how complicated, is made up of the same essential parts (Fig. 23-9). There must be a source of electrical pressure or voltage—in this illustration a 12-volt automotive battery. There is always resistance to current flow, in this case the light bulb. There must be a switch to turn the current flow in the circuit on or off. Wires or conductors connect the battery, switch, and light bulb. A circuit, then, has a voltage source (battery), a resistance unit (light bulb), and a switch, connected by conductors (wires).

In order for current to flow in a circuit the path must be unbroken. In fact, the term *circuit* means circle. In the circuit shown in Figure 23-9, current cannot flow because the open switch does not allow the current a complete path back to the battery. This is called an open circuit. Any time there is a break in the circuit, either by design or by accident, current cannot flow.

If we close the switch, we provide a complete path for current to flow. The electrical energy created by the battery causes electrons to flow through the conductors through the light bulb and back to the battery. The bulb lights up (Fig. 23-10). This is a complete or closed circuit.

23.19 Types of Circuits

Three types of circuits are used in automotive electricity: series circuits, parallel circuits, and series-parallel circuits. In a series circuit (Fig. 23-11), the current flows in one path. Current flows from the battery through the switch and then through the two light bulbs. The current then returns to the battery.

When the current goes through the first light bulb, part of it is used up. This leaves only a part of the current to pass through the second light bulb. When the resistance of the two light bulbs is added together, current flow is reduced so that neither bulb burns very bright. If one of the bulbs burns out or is

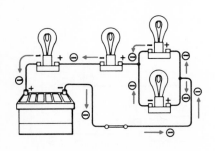

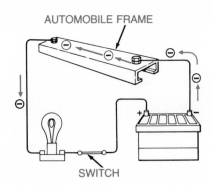

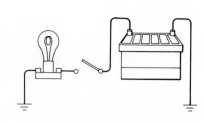

Fig. 23-13 Series parallel circuit.

Fig. 23-14 Single wire circuit.

Fig. 23-15 Ground symbols used in single wire system schematic.

removed from its socket, the circuit is broken and no current flows. In all series circuits, the current must pass through all the electrical devices, one after the other. If any device fails to work, it will act as a switch and open the whole circuit.

A parallel circuit provides two or more paths for current flow (Fig. 23-12). Both of the light bulbs in the illustration receive the same amount of current, so they both burn bright. If one bulb burns out or is removed from its socket the current still goes through the other bulb. It burns normally.

Most automotive electrical circuits use a series-parallel circuit. This is a combination of a series and a parallel circuit, as shown in Figure 23-13. Notice that one pair of light bulbs in the illustration is connected in series and the other pair in parallel. The parallel part of the circuit acts like the parallel circuit described above. The series part of the circuit works like the series circuit, as shown in Figure 23-11.

23.20 Single-wire Systems

Up to this point we have studied circuits that use one wire to carry current to an electrical device and another wire to return the current to the battery. Since the automobile frame and body is made from metal, it can be used as a conductor. This allows circuits to be made from a single wire.

In a single-wire system (Fig. 23-14), when the switch is closed, current flows from the battery through the automobile frame to the insulated wire, then through the light and switch back to the battery. This means that when a driver turns on the headlights or other electrical devices, current flows from the

battery through the engine block and body to the electrical device. It returns through the insulated wiring.

Wiring diagrams, schematics, or maps of electrical circuits do not show the automobile frame or body. Instead they use a symbol called the ground symbol (Fig. 23-15) to show that the units are connected or grounded to the automobile. Since wiring diagrams picture only the insulated wires, it is easier to understand and follow the diagrams if the mechanic visualizes the current flowing through the insulated wires first and then back to the battery through the grounded part of the circuit. This is the way current flow will be explained in this book.

23.21 MAGNETISM

Magnetism is a force involved in the operation of many types of electrical equipment. The ignition coil, starter motor, alternator, and voltage regulator are just a few examples of electrical equipment that use the principles of magnetism.

23.22 What Is a Magnet?

Magnetism was first observed when loadstone, an iron ore, was found to attract other pieces of iron. Lodestone is a natural magnet. A piece of lodestone suspended by a string lines up in a north and south direction. Ancient man used a lodestone compass to find the way over deserts and oceans.

Although magnetism has been used for centuries, exactly what it is and how it works is still not completely understood. One theory says that each electron has a circle of magnetic force around it. In an

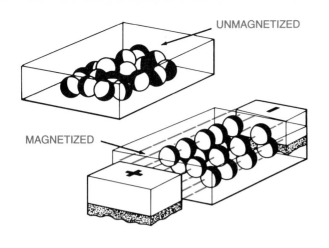

Fig. 23-16   Magnetism is the alignment of electron orbits.

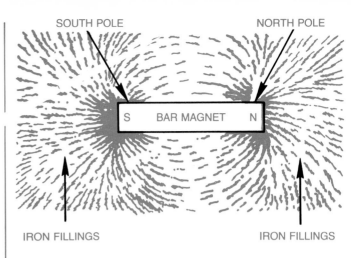

Fig. 23-17   Iron filings used to show a magnetic field.

unmagnetized piece of iron the electron orbits are not arranged in any pattern. In a magnetized piece of iron the electron orbits are lined up so that their circles of magnetic force add together (Fig. 23-16). This causes the metal to be magnetized.

Some metals may easily be magnetized. A piece of iron rubbed with another piece of iron that is already magnetized will become magnetized. A piece of iron placed near a strong magnet will also become magnetized. The orbits of the electrons in the iron are affected by the strong magnet and line up. Some metals hold their magnetism for a long time. Others are called temporary magnets because they quickly become unmagnetized. Many metals and materials are nonmagnetic. Copper, aluminum, wood, glass, plastic, and rubber never show any of the properties of magnetism.

23.23   Magnetic Fields

Almost everyone has used an ordinary bar magnet to pick up small metal objects. The force which allows the magnet to pick up objects is described as a field. The field surrounding a magnet is invisible, but it may be observed by a simple experiment. If a piece of paper is placed on top of a bar magnet and iron filings are sprinkled on the paper, the filings will align themselves in a line pattern around the bar magnet (Fig. 23-17).

The pattern of the iron filings will show that the magnetic force is strongest at or near the ends of the magnet. These areas are called magnetic poles. Since one end of the magnet points north, it is called the north pole. The other end is called the south pole. If the bar magnet was broken into two, each piece would

have its own north and south pole. This would be true no matter how many times the bar magnet was broken.

The experiment with the iron filings leads to some other important rules about magnetic fields. The filings show that the magnetic lines are closed loops that do not cross each other. The experiment also shows that the magnetic field will pass through paper. In fact, they will pass through any material. There is no known insulator for magnetic lines of force. Some materials, however, will allow the lines of force to pass through more easily than others. Material that will not pass lines of magnetic force easily has what is called a high reluctance. A material that will allow the easy passage of the lines of force has a low reluctance. Iron has a low reluctance. Air has a high reluctance.

If two bar magnets are placed close to each other, there is a force of attraction between the two unlike poles. On the other hand, there is a force of repulsion between two like poles. Unlike poles attract each other and like poles repel each other, as shown in Figure 23-18.

23.24   Electromagnetism

In the early 1800s, a connection was discovered between electricity and magnetism which is known as electromagnetism. A conductor that has current passing through it develops a magnetic field. This may be shown by a simple experiment (Fig. 23-19). A battery is connected to a conductor so that current may flow. The conductor is directed through a piece of cardboard on which some iron filings are sprinkled. The iron filings arrange themselves in a pattern

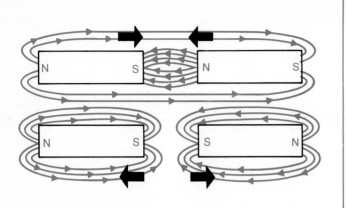

Fig. 23-18 Unlike poles attract and like poles repel.

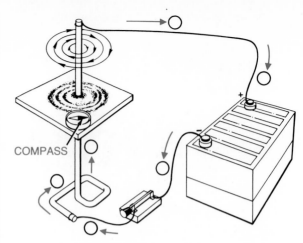

COMPASS

Fig. 23-19 A magnetic field surrounds a current carrying conductor.

around the wire just as they do when affected by a magnet.

If a small compass is placed on the cardboard, the needle will always point in a direction parallel to the magnetic lines. If the battery is connected to the conductor so that current flows in the opposite direction, the compass needle will point in the opposite direction (Fig. 23-20). This experiment demonstrates an important rule of magnetism: in a magnetic field created around a current-carrying conductor, the direction of the magnetic lines depends upon the direction of the current through the conductor.

Look at Figure 23-21. If two conductors carrying current in the same direction are placed next to each other, their magnetic fields combine. On the other hand, if the two conductors carry current in opposite directions, the two fields do not combine. They oppose each other, and the conductors tend to move apart. Similarly, if a current-carrying conductor is placed in a field created by a magnet, the two magnetic fields oppose each other. A strong magnetic field is created on one side of the conductor and a weak field on the other side. The conductor will be pushed in the direction of the weak field. The more current flowing in the conductor, the stronger the push. The stronger the magnetic field of the magnets, the stronger the push. This push or force on the conductor may be used to perform work. This principle is used in electric motors such as the starter motor on an automobile.

When electric current is passed through a conductor that is formed into a loop, a weak magnet with a north and south pole is created. If several loops are formed in the conductor so that it becomes a coil (Fig. 23-22), a stronger magnetic field is created. The

strength of the field around the coil may be increased in several ways: by increasing the number of coils or turns, by increasing the amount of current in the coils, or by increasing both the number of turns and the amount of current.

Another way of increasing the magnetic field surrounding a coil is to place a soft iron bar called a core inside the coil, as shown in Figure 23-23. Since the soft iron has less reluctance than air, the strength of the magnetic field is greatly increased. The magnet formed by a coil of wire around an iron core is called an electromagnet. Electromagnets are used in many types of automotive electrical equipment, such as ignition coils, solenoids, and voltage regulators.

23.25 Induction

The principles of induction depend upon the relationship between magnetic fields and conductors. Induction is the transfer of energy from one object to another without the objects physically touching. One important principle of induction is that voltage is created in a conductor moving across a magnetic field (Fig. 23-24).

This principle may be illustrated by connecting a voltage measuring device, called a voltmeter, to the ends of a conductor. If the conductor is moved between the poles of a permanent magnet fast enough to cut the magnetic field, a voltage is created that causes a current flow in the conductor. When the direction of motion of the conductor is changed, the direction of current flow through the conductor is also changed. This type of induction, called generated voltage, is used in automotive alternators.

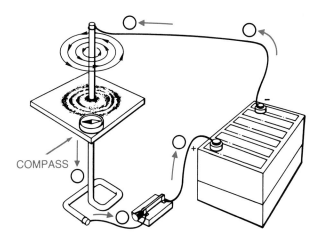

Fig. 23-20 Reversing current reverses the magnetic field.

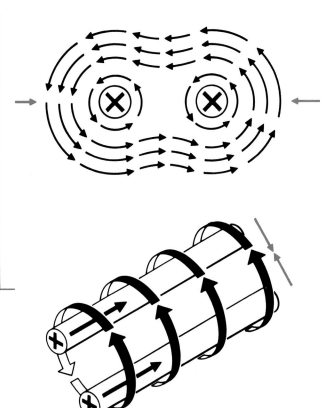

MAGNETIC FIELDS COMBINE WHEN CURRENT FLOWS IN THE SAME DIRECTION

Another important use of induction is in coils. A magnetic field surrounds a current-carrying coil. If such a coil is placed near another coil without current, as shown in Figure 23-25 (a), the bulb connected to the second coil will not light. If the switch is opened [Fig. 23-25 (b)], the field around the first coil will collapse and jump over to the second coil. This collapsing magnetic field will cause current to flow briefly in the second coil. The light connected to the second coil will light for a fraction of a second. This kind of induction is used in automotive ignition coils.

23.26   ELECTRONICS AND SEMICONDUCTORS

Electronics is a branch of electricity concerned with the flow of electrons through semiconductor material. The field of electronics has undergone great change in the past thirty years. Large, delicate vacuum tubes have been replaced by tiny devices constructed from silicon chips. In the last twenty years, electronic technology has developed to the point that low cost and high reliability has made it suitable for many applications in the automobile electrical system. In this section we will describe the electronic devices used in automotive applications.

Semiconductors are tiny solid state devices made from crystals of germanium, silicon, boron, and phosphorus. These crystals in their pure form are not good conductors of electricity. When the crystals are changed by adding an impurity, they become semiconductors. Under certain conditions, semiconductors act like conductors, and under other

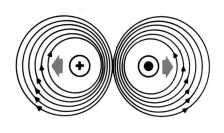

MAGNETIC FIELDS OPPOSE AND PUSH THE CONDUCTORS APART IF CURRENT FLOWS IN OPPOSITE DIRECTIONS

Fig. 23-21 Magnetic fields oppose and push the conductors apart if current flows in opposite directions.

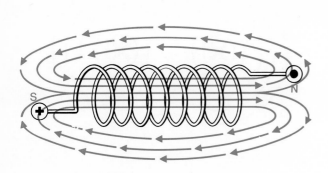

Fig. 23-22 Current in a coil forms a magnet.

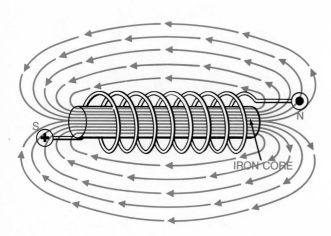

Fig. 23-23 An iron core increases the magnetic field of a coil.

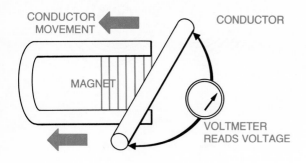

CONDUCTOR MOVEMENT

CONDUCTOR

MAGNET

VOLTMETER READS VOLTAGE

Fig. 23-24 Moving a conductor through a magnetic field creates voltage.

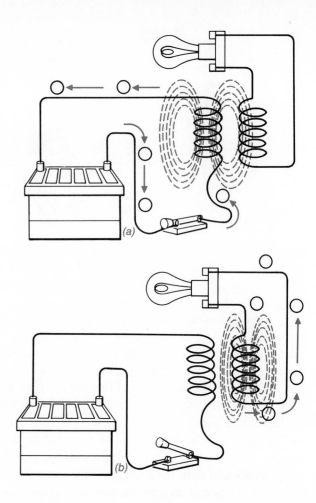

(a)

(b)

Fig. 23-25 A collapsing magnetic field can induce a current in a coil.

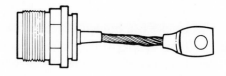

Fig. 23-26 Diode.

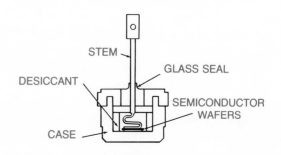

STEM

GLASS SEAL

DESICCANT

SEMICONDUCTOR WAFERS

CASE

Fig. 23-27 Cross section of a diode.

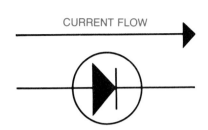

CURRENT FLOW

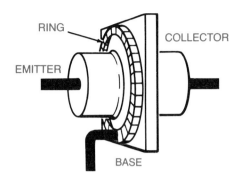

RING COLLECTOR

EMITTER

BASE

Fig. 23-28 Wiring diagram symbol for a diode.   **Fig. 23-29** Transistor.   **Fig. 23-30** Construction of a transistor.

conditions they act like insulators. Two types of semiconductors are commonly used in automotive electrical systems: the diode and the transistor.

23.27   Diode

A diode (Fig. 23-26) is a tiny semiconductor that allows current to flow freely in one direction but offers extremely high resistance to current flow in the opposite direction. Diodes are used in automobile charging systems to control the direction of current flow.

A diode is constructed from two wafer-thin chips of semiconductor material (Fig. 23-27). One of the wafers is usually silicon with phosphorus added as an impurity. The other wafer is usually silicon with boron added as an impurity. The two wafers are joined together by a diffusion process and mounted in a copper case. A stem attached to the semiconductor at one end goes out of the case for connection into an electrical circuit. The other wafer of semiconductor material is attached to the bottom of the diode case.

Since moisture can ruin the semiconductor, a moisture-absorbing material called a desiccant is located inside the case. A glass seal around the diode stem also prevents moisture from entering. The diode case is often mounted in a metal heat sink. The heat sink provides a way of removing the heat developed during operation.

The diode symbol used in wiring diagrams is shown in Figure 23-28. The arrow on the symbol shows the direction the diode will permit current flow. Current will not flow through the diode semiconductor material in the other direction. Electrically,

one of the semiconductor wafers inside the diode is connected into a circuit through the stem. This makes up half the diode circuit. The other wafer, connected to the case of the diode, forms the other side of the circuit.

23.28   Transistors

A transistor (Fig. 23-29) is a semiconductor device used to control current flow. It consists of two diodes back to back or two diodes sharing a common base material (Fig. 23-30). It is constructed from small pieces of semiconductor material, usually germanium, with an impurity such as idium and antimony added. The transistor has a very thin base to which a metallic ring is connected. One of the transistor circuit connections is attached to the ring. On each side of the base is another small piece of semiconductor material. One side is called the emitter and the other the collector. The semiconductor materials are housed in a small case. Three small connectors go out of the case from the emitter, base, and collector. The electrical symbol for a transistor is shown in Figure 23-31.

The transistor has a special characteristic that makes it useful in controlling current flow. The main current in a circuit cannot pass through the emitter to the collector unless a small amount of current is allowed to pass through the emitter to base circuit. In other words a small amount of current may be used to trigger or switch a large amount of current.

The best way to understand how a transistor controls current flow is to put a transistor into a simple circuit. The circuit shown in Figure 23-33 has a battery, a light bulb, a transistor, and two switches.

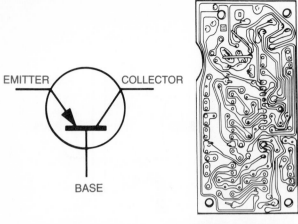

Fig. 23-31 Electrical symbol for a transistor.

Fig. 23-32 A PC or printed circuit board. (Ford Motor Company)

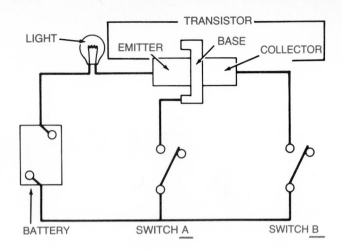

Fig. 23-33 No current flow with both switches open.

When switches A and B are open, current will not flow in the circuit to light the bulb. When switch B is closed, current will not flow across the transistor to light the bulb (Fig. 23-34). When switch A and switch B are closed (Fig. 23-35), a very small amount of current flows across the emitter to the base circuit in the transistor. This affects the semiconductor material so that full battery current flows from the emitter across the base to the collector to light the bulb.

This characteristic of a transistor makes it useful as a relay or switch. It has a big advantage over other switches in that it contains no moving parts. In later chapters we will study circuits in which transistors control current flow.

23.29 Printed Circuit Boards

Because of the smaller size of electronic components, they can be connected together on a printed circuit board or PC board (Fig. 23-32). The PC board is an etching made on a board that is an insulator. The circuit is a "map" of conductors, flowing from component to component just as wire conductors did. Components are attached to the board and their connectors soldered to the etched conductors at the appropriate places.

Many automotive circuits make use of PC boards. Always handle printed circuits with care! A panel that is bent or cracked can alter or destroy components connected to it, or destroy the board itself.

23.30 Microelectronics

The field of electronics has evolved into the field of microelectronics. Microelectronics involves making electronic circuits smaller and smaller. Microelectronic circuits are smaller, lighter, and in many cases can be manufactured less expensively than standard electronic components.

The use of the circuit board has evolved to the point where conducting material can be sprayed on parts of tiny silicon wafers. The circuits created are called *integrated circuits*.

The microelectronic chip is the equivalent of a printed circuit on a tiny slice of silicon. A silicon integrated circuit is produced by building layers of chemicals on a silicon slice (about 2mm square and 0.2mm thick), each layer acting as an electrical microcircuit. The surface of the slice is specially treated so that the silicon atoms either liberate an electron or lose one. The regions in each layer combine to act as transistors (which amplify current), and resistors or capacitors (which store it).

Microelectronic chips are now found in all types of equipment, from pocket calculators to watches to TV games to automotive control systems. Some are so small they cannot even be examined without the help of a microscope.

Microelectronic components are used in the microprocessor. The microprocessor is the computer used in most late model cars to provide electronic engine control. We will describe the electronic control system in later chapters.

NEW TERMS

Atom the small particle which is the basis of all matter.

Circuit A complete path for electrical current flow.

Conductor A material that allows electrical current flow.

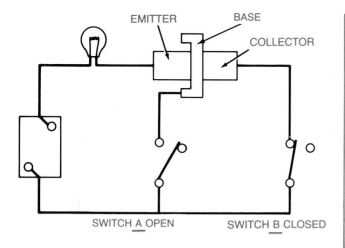

Fig. 23-34 No current flow with one switch open.

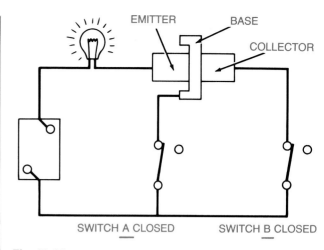

Fig. 23-35 Small current across emitter base circuit allows main current to pass through transistor.

Charging system The system that provides electrical energy for the automobile.

Current The flow of electrons in an electrical circuit.

Diode A semiconductor that allows current flow in only one direction.

Electrical system The system that provides electrical energy to both start and operate the engine as well as to power all the electrical equipment.

Electricity The flow of electrons from one atom to another.

Electromagnetism Magnetism produced by an electric current.

Electronics A branch of electricity concerned with the flow of electrons through vacuum tubes and semiconductors.

Electron theory Rules used to explain electricity.

Induction The transfer of energy from one object to another without the objects touching.

Ignition system The electrical system that provides the high-voltage spark to ignite the air-fuel mixture in the cylinder.

Insulator A material that prevents the flow of electricity.

Lighting and accessory circuit The circuit that provides electrical power for lights and other accessories.

Magnetic field An area of force surrounding a magnet.

Matter Anything that has weight and takes up space.

Printed Circuit: Printed board which, in place of wiring, has thin metallic conductors on one side.

Resistance The opposition offered to the free flow of electrons; measured in ohms and abbreviated R.

Starting system The electrical system that provides the power for starting the engine.

Transistor A semiconductor device used to control current flow.

Voltage The source of potential energy in an electrical system; measured in volts and abbreviated E.

CHAPTER REVIEW

1. List the four main systems of the automobile electrical system.
2. Describe an atom.
3. What are bound and free electrons?
4. Define electricity.
5. What is voltage?
6. What is current?
7. What is resistance?
8. Explain what an electrical circuit is.
9. Describe the single-wire system used in an automobile.
10. What are some nonmagnetic materials?
11. Describe a magnetic field.
12. What is an electromagnet?
13. What is induction?
14. What is a diode?
15. What is a transistor?

DISCUSSION TOPICS AND ACTIVITIES

1. Make a list of all the electrical equipment you can recognize on an automobile. Group the equipment under the main circuits we have studied in the chapter.
2. Write a definition of electricity in your own words.
3. Use a battery, wires, switch, and light to build a simple circuit. Can you make the light work?

Storage Battery

The automotive electrical system must have a source of stored energy ready for immediate use to power the electrical components. A lead-acid storage battery is used to store chemical energy and change it into electrical energy.

The storage battery provides all of the electrical power for the automobile when the engine is not running. It is the storage battery that provides the energy to power the starter motor and ignition system so that the engine may be cranked and started. When the engine is running, the charging system provides most of the energy to power the electrical system and to restore the chemical energy used by the battery. However, when electrical demand is higher than the output of the charging system, the storage battery will supply energy to help out the charging system.

OBJECTIVES

After studying this chapter, you should be able to do the following:

1. Describe the purpose of an automotive storage battery.
2. Understand how electricity is developed through chemistry.
3. Identify the main components of a battery.
4. Explain the performance ratings that are used on batteries.
5. Describe the causes of battery failure.

24.1 ELECTRICITY THROUGH CHEMISTRY

When two strips of different metals or conductors are placed in an acid solution that is also a conductor, the acid attacks one of the strips of metal. As the metal is eaten away, electrons are released that become attached to the other strip of metal. It was this discovery that led to the development of the battery.

A small battery or cell may be constructed from a container filled with electrolyte (Fig. 24-1). The electrolyte is made from sulphuric acid mixed with water. When two plates of different kinds of lead are placed in the electrolyte, the acid attacks the material in one of the plates. This releases electrons which go to the other plate. The plate that gains electrons is called the negative plate. The plate that loses electrons is called the positive plate.

When the negative plate is full of electrons, the battery is charged. For the negative plate is full of electrons ready to flow to atoms that are short of electrons. The battery, in other words, has an electrical potential or voltage.

If the battery is connected into a simple circuit (Fig. 24-2), its potential or voltage causes electrons to flow through the circuit and light the light bulb. As electrons are pulled away from the negative plate, the battery becomes weaker and weaker. Soon the light bulb will go out because the battery is discharged.

The discharged battery can be recharged by reversing the process. During recharging, a direct current forced through the battery supplies lost electrons to the positive plate. The positive and negative plates become different materials again. This chemical action builds up the electrolyte as well as the

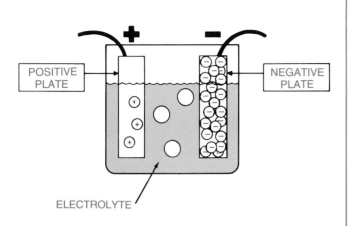

Fig. 24-1 A simple cell or battery.

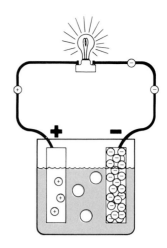

Fig. 24-2 A battery supplies electrons to power a light bulb.

plates to their original condition.

As we will see later, some battery service jobs require an inspection of the battery chemicals. For this reason, a mechanic must understand the chemical changes that take place in a battery during charging and discharging. The active material in the positive battery plate is lead peroxide. Its chemical symbol is PbO_2. The active material in the negative plate is spongy lead, whose symbol is Pb. The electrolyte in a fully charged battery is a mixture of about 36 percent sulphuric acid (H_2SO_4) and about 64 percent water (H_2O).

The chemistry of a fully charged battery is shown in Figure 24-3 (a). When the battery is connected to a load it begins to discharge [Fig. 24-3 (b)]. The positive plate (PbO_2) gives up oxygen (O_2) which combines with the hydrogen (H_2) in the electrolyte. This forms water (H_2O). At the same time lead (Pb) in both plates combines with the sulfate (SO_4) in the electrolyte to form lead sulfate ($PbSO_4$).

The chemistry of a discharged battery is shown in Figure 24-3 (c). Both plates are chemically similar. They are covered with lead sulfate ($PbSO_4$). The electrolyte has changed to water (H_2O). This fact will become important to the battery service mechanic. The state of charge of a battery may be measured with a hydrometer to test whether the electrolyte has been changed to water.

The chemical reaction during charging [Fig. 24-3 (d)] separates the lead sulfate on the positive and negative plates into lead (Pb) and sulphate (SO_4). The sulphate returns to the electrolyte to form sulphuric acid (H_2SO_4). The oxygen (O) in the electrolyte combines with the lead (Pb) at the positive plate to form lead peroxide (PbO_2). The negative plate becomes lead (Pb). The battery again has potential.

The chemical process can begin all over again.

During charging, hydrogen and oxygen travel freely through the electrolyte. In vented batteries, some of this hydrogen and oxygen can escape in the form of a gas. **Safety Caution: The hydrogen gas is explosive. An electrical spark or a burning cigarette close to the battery could cause an explosion.** As hydrogen and oxygen escape from the battery, the water in the electrolyte is used up.

24.2 BATTERY CONSTRUCTION

A simple battery constructed from two strips of metal placed in a container of acid cannot provide the electrical potential required by a modern automobile. An automobile battery operates on the same principles as the simple battery, but it has more active material in contact with more electrolyte.

24.3 Plates

The plates of an automotive strorage battery are flat, rectangular lead castings. They have a number of horizontal and rectangular strips, called grids, on which active material is spread or pasted.

On batteries that require the regular addition of water, the grids are made of lead and antimony. Antimony in a grid reacts chemically to require the periodic addition of water. Maintenance-free batteries have grids manufactured from lead-calcium. The use of calcium results in a grid in which water usage is greatly reduced. The active material on the negative plates is gray sponge lead. The active material on the positive plates is brown lead peroxide.

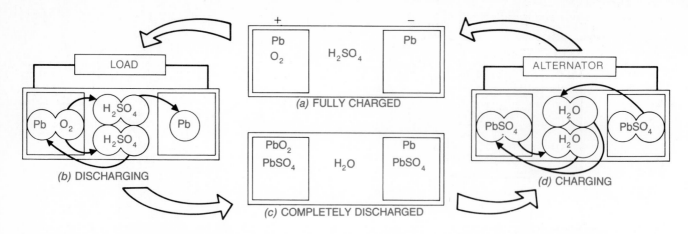

Fig. 24-3 Chemical action in a battery cell.

A number of positive plates are connected together by soldering them to a small lead casting called a plate strap. A number of negative plates are connected together in the same way. A group of plates puts much more active material in contact with the electrolyte than simple strips of metal.

The negative and positive plate group are assembled so that each negative plate is next to a positive plate. Both outside plates are negative, because this has been found to improve battery performance.

When the two plate groups are placed together, they are very close. If a positive plate were to touch a negative plate, there would be an electrical short and the cell would fail to work. To prevent them from touching, thin sheets of porous insulation material called separators are placed between the plates (Fig. 24-4). The separators are porous enough so that the electrolyte flows through. In addition, there may be ribs on the side of the separators that face a positive plate to hold a reservoir of electrolyte next to the positive plate. Materials used to make separators include polyvinylchloride, microporous rubber, purified wood and fiber glass.

24.4   Elements and Cells

The positive and negative plate group, together with the separators, are called an element (Fig. 24-5). An element becomes a cell when it is installed in a container filled with electrolyte (Fig. 24-6). No matter how large it may be, one cell can develop only about 2 volts of electrical potential. Since most automotive electrical systems require 12 volts, a battery container, called a case, is made to hold six cells (Fig. 24-7). Six cells connected together in a series add up to 12 volts.

24.5   Case

The battery case is made of hard plastic with partitions that separate the cells. The elements rest on steps in the bottom of the case. The steps provide an area for sediment to build up below the plates.

24.6   Connections

After the plate groups are in place in the case, the elements are connected in series from a terminal soldered to each set of plates. On older batteries the cell connectors were visible on the top of the battery. Newer batteries use connectors that pass through sealed holes in the partitions between the cells (Fig. 24-8). The lead connectors are soldered to the plate group terminals.

The cell on each end of the battery has a large terminal connected to it (Fig. 24-9). From these two terminals, the battery is connected into the automobile electrical circuit. One of the terminals is connected to a positive plate group and the other to a negative plate group. The terminals are identified as positive or negative by the symbols + or − or by the abbreviations *pos.* or *neg.* stamped on the case near the terminal.

24.7   Cover

The top of the battery is covered with a one-piece plastic cover bonded to the case with sealing compound. The cover may have threaded or tapered holes over each cell for a vent cap. The cap may be removed for inspection and refilling of the water in the electrolyte. The cap which screws or presses into the cover

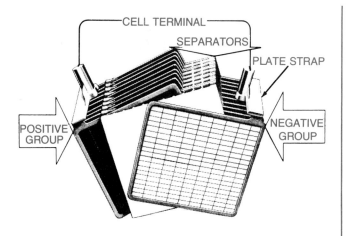

Fig. 24-4 Plate groups and separators.
(Chevrolet Motor Division, GMC)

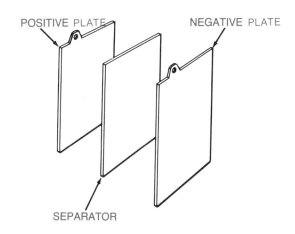

Fig. 24-5 Battery element. (Chevrolet Motor Division, GMC)

also has a vent to allow hydrogen and oxygen gas to escape during charging. The vent caps usually have a small cylinder where much of the hydrogen and oxygen may condense and run back into the cell. This design minimizes water loss.

The maintenance-free battery (Fig. 24-10) does not have cell vent caps. It is commonly called a sealed-top battery. Some batteries have a pry-off cover for access to the cells. The small amount of gas produced goes out through vents with flame arrestors to prevent battery explosion. A liquid-vapor separator drains the electrolyte back into the case.

24.8 BATTERY PERFORMANCE RATINGS

How well a battery works is determined by tests or rating procedures established by the battery manufacturers. Each manufacturer uses the same laboratory testing procedures so that one manufacturer's battery may be compared with another manufacturer's battery. A replacement battery must have the same performance rating as the original.

24.9 Voltage Ratings

Each cell of a battery can develop approximately 2 volts of electrical potential. Early automobiles used a 6-volt battery consisting of three cells connected in series. A 12-volt battery consisting of six cells connected in series is now standard on almost all automotive applications. On large industrial equipment that needs higher voltages, two 12-volt batteries are connected together in series for 24 volts (Fig. 24-11).

24.10 Capacity Rating

All six-cell storage batteries have the same voltage, but they may have a different capacity. Capacity is a measure of how long a battery can supply current. It is determined by the amount of active material and electrolyte in each cell. A battery with a few small plates will become discharged very quickly when supplying a high current demand. On the other hand, one with many large plates can supply current for a longer period of time. Several different tests are used to determine battery capacity.

One common test is called the 20-hour rating. This test shows the lighting and accessory load capacity of the battery. The test involves discharging the battery at a constant rate and a constant temperature of 80°F (27°C) for 20 hours. At the end of 20 hours the cell voltage should be 1.75 volts or more. The more current, measured in ampere = hours, that a battery is capable of supplying for 20 hours, the greater its capacity. If, for example, the battery can supply 5 amperes for 20 hours it gets a rating of 100 ampere-hours (5 amperes × 20 hours = 100 ampere-hours). A battery able to supply only 3 amperes for 20 hours would have a 60 ampere-hour rating.

The ability of a battery to supply current in cold weather is determined by the cold cranking test. In this test, the battery supplies current for 30 seconds while maintaining a minimum of 1.2 volts per cell. Two separate current ratings are made, one at 0°F (− 18°C) and another at −20°F (− 7°C). The battery is rated according to the amount of current in amperes it can supply under these conditions.

The reserve capacity test measures the time in minutes that the battery can supply current at night if the alternator should fail. A fully charged battery is

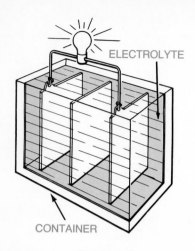

Fig. 24-6 Battery cell.
(Chevrolet Motor Division, GMC)

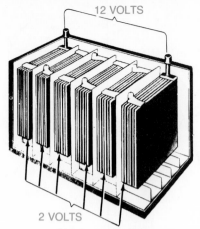

Fig. 24-7 Six cells provide 12 volts.
(Chevrolet Motor Division, GMC)

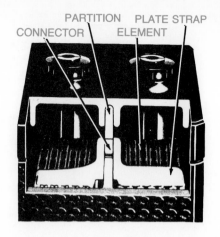

Fig. 24-8 Cells connected through the case partition. (Delco-Remy Division, GMC)

discharged at a constant 25 amperes at a temperature of 80°F (27°C) until the cell voltage drops to 1.75 volts. The longer the battery can supply this 25 amperes, the higher the reserve capacity of the battery.

24.11 Power Rating

In recent years, a new testing procedure for batteries has been developed based upon wattage. A watt (W) is a unit of electrical power equal to voltage (E) multiplied by amperage (I). Since this formula includes both voltage and capacity (current), a rating in watts is very useful in comparing battery performance. The rating is the highest wattage the battery can achieve under carefully controlled laboratory conditions. The higher the wattage rating, the more power or cranking ability the battery has.

24.12 BATTERY FAILURE

The typical battery will function properly for two or three years before it must be replaced. A number of conditions lead to early battery failure.

24.13 Deep Cycling

A battery cycle is a discharge and a recharge. In deep cycle, a battery is severely discharged before it is recharged. If a battery is subjected to repeated deep cycling, its life will be shortened. Repeated deep cycling causes the active material on the positive plate to shed and fall into the sediment chamber in the case. Deep cycling often occurs on a vehicle that is hard to start. When the operator must crank the engine for long periods of time to get it started, there is a rapid, high discharge.

24.14 Undercharging

Many automobiles are used for short trip, stop-and-start driving. Power is drawn from the battery to start the engine, but the automobile is not operated long enough for the charging system to recharge the battery. Thus, the battery is constantly in a state of undercharge. It was pointed out that in a discharged battery, lead sulphate ($PbSO_4$) forms on the plates. If the lead sulphate remains on the plates for a long period of time, it will crystallize. A battery in this condition is described as sulphated. If the sulfation crystals are allowed to remain on the plates very long, they are difficult to break down by normal recharging. The battery must often be replaced.

24.15 Overcharging

A battery may be overcharged or charged at too high a rate in one of two ways. First, a problem in the charging system can cause a battery to be overcharged. Second, a battery can be overcharged with a battery charger during a service operation. When a battery is overcharged, a violent chemical action in the cell rapidly breaks down the electrolyte into hydrogen and oxygen gas. The violent gassing causes a rapid water loss from the cell and washes active material off the plates. This greatly shortens the life of the battery. Overcharging also produces heat that can oxidize the positive plate grids and even buckle the plates. This, of course, will lead to early battery failure.

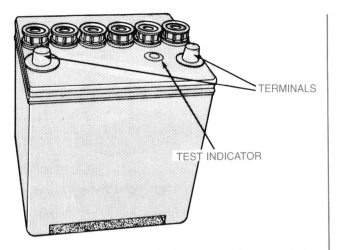

Fig. 24-9 The battery terminals are used to connect the battery into the circuit. (Chrysler Corporation)

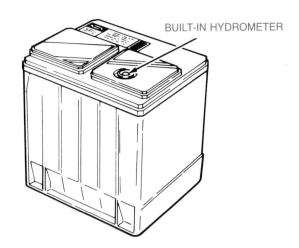

BUILT-IN HYDROMETER

Fig. 24-10 Maintenance-free battery. (General Motors Corporation)

24.16　　Improper Electrolyte Level

During charging, water is lost from the cell in the form of hydrogen and oxygen gas. In a vented battery this means that the level of the electrolyte in the cell will drop. If the level drops below the top of the plates, active material is exposed. Active material that is not in electrolyte hardens and becomes chemically inactive. As water is lost from the cell the percentage of sulphuric acid in the remaining electrolyte becomes so high it may cause the plates to break down rapidly.

Overfilling removes sulphuric acid from the cell. This dilutes the chemical process in the cell and leads to poor performance. The spillage over the battery top and around terminal connections also causes corrosion.

24.17　　Effects of Temperature

The effects of too high a temperature were mentioned in connection with overcharging. Too high a temperature shortens battery life. Low temperatures due to cold climate and winter operation can freeze the electrolyte in a battery cell. The freezing electrolyte expands and breaks the case, ruining the battery. The temperature at which the electrolyte freezes depends upon the battery's state of charge. A fully charged battery has a strong enough concentration of sulphuric acid so that the electrolyte will not freeze at $-50°F$ ($-46°C$). A discharged battery whose electrolyte is mostly water can freeze at $18°F$ ($-8°C$). To prevent freezing, a battery must be kept charged in cold weather.

The colder the weather the thicker the engine oil and the harder the engine is to crank over. But low temperatures also slow down the chemical activity in the cell. Figure 24-12 shows that battery power decreases while the need for engine cranking power increases as it gets colder.

24.18　　Vibration

Vibration occurs when the battery is bounced or shook violently as the vehicle goes over rough roads. Vibration is especially bad if the battery is not held tightly in its mount by the proper bracket. Active material shakes loose from the plate grids and falls into the sediment chamber at the bottom of the case. The life of the battery is shortened considerably.

24.19　　Corrosion

Electrolyte that spills or splashes outside the battery can form a green buildup called corrosion. Corrosion may build up on metal parts near the battery, usually the hold-down bracket and terminal connections. It will eventually eat away brackets and terminals. Corrosion on the terminal connections works its way between the battery terminal and the cable connection. This will soon increase resistance at the terminal so that the battery cannot supply enough power to crank the engine.

NEW TERMS

Acid　A mixture of water and sulphuric acid used in a battery cell.
Active material　Sponge lead and lead peroxide used in the plates of a battery.

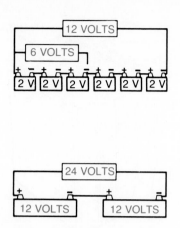

Fig. 24-11   Battery voltage is determined by the number of 2-volt cells connected in series.

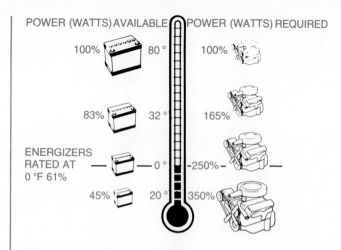

Fig. 24-12   Battery power decreases while need increases with failing temperature.

Capacity rating   A rating of how long a battery can supply current.

Cell   A basic unit of the battery capable of developing about 2 volts.

Cold cranking test   A test of the battery's ability to supply current in cold weather.

Deep cycling   A condition in which the battery is severely discharged before it is recharged.

Electrolyte   The acid solution in a battery cell.

Lead peroxide   The active material on the positive plate.

Maintenance-free battery   A battery that does not have cell caps for periodic refilling with water.

Negative plates   The group of plates in a battery negatively charged with electrons.

Overcharging   A condition in which the battery is charged at too high a rate.

Plate   The part of the battery on which the active material is spread.

Positive plates   The group of plates in a battery that give off electrons.

Reserve capacity test   A test to find out how long the battery can supply current at night if the alternator should fail.

Separators   Sheets of insulation placed between the plates of a battery.

Sponge lead   The active material on the negative plates in a cell.

Storage battery   A battery used to store electrical energy in chemical form.

Twenty-hour rating   A test of a battery's capacity to deliver current for twenty hours.

Undercharging   A condition in which a battery is not provided with a full charge.

Voltage rating   A rating of how many volts the battery can deliver.

Watt   An electrical unit of power computed by multiplying volts times amperes.

CHAPTER REVIEW

1. Why does a battery discharge?
2. How can a battery be charged?
3. Why is the hydrogen gas in a battery dangerous?
4. Why is it necessary to add water to a vented battery?
5. Explain how the plates of a battery are made.
6. What is a battery element?
7. What is a battery cell?
8. How are the terminals on the battery identified?
9. Explain what a battery voltage rating is.
10. How many cells does a 12-volt vattery have?
11. How is a battery's 20-hour rating determined?
12. What is a power rating for a battery?
13. Define *watt*.
14. Describe the condition of deep cycling.
15. What is undercharging and why is it bad for a battery?

DISCUSSION TOPICS AND ACTIVITIES

1. Describe the chemistry involved in creating electricity.
2. Study a cutaway battery in the shop. Can you identify the major parts?

Storage Battery Service

The usual result of battery troubles is that the engine does not crank over fast enough to start or does not crank over at all. Either condition may also be caused by a problem in a part other than the battery. A careful diagnosis of battery condition is necessary to find out the problem and avoid servicing the wrong part. Battery testing determines whether the battery is in satisfactory condition, requires recharging, or is defective and needs to be replaced.

OBJECTIVES

After studying this chapter, you should be able to do the following:

1. Recognize the dangers involved in battery service.
2. Describe the troubleshooting steps to find out what is wrong with a battery.
3. Explain the preventive maintenance jobs necessary to prevent battery failure.
4. Explain how batteries are charged.
5. Describe how to install a new battery.

25.1   BATTERY SAFETY

Battery servicing can be dangerous unless the mechanic takes certain safety precautions. Since electrolyte contains sulphuric acid, if it is spilled, it will damage clothing, upholstery, or paint. More important, it is extremely harmful if spilled on the skin or splashed in the eyes. Safety glasses must always be worn when servicing batteries. If electrolyte is splashed in the eyes, flush them with cool clean water immediately for about five minutes and notify a doctor.

Electrolyte on the skin or clothing can be neutralized with a solution of baking soda and water. A container of baking soda should always be present where batteries are serviced.

The gas that forms in the battery cell during charging is explosive. On vented batteries some of this gas escapes through the vent plugs. If ventilation around the battery is poor, an explosive mixture can remain around the battery for several hours after it has been charged. A spark or flame can ignite the mixture and cause an explosion.

Charge and service batteries in a well ventilated area. Avoid breaking any live circuits that may cause a spark around the battery. Attach booster or jumper cables, tester, and charger leads carefully to avoid a loose connection that could cause a spark. Do not smoke near a battery.

25.2   TROUBLESHOOTING

The first step in troubleshooting a battery is to look for damage (Fig. 25-1) such as a cracked case or loose or broken battery terminals. If any of these conditions are found, the battery should be replaced.

25.3   Visual Inspection

Inspect the battery cables and terminals for breaks, loose connections, or corrosion. Inspect the top of the battery for dirt or electrolyte. Too much electrolyte on the top of the battery may be the result of overfilling. If the top of the battery is not clean,

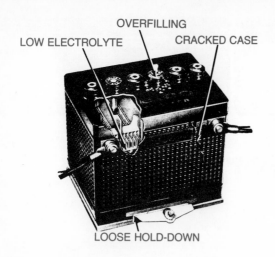

LOW ELECTROLYTE
OVERFILLING
CRACKED CASE
LOOSE HOLD-DOWN

Fig. 25-1 Battery visual checks. (Delco Remy Division, GMC)

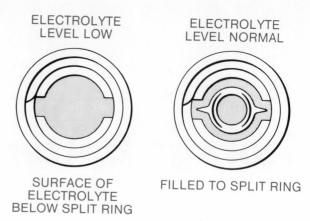

ELECTROLYTE
LEVEL LOW

SURFACE OF
ELECTROLYTE
BELOW SPLIT RING

ELECTROLYTE
LEVEL NORMAL

FILLED TO SPLIT RING

Fig. 25-2 The split ring is used to determine electrolyte level.

current can flow across the foreign material. This will cause the battery to discharge by itself when the vehicle is idle. Check the battery hold-down to be sure it is tight. A loose hold-down could mean the active material has vibrated off the plates. Finally, remove the cell vent caps to inspect the electrolyte level. If the electrolyte level is not above the top of the plates, add water (preferably distilled) to the cell before any further testing, as shown in Figure 25-2.

25.4   Specific Gravity Testing

The next test procedure is to measure the electrolyte specific gravity. As the battery is discharged, sulphuric acid in the electrolyte combines with the active material on the plates. As the sulphuric acid leaves, the remaining electrolyte is nearly pure water. The specific gravity test tells the amount of sulfuric acid and of water in the electrolyte. This is a measure of whether the battery is charged or discharged.

The tool used to measure specific gravity is called a hydrometer (Fig. 25-3). The hydrometer is a glass tube with a squeeze bulb at the top. Place the hydrometer into the cell through the vent cap hole. Squeeze the bulb and release to suck electrolyte into the glass tube. If the electrolyte has a high sulphuric acid content, the float in the tube will not sink very far below the electrolyte level. If the electrolyte is mostly water, the float will sink further. The reason for this is that water is less dense or has a lower specific gravity than water mixed with sulphuric acid.

Numbered marks on the float allow the mechanic to note its level. On the specific gravity scale, pure water is 1.000. Numbers bigger than 1.000 mean a higher specific gravity or more sulphuric acid. Most hydrometer scales read from 1.160 to 1.320 in gradations of .005.

The electrolyte level of the battery must be normal before a specific gravity test. If water is added, it must be mixed thoroughly with the electrolyte by charging the battery before a reading is taken. To read a hydrometer, hold it vertically and carefully suck electrolyte into the hydrometer about halfway up the glass tube. Then sight directly across the electrolyte level to the marking on the float that lines up with the electrolyte level. Note and record the number on the float. Repeat this procedure for each of the other cells.

The specific gravity of the electrolyte changes not only with acid strength but also with temperature. Hydrometer floats are made to be read at a temperature of 80°F (27°C). As its temperature rises, the electrolyte's specific gravity is reduced. As temperature falls, the electrolyte gets thicker and its specific gravity increases. Specific gravity changes caused by temperatures above or below 80°F (27°C) must be corrected to a true reading.

Most hydrometers have a thermometer built into the side. When measuring the specific gravity, also note the temperature on the thermometer. If it is above or below 80°F (27°C), the reading must be corrected. Add .004 specific gravity for every 10 degrees over 80°F (5.6 degrees over 27°C). Subtract .004 specific gravity for every 10 degrees under 80°F (5.6 degrees over 27°C). A correction chart (Fig. 25-5) may be used to calculate the correction. Two correction examples follow.

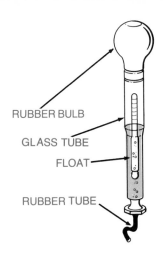

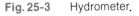

Fig. 25-3 Hydrometer.

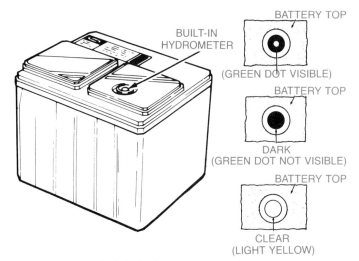

Fig. 25-4 Built-in hydrometer. (Chevrolet Motor Division, GMC)

Example 1

Acid Temperature	20 degrees Fahrenheit
Hydrometer Reading	1.260
Subtract Specific Gravity	−.024
Correct Specific Gravity	1.236

Example 2

Acid Temperature	37.8 degrees Celsius
Hydrometer Reading	1.255
Add Specific Gravity	+.008
Corrected Specific Gravity	1.263

With a corrected specific gravity reading for each cell, the mechanic is ready to find out if the battery is charged. The scale below shows some common readings:

Specific Gravity Reading	State of Charge of Battery
1.260 and above	Fully charged
1.250	75% charged
1.220	50% charged
1.190	25% charged
1.130 and below	Discharged

As this scale shows, a specific gravity of 1.260 or above in all the cells shows a fully charged battery. A reading of 1.130 and below shows a completely discharged battery. A variation of 0.050 or more between the highest and lowest cell indicates internal damage in the battery. The battery must be replaced.

A battery with uniform specific gravity readings below 1.250 must be charged before any further testing. Charge the battery, following the procedure outlined under Section 25.11 on battery charging. A battery with uniform specific gravity readings above 1.250 may be tested further as outlined below.

Many maintenance-free batteries have a built-in hydrometer (Fig. 25-4). It consists of a glass rod with a green ball in a cage at the bottom of the rod. When the charge is 65 percent or greater, the ball rises, touches the bottom of the rod, and the window in the top of the battery appears green. At a lower charge, the ball sinks and the window is dark. If the electrolyte level is low it will be below the end of the rod, and the window will be yellow.

25.5   Capacity or Load Testing

The next test for a battery that has a uniform specific gravity above 1.250 is a capacity test (Fig. 25-6). This is often called a load test because the battery is connected to a load that discharges it at a high rate. There are a number of different types of capacity testers. The programmed tester uses a programmed procedure consisting of a series of timed discharge and charge cycles to indicate whether the battery is in satisfactory condition or should be replaced.

If the programmed test unit is not available, use a standard battery starter tester. This tester consists of a test voltmeter, a test ammeter, and a loading device called a carbon pile load. Before making any connections, turn off the load knob and set the voltage selector switch on the correct voltage. Connect the positive ammeter and voltmeter leads to the positive battery terminal. Connect the negative voltmeter and ammeter leads to the negative battery terminal.

TEMP. °C	TEMP. °F	GRAVITY POINTS TO ADD OR SUBTRACT		TEMP. °F	TEMP. °C
			+ 2		
71.1	160	+32	0	80	26.7
		+30	− 2		
65.6	150	+28	− 4	70	21.1
		+26	− 6		
60.0	140	+24	− 8	60	15.6
		+22	−10		
54.4	130	+20	−12	50	10.0
		+18	−14		
48.9	120	+16	−16	40	4.4
		+14	−18		
43.3	110	+12	−20	30	−1.1
		+10	−22		
37.8	100	+ 8	−24	20	−6.7
		+ 6	−26		
32.2	90	+ 4	−28	10	−12.2

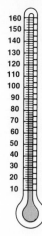

Fig. 25-5 Specific gravity correction chart.

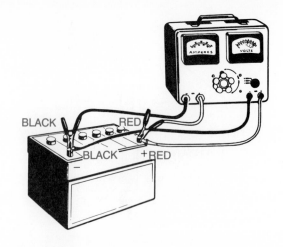

Fig. 25-6 Battery capacity test. (Chrysler Corporation)

The voltmeter clips must be attached to the battery terminals, not the cable clamps or ammeter lead clips. Batteries with side terminals require special adapters (Fig. 25-7) when testing outside the vehicle. Since temperature can change capacity, the battery temperature should approximate 80°F. Turn the load knob clockwise until the ammeter reading is three times the ampere-hour rating of the battery. If the battery is rated at 100 ampere-hours, the load setting should be 300 amperes (100 × 3 = 300). Hold the load for 15 seconds while watching the voltmeter. If a 12-volt battery has enough capacity, the voltmeter will not drop below 9.5 volts. After 15 seconds, return the load knob to the off position.

If the battery passes the capacity test, it can supply current and hold the necessary voltage. The battery is in satisfactory condition. If the engine is not cranking fast enough to start, the problem is in some other part. Troubleshooting the other parts of the starting system is explained in Chapter 27. A battery that fails the capacity test should be replaced.

25.6 PREVENTIVE MAINTENANCE

Battery life can be improved by simple periodic maintenance. Battery maintenance should be a regular part of the automobile's maintenance schedule.

25.7 Electrolyte Level

Batteries with cell vent plugs should be inspected for proper electrolyte level. Check electrolyte level monthly during cool weather driving and even more often during warm weather. The higher the battery temperature and the higher the charge rate, the more gas that is developed and the faster the water loss. Long trips in hot weather subject the cells to high temperatures and high charging rates. These conditions mean that the electrolyte level must be checked often.

Remove each of the cell vent plugs. The electrolyte level should be well above the plates. Most manufacturers have a guide ring built into the top of the case above the cell. The electrolyte level should be filled to the level of the guide ring. One manufacturer uses a vent plug with a transparent rod extending through the center. When electrolyte is at the right level, the lower tip of the rod is covered and the top of the rod, visible in the vent cap, appears very dark. When the level falls below the tip of the rod, the top of the rod glows. This allows a mechanic to tell at a glance that the cell needs water.

If the electrolyte level is low, add water to the cell. Since regular tap water may have a high salt and mineral content, it is best to use distilled water. The water should be added with a plastic or rubber tool (see Fig. 25-8 for service tools) made for battery filling, not a metal funnel. A metal object could cause a short between the plates. Take care not to overfill the cell. This would dilute the electrolyte strength and cause an acid buildup on the outside of the battery.

25.8 Cleaning the Battery

The outside of the battery should be cleaned periodically. Dirt, moisture, and corrosion on the top of the battery provide a path for current flow between the battery terminals. This can cause the battery to self-discharge. Install the cell vent plugs tightly before cleaning the battery. Brush a solution of baking

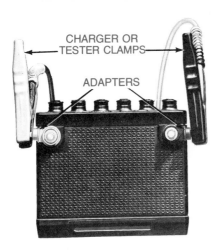

Fig. 25-7 Adapters used with side terminals.
(Delco Remy Division, GMC)

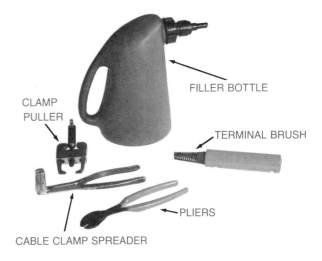

Fig. 25-8 Battery service tools.

soda and water over the battery to neutralize any acid buildup (Fig. 25-9). Then flush the battery with clean water. Be careful not to allow the cleaning solution to enter the vent caps and get into the cell.

25.9   Cleaning the Cables

A good electrical contact is necessary between the battery terminals and the battery cables. Batteries without sealed terminals often develop corrosion on the terminals that increases the resistance between the cable and the battery. This may cause starting difficulties. Eventually, the corrosion will destroy the cable connections.

If the terminals are corroded, disconnect the cables. After loosening the cable clamp, use a battery cable puller to remove it from the terminal. Never pry a cable clamp off a terminal. This could ruin the terminal connection inside the battery. If corrosion has attacked the cable clamp bolt, use battery pliers to loosen the clamp bolt.

The cable clamp and battery terminal may be cleaned with a special wire brush. One side of the brush is designed to clean inside the cable clamp. The other side is designed to fit over and clean the battery terminal (Fig. 25-10). A solution of baking soda and water can also be used to neutralize corrosion. When the terminal and cable clamp are clean, they can be reconnected. To prevent corrosion buildup, apply a thin coat of petroleum jelly.

25.10   Carrier and Hold-Down

The carrier and hold-down should also be cleaned and inspected periodically. A loose hold-down can allow the battery to vibrate and lose active material from the plates. Proper torque on the hold-down bolts is necessary to prevent excessive strain on the battery case.

25.11   BATTERY SERVICE

When the specific gravity reading shows that the battery is at less than a full charge, it must be recharged before being returned to service. A battery may be charged in or out of a vehicle. If it is charged in the vehicle, both cables must be disconnected prior to connecting a charger. Failure to do this may damage the vehicle's charging system. Battery charging involves applying a current through the battery to restore its chemical potential. A battery must be charged with the correct amount of current, called rate, and for the correct length of time.

25.12   Fast Charging

A unit known as a fast charger (Fig. 25-11) charges at the high rate of 40–50 amperes. The fast charger is used when there is not enough time for a slow charge. A fast charge will provide enough charge in about an hour for the battery to handle the vehicle electrical load. The fast charger may also be used for an emergency boost charge to crank start the engine. Batteries that do not have uniform specific gravity readings and batteries that have been discharged for a long time should *not* be fast charged.

To use a fast charger, connect the positive lead of the charger to the battery positive terminal and the negative lead of the charger to the battery negative terminal. Most fast chargers do not have a rate

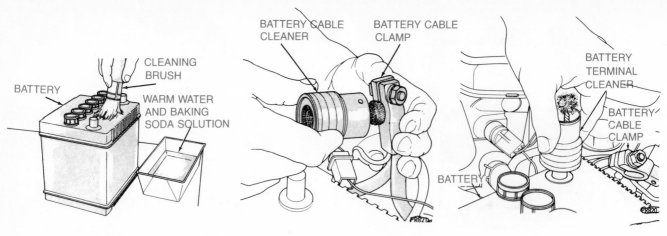

Fig. 25-9 Cleaning the battery with baking soda and water. (Chrysler Corporation)

Fig. 25-10 Cleaning battery cable clamps and terminals with a wire battery brush. (Chrysler Corporation)

selector. The charging rate of 40–50 amperes is preset. Set the voltage selector to either 6 or 12 volts, depending upon the battery voltage. Most chargers have a timer that can be set according to the battery's specific gravity. The following table may be used as a guide:

Specific Gravity	Fast Charging Time
1.150 or less	one hour
1.150 to 1.175	3/4 hour
1.175 to 1.200	1/2 hour
1.200 to 1.225	1/4 hour

Above 1.225 do not fast charge (Fig. 25-12).

If the battery is not removed from the vehicle, disconnect the cables during charging. Check the battery electrolyte temperature during charging. It must never be allowed to get higher than 125°F (52°C). If the temperature is too high, cool the battery by reducing the charging rate or turning off the charger. As the level of charge in the battery increases, the cells will begin to bubble. If too much gassing is observed, lower the charging rate or turn off the charger. Do not fast charge a battery longer than an hour.

25.13 Slow Charging

High charging rates are not good for completely charging a battery. To completely charge a battery or to charge a completely discharged battery, a slow charger with a rate of 3–20 amperes is required. Slow chargers are made as separate units or as a part of a fast charger.

A discharged or a sulphated battery may often be brought back to satisfactory condition by slow charging. Connect the slow charger to the battery by hooking the negative lead of the charger to the negative battery terminal and the positive lead of the charger to the positive terminal. Set the voltage switch to 6 or 12 volts, depending upon battery voltage. Many slow chargers have a rate switch. Few have a time selector. The charging time will have to be observed by the mechanic.

The battery should be tested with a hydrometer at regular intervals throughout the charge. The specific gravity readings for each cell should be written down. The correct slow charging rate may be found in two ways. The manufacturer's specifications for the battery will show the number of positive plates in each cell as well as the ampere-hour rating of the battery. Either figure can be used to find the slow charging rate. A charging rate of one ampere per positive plate per cell or 7 percent of the ampere-hour rating is correct for most batteries. A battery that has been discharged for a long period of time and is suspected of being sulphated should be charged at half this rate to break up the sulphate crystals on the plates.

The average length of time necessary to slow charge a battery ranges from 12 to 16 hours. The battery is fully charged when each cell is gassing freely and when there is no further rise in specific gravity after three successive readings taken at hourly intervals. Watch temperature carefully and lower the charging rate if a cell temperature reaches 110°F.

As the battery gets near full charge, its chemical potential increases the battery's voltage. This higher voltage opposes the voltage of the battery charger. This opposing voltage is called counter elecrotomotive force, abbreviated CEMF. The internal resistance of the battery also increases as the battery nears full charge because an obstructive gas film is formed on

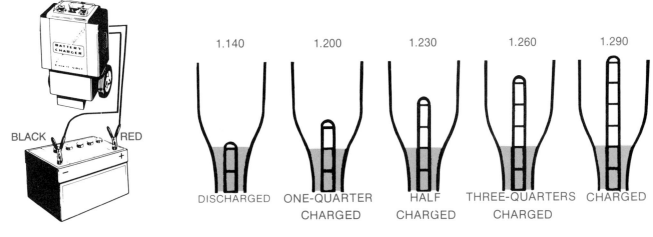

Fig. 25-11 Charging a battery.
(Chrysler Corporation)

Fig. 25-12 Various specific-gravity readings.

1.140 DISCHARGED
1.200 ONE-QUARTER CHARGED
1.230 HALF CHARGED
1.260 THREE-QUARTERS CHARGED
1.290 CHARGED

the surface of the plates. The combination of CEMF and internal resistance results in the battery limiting its own charge rate as it nears full charge. A lower charge rate will be shown on the slow charger ammeter as the battery reaches full charge.

25.14 EMERGENCY JUMP STARTING

It is sometimes necessary to jump start a vehicle with a dead battery. This is an emergency procedure when the discharged battery cannot be given a boost charge with a battery charger. Jump starting is dangerous. If not done properly, it may cause a battery explosion or damage to the electrical system. The mechanic must be careful when making connections to avoid sparks that may cause an explosion. **Safety Caution: Always wear eye protection when connecting or disconnecting booster batteries.**

Set the parking brake on both the vehicle with the discharged battery and the one with the booster battery. Put the gear selector in park for an automatic transmission or in neutral for a manual transmission. **The vehicles should not touch each other because this could cause a ground connection.** Place a fire blanket across the top of both the discharged and the booster battery to reduce the possibility of an explosion.

The proper way to connect a booster battery to a discharged battery (with a negative ground system) is shown in Figure 25-13.

Attach one end of one jumper cable to the positive terminal of the booster battery and the other end to the positive terminal of the discharged battery. Attach one end of the other cable to the negative terminal of the booster battery and the other

end to a ground at least 12 inches (305 mm) from the battery filter caps of the vehicle being started. **Do not connect directly to the negative terminal of the dead battery.** See Figure 25-13.

If the vehicles have a positive grounded system, attach one end of one jumper cable to the negative terminal of the booster battery and the other end to the negative terminal of the discharged battery. Attach one end of the other cable to the positive terminal of the booster battery and the other end to a ground at least 12 inches (305 mm) from the battery filler caps of the vehicle being started. **Do not connect directly to the positive terminal of the dead battery.**

Make sure that the clamps of one cable do not touch the clamps of the other cable. Be careful not to lean over the battery when making the connections. Start the vehicle with the discharged battery. Disconnect the booster cables by removing the connections at the negative terminals first, then at the positive terminals.

25.15 INSTALLING A NEW BATTERY

When a battery replacement is indicated, the mechanic has two choices for a replacement battery. The mechanic may use a wet-charge or a dry-charge battery. The two types have specific advantages and disadvantages which are explained in the following sections.

25.16 Wet-charge and Dry-charge

When testing shows a defective battery, install a new battery. Replacement batteries are sold as either wet- or dry-charged. A wet-charged battery is

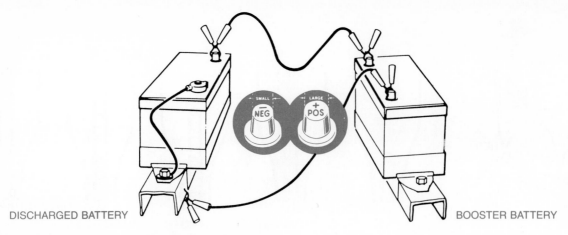

Fig. 25-13   Proper connection for booster or jumper cables.

full of electrolyte when it leaves the factory. If not properly cared for, the wet-charged battery can self-discharge. Wet-charged batteries must be stored connected to a charger to hold a full charge.

Problems in storage and handling of the wet-charge battery led to the development of the dry-charge battery. The dry-charge battery has electrolyte added at the factory so that the battery can receive a forming charge. The forming charge determines the chemical makeup of the plates and establishes the battery's polarity. The electrolyte is then removed from the cells, the cells are sealed, and the battery is shipped to be sold dry. Since there is no electrolyte in the cells, there is no problem with self-discharge. Dry-charge batteries do not have to be stored on a charger.

25.17   Electrical Rating

A battery's electrical rating must at least equal that of the original equipment battery. The automobile manufacturer's service manual specifies the recommended battery rating as a capacity rating, a wattage rating, or both. An undersized battery may result in poor performance and early failure. A battery with a higher rating may be used if the electrical load has been increased through the addition of accessories or if the operator's driving habits prevent the charging system from keeping the battery charged.

25.18   Installation Procedures

A wet-charged battery is ready for installation right off the shelf. A dry-charged battery must be activated before installation by adding electrolyte to the cells. **Safety Caution: Handle electrolyte carefully and wear eye protection.** Fill the cells to the proper level with the electrolyte as shown in Figure 25-14. Directions attached to the battery usually say that an activation charge is necessary after adding the electrolyte to mix the electrolyte chemicals.

When installing the new battery, there are several things to watch out for. Look at the ground polarity of the present battery. In most cases the negative termimal of the battery is connected through a cable to ground. Some older vehicles and some European vehicles use positive grounding. The battery must be installed with the correct polarity.

When removing a battery from the circuit, always remove the grounded terminal connection first. During installation, always connect the grounded terminal last. The grounded terminal is less likely to cause a spark which could result in a short circuit or an explosion (Fig. 25-15).

After the defective battery is removed, clean the carrier assembly with baking soda and water. Make sure the bottom of the carrier is clean and in good condition so that the new battery will rest properly in it. Clean and tighten the cable connections and protect them with petroleum jelly. Follow recommended tightening torques for the terminal studs and hold-down bolts. Finally, test drive the vehicle.

NEW TERMS

Capacity test   A battery capacity test that uses a load to discharge the battery at a high rate.
Carrier   The box in the engine compartment that holds the battery.
Counter electromotive force   Battery voltage that opposes the voltage of a battery charger during charging; abbreviated CEMF.

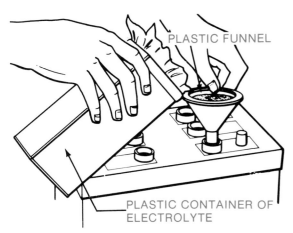

Fig. 25-14   Filling a dry-charged battery with electrolyte.

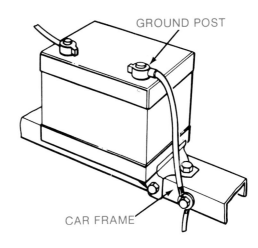

Fig. 25-15   The grounded terminal is always connected last.

Dry-charged battery   A new battery that is empty of electrolyte; electrolyte must be added to activate it.

Electrolyte level   The height of the electrolyte in the cells.

Fast charging   Applying a current through the battery at a high rate to restore its potential.

Hold-down   The bracket that holds the battery in the carrier.

Hydrometer   A tool to measure the specific gravity of the electrolyte.

Jump starting   Using another battery to start an engine with a discharged battery.

Jumper cables   Long heavy cables used to connect two batteries for jump starting.

Load testing   Same as *capacity testing*.

Slow charging   Applying a current through the battery at a slow rate to restore its potential.

Specific gravity   A measure of the strength of the electrolyte in a battery cell.

Specific gravity test   A test of the specific gravity in the cells that uses a hydrometer to find out if the battery is charged.

Wet-charged battery   A new battery that has electrolyte in the cells.

CHAPTER REVIEW

1. Why is electrolyte dangerous?
2. Why should batteries be charged in a well ventilated area?
3. List the visual checks made to locate battery trouble.

4. Explain how to use a hydrometer to measure specific gravity.
5. What effect does temperature have on specific gravity?
6. How are temperature corrections made to specific gravity readings?
7. What does the load test tell about a battery?
8. If the electrolyte level is low, what is added to the cell?
9. Explain how to clean the outside of the battery.
10. Describe how to clean battery cables.
11. What is a fast battery charger?
12. Describe how to fast charge a battery.
13. What is a slow battery charger?
14. Describe the hookup for emergency jump starting.
15. What is the difference between a wet- and a dry-charged battery?

DISCUSSION TOPICS AND ACTIVITIES

1. Use a hydrometer to measure the specific gravity of a battery. Record your results. Is the battery charged or discharged?
2. Charge a battery with a fast and slow charger. Follow the correct procedure. How can you tell when the battery is fully charged?
3. Connect the batteries from two vehicles with jumper cables for jump starting. What precautions must be observed?

The Starting System

CHAPTER PREVIEW

In order to start the engine, the crankshaft has to be rotated at a fairly high speed. On early automobiles, the driver started the engine by engaging a crank to the crankshaft where it sticks through the front of the engine. The driver then tried to rotate the crankshaft by hand fast enough to get the engine started. The development of an electric starter was a giant step forward for the automobile industry.

OBJECTIVES

After studying this chapter, you should be able to do the following:

1. Explain the operation of the starter motor.
2. Describe the construction of the starter motor.
3. Recognize the several different starter motor circuits.
4. Explain the operation of inertia and overrunning clutch starter motor drives.
5. Describe the operation of the solenoids used in starting systems.

26.1 STARTER MOTOR OPERATION

The starter motor has two major parts, a field winding assembly and an armature assembly. The field winding assembly has a number of large magnets mounted to the starter housing or field frame. The magnets, called pole pieces, create a magnetic field between them (Fig. 26-1). A wire called a field winding is wrapped around the pole pieces. Current is directed through the field winding to increase the strength of the magnetic field (Fig. 26-2).

If a loop of wire carrying current is placed in the magnetic field, the magnetic field around the wire and the field between the pole pieces repel each other, forcing the loop to turn (Fig. 26-3). An armature contains a number of loops of wire. Metal segments attached to each end of the loops form a contact surface called a commutator. Sliding contacts called brushes allow battery current to enter the rotating armature assembly (Fig. 26-4).

26.2 STARTER MOTOR CONSTRUCTION

A 3-piece housing holds the starter motor (Figs. 26-5 and 26-6). The tubular center housing, called the field frame assembly, contains the pole shoes and field windings. Attached to it at one end is the drive end frame. The commutator end frame is placed at the other end. Bearings or bushings in the end frames support the armature. The bushings are made from a porous bronze alloy whose pores retain oil. The bushings, oiled during manufacturing, do not require periodic oiling in service. Long through bolts hold the 3-piece housing together.

The armature assembly (Fig. 26-7) is made up of several parts. Each of the loops of wire is held in place by a core made from a number of thin iron plates called laminations. The laminations are insulated with thin sheets of paper or special insulation varnish. The iron core helps concentrate and direct the magnetic lines of force.

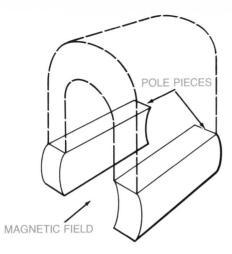

Fig. 26-1   Pole pieces create a magnetic field.

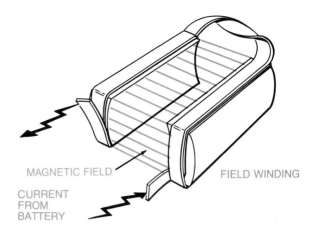

Fig. 26-2   Field winding increases the magnetic field.

The loops of wire are connected to commutator segments insulated from each other with a material called mica. The segments are constructed from a good conductor, usually copper. A hardened steel shaft pressed through the core laminations supports the armature in the starter housing and allows it to rotate. A drive assembly is attached to the front end of the shaft. The armature loops and commutator are insulated from the shaft.

Sliding contacts called brushes riding on the commutator, direct full battery current into the armature. The brushes are made of a material that provides good electrical contact, usually made from various alloys of copper. They are held in place over the commutator by brush holders (Fig. 26-8) attached to the commutator end frame or to the starter field frame assembly. A small spring attached to the holder pushes the brushes firmly against the commutator. Wires attached to the brushes direct current into and out of the armature.

The field coil and pole shoe assembly are mounted to the starter housing by large screws. The field windings are protected by an insulation wrapping. The field coils and the brushes are connected electrically to a terminal usually located at the top rear of the starter housing. A number of different wiring arrangements are used.

26.3   STARTER MOTOR CIRCUITS

On most starter motors, all the current passes through the field windings and the armature in series. This arrangement, called a series-wound motor (Fig.

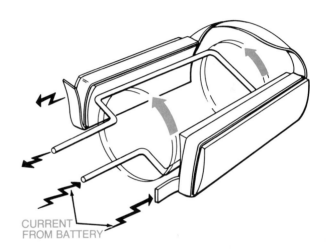

Fig. 26-3   Loop carrying current in the magnetic field is forced to turn.

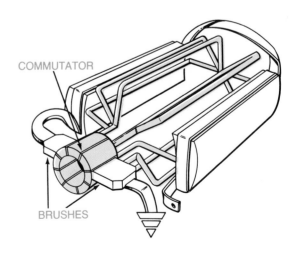

Fig. 26-4   Armature and brush assembly

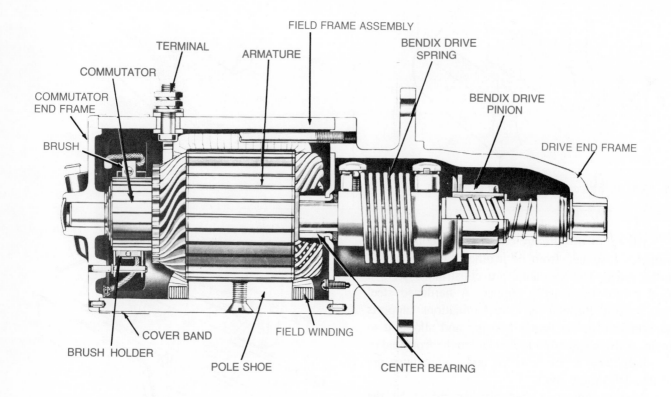

Fig. 26-5 Sectional view of starter motor with drive mechanism. (Delco-Remy Division, GMC)

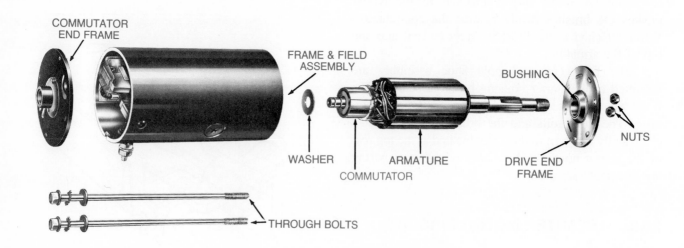

Fig. 26-6 Exploded view of starter motor parts.
(Delco-Remy Division, GMC)

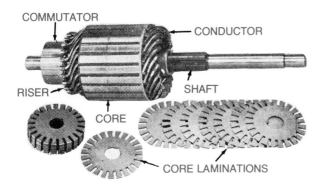

Fig. 26-7 Armature assembly. (Delco-Remy Division, GMC)

26-9), provides a great deal of cranking power. Current enters the starter motor from the battery at the terminal, passes through the field coils and enters the armature through the two insulated brushes. Current leaves the armature through the two grounded brushes.

The starter circuit (see Fig. 26-10) described above, with 4-field poles and 2-field windings, is referred to as a two-field, four-brush circuit. Since it uses only 2-field windings, its low resistance permits high current flow. The higher the current flow, the more power developed by the starter motor. Starter motors with four field windings are called 4-field, 4-brush circuits. These circuits provide a stronger magnetic field, for greater torque or cranking ability.

For heavy-duty diesel use, starter circuits may have as many as 6-field windings and 6 brushes. Most of these units use voltages higher than 12 volts. Regardless of the circuit design, all the conductors are constructed of heavy copper ribbon for low resistance and high current flow.

26.4   STARTER MOTOR DRIVES

When the engine is cranked, a small pinion gear mounted on the end of the starter armature shaft meshes with the teeth on the engine's flywheel ring gear (Fig. 26-11). The number of pinion teeth in relation to the number of ring gear teeth is given as a ratio. Usually, the ratio is 15:1. This means that the ring gear has 15 teeth for every tooth on the pinion. With this ratio, the starter motor can turn very fast and develop a great deal of turning effort or torque to crank the engine. Some high-compression engines require a higher ratio. This may be obtained with another set of gears in the starter motor.

VIEW WITH BRUSH HOLDER IN PLACE

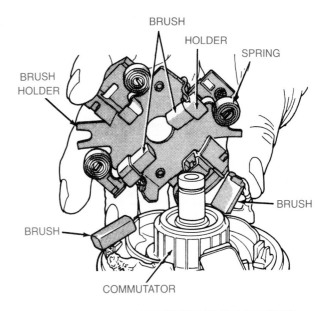

VIEW WITH BRUSH HOLDER REMOVED

Fig. 26-8   End frame and brush holder assembly. (Chrysler Corporation)

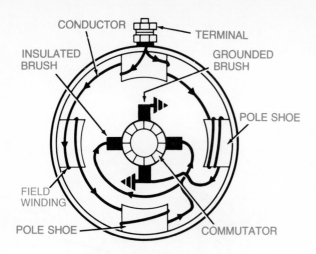

Fig. 26-9 Electrical schematic of a starter motor.

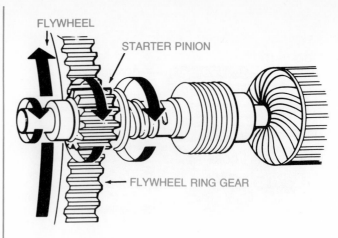

Fig. 26-11 Pinion meshes with flywheel ring gear.

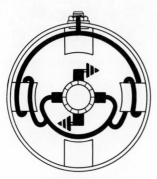

2 FIELD, 4 BRUSH

4 FIELD, 4 BRUSH

6 FIELD, 6 BRUSH

Fig. 26-10 Starter motor circuits (Delco-Remy Division, GMC)

The starter motor drive assembly gets the pinion into mesh with the flywheel ring gear to crank the engine and out of mesh when the engine begins to run. A 15:1 gear ratio is desirable when the pinion is turning the flywheel, but when the engine begins to run, the flywheel turns the pinion gear. The high gear ratio plus high engine speed would rotate the pinion and starter armature fast enough to destroy the starter motor. The starter motor drive assembly gets the pinion gear out of mesh or disconnects it from the armature shaft to protect the starter motor.

There are two types of starter motor drives for automotive use: The inertia drive and the overrunning clutch drive.

26.5   Inertia Drive

The inertia drive, sometimes called a Bendix drive, uses inertia to provide meshing and unmeshing of the pinion with the engine flywheel ring gear. The unit consists of a drive pinion, sleeve, spring and drive head (Fig. 26-12). The drive pinion has screw threads machined on its inner bore to match screw threads machined on the outside diameter of the hollow sleeve. The sleeve is placed loosely over the starter motor armature shaft. It is connected through the spring to the drive head, which is keyed to the armature shaft. This allows the sleeve to turn on the armature shaft within the limits permitted by flexing of the spring.

When the starter motor switch is closed, the armature shaft accelerates rapidly. The rotational force is transmitted from the armature to the drive head and through the spring to the sleeve. The pinion, which fits loosely on the threads of the sleeve, is

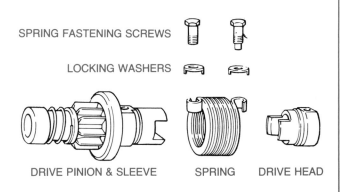

Fig. 26-12 Parts of the inertia drive. (Delco-Remy Division, GMC)

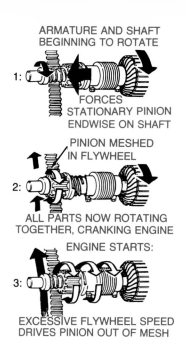

Fig. 26-13 Operation of the inertia drive. (Delco-Remy Division, GMC)

counterbalanced or unbalanced to prevent it from rotating. The threads between the pinion and the sleeve rotating inside the pinion cause the pinion to travel forward on the sleeve and into mesh with the flywheel ring gear.

When the pinion reaches the end of its travel, it contacts a stop on the sleeve. In this position there are no longer any threads for the pinion to slide on. It begins to rotate with the armature. In mesh with the flywheel ring gear, the pinion can crank the flywheel to start the engine.

When the engine starts, the pinion, in mesh with the flywheel ring gear, is driven at a higher speed than the armature and sleeve. The threads between the sleeve and pinion allow the pinion to travel back down the sleeve out of mesh with the flywheel ring gear. Figure 26-13 illustrates these stages of operation.

Several different kinds of inertia drive are in use. In the barrel inertia drive (Fig. 26-14), the pinion operates directly on the pinion shaft. This allows the use of a smaller pinion gear and a larger gear ratio between the pinion and flywheel ring gear for increased cranking torque. The inertia drive is made in an inboard and an outboard version with either right-hand or left-hand rotation.

26.6 Overrunning Clutch Drive

The overrunning clutch drive gets its name from a clutch it uses to protect the starter motor when the engine starts. The overrunning clutch drive uses a shift lever, operated electrically, to work the drive pinion. The pinion and overrunning clutch assembly are moved along the armature shaft into or out of mesh with the flywheel ring gear.

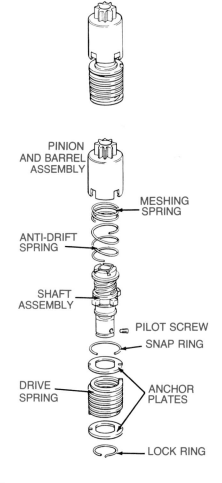

Fig. 26-14 Parts of the barrel inertia drive. (Delco-Remy Division, GMC)

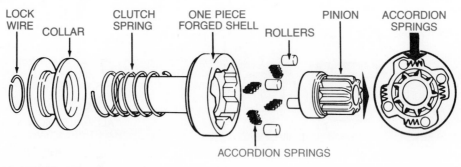

Fig. 26-15 Exploded view of overrunning clutch drive.
(Delco-Remy Division, GMC)

The shift lever engages a collar which pushes on the pinion and clutch assembly through a clutch spring. When the starter motor is energized, the clutch and pinion assembly moves along the armature shaft, pushed by the collar and spring. If the teeth of the flywheel and pinion do not line up, the pinion will not go into mesh. The spring on the drive will compress. When the pinion begins to rotate, the spring forces the pinion into mesh with the flywheel ring gear. When the engine starts, the armature must be protected from overspeeding until the pinion is unmeshed. This is the job of the overrunning clutch.

The overrunning clutch (Figs. 26-15 and 26-16) transmits the rotating force of the starter motor armature to the drive pinion to crank the engine. After the engine starts, it allows the drive pinion to rotate freely with respect to the drive assembly and the armature. The unit is constructed of a shell and sleeve assembly with internal splines that mesh with another set of splines on the armature shaft. The pinion is attached solidly to a collar that fits inside the shell. Notches in the shell contain hardened steel rollers that wedge between the collar and shell during cranking. The rollers force the pinion to rotate with the shell to crank the engine.

When the running engine drives the pinion faster than the armature can rotate, the rollers move into a larger part of the notch. Here they do not wedge the shell to the collar. The pinion can rotate freely without driving the armature. Small accordion or coil springs hold the rollers in the large section of the notch. When the starter motor switch is released, the shift mechanism pulls the pinion and overrunning clutch assembly back along the splines of the armature out of mesh with the flywheel ring gear.

26.7   SOLENOID

The solenoid (Figs. 26-17 and 26-18) is a magnetically operated switch that controls the circuit between the battery and the starter motor. Since the starter motor requires full battery current to operate, large cables must be used for current from the battery. These cables could go to the starter key switch on the steering column. However, their great length would add a high resistance to the circuit. Instead, the solenoid in the engine compartment acts as a remote control switch. When an overrunning clutch drive is used, the solenoid also shifts the pinion into and out of mesh with the flywheel ring gear.

26.8   Solenoid Operation

The solenoid is made up of a hollow coil wound around a movable plunger (Fig. 26-19). The unit is usually mounted on the top of the starter motor. When the driver turns the key switch to the start position, battery current goes to energize the solenoid. With the starter switch closed, battery current flows through two separate windings in the solenoid coil. One of the windings is called a pull-in, the other a hold-in winding. The two windings produce a magnetic field strong enough to pull in the plunger. Movement of the plunger shifts the pinion and closes the main contacts in the solenoid. When these contacts are closed, full battery current enters the starter motor.

Current from the starter switch enters the rear of the solenoid through a small terminal and flows through the pull-in and hold-in windings. The two windings have about the same number of turns, but the pull-in winding is a heavier wire. It must create a

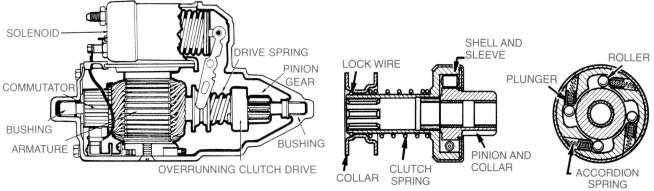

Fig. 26-16 Parts of overrunning clutch drive.
(Delco-Remy Division, GMC)

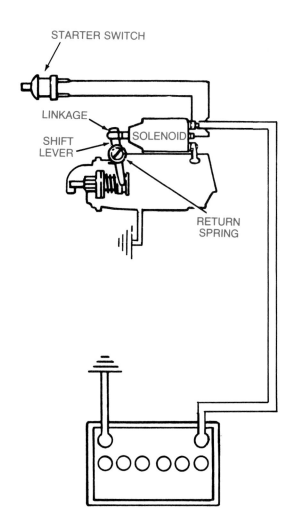

Fig. 26-17 Starter motor solenoid circuit.

strong enough magnetic field to pull the plunger into the coil. The air gap between the coil and plunger is small enough that the hold-in winding can hold the plunger in position. The pull-in winding is connected across the main contacts so that once the plunger is in, the heavy current draw through the pull-in winding is shorted out.

The plunger is attached by linkage to a shift lever that rides in the collar of the overrunning clutch drive. As the plunger is pulled in, it moves the shift lever, which pushes the drive assembly forward so the pinion meshes with the flywheel ring gear.

Plunger movement also closes the main solenoid contacts. At the rear of the solenoid (Fig. 26-20) are two large terminals. One terminal is connected to a short, heavy wire that enters the starter motor. The other terminal is connected to a heavy battery cable. Each of the terminals is attached to a large contact in the solenoid. When the plunger is pulled in, it pushes a copper disk back against the two large contacts. This closes the circuit between the two contacts. Battery current can flow across the disk and into the starter motor. The starter motor can then crank the engine.

When the engine starts, the driver moves the key switch to the run position. The circuit between the battery and the solenoid coil is broken. A return spring on the shift lever pulls the plunger out of the solenoid coil. A spring on the disk pulls it away from the contacts. The circuit between the battery and starter motor is broken.

26.9 Solenoids Used with Inertia Drive

Solenoids used on starter motors with inertia drive units do not shift the pinion into mesh. Their only job is to close the circuit between the battery and

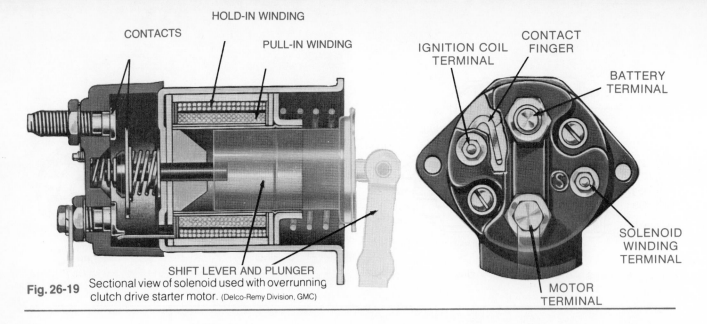

Fig. 26-19 Sectional view of solenoid used with overrunning clutch drive starter motor. (Delco-Remy Division, GMC)

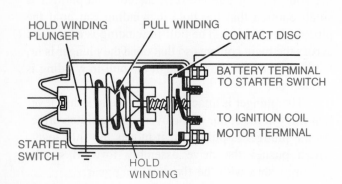

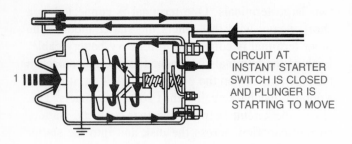

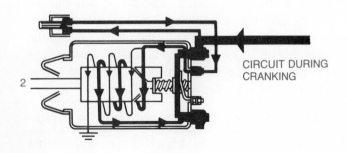

Fig. 26-18 Operation of a solenoid.

the starter motor. The solenoid for this kind of drive can be a simple magnetic switch mounted anywhere in the engine compartment (Fig. 26-21).

Many solenoids of this type use a single coil winding connected to the starter switch through a small terminal on the side of the unit. A large terminal is connected to the battery with a large cable. Another large terminal connects a heavy cable to the starter motor. The terminals are attached to large contacts inside the solenoid. When the key switch is turned to start, the coil inside the solenoid is energized. A small plunger is pulled into the magnetic field created by the coil. A contact disk attached to the plunger closes the circuit between the two contacts. Battery current flows in one terminal, across the disk, and out the terminal to the starter motor. The starter motor spins to crank the engine.

When the key switch is turned away from start, the magnetic field in the solenoid coil collapses. A return spring moves the plunger out of the coil. The contact disk is moved away from the contacts, breaking the circuit between the starter motor and battery.

26.10   STARTER MOTOR CONTROL SWITCHES

The driver controls the operation of the solenoid with the ignition key switch. The typical starting system also incorporates a neutral or clutch switch to prevent the engine from being started when the transmission is in gear.

The ignition switch is a multiple-purpose control device. As the name implies, its main function is to control the ignition circuit, but it also controls the starting system as well as providing power for

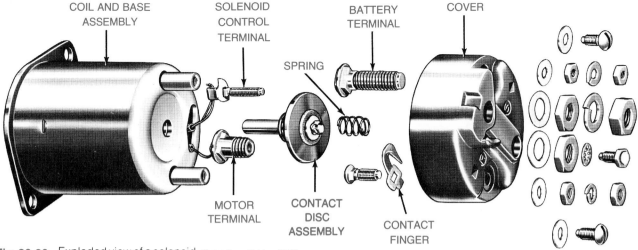

Fig. 26-20 Exploded view of a solenoid. (Delco-Remy Division, GMC)

the instruments and vehicle accessories. There are two types of ignition switches in use. The older type was a rotating contact switch, directly operated by the ignition key and physically located in the instrument panel. The newer switch, which is used with the locking-type of steering column, is usually mounted on the column and operated remotely from the ignition key through a linking rod. With this remote switch, connections are made by means of contacts which slide as the key is rotated through its detented positions.

The neutral switch is located between the ignition switch and the solenoid. When the vehicle is in gear, the safety switch is open so that the cranking motor will not operate. When the vehicle is in neutral or park, the neutral safety switch is closed so that the cranking motor can operate. For automatic transmissions, the vehicle will start only in neutral or park. The neutral safety switch is located either on the steering column or on the engine side of the firewall.

The neutral or clutch start switch on manual transmissions operates the same way as the safety switch on automatic transmissions. It is located either under the dashboard, or it is attached to the clutch linkage under the vehicle.

26.11 DIESEL STARTING SYSTEMS

The diesel engine, because of its compression ignition, has a problem with cold starts. When the engine is first cranked, the air entering the engine is cold. The compression stroke increases the air temperature, but the cold combustion chamber absorbs a great deal of the heat. The result may be

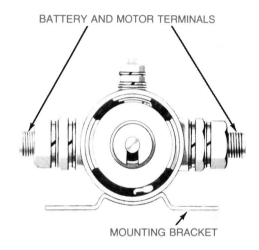

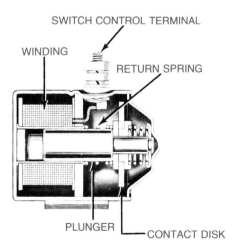

Fig. 26-21 Sectional view of magnetic switch used with inertia drive starter motor. (Delco-Remy Division, GMC)

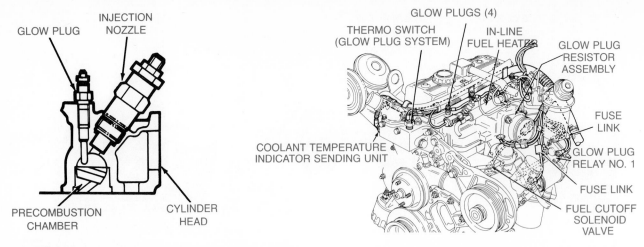

Fig. 26-22 Cross-sectional view of cylinder head showing a glow plug. (Ford Motor Company)

Fig. 26-23 Glow plug electrical system. (Ford Motor Company)

that the air temperature is still lower than that required for ignition. This problem is, of course, much worse in cold weather conditions.

A common solution to the cold start problem is to use a preheating system. A preheating system incorporates a set of glow plugs. The glow plug is an electrically heated wire filament that fits into the combustion chamber as shown in the cylinder head cross section in Figure 26-22. The heating element is enclosed in a tube of heat-resistant steel. The element is insulated in a fine magnesium oxide powder.

A glow plug is used in each cylinder of the engine. They are connected electrically as shown in Figure 26-23. When the driver turns the ignition key to *run*, a wait lamp lights up on the instrument panel. During this time, the glow plugs are supplied current and heat up to a cherry red. The combustion chamber area is heated. When the wait lamp goes off, the combustion chambers are warm enough for starting. After the engine is started, the glow plugs remain on for a short time, then automatically turn off.

NEW TERMS

Armature assembly   A part of the starter motor that is rotated by a magnetic field.

Brushes   The sliding contacts that deliver battery current into the rotating armature.

Field winding   The part of the starter motor that creates a magnetic field.

Glow plugs   Heating elements installed in the combustion chamber of a diesel engine to warm the combustion chamber and help the engine start.

Overrunning clutch drive   A starter motor drive that uses an overrunning clutch to disconnect the drive pinion from the flywheel ring gear.

Pinion   The gear driven by the starter motor that rotates the flywheel.

Ring gear   The gear formed by the teeth on the outside of the flywheel.

Solenoid   A magnetic switch that controls the circuit between the starter motor and battery.

Starter motor   The electric motor powered by the battery that cranks the engine to start it.

Starter motor drive   The system that disconnects the starter from the engine flywheel when the engine is running.

Starting system   The system that cranks the engine to start it.

CHAPTER REVIEW

1. What are the two major parts of a starter motor?
2. What is the purpose of the field winding assembly?
3. What is the purpose of the armature assembly?
4. What is a commutator?
5. How are the brushes held against the commutator?
6. Why is the starter motor called a series-wound motor?
7. What is the advantage of a 4-field, 4-brush starter circuit?

DISCUSSION TOPICS AND ACTIVITIES

1. Disassemble a starter motor and identify all the parts.
2. Disassemble a solenoid. Try to identify the parts and explain its operation.

CHAPTER 27

Starting System Service

CHAPTER PREVIEW

Starting system troubles are indicated by three conditions: the starter motor spins but does not crank the engine; the starter motor cranks the engine too slowly; the starter motor will not crank over the engine.

If a starter motor spins but will not crank the engine, the problem is in the drive mechanism. Other signs of starter drive problems are noisy engagement or a starter motor that will not disengage after the engine is started. The starter motor must be removed from the engine for inspection of the drive assembly.

OBJECTIVES

After studying this chapter, you should be able to do the following:

1. Follow troubleshooting procedures to find out what is wrong with a starting system.
2. Describe how starter motors are tested.
3. Explain the disassembly, repair, and reassembly procedures for starter motors.
4. Describe how starter motor drives are inspected and serviced.
5. Explain the steps in servicing a solenoid.

27.1   TROUBLESHOOTING

A step-by-step check of the starting system is required if the starter motor will not crank the engine at all or if it cranks too slowly. A number of visual and electrical checks should be made to locate the trouble before removing any unit.

27.2   Battery

The battery is the heart of the starting system. A defective, discharged, or undersized battery will cause starting system difficulties. The battery must be thoroughly tested and inspected following the procedures in Chapter 25 on the storage battery.

27.3   Wiring and Cables

The starting system wiring should be inspected for broken insulation or other damage. Inspect all connections at the starter motor, solenoid, and key switch. Clean and tighten as required. Replace all bad wiring. Inspect the battery cables for corrosion. Poor cable contact cuts off current to the starter. Clean, tighten, or replace the cables as necessary. Most starter testers provide insulated circuit test and the ground circuit test procedures. These test the resistance in the wiring and cables.

27.4   Solenoid and Control Switches

A bad solenoid or starter key switch with too much resistance can prevent the starting system from working. Most vehicles with automatic transmission have a neutral safety switch mounted between the starter key switch and the starter solenoid. While the transmission selector lever is in gear, this switch will not allow the starter circuit to be completed. A broken or incorrectly adjusted neutral safety switch can prevent the engine from cranking.

The quickest way to test whether a switch is the cause of a problem is to bypass it. Connect a jumper

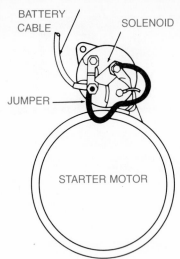

Fig. 27-1   Bypassing a solenoid to test it.

Fig. 27-2   Starter motor amperage draw tester.
(Sun Electric Corporation)

lead around any control switch suspected of being defective. If the system operates properly when the switch is bypassed, replace or repair the switch. If the starter motor will not crank the engine at all, the problem may be too much resistance in the solenoid contacts. Bypass the solenoid by connecting a heavy jumper lead across the main terminals (Fig. 27-1). Attach one end of the jumper to the battery terminal of the solenoid, the other at the starter motor terminal. This will allow battery current to flow directly into the starter motor. If the motor spins, the solenoid will have to be repaired or replaced.

27.5   Starter Motor

The first step in checking the starter motor is a visual inspection. Make sure that the starter motor is solidly mounted to the engine. If possible, remove the starter motor cover band and inspect for thrown solder, loose connections, worn brushes, or dirty commutator. If any of these conditions are found, remove the starter motor for service.

If the engine will not crank at all and all the checks described above fail to uncover the problem, remove the starter motor for further testing. If the engine cranks too slowly, the starter motor may be tested on the vehicle.

27.6   STARTER MOTOR TESTING

The condition of the starter motor may be found by the starter motor amperage draw test. The amperage draw test measures how much current the starter motor uses or draws. The amount of current a starter motor should draw may be found in the service specification for the vehicle being serviced. In general, starter motors for small engines draw around 100–150 amps. Starter motors for large engines draw as much as 300 amps.

Several electrical test equipment manufacturers make a starter motor amperage draw tester (Fig. 27-2). It is usually combined with a battery load tester. The tester consists of an ammeter, a voltmeter, and a loading device called a carbon pile along with instructions for hookup and test procedure. The starter motor is operated and the amount of current it uses is noted on the tester's ammeter. The starter motor should never be operated any longer than 15 seconds at a time without pausing to allow it to cool for at least 2 minutes. Too much cranking can cause overheating and serious damage to the starter motor.

The starter motor amperage draw test may be done with the starter motor on or off the vehicle. When it is tested on the automobile, the engine must be at normal operating temperature. Any mechanical problem with the engine that would make it hard to crank would affect the test. If such a problem is suspected, try to rotate the engine by hand.

The starter motor amperage draw may be measured with the starter motor off the vehicle. This test, called free running or no-load amperage draw, is useful in troubleshooting a problem in the starter motor or checking an overhauled starter motor. Manufacturer's specifications for this test will, of course, be different from those used when the starter motor is mounted to the engine. When the starter motor is removed from the engine, check the armature shaft for freedom of operation by turning the pinion by hand. Dirty or worn bearings, bent armature shaft, or a loose pole shoe screw will make the armature

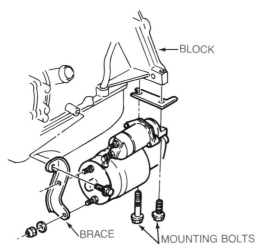

Fig. 27-3 Removing the starter motor. (Chevrolet Motor Division, GMC)

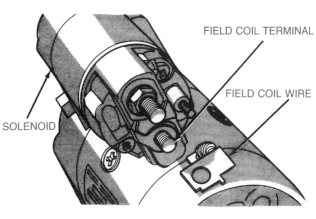

Fig. 27-4 Disconnecting the field coil wire. (Chrysler Corporation)

drag. If the armature shaft does not turn freely, the starter motor need not be tested. It should be disassembled for repair.

High amperage draw may indicate a mechanical or an electrical problem. Any condition that prevents free armature rotation, such as a bent shaft, worn bearings, or loose pole shoes, will cause the unit to draw excessive current. A shorted armature or field circuit is a typical electrical problem that causes a high amperage draw. A starter motor may draw excessive current but not rotate on the free running test. This is often the result of a direct ground at the brushes or at the field connections.

An unusually low amperage draw along with slow cranking speed is a sign of high resistance within the starter motor. One of the field windings may be open, reducing the amount of current draw. This also reduces the magnetic field so that not enough turning effort or torque is developed. A starter motor that does not operate and does not draw any current has an open circuit. The open may be in the fields, in the armature, at the connections of the brushes, or between the brushes and commutator.

27.7 STARTER MOTOR SERVICE

High or low amperage draw means the starter motor must be disassembled for service. Disassembly and reassembly procedures are different for different starter motors. Following are general instructions for overrunning clutch starter motors. Manufacturer's service procedures and specifications should be located and followed.

27.8 Starter Motor Removal

Use battery pliers and a terminal puller to remove the ground cable from the battery. If necessary, lift the vehicle with a hydraulic jack and stands or a hydraulic lift. **Safety Caution: Do not work on the starter until the battery is disconnected or you could be injured by an accidental cranking.**

If there is a heat shield on the side of the motor, you must remove it. Remove the cables and wires from the solenoid. Put the nuts back onto the terminals so you will not lose them. Remove the mounting bolts from the cranking motor and remove any brackets (Fig. 27-3). Remove the cranking motor by pulling the front end down slightly, then pull the cranking motor forward and out.

27.9 Starter Motor Disassembly

The solenoid must be removed from the starter motor. The solenoid terminal nut or screw must be removed and the wire disconnected before you can remove the solenoid from the starter motor (Fig. 27-4). Use a screwdriver to remove the mounting screws from the solenoid (Fig. 27-5). Rotate the solenoid about one-fourth of a circle in either direction. Disconnect the solenoid from the cranking motor by working the solenoid hook off the starter shift lever.

Remove the two screws and remove the end frame bearing cap, if used. Then remove the end frame bearing washer or washers. Remove two starter through bolts and then pull off the end frame (Fig. 27-6). Locate the two brushes which are connected to the field windings. Disengage the brush

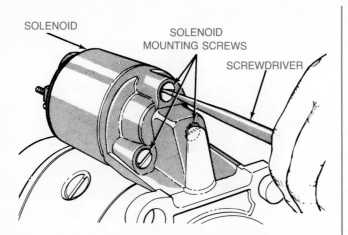

Fig. 27-5 Removing the solenoid mounting screws. (Chrysler Corporation)

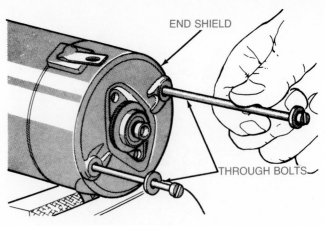

Fig. 27-6 Removing the through bolts. (Chrysler Corporation)

springs, then pull the two brushes out of their holders. Pull the brush plate off the commutator. Leave the ground brushes in their holders. Slide the field frame assembly (center housing) off the starter motor armature as shown in Figure 27-7.

Remove the clutch shift lever pivot bolt from the drive end housing as shown in Figure 27-8. Remove the overrunning clutch drive snap ring with snap ring pliers. Remove the overrunning clutch drive from the armature shaft as shown in Figure 27-9. Pull the drive end housing off the armature.

27.10   Starter Motor Inspection and Repair

Visually inspect the starter motor brushes for wear. If they are worn down to half their original length (compare with a new brush), they should be replaced. Make sure the brush holders are clean and the brushes are not binding in the holders. The full brush surface should ride on the commutator with proper spring tension (refer to test specifications) to give good, firm contact. Brush leads and screws should be tight and clean.

The armature should be checked for three common electrical problems, short circuits, opens, and grounds.

Short circuits in the armature are located by rotating the armature in a growler with a steel strip such as a hacksaw blade held on the armature (Fig. 27-10). The steel strip will vibrate on the area of the short circuit. Shorts between segments are sometimes produced by brush dust or copper between

them. Undercutting the insulation will eliminate these shorts.

Opens may be located by inspecting the points where the conductors are joined to the commutator for loose connections. Poor connections cause arcing and burning of the commutator. If the segments are not badly burned, resolder the leads in the riser segments and turn the commutator down in a lathe. Then undercut the insulation between the commutator segments 1/32 inch.

Grounds in the armature can be detected with a test lamp. If the lamp lights with one test prod on the commutator and the other test prod on the armature core or shaft, the armature is grounded (Fig. 27-11). If the commutator is worn, dirty, out of round, or has high insulation, the commutator should be turned down and undercut.

The field coils should be checked for grounds and opens with a test lamp. Disconnect field coil ground connections. Connect one test prod to the field frame and the other to the field connector. If the lamp lights, the field coils are grounded and must be repaired or replaced.

Connect test lamp prods to the ends of the field coils. If the lamp does not light, the field coils are open. To remove them for repair or replacement, use a pole shoe spreader and pole shoe screwdriver. Care should be taken in replacing the field coils to prevent grounding or shorting them as they are tightened into place. Where the pole has a long lip on the side, it should be assembled in the direction of armature rotation.

The armature and field windings must not be cleaned in any grease-dissolving solution or by any

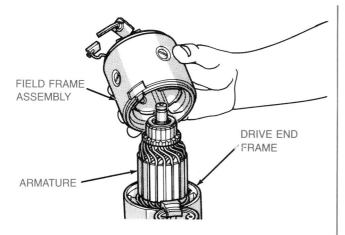

Fig. 27-7 Removing the field frame assembly. (Chrysler Corporation)

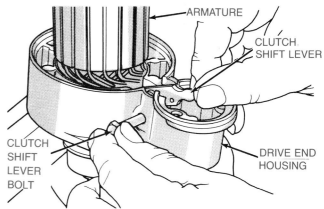

Fig. 27-8 Removing the shift lever bolt. (Chrysler Corporation)

high-temperature grease-removing method, since this will damage the insulation. Special solvents are available for cleaning electrical components.

27.11 Starter Drive Inspection and Service

A defective drive may be the problem if the starter motor spins but does not crank the engine. Other signs of starter motor drive problems are noisy engagement or a starter motor that will not disengage after the engine is started. If any of these problems occur, the starter motor must be removed from the engine for inspection.

Clean the drive assembly by wiping with a dry rag. The overrunning clutch has a high-temperature lubricant packed into it during manufacture. Cleaning the unit with high-temperature or grease-removing methods would remove the lubricant and cause rapid clutch failure.

After cleaning, inspect each part of the drive assembly. If there are any chipped teeth on the pinion, inspect the ring gear on the flywheel. A damaged ring gear must be replaced. This requires removal of the transmission. The overrunning clutch may be tested by rotating the pinion. It should turn freely in one direction and lock up in the other. Any roughness in the clutch means too much wear. The clutch cannot be rebuilt. It must be replaced.

The most common source of problems in the inertia drive assembly is the drive spring. If an engine backfires with the pinion in mesh with the flywheel, the inertia spring is often broken or distorted. Another common problem occurs when the driver

has difficulty starting the engine. When the engine starts and then quits, it throws the inertia drive pinion out of mesh. As the engine stops, it often rocks back or rotates in the reverse direction for part of a revolution. Should the driver reengage the drive mechanism while the engine is rocking back, the inertia spring will be damaged. It is good practice to allow at least five seconds between attempts to crank.

Starter motor drive parts that show signs of wear must be replaced. Replacement parts are available for some drive mechanisms. Others must be replaced as a complete unit. Disassembly and reassembly procedures for the drive mechanism are in the manufacturer's service manuals.

After reassembly, the overrunning clutch drive requires a pinion clearance adjustment. The pinion clearance is the space between the pinion and the pinion retainer. Incorrect adjustment could cause the pinion to hang up or not mesh properly with the flywheel ring gear. On some units the adjustment is made by sliding the solenoid backward or forward on its mounting bolts. Other starter motors use a threaded solenoid plunger. Refer to the manufacturer's service manual for specifications and adjustment procedures.

27.12 Starter Motor Reassembly

Install the drive end housing over the armature. Install the overrunning clutch drive with a new snap ring. Install the clutch shift lever assembly with the pivot bolt.

Slide the field frame (center housing) over the armature. Install new grounded brushes and the

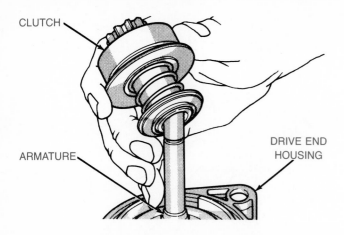

Fig. 27-9 Removing the overrunning clutch drive. (Chrysler Corporation)

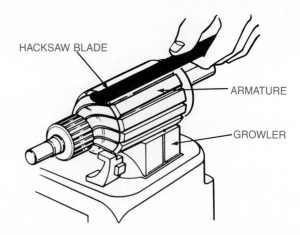

Fig. 27-10 Checking armature for short circuits on a growler.

brush plate over the commutator. Put in new field brushes and connect them. Install the end frame and through bolts and torque them to specifications. Install the end frame bearing washer or washers and the new "C" washer as shown in Figure 27-12. Install the end frame bearing cap.

Put the solenoid in position on the starter and hook the plunger on the shift lever. Install and tighten the two mounting screws with a screwdriver. Replace the terminal nut or screw. Seal the surface where the solenoid fits next to the starter with silicone compound.

27.13   Starter Motor Reinstallation

Put the cranking motor in place, and install the bolts and/or brackets. Torque the bolts to specifications. Reconnect the wires and the cables. If you removed a heat shield, put it back in place. Reconnect the ground battery cable. Check the starting motor for proper operation.

27.14   SOLENOID SERVICE

A bad solenoid can prevent full battery current from reaching the starter motor. On overrunning clutch starter motors a bad solenoid may prevent the pinion from being shifted into mesh with the flywheel ring gear. The solenoid may be bypassed with a jumper lead for troubleshooting (see Section 27-4). Most battery-starter testers include a test for solenoid circuit resistance. Manufacturers of solenoids usually provide procedures for testing the solenoid circuits with a voltmeter.

A common problem with solenoids is high resistance between the contact disk and the main contacts.

On some solenoids, the body may be disassembled and the disk and contacts removed and replaced. Many solenoids, however, are not rebuildable and must be replaced as a complete unit. Low system voltage or an open circuit in a hold-in winding may cause the plunger to oscillate or chatter. If this occurs, a check should be made for a complete circuit in the hold-in winding, and the battery condition should also be rechecked. Windings are nonreplaceable on most solenoids. A problem in the pull-in or hold-in winding will mean replacement of the solenoid.

NEW TERMS

Amperage draw test   A test of the amount of amperage that a starter motor draws or uses to crank the engine, indicating whether the starter motor is operating correctly.

Amperage draw tester   An electrical tester used to measure starter motor amperage draw.

Ground   An electrical problem in which current bypasses the normal circuit and goes directly to ground.

Open   A break or interruption in an electrical circuit.

Short   An electrical problem in which a circuit is completed so that current bypasses part of the normal circuit.

CHAPTER REVIEW

1. List the three conditions that may result from starting system problems.
2. Why must the battery be checked during a starting system test?

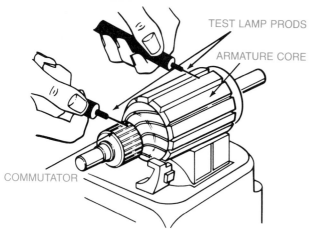

TEST LAMP PRODS

ARMATURE CORE

COMMUTATOR

Fig. 27-11 Testing the armature for grounds. (Delco-Remy Division, GMC)

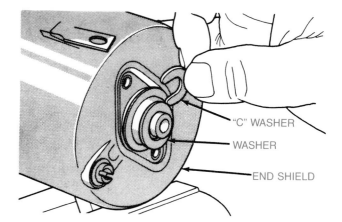

"C" WASHER

WASHER

END SHIELD

Fig. 27-12 Installing the new "C" washer. (Chrysler Corporation)

3. Why should wiring and cables be checked if there is a starting system problem?

4. What is the neutral safety switch?

5. Explain how to bypass a solenoid with a jumper to check it.

6. What is the first step in checking a starter motor?

7. What is a starter motor amperage draw test?

8. Why should a starter motor not be operated longer than 15 seconds when testing?

9. List the causes of a high amperage draw.

10. List the causes of a low amperage draw.

11. How can you tell whether starter motor brushes need replacing?

12. What is an electrical open?

13. What is an electrical short?

14. What is an electrical ground?

15. What is a common problem with solenoids?

DISCUSSION TOPICS AND ACTIVITIES

1. List the troubleshooting steps to find a problem in a starting system.

2. Use a shop engine and tester to measure the amperage draw of a starter motor. What were the results?

3. Disassemble a defective starter and try to locate the problem. Could you fix it?

The Charging System

The engine's charging system provides current to recharge the battery. It also develops electricity to power all the electrical components when the engine is running. The charging system consists of an alternator or A-C generator and a voltage regulator. The alternator generates the electricity required and the regulator controls the system.

OBJECTIVES

After studying this chapter, you should be able to do the following:

1. Identify the main components and explain the purpose of the alternator.
2. Describe how alternating current is changed to direct current in an alternator.
3. Explain how current is regulated in the charging system.
4. Explain how voltage is regulated in the charging system.
5. Describe the operation of the mechanical, transistorized, and integral charging system regulators.

28.1   ALTERNATOR OPERATION

A simple alternator may be constructed from a conductor and a bar magnet. A conductor, called a stator because it is stationary, is formed into a loop and connected to a light bulb (Fig. 28-1). A voltage is induced in the stator by placing a magnet in its center

(Fig. 28-2). As the magnet is rotated, the magnetic lines of force cut across the conductor. A voltage is induced in the stator that lights the bulb. Since the magnet in an alternator rotates, it is called a rotor.

28.2   Principles of Operation

As the rotor turns inside the stator, current flows to the light bulb first in one direction and then in the other. As shown in Figure 28-3 (a), when the magnet's south pole is directly under the top of the loop and its North pole is directly over the bottom, the induced voltage causes current to flow through the loop in the direction shown by the arrows. Since current flows from negative to positive through the light bulb, the end of the wire marked "A" will be positive (+), and the end marked "B" will be negative (−).

When the rotor has moved through one-half revolution, as shown in Figure 28-3 (b), the North pole is directly under the top of the loop and the South pole directly over the bottom. The induced voltage now causes current to flow in the opposite direction. The end of the wire marked "A" is now negative (−), and the end marked "B" is positive (+). After a second one-half revolution, the magnet is back at the starting point where "A" is positive (+) and "B" is negative (−).

When current flows in just one direction through a wire it is called direct current, abbreviated DC. The current developed by our simplified alternator is alternating current, abbreviated AC. Since automobile electrical equipment is designed to operate on direct current, the alternating current developed by the alternator must be changed to direct current. The

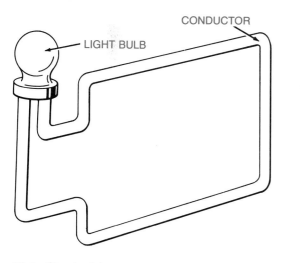

Fig. 28-1 Simple stator

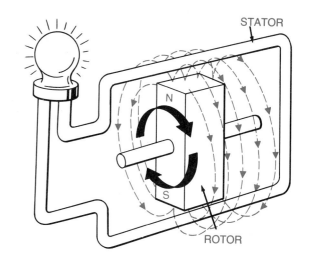

Fig. 28-2 The rotor and stator generate voltage.

changing of alternating current to direct current is called rectification.

28.3 Boosting Voltage

In order to power all the electrical equipment on an automobile, an alternator must develop much more voltage than our simple model. There are a number of ways to make the alternator more efficient. One is to wrap wire around the rotor magnet and send current through the wire to make the rotor an electromagnet (Fig. 28-4). The wire wrapped around the magnet is called the field winding. Since the rotor turns, current from the battery enters the field winding through sliding contacts called brushes. The brushes ride on round conductors called slip rings. Each end of the field winding is attached to a slip ring. Current from the battery flows through one brush and slip ring, through the field winding, and then to the battery through the other slip ring and brush. The more turns, or times the wire is wrapped around the magnet, the stronger the magnetic field.

The operation of the alternator is improved by placing the stator and the rotor assembly inside an iron frame or housing (Fig. 28-5). The frame provides a conducting path for the magnetic lines of force. Without it, magnetism leaving the N pole of the rotor must travel through air to get to the S pole. Because air has a high reluctance, much of the force coming out of the North pole is lost. Surrounding the rotor and stator with a housing decreases the reluctance. More lines of force cut the conductor and more voltage is developed.

Figure 28-6 shows the different positions of the rotor through one complete cycle or revolution. The

(a) FIRST HALF REVOLUTION

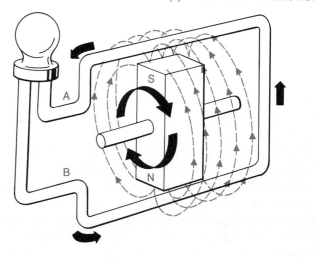

(b) SECOND HALF REVOLUTION

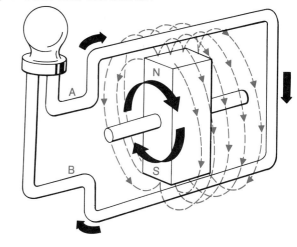

Fig. 28-3 Current flows first one direction and then the other.

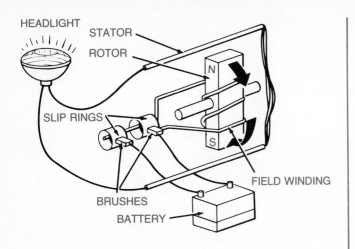

Fig. 28-4 Simple alternator with a field winding.

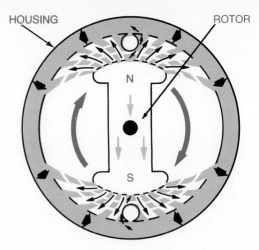

Fig. 28-5 Iron housing increases magnetic lines of force. (Ford Motor Company)

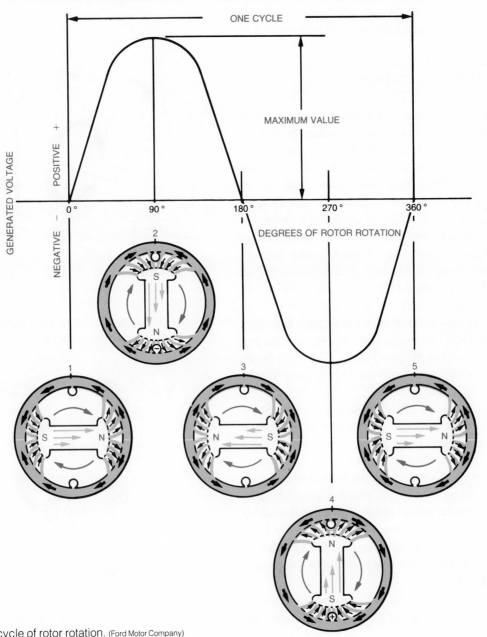

Fig. 28-6 One cycle of rotor rotation. (Ford Motor Company)

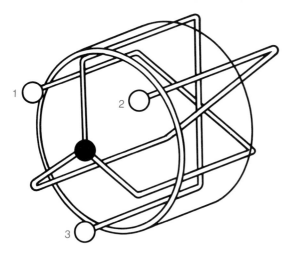

Fig. 28-7 Three-phase stator. (Ford Motor Company)

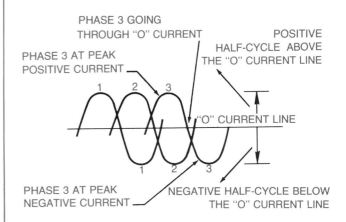

Fig. 28-8 Output from a three-phase stator. (Ford Motor Company)

curve at the top of the illustration shows the amount of generated voltage. When the rotor is in position (1), no voltage is generated in the stator because no magnetic lines of force are being cut. As the rotor turns toward position (2), the weak magnetic field at the edge of the rotor starts to cut across the conductor and voltage increases. When the rotor reaches position (2), the generated voltage has reached its peak. In this position, the stator is being cut by the largest number of magnetic lines of force.

As the rotor continues its revolution, the voltage drops off until at position (3) it again becomes zero. When the rotor turns from position (3) to position (4), voltage is again developed. Since the North pole of the rotor is now passing under the top of the stator, the current flow changes direction. This is shown by the voltage curve's change of direction.

Up to this point, the stator of the simplified alternator has been made of one loop or winding of wire. The voltage can be greatly increased if the stator winding is formed into many coils or turns. A stator consisting of one winding, regardless of the number of coils of wire in that winding, is called a single-phase stator. Another way to improve alternator performance is to have more than one winding spaced around the stator. This allows the magnetic lines of force of the rotor to cut across a stator winding more times during each revolution. Most alternators use three windings, which is called a three-phase stator (Fig. 28-7). Each stator winding is called a phase. Since the connection of the windings is shaped like a Y, the stator winding is called a three-phase, Y-connected stator.

The three-phase stator develops current in each of the three windings as shown in the voltage graph in Figure 28-8. With a three-phase stator, therefore, more voltage can be developed during each revolution of the rotor. Another advantage of the three windings is that voltage is more even between phases. The windings are so placed that each phase reaches its highest voltage at a different time.

Rotor speed affects the amount of voltage created in an alternator. The faster the rotor turns, the more voltage is induced in the stator because lines of force from the rotor cut across the stator windings more often in a given period of time.

28.4 ALTERNATOR CONSTRUCTION

An alternator (Figs. 28-9 and 28-10) consists of a rotor assembly, a stator assembly, and a rectifier mounted in a housing. The housing is usually made up of two pieces of die-cast aluminum. Aluminum is used because it is a nonmagnetic, lightweight material that provides good heat dissipation. Bearings supporting the rotor assembly are mounted in the front and rear housing. The front bearing is usually pressed into the front housing or onto the rotor shaft. It is usually a factory-lubricated ball bearing. The rear bearing is usually installed with a light press fit in the rear housing.

The stator is clamped between the front and the rear housing. A number of steel stampings are riveted together to form its frame. Three windings around the stator frame are arranged in layers in each of the slots on the frame. The three windings are joined together at one end. At the other end, identified in Figure 28-11 as A, B, and C, they are connected into the rectification assembly.

The rotor assembly (Fig. 28-12) consists of a rotor shaft, a winding around an iron core, two pole

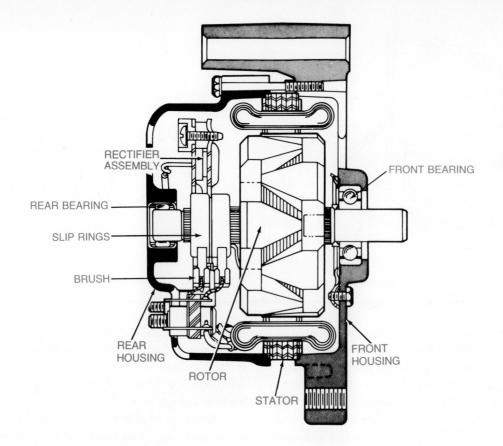

Fig. 28-9 Sectional view of an alternator. (Ford Motor Company)

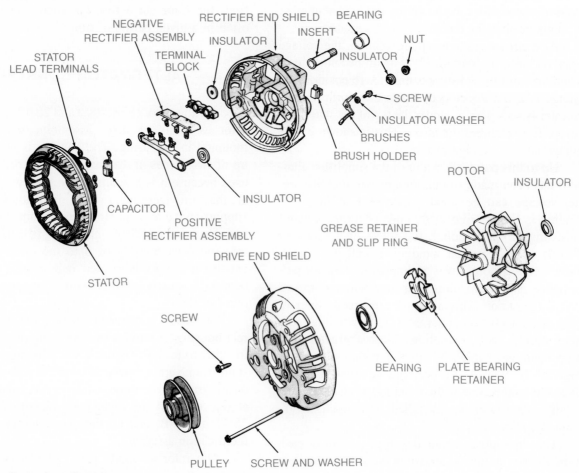

Fig. 28-10 Parts of an alternator. (Chrysler Corporation)

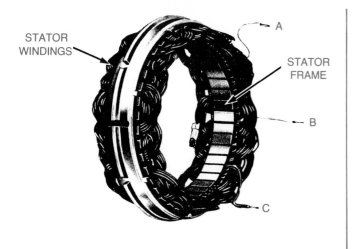

Fig. 28-11 Stator assembly. (Delco-Remy Division, GMC)

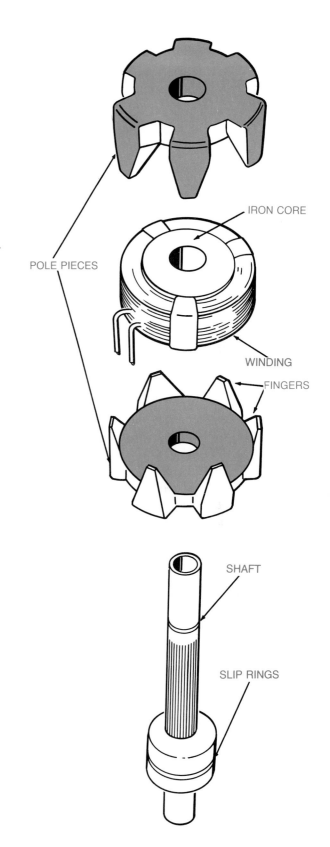

Fig. 28-12 Rotor assembly. (Ford Motor Company)

pieces, and slip rings. The rotor shaft is pressed into the core. Six-fingered, malleable, iron pole pieces are pressed onto the shaft against each end of the winding core. They are placed so that the fingers mesh but do not touch. When direct current is passed through the field coil winding, the fingers become alternately north and south poles. A slip ring assembly is pressed onto the rear end of the rotor shaft and connected to the two ends of the field winding.

Two brushes are held against the slip rings by springs, usually mounted in plastic brush holders that support the brushes and prevent brush sticking. Each brush is connected into the circuit by a flexible copper lead wire. The brushes ride on the slip rings and are connected through a switch to the battery (Fig. 28-13). When the switch is closed, current from the battery passes through one brush, through the slip ring, and then through the field winding. After leaving the field winding, current flows through the other slip ring and brush before returning to the battery through the ground return path. The flow of electrical energy through the field winding, called field current, creates the magnetic field for the rotor.

The rectifier assembly consists of six diodes mounted either in the rear housing or in a separate small housing called a rectifier bridge. Three of the diodes are connected to ground and three are mounted in an insulator. Since the mounting assembly carries off heat caused by diode operation, it is often called a heat sink.

A fan and pulley assembly is either pressed onto the rotor shaft or held with a nut. The pulley drives the rotor through an engine accessory drive belt. The fan behind the alternator pulley pulls air in through vents at the rear of the alternator to cool the diodes (Fig. 28-14).

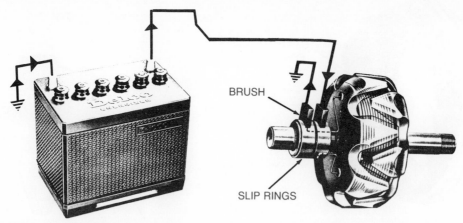

Fig. 28-13 Current flow from battery into the field. (Delco-Remy Division, GMC)

BRUSH

SLIP RINGS

28.5 CHANGING ALTERNATING CURRENT TO DIRECT CURRENT

Automotive electrical equipment is made to operate on direct current. The alternating current developed by the alternator must therefore be changed or rectified to direct current. The rectifier system of an alternator consists of six diodes. A diode, discussed in chapter 23, is a tiny semiconductor device that allows current to flow freely in one direction but offers extremely high resistance to current flow in the opposite direction.

Figure 28-15 shows a diode in a simple circuit with an alternator and a light bulb. When current flows from the alternator in the direction shown in Figure 28-15 (a), the diode allows the current to complete its path back to the alternator. The complete circuit lights the bulb. Further rotation of the rotor inside the alternator induces current in the opposite direction. Since the diode does not allow current flow in this direction, there is not a complete circuit and the light bulb does not light, as shown in Figure 28-15 (b).

The alternating current from a three-phase stator could be connected to a rectifier that would allow current flowing in one direction to go to the battery but prevent current flow in the other direction. This would be called half-wave rectification because only half of the current developed by the alternator would be used.

In order to use all the current developed, alternators are designed to use full-wave rectification. Full-wave rectification is made possible by connecting two diodes to each of the three-stator windings (Fig. 28-16). A complete rectifier has six diodes.

Three of the diodes are negative and are connected to ground. The other three diodes are positive and are connected to the battery through the output terminal at the rear of the alternator.

To understand how the rectification takes place it will be necessary to study a wiring diagram of a stator and rectifier connected to a battery. The diagram of a stator winding shown in Figure 28-17 is the standard symbol for the windings of a three-phase Y-connected stator.

A complete stator and rectifier circuit connected to a battery is shown in Figure 28-18. The diagram identifies the negative diodes in the rectifier as N1, N2, N3, and the positive diodes as P1, P2, and P3. Figure 28-19 shows one phase of the stator being cut by a pair of rotor poles. At this point in the rotor's rotation, current is induced to flow away from the Y connection toward the diodes. This stator phase is connected to the terminal lead of one positive diode (P2) and one negative diode (N2). The current is blocked by the negative diode and must pass through the positive diode. The other two positive diodes (P1 and P3) prevent the current from reversing itself, so that all the current must pass through the output terminal and into the battery.

In order to have a complete circuit the current must return where it started; to the Y connection, the current passes through ground to the alternator housing. From this point, the current flows to the cases of three negative diodes. Current cannot pass through the negative diode (N2) because of the equal voltage acting on both sides of the N2 diode. Since the current cannot pass through the center diode, it must return through the two outside diodes, N1 and N3. The current flowing through diodes N1 and N3 is blocked

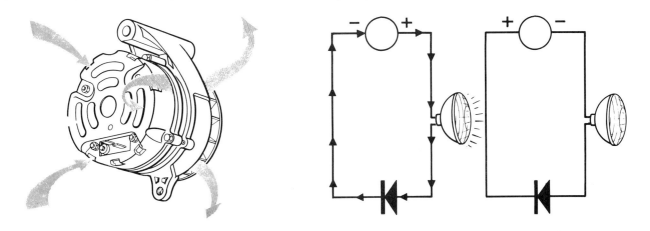

Fig. 28-14 Air flow from fan cools the diodes.
(Ford Motor Company)

Fig. 28-15 Diode allows current flow in only one direction.

TYPICAL STATOR WITH ONE
OF THREE WINDINGS INSTALLED

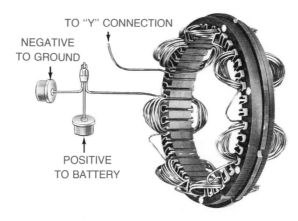

Fig. 28-16 Diodes connected to one stator winding.
(Chevrolet Motor Division, GMC)

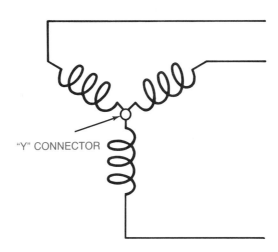

Fig. 28-17 Stator diagram. (Chevrolet Motor Division, GMC)

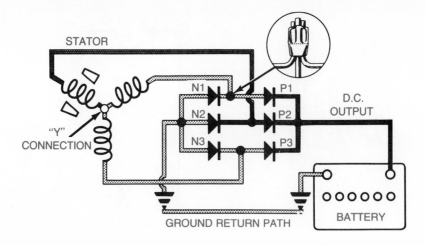

STATUS

N1 P1

N2 P2 D.C. OUTPUT

N3 P3

"Y" CONNECTION

GROUND RETURN PATH BATTERY

Fig. 28-18 One half phase of output. (Chevrolet Motor Division, GMC)

from passing through the positive diodes because of the voltage on both sides of the positive diodes. The two remaining stator phases act as the return path to the Y connection.

In Figure 28-19 the rotor has advanced until the north and south poles now affect the opposite sides of the stator winding. The induced current flow is now in the opposite direction toward the Y connection. The current flows through either or both of the remaining two stator windings and through the two outer positive diodes P1 and P3. From these diodes, the current passes to the battery output terminal and on to the battery. The current returns through the ground path and into the housing. At this point the return flow is blocked at the N1 and N3 negative diodes by the voltage on the opposite side. The only path available for the current is through the remaining diode N2 and back to where it began.

The operation described above completes one cycle of current flow. All three phases of the stator windings work together with all the poles of the rotor. The three phases and sets of rotor poles result in current that rises to its maximum value 21 times in each direction with every revolution of the rotor. The current developed in each phase overlaps with the output of the other phases. With both halves of the alternating cycle rectified by the diodes, the result is an almost constant flow of direct current at the output terminal (Fig. 28-20).

On some alternators, a condenser or capacitor is mounted in the rear housing and connected to the output terminal. The capacitor absorbs voltage surges induced in the stator windings each time the direction of current flow through these windings reverses.

28.6 REGULATION

The alternator develops voltage that causes current to flow. Too much current or voltage could damage the automobile's electrical system.

28.7 Current Regulation

The current developed by an alternator is regulated automatically using the principles of induction. Induction, as explained earlier, involves the transfer of energy from one object to another without the objects physically touching. When current flows through a coil, the lines of force cut across any coil next to that coil. If the current flow is stopped, the lines of force will induce a voltage in the other coil. The voltage induced is *opposite* to that in the first coil.

Two stator windings next to each other are shown in Figure 28-21. The main current flow developed by the rotor field cutting the stator windings is shown by the large arrows. The main current flow changes direction many times per second as the alternator develops current. The changing direction of the main current causes the lines of force to induce a voltage in the other windings. This smaller voltage is induced in a direction opposite to the main current flow. This opposing voltage limiting the amount of current that can flow is called inductive reactance.

The faster the current changes direction in the stator windings the more rapid the buildup and collapse of the induced magnetic field. This in turn increases the inductive reactance opposing current flow. The faster the rotor turns, the faster the current

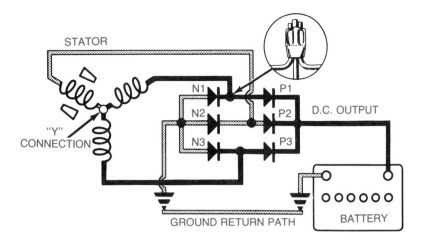

alternates in the stator windings and the more inductive reactance is created to oppose current flow. Increased rotor speed generates a higher voltage and tends to increase current flow in the stator windings. But, since inductive reactance also increases with rotor speed, the current output of the alternator is controlled automatically.

28.8 Voltage Regulation

The voltage developed by an alternator increases with the speed of the rotor. Enough voltage must be developed at low speeds to charge the battery and power all the electrical accessories. This voltage would increase enough at high speeds to overcharge the battery and damage the accessories. The job of the charging system regulator is to limit the alternator voltage.

The voltage regulator unit limits voltage by controlling the amount of rotor field current in the alternator. The more current that flows in the rotor field winding, the stronger the rotor's magnetic field. The stronger the magnetic field, the more lines of force that cut across the stator winding and the more voltage is induced. If the amount of field current is decreased at any given rotor speed, the voltage is decreased. If the field current is decreased as the alternator speed increases, a nearly constant voltage is produced.

A simplified circuit with a voltage regulator is shown in Figure 28-22. Current flow from the battery passes through the ignition switch and into the voltage regulator. The regulator determines the amount of current that enters the rotor field windings through the

brush and slip ring assembly. The more current the regulator allows to enter the rotor, the higher the alternator voltage. While all voltage regulators limit field current, there are three different types of regulators and regulator circuits: mechanical regulators, transistorized regulators, and integral regulators.

28.9 Mechanical Voltage Regulator

The mechanical voltage regulator (Fig. 28-23) controls alternator voltage by regulating current flow through the rotor windings. It consists of a magnetically operated switch that directs rotor field current through a resistance in order to lower alternator voltage. All current mechanical regulators use double contact points and are sometimes referred to as double-contact voltage regulators.

28.10 Field Relay

Many regulator units contain two magnetic switches, one for voltage regulation and another called a field relay (Fig. 28-24). The field relay is a single contact switch with a winding and armature assembly similar to that used on the voltage regulator. It closes a set of contacts when the field relay winding is working. A spring located between a movable armature and an iron frame causes the contacts to separate when the winding is not working. The purpose of the field relay is to disconnect the alternator field from the battery when the ignition switch is turned off.

When the engine ignition switch is turned off, spring tension on the relay armature separates the

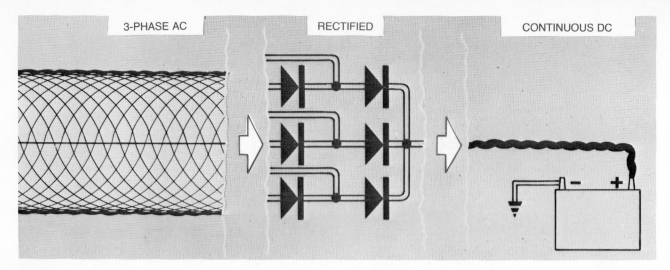

Fig. 28-20 Full-wave rectification. <small>(Chevrolet Motor Division, GMC)</small>

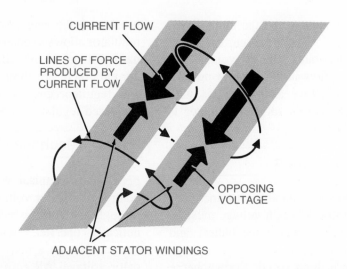

Fig. 28-21 Inductive reactance limits current flow.

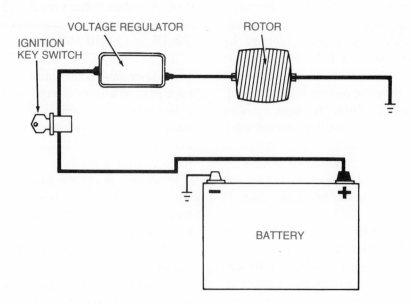

Fig. 28-22 Voltage regulator limits rotor field current.

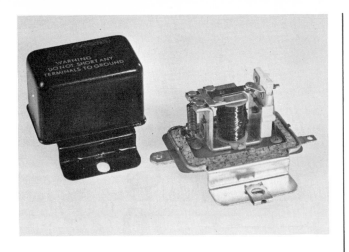

Fig. 28-23 Mechanical voltage regulator.

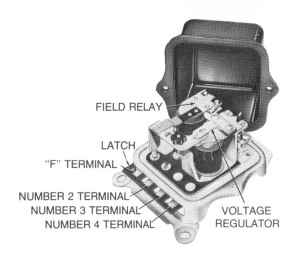

Fig. 28-24 Regulator with field relay. (Delco-Remy Division, GMC)

contact points. Battery current is prevented from passing through the relay and into the voltage regulator. When the ignition switch is turned on, current flows into the relay coil. The magnetic field surrounding the coil pulls the hinged armature down, closing the contact points. Current is then able to flow into the voltage regulator.

28.11   Transistorized Regulator

A mechanical regulator has some limitations. Vibrating contacts wear out after a period of time, so the regulator must be serviced or replaced periodically. The use of contacts also limits the amount of field current, which limits the output of the alternator. High current flow can cause arcing of the contacts, resulting in very short contact life. The transistorized regulator (Fig. 28-25) eliminates these problems because it has no moving parts. Instead, a number of transistors and diodes are used to limit the alternator field circuit.

28.12   Integral Regulator

An integral regulator (Fig. 28-26) is a voltage regulator mounted inside an alternator. Microminiature electronic equipment with parts too small to be seen without a microscope is used to make a voltage regulator small enough to be mounted inside the alternator. Since the unit is mounted inside the alternator, it is described as an integral regulator.

The unit is mounted in the rear housing of the alternator. Circuitry inside the integral regulator is essentially the same as in transistorized regulators. The regulator limits the generator voltage to a safe

amount by controlling the alternator field current. Like the transistorized regulator, it operates electronically to turn off and turn on the voltage in the field winding. This electronic switching can occur at a rate as low as 10 times per second and as high as 7,000 times per second. The integral regulator is capable of limiting the alternator output under all conditions of speed and electrical demand.

The chief advantage of an integral regulator is that a considerable amount of external wiring is eliminated. The mounting of the regulator inside the alternator also protects it from the moisture and oil in the engine compartment.

NEW TERMS

Alternating current   Electrical current that flows first in one direction and then the other.

Charging system   The automobile electrical system that charges the battery and provides the electrical power when the engine is running.

Current regulation   The limiting of the current developed by the alternator.

Direct current   Electrical current that flows in one direction.

Field relay   A magnetic switch in the regulator that controls the circuit between the voltage regulator and the battery.

Inductive reactance   An induced voltage that opposes current flow in the stator windings.

Integral regulator   A voltage regulator mounted inside the alternator.

Mechanical voltage regulator   A voltage regulator that uses magnetically controlled switches to control voltage.

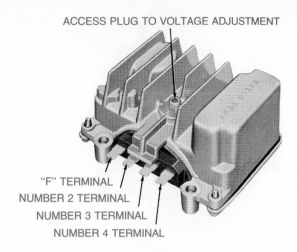

ACCESS PLUG TO VOLTAGE ADJUSTMENT

"F" TERMINAL
NUMBER 2 TERMINAL
NUMBER 3 TERMINAL
NUMBER 4 TERMINAL

Fig. 28-25 Transistorized regulator. (Delco-Remy Division, GMC)

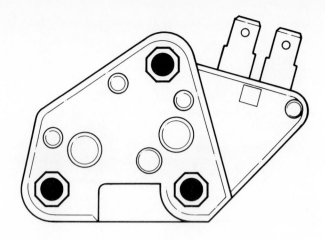

Fig. 28-26 Integral regulator. (Delco-Remy Division, GMC)

Rectifier The part of an alternator that changes alternating current to direct current.

Rotor assembly One of the major parts of an alternator in which a magnetic field is developed by a rotating magnet.

Slip rings A part of the rotor assembly on which brushes ride.

Stator assembly One of the major parts of an alternator in which the current is developed in a stationary coil.

Transistorized voltage regulator A voltage regulator that uses solid state components to limit voltage.

Voltage regulation The limiting of alternator output to a safe voltage.

CHAPTER REVIEW

1. What is the purpose of the charging system?
2. What is alternating current?
3. What is direct current?
4. What kind of current does the alternator develop?
5. Why is a three-phase stator used in the alternator?

6. What is the main job of the rotor in an alternator?
7. What is the main job of the stator in an alternator?
8. Where are the diodes located in an alternator?
9. What do the diodes do?
10. Explain how current is regulated inside the alternator.
11. What is the purpose of the voltage regulator?
12. How does the voltage regulator limit voltage?
13. Explain how a mechanical voltage regulator works.
14. What is a transistorized voltage regulator?
15. What is an integral voltage regulator?

DISCUSSION TOPICS AND ACTIVITIES

1. Explain how alternating current is changed to direct current in an alternator.
2. Disassemble a shop alternator. Can you identify the main parts?
3. Remove the cover from a shop mechanical voltage regulator. Find the voltage regulator switch. Work the switch by hand.

Charging System Service

The following conditions indicate problems in the charging system: a battery that is undercharged; a battery that is overcharged by the charging system; a charging system indicator lamp that stays on when the engine is running. This chapter will present the trouble-shooting testing, and service procedures necessary to repair the charging system.

OBJECTIVES

After studying this chapter, you should be able to do the following:

1. List the steps to find out what is wrong with the charging system.
2. Recognize the precautions that must be taken when servicing the charging system.
3. Explain how to test an alternator for output.
4. Describe the test procedures for charging system regulators.
5. Describe the service procedures for the alternator and regulator.

29.1   TROUBLESHOOTING

An undercharged battery cranks the engine too slowly. Specific gravity readings taken on the battery will be low. An undercharged condition may be caused by a problem in the charging system, but it may also be caused by a bad battery. For this reason, it is important to test the battery. Another possible cause for this condition is an unusual battery drain. A partly shorted wire or a bad switch or accessory may drain or discharge the battery when the automobile is parked. Most battery charging system testers have a test for finding out if there is a discharge current flowing when all accessories and lights are off.

A battery that is being overcharged will use large amounts of water. If water must be added to the battery very often, it is probably being overcharged. Overcharging causes violent gassing in the battery cells that results in rapid water loss and the strong smell of battery gas near the battery. A cracked battery case may also cause water loss but would probably not result in all the battery cells losing water.

The charging system indicator lamp lights up when the charging system is not working. If the light comes on when the engine is running, the driver is warned that there is a problem in the charging system, that the battery is not being charged. The charging system must be tested to find the source of the problem. It is also possible that the indicator lamp circuit itself may be bad.

When a vehicle has any of these problems, a systematic checkout of the charging system will be necessary. A number of checks, both visual and electrical, must be made to trace the trouble to a particular unit before removing any unit.

29.2   Alternator Drive Belt

A loose alternator drive belt can slip, causing the alternator to run at a lower speed and reduced output. Glazed, frayed, or worn spots on the belt also cause reduced output. Inspect the belt and replace or adjust as necessary.

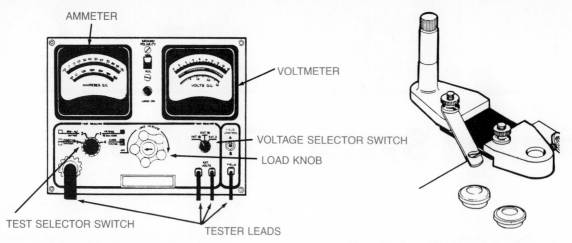

Fig. 29-1 Volt-amp charging system tester. (Sun Electric Corporation)

Fig. 29-2 Battery post adapter. (Sun Electric Corporation)

29.3 Wires and Wiring

Check the wires to the alternator and regulator to make sure they are properly connected and in good shape. Wires are sometimes pinched under sheet metal edges or under screw heads. Worn insulation is common where a loose wire is rubbing against a rough metal surface or the threads of a screw. Check battery cables also for tightness and corrosion.

29.4 Alternator Visual Inspection

Check the alternator for external damage. A cracked alternator housing may allow the rear bearing to move out of alignment so that the rotor rubs on the stator core. A broken mounting bracket can move the alternator out of alignment with the drive belt. Either of these conditions may cause low output.

29.5 Battery

Charging system problems usually show up as battery problems. Test the battery thoroughly before any electrical testing of the alternator or regulator. The battery must pass a visual inspection, a specific gravity test, and a load test, following the procedures outlined in Chapter 25 on storage batteries.

29.6 Indicator Lamp Circuit

If the indicator lamp stays on when the engine is running and there are no other signs of a charging system problem, test the indicator lamp circuit. The circuit is wired so that alternator output makes the indicator light go out. The circuit usually includes a fuse. If the fuse burns out, the light will operate on battery current and stay on. Locate the fuse for the light. If it is blown, replace it.

29.7 Alternator and Regulator

If the visual inspection and battery tests fail to locate the problem, the alternator and regulator should be tested electrically.

29.8 ALTERNATOR SYSTEM PRECAUTIONS

Several special precautions must be observed when servicing a charging system. Otherwise the charging system components may be damaged.

Do not short across or ground any of the terminals in the charging system. Shorting or grounding may overload the diodes and damage them. This may occur even when the system is not in operation, since there is always battery voltage at the alternator output terminal.

Observe polarity when installing a battery in a vehicle. If a battery is connected into the vehicle in the wrong polarity, the diode rectifier can be damaged.

Disconnect both battery cables before connecting a battery charger. Connecting or disconnecting a battery charger and a battery that is connected into a circuit may cause sparking or arcing. The resulting voltage surge could damage the rectifier circuit.

Observe polarity on testers and booster batteries. Anytime a tester or booster battery is connected

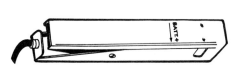

Fig. 29-3 Inductive type clamp on pickup. (Sun Electric Corporation)

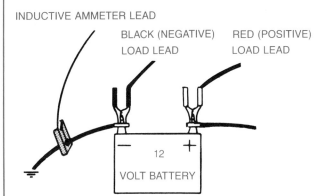

INDUCTIVE AMMETER LEAD

BLACK (NEGATIVE) LOAD LEAD   RED (POSITIVE) LOAD LEAD

12 VOLT BATTERY

Fig. 29-4 Typical connections for checking alternator output. (Sun Electric Corporation)

to a battery in a charging circuit, the polarity must be observed. Connect negative to negative and positive to positive. Failure to observe the proper polarity may damage the rectifier circuit.

Never operate an alternator on open circuit. The alternator must never be operated with the output terminal disconnected when the rotor (field) is energized. This allows the alternator to operate without any resistance, which could lead to damage from too much output.

29.9 ALTERNATOR TESTS

Alternators are tested electrically in one of two ways. The alternator may be removed from the vehicle and installed on a test bench. The other method is to use a portable tester called a volt-amp tester and leave the alternator mounted on the engine. In either case the same tests are performed. A typical volt-amp charging system tester has a voltmeter, ammeter, and load knob (Fig. 29-1). Smaller testers perform the voltage and amperage testing on one scale. The ammeter measures the amount of current flowing in the circuit being tested. The voltmeter registers the number of volts produced by the charging system.

Older models of the testers required the installation of a battery post adapter (Fig. 29-2) to allow breaking into the charging system circuit. Newer testers use an inductive clamp-around probe (Fig. 29-3). This type of probe is recommended for use on electronic-type ignition systems. The clamp probe makes it unnecessary to break a circuit or use a battery post adapter.

29.10 Output Test

Alternators are rated by the current they can deliver at a specified speed and voltage. The alternator output test measures the ability of the alternator to produce its rated output. The vehicle manufacturer provides output specifications in the service manual. Output is specified at a certain engine rpm and voltage because these will affect the amount of current an alternator can deliver.

To conduct the test, connect an alternator tester to the charging circuit. Typical connections are shown in Figure 29-4. On most testers, connect the positive load lead to the positive (+) battery terminal. Connect the negative load lead to the battery negative (−) terminal. Clamp the amps inductive ammeter lead around the negative ground cable. (Be sure to clamp it in correct direction as specified on the clamp.) The tester manual will explain the proper connections as well as the test procedure. Different connections are required for different wiring systems. The test involves setting the engine rpm to a specified amount measured with a tachometer. Then a carbon pile loading device on the tester draws or absorbs current from the alternator. The load is adjusted to a specified voltage on a voltmeter, and the current output is read on an ammeter.

An output 2 to 8 amperes below the specified rating usually indicates an open diode in the rectifier. A slipping drive belt can also cause this same reading. Recheck the belt. An output 10 to 15 amperes below the specified rating usually indicates a shorted diode. An alternator with a shorted diode often has a bad whine at idle speeds. An output very much lower than

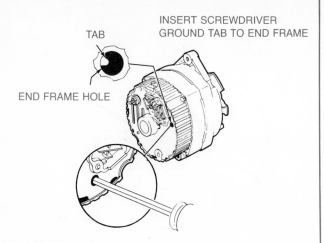

Fig. 29-5 Grounding the field in the alternator. (Chevrolet Motor Division, GMC)

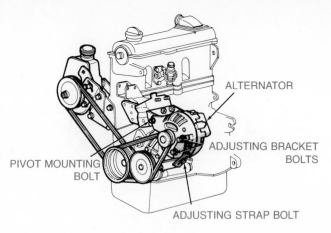

Fig. 29-6 Typical alternator mounting. (Chrysler Corporation)

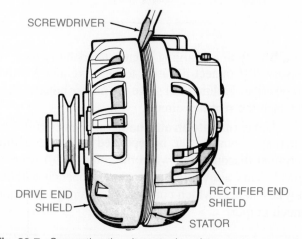

Fig. 29-7 Separating the alternator housings. (Chrysler Corporation)

specifications may signal a shorted rectifier system or other internal problems. Any test showing an alternator problem should be followed by a circuit resistance test to find out whether the circuit is faulty or whether the alternator should be removed from the vehicle for servicing.

If the output test shows that the alternator delivers the correct amount of current, it is in satisfactory condition. The mechanic must look somewhere else for the problem. An over- or undercharged battery may be caused by faulty wiring or a faulty regulator. Test the regulator following the procedures outlined in the next section.

29.11 Circuit Resistance Test

Most alternator testers provide a procedure for measuring the resistance of the insulated wires and the ground connections in the charging circuit. These tests, called insulated circuit resistance and ground circuit resistance, measure resistance with the alternator operating at a specified rpm and current flow.

Specifications for the circuit resistance tests are available in the manufacturer's service manual. Too much resistance can be caused in the insulated circuit by loose or corroded connections at the alternator output terminal or battery terminals or cables and by faulty wiring from alternator to regulator. High resistance in the ground circuit may be due to loose mounting bolts or corroded ground straps. Inspect and clean all the ground connections.

If the circuit resistance is satisfactory and the alternator output is below specifications, the alternator will have to be removed from the vehicle for service.

29.12 REGULATOR TESTING

Regulator testing is usually done with the same tester that is used for alternators. The testing may be done on the vehicle or on an alternator regulator test bench. The tester usually has a regulator test selector switch to check regulator operation. Test connections and specifications differ for different regulators. Both the tester operator's manual and the regulator manufacturer's test procedures must be followed closely. The following are some common tests required on most regulators.

29.13 Field Relay Tests

Many regulators, even those that are transistorized, use a mechanical field relay. Test the field relay before testing the voltage regulator unit. If it is not working when the engine is running, the alternator will produce little or no output current. Most testers provide a procedure to find out whether the relay contacts are closing at the proper voltage.

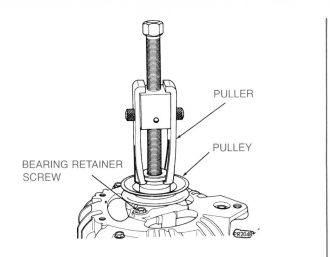

Fig. 29-8 Using a puller to remove the pulley. (Chrysler Corporation)

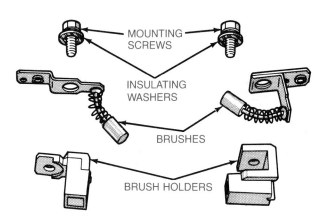

Fig. 29-9 Brush holders and brushes. (Chrysler Corporation)

The specifications show the voltage required to pull the contacts together. An adjustable resistance in the tester, called a rheostat, sends current through the relay winding. Check a voltmeter at the moment the relay closes. If the closing voltage is not correct, the relay may need to be adjusted. If the relay fails to close at all, it must be replaced.

29.14 Voltage Regulator Tests

Voltage regulator tests tell whether the voltage regulator is limiting the alternator field current properly. A voltage regulator with a short, a ground, or an open will not operate properly. Mechanical regulators are checked for proper operation in all three contact point positions. Transistorized regulators are tested for proper adjustment or voltage setting. Both mechanical and transistorized regulators have adjustable voltage settings.

Voltage regulator testing involves some special procedures for accuracy. The regulator must be normalized at the proper operating temperature. Since temperature affects the regulator setting, a temperature measurement may be required as part of the test procedures. The magnetic field inside mechanical regulators is affected by the metal regulator cover. Test specifications may specify that the regulator cover be on or off for testing. The regulator must often be cycled by turning off the engine and then restarting it to interrupt the field current.

Many alternators with internal regulators have a test hole in the rear of the alternator for regulator testing. These regulators are tested with the same hookup and volt-amp tester procedure as was described for alternator output. Start the engine and set the engine speed between 1500-2000 rpm. Ad-

just the tester load knob to obtain maximum current output. When maximum current output is obtained, insert the tip of a screwdriver into the end frame hole so that it touches both the side of the hole and the tab within the hole (Fig. 29-5). This will ground the field in the alternator. Check the volt-amp tester reading for total output of the alternator and compare it with the rated output. If the output is not within 10 amperes of rated output, the alternator is defective. If the output is within 10 amperes of rated output, the regulator is defective.

29.15 ALTERNATOR SERVICE

An alternator whose current output is below specifications must be removed from the vehicle for service. The following procedures are typical. The vehicle manufacturer's service procedures and specifications should be located and followed.

29.16 Alternator Removal

The output terminal of the alternator always has battery voltage connected to it. Grounding the output terminal or the wire connected to it can result in a wiring harness burnout or damage to the alternator. To prevent these problems, the battery ground cable must be disconnected before removing the alternator:

Disconnect the battery ground cable from the battery ground terminal. Find the wire leads to the alternator and disconnect them from the alternator. Identify these wires by marking them where they originally attached. Loosen and remove the alternator adjusting bolt (Fig. 29-6). Loosen the alternator pivot or mounting bolt. Move the alternator toward the engine and remove the alternator belt

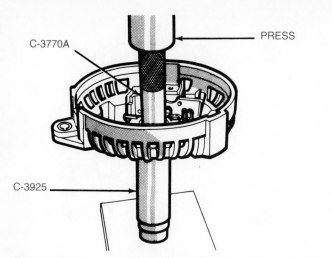

Fig. 29-10 Pressing out the rear bearing. (Chrysler Corporation)

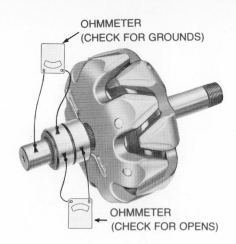

Fig. 29-11 Testing the rotor for opens, shorts, and excessive resistance. (Delco-Remy Division, GMC)

from the alternator pulley. Remove the alternator pivot or mounting bolt. Remove the alternator from the engine.

29.17 Disassembly

Make scribe marks on the two end frames (housings) to help you reassemble. Remove the through bolts and pry between the stator and drive end frame with the blade of a screwdriver as shown in Figure 29-7. Carefully separate the drive end frame, pulley, and rotor assembly away from stator and rectifier end frame assembly.

To remove the drive end housing from the rotor, place the housing in a vise and tighten only enough to permit removal of the shaft nut. On some models, you can use a large Allen wrench to prevent the rotor from turning while loosening the pulley nut with a wrench. Remove the pulley nut, lockwasher, pulley, fan, and collar. Some models of alternators have a pulley which is pressed into place. A puller must be used to remove the pulley as shown in Figure 29-8.

Separate the front end housing from the rotor shaft. Remove three stator winding attaching nuts and washers and remove the stator windings from the bridge rectifier terminals. Separate the stator from the rear housing. Remove the diode trio strap terminal attaching screw from the brush holder and remove the diode trio. Remove the capacitor holddown screw. Remove the bridge rectifier attaching screws and battery wire terminal screw. Remove the bridge rectifier. Note the insulator located between heat sink and rear housing.

Remove the brush holder screws. Note the position of all insulator washers to facilitate correct assembly. Remove the brush holder and brushes. Carefully note the position of parts for assembly (Fig. 29-9). Remove the voltage regulator if the alternator has an integral type. Remove the front bearing retainer plate screws, retainer plate, and inner collar.

Press out the front bearing and slinger from the front housing with a suitable tube or collar. Press out the rear bearing using a tube or collar that fits inside the rear housing (Fig. 29-10). Press from inside of the housing toward the outside.

29.18 Cleaning and Inspection

Clean the rotor poles with cleaning solvent. Inspect the slip rings for dirt and roughness and clean with solvent. If necessary, clean and finish the slip rings with commutator paper, or 400 grit polishing cloth. Do not use metal-oxide paper. Spin the rotor in a lathe or other support while holding the abrasive against the rings. When using an abrasive, support the rotor while spinning to clean slip rings evenly. Cleaning the slip rings without support may result in flat spots on the slip rings. This will cause brush noise and premature brush wear. Wipe or brush the stator. Do not soak it in cleaning solvent.

Inspect brush springs for evidence of damage or corrosion. Replace the springs if there is any doubt about their condition. Inspect brushes for wear or contamination. If the brushes are to be reused, clean with a soft, dry cloth until completely free of lubricant.

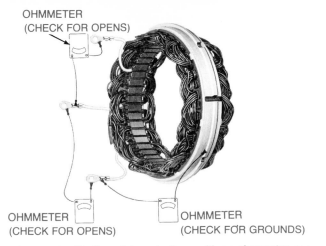

Fig. 29-12 Testing stator windings with an ohmmeter. (Delco-Remy Division, GMC)

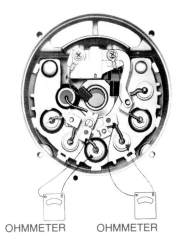

Fig. 29-13 Testing diodes. (Delco-Remy Division, GMC)

29.19 Testing the Rotor Field Windings

Low alternator output may be caused by an open circuit or a grounded circuit. Use an ohmmeter to test for an open. Connect one of the test leads on the ohmmeter to one of the slip rings and the other lead to the other slip ring (Fig. 29-11). If the ohmmeter reading is high (infinite), the winding is open.

To test for a ground, connect the one lead of the ohmmeter to the rotor shaft and the other lead to one of the slip rings (Fig. 29-11). If you get a reading, the winding is grounded and must be replaced. You should read infinite resistance.

29.20 Testing the Stator

The stator windings may be tested with an ohmmeter (Fig. 29-12). On some alternators, the stator windings are held by screws. If they are soldered in place, the connection will have to be cut and resoldered after testing. To test for grounds, connect one lead of the ohmmeter to the stator frame and the other lead to any one of the three stator windings. The ohmmeter should register a high (infinite) value. If the meter reading is low, the windings are grounded.

Connect the ohmmeter leads between two adjoining stator leads to test for opens. The meter should indicate continuity between any two stator windings. A high ohmmeter reading indicates an open winding.

The low resistance in the stator windings makes it difficult to locate a short circuit without laboratory equipment. If all other electrical checks on the rotor,

stator, and rectifier assembly prove normal, shorted stator windings may be the problem.

29.21 Testing the Rectifier

In some alternators, each of the diodes is accessible in the rear housing. In other alternators, the entire rectifier assembly is mounted in a small unit called a bridge attached to the rear alternator housing. When the diodes are accessible, they may be checked individually with an ohmmeter. Never use a 110 volt test lamp to test diodes. This high voltage would damage the diode.

To test the diodes, the stator winding leads must be disconnected. Test the diodes mounted in the heat sink by connecting one of the ohmmeter leads to the heat sink and the other lead to the diode lead (Fig. 29-13). Note the reading. Then reverse the ohmmeter leads and note the reading. A good diode will give one high and one low reading. If both readings are very low or very high the diode is bad. Test the other two heat sink diodes in the same way.

Check diodes mounted in the housing in the same way. Connect one ohmmeter lead to the housing and the other lead to the diode lead. Note the reading. Reverse the ohmmeter connections and note this reading. Again, a good diode will give one high and one low reading. If both readings are high or low, the diode is defective.

A rectifier bridge assembly may also be tested with an ohmmeter. The rectifier bridge has a grounded heat sink and an insulated heat sink connected to the output terminal. To check the rectifier bridge, connect the ohmmeter as shown in Figure

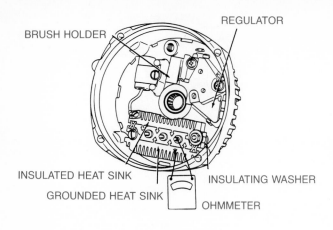

Fig. 29-14 Testing the rectifier bridge. (Chevrolet Motor Division, GMC)

Fig. 29-15 Alternator test bench. (Sun Electric Corporation)

29-14, pressing down very firmly onto the flat metal connector, not onto the threaded stud. Then reverse the lead connections to the grounded heat sink and same terminal. There should be one high and one low reading. If both readings are the same, replace the rectifier bridge.

29.22 Reassembly

Press in any bearings to be replaced with a suitable tube or collar that fits over the outer bearing race. Install the inner collar retainer plate and screws. Position the housing, the outer collar, fan, pulley, and washer on the rotor shaft and install the pulley nut.

Place the housing in a vise. Tighten the vise only enough to permit tightening of the pulley nut. Tighten the nut to specifications. Use an Allen wrench to prevent the rotor from turning while tightening the nut with the wrench.

Install springs and brushes into the brush holder. Brushes should slide in and out of the brush holder without binding. Install the integral voltage regulator if used on this model alternator. Attach the brush holder to the rear housing. Carefully note the position of insulating washers. Install the diode trio terminal strap attaching screw and insulating washer. Tighten the remaining two brush holder screws securely. Position the bridge rectifier on the rear housing with the insulator inserted between the insulated heat sink and the rear housing.

Install the bridge rectifier attaching screw and battery wire terminal screw. Position the diode trio strap terminals on the bridge rectifier terminal studs. Install the stator in the rear housing. Attach the stator windings to the bridge rectifier terminal studs.

Secure with washers and nuts. Join the front housing and rear housing together with the scribe mark aligned. Install the through bolts and tighten them to specifications.

29.23 Bench Testing

If equipment is available, it is a good idea to bench test the alternator before it is reinstalled on the vehicle. Several testing equipment manufacturers make an alternator test bench (Fig. 29-15). Mount the alternator to the test bench. The test bench has a motor and belt assembly that is connected to the alternator so that it may be driven at a specified rpm. A voltmeter, ohmmeter, and carbon pile load mounted in the tester is connected to the alternator. Drive the alternator at specified rpm with a voltage load and measure its current output. If the alternator can deliver the specified current output, it is ready to be reinstalled on the vehicle.

29.24 Alternator Installation

To install the alternator, place the alternator in position in the vehicle. Slide the pivot attaching bolt back in place. Install the alternator belt over the alternator pulley. Check the alignment of the belt and the pulley to the water pump pulley and the crankshaft pulley. Put the alternator adjusting bolt back into the adjustment bracket.

Use a belt tension gauge to adjust the belt tension to the manufacturer's specifications. To adjust, use a pry bar to pry the alternator away from the engine and tighten the adjusting bolt. Then tighten the pivot or mounting bolt. Be sure to place the pry

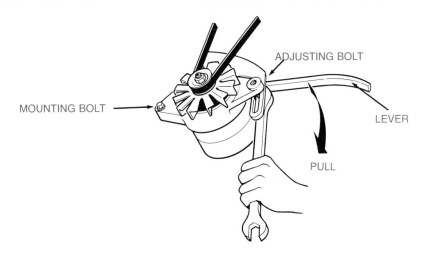

ADJUSTING BOLT

MOUNTING BOLT

LEVER

PULL

Fig. 29-16   Adjusting the alternator belt.

bar against that part of the alternator where the two halves join. This is the most solid part of the alternator (Fig. 29-16). Reconnect the wire leads to the alternator. Be sure they are connected to the correct terminals. Reconnect the battery ground cable to the battery terminal.

29.25   REGULATOR SERVICE

The service procedures on charging system regulators are mostly adjustments. If, during testing, the voltage regulator fails to deliver current to the alternator field winding, it must be replaced. Replacement parts for regulators are not generally available. Problems such as open resistors and shorted shunt windings require regulator replacement. If, however, the problem found during testing is an incorrect voltage setting, the regulator can be adjusted.

NEW TERMS

Circuit resistance test   A test to determine the amount of resistance in the charging system circuit.
Closing voltage   A field relay test that tells at what voltage the contact points close.
Ground circuit resistance   The resistance of all the ground connections in the charging system circuit.
Insulated circuit resistance   The resistance of all the insulated wiring in the charging system circuit.
Open diode   An alternator problem in which a diode has an open circuit.

Shorted diode   An alternator problem in which a diode has a shorted circuit.
Voltage setting   The adjustment of a voltage regulator that determines the voltage limit of the alternator.

CHAPTER REVIEW

1. How can you tell if a battery is being overcharged?
2. What does the charging system indicator light do?
3. What happens to alternator output if the drive belt slips?
4. Why must polarity be observed when connecting a battery into a vehicle?
5. Why should a battery be disconnected from the vehicle before connecting it to a charger?
6. What is an alternator output test?
7. What is a circuit resistance test?
8. Explain how a voltage regulator is tested.
9. Describe how a rotor field winding is tested.
10. Describe how a stator is tested.

DISCUSSION TOPICS AND ACTIVITIES

1. List the steps to locate a problem in the charging circuit.
2. Look up the output specifications for an alternator. How could you find out if the alternator meets these specifications?
3. Look up the voltage regulator voltage setting for any automobile. Is the voltage setting adjustable?

The Ignition System

CHAPTER PREVIEW

The ignition system (Fig. 30-1) provides a high voltage spark to each cylinder so the air-fuel mixture is ignited at precisely the right time. Twelve volts in the primary circuit are boosted by the coil to 30,000 or more volts at the spark plug. Older systems use breaker points, which last about one year. Late model cars all use solid state switching for longer life.

OBJECTIVES

After studying this chapter, you should be able to do the following:

1. Describe the construction and operation of the ignition primary system.
2. Describe the construction and operation of the ignition secondary system.
3. Explain the operation of ignition timing systems.
4. Understand the function and operation of spark plugs.
5. Describe the operation of solid state inductive and capacitive discharge ignition systems.

30.1   IGNITION COIL CONSTRUCTION

The ignition coil (Fig. 30-2) steps up the low voltage of the battery or alternator to a voltage high enough to jump an air gap at the spark plug. The coil's primary winding has approximately 200 turns of relatively heavy copper wire. The secondary winding in the center of the primary winding has as many as 21,000 turns of very fine copper wire. The primary and secondary windings are wound around a laminated iron core and enclosed by a soft iron shell. The lamination and shell concentrate the magnetic field. This assembly is placed into a one-piece steel case. A coil cap of molded insulating material which contains the primary and secondary terminals is mounted to the top of the case. A porcelain insulator prevents the winding assembly from touching the grounded case.

When the coil is made it is filled with oil, tar, or epoxy. They completely remove air from the exposed turns of the winding. The entire unit is then sealed to prevent air or moisture from getting in.

30.2   IGNITION COIL OPERATION

When the driver turns the key switch on, the distributor contact points are closed. Current flows from the power source through the key switch into the coil primary terminal and through the coil primary winding. Current goes out of the coil through the second primary terminal and flows through the ignition wire into the distributor (Fig. 30-3). The current flow in the primary winding creates a magnetic field inside the coil. The field is concentrated by the laminated core and the shell. In a fraction of a second, called saturation or buildup time, the current flow and the magnetic field both reach their maximum. The reason that they require buildup time is self-induction. Self-induction causes a momentary countervoltage in the coil that opposes any change in the amount of current flowing. This countervoltage must be overcome by the battery voltage so that the current can increase to its maximum.

When the distributor contact points remain closed so that the flow of current is increasing, energy is

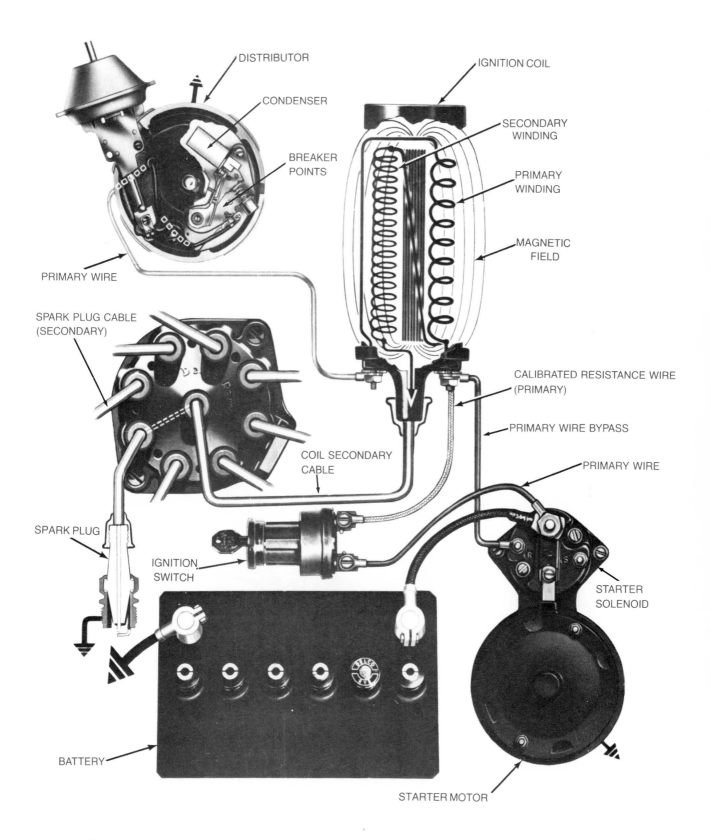

Fig. 30-1 The ignition system. (Chevrolet Motor Division, GMC)

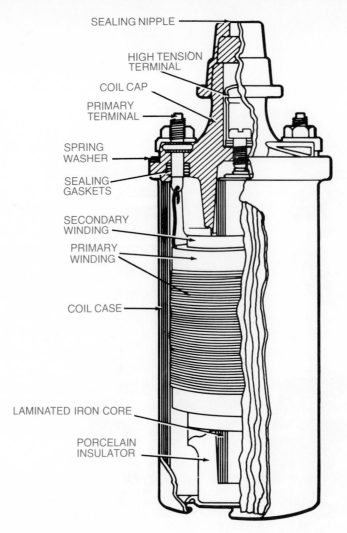

SEALING NIPPLE

HIGH TENSION TERMINAL

COIL CAP

PRIMARY TERMINAL

SPRING WASHER

SEALING GASKETS

SECONDARY WINDING

PRIMARY WINDING

COIL CASE

LAMINATED IRON CORE

PORCELAIN INSULATOR

Fig. 30-2 Coil construction. (Delco-Remy Division, GMC)

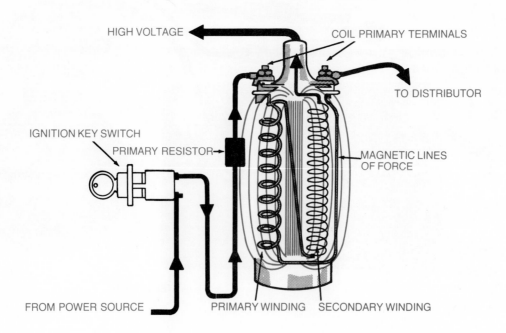

HIGH VOLTAGE

COIL PRIMARY TERMINALS

TO DISTRIBUTOR

IGNITION KEY SWITCH

PRIMARY RESISTOR

MAGNETIC LINES OF FORCE

FROM POWER SOURCE

PRIMARY WINDING

SECONDARY WINDING

Fig. 30-3 Current flow through coil circuit.

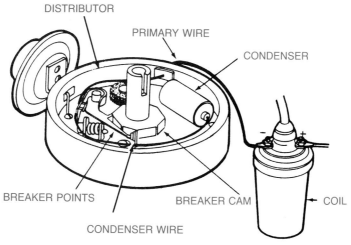

Fig. 30-4 Parts of mechanical breaker point primary circuit in distributor.

being stored in the coil. Further rotation of the breaker cam in the distributor opens the contact points as the flow of current is stopped. The magnetic field which depends upon this flow of current rapidly collapses, inducing a high voltage in every turn of both the primary and secondary windings. In the primary winding the voltage may reach 300 volts. In the secondary winding, which has up to 100 times as many turns of wire, the voltage may reach 30,000 volts or more. This high voltage goes out the secondary center terminal of the coil to the distributor cap.

Under most operating conditions, the voltage created by the coil does not reach 30,000 volts. The coil produces only the amount of voltage necessary to produce a spark at the air gap of the spark plug. This is usually between 6,000 and 20,000 volts, depending upon engine compression, air-fuel ratio, width of the spark plug air gap, resistance of the ignition cables, width of the rotor, and spark plug operating temperature.

Coil voltage also depends upon saturation or buildup time. Under any conditions saturation time is only a fraction of a second. At high engine speed, the distributor contact points remain closed a very short time. The current and the magnetic field in the coil cannot increase to their highest amount. Coils must provide the necessary voltage with a short saturation time.

30.3 DISTRIBUTOR PRIMARY SYSTEM CONSTRUCTION

The fast buildup and collapse of the coil primary winding is made possible by the switching action inside the primary section of the distributor (Fig. 30-4).

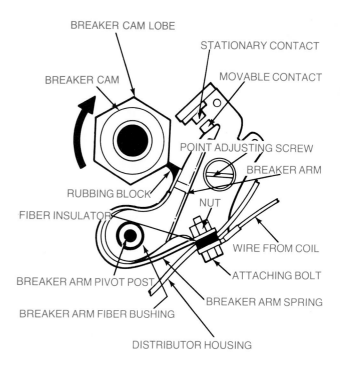

Fig. 30-5 Breaker point assembly.

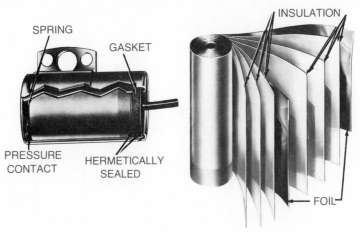

Fig. 30-6 Inside a condenser. (Chevrolet Motor Division, GMC)

30.4   Mechanical Breaker Point Assembly

The primary circuit on older cars is opened and closed by a mechanical breaker point assembly (Fig. 30-5). The assembly is opened and closed by a breaker cam rotated by the distributor shaft. The shaft is driven by gearing within the engine, usually in connection with the engine camshaft. The distributor shaft and breaker cam are rotated at half the engine speed because ignition must occur during only one stroke of the four-stroke cycle.

The breaker cam has the same number of lobes as there are cylinders in the engine. A laminated phenolic rubbing block riding on the breaker cam is attached to the contact point set. There are two contact points. The stationary or grounded contact does not move during operation. The movable contact is mounted on a bushing. Rotation of the breaker cam pushes a lobe on the rubbing block which causes the movable contact to pivot on its bushing and separate from the stationary contact. Further rotation of the breaker cam allows the lobe to pass by the rubbing block. A spring, usually made from stainless steel with a copper conductor strip attached, closes the contact points.

At 60 miles per hour the contact points open and close over 150 times per second.

30.5   Condenser

Proper contact point operation requires a condenser, sometimes referred to as a capacitor, which is mounted close to the breaker point assembly. Without the ignition condenser, current would continue to flow between the separating contact points. This current would form an arc which would burn the points and drain away most of the energy stored in the coil.

The condenser prevents arcing by providing a place where current can flow until the points are completely separated. The condenser consists of two long sheets of conductor foil separated by several sheets of insulated paper. The foil and the insulation are wound into a tight roll (Fig. 30-6) and installed in a small metal canister. An insulated end piece through which runs a small insulated wire lead or pigtail is placed on top of the canister. The end of the canister is crimped over the insulated end piece. A gasket is located between the end piece and the foil sheets. A spring is sometimes used at the bottom of the canister to maintain pressure on the end piece gasket.

Very small amounts of moisture can affect the paper insulation, leading to early condenser failure. For this reason, air and moisture are removed under heat and vacuum in a process known as hermetically sealing. The spring, gasket, and end piece maintain the hermetic seal through the service life of the condenser.

30.6   DISTRIBUTOR PRIMARY SYSTEM OPERATION

When the driver turns the ignition key switch on and the distributor breaker points are closed, current flows from the battery through the coil primary wind-

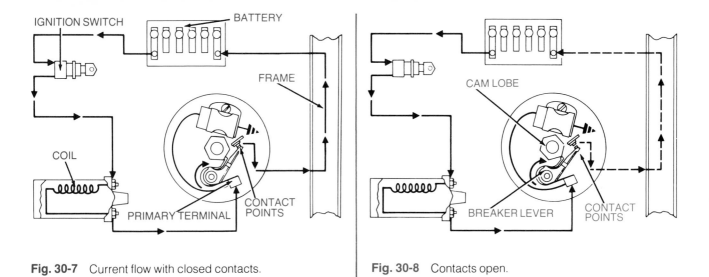

Fig. 30-7 Current flow with closed contacts.

Fig. 30-8 Contacts open.

ing and into the distributor (Fig. 30-7). Current entering the distributor primary terminal flows through the movable contact spring across the movable contact to the grounded stationary contact. Current returns to the battery through ground. This complete circuit allows current to flow and the magnetic field in the coil primary to build. Rotation of the breaker cam causes a cam lobe to strike the rubbing block and separate the breaker points (Fig. 30-8).

As shown in Figure 30-9, the ignition condenser provides a place where current can flow during the first instant the points begin to open. The condenser provides a storage chamber for the electrical energy which quickly brings the flow of current in the primary circuit to a stop. This quick collapse, sometimes referred to as the condenser effect, allows the coil to induce secondary current.

The condenser can store and discharge high voltages because of its foil sheets. The condenser symbol in Figure 30-10 shows that one of the rolls of foil is connected to ground through the condenser housing. The other foil sheet is connected to the wire lead. Since the condenser is connected between the insulated contact and ground, current flows into the condenser, creating a difference in voltage between the two foil sheets. A complete circuit is available only through the coil primary winding and battery to ground. The condenser voltage forces current to flow back through this circuit. The grounded foil then becomes charged to a higher voltage than the insulated foil. The direction of current flow again reverses. This oscillating process continues until all the remaining coil energy is used up. Further rotation of the breaker cam allows the contact points to close so that the cycle of primary buildup and collapse begins once again.

30.7 RESISTOR BYPASS CIRCUIT

Most ignition systems use a resistor bypass circuit (Fig. 30-11) to provide a low-resistance path for primary current when the engine is being started and a higher-resistance path when the engine is running. The ignition key switch has three wires connected to it. One wire is connected to the battery cable, allowing full battery voltage to enter the switch. The other two terminals on the switch provide two different paths for current flow into the coil primary winding.

When the driver turns the ignition key to the Start position, the starting system is activated to crank the engine. The starter motor draws current from the battery, dropping battery voltage from 12 volts to around 9.5 volts. Ignition primary current is routed through a low-resistance wire called a bypass wire directly into the coil primary. Coils used on resistor bypass circuits are designed to provide enough secondary current on 9 volts.

After the engine is started, the driver turns the key to the Run position with the starter motor disengaged. The voltage at the ignition key switch immediately returns to 12 or more volts. If the coil, designed for 9 volts, received the full 12 volts, it could overheat and fail. This high voltage could also cause the contact point set to fail in a short time. For these reasons, when the ignition key switch is in the Run position, current flows into the coil through a second wire. The resistor in this circuit reduces the voltage to the coil to about 9 volts.

Many automobiles use a ballast resistor to provide a certain resistance regardless of temperature.

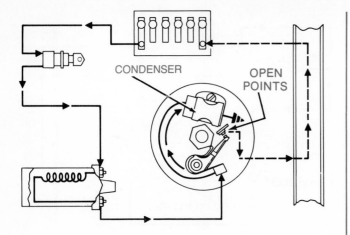

Fig. 30-9 Condenser provides place for primary circuit to flow.

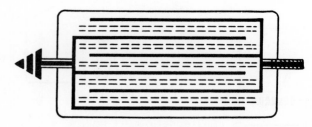

Fig. 30-10 Condenser symbol.

This allows the resistor to remove heat. Most ballast resistors are mounted on or near the coil.

Other ignition systems use a unit whose resistance changes with temperature. At low engine speeds the contact points are closed for a relatively long period of time, causing the resistor to get very hot. The hotter the resistor gets, the more it restricts the flow of current. As engine speed increases, the contact points are closed for a much shorter period of time. The resistor then operates at a cooler temperature with less resistance. At higher engine speeds less resistance is desirable because there is less time for coil saturation. This type of resistor may be separately mounted, or it may be a special resistance wire in the ignition circuit or inside the coil.

30.8   DISTRIBUTOR SECONDARY SYSTEM CONSTRUCTION

The secondary system distributes the high voltage developed by the coil to the correct spark plug. Its rotor cap is mounted on top of the distributor, usually with two spring clips or spring-loaded screws. The rotor is mounted on and keyed to the distributor shaft directly under the distributor cap.

The distributor cap (Fig. 30-12), molded from bakelite or some similar insulating material, contains 4, 6, or 8 high-voltage contacts, one for each cylinder. The contacts, permanently attached to the cap, are made from brass or aluminum. Small towers molded into the cap above each contact are used to plug in an ignition cable to touch the contacts. A center tower and contact in the cap is used to plug in

the high-voltage secondary lead from the coil. The center contact assembly has a carbon button that contacts the rotor. A groove or key in the side of the rotor cap allows it to be mounted to the distributor in only one position.

The rotor (Fig. 30-13) is molded from an insulation material similar to that of the distributor cap. A contact blade made of a good conductor such as brass is attached by a rivet molded into the rotor. Since the blade must withstand high-voltage surges, it is sometimes manufactured with a tungsten tip. When the rotor and rotor cap are in place on the distributor, the stainless steel rotor spring bears against the carbon button in the distributor cap. Some rotors have a resistor between the spring and blade contact to reduce radio and television interference. A key or groove molded in the rotor allows it to be mounted on and locked to the distributor shaft in only one direction.

30.9   DISTRIBUTOR SECONDARY SYSTEM OPERATION

A simplified secondary circuit for a 2-cylinder engine is illustrated in Figure 30-14. When the contact points open, a high voltage is induced in the coil secondary winding. This current is directed through a high-voltage secondary wire into the center terminal of the distributor cap. Current flows down the center cap insert, into the carbon button, into the spring, and then into the rotor blade. At this instant the rotor blade is in place under the cap insert for the number one spark plug. There is a small gap between the rotor

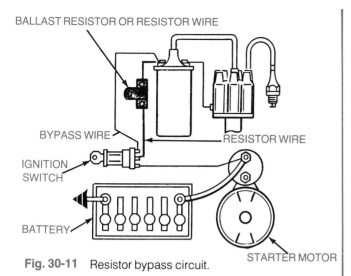

Fig. 30-11 Resistor bypass circuit.

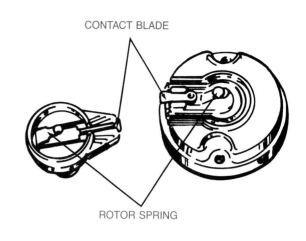

Fig. 30-13 Two kinds of rotors.

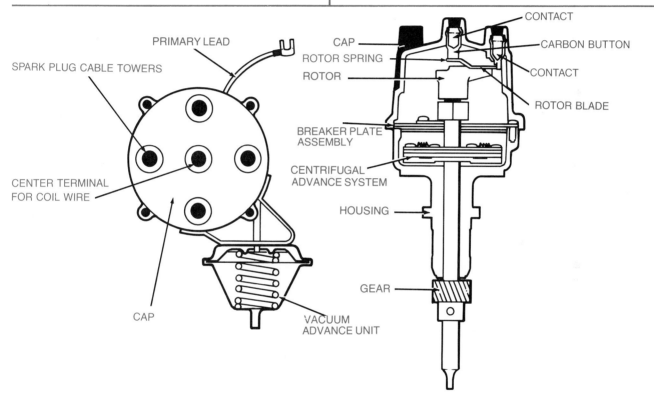

Fig. 30-12 Sectional view of distributor.

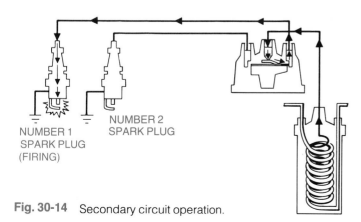

Fig. 30-14 Secondary circuit operation.

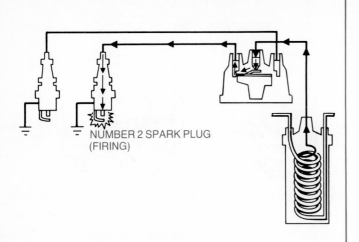

Fig. 30-15 Rotor turned to fire spark plug number 2.

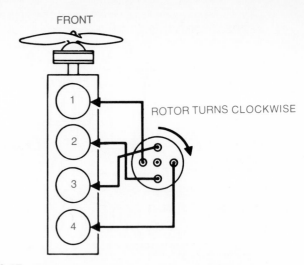

Fig. 30-17 Distributor cap wiring for 1, 3, 4, 2 firing order.

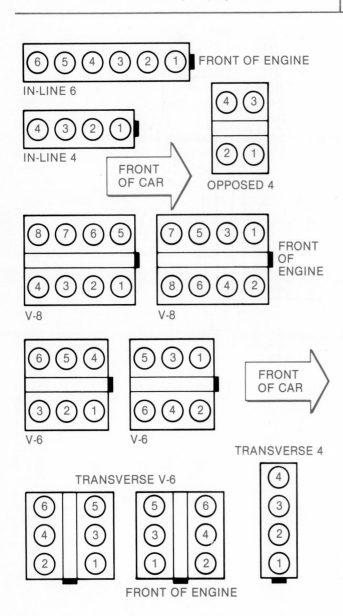

Fig. 30-16 Typical cylinder numbering arrangement.

blade and the cap terminal insert in the distributor cap which the current jumps. Current then flows through an ignition cable to the number 1 spark plug where a spark is created to burn the air-fuel mixture in the combustion chamber.

Distributor shaft rotation closes the contact points to build another magnetic field in the coil. Further rotation of the shaft causes the breaker cam to open the contacts again, inducing another high-voltage surge in the coil secondary winding. The rotor, turning with the distributor shaft, is in position to fire the number 2 spark plug (Fig. 30-15). Current flows through the coil high tension wire into the center contact and button through the rotor. The current jumps the rotor gap into the cap terminal insert and flows to the number 2 spark plug.

In a 4-stroke-cycle engine, the spark must be delivered to each cylinder when its piston is in firing position. The arrangement of the secondary wires in the distributor cap is based upon the manufacturer's cylinder numbering system and firing order. The numbering method is fairly standard on in-line 4- and 6-cylinder engines. The cylinders are numbered consecutively from the front of the automobile (see Fig. 30-16). The numbering of the cylinders in a V-8 engine differs from one manufacturer to another.

The firing order, the order in which the cylinders deliver their power stroke, is designed to reduce vibration and provide an even flow of power. The crankshaft on an in-line 4-cylinder engine is arranged with crank throws 180° apart so that when the number 1 piston moves down on a power stroke, the number 4 piston is moving down on intake. At the same time, the number 2 and 3 pistons are moving up, one on exhaust, the other on compression. Two firing orders

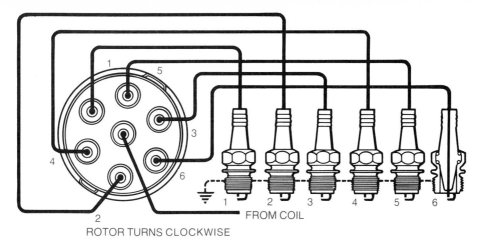

Fig. 30-18 Six-cylinder wiring system for 1, 5, 3, 6, 2, 4 firing order.

can be used: 1, 2, 4, 3 or 1, 3, 4, 2 (Fig. 30-17). The distributor cap wiring system must be arranged so that the rotor, as it turns, delivers the secondary voltage to the correct cylinder in its firing order. The rotor may be geared to turn either clockwise or counterclockwise, but clockwise is more common.

The in-line 6-cylinder engine's crankshaft throws are 120° apart. The cylinders provide a power stroke every one-third revolution of the crankshaft, reducing stress on any one part of the crankshaft by scattering power strokes over the length of the crankshaft. When an end cylinder fires, the next cylinder to fire should be in the middle or toward the other end of the crankshaft. Two common firing orders are used with 6-cylinder in-line engines: 1, 5, 3, 6, 2, 4 (Fig. 30-18) and 1, 4, 2, 6, 3, 5.

V-engine firing orders alternate firing between ends of the crankshaft and each bank of cylinders. This allows the forces to be distributed over the entire engine rather than on any one area of the crankshaft. Crank throws in a V-8 engine are 90° apart. One common firing order is 1, 8, 4, 3, 6, 5, 7, 2 (Fig. 30-19). Other firing orders are 1, 6, 2, 5, 8, 3, 7, 4; 1, 5, 4, 2, 6, 3, 7, 8; and 1, 8, 7, 3, 6, 5, 4, 2.

In any wiring system, the manufacturer decides which of the distributor cap terminals should be routed to the number 1 cylinder. The distributor is meshed with the camshaft so that the rotor is in position to deliver current to the number 1 cylinder when it is ready for a power stroke. The drive gear attached to the distributor shaft may be meshed with the camshaft in a number of different ways. When a distributor is removed it must be replaced so that the rotor is in the correct position when the number 1 cylinder is ready for a power stroke.

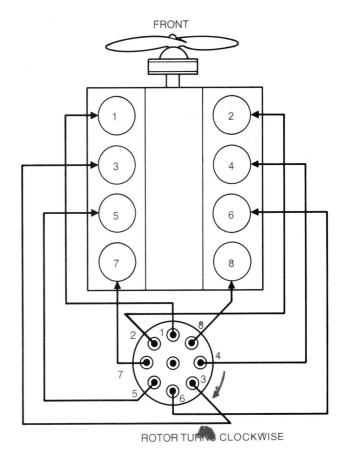

Fig. 30-19 V-8 wiring system for 1, 8, 4, 3, 6, 5, 7, 2 firing order.

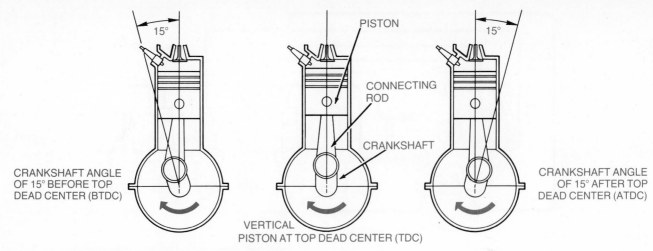

Fig. 30-20 Crankshaft and connecting rod angles and ignition timing.

30.10   IGNITION TIMING

The exact time at which ignition should occur in a combustion chamber depends upon how long it takes to burn the air-fuel mixture in the cylinder. The time required for complete combustion is affected by several engine design features: combustion chamber shape, spark plug position, and bore diameter. Besides engine design, several other things affect ignition timing. A proper air-fuel mixture burns much faster than one that is too rich or too lean. Gasoline with a high octane rating burns much slower than gasoline with a low octane. Highly volatile gasoline burns much faster than less volatile gasoline.

The time required for combustion also depends upon the engine's operating conditions. When the engine is operating at a low rpm there is enough time for the spark to burn the air-fuel mixture completely. At higher engine speeds, however, the air-fuel mixture must ignite, burn, and provide power to the piston in a shorter time. How hard the engine is working also affects combustion time. When the vehicle is under hard acceleration or climbing a hill, it is under a heavy load. Under these conditions, a rich air-fuel mixture is tightly packed in the cylinder. Combustion in the cylinder is fairly rapid. When the automobile is operated at medium speed on a level road, the engine is under a light load. Under these conditions, the carburetor provides a lean air-fuel mixture less tightly packed in the combustion chamber. Combustion is then slower.

Finally, engine operating temperature affects combustion time. Combustion is slower when the combustion chamber area is cold. As the engine heats up, the metal of the combustion chamber reaches a temperature which helps speed combustion.

When combustion takes a long time, the ignition system must deliver a spark to the cylinder earlier. This will provide enough time for a complete burning of the air-fuel mixture. When operating conditions allow faster combustion, the spark may be sent to the cylinder later.

When the piston is at top dead center (Fig. 30-20), the crankshaft and connecting rod are lined up vertically. The crankshaft is at an angle to this vertical line when the piston is at a point before or after top dead center. This angle, measured in degrees, is the method used to describe when ignition occurs. The letters BTDC indicate angles before top dead center and ATDC angles after top dead center.

When ignition occurs in relation to crankshaft movement, it is determined by three distributor advance systems: the initial or basic advance system, the centrifugal advance system, and the vacuum advance system. The purpose of the advance systems is to adjust ignition timing to engine operating conditions.

The ignition timing system is incorporated in the distributor on older vehicles and in the engine control computer on late model vehicles.

30.11   Initial or Basic Timing

The distributor cam is connected through the distributor shaft to the camshaft in the engine. The distributor contact points are mounted to a breaker plate attached to the distributor housing. The housing of the distributor is held in position on the engine by a hold-down bolt and clamp arrangement. When the hold-down bolt is loosened, the distributor housing and contact points may be rotated in relation to the breaker cam. Rotating the distributor housing in a

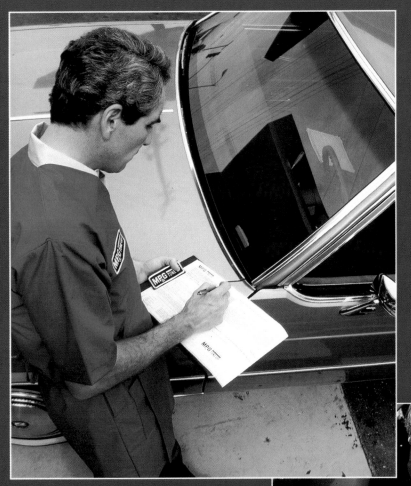

Left
When a car comes in for repair, enter on the repair order the usual data about the car owner and his car, and be sure you include the vehicle identification number behind the windshield. (Atlantic Richfield Company)

Below
Before getting into the car, protect the floor with a cover. (Atlantic Richfield Company)

Protect the fender with a cover to avoid belt buckle scratches or grease stains on the paint. (Atlantic Richfield Company)

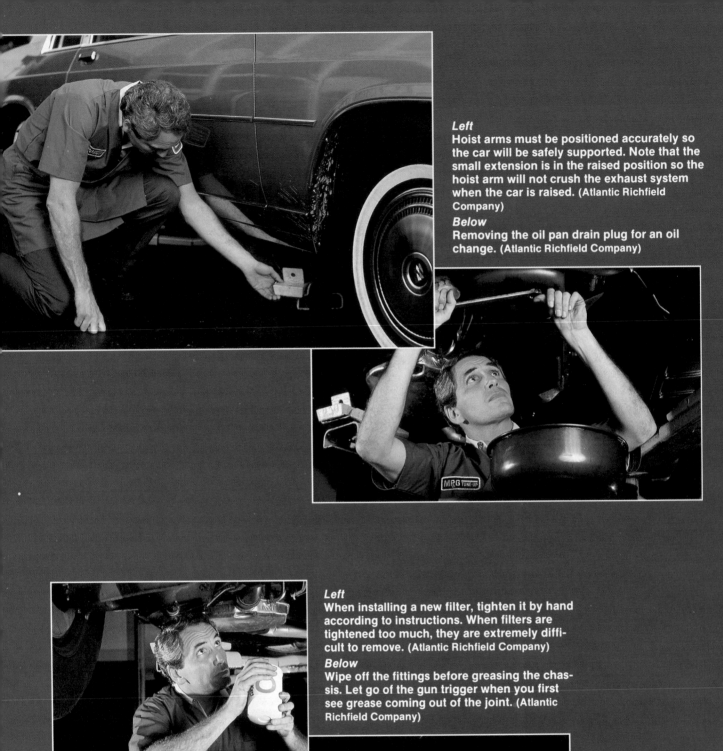

Left
Hoist arms must be positioned accurately so the car will be safely supported. Note that the small extension is in the raised position so the hoist arm will not crush the exhaust system when the car is raised. (Atlantic Richfield Company)

Below
Removing the oil pan drain plug for an oil change. (Atlantic Richfield Company)

Left
When installing a new filter, tighten it by hand according to instructions. When filters are tightened too much, they are extremely difficult to remove. (Atlantic Richfield Company)

Below
Wipe off the fittings before greasing the chassis. Let go of the gun trigger when you first see grease coming out of the joint. (Atlantic Richfield Company)

Before filling with oil, think: Did I put the plug back into the oil pan? (Atlantic Richfield Company)

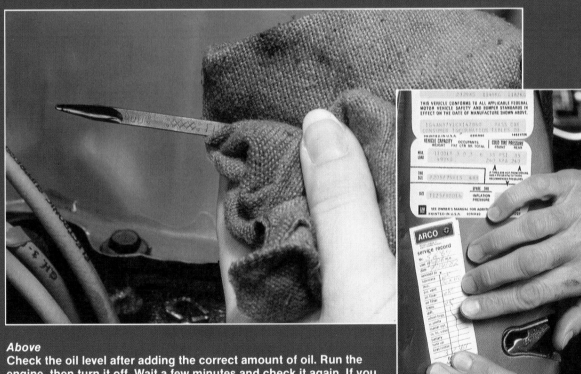

Above
Check the oil level after adding the correct amount of oil. Run the engine, then turn it off. Wait a few minutes and check it again. If you changed the oil filter, you will probably have to add more oil because the filter fills up with about one quart. (Atlantic Richfield Company)

Right
Enter the mileage and service performed on the lubrication sticker and install it on the door jamb. (Atlantic Richfield Company)

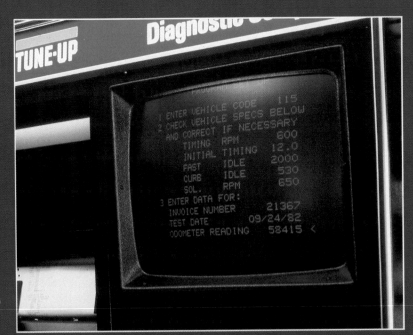

A modern engine analyzer gives instructions on the screen, and takes you step-by-step through the complete analysis. The computer knows whether you have hooked the leads up correctly, and will tell you if you have done it wrong. (Atlantic Richfield Company)

Above
Computer analyzers have a memory that knows the specifications for several years of cars. Just enter the vehicle, model, and engine size and type. The computer will show you the engine specifications on the screen. (Atlantic Richfield Company)

Right
Insert the hose into the exhaust pipe, and a two-gas analyzer will measure the amounts of hydrocarbon and carbon monoxide in the exhaust of a running engine. A four-gas analyzer will also measure the carbon dioxide and oxygen in the exhaust. (Atlantic Richfield Company)

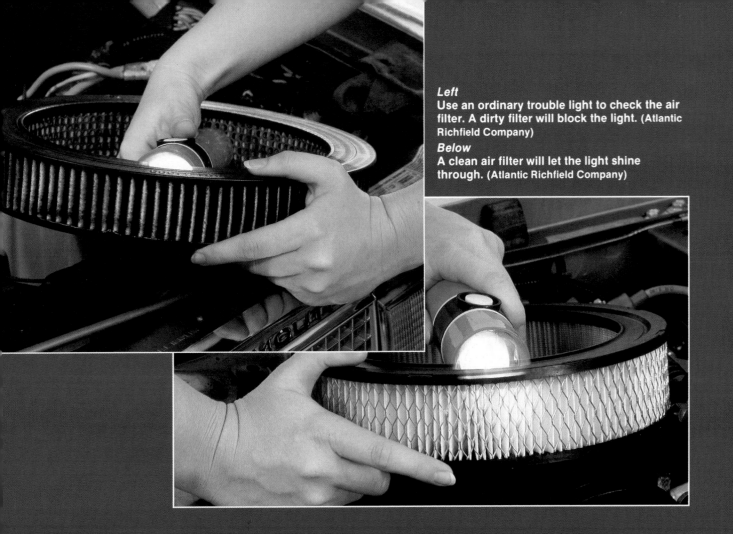

Left
Use an ordinary trouble light to check the air filter. A dirty filter will block the light. (Atlantic Richfield Company)

Below
A clean air filter will let the light shine through. (Atlantic Richfield Company)

Look the engine compartment over carefully for disconnected hoses, loose wire, or other things that might cause trouble. (Photo by Von Dem Bussche, Image Bank)

Squeeze the radiator hose to see if it is soft and deteriorated. If the engine is still warm, pressure in the hose may prevent squeezing it. Do not remove the radiator cap until the engine cools off. (Atlantic Richfield Company)

Left
With the engine dead, turn the belts over with your finger to see if they are cracked or worn. (Atlantic Richfield Company)

Below
With the engine cool, remove the radiator cap and check the coolant level. Engines with a coolant recovery tank should have their radiators filled, without any air space. (Atlantic Richfield Company)

When checking the power steering fluid, note that there are usually two marks on the dip-stick, one for hot fluid, and one for when the fluid is cold. Overfilling the power steering may cause the reservoir to overflow. (Atlantic Richfield Company)

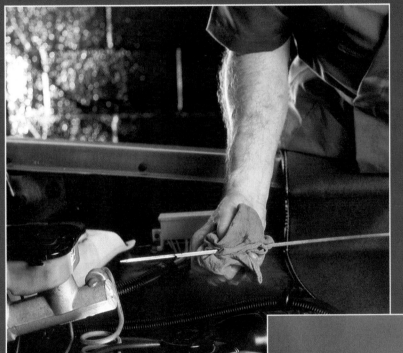

Left
Check the automatic transmission with the engine running, the shift lever in PARK, and the parking brake on. (Atlantic Richfield Company)

Below
Check the engine oil after the engine has been off for a few minutes to allow the oil to drain down into the oil pan. If you check it imme-diately after shutting the engine off, the read-ing will be low. (Atlantic Richfield Company)

Above
A corroded battery post and cable. If allowed to continue, the corrosion will build up between the post and cable, preventing the car from starting. (Atlantic Richfield Company)

Right
Scrape the corrosion off, then remove the cable and clean both the post and cable thoroughly. (Atlantic Richfield Company)

Below
A cable that has been removed, cleaned, and installed on a clean battery post. Oil or grease on the post and cable will help reduce corrosion. (Atlantic Richfield Company)

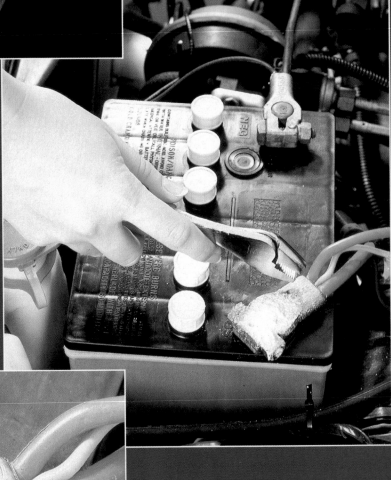

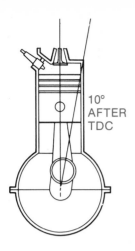

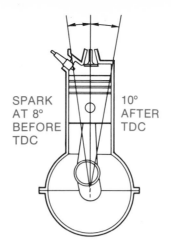

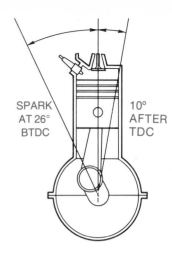

Fig. 30-21 Maximum pressure developed between 10 and 20 degrees after top dead center.

Fig. 30-22 Engine operating at 1,000 rpm.

Fig. 30-23 Engine operating at 2,000 rpm.

direction opposite that of cam rotation causes the contact points to open sooner. This causes ignition to advance or to occur sooner in the cylinder. Moving the distributor housing in the same direction as cam rotation causes the contact points to open later. This causes ignition to be retarded or to occur later in each of the cylinders.

Initial or basic timing is the positioning of the distributor housing in relation to the distributor cam. Initial timing is adjusted to manufacturer's specifications each time the ignition system is serviced. Specifications for most engines call for initial timing to be advanced several degrees before top dead center (BTDC). Some engines with emission control equipment are set when idling at top dead center (TDC) or even retarded several degrees after top dead center (ATDC).

Most engines have a stationary pointer above a pulley on the front of the crankshaft. Marks on the crankshaft pulley relate to degrees of advance or retard for the number 1 cylinder. Using a timing light, a mechanic can move the distributor housing when the engine is idling to set the proper amount of initial advance for the number 1 cylinder. The setting for the number 1 cylinder adjusts the initial timing for the entire engine.

30.12 Centrifugal or Speed Advance

When the engine is idling, ignition is usually timed to occur just before the piston reaches top dead center. At higher engine speeds, however, a shorter time is available for the air-fuel mixture to ignite, burn, and provide power to the piston. In order to get the most power from the mixture at higher engine speeds, the high-voltage spark must reach the cylinder earlier in the cycle.

The burning time for air-fuel mixture in an automotive engine is approximately 0.003 second. To obtain full power from combustion, maximum pressure must be reached while the piston is between 10 degrees and 20 degrees after top dead center (see Fig. 30-21). This maximum pressure point is fixed and does not change with engine speed. When the engine is operating at 1,000 revolutions per minute (rpm), the crankshaft travels through 18 degrees in 0.003 second. As shown in Figure 30-22, the spark must therefore occur at 8 degrees before top dead center if the air-fuel mixture is to be burned by 10 degrees after top dead center.

When engine speed increases, the crankshaft travels further in 0.003 second. At 2,000 rpm the crankshaft travels through 36 degrees of rotation in 0.003 second (Fig. 30-23). For complete combustion by 10 degrees after top dead center, ignition must therefore occur at 26 degrees before top dead center. At engine speeds higher than 2,000 rpm, the ignition must be advanced even further.

The timing of ignition to engine speed is done by the centrifugal advance mechanism in the distributor housing under the breaker plate. It consists of two centrifugal weights and two springs connected to the distributor cam assembly. The centrifugal weights, mounted on the distributor shaft, are held together or in a closed or inward position by the springs. The weights are connected to and drive the breaker cam assembly. When the engine is running, the distributor shaft and weight assembly rotate. As engine speed increases, the two weights move outward from centrifugal force, turning the breaker cam in an advance direction (Fig. 30-24). As a result, the cam lobes on

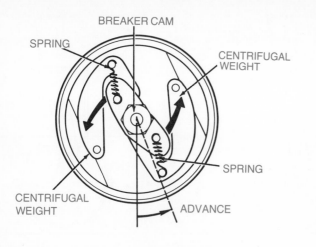
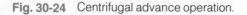

Fig. 30-24 Centrifugal advance operation.

Fig. 30-25 Two extremes of centrifugal advance.

the breaker cam contact the rubbing block on the contact set earlier. This causes the spark to occur sooner at the spark plug.

As engine speed continues to increase, the weights are forced further outward. This continues to advance the timing until the weights reach the end of their travel. On most engines, the centrifugal advance continues until it reaches approximately 30 degrees before top dead center. As engine speed decreases, there is less centrifugal force on the two weights and the spring tension starts to return the weights inward to their original position. As the weights move inward, timing is retarded. Figure 30-25 shows the two extremes of full and no advance.

30.13 Vacuum Advance

When the engine is operated at part throttle, a high vacuum is developed in the intake manifold and a smaller amount of air-fuel mixture is pulled into the cylinders. Since the mixture in the cylinders is leaner and less compressed, it burns slower. Under these conditions, spark advance is necessary beyond that provided by the centrifugal advance mechanism. Increasing the advance at part throttle will increase the time for combustion and result in increased fuel economy. Figure 30-26 compares full and part throttle advance requirements.

The vacuum advance (Fig. 30-27) advances the ignition at part throttle. The vacuum advance has a spring-loaded diaphragm connected by linkage to the distributor breaker plate. The airtight spring-loaded side of the diaphragm is connected by a vacuum

passage to an opening in the carburetor. This opening is on the atmospheric side of the throttle plate when the throttle is in idling position. In this position, there is no vacuum in the passage. When the throttle is partly opened, it swings past the opening of the vacuum passage. Intake manifold vacuum draws air from the airtight chamber in the vacuum advance mechanism, moving the diaphragm against the spring. This motion is transferred by mechanical linkage to the distributor breaker plate. The linkage is connected inside the housing so that it moves back and forth in relation to the breaker cam. When the breaker plate is rotated, the contact points mounted on it are positioned to be opened earlier by the distributor cam, and the ignition is advanced.

When engine load increases, intake manifold vacuum decreases and the spring returns the diaphragm and linkage to the original position. The breaker plate returns to a position where the cam contacts the contact point rubbing block later, retarding the ignition. The relationship between the contact points and distributor cam under high and low vacuum is shown in Figure 30-28.

30.14 IGNITION CABLES

The high-voltage wires which route current from the coil to the distributor cap and from the distributor cap to the spark plugs are called secondary wires, high-voltage wires, spark plug wires, high-tension wires, or ignition cables. They must be able to handle high voltage without leakage and withstand high

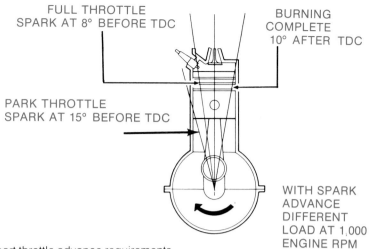

Fig. 30-26 Full and part throttle advance requirements.

FULL THROTTLE
SPARK AT 8° BEFORE TDC

BURNING
COMPLETE
10° AFTER TDC

PARK THROTTLE
SPARK AT 15° BEFORE TDC

WITH SPARK
ADVANCE
DIFFERENT
LOAD AT 1,000
ENGINE RPM

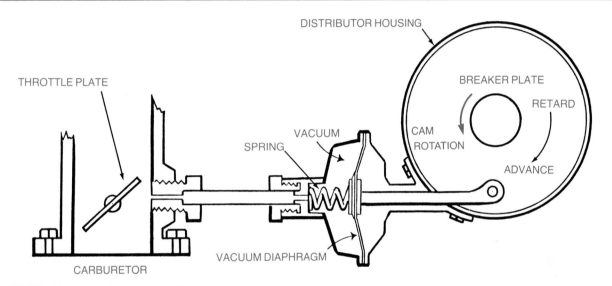

Fig. 30-27 Vacuum advance operation.

DISTRIBUTOR HOUSING

THROTTLE PLATE

BREAKER PLATE

RETARD

CAM ROTATION

ADVANCE

VACUUM

SPRING

CARBURETOR

VACUUM DIAPHRAGM

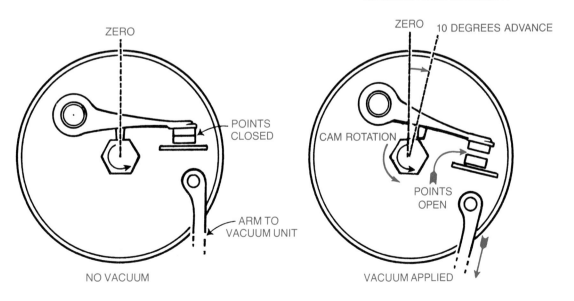

Fig. 30-28 Relationship of contact points to breaker cam.

BREAKER PLATE MOVEMENT

ZERO

ZERO   10 DEGREES ADVANCE

POINTS CLOSED

CAM ROTATION

POINTS OPEN

ARM TO VACUUM UNIT

NO VACUUM

VACUUM APPLIED

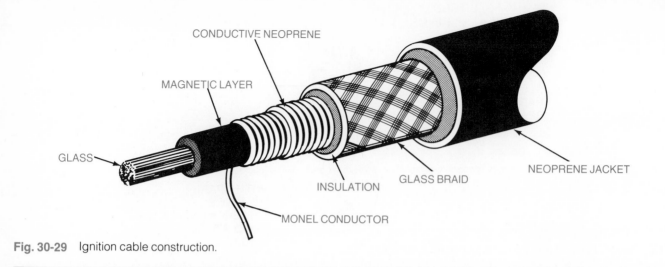

Fig. 30-29 Ignition cable construction.

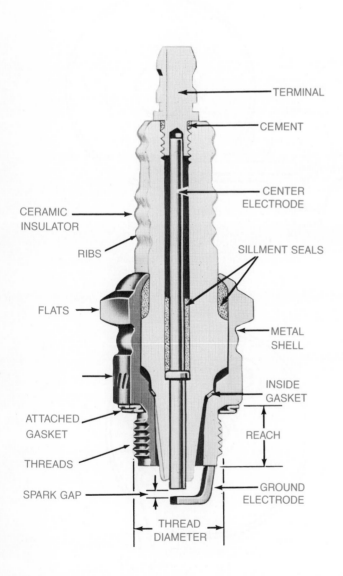

Fig. 30-30

under-hood temperatures (up to 200°F or 93°C) as well as water, oil, vibration, and abrasion.

For many years automotive ignition cables constructed from stainless steel or copper cores insulated with rubber gave satisfactory service. In the early 1960s, suppression spark plug cables were introduced to reduce interference with radio and television reception from high-frequency ignition waves. The first suppression cables were constructed with a core of linen thread saturated with graphite. Constantly changing under-hood temperatures caused the linen wire to become brittle. Handling the wires during a repair job often led to breakage. An improved ignition cable using a glass yarn core (Fig. 30-29) solved this problem. The glass core does not conduct voltage but provides mechanical strength for the wire. Conductive neoprene and monel surround the glass yarn and carry the current. Several layers of insulation to prevent leakage and glass braid to add strength are formed around the conductive materials. This wire provides the necessary radio and television suppression without loss of strength. The initials TVRS (television radio suppression) or the words electronic suppression, radio GM, or radio Ford are commonly printed on the jacket of ordinary resistance wire.

The suppression qualities result from high resistance offered by the wire. This high resistance does not reduce the effectiveness of the ignition because of the high voltage. In fact, the higher resistance in the cables may lead to longer spark plug life. Other means of television and radio suppression, such as resistorized rotors and resistorized spark plugs, should not be mixed. Together they could add excessive resistance to the secondary system. Distributor caps used with suppression wire must have aluminum cap inserts.

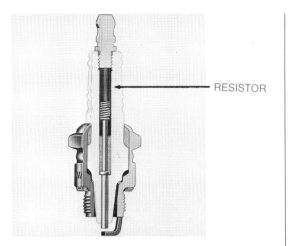

Fig. 30-31 Spark plug with resistor in center electrode. (Champion Spark Plug Company)

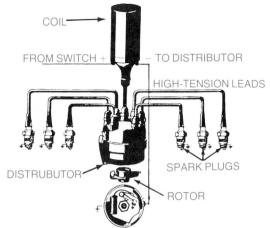

Fig. 30-32 Proper coil polarity for 12-volt negative ground system. (Champion Spark Plug Company)

Caps with copper inserts will react with the suppression wire to form high-resistance corrosion.

30.15   SPARK PLUGS

The spark plug provides an air gap in the engine's combustion chamber which the secondary voltage jumps, creating a spark to ignite the air-fuel mixture. But the spark plug is subjected to very difficult conditions. It must insulate the flow of thousands of volts of secondary current into the cylinder many times per second. While operating, the terminal end of the spark plug may be ice cold as the firing end three inches away is subjected to flame temperatures in excess of 2,000°F (1,093°C). The spark plug must be able to seal high pressures and resist the erosion caused by millions of spark discharges. If the spark plug and the rest of the ignition system perform satisfactorily, the air-fuel mixture in the cylinder will be burned smoothly, developing a great deal of power with very little pollution.

30.16   Spark Plug Construction

A spark plug is a wire with an air gap at the bottom that will fit into the engine's combustion chamber (Fig. 30-30). The wire which conducts high voltage into the cylinder is called the center electrode. A terminal is attached to the top of the center electrode to attach a connector from an ignition cable.

Since the center electrode must carry high voltage into the cylinder, it must be well insulated. The ceramic insulator formed around the center electrode has ribs on its outside diameter to increase the distance between the terminal and the nearest ground.

This helps eliminate current leakage or flashover, especially when the outside of the ceramic is dirty or wet.

The center electrode and ceramic insulator assembly is joined to a metal shell. The shell, insulated from the center electrode by the ceramic, has threads that allow the spark plug to be screwed into the combustion chamber. Flats on the outside of the shell allow a wrench to be used on the spark plug for installation and removal. A side or ground electrode is attached to the shell a small distance away from the center electrode. This distance is the air gap or spark plug gap that the current jumps to create a spark.

The spark plug, mounted in the combustion chamber, is subjected to extremely high pressures. Seals between the shell and ceramic insulator and between the center electrode and the ceramic insulator prevent leakage of combustion pressures. Either a copper gasket or a special taper seat is used to prevent leakage of combustion pressures around the shell threads.

Most spark plug manufacturers offer a spark plug designed to suppress radio and television interference. These spark plugs use a resistor in the center electrode (Fig. 30-31). Voltage requirements of resistorized and regular spark plugs are about the same. The resistor changes ignition oscillating frequency at the instant the arc is established across the electrodes. This change in frequency moves the ignition system out of television and radio frequencies.

30.17   Spark Plug Operation

Secondary high voltage flows from the ignition coil to the distributor cap to the rotor and back out of

Fig. 30-33 Spark plug thread dimensions.
(Champion Spark Plug Company)

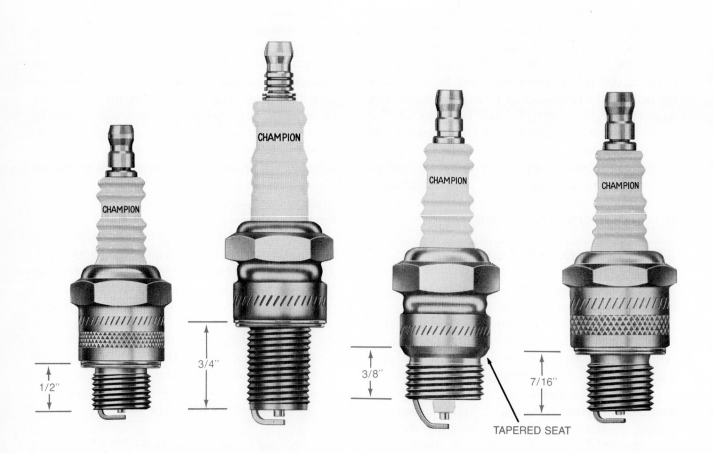

TAPERED SEAT

Fig. 30-34 Spark plug reaches. (Champion Spark Plug Company)

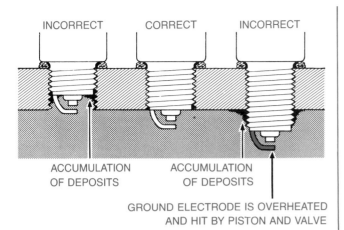

INCORRECT   CORRECT   INCORRECT

ACCUMULATION
OF DEPOSITS

ACCUMULATION
OF DEPOSITS

GROUND ELECTRODE IS OVERHEATED
AND HIT BY PISTON AND VALVE

Fig. 30-35   Comparison of correct and incorrect reach spark plugs in a cylinder head. (NGK Spark Plugs)

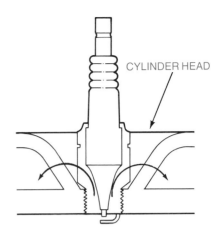

CYLINDER HEAD

Fig. 30-36   Heat flow away from firing end.

the cap through the high-voltage ignition cables. The voltage enters the spark plug at the terminal end of the center electrode and flows down the center electrode to the air gap located in the engine's combustion chamber. The current overcomes the resistance of the air-fuel mixture and jumps the air gap to the side electrode. The spark created as the current jumps the gap ignites the combustible mixture.

The voltage required to overcome the resistance of the air-fuel mixture varies under different conditions. The wider the air gap, the higher the required voltage. The condition of the spark plug electrodes is also very important. Much less voltage is required to jump from clean, sharp electrodes than dirty, eroded ones. The higher the compression pressures, the higher the voltage required to overcome the air gap.

In order for current to jump the gap from the center to the side electrode, the electrodes must have the correct polarity. The polarity should be negative at the spark plug terminal to decrease voltage required to jump the gap. The center electrode operates at much higher temperatures than the side electrode, and electrons will leave the hotter surface at a lower voltage.

The polarity at the electrodes is determined by the direction current flows through the primary winding of the coil. Most vehicles use a 12-volt negative ground electrical system. The primary terminals on the coil may be identified as *pos* or + for positive and *neg* or − for negative. The negative lead should always be connected to the distributor terminal (Fig. 30-32). If these leads are reversed, much higher voltages are required to operate the ignition. The system operates, but at reduced efficiency. To avoid reversed polarity, many coil manufacturers identify the terminal that should be connected to the distributor with the abbreviation *dist.* or *bat.* for battery.

30.18   Spark Plug Sizes

The spark plug must be the right size for the combustion chamber. Different sizes of spark plugs are required for different engine designs. Spark plugs are made with different shell thread diameters. The threads in metric sizes are measured in millimetres. Using a metric thread allows the plugs to be used in both foreign and American automobiles. The two most common thread sizes are 16 mm and 18 mm (see Fig. 30-33).

The threaded section of the shell is also made in different lengths or reaches (Fig. 30-34). There are several common reach dimensions: 3/8 inch, 7/16 inch, 1/2 inch, and 3/4 inch. The thickness of the combustion chamber determines the reach of the spark plug. The reach must not be too short or too long, as shown in Figure 30-35.

30.19   Heat Range

The spark plug tip or electrode area, mounted in the combustion chamber, is subjected to temperatures that may exceed 2,000°F (1,093°C). The firing end of the spark plug removes this heat through the cylinder head (Fig. 30-36). Heat moves up the ceramic insulator to the metal shell, out into the cylinder head, and into the cooling system.

Spark plugs must operate within a specific temperature range. The heat range or the ability of a spark plug to conduct heat away from the firing end is determined by the distance the heat must flow from the firing end to the shell (Fig. 30-37). This is determined by the length of the insulator firing end. If the path is long, the firing end remains at a high temperature. This is referred to as a hot spark plug. If the path

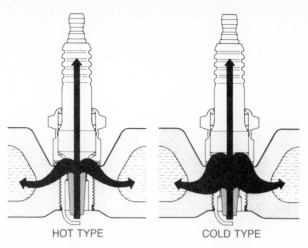

HOT TYPE   COLD TYPE

Fig. 30-37 Heat flow in a hot and cold spark plug. (NGK Spark Plugs)

for heat flow is short, heat is removed easier from the firing end and the spark plug operates cooler. This type of spark plug is referred to as a cold spark plug.

The spark plug tip must operate between carbon and oil fouling temperatures and preignition and electrode burning temperatures. If the temperature of the tip of the spark plug is too cold, carbon and oil will burn off the electrodes. Deposits will soon build up on the electrodes and cause misfire. If the tip area is too hot, the insulator end may ignite the air-fuel mixture, causing preignition. Excessive heat at the tip end will also speed up electrode burning and erosion, reducing the useful life of the spark plug.

Since different engines have different temperature characteristics, spark plugs with different heat ranges must be manufactured. Figure 30-38 shows the tip temperature of three spark plugs at different engine speeds. Notice that the tip temperature of all three spark plugs increases as the engine speed increases from idle to full throttle. Spark plug number 1 is too hot. At full throttle the tip temperature is in the preignition and electrode burning area. Spark plugs number 3 is too cold. At idle speeds its tip allows carbon and oil fouling. The correct spark plug for this engine is number 2. At idle its tip temperature is high enough to prevent carbon and oil fouling; at full throttle it does not reach preignition temperatures.

Some spark plug insulator noses and electrodes extend deeper into the combustion chamber (Fig. 30-39). These extended tip spark plugs use charge cooling at higher engine speeds (Fig. 30-40). The incoming air-fuel mixture hits the extended tip at high speeds, reducing the temperature of the tip and the electrodes. This provides protection against overheat-

ing at high speeds while keeping the plug hot enough to provide low-speed fouling protection.

Spark plug and engine manufacturers work together to determine the best spark plug heat range for a particular engine. In many cases application charts suggest several spark plugs with different heat ranges for a vehicle. The mechanic should select the best heat range for driving conditions. A vehicle operated most of the time at high speed needs a cold plug. One operated in stop-and-go traffic may require a hotter plug.

30.20   Spark Plug Codes

To be correctly matched to an engine, a spark plug must have the correct thread diameter, gasket or tapered seat, heat range resistor, and reach. Spark plug manufacturers identify these items on their spark plugs with a code printed on the ceramic insulator of the spark plug. There is no universally adopted code. All spark plug manufacturers use their own code system. On the code system shown in Figure 30-41, the letter identifies the spark plug reach. For example, the J indicates plugs with a 3/8-inch reach and L plugs with a 3/4-inch reach. Another letter, such as R or X, may identify a resistor spark plug. Thread sizes and gasket or tapered seat plugs are identified by numbers. Since each spark plug manufacturer's code is different, a mechanic must look at an application chart to find out the correct plug for any vehicle. Most of these charts also provide a cross reference so that one manufacturer's spark plug can be correctly replaced with another.

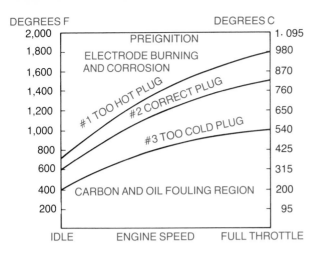

DEGREES F

2,000 — PREIGNITION
1,800 — ELECTRODE BURNING
1,600 — AND CORROSION
1,400 — #1 TOO HOT PLUG
1,200 — #2 CORRECT PLUG
1,000 — #3 TOO COLD PLUG
800 —
600 —
400 — CARBON AND OIL FOULING REGION
200 —

DEGREES C

1 095
980
870
760
650
540
425
315
200
95

IDLE   ENGINE SPEED   FULL THROTTLE

Fig. 30-38 Proper spark plug heat range.

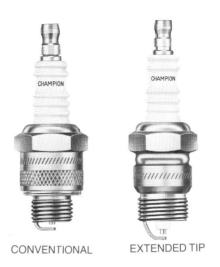

CONVENTIONAL   EXTENDED TIP

Fig. 30-39 Conventional and extended tip spark plug. (Champion Spark Plug Company)

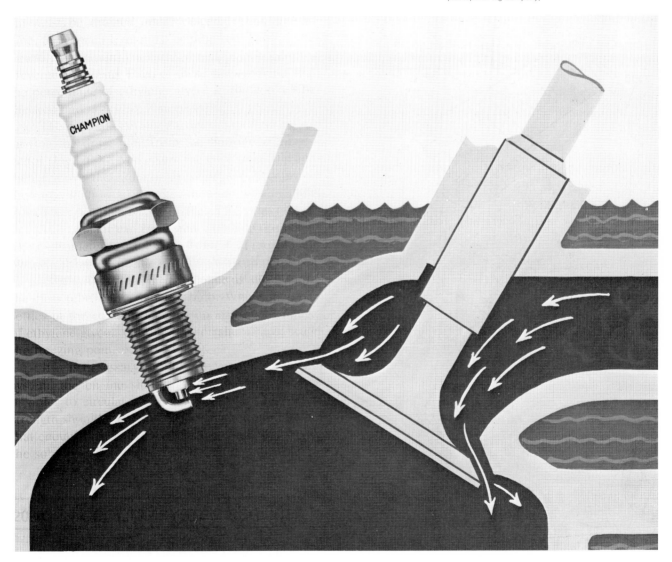

Fig. 30-40 Charge cooling the spark plug.
(Champion Spark Plug Company)

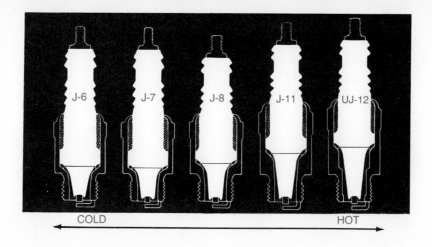

COLD ← → HOT

J-6   J-7   J-8   J-11   UJ-12

Fig. 30-41   Heat range codes. (Champion Spark Plug Company)

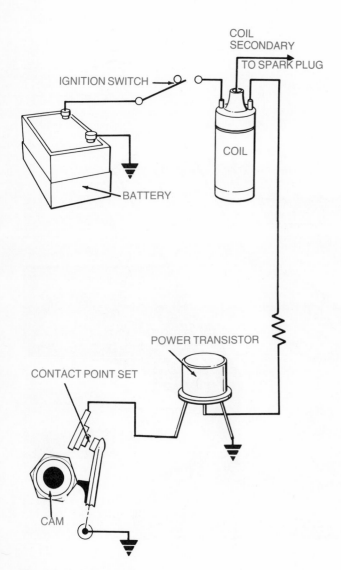

IGNITION SWITCH

BATTERY

COIL
SECONDARY
TO SPARK PLUG

COIL

POWER TRANSISTOR

CONTACT POINT SET

CAM

Fig. 30-42   Contact-triggered solid state ignition system.

30.21   SOLID STATE IGNITION SYSTEMS

The solid state ignition system may be called an electronic ignition, transistorized ignition, breakerless ignition, or high-energy ignition. It is designed to overcome a number of problems with the conventional ignition system. The performance of the conventional ignition has always been restricted because of some of the following limitations of the contact points:

1. *Limited contact point life.* Contact points begin to wear from the moment they are installed. After ten thousand miles or so the contact points are worn out and ignition failure may result.

2. *Changes in ignition timing.* The wear of the contact points and rubbing block changes the time at which the contact points open. This changes the ignition timing and may result in poor engine operation.

3. *Periodic maintenance.* Contact point and rubbing block wear make it necessary to change the contact points to guard against system failure.

4. *Current handling limitations.* Contact points can handle only a limited amount of current. This limits the output from the coil.

5. *High engine speed effects.* At high engine speeds the time the contact points are closed to store energy in the coil is very short. This short time for current flow results in low-voltage output.

6. *Temperature effects.* The current flow across the contact points is affected by temperature. High contact point operating temperatures increase resistance and limit system operation. Low operating

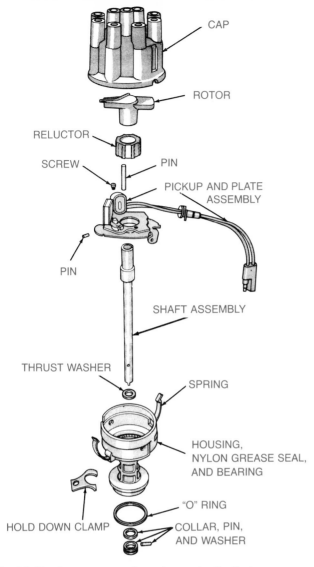

Fig. 30-43 Components of an electronic distributor. (Chrysler Corporation)

Labels in figure:
CAP
ROTOR
RELUCTOR
SCREW
PIN
PICKUP AND PLATE ASSEMBLY
PIN
SHAFT ASSEMBLY
THRUST WASHER
SPRING
HOUSING, NYLON GREASE SEAL, AND BEARING
"O" RING
HOLD DOWN CLAMP
COLLAR, PIN, AND WASHER

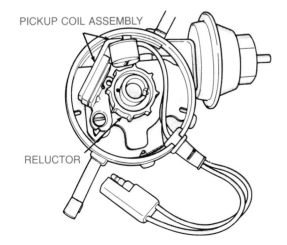

Fig. 30-44 Main parts of the electronic distributor are the pickup coil and reluctor. (Chrysler Corporation)

Labels in figure:
PICKUP COIL ASSEMBLY
RELUCTOR

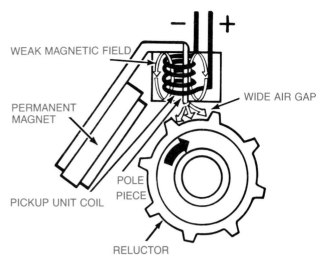

Fig. 30-45 The wide air gap provides resistance to the magnetic field. (Chrysler Corporation)

Labels in figure:
WEAK MAGNETIC FIELD
PERMANENT MAGNET
PICKUP UNIT COIL
WIDE AIR GAP
POLE PIECE
RELUCTOR

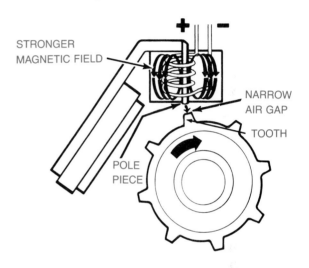

Fig. 30-46 When tooth and pole piece align, there is a stronger magnetic field and a positive voltage. (Chrysler Corporation)

Labels in figure:
STRONGER MAGNETIC FIELD
NARROW AIR GAP
TOOTH
POLE PIECE

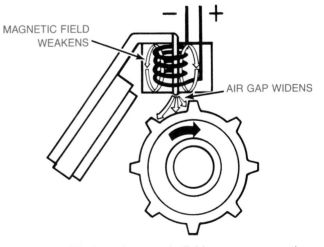

Fig. 30-47 Weakened magnetic field causes a negative voltage. (Chrysler Corporation)

Labels in figure:
MAGNETIC FIELD WEAKENS
AIR GAP WIDENS

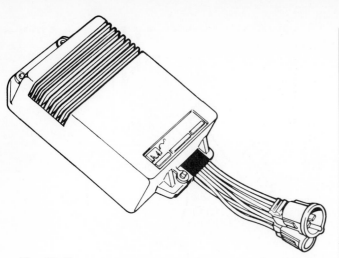

Fig. 30-48 An electronic control unit or module. (Ford Motor Company)

temperatures decrease circuit resistance, allowing an increase in current flow. A high current flow across the contact points may result in burned contact points.

The solid state ignition system was developed to overcome these problems and to reduce exhaust emissions. Solid state systems may be divided into inductive discharge systems, Hall effect, and capacitive discharge systems.

30.22 INDUCTIVE DISCHARGE SYSTEMS

An inductive discharge system uses the energy stored in a coil or inductor for ignition. The conventional ignition system is an inductive discharge system, and so are most solid state ignition systems. There are three types of solid state inductive discharge systems: contact-triggered, magnetically triggered, and light-triggered systems.

30.23 Contact-Triggered Inductive Discharge Systems

Because of the many problems with contact points, an ignition system using a transistor as a switch was developed to take the burden off the points. The earliest solid state ignition did this by using the points to control a power transistor. The transistor handles the switching of the primary current for the coil. Contact-triggered systems were developed in the 1950s and were used on production automobiles in the 1960s.

A simplified drawing of a contact-triggered

system is shown in Figure 30-42. A power transistor is used in the primary circuit between the contact points and the coil. The rotation of the distributor cam opens and closes the contact points just as in a conventional system. In this system, however, only a small amount of the current of a conventional system goes across the points. The opening and closing of the points is used to switch the bias current to the base-emitter junction of the transistor. The transistor does the switching of the coil primary through its collector-emitter junction. Since the contact points handle a small amount of current, they last much longer.

This system is very similar to the conventional system except for the addition of the transistor and the removal of the condenser. The transistor makes possible a higher current flow to the coil primary. With more current available, ignition coils for these systems could be designed for higher secondary voltages.

The power transistor is located in an aluminum heat sink mounted in a cool area under the hood. The rest of the components are similar to a conventional system with the exception that the breaker points use no condenser.

30.24 Magnetically Triggered Inductive Discharge Systems

In the middle and late 1960s an inductive discharge system was developed that eliminated contact points entirely. A magnetic trigger device in the distributor replaced the contact points in working the power transistor. The magnetically triggered unit proved so successful that it has replaced contact-triggered units on all new vehicles.

The battery, resistor, switch, ignition cables, and spark plugs of this system are the same as those used in the conventional system. The ignition coil, which may be similar in appearance to the conventional ignition coil, is different electrically. It has a different number of turns of wire in both the primary and secondary windings because the primary current is greater than in the conventional system.

Many components of the electronic ignition distributor (Fig. 30-43) are the same as those for a breaker point distributor. Both ignition systems use the same type of ignition coil and spark plugs. The main difference between the two distributors is that the breaker point assembly in the breaker point distributor is replaced with a pickup unit in the electronic distributor, and the cam is replaced with a reluctor (Fig. 30-44).

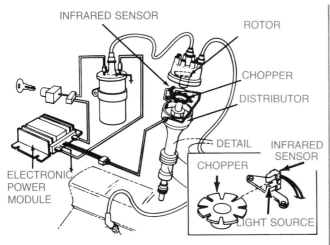

Fig. 30-49 Parts of a light-triggered inductive discharge system

The pickup unit consists of a permanent magnet and a coil that is wound around a pole piece. The pole piece is an extension of the mounting bracket and is attached to the permanent magnet. Because of this arrangement, the pickup unit resembles a horseshoe-type magnet, with the reluctor end of the pole piece acting as one of the poles.

The reluctor is a gear-like component that is attached to the distributor shaft in the same position as the cam in a breaker point distributor. The reluctor is not a magnet, but it does provide a better magnetic path than air. In other words, it is capable of reducing reluctance (resistance to the flow of magnetic lines of force). The reluctor may be called a trigger wheel (AMC), reluctor (Chrysler), armature (Ford), or timer core (GM). The magnetic pickup may be called a sensor (AMC), magnetic pickup (Chrysler), stator (Ford), or pickup coil assembly (GM).

The reluctor and the pickup unit in an electronic ignition distributor do electrically what the cam and rubbing block do mechanically in a breaker point distributor. Although the electronic distributor components replace the cam and breaker points, they operate quite differently. In a breaker point distributor, the current flowing through the primary winding of the ignition coil is interrupted when the breaker points are opened by the rotating cam. The collapsing magnetic field in the primary winding induces enough voltage in the secondary winding to fire the spark plugs. In the electronic ignition distributor, a permanent magnet in the pickup unit provides a magnetic field from the pole piece to the permanent magnet. This permanent magnetic field passes through the pickup unit coil that is wound around the pole piece. The magnetic field is relatively weak, because the wide air gap (Fig. 30-45) between the pole piece and the permanent magnet does not provide a good magnetic path.

As a tooth of the reluctor approaches the pole piece (Fig. 30-46), it provides a better path than the wide air gap provides, and the strength of the magnetic field in the pickup unit is increased. Increasing the magnetic field strength at the pickup unit coil induces a positive ($+$) voltage at one terminal of the coil. This voltage is induced as a result of the changing (increasing) magnetic field strength. It is not caused by the physical movement of the magnetic field or the pickup unit coil. The positive ($+$) voltage continues to build until the reluctor tooth is exactly opposite the pole piece.

As soon as the reluctor tooth passes the pole piece (Fig. 30-47), the air gap widens and the magnetic field weakens once again. The weakened magnetic field through the coil induces a negative ($-$) voltage at the same terminal of the pickup unit coil winding. Again, the voltage is induced by the change (reduction) in magnetic field strength. No voltage is induced in the pickup unit coil unless the reluctor is moving. The rapid increase and decrease of the magnetic field as the rotating reluctor teeth approach and pass the pole piece induces the positive ($+$) and then the negative ($-$) voltage.

The induced voltage is a very small electrical signal that is fed into the electronic control unit (Fig. 30-48). The control unit is an electronic switching circuit which turns the primary circuit off and on in response to a voltage pulse received from the reluctor and pickup coil. The ignition control module is called the control unit (AMC and Chrysler), modulator assembly (Ford), or module (GM).

The control unit switches off the flow of current to the coil primary windings, inducing the secondary windings to build up a high voltage charge which is distributed to the spark plugs exactly as in the breaker type ignition system. The control unit contains timing circuits which then close the primary circuit allowing it to build up a charge sufficient to enable the secondary windings to produce the high voltage required to fire the next cylinder. In effect, this timing action sets the dwell, or period corresponding to the time the breaker points are closed in the breaker type ignition system. Thus, electronic ignition systems never need dwell adjustments.

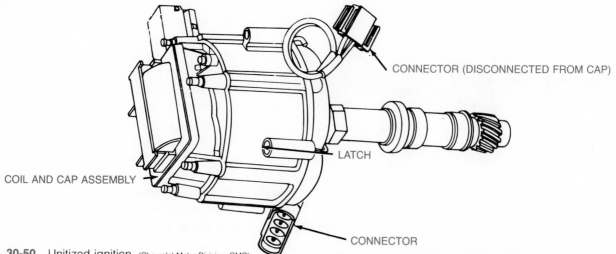

Fig. 30-50 Unitized ignition. (Chevrolet Motor Division, GMC)

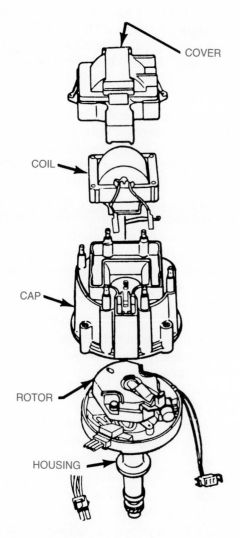

Fig. 30-51 Exploded view of unitized ignition. (Chevrolet Motor Division, GMC)

30.25 Light-Triggered Inductive Discharge System

The light-triggered system (Fig. 30-49) operates in much the same way as the magnetically triggered system. The difference is the method used to trigger the coil. A beam of infrared light is interrupted instead of a magnetic field. Again, a rotating toothed wheel is used. In most units it is called a chopper. By passing the teeth between a light source and a light sensor, a signal is produced for the control or power module. The control module operates the coil just as in the other systems.

30.26 Unitized Ignition System

Since 1975, most General Motors vehicles have been equipped with a high-energy unitized ignition system (Figs. 30-50 and 30-51). This system is called unitized because the coil and control unit are housed together in the distributor. The system works the same as the magnetically triggered system. A number of components used in the unitized system appear to be quite different, however.

The system uses a built-in ignition coil, an electronic module, and a magnetic pickup assembly. The module and pickup assembly take the place of the conventional contact points and condenser. The magnetic pickup assembly over the shaft contains a permanent magnet, a pole piece with internal teeth, and a pickup coil (Fig. 30-52). When the teeth of the timer core line up with the teeth of the pole piece, an induced voltage in the pickup coil signals

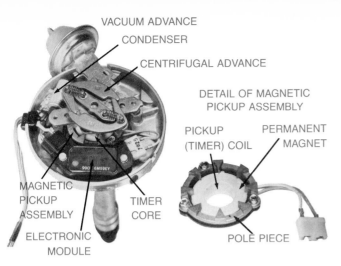

Fig. 30-52   Inside the unitized distributor and detail of magnetic pickup assembly.

VACUUM ADVANCE
CONDENSER
CENTRIFUGAL ADVANCE
DETAIL OF MAGNETIC PICKUP ASSEMBLY
PICKUP (TIMER) COIL
PERMANENT MAGNET
MAGNETIC PICKUP ASSEMBLY
TIMER CORE
ELECTRONIC MODULE
POLE PIECE

Fig. 30-53   Electronic module.

990 6M59EY

the electronic module to interrupt the coil primary circuit. The standard vacuum and centrifugal advance systems are utilized.

The module (Fig. 30-53) mounted inside the distributor has been miniaturized. It contains a microminiature electrical circuit with components so small that they cannot be seen even with a magnifying glass. When the module receives a signal from the pickup coil, it allows the ignition coil primary to flow. When the timer core teeth move away from the pole piece teeth, the voltage signal disappears and the module turns the primary current off, inducing a high voltage in the coil secondary.

The unitized system coil (Fig. 30-54) is mounted on top of the distributor cap. It consists of an iron frame and a primary and secondary winding covered with epoxy for insulation. The center lead of the coil is connected under one of the mounting screws. When the connector on the distributor is attached to the terminals, the coil iron frame is grounded to the distributor base. This allows any electrical charge that builds up on the coil frame to drain off to ground, preventing possible arc-over and radio noise. The coil circuit is the same as that of a conventional unit. The coil, rotor cap, and spark plug wiring harness assembly are attached to the distributor housing with two bolts.

30.27   HALL EFFECT IGNITION SYSTEMS

In recent years, automotive manufacturers have developed an ignition system based upon the Hall effect. This system operates with a different prin-

ciple than the magnetically triggered system used previously. The Hall effect system has all the advantages of other solid state ignitions. In addition, the Hall effect system can be manufactured less expensively than other systems and blends easily into a complete electronic engine control system.

30.28   Hall Effect Principle

The Hall effect was discovered by Edward H. Hall of Johns Hopkins University in 1879. He found that when a thin rectangular conductor carrying an electric current is crossed at right angles by a magnetic field, a difference in voltage can be detected at the conductor's edges (Fig. 30-55). Further, he found that the stronger the current flowing through the conductor, and the strength of the magnetic field, the higher the voltage output.

Whenever an electron moves through a magnet field, a force is exerted on the electron. This force is called the Lorentz force. This force will move the electron at right angles to the magnetic field and at right angles to the direction of the current flow. The Lorentz force is proportional to the strength of the magnetic field and to the speed of the electron.

The Lorentz force in the Hall effect element causes the electrons to move perpendicular to the current flow and perpendicular to the magnetic field. As the strength of the magnetic flux is increased, more electrons will be deflected downward toward the edge of the thin slab of gold or semiconductor material. Hall effect voltages tend to be weak, so an amplifier is used in the circuit.

A system using the Hall effect principle is capable of delivering higher energy with lower aver-

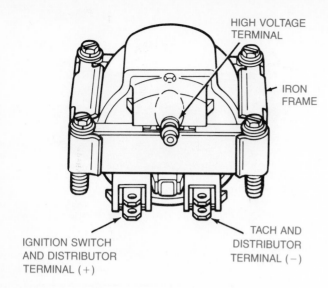

Fig. 30-54 Unitized coil. (American Motors Corporation)

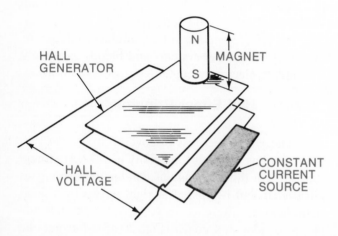

Fig. 30-55 The Hall effect principle.

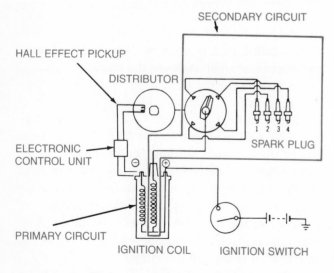

Fig. 30-56 Hall effect primary and secondary circuit schematic. (Chrysler Corporation)

age current flow at lower rpm than conventional solid state ignition systems. Since engines require highest spark plug voltage at lowest engine rpm, the Hall effect ignition system has distinct advantages over conventional electronic ignition systems.

30.29 Components and Operation

An electrical schematic of the primary and secondary circuit is shown in Figure 30-56. The primary circuit consists of the ignition switch feed, an electronic control unit, a Hall effect pickup assembly (including the underside parts of a rotor), and the primary circuit of the ignition coil. On models without electronic spark control, the primary circuit is also controlled by speed (centrifugal) and load (vacuum) advance mechanisms.

The secondary circuit consists of the secondary circuit of the ignition coil, a high output cable to the distributor cap, the upper part of the rotor, distributor secondary terminals and cables, and the grounded spark plugs. The ignition coil assembly is shared by both circuits, as is the distributor assembly.

The circuit containing the Hall effect element and a signal conditioner are part of the pickup module attached to the distributor plate (Fig. 30-57). A permanent magnet is also mounted on the plate facing the sensor, with a small air gap between the two. A circular ring of four iron alloy "shutters" is attached to a distributor rotor so that the shutters rotate through the air gap when the distributor shaft turns (Fig. 30-58). This alternately turns the magnet field on and off, causing a change in the Hall voltage in the sensor directly related to the position of the distributor rotor.

The Hall voltage signal is converted into a sharp "on/off" signal by the signal conditioner. The length of time the primary circuit is closed (called *dwell*) is controlled by the design of the shutters on the distributor rotor. This allows maximum high rpm output with minimum low rpm coil heating. All that is needed to switch the ignition coil primary current is power amplification, which is provided by the electronic control unit or electronic control computer.

The electronic control unit (Fig. 30-59) powers the Hall effect sensor. An electronic switch called the electronic control unit (ECU) receives a signal from the Hall sensor in the distributor. The signal is received each time a rotor shutter passes the magnet and sensor. Current (amperage) that flows through the ignition coil primary windings also flows through the ECU. When a signal from the distrib-

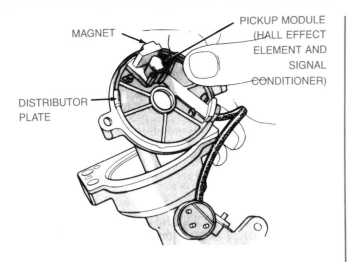

Fig. 30-57 Hall effect pickup assembly. (Chrysler Corporation)

utor is sent to the ECU, the coil primary current is temporarily stopped causing the coil secondary circuit to discharge voltage to the distributor and spark plugs.

30.30 CAPACITIVE DISCHARGE IGNITION SYSTEMS

The capacitive discharge (CD) ignition system stores and discharges energy from a condenser or capacitor. A reliable capacitive discharge system was not developed until the beginning of solid state electronics in the 1960s. While this system is not standard equipment on any American automobile, several companies manufacture after-market or add-on capacitive discharge systems.

Like the conventional ignition system, a condenser or capacitor is made of two parallel plates separated by an insulator. When current enters the capacitor, electrons build up on one plate, and their negative charge repels a like number of electrons on the other plate. In this condition the capacitor is said to be charged. Energy is stored in the capacitor. When the current flow is stopped the energy remains in the capacitor. Only when a conductor is connected across the two plates will it discharge or regain electron balance. A small capacitor is capable of storing a large electron charge and providing a big discharge.

In a capacitive discharge system a charged capacitor is placed across the primary winding of an ignition coil. As the capacitor discharges into the primary winding, a strong magnetic field is established that cuts the secondary winding, inducing a high voltage. Energy is not stored in the coil, but is

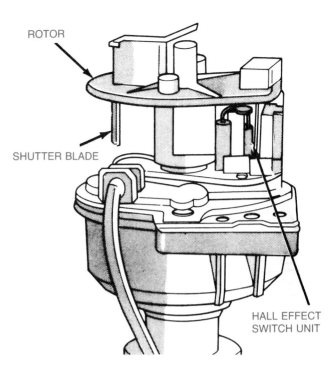

Fig. 30-58 Shutters rotate past the Hall effect switch. (Chrysler Corporation)

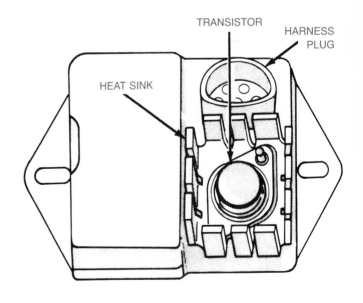

Fig. 30-59 Electronic control unit for the Hall effect system. (Chrysler Corporation)

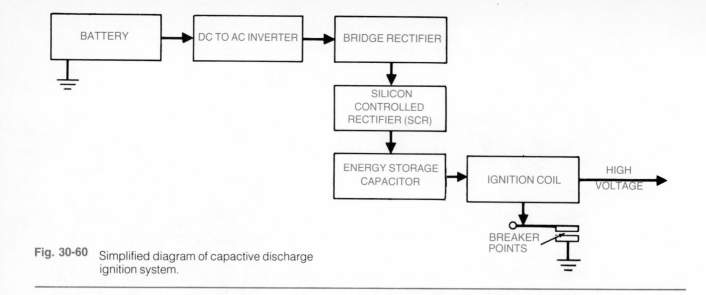

Fig. 30-60 Simplified diagram of capacitive discharge ignition system.

used only to step up the voltage from the capacitor. More energy is developed in this way than in a conventional ignition. The capacitor is then disconnected from the coil and recharged so that the discharge into the primary can occur again for the next firing cycle. The charging of the capacitor requires a voltage higher than the 12 volts available from the battery or alternator.

A simplified diagram of a capacitive discharge system is shown in Figure 30-60. Because of the very short time interval, around 5 milliseconds, to charge the capacitor even at low engine speeds, an inverter is used to quickly build up a charge in the energy storage capacitor. The inverter changes the low voltage direct current from the battery or alternator to an alternating current. The alternating current transformed by the inverter is changed back to direct current by the bridge rectifier. The output of the inverter and rectifier is approximately 400 volts.

The 400 volts stored in the capacitor must be discharged into the coil primary at just the right time for ignition. The conventional distributor and contact points may be used as a trigger. The contact point opening supplies a signal to a switching device called a silicon controlled rectifier (SCR). When the SCR gets the signal from the contact points, it switches the circuit so that the capacitor discharges into the coil primary. A high voltage induced in the secondary is directed to the rotor cap and rotor system. The SCR then switches the circuitry back to allow the capacitor to charge for the next discharge.

In the control unit of a capacitive discharge ignition system (Fig. 30-61), the distributor may utilize contact points or a magnetic pickup to provide the SCR signal. In either case, the conventional vacuum and centrifugal timing mechanisms are used. The control unit is the only thing that looks different from a conventional ignition. The control unit houses the inverter, bridge rectifier, SCR, and energy storer capacitor.

NEW TERMS

Capacitor An electrical device that stores or soaks up a surge of electricity.

Capacitive discharge ignition system An ignition system that uses the energy stored in a capacitor to develop high voltage.

Centrifugal advance An ignition timing system that uses a set of weights controlled by centrifugal force.

Coil An electrical device that steps up voltage for ignition.

Condenser The capacitor in the ignition primary that prevents contact point arcing.

Contact points The switch in the ignition primary system that controls coil operation.

Ground electrode The spark plug electrode that is connected to ground.

Distributor The part that distributes ignition current to the correct cylinder at the correct time.

Hall effect ignition Breakerless electronic control switch, the operation of which is based upon the Hall effect. In the case of electronic ignition systems, it is used as a pulse generator.

Heat range How hot the plug gets in operation.

Ignition cables High-voltage ignition cables used to carry secondary voltage.

Ignition timing Providing the spark to the correct cylinder at the correct time for combustion.

Fig. 30-61 Control unit for capacitive discharge ignition.
(Delta Products)

Inductive discharge system An ignition system that uses the energy stored in a coil for ignition.

Initial timing Timing adjusted by the position of the distributor in the engine.

Light-triggered inductive discharge system An ignition system that uses a beam of light to trigger the coil.

Magnetically triggered inductive discharge system An ignition system that uses a magnetic pulse to trigger the coil.

Primary system The ignition circuit that carries the low-voltage ignition current.

Primary winding A winding in the coil consisting of heavy wire.

Resistor bypass circuit The circuit that sends ignition current through a resistor when the vehicle is started.

Rotor The contact that distributes high voltage to the cylinders.

Rotor cap Cap on top of distributor in which ignition cables are placed.

Secondary system The ignition circuit that carries the high voltage required for ignition.

Secondary winding The coil winding consisting of fine wire.

Solid state ignition An ignition system that uses solid state components instead of contact points to develop high voltage.

Spark plugs Ignition system part that creates a spark in the combustion chamber.

Unitized ignition An ignition system that combines the coil and distributor in one unit.

Vacuum advance The timing system that uses engine vacuum to advance the timing.

CHAPTER REVIEW

1. What is the purpose of the ignition system?
2. What does the ignition coil do?
3. What is coil saturation?
4. How high is the voltage created by the coil?
5. What do the contact points inside the distributor do?
6. Why is a condenser needed in the distributor?
7. Explain how the distributor primary system works to develop high voltage.
8. What is the resistor bypass circuit?
9. Describe how the distributor secondary system works.
10. What is the purpose of the rotor and rotor cap?
11. What is firing order?
12. Define ignition timing.
13. List the three distributor advance systems.
14. What is initial timing?
15. Describe how the centrifugal advance system operates.
16. Describe how the vacuum advance system operates.
17. Why is suppression wire used for ignition cables?
18. What is the purpose of the spark plug?
19. What is the heat range of a spark plug?
20. Why were solid state ignition systems developed?
21. List the three main types of solid state ignition systems.
22. List the three ways inductive discharge systems may be triggered.
23. Describe a unitized ignition system.
24. What is the Hall effect?
25. How is the energy in a capacitor used in a capacitive discharge ignition system?

DISCUSSION TOPICS AND ACTIVITIES

1. Identify the components of an ignition system on a shop engine. What parts belong to the primary and what parts belong to the secondary system? Do any parts work in both the primary and secondary?
2. Remove the distributor cap from a shop distributor. Turn the shaft of the distributor. What happens to the contact points? Why?
3. Find a vehicle with a late model solid state ignition system. What type is it? Can you identify the main components?

Ignition System Service

A tune-up involves replacing worn ignition parts such as contact points, condenser, rotor, distributor cap, ignition cables, and spark plugs. The elimination of some of these wearing parts in late-model vehicles has increased the interval between tune-ups. But recent emphasis on fuel economy and emissions has made tune-ups even more important. In this chapter we will study the repair procedures used to tune an engine's ignition system.

OBJECTIVES

After studying this chapter, you should be able to do the following:

1. List the steps in finding a problem with the ignition system.
2. Explain the use of the oscilloscope in diagnosing ignition system problems.
3. Describe the procedures used to service the distributor.
4. Explain how to use a dwell meter and timing light.
5. List the steps in servicing spark plugs.

31.1   TROUBLESHOOTING

The ignition system provides a high-voltage spark in each of the engine's cylinders at the correct time to burn the air-fuel mixture. An engine that cranks over fast enough to run, but will not start, may have ignition trouble. An automobile that loses power and quits on the road is also likely to have ignition problems. When either of these problems occurs, first eliminate the obvious. Check the fuel gauge to make sure the vehicle is not out of gasoline. Open the hood and look the engine over carefully. Give the carburetor and fuel pump a quick look to see if they are in satisfactory condition. Smell for gasoline. If everything looks okay, begin a step-by-step inspection of the ignition system.

Begin by looking over all of the ignition wiring very carefully. A coil wire may have fallen out or one of the primary leads to the coil or distributor may have come loose. If the wiring looks okay, pull off one of the spark plug wires at the spark plug. Insert the blade of a small screwdriver into the boot that covers the spark plug so that it touches the metal connector. Prop the screwdriver up so that the rest of the blade is about half an inch away from any metal part of the engine (Fig. 31-1). Have someone crank the engine. **Safety Caution: To avoid a shock always handle spark plug cables with insulated pliers.** If the ignition system is working properly, a good, strong spark should jump from the screwdriver to the metal. If the ignition system is okay, proceed to the fuel system checks.

No spark at the spark plug wire, however, means the ignition system is at fault. Pull the secondary coil wire out of the middle of the distributor cap. Position this wire about half an inch away from a metal part of the engine (Fig. 31-2). Have someone crank the engine. Look for a spark to jump from the coil wire to the metal. If several strong sparks jump every time the engine cranks over, the primary system and the coil are working. The problem must be in the ignition secondary system—the rotor or the distributor cap.

Remove the distributor cap from the distributor and look inside the cap. It may be cracked or have

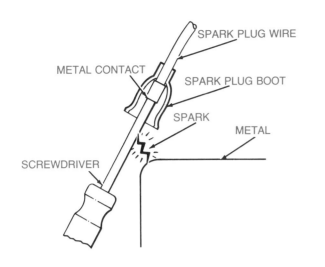

Fig. 31-1 Checking for spark at spark plug wire.

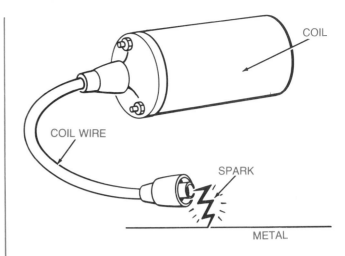

Fig. 31-2 Checking for spark at coil.

water or dirt in it that would disrupt current flow. Wipe the cap with a clean rag. Inspect the center contact in the cap that touches the rotor. These sometimes break off. If the cap is clean and the contacts are okay, check out the rotor. Try to turn the rotor on the distributor shaft. It should not turn. If it does, the key—the small projection inside the rotor hole that fits into a groove on the shaft and holds the rotor stationary—is broken. Check out the contact on the rotor to make sure it is one piece. If either the rotor or distributor cap is damaged, replace it.

Ignition primary problems are common on older cars with mechanical breaker points. If the car has breaker points and you do not have any spark at the coil wire, make a quick check of the breaker points. Leave the coil wire in position to check for a spark. A common problem is contact point surfaces that are too dirty or burned to work correctly. Have someone crank the engine one crank at a time until the contact points are closed. Turn on the ignition key switch. Touch a screwdriver blade between the contact point wire terminal and a metal part of the distributor. There should be a small spark, indicating that current is getting to the points. Use a screwdriver to open and close the contact points by pushing on the movable contact point (Fig. 31-3). Do not touch any other metal with the screwdriver when doing this. If the contact points are okay, each time they are opened a spark will jump from the coil wire to the metal.

If there is no spark at the coil when the contact points are opened and closed with a screwdriver, the contact points are probably to blame. Their surfaces will have to be cleaned with a small file, called an ignition point file. In an emergency, the points can be

cleaned with a fingernail file or simply scraped with a screwdriver. Both contact point surfaces must be filed clean. Make the contact point check again with the screwdriver. They should work now and the engine should start and run. Remember that any ignition difficulty of this type indicates that the car is overdue for an electrical tune-up.

31.2 Using an Oscilloscope for Troubleshooting

The automotive oscilloscope is the standard troubleshooting tool for ignition systems. When connected to an automotive ignition system, a cathode ray oscilloscope will show a graph of the changing voltage in the system as a pattern on a television-like screen. A mechanic can determine from the pattern what, if any, ignition component is working incorrectly (Fig. 31-4).

31.3 Oscilloscope Pattern

The pattern of light traced on the oscilloscope screen is called a pattern, a trace, or a display. It is a graph showing voltage in relation to time. The vertical height of the pattern from the zero line shows voltage at any instant along the zero line, which represents time. Most oscilloscopes are designed to display a primary pattern from the distributor primary terminal or a secondary pattern from the secondary terminal. The secondary pattern (Fig. 31-5) is more generally used for showing overall ignition system operation. Each section of the pattern represents a specific part of

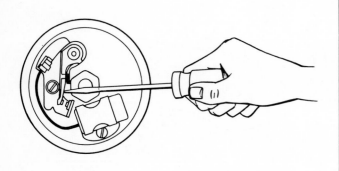

Fig. 31-3 Checking for spark at contact points.

Fig. 31—4 An oscilloscope. (Sun Electric Corporation)

ignition system operation: the firing section, the intermediate section, and the dwell section.

The firing section shows a voltage picture of the firing of the spark plug. It is made up of two lines, the firing line and the spark line. The vertical firing line shows the voltage required to overcome the rotor and spark plug gap. The horizontal spark line shows the voltage required to maintain the spark. The firing of the spark plug involves two separate events. The first of these is the creation of the peak, firing, or ionization voltage. The second event is the arc-maintaining voltage or spark line. Once the plug fires there is a drop in secondary voltage. As the spark continues to cross the electrode gap, the spark voltage remains fairly constant until the spark quits at the beginning of the intermediate section.

The intermediate section is a series of wavy lines or oscillations which disappear at the beginning of the dwell section. It shows the dissipation of the energy remaining in the coil and condenser after the spark plug has stopped firing. The number of oscillations depends on dwell angle, engine speed, duration of spark, degree of coil saturation, and coil and condenser condition.

The dwell section covers the period from the time the distributor contact points close until the contacts open to fire the next cylinder. Closing the points causes a short downward line followed by a series of small oscillations showing condenser operation.

The oscilloscope pattern for a solid state ignition is compared to a conventional pattern in Figure 31-6. The patterns are similar except that the solid state system gives no signal corresponding to condenser oscillations. The firing and spark lines are the same in both patterns. An oscillation after the spark line shows the transistor turning on, and the end of the pattern shows the transistor turning off.

31.4 SERVICING THE DISTRIBUTOR PRIMARY SYSTEM

On older cars with mechanical breaker points, the contact points act as the switch that triggers the high voltage buildup in the coil. After a period of time, current flow across the contact points breaks down the contact surfaces. The destruction of the contact surfaces can become severe enough to affect current buildup in the coil. The engine begins to lose power and waste gasoline. If the contact points are not serviced, they may get bad enough so the car stops running altogether. For these reasons, the contact points are changed regularly.

The condenser's job is to protect the contact points and improve coil operation, by soaking up excessive current that tries to jump across open contact points. If the condenser fails, the engine could fail to run. To prevent condenser failure, a new condenser is installed each time the contact points are replaced. The contact points and condenser usually come in the same kit.

To change the contact points and condenser, the distributor cap must be removed. Most distributors have spring clips on each side of the cap, which are unsnapped to free the cap. Some distributors use spring-loaded hold-down screws. Lift the cap off far enough to work inside the distributor.

The next thing to be removed is the rotor, which turns with the distributor shaft and distributes high

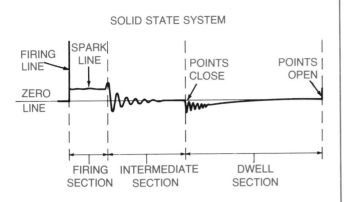

Fig. 31-5 Basic secondary oscilloscope pattern.
(Chevrolet Motor Division, GMC)

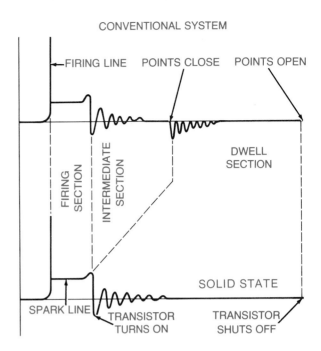

Fig. 31-6 Comparison of solid state and conventional pattern.

voltage to each of the contacts in the distributor cap. The rotor can be removed from the shaft by pulling it straight up. Examine the contact surface on the end of the rotor. If there is any evidence of burning, it should be replaced.

With the distributor cap and rotor removed, the contact points should be visible. Some cars have a metal shield covering the contact points. It is removed by loosening the screws which mount it to the distributor. Look at the contact points. Notice where the rubbing block is in relation to the distributor cam lobes. The points must be in the open position (Fig. 31-7) for servicing. This means that the rubbing block on the movable contact must be resting on the top of a cam lobe. If the contacts are not open, have someone crank the engine a little at a time until they are.

When the points are open, they can be inspected. Use a small screwdriver to gently pry the contact points apart enough to see the contact surfaces. If they show any sign of pitting or burning, they should be replaced. Before disassembling anything, carefully examine the wires connected to the contact points. One wire connected from the points to the distributor terminal brings primary current into the distributor from the coil. Another wire is connected from the condenser to the contact points. Both of these wires are protected from touching any metal that is grounded. If either of these wires is grounded the vehicle will not run. Make a careful sketch of the way the wires are connected so they can be reinstalled correctly.

Remove the small screws that hold the contact points down. Remove the screws that hold down the condenser. Disconnect the wires from the distributor to the contact points. Lift the point assembly out of

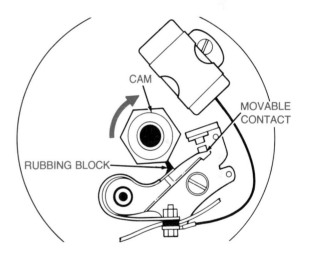

Fig. 31-7 Contact points in open position.

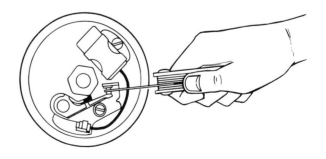

Fig. 31-8 Checking contact point spacing with feeler gauge.

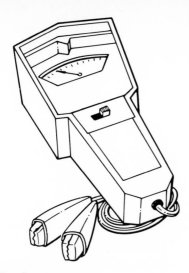

Fig. 31-9 Dwell meter.

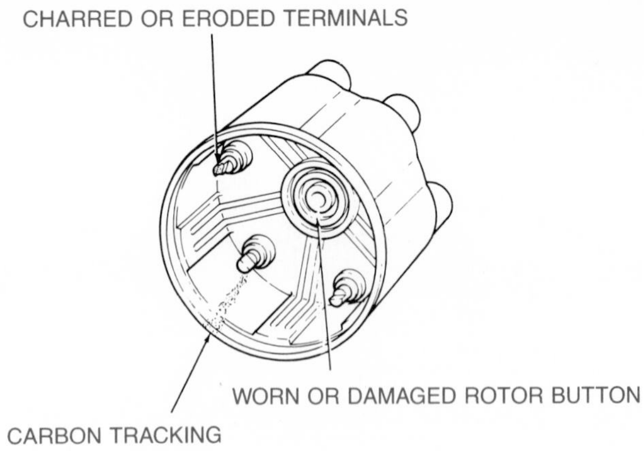

CHARRED OR ERODED TERMINALS

WORN OR DAMAGED ROTOR BUTTON

CARBON TRACKING

Fig. 31-10 Inspecting the distributor cap. (American Motors Corporation)

the distributor. Wipe any dirt or oil out of the distributor with a clean rag.

Most new contact point sets come with a small tube of distributor cam lubricant. This is special high-temperature grease. Put a small amount of the grease on the distributor cam to prevent wear to the rubbing block on the contact points. Never use any other kind of grease for this purpose.

Remove the new contact point set from the package. Do not touch the point surfaces. Oil from the skin can coat the points and cause quick burning of the points.

Position the new contact point set in the distributor. Start the screws but do not tighten them. Mount the new condenser. Reinstall the wires just as they were. Make sure the rubbing block of the new contact set is positioned on top of the cam lobe. Check the service manual for the correct spacing of the points. The dimension will be given in thousandths of an inch or millimeters. Choose the flat feeler gauge of the correct size and make sure it is perfectly clean. Slide it between the contact points. If the gap is accurate, there will be a slight drag (Fig. 31-8).

If the gap is too wide or too narrow, adjust the points by sliding the contact set around. When the adjustment is correct, tighten the contact point mounting screws. Recheck the spacing with the feeler gauge. Recheck the wiring. If everything looks good, the shield, rotor, and cap can be replaced. The rotor is keyed to the distributor shaft so that it will fit in only one position. Look at the underside of the rotor for the key or groove. Push the rotor on the distributor shaft and turn it until it engages the key. Replace the distributor cap. It is also keyed or grooved so that it fits properly on the distributor. Move it back and forth

until it drops into position. Reinstall the spring clips or hold-down screws. Replace the coil wire. Check all the plug wires to make sure none have pulled out when the distributor cap was moved around. The engine is ready to run again.

31.5   Using a Dwell Meter

Setting the contact point spacing with a feeler gauge gives satisfactory performance from most engines. A more accurate contact point adjustment can be done with a dwell meter, which electronically measures the time that the contact points are closed for coil saturation. It makes possible very precise adjustments (Fig. 31-9).

If a dwell meter is used, the contact points are still installed and adjusted with a feeler gauge. The distributor is put back together so the engine will run. The dwell meter is connected to the engine according to the directions provided with the meter.

The dwell meter must be calibrated and set for the proper number of engine cylinders. This procedure will be outlined in the dwell meter instruction booklet. The engine is then started. The needle points to degree numbers on the face of the dwell meter. The proper dwell for the car can usually be found in the owner's manual or shop service manual.

If the dwell is incorrect, the contact spacing must be changed. If the dwell is too high, the contact spacing is too narrow and the points should be adjusted slightly wider. If the dwell is too low, the points are adjusted too wide and must be closed up slightly. The distributor cap will have to be removed and a small adjustment made. The cap will have to be reinstalled and the engine restarted to check the adjustment.

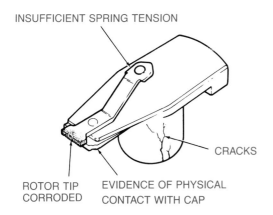

Fig. 31-11 Inspecting the rotor. (American Motors Corporation)

INSUFFICIENT SPRING TENSION

CRACKS

ROTOR TIP CORRODED

EVIDENCE OF PHYSICAL CONTACT WITH CAP

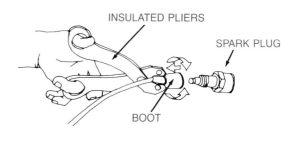

Fig. 31-12 Use insulated pliers to remove a spark plug cable from the spark plug.

INSULATED PLIERS

SPARK PLUG

BOOT

31.6 SERVICING THE DISTRIBUTOR SECONDARY SYSTEM

The servicing of distributor secondary circuit components is the same for electronic and mechanical breaker point distributors.

Remove the distributor cap by unsnapping the spring arms or disengaging the screws. A cap that is greasy or dirty on the outside creates a path that can allow the high voltage current to escape. The current may travel or "flashover" to another terminal or to ground. Flashover most often happens when the wire connections are loose. Also check the distributor cap for cracks.

Check the inside of the distributor cap for carbon tracking, which is caused by flashover from one terminal to another (Fig. 31-10). Grease and dirt inside the cap can also cause flashover to another terminal. In both cases, the cap should be replaced because erosion and damage to the cap have started.

If the rotor contact at the center of the distributor cap is burned away, the cap should be replaced. If the terminal posts are burned or badly grooved, the cap should be replaced. Check the rotor resistance rod, if there is one, to see if it is broken or burned out. Check the contact spring to see if it is broken or has excessive burning on the tip (Fig. 31-11). If any of these defects are found, the rotor should be replaced. Install the rotor on the shaft. Be sure the rotor groove, flats, or tabs match the distributor shaft groove or the advance mechanism openings. Mark the location of the number 1 spark plug cable on the old distributor cap.

Remove the old cap from the distributor and move it to one side. Do not remove the spark plug cables at this time. Install the new distributor cap onto the distributor. Be sure the distributor cap is centered over the rotor and fits squarely down on the distributor. Transfer one spark plug cable at a time to the new distributor cap, starting with the number 1 spark plug cable. Check the installed cables against the firing order.

Start the engine and check for proper operation. If the engine misfires you may have installed the cables incorrectly. Recheck the firing order.

31.7 Inspecting and Servicing Spark Plug Cables

The spark plug cables carry the high secondary voltage from the distributor cap to the spark plugs. High underhood temperatures eventually break down the cable insulation. The cables must be inspected and, if necessary, replaced at regular intervals.

Using a pair of insulated spark plug cable pliers, remove the spark plug end of one spark plug cable by first twisting the rubberlike boot back and forth. This breaks the seal that the protective boot forms around the top of the spark plug. Be sure you twist the boot and not the wire. Then, gripping the end of the boot, pull or snap the cable straight out away from the spark plug (Fig. 31-12). Repeat this procedure for each of the spark plug cables. Before removing any cables from the distributor cap, mark the location of the number 1 cable distributor cap terminal with a piece of chalk.

Remove the same cable that you disconnected at the spark plug. Again, break loose the rubberlike nipple from the distributor cap tower. To do this,

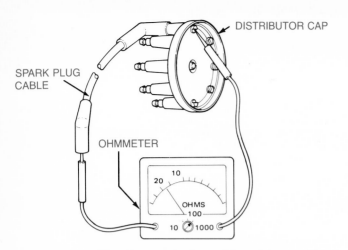

Fig. 31-13 Checking spark plug cable resistance with an ohmmeter. (Ford Motor Company)

Fig. 31-14 Timing marks on the pointer are lined up with a notch on the pulley. (Chevrolet Motor Division, GMC)

peel the nipple back from around the tower of the distributor cap. Then, grip the upper part of the nipple and the cable. Pull the spark plug cable straight out, away from the distributor cap. Visually check each spark plug cable for dry, cracked insulation, cuts and breaks in the wires. Wires that are oil or grease-soaked, dirty, or salt-encrusted should be replaced unless they can be cleaned satisfactorily with a damp cloth and a mild detergent.

Each cable should be tested for resistance with an ohmmeter. Calibrate the ohmmeter to the × 1000 scale. Connect one tester lead to the spark plug end of the cable. Touch the other tester lead to the terminal on the distributor cap end of the cable. Check your readings against specifications to determine if the cables should be replaced. You should twist the wire while you are watching the reading on the ohmmeter. If the needle fluctuates, replace the wire because the fluctuation indicates a broken or partially separated conductor within the wire. This test can also be done without removing the wires from the cap, as shown in Figure 31-13.

To replace the cables, start with the number 1 spark plug wire of the firing order. Lay the old wire alongside the new one; match the cable lengths to be sure you have the right length for the cylinder you are working on. Route the new cable on the engine in the place of the old. In some instances, the wire must be routed through small, tight passages. Do not force, yank, or pull the cable because this will damage it.

Set the cable into the clips or "looms" that support the wire and keep it apart from the other cables. Always make sure that the cables are as short as possible. Do not make any sharp bends in them

or let them come into contact with heated, vibrating, or moving parts.

Spark plug cables should be routed properly to prevent inductive cross-firing. Cross-firing occurs when the spark from one spark plug wire induces a current in the wire lying next to it. It causes the wrong spark plug to fire in the wrong cylinder at the wrong time. Cross-firing happens when the spark plug cables are parallel over long distances, particularly those cables that connect to the spark plugs or cylinders that are side by side. Push the spark plug boots firmly over each spark plug and push each distributor cap terminal and boot firmly into place.

Check the cable installation with the firing order to make sure no cables are out of order. Start the engine and check for proper operation.

31.8 Adjusting the Timing

The initial timing determines when the spark plugs receive the spark from the distributor. Changing the contact points also changes the relationship between the rubbing block and the distributor cam, which affects the ignition timing. Each time the contact points are changed and adjusted, ignition timing must be checked. The timing should also be checked and if necessary adjusted when you are doing a tune-up on a car with an electronic ignition.

After the contact points are adjusted properly, the engine should be allowed to run for a while until it is warm. While the engine is warming up, check the timing specifications in the owner's manual. The specifications will say how many degrees the spark should be set before or after top dead center at idle speed. The degrees refer to degrees of crankshaft

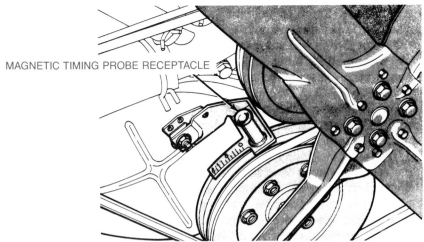

MAGNETIC TIMING PROBE RECEPTACLE

Fig. 31-15 Receptacle for a magnetic probe timing tester.
(Chrysler Corporation)

rotation. Top dead center means that the piston in the number 1 cylinder is at the top of its stroke. For example, the specifications may read that the timing should be set at five degrees before top dead center. This means that the spark should enter the cylinder five crankshaft degrees before the piston reaches top dead center.

Timing is checked with a timing light which comes with instructions that explain how it is to be hooked up. The light is connected to a power source and to the engine's number 1 spark plug wire (identified in the service manual). When the engine is running, the high voltage in the number 1 spark plug wire makes the timing light flash, producing a strobe light effect in time with the ignition firing.

The timing light is aimed at timing marks on the crankshaft front pulley. A stationary pointer is mounted to the engine block near the pulley. The timing marks may be on the pulley or there may be a notch on the pulley and timing marks on the stationary pointer (Fig. 31-14). When the timing light is flashing, the timing marks and pointer will be visible. The shop service manual will explain what the marks on the crank pulley mean. Typically, there is a center mark for top dead center and a number of marks for degrees before and after top dead center.

Many late-model vehicles are equipped with a magnetic probe receptacle (Fig. 31-15) to accommodate a magnetic timing tester which senses engine crankshaft position. The magnetic probe timing system is much more accurate because the tester displays a digital reading of ignition timing.

When the engine is warmed up, turn it off and connect the timing light. Wipe off the timing marks on the crankshaft pulley so they are visible. Change the timing by moving the distributor housing back and forth, after loosening the hold-down clamp by turning the clamp bolt counterclockwise.

Restart the engine. On some older cars specifications will indicate that the timing is checked with the vacuum advance disconnected. If necessary, locate the vacuum advance on the side of the distributor and pull off the vacuum line connected to it. Shine the timing light down at the pointer, taking care not to get the timing light wires caught in the fan or belts. One of the marks on the moving crank pulley will line up with the stationary pointer. If the pointer and crank pulley scale are not aligned to the proper mark, move the distributor a small distance to get them aligned. When they are aligned, tighten the distributor hold-down clamp by turning the bolt clockwise. Recheck the timing. If it is still in alignment, stop the engine and disconnect the timing light. If it was disconnected, reconnect the vacuum line. See chapter 54 for timing adjustment procedures on computer-controlled engines.

31.9 SPARK PLUG SERVICE

Spark plug removal and service is an important part of every electrical tune-up. Spark plug firing voltages are best checked under actual engine operation with an oscilloscope. Whether or not an oscilloscope is available, remove the spark plugs to determine their condition. A close look at the spark plug can also provide the mechanic with valuable clues to the condition of the engine and its systems.

31.10 Spark Plug Removal

Spark plug removal is sometimes difficult because of their location on the engine and the engine

NORMAL

Brown to grayish tan color and slight electrode wear. Correct heat range for engine and operating conditions.

RECOMMENDATION. Properly service and reinstall. Replace if over 10,000 miles of service.

SPLASHED DEPOSITS

Spotted deposits. Occurs shortly after long delayed tune-up. After a long period of misfiring, deposits may be loosened when normal combustion temperatures are restored by tune-up. During a high-speed run, these materials shed off the piston and head and are thrown against the hot insulator.

RECOMMENDATION. Clean and service the plugs properly and reinstall.

CARBON DEPOSITS

Dry soot.

RECOMMENDATION. Dry deposits indicate rich mixture or weak ignition. Check for clogged air cleaner, high float level, sticky choke or worn breaker contacts. Hotter plugs will temporarily provide additional fouling protection.

HIGH SPEED GLAZING

Insulator has yellowish, varnish-like color. Indicates combustion chamber temperatures have risen during hard, fast acceleration. Normal deposits do not get a chance to blow off, instead they melt to form a conductive coating.

RECOMMENDATION. If condition recurs, use plug type one step colder.

OIL DEPOSITS

Oily coating.

RECOMMENDATION. Caused by poor oil control. Oil is leaking past worn valve guides or piston rings into the combustion chamber. Hotter spark plug may temporarily relieve problem, but positive cure is to correct the condition with necessary repairs.

ASH DEPOSITS

Light brown to white colored deposits encrusted on the side or center electrodes or both. Derived from oil and/or fuel additives. While non-conductive, excessive amounts may mask the spark, causing misfire.

RECOMMENDATION. If excessive deposits accumulate in short mileage, corrective measures may include installation of valve guide seals to prevent seepage of oil into combustion chamber.

TOO HOT

Blistered, white insulator, eroded electrodes and absence of deposits.

RECOMMENDATION. Check for correct plug heat range, overadvanced ignition timing, cooling system level and/or stoppages, lean fuel/air mixtures, leaking intake manifold, sticking valves, and if car is driven at high speeds most of the time.

MECHANICAL DAMAGE

Mechanical Damage to the plug's firing end is caused by some foreign object in the combustion chamber. It may also be due to the piston striking the firing tip of improper reach plugs. When working on an engine, be sure to keep the carburetor throat and any open plug holes covered. Consult the catalog for proper reach plugs.

Fig. 31-16 Spark plug analysis chart.
(Champion Spark Plug Company)

Fig. 31-17　Flashover is caused by dirty insulator or wide electrode gap. (Chevrolet Motor Division, GMC)

Fig. 31-18　Used spark plug. (Champion Spark Plug Company)

accessories that are sometimes in the way. Special tools, such as a spark plug socket with a hex at the drive end and a flexible head ratchet, make most difficult jobs easy. Use a 6-point deep spark plug socket for spark plug removal and installation. Spark plug sockets are designed to hold the spark plug firmly so that it may be placed in the socket and started into the cylinder head by hand.

Since the condition of each spark plug tells a story about the cylinder it was removed from, it is a good idea to keep the plugs in order. An easy method of doing this is to make a spark plug holder from a block of wood. Placing the plugs in the holder with the terminal end down allows them to be inspected without removing them from the holder.

Inspect the appearance and condition of both ends of the insulator, the electrodes, seat gasket, and the shell of the plug. This will tell you how efficiently the engine has been operating and how suitable the spark plug is for the type of operation. Frequently the same type of spark plug used in two engines of the same make and model may show a big difference in appearance. The causes of these differences are the condition of the engine, its piston rings, carburetor setting, kind of fuel used, and conditions under which the engine is operated.

31.11　Gasket Inspection

After removing the spark plug, examine the engine seat gasket of each plug. The gasket performs two important jobs. It conducts away much of the heat absorbed by the spark plug insulator tip from the burning fuel in the combustion chamber. Secondly, it maintains a gas-tight seal between the plug and its seat in the cylinder head. If a spark plug gasket is not tightly seated, leaking combustion gases will cause overheating of the plug. This not only shortens the life of the plug because of excessive wear of the overheated electrodes, but it may also lead to preignition.

If the gasket is flattened too much, the spark plug shell may be distorted or cracked and the plug gap may be changed by the excess torque.

A new spark plug gasket should be used every time a new or cleaned spark plug is installed for better performance and longer spark plug life.

31.12　Spark Plug Examination

Each spark plug should be compared to an analysis chart like that shown in Figure 31-16. Under normal operating conditions, spark plugs wear out from intense heat, from the action of sulphur and lead compounds in the fuel, and from the erosion caused by the electric spark on the electrodes. Plugs that have been in operation for a long period of service should be replaced. Worn plugs cause loss of power, loss of speed, hard starting, and sluggish performance.

Brown to grayish-tan deposits and slight electrode wear are signs of spark plug wear, correct spark plug heat range, and mixed periods of high- and low-speed driving. Spark plugs that look like this may be cleaned, regapped, and reinstalled.

One of the most frequent causes of spark plug misfiring is dirt on the top of the insulator. When combined with moisture, the dirt allows high voltage to go across the insulator top to the shell and away from the firing end. This dirt should be cleaned off with a suitable solvent.

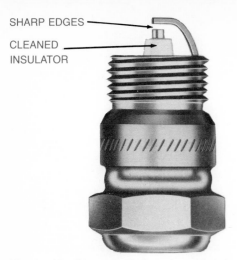

SHARP EDGES

CLEANED
INSULATOR

Fig. 31-19 Cleaned, filed, and regapped spark plug. (Champion Spark Plug Company)

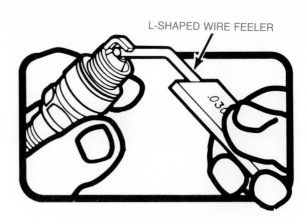

L-SHAPED WIRE FEELER

.030

Fig. 31-20 Using a wire feeler gauge to measure spark plug gap. (Sun Electric Corporation)

Soft, fluffy, dry, black carbon deposits mean too much fuel in the combustion chamber. This can result from operating the engine at low speeds or from too-rich fuel mixture, excessive idling, stuck manifold heat riser, restricted air cleaner, or improperly operating automatic choke. Using "too cold" a plug will also allow excessive carbon buildup. If the fouling continues, a change to a plug one or two steps hotter may be necessary.

Red, brown, yellow, and white coatings on the insulator are byproducts of combustion from the fuel and lubricating oil. Under severe operating conditions, these deposits may cause missing—especially at high speeds and on hard pulls. If the insulator is not too heavily coated, these deposits can be removed by abrasive cleaning. If deposits are packed between the insulator and the shell of the plug, they cannot be completely removed. In this case, the spark plug should be replaced.

The combined action of intense heat, pressure, and corrosive gases within the combustion chamber together with the spark discharges, causes the spark plug gap to widen. A great deal of gap wear at low mileage means that the engine is operating under very high loads or that the wrong plug (too hot) is being used. Before changing to a cooler plug, check the heat range. If the plug showing rapid electrode wear is the correct type, check the seat gasket. If the gasket is in good condition, install spark plugs at least one step colder.

The spark plug conducts electrical energy of several thousand volts to the spark gap in the combustion chamber. This electrical energy will always take the path of least resistance. Several things may cause this electrical energy to take a path away from the spark plug. A shorted upper insulator, causing

flashover, results from a dirty or oily upper insulator (Fig. 31-17). A gap that is too wide as a result of wear or improper setting when the plug was installed is another cause. Sparking through the insulator to the shell results from a break in the insulator. This is caused by careless removal or installation of the spark plug. A fractured plug must be replaced.

A broken lower insulator is generally visible, especially after the spark plug has been cleaned. One cause of this is carelessness in regapping: never bend the center electrode to adjust the gap. Never allow the gapping tool to push too hard against the tip of the center electrode or insulator when bending the side electrode to adjust the gap. If the lower insulator is broken, replace the spark plug.

A break in the lower insulator may also occur if the engine has been operated for long periods with heavy detonation or preignition. This "heat shock failure" is usually the result of over-advanced ignition timing and the use of low-octane fuel. Rapid increase in tip temperature under severe operating conditions causes the heat shock and the break. A colder spark plug may correct the operation. Check the type being used against the specification chart. A plug that is hotter than recommended might result in this problem. If the type recommended is being used, install a colder type.

31.13 Cleaning and Gapping Spark Plugs

Considering the time required to remove and replace spark plugs it is always better to remove old spark plugs and replace them with new ones. There

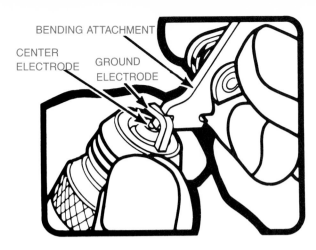

BENDING ATTACHMENT

CENTER ELECTRODE

GROUND ELECTRODE

Fig. 31-21 Gap adjustments are made by bending the ground electrode. (Sun Electric Corporation)

are times when it is necessary to clean and gap a spark plug and to reuse it.

Spark plugs coated with carbon or oxide deposits (Fig. 31-18) can be cleaned in a blast cleaner. Follow the instructions of the cleaner manufacturer carefully. Plugs should be cleaned until the inside of the shell, the entire insulator, and the electrodes are clean. However, blast cleaning for too long will wear down the insulation and damage the plug. Plugs which cannot be completely cleaned with a reasonable amount of blasting should be replaced. Plugs with an oily or wet deposit should be cleaned in a non-flammable degreasing solution and thoroughly dried before blast cleaning to prevent the cleaning compound from packing into the shell. Spark plug service also includes cleaning the top insulator and terminal with a cleaning solvent to remove all oil and dirt.

After cleaning, inspect the plug carefully for cracks or other defects which may not have been visible before. If the plug appears to be in good condition, the end of the center electrode should be filed lightly to provide a flat, square surface (Fig. 31-19). Also, if blast cleaning has not removed all deposits form the electrodes, they should be cleaned with several strokes of *fine* abrasive or a file.

After cleaning the plug, look at the threads for carbon deposits. Clean them with a hand wire brush, taking care not to injure the electrodes or the insulator tip. Clean threads allow easier installation and proper seating of the plug when it is reinstalled in the engine. Plugs with badly nicked or damaged threads should be replaced.

The gap of each spark plug must be checked and if necessary adjusted before the spark plug is installed. The gap must be checked even if you are installing new spark plugs. First look up the specified gap in a shop service manual. Select a wire feeler gauge of the correct thickness to measure the gap. Never use a flat feeler gauge for this job as it will be inaccurate for measuring used spark plug gaps.

Slide the wire feeler gauge between the spark plug electrodes as shown in Figure 31-20. The wire should fit between the electrodes with a light drag. If the gap is too wide or too narrow it must be adjusted.

An electrode adjusting tool is included in most spark plug wire feeler gauge sets. The notch on the adjusting tool is inserted around the spark plug ground electrode. The tool is then used to bend the ground electrode closer to or away from the center electrode (Fig. 31-21). Never attempt to bend the center electrode.

31.14   Installing Spark Plugs

A new spark plug seat gasket must be used with each new or cleaned plug. Be sure the cylinder head threads and plug seats are clean and free from any dirt which would prevent proper seating of the plug and gasket. Dirty cylinder head threads should be cleaned with a greased thread chaser of the proper size.

When using any spark plug different from the original, be sure that the new plug has the same reach or length of thread as the original equipment plug. If the new plug threads are too long, the threads exposed inside the combustion chamber will become corroded and covered with carbon. This may damage the threads in the cylinder head when the plug is removed. If a plug with short threads is used, the exposed cylinder head threads may become carboned up or partially burned away, preventing proper installation of a plug with the correct reach. Extended reach spark plugs, when used in some engines, may interfere with the pistons and cause a great deal of engine damage.

Screw the plug by hand all the way down until it seats on the gasket finger-tight. Then use a torque wrench and torque to the specification in the service manual. This specification is given for new gaskets, with spark plug and engine threads thoroughly clean.

Since spark plug torquing is frequently difficult because of inaccessibility, the following rule of thumb will produce plug installations that are neither too tight nor too loose. Tighten the spark plug finger-tight and then turn it with a spark plug wrench 1/2 to 3/4 turn.

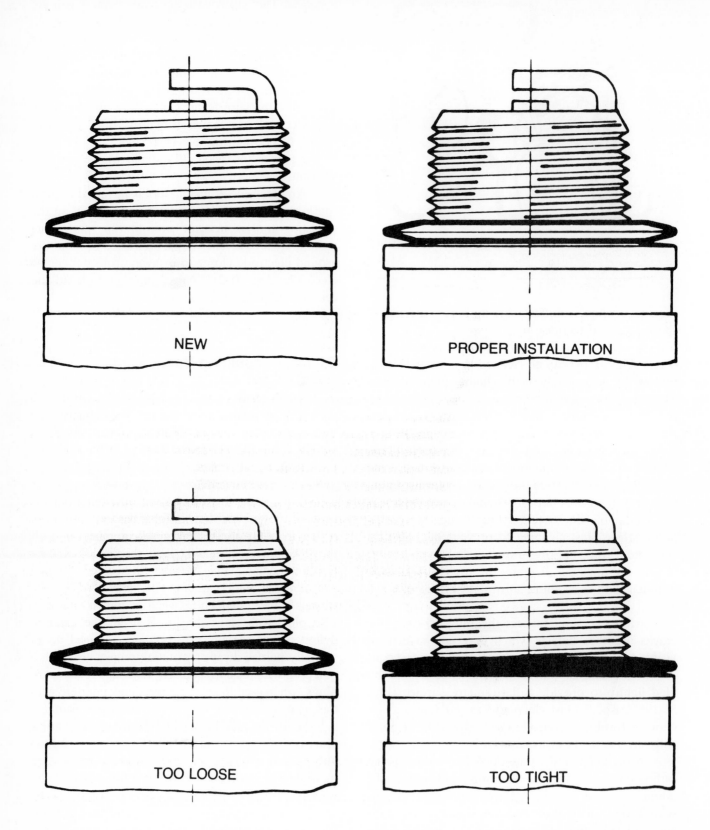

Fig. 31-22 Spark plug gasket inspection.
(Chevrolet Motor Division, GMC)

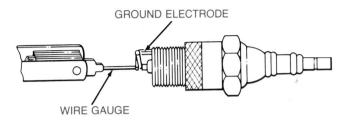

GROUND ELECTRODE

WIRE GAUGE

Fig. 31-23

NEW TERMS

Dwell The length of time, measured in crankshaft degrees, that the contact points are closed for coil saturation.

Dwell meter A tool used to measure the amount of dwell in an ignition system.

Oscilloscope A tool that displays an electrical image of the ignition system on a television-like screen.

Primary pattern An oscilloscope pattern showing the operation of the ignition primary circuit.

Secondary pattern An oscilloscope pattern showing the operation of the secondary ignition circuit.

Spark plug analysis chart A chart showing common problems of spark plugs.

Spark plug socket A special socket made to remove spark plugs without damaging them.

Timing light A tool made to measure the initial timing of an ignition system.

Tune-up The replacing of worn ignition parts and adjustment of other systems to get the best performance from an engine.

CHAPTER REVIEW

1. Describe how to find out whether the ignition system is providing a spark.
2. Describe how to troubleshoot the primary circuit.

3. What does the firing section of an oscilloscope pattern show about an ignition system?
4. What does the dwell section show about the ignition?
5. Explain how to install a new set of contact points.
6. Describe how to adjust contact points with a dwell meter.
7. Explain how to adjust ignition timing.
8. Describe how to remove a set of spark plugs.
9. What do soft, fluffy, dry black carbon deposits on a spark plug mean?
10. What happens to the spark plug gap after it has been in the engine for a long period of time?
11. What is a spark plug analysis chart used for?
12. What can cause a broken lower spark plug insulator?
13. Explain how to clean a spark plug.
14. Describe how to gap a spark plug.
15. Explain how to install a set of spark plugs.

DISCUSSION TOPICS AND ACTIVITIES

1. List the steps in locating a problem in the ignition system.
2. Visit a shop that uses an oscilloscope. Report on what you see.
3. Match up a collection of used shop spark plugs with a spark plug analysis chart. What problems can you identify?

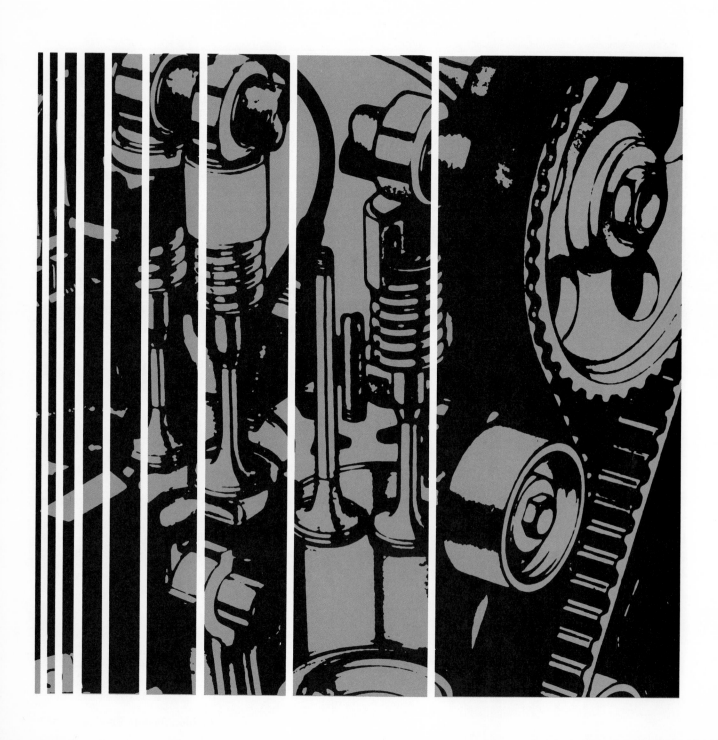

Automobile Power Train

PART 5

Manually Operated Clutch

The power developed by the engine is delivered to the driving wheels of the automobile by the power train. The transmission, a major part of the power train, may be shifted with a manually operated clutch or it may be fully automatic. In either case, the transmission's job is to multiply the turning effort or torque developed by the engine to get the automobile moving.

The purpose of the manually operated clutch is to couple and uncouple the engine from the power train. The engine must be disconnected from the power train in order to crank the engine for starting. In addition, uncoupling the engine from the power train makes shifting the transmission easier and allows the engine to run with the transmission in gear while stopped.

OBJECTIVES

After studying this chapter, you should be able to do the following:

1. Explain the operation of the manually operated clutch during engagement.
2. Describe the operation of the manually operated clutch during disengagement.
3. Identify the different types of automotive clutches.
4. Describe the construction of automotive clutches.
5. Explain how the clutch linkage operates.

32.1 CLUTCH OPERATION

The manual clutch disconnects the engine from the power train when the driver pushes down the clutch pedal. As the driver allows the pedal to come up, the engine is connected to the power train and the automobile can move. The components which make this possible are a friction disc and pressure plate assembly.

The transmission has a splined input shaft and a smooth, round pilot that fits in a bearing in the engine crankshaft or flywheel. This support, or pilot bearing, is necessary to maintain clutch disc alignment with the flywheel. A clutch disc with an internal spline fits on the transmission input shaft and rotates with the input shaft. The straight splines let the clutch disc move back and forth on the input shaft.

If the clutch disc is held against the rotating engine flywheel with enough force, the disc will rotate with the flywheel (Fig. 32-1). A friction facing is riveted or bonded to the front and rear sides of the clutch disc to withstand the wear and heat developed during engagement.

To get the clutch disc and transmission input shaft turning, a pressure or force must be applied to press the clutch disc against the engine flywheel. This is done by pressure plate assembly (Fig. 32-2). The pressure plate assembly is made up of a cast iron plate, a heavy stamped cover, heavy springs between the plate and the cover, release levers, and links. The cover and plate assembly is bolted to and rotates with the engine flywheel. It squeezes the clutch disc between the flywheel and the pressure plate, forcing it to turn with them. Since the clutch disc is mechanically connected to the transmission input shaft, a solid connection is now formed from the engine to the transmission.

When the pressure plate is in an engaged position, the springs squeeze the disc against the flywheel (Fig. 32-3) with a force of 1,000 to 3,000 pounds (4 448 to 13 344 N), depending on the type

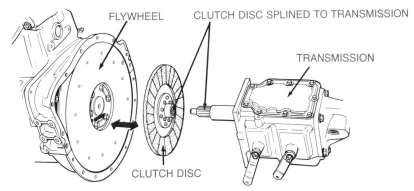

Fig. 32-1 Clutch disc driven by engine flywheel when held against flywheel. (Ford Motor Company)

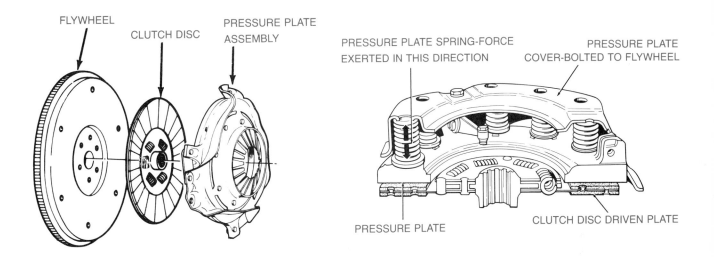

Fig. 32-2 The clutch disc held against flywheel by pressure plate assembly. (American Motors Corporation)

Fig. 32-3 Springs exert pressure to squeeze disc against flywheel. (Ford Motor Company)

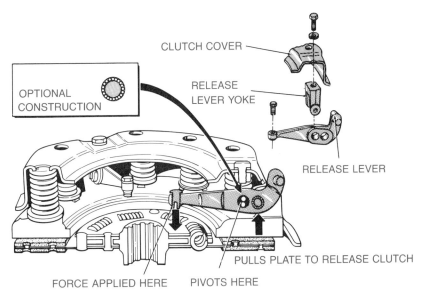

Fig. 32-4 Clutch release. (Ford Motor Company)

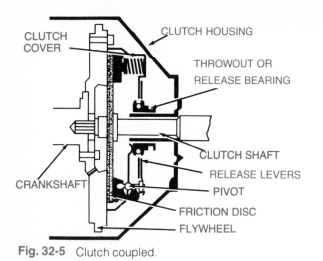

Fig. 32-5 Clutch coupled.

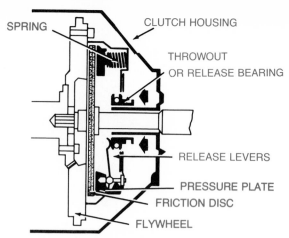

Fig. 32-6 Clutch uncoupled or released with throwout bearing.

of clutch. The clutch pressure plate springs are under pressure when the clutch cover is assembled to the pressure plate. They are compressed even further when the assembly is bolted to the flywheel.

Removing the spring pressure from the disc releases or uncouples the clutch. A number of equally spaced clutch release levers are fastened to the clutch pressure plate cover so that they pivot on the cover attachment. A short distance beyond this pivot point is a second attaching hole that is fastened to the pressure plate.

When a force is applied in a forward direction to the inner end of the release levers, the outer ends must move in the opposite direction because the levers are held between these two points. The pressure plate, attached to the outer end of the release levers, moves away from the flywheel. This takes the pressure away from the clutch disc and allows it to rotate at a speed independent of the flywheel and pressure plate (Fig. 32-4).

Whenever the driver's foot is off the clutch pedal, the pressure plate springs push on the pressure plate and squeeze the disc against the flywheel. The engine is coupled to the transmission (Fig. 32-5).

When the driver depresses the clutch pedal, this movement is transferred into the clutch through a linkage attached to a throwout bearing or release bearing behind the pressure plate assembly. As the throwout bearing is moved toward the pressure plate assembly, it contacts the release levers attached to the pressure plate. When the levers are moved, the pressure plate is pulled away from the friction disc. The disc is no longer driven by the flywheel, so the clutch is uncoupled (Fig. 32-6).

The release or throwout bearing is designed so that it can push on the levers as it rotates with them. The bearing is usually made from two parts: a collar or sleeve attached to the linkage and a rotating bearing assembly mounted on the collar. The throwout bearing assembly is moved by a throwout lever or clutch fork connected to the pedal linkage.

32.2 TYPES OF AUTOMOTIVE CLUTCHES

Most automotive clutches use a single dry friction disc. Automatic transmissions and motorcycles use clutches with several friction discs in oil.

There are several types of single dry disc clutches. They are classified by the type and number of springs used in the pressure plate assembly. The pressure plate assembly described earlier is called a coil spring pressure plate because coil or helical springs are used to push on the friction disc. There are many designs of coil spring pressure plates. Some use three large coil springs; others use nine or twelve smaller springs.

The diaphragm or conical spring pressure plate uses one large spring. The diaphragm spring is a conical piece of spring steel punched to give it greater flexibility. The diaphragm is placed between the cover and the pressure plate so that the diaphragm spring is nearly flat when the clutch is in the engaged position. The action of this type of spring can be demonstrated with an oil can. When you push in on the center of the top of the can, the outside rim moves out. When you release the pressure the outside rim moves back in.

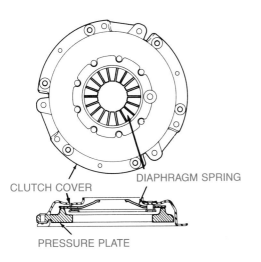

Fig. 32-7   Parts of the diaphragm clutch. (American Motors Corporation)

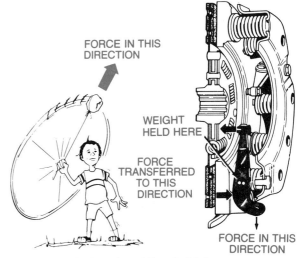

FORCE IN THIS DIRECTION

WEIGHT HELD HERE

FORCE TRANSFERRED TO THIS DIRECTION

FORCE IN THIS DIRECTION

Fig. 32-8   Action of centrifugal clutch. (Ford Motor Company)

CLUTCH COVER

DIAPHRAGM SPRING

PRESSURE PLATE

The outer rim of the diaphragm is hooked to the pressure plate and pivoted on rings approximately one inch from the outer edge (Fig. 32-7). The application of pressure at the inner section moves the outer rim away from the flywheel and draws the pressure plate away from the clutch disc, releasing or disengaging the clutch. When the pressure is released from the inner section, it moves out, and the outer rim moves in, forcing the pressure plate against the clutch disc and engaging the clutch.

Semi-centrifugal clutches use centrifugal force to increase the spring pressure against the friction disc. An added force can be gained by reshaping the release levers and adding a weight to their outer ends. As the speed of the engine increases, centrifugal force acting on the weights of the release levers tends to throw the weights out to a greater diameter. The weights are held, however, and pivoted at a point revolving around the lever pivot point. Since the weights and pivot points are not on the same plane as the flywheel, the centrifugal force applies additional pressure to the pressure plate. This results in more grip on the clutch disc and a greater torque-carrying ability of the clutch (Fig. 32-8).

In clutches used for large trucks and racing automobiles, where additional gripping force is necessary but diameter is limited, more than one friction disc may be used. By adding friction disc area, this design provides more clutch torque-carrying ability. A flywheel with a recess in the rear face and notches or pins in the rear flange is used to fit the additional pressure plate and clutch disc. A double-disc clutch (Fig. 32-9) uses two pressure plates and two friction discs, doubling the friction area. With double the friction area there is much greater gripping strength.

32.3   CLUTCH CONSTRUCTION

The friction disc (Fig. 32-10) has a splined hub which is free to slide lengthwise along the splines of the clutch shaft but which drives the shaft through these same splines. Grooves on both sides of the disc lining prevent the disc from sticking to the flywheel and the pressure plate from disengaging as a result of vacuum between the parts. The clutch disc is usually made of spring steel in the shape of a single flat disc with a number of flat segments. Frictional facings are attached to each side of the disc with brass rivets. These facings must be heat resistant, since friction produces heat. The most commonly used facings are made of cotton and asbestos fibers woven or molded together with resins.

To eliminate chatter during clutch engagement, the steel segments attached to the splined hub are slightly waved. The waved segments are called cushion springs. The facings make gradual contact with the flywheel and pressure plate as the waved cushion springs flatten out.

The clutch disc usually has a flexible center to absorb the torsional vibration of the crankshaft. Torsional vibration would be transferred to the power train unless it were eliminated. The flexible center is made from torsional coil springs placed between the hub and the steel plate. The springs allow the disc to rotate slightly in relation to its hub until the springs are fully compressed and relative motion stops. Then the disc can rotate slightly backward as the springs decompress. This slight backward and forward rotation allows the clutch shaft to rotate at a more uniform rate than the crankshaft and eliminates some of the torsional vibration from the crankshaft.

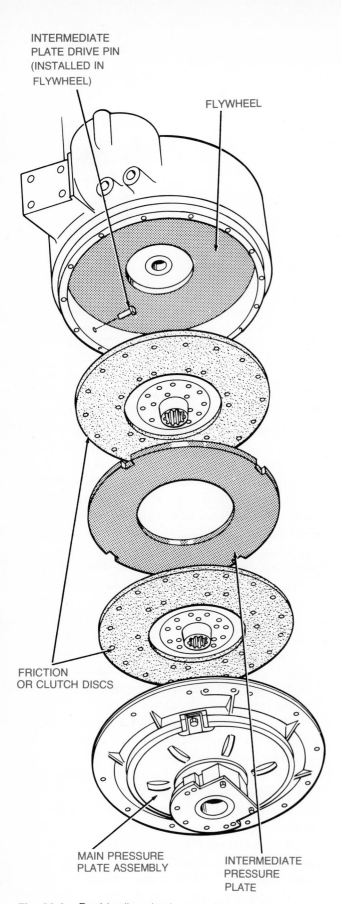

Fig. 32-9 Double-disc clutch assembly. (Borg-Warner Corporation)

INTERMEDIATE
PLATE DRIVE PIN
(INSTALLED IN
FLYWHEEL)

FLYWHEEL

FRICTION
OR CLUTCH DISCS

MAIN PRESSURE
PLATE ASSEMBLY

INTERMEDIATE
PRESSURE
PLATE

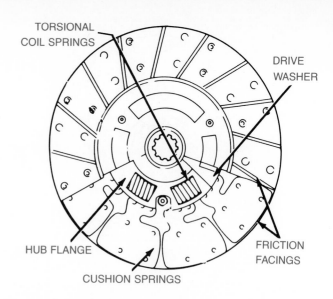

Fig. 32-10 Sectional view of clutch disc. (General Motors Corporation)

TORSIONAL
COIL SPRINGS

DRIVE
WASHER

HUB FLANGE

CUSHION SPRINGS

FRICTION
FACINGS

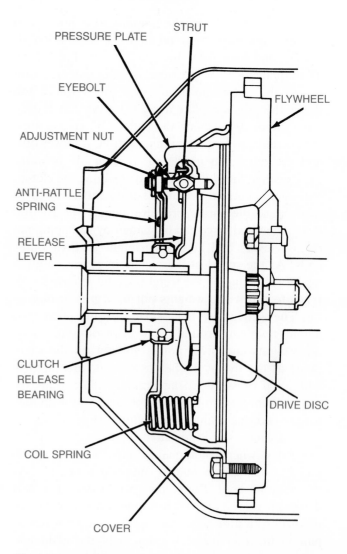

Fig. 32-11 A sectional view of a clutch with a coil spring pressure plate assembly. (General Motors Corporation)

PRESSURE PLATE

STRUT

EYEBOLT

FLYWHEEL

ADJUSTMENT NUT

ANTI-RATTLE
SPRING

RELEASE
LEVER

CLUTCH
RELEASE
BEARING

DRIVE DISC

COIL SPRING

COVER

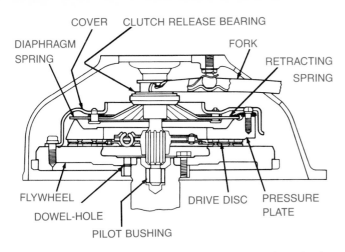

Fig. 32-12 Sectional view of a diaphragm spring clutch assembly. (General Motors Corporation)

Labels in figure: COVER · CLUTCH RELEASE BEARING · DIAPHRAGM SPRING · FORK · RETRACTING SPRING · FLYWHEEL · DOWEL-HOLE · PILOT BUSHING · DRIVE DISC · PRESSURE PLATE

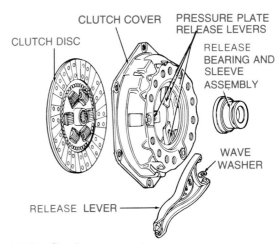

Fig. 32-13 Clutch components. (American Motors Corporation)

Labels in figure: CLUTCH COVER · PRESSURE PLATE RELEASE LEVERS · CLUTCH DISC · RELEASE BEARING AND SLEEVE ASSEMBLY · WAVE WASHER · RELEASE LEVER

As described earlier, the pressure plate assembly may contain a diaphragm spring or a number of coil springs. The springs are connected at one end to a steel cover. At the other end they are connected to a heavy flat ring with one ground contact surface, the pressure plate. The pressure plate and flywheel surfaces are usually machined and ground from nodular iron. Nodular iron contains enough graphite to provide some lubrication when the clutch is slipping during engagement. A sectional view of a clutch with a coil spring pressure plate is shown in Figure 32-11. A sectional view of a clutch with a diaphragm spring pressure plate is shown in Figure 32-12.

The clutch release or throwout bearing is a ball thrust bearing within the clutch housing mounted on a sleeve attached to the front of the transmission case. The release bearing is connected through linkage to the clutch pedal. The release fork engages the release levers and moves the pressure plate to the rear, separating the clutch pressure plate from the clutch disc when the clutch pedal is depressed by the driver (Fig. 32-13).

The bearing assembly normally operates in a housing filled with high-temperature lubricant. On most units this lubrication is installed when the bearing is manufactured. Since there is no way to add new lubrication, a throwout bearing must never be soaked in solvent or in any other fluid that would ruin the lubricant.

32.4   CLUTCH LINKAGE

The clutch linkage allows the driver to engage and disengage the clutch with a pedal. Two types of linkage are used: mechanical and hydraulic.

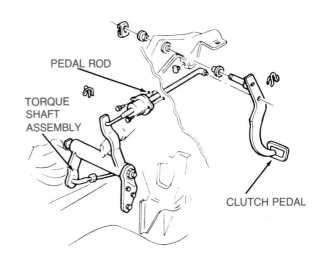

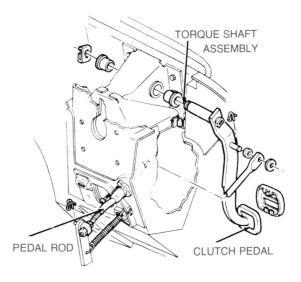

Fig. 32-14 Mechanical clutch linkage. (Chevrolet Motor Division, GMC)

Labels in figures: PEDAL ROD · TORQUE SHAFT ASSEMBLY · CLUTCH PEDAL

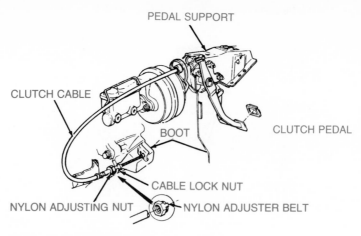

Fig. 32-15 Mechanical clutch linkage using a cable. (Ford Motor Company)

Most pressure plate assemblies require about 600 pounds (2700 N) of force to depress the release levers. The mechanical clutch linkage (Fig. 32-14). has a system of levers that provides a force of approximately 40 pounds (180 N) at the clutch pedal to release the clutch. A relatively great distance and light force at the clutch pedal is changed to a short distance and increased force at the clutch pressure plate. A strong over-center spring returns the clutch pedal. The return spring also preloads clutch linkage, removing looseness due to wear, and keeps the release bearing clear of the release levers.

Many compact automobiles use a cable (Fig. 32-15) instead of rods to pull on the clutch fork. The cable, which may be routed through a small area, is used where space is a problem.

Another way of getting motion from the clutch pedal to the pressure plate is through the use of hydraulic pressure (Fig. 32-16). A master cylinder at the clutch pedal is connected to a slave cylinder at the pressure plate release lever. The operation of master and slave cylinders in presented in Chapter 46.

Regardless of the linkage, most late-model vehicles use a clutch safety switch. This switch, connected to the linkage, prevents ignition if the clutch pedal is not depressed. This prevents the vehicle from starting with the pedal engaged and the vehicle in gear (Fig. 32-17).

NEW TERMS

Clutch disc assembly   The part of the clutch assembly that is connected to the transmission.
Clutch linkage   The rods and levers that allow the driver to operate the clutch.

Clutch pedal   The pedal used by the driver to operate the clutch.
Coil spring pressure plate   A pressure plate that uses coil springs.
Diaphragm spring pressure plate   A pressure plate that uses a diaphragm spring.
Multiple-plate clutch   A clutch that uses more than one disc.
Pressure plate assembly   The part of the clutch connected to the engine.
Release bearing   A bearing operated by the clutch linkage used to disengage the clutch.
Semi-centrifugal clutch   A clutch that uses centrifugal force during application.

CHAPTER REVIEW

1. What is the purpose of the clutch?
2. What types of automobiles usually have a manually operated clutch?
3. Describe the operation of the clutch during engagement.
4. Explain the operation of the clutch during disengagement or release.
5. What is the purpose of the pressure plate?
6. What is the purpose of the clutch disc?
7. What is the purpose of the throwout bearing?
8. What are the two parts that make up the throwout bearing?
9. What is the single dry disc clutch?
10. What two types of pressure plates are in common use?
11. What is a semi-centrifugal clutch?
12. Why does the clutch disc have a flexible center?

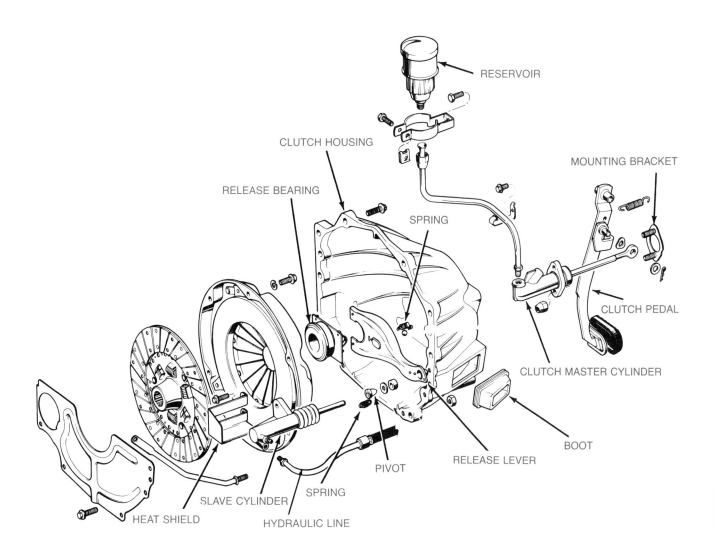

RESERVOIR

CLUTCH HOUSING

MOUNTING BRACKET

RELEASE BEARING

SPRING

CLUTCH PEDAL

CLUTCH MASTER CYLINDER

BOOT

RELEASE LEVER

PIVOT

SLAVE CYLINDER

SPRING

HEAT SHIELD

HYDRAULIC LINE

Fig. 32-16 Hydraulic clutch linkage. (American Motors Corporation)

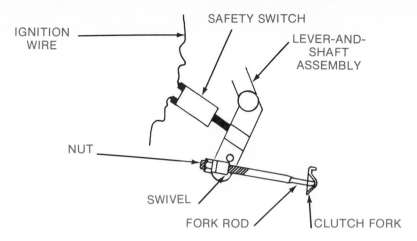

IGNITION WIRE

SAFETY SWITCH

LEVER-AND-SHAFT ASSEMBLY

NUT

SWIVEL

FORK ROD

CLUTCH FORK

Fig. 32-17 The clutch safety switch prevents ignition unless the clutch is depressed.

13. What do the pressure plate springs push on?

14. What happens to the pressure plate springs when the driver depresses the clutch pedal?

15. What are the two common types of clutch linkage?

DISCUSSION TOPICS AND ACTIVITIES

1. Examine a shop cutaway model of a clutch assembly. Can you explain the operation of the clutch during engagement and disengagement?

2. Study several different types of pressure plates found around the shop. What are the differences between them?

3. Study the clutch linkage on the automobile of your choice. Is it mechanical or hydraulic? How does it work?

CHAPTER 33

Clutch Service

CHAPTER PREVIEW

Of all the drive line components, the manually operated clutch gets the most abuse. Power transmission problems are often the result of clutch failure. A mechanic must be able to recognize and correct these problems. In this chapter we will present the troubleshooting, preventive maintenance, and service procedures for automotive clutches.

OBJECTIVES

After studying this chapter, you should be able to do the following:

1. List the steps to find out what is wrong with the clutch.
2. Describe the preventive maintenance procedures used on the clutch.
3. Explain the removal of the clutch assembly.
4. Describe how to clean and inspect the clutch components for wear.
5. Explain how to install the clutch assembly.

33.1 TROUBLESHOOTING

Clutch problems generally fall into one of the following categories:

Clutch chatter
Clutch slippage
Clutch drag
Clutch pedal pulsation
Clutch-related vibration
Clutch area noises

Troubleshooting procedures for each of these categories are explained in the following sections.

33.2 Clutch Chatter

Clutch chatter can be described as a shaking or shuddering that is felt throughout the automobile. Chatter usually develops when the clutch cover pressure plate first makes contact with the clutch disc and stops when the clutch is fully engaged (clutch pedal released). The following test of clutch operation requires clutch engagement to the point of vehicle movement. **Safety Caution: The area to front and rear of automobile must be clear.**

Start the engine, push down the clutch pedal, and shift the transmission into first gear. Increase the engine speed to 1200–1500 rpm and slowly release the clutch pedal. When the pressure plate first makes contact with the clutch disc, watch clutch operation. Depress clutch pedal and reduce engine speed. Shift the transmission into reverse and repeat the procedure. If there is no clutch chatter, increase engine speed to 1700–2200 rpm and repeat the test.

If there is no clutch chatter during the tests outlined, the problem may be improper operation by the owner. If there is clutch chatter, raise the vehicle on a hoist. Check for loose or broken front or rear engine support cushions. Tighten or replace as necessary. Check for loose clutch housing-to-engine and clutch housing-to-transmission attaching bolts. Tighten as necessary. Refer to torque specifications in the service manual. Check for binding, worn, bent, or broken clutch linkage components. Lubricate or replace them as necessary.

Fig. 33-1   If a clutch slips too long it may be destroyed.

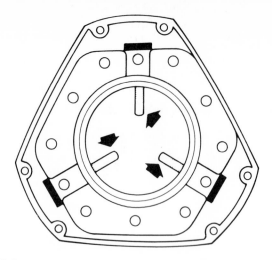

Fig. 33-2   Excessive lever wear can cause pulsation.

If components inspected were in good condition, or if one or more problems were discovered and corrected, lower the automobile and repeat the test. If chatter still shows up, remove the transmission and inspect the clutch components as explained later.

33.3   Clutch Slippage

Clutch slippage is a condition in which the engine overspeeds (overrevs) but does not provide any power to the rear wheels. Slippage occurs when the clutch disc is not gripped firmly between the flywheel and clutch cover pressure plate and rotates or slips between them at high torque. Clutch slippage can occur during initial acceleration or during gear shifts.

Drive the vehicle long enough to allow the clutch to warm up. Listen for signs of overreving during shifting or acceleration (Fig. 33-1).

33.4   Clutch Drag

Clutch drag is a condition in which the clutch disc and the transmission clutch shaft do not come to a complete stop after the clutch pedal is pushed down (clutch disengaged). Clutch drag can cause gear clash when shifting into reverse or hard or difficult shifting. Check clutch operation as follows: Start the engine, depress the clutch pedal fully, and shift the transmission into first gear. Shift the transmission into neutral but DO NOT release clutch pedal. Wait 5 to 10 seconds and shift transmission into reverse. If shift is smooth with no gear clash, clutch operation is normal. If shifting into reverse causes gear clash, raise the vehicle on hoist. Check clutch linkage for

binding, worn, broken or bent components. Lubricate or replace as necessary. If components are in good operating condition, or if one or more problems were discovered and repaired, lower the vehicle and repeat the test. If clutch still drags, remove the transmission and inspect clutch components as explained later.

33.5   Clutch Pedal Pulsation

Clutch pedal pulsation is a rapid up-and-down (pumping) movement of the pedal without any noise. This pedal movement is usually slight, but can be felt by the driver. On occasion, pedal movement is great enough to be visually observed (Fig. 33-2).

Clutch pedal pulsation occurs when the release bearing first makes contact with the clutch cover release levers (clutch partially disengaged) or at any time the release bearing is in contact with the release levers. Pulsation is usually caused by incorrect clutch release lever height or clutch housing misalignment. Check clutch operation as follows: start the engine, slowly depress clutch pedal until release bearing first makes contact with clutch release levers, and check for pulsation. Continue to depress clutch pedal while checking for pulsation until pedal is fully depressed. If there is no pulsation or it is minor, stop the repair. If pulsation is very rapid and can be felt throughout the automobile, refer to the following section. If there is a good deal of pulsation, the transmission and clutch must be removed for inspection.

33.6   Clutch-Related Vibrations

Clutch-related vibrations are different from pedal pulsations. They can be felt throughout the vehicle.

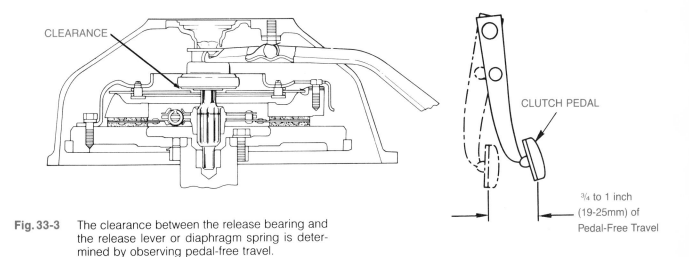

CLEARANCE

CLUTCH PEDAL

¾ to 1 inch
(19-25mm) of
Pedal-Free Travel

Fig. 33-3 The clearance between the release bearing and the release lever or diaphragm spring is determined by observing pedal-free travel.

Clutch vibrations usually occur at a relatively high engine speed (over 1500 rpm) regardless of clutch pedal position.

Raise the vehicle on a hoist and check whether any engine components such as exhaust manifold or valve cover touch the body or frame. If one of these components is touching, repair and check for vibration. If vibration stops, discontinue the repair.

If vibration continues, lower the vehicle, disconnect accessory drive belts one at a time, and check for vibration. If vibration is corrected after taking off a drive belt, the cause of vibration is the accessory driven by the belt or the belt itself. Repair as necessary. If vibration continues, check the following areas:

Loose flywheel mounting bolts
Excessive flywheel face runout
Damaged crankshaft vibration damper
Clutch cover imbalance

33.7   Clutch Area Noises

Clutch throwout bearing noises are whirring, grating, or grinding noises that occur when the clutch pedal is pushed down. These noises usually continue until the clutch pedal is fully released (clutch engaged) and the bearing is no longer in contact with the clutch cover release levers. Throwout bearing noise is corrected by replacing the bearing and sleeve, as explained later.

Clutch shaft or counterpart bearing noises are whirring, grating, or grinding noises that stop when the clutch pedal is pushed down (clutch disengaged) or when the transmission is shifted into gear. These noises are most noticeable when the clutch pedal is

fully released and the transmission is in neutral. To correct these noises, remove the transmission and replace the problem bearing(s).

Pilot bushing noises are squealing, howling, or trumpeting noises most noticeable when the engine is cold. These noises occur during the first few inches of clutch pedal travel as the pedal is being released (partial clutch engagement) with the transmission in gear. They can also occur in very cold weather when the pedal is fully pushed down (clutch disengaged) and the engine is started with the transmission in neutral. To correct pilot bushing noise, replace the bushing.

33.8   PREVENTIVE MAINTENANCE

Preventive maintenance on the clutch consists of periodic lubrication of the clutch linkage and adjusting the clutch pedal free play. The clutch linkage should be lubricated each time the vehicle has a chassis lubrication.

A clutch pedal free play or free travel adjustment is necessary whenever the clutch does not disengage or engage properly, or when new clutch parts are installed. Improper adjustment of the clutch pedal free travel is often a cause of clutch failure and can be a factor in some transmission failures (Fig. 33-3).

To check and adjust the pedal free travel, first measure and note the distance from the floor pan to the top of the pedal. Then depress the pedal slowly until the clutch release levers contact the clutch release bearing. Note the reading on the tape. The difference between the reading with the pedal in the depressed position and the reading with the pedal in the fully released position is the pedal free travel.

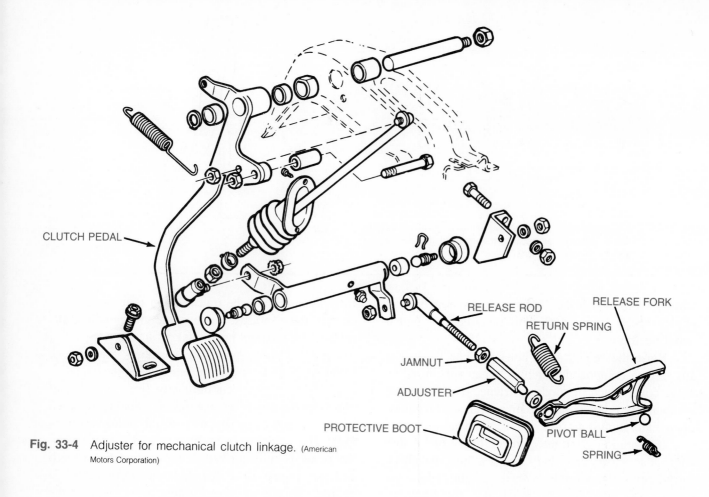

Fig. 33-4 Adjuster for mechanical clutch linkage. (American Motors Corporation)

CLUTCH PEDAL

RELEASE ROD

RELEASE FORK

RETURN SPRING

JAMNUT

ADJUSTER

PROTECTIVE BOOT

PIVOT BALL

SPRING

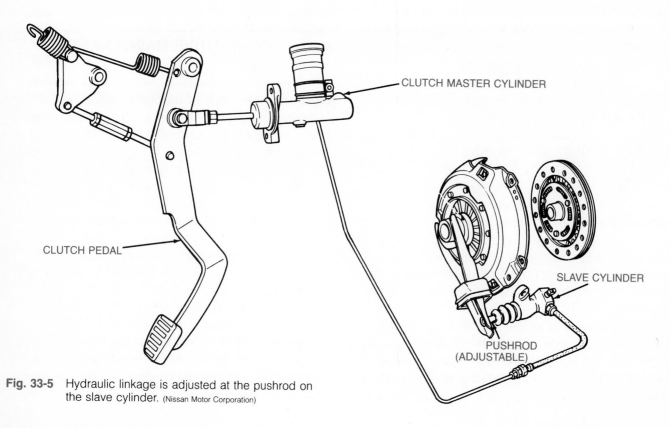

Fig. 33-5 Hydraulic linkage is adjusted at the pushrod on the slave cylinder. (Nissan Motor Corporation)

CLUTCH MASTER CYLINDER

CLUTCH PEDAL

SLAVE CYLINDER

PUSHROD (ADJUSTABLE)

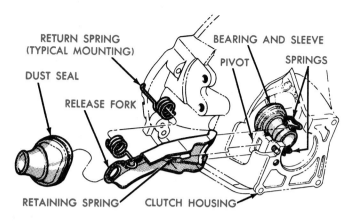

Fig. 33-6 Removing clutch release bearing and sleeve assembly from clutch housing. (Chrysler Corporation)

If the free travel is not correct according to specifications, the clutch linkage will require adjustment. First, locate the adjuster on the linkage. Usually the release rod connected to the release fork is constructed in two threaded pieces so that it can be made longer or shorter. An adjuster is shown on the mechanical linkage in Figure 33-4. Hydraulic clutch linkage free travel is adjusted by lengthening or shortening the pushrod at the clutch slave cylinder shown in Figure 33-5.

The adjustment is made by loosening the jam nut and lengthening or shortening the release rod as required. Some adjusters must be disconnected from the linkage before they can be adjusted. Check the adjustment by measuring the free travel as explained earlier.

33.9   CLUTCH SERVICE

When the troubleshooting procedures show a problem with the clutch, it must be disassembled for inspection, service, or replacement. In this section, we will present the service procedures for most automotive clutches.

33.10   Clutch Removal

On front-engine rear drive vehicles, the transmission and drive shaft must be removed before removing the clutch. On front drive vehicles, the engine or transaxle must be removed to service the clutch. Transmission removal procedures are presented in the chapters on transmission service.

When the transmission has been removed, remove the clutch release bearing and sleeve assembly from the clutch release fork (Fig. 33-6). Mark the clutch cover and flywheel (Fig. 33-7) so that they may be installed in the same place. Loosen and back off each of the clutch cover attaching bolts, one or two turns at a time, to avoid bending the cover flange. Remove the clutch assembly and disc from the clutch housing. **Safety Caution: Handle clutch and disc carefully to avoid contaminating the friction surfaces.**

33.11   Cleaning and Inspection

Clean dust out of the clutch housing. **Safety Caution: Clutch dust may contain asbestos. Do not blow the dust into the air with compressed air because it is dangerous to breathe in asbestos.** Inspect for oil leakage through the engine rear main bearing oil seal and transmission input clutch shaft seal. If there is leakage, correct it at this time.

The friction face of the flywheel should have a uniform appearance throughout the entire disc contact area. If there is heavy contact on one part of the wear circle and very light contact 180 degrees from that part, the flywheel may be improperly mounted or sprung. In either case, a dial indicator mounted on the clutch housing with the plunger in contact with the wear circle should show no more than 0.003 (0.08 mm) inch runout throughout a complete rotation of the flywheel. The friction face of the flywheel should also be free from discoloration, burned areas, small heat cracks, grooves, and ridges.

The pilot bushing or bearing pressed in the rear end of the crankshaft should be smooth and show no excessive wear. A new transmission input clutch

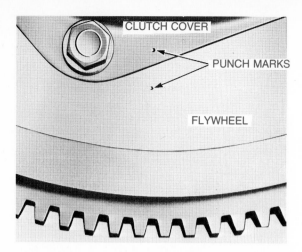

Fig. 33-7 Mark clutch cover and flyweel. (Chrysler Corporation)

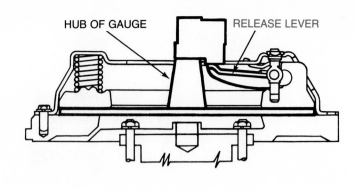

Fig. 33-8 Checking height of release levers. (American Motors Corporation)

shaft can be used to gauge the size of the bushing. The end of the transmission input clutch shaft should be smooth and bright, without grooves and ridges.

The disc assembly should be handled without touching facings. Replace the disc if facings show evidence of grease or oil soakage or if there is wear to within less than 0.015 inch (0.38 mm) of the rivet heads. The hub splines and splines on the clutch shaft should be a snug fit without signs of excessive wear. Metallic parts of the disc assembly should be dry and clean and show no evidence of having been hot. Each of the arched springs between facings should be unbroken, and all rivets should be tight.

Wipe the friction surface of pressure plate with a solvent. Using a straightedge, check the pressure plate for flatness. The pressure plate friction area should be flat within 0.015 inch (0.38 mm) and free from discoloration, burned areas, cracks, grooves, or ridges. Inner ends of release levers should have a uniform wear pattern. Using a surface plate, test the cover for flatness. All sections around attaching bolt holes should be within 0.015 inch (0.38 mm) of contact with the surface plate. A gauge is available (Fig. 33-8) for checking the height of each of the release levers. This is usually done with the pressure plate mounted to the flywheel. If the fingers are not uniform, they may be adjusted on some units, but in most cases the pressure plate assemby is replaced.

Examine the condition of clutch throwout bearing. The clutch release bearing is a prelubricated, sealed thrust bearing that should not be soaked in solvent. The bearing should turn freely when held in the hands under light thrust load and show no evidence of roughness.

33.12 Replacing Release Bearing

The bearing is retained on the sleeve with a press fit. Support the bearing and sleeve in a vise or press and carefully press out the sleeve.

Clean the sleeve in solvent and remove all old lubricant. Do not get solvent on the new release bearing. The solvent could contaminate the lubricant in the bearing. Never drive the bearing on the sleeve with a hammer. Place the new bearing on the sleeve and place the old bearing against the face of the new bearing. Support parts in a vise and carefully press the new bearing on the sleeve (Fig. 33-9). Make sure the bearing is seated on the shoulder of the bearing sleeve. Rotate bearings as they are pressed together.

33.13 Installing the Clutch

Lubricate the transmission input clutch shaft bushing in the end of crankshaft with a small amount of grease. Place the lubricant in the radius in back of the bushing. Clean the surfaces of flywheel and pressure plate thoroughly with fine sandpaper or crocus cloth and make certain that all oil or grease has been removed.

Hold the clutch disc, pressure plate and cover in mounting position, with springs on disc damper facing away from the flywheel. Do not touch disc facings, as dirt or grease may result in clutch chatter. Insert a clutch disc aligning arbor through the hub of the disc and into the bushing (Fig. 33-10). If an arbor is not available, use a spare transmission input clutch shaft.

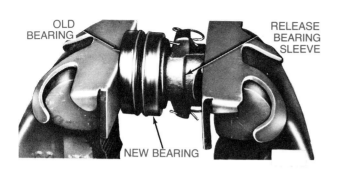

Fig. 33-9 Using vise and old bearing to install new bearing on sleeve. (Chrysler Corporation)

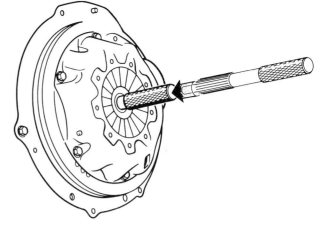

Fig. 33-10 An aligning arbor is used to center the clutch disc with the pilot bearing. (Nissan Motor Corporation)

Install clutch cover attaching bolts (after aligning balance punch marks), but do not tighten them. To avoid bending the clutch cover, bolts should be tightened a few turns at a time (alternately) until they are all snug. Tighten bolts to specification with a torque wrench.

Reassemble the clutch fork and release bearing assembly. Lubricate these components as required by the manufacturer. Install the transmission and drive shaft and adjust the clutch free travel.

NEW TERMS

Clutch chatter   A shaking or shuddering of the vehicle as the clutch is operated.

Clutch disc aligning arbor   A tool used to line up the clutch disc with the pressure plate.

Clutch drag   A problem in which the clutch disc does not come to a complete stop after the clutch pedal is depressed.

Clutch slippage   A condition in which the engine overrevs during shifting or acceleration.

Pedal free play   The free movement of the clutch pedal before the throwout bearing works the release fingers.

Pedal pulsation   A rapid up-and-down movement of the clutch pedal during operation.

Pedal travel   Same as pedal free play.

CHAPTER REVIEW

1. What is clutch chatter?
2. Explain how to check for clutch chatter.
3. What is clutch slippage?
4. What is clutch drag?
5. Explain how to check for clutch drag.
6. What is clutch pedal pulsation?
7. What causes clutch pedal pulsation?
8. List four causes of clutch vibrations.
9. Explain how to check for clutch area noises.
10. What is clutch pedal free play?
11. How is clutch pedal free play measured?
12. Explain how the clutch is removed.
13. Explain how the clutch parts are cleaned and inspected.
14. Describe how a throwout bearing is replaced.
15. Describe how the clutch is installed.

DISCUSSION TOPICS AND ACTIVITIES

1. Make a list of the common clutch problems described in the chapter. Describe the steps you would follow to find the trouble.
2. Look up the clutch pedal free play specifications for the automobile of your choice. Measure the free play and compare it with the specifications.

Manually Operated Transaxle and Transmission

CHAPTER PREVIEW

A transmission contains gears which increase the engine's turning effort, or torque, to get the car moving, and allow it to back up. A front-engine, rear-drive vehicle has a transmission at the back of the engine, and a differential or rear axle at the rear, connected by a drive shaft. A front-engine, front-drive vehicle uses a transaxle, which is a combination of transmission and rear axle in the same housing.

OBJECTIVES

After studying this chapter, you should be able to do the following:

1. Understand the purpose of gears and gearing.
2. Identify the major parts of a manually operated transmission.
3. Name and identify the different types of transmissions in use.
4. Describe the powerflow through a manual transaxle.
5. Explain the power flow through a three- and four-speed transmission.

34.1 GEARING AND TORQUE

An automotive engine develops low torque at low rpm. Without some way of increasing this torque, the typical 3,000-pound automobile could not be moved from a standstill. It is possible to increase torque by connecting the engine to a small gear and the rear wheels to a large gear. When a small gear turns a larger one, the effect is the same as using a larger wrench to tighten a nut or bolt (Fig. 34-1). More turning effort or torque is possible. The larger gear provides more leverage to turn the driving wheels with more torque.

When a small gear turns a large one, the small gear turns around several times before the big one has made a complete revolution. This means that the engine, connected to a small gear, turns at a higher rpm than the rear wheels. The speed difference, as well as the torque increase through a gear mechanism, depends on the number of teeth on the gears. If two gears in mesh have the same number of teeth, they will turn at the same speed and will not multiply torque (Fig. 34-2). The gear ratio is determined by dividing the number of teeth on the large gear by the number of teeth on the small gear. Thus, if a gear with 24 teeth turns a gear with 12 teeth, the ratio is 2:1.

An automotive transmission provides the driver with a way of changing the gear ratio between the engine and the rear wheels (Fig. 34-3). Gear ratios are different for different automobiles, but in low gear the ratio through the transmission is about 3:1. In second gear, the ratio is about 2:1. When the vehicle is moving fast enough, torque multiplication through the transmission is no longer required. The driver shifts into high gear, which has a 1:1 ratio. With a three-speed transmission (Fig. 34-4), the driver can select three ratios. A four-speed offers four possible ratios. In addition, there is always a reverse gear.

34.2 TRANSMISSION COMPONENTS

The manual transmission (Fig. 34-5) is a buildup of several gear assemblies. The top row of gears is

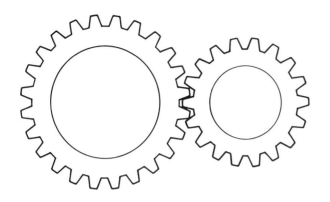

Fig. 34-1 When small gear turns large gear, torque is multiplied.

Fig. 34-2 Two gears the same size do not multiply torque.

called the mainshaft or mainshaft assembly. The bottom row is called the countergear or countershaft assembly. A reverse idler assembly is placed off to the side. The clutch disc is attached to an input or clutch shaft that enters the transmission. The engine's power enters the transmission when the driver's foot releases the clutch pedal.

The clutch shaft is attached to the clutch gear, or main drive gear, which always turns when the clutch shaft turns. The countershaft, along with several other gears permanently attached to it, turns as a unit. The countershaft of a three-speed transmission has a drive gear, a second gear, a low gear, and a reverse gear.

The gears on the countershaft (second, low, and reverse) are in mesh with gears on the mainshaft. The end of the mainshaft at the rear of the transmission, called the output shaft, delivers power to the drive line after it has passed through the transmission. Each of the mainshaft gears is free to rotate until the driver shifts to that gear. Then it is locked to the mainshaft.

34.3   SYNCHRONIZERS

Which gears will be used is determined by the driver's positioning of the shift lever. Gear shifting on older transmissions moved the gears in and out of mesh with each other. Careful driving technique was needed to avoid clashing of gears. All current car transmissions use synchronizers for shifting. The gears remain in constant mesh with each other. When a particular gear is selected, a synchronizer locks mainshaft gears to the mainshaft so that engine power can be transferred through them. The unit synchronizes the speed of the shaft and the gear so they may be locked up without any clashing.

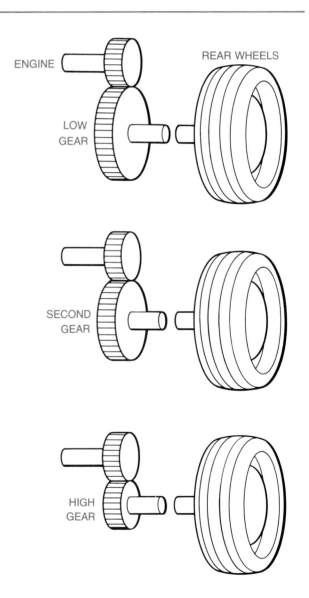

Fig. 34-3 Driver uses transmission to vary gear ratio between engine and rear wheels.

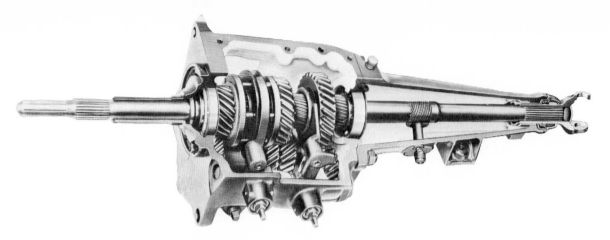

Fig. 34-4 Cutaway view of three-speed transmission.
(Dodge/Chrysler Corporation)

The synchronizer (Fig. 36-6) consists of a sleeve that is moved back and forth on a hub attached to the main shaft. A bronze synchronizer ring with a coned or tapered inside surface is matched on the gear with which the synchronizer works. The driver moves the shift linkage to lock up a gear. The sleeve is moved toward the gear on the teeth of the hub until it begins to contact the synchronizer ring. The ring is pushed in contact with the gear. The matching surfaces of the ring and gear act as a clutch. As soon as they touch, the gear and mainshaft begin to turn at the same speed. The sleeve can then be moved far enough to lock onto the gear, which is locked to the sleeve and, through the hub, to the mainshaft. The operation of the synchronizer is shown in Figure 34-7. The separate components are shown in Figure 34-8.

Each of the gears to be synchronized—main drive gear, second-speed gear, and first-speed gear—has a cone surface. The hub and the gear carrier is tightly splined to the mainshaft. The main drive gear and first- and second-speed mainshaft gears can turn in relation to the mainshaft.

Three keys (Fig. 34-9) slide in slots of the hub. These keys are spring loaded by two synchronizer springs (Fig. 34-10). The synchronizer ring has three slots in which the keys engage, and is thereby moved along with the sleeve. The slots in the synchronizer ring are wider than the keys, so that the synchronizer ring can rotate slightly relative to the hub.

The internally splined mainshaft first and reverse synchronizer sleeve slides along the external splines of the hub. The first speed gear clutch sleeve splines have a shallow groove (Fig. 34-8) in which the raised part of the key rests when in neutral position. Each

spline of the first and reverse speed gear clutch sleeve and each tooth of the synchronizer ring has a wedge angle on both sides. Through the press of these wedge angles, the engagement of the gears is prevented until the synchronizer ring has brought the mainshaft first speed gear to the speed of the hub. Gear clash in a synchronized transmission usually means that the synchronizers are worn and the parts should be replaced.

34.4 POWER FLOW THROUGH A THREE-SPEED TRANSMISSION

To get the automobile moving from a stop, the driver selects low gear (Fig. 34-11). The shift linkage allows a synchronizer to lock low gear to the mainshaft. As the driver lets up on the clutch pedal, engine power entering the transmission turns the clutch gear and countershaft assembly. The countershaft turns all the gears in mesh with it, but only the low gear is locked to the mainshaft. The power goes through the low gear on the countershaft to the low gear on the mainshaft. Since the countershaft low gear is small and the mainshaft low gear is large, the mainshaft is driven with a torque increase.

After the automobile is under way, the driver selects second gear, pushing down on the clutch pedal as he shifts (Fig. 34-12). This momentarily disconnects the engine from the transmission, making the job of the synchronizers easier. When second is engaged, the power flows through the clutch gear and countershaft, across the countershaft second gear, and through the mainshaft second gear. Since there is some difference in size between these two gears, there is some gear reduction and torque increase.

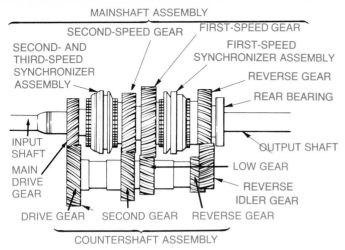

Fig. 34-5 Basic parts of manually operated transmission.
(Buick Motor Division, GMC)

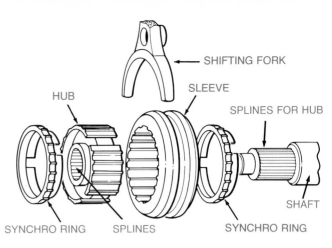

Fig. 34-6 Simplified synchronizer assembly.

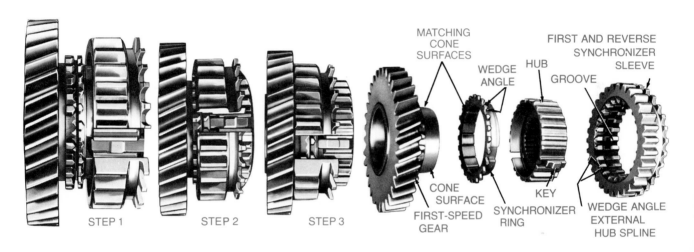

Fig. 34-7 Synchronizer operation. (Chevrolet Motor Division, GMC)

Fig. 34-8 Synchronizer components. (Chevrolet Motor Division, GMC)

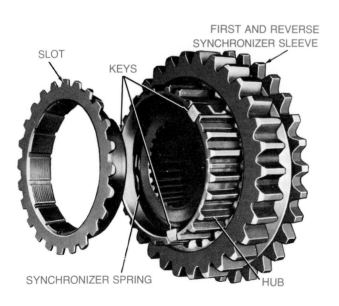

Fig. 34-9 Synchronizer hub and sleeve.
(Chevrolet Motor Division, GMC)

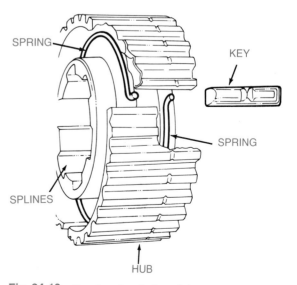

Fig. 34-10 Synchronizer hub and ring. (American Motors Corporation)

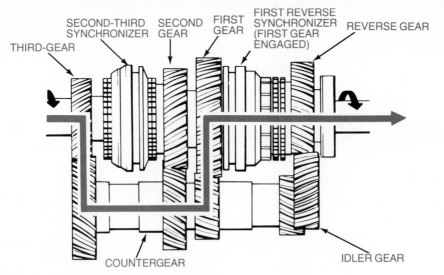

Fig. 34-11 Power flow in low gear.

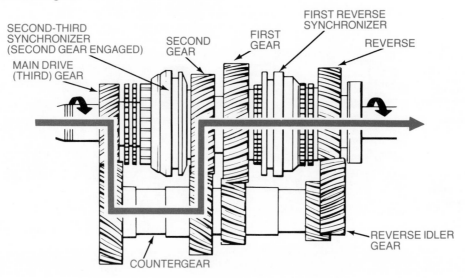

Fig. 34-12 Power flow in second gear.

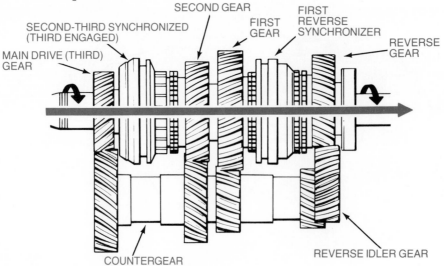

Fig. 34-13 Power flow in direct drive or high gear.

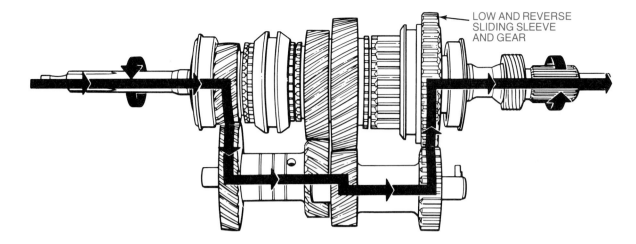

Fig. 34-14 Low reverse sliding gear in reverse.

In high gear (Fig. 34-13), no torque multiplication through the transmission is needed. The easiest connection for a 1:1 gear ratio is to hook the clutch shaft directly to the mainshaft. A synchronizer placed between the two shafts disengages second gear and connects the two shafts. Power flows through the clutch shaft and into the mainshaft. With no gears used, there is no gear reduction or torque increase.

If the driver wishes to back up, he or she shifts into reverse (Fig. 34-14). When reverse is selected, a reverse gear is locked to the mainshaft. The reverse gear is also in mesh with a reverse idler gear. Power flows through the clutch gear to the countershaft reverse gear, is transferred to the reverse idler, and passes to the mainshaft reverse gear. Adding another gear to the system reverses the mainshaft's direction of rotation so that the automobile can be backed up.

When the driver wants the automobile to idle without the clutch pedal down, he shifts to neutral (Fig. 34-15). In neutral, all the gears on the mainshaft are unlocked. The clutch gear turns the countershaft, which in turn drives the gears on the mainshaft. With the gears on the mainshaft disengaged, no power goes to the mainshaft. The gears turn, but the automobile does not move.

34.5 GEAR SHIFTING

Gear shifting is done in the transmission by moving the synchronizer assemblies with shifting forks (Fig. 34-16). The shifting forks, often mounted in a top or side cover, are moved into position by linkage controlled by the driver. An interlock cam prevents two gears from being meshed at one time.

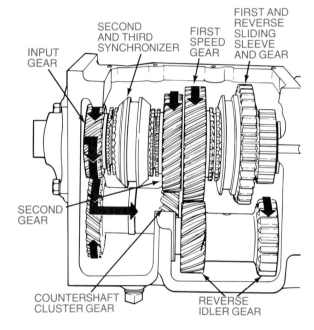

Fig. 34-15 Power flow in neutral.

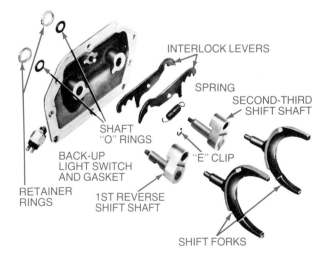

Fig. 34-16 Exploded view of shift levers and side cover.
(Chrysler Corporation)

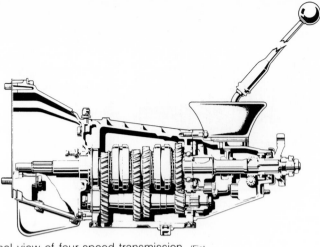

Fig. 34-17 Sectional view of four-speed transmission. (Fiat Motors of North America)

Most current cars use a gear shift lever assembly which is on the floor. The shift assembly may be mounted on the rear of the transmission and linkage used to transfer the movement to the side of the transmission. More commonly the shift mechanism goes directly into a top mounted shift cover.

34.6   TYPES OF TRANSMISSIONS

We have explained the parts and operation of three-speed manual transmission. Most cars use manual transmissions with more than three speeds. The smaller engines now in use require four- or five-speed transmissions.

34.7   Four-Speed Transmission

The four-speed transmission (Fig. 34-17) is frequently used in small automobiles and performance vehicles to provide a better match between the engine and the vehicle's torque requirements. It adds another gear on the countergear and mainshaft assemblies.

The power flow through the four-speed transmission is similar to that of the three-speed except that an additional set of gears is used. In neutral, with engine clutch engaged, the main drive gear turns the countergear. The countergear then turns the third, second, first, and reverse idler gears. But, because the third-fourth and first-second speed synchronizers are in neutral position and the reverse speed gear is positioned at rear, away from the reverse idler gear, power will not flow through the mainshaft (Fig. 34-18).

In first speed, the first- and second-speed clutch (sleeve) is moved rearward to engage the first speed gear, which is being turned by the countergear. Because the first- and second-speed clutch (hub) is splined to the mainshaft, torque is applied to the mainshaft from the first-speed gear through the clutch assembly (Fig. 34-19).

In second speed, the first- and second-speed synchronizer is moved forward to engage the second-speed gear, which is being turned by the countergear. This engagement of the synchronizer with the second-speed gear applies torque to the mainshaft because the first- and second-speed synchronizer is splined to the mainshaft (Fig. 34-20).

In third speed, the first- and second-speed synchronizer is in a neutral position. The third- and fourth-speed synchronizer moves rearward to engage the third-speed gear, which is being turned by the countergear. Because the third- and fourth-speed synchronizer is splined to the mainshaft, torque is applied to the mainshaft from the third-speed gear through the clutch assembly (Fig. 34-21).

In fourth speed, direct drive, the third- and fourth-speed synchronizer is moved forward to engage the main drive gear and the first- and second-speed clutch remains in a neutral position. This engagement of the main drive gear with the third- and fourth-speed synchronizer applies torque directly to the mainshaft (Fig. 34-22).

In reverse, both synchronizers are in neutral position. The reverse speed gear is moved forward to engage the rear reverse idler gear, which is being turned by the countergear. Because the reverse-speed gear is splined to the mainshaft, this engagement causes the mainshaft to turn. However, because power flows from main drive gear to countergear and through reverse-idler gear to reverse-speed gear, it turns in a reverse direction (Fig. 34-23).

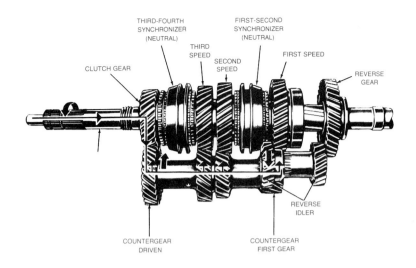

THIRD-FOURTH
SYNCHRONIZER
(NEUTRAL)

FIRST-SECOND
SYNCHRONIZER
(NEUTRAL)

THIRD
SPEED

FIRST SPEED

CLUTCH GEAR

SECOND
SPEED

REVERSE
GEAR

REVERSE
IDLER

COUNTERGEAR
DRIVEN

COUNTERGEAR
FIRST GEAR

Fig. 34-18 Neutral gear in a four-speed. (Chevrolet Motor Division, GMC)

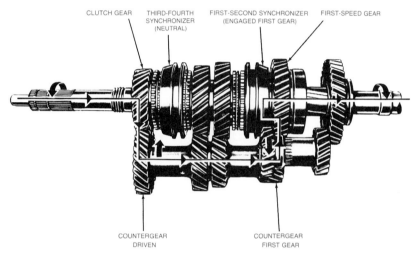

CLUTCH GEAR

THIRD-FOURTH
SYNCHRONIZER
(NEUTRAL)

FIRST-SECOND SYNCHRONIZER
(ENGAGED FIRST GEAR)

FIRST-SPEED GEAR

COUNTERGEAR
DRIVEN

COUNTERGEAR
FIRST GEAR

Fig. 34-19 First gear in a four-speed. (Chevrolet Motor Division, GMC)

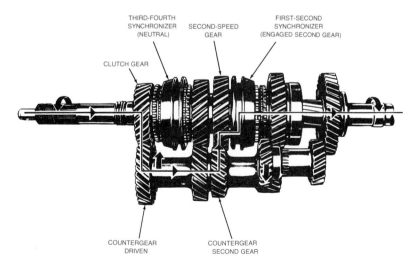

THIRD-FOURTH
SYNCHRONIZER
(NEUTRAL)

SECOND-SPEED
GEAR

FIRST-SECOND
SYNCHRONIZER
(ENGAGED SECOND GEAR)

CLUTCH GEAR

COUNTERGEAR
DRIVEN

COUNTERGEAR
SECOND GEAR

Fig. 34-20 Second gear in a four-speed. (Chevrolet Motor Division, GMC)

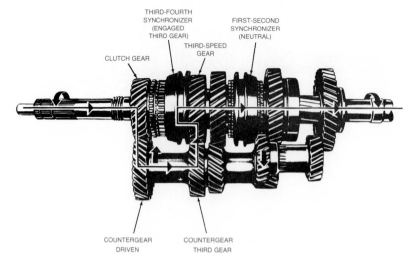

Fig. 34-21 Third gear in a four-speed. (Chevrolet Motor Division, GMC)

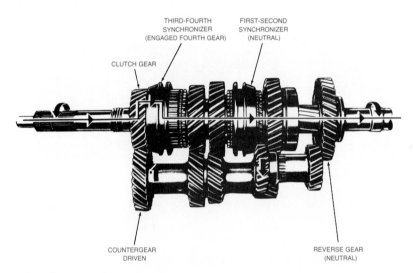

Fig. 34-22 Fourth gear in a four-speed. (Chevrolet Motor Division, GMC)

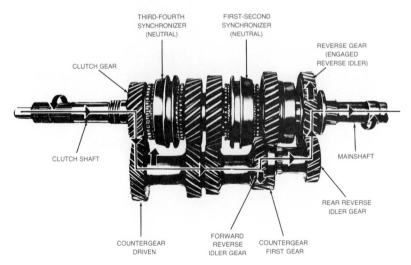

Fig. 34-23 Reverse gear in a four-speed. (Chevrolet Motor Division, GMC)

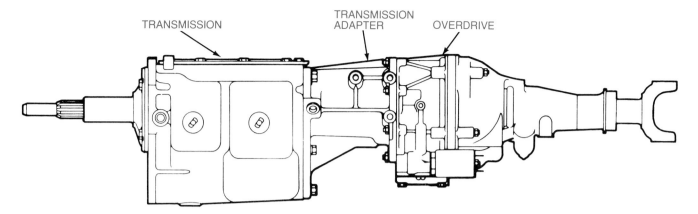

Fig. 34-24 Transmission and overdrive unit.

34.8 Five-Speed and Overdrive Transmissions

An overdrive transmission provides a gear ratio higher than 1:1. There are two main advantages of an overdrive. In overdrive, the engine turns slower for any given speed, which can result in longer engine life. A second advantage is that when the engine turns slower, it uses less fuel. Gasoline mileage can be greatly increased when the vehicle is in overdrive.

There are two overdrive systems in use. One (Fig. 34-24) uses an extra gear housing. This unit consists of a planetary gear system that increases the output shaft ratio beyond that of the transmission. The operation of planetary gears is explained in Chapter 36. The planetary gears are engaged by the driver through electrical or manual controls. This overdrive system, with an adapter, can be mounted to the rear of many transmissions.

Another type of overdrive transmission (Fig. 34-25) is a five-speed. The first four speeds provide ratios similar to a four-speed. The fifth speed is an overdrive ratio. The gear ratios are as follows:

1st	2nd	3rd	4th	5th	R
3.41	2.08	1.40	1.00	.80	3.36

The .80 ratio in fifth gear provides a 20 percent reduction in engine speed over the 1:1 ratio of fourth gear. Five-speed transmissions are standard equipment on some automobiles.

34.9 Transaxle

Automobiles with front-engine and front-wheel drive or rear-engine and rear-wheel drive normally combine the transmission and differential assembly into one unit (Fig. 34-26). The difference in the transmission is that the output shaft is connected directly into the differential assembly.

34.10 Manual Transaxle Components

The main two sections of the manual transaxle are shown in Figure 34-26. The transmission section which fits between the clutch and differential provide four forward gear ratios and one reverse gear ratio. The differential section which fits between the transmission and constant velocity joints and front wheels allows one wheel and axle to rotate faster than the other when the vehicle is turning. We will explain how this section works in Chapter 40.

The input cluster shaft receives engine power and transfers it to the mainshaft assembly. Reverse idler gear engages the reverse gear on the input cluster shaft and the reverse sliding gear on the mainshaft when a shift to reverse is made. This provides for the correct rotation for reverse operation. The final drive ring gear driven by main shaft transfers power to the differential case. Synchronizers are operated by the two forks of the shift mechanism. The synchronizers engage first through fourth gears without clashing.

34.11 Manual Transaxle Powerflow

The powerflow through a transaxle is similar to that described previously for a transmission. In addition, the synchronizer operation is the same. In neutral (Fig. 34-27), engine power drives the input cluster shaft, turning the input shaft gears. The synchro sleeves are centered. Mating gears on the

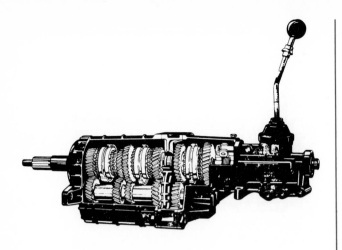

Fig. 34-25 Five-speed overdrive transmission. (Borg-Warner Corporation)

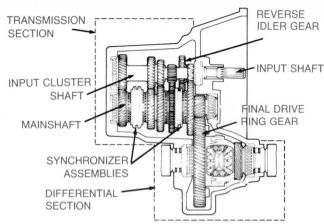

Fig. 34-26 Main sections and components of a manual transaxle. (Ford Motor Company)

mainshaft, not engaged to the mainshaft, turn freely. The mainshaft is stationary and there is no power flow to differential.

When the driver shifts to first gear (Fig. 34-28), the engine power drives the input cluster shaft. First and second gear synchronizer is engaged to first gear. The synchronizer hub is engaged to the mainshaft. First gear on the input shaft drives first gear on the mainshaft. The mainshaft drives the differential ring gear. Power flows through side and pinion gears to the stub shaft on one side and directly to the stub shaft on the other.

When the driver shifts to second gear (Fig. 34-29), the engine power drives the input cluster shaft. The first and second gear synchronizer is engaged to second gear. The synchronizer hub is engaged to the mainshaft. The second gear on the input shaft drives the second gear on the mainshaft. The mainshaft drives the differential ring gear. Power flows through side and pinion gears to the stub shaft on one side and directly to the stub shaft on the other.

The powerflow in third gear is shown in Figure 34-30. The engine power drives the input cluster shaft. Third and fourth gear synchronizer is engaged to the third gear. The synchronizer hub is engaged to the mainshaft. The third gear on the input shaft drives the third gear on the mainshaft. The mainshaft drives the differential ring gear. Power flows through side and pinion gears to the stub shaft on one side and directly to the stub shaft on the other.

When the driver shifts into fourth gear (Fig. 34-31), the engine power drives the input cluster shaft. The third and fourth gear synchronizer is engaged to the fourth gear. The synchronizer hub is engaged to the mainshaft. The mainshaft drives the

differential ring gear. Power flows through side and pinion gears to the stub shaft on one side and directly to the stub shaft on the other.

When the driver shifts into reverse (Fig. 34-32), the engine power drives the input cluster shaft which drives the reverse idler gear. The reverse idler gear drives the mainshaft through the reverse sliding gear and provides the correct direction of rotation for reverse operations. The mainshaft drives the final drive ring gear. Power flows through side and pinion gears to the stub shaft on either side.

34.12 TRANSMISSION ACCESSORIES

The manually operated transmission may be connected to several accessory systems on the automobile. One such accessory is the speedometer drive. A small gear housed on the rear of the transmission case meshes with a gear on the transmission output shaft. A cable connected to the gear in the housing drives the speedometer mechanism on the instrument panel.

A backup light switch is sometimes worked by the shift linkage on the transmission. When the driver shifts the transmission linkage into reverse, a switch is closed to light a set of backup warning lights at the rear of the automobile.

The transmission may also be a part of the vehicle's emission control system. A transmission-controlled spark switch (Fig. 34-33) is installed in many late model transmissions. This switch is closed in all gears but high, grounding an electrical circuit in the emission control system. This has the effect of retarding the ignition.

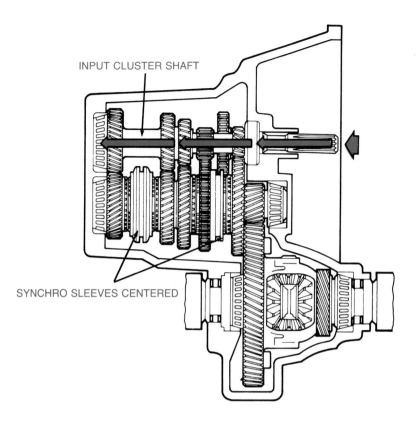

INPUT CLUSTER SHAFT

SYNCHRO SLEEVES CENTERED

Fig. 34-27 Powerflow through a manual transaxle in neutral. (Ford Motor Company)

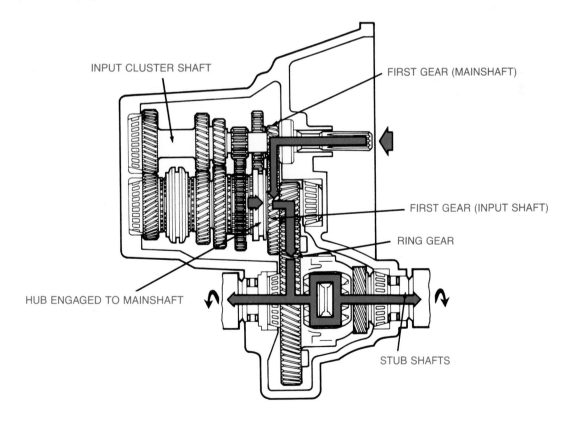

INPUT CLUSTER SHAFT

FIRST GEAR (MAINSHAFT)

FIRST GEAR (INPUT SHAFT)

RING GEAR

HUB ENGAGED TO MAINSHAFT

STUB SHAFTS

Fig. 34-28 Powerflow through a manual transaxle in first gear. (Ford Motor Company)

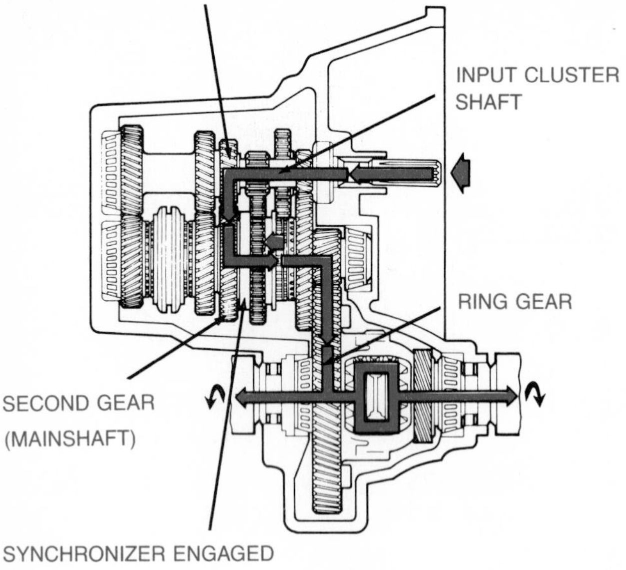

SECOND GEAR (CLUSTER SHAFT)

INPUT CLUSTER
SHAFT

RING GEAR

SECOND GEAR
(MAINSHAFT)

SYNCHRONIZER ENGAGED

Fig. 34-29 Powerflow through a manual transaxle in second gear. (Ford Motor Company)

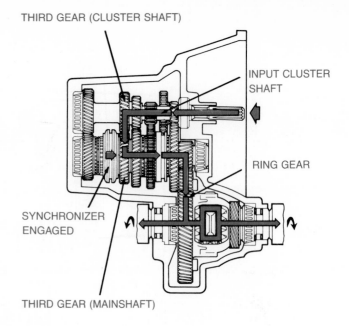

THIRD GEAR (CLUSTER SHAFT)

INPUT CLUSTER
SHAFT

RING GEAR

SYNCHRONIZER
ENGAGED

THIRD GEAR (MAINSHAFT)

Fig. 34-30 Powerflow through a manual transaxle in third gear. (Ford Motor Company)

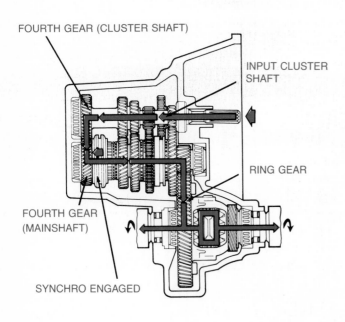

FOURTH GEAR (CLUSTER SHAFT)

INPUT CLUSTER
SHAFT

RING GEAR

FOURTH GEAR
(MAINSHAFT)

SYNCHRO ENGAGED

Fig. 34-31 Powerflow through a manual transaxle in fourth gear. (Ford Motor Company)

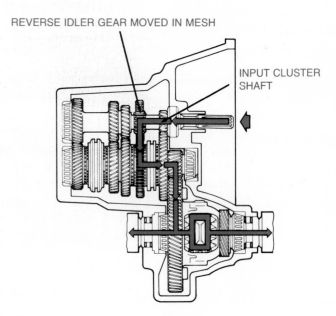

REVERSE IDLER GEAR MOVED IN MESH

INPUT CLUSTER
SHAFT

Fig. 34-32 Powerflow through a manual transaxle in reverse. (Ford Motor Company)

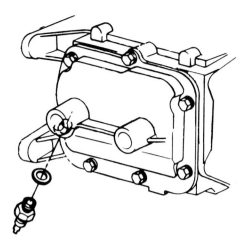

Fig. 34-33 Transmission-controlled spark switch. (Pontiac Motor Division, GMC)

NEW TERMS

Control linkage The floor or steering column linkage used by the driver to select the transmission gears.

Five-speed transmission A transmission with five forward speeds or gear ratios.

Four-speed transmission A transmission with four forward speeds or gear ratios.

Gear A wheel with teeth that engage or mesh with teeth of another wheel.

Gear ratio The ratio of the number of teeth on two gears in mesh with each other.

Manually operated transmission A transmission that is shifted from one speed to another by the driver.

Overdrive transmission A transmission that provides a gear ratio higher than one to one.

Synchronizer A device that synchronizes the speed of gears and shafts so they can be meshed without clashing.

Three-speed transmission A transmission with three forward speeds or gear ratios.

Transaxle An axle assembly and transmission combined into one housing.

Transmission A housing containing a number of gears used to increase the engine's turning effort.

CHAPTER REVIEW

1. What is the purpose of the transmission?

2. What happens when a small gear is used to turn a large one?

3. What is gear ratio?

4. If a small gear with 12 teeth turns a large one with 24 teeth, what is the gear ratio?

5. What is the top row of gears in a transmission called?

6. What is the bottom row of gears in a transmission called?

7. Why are synchronizers used in transmissions?

8. Describe the operation of synchronizer

9. Describe the power flow through a manual transaxle in first gear.

10. Describe the power flow through a manual transaxle in second gear.

11. Describe the power flow through a manual transaxle in third gear.

12. Describe the power flow through a manual transaxle in fourth gear.

13. Describe the power flow through a manual transaxle in reverse.

14. What is an overdrive transmission?

15. Where is the speedometer drive mounted?

DISCUSSION TOPICS AND ACTIVITIES

1. Using a shop transmission, demonstrate all shift positions for a three-speed transmission. Describe the flow of power in each position.

2. Calculate the gear ratios in the three forward speeds as well as the reverse speed of the transmission.

3. Take apart a shop synchronizer unit. Try to explain how it works.

CHAPTER 35

Manual Transmission and Transaxle Service

CHAPTER PREVIEW

A manual transmission or transaxle normally runs thousands of miles before it needs major service. For major service, a manual transmission or transaxle must be removed from the vehicle and disassembled. Because of the complexity of modern transmission and transaxles, the mechanic must follow an up-to-date service manual. In this chapter, we will present general troubleshooting, maintenance, and service procedures.

OBJECTIVES

After studying this chapter, you should be able to do the following:

1. List the steps in troubleshooting a manual transmission or transaxle.
2. Describe preventive maintenance procedures for a manually operated transmission or transaxle.
3. Explain the removal and disassembly steps in servicing a manual transmission or transaxle.
4. Describe the cleaning and inspection procedures in servicing a manual transmission or transaxle.
5. Explain the reassembly and installation procedures used on a manual transmission or transaxle.

35.1   TROUBLESHOOTING

Manual transmission or transaxle problems can be divided into five categories:

1. The transmission or transaxle shifts hard.
2. The gears clash when shifting.
3. The transmission or transaxle is noisy.
4. The transmission or transaxle jumps out of gear.
5. The transmission or transaxle is locked in one gear and cannot be shifted out of that gear.

35.2   Transmission Shifts Hard

When a transmission or transaxle shifts hard, check the clutch for incorrect clutch adjustment or binding clutch linkage. If the clutch operates satisfactorily, the gearshift linkage may be incorrectly adjusted, bent, or binding. There may be an internal bind in the transmission at the shift rails, interlocks, shift forks, or synchronizer teeth.

35.3   Gear Clash

Gear clash when shifting from one forward gear to another may also be caused by an incorrect clutch adjustment, by binding clutch linkage, or by gear shift linkage incorrectly adjusted, bent, or binding. Inside the transmission, damaged or worn shift forks, synchronizers, shift rails, and interlocks may cause gear clash. Excessive end play from worn thrust washers can also cause this problem.

35.4   Transmission Noisy

When a transmission or transaxle is noisy, first check the transmission lubricant. A lubricant level that is too low, an incorrect lubricant, or dirt or metal in the lubricant will cause noise. Loose housing bolts or gearshift linkage that is incorrectly adjusted, bent,

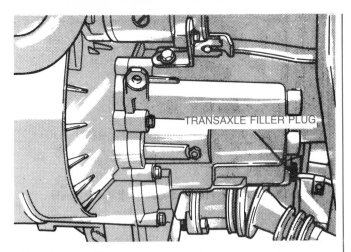

Fig. 35-1   A filler plug on the side of a transaxle. (Chrysler Corporation)

Fig. 35-2   Removing the transmission-to-engine bolts. (Chevrolet Motor Division, GMC)

or binding can also cause noise. Worn internal parts which can cause noise include front and rear bearings, clutch and countershaft bearings, worn or damaged gear teeth or synchronizer components.

35.5   Jumps Out of Gear

When a transmission or transaxle jumps out of gear, inspect the linkage. The linkage may be incorrectly adjusted, bent, or binding. A worn clutch pilot bearing may also be the cause. Inside the transmission or transaxle look for worn synchronizer parts or worn tapered gear teeth. Worn shifter forks, shift rails, or detents and excessive end play in any of the gear assemblies can cause this problem.

35.6   Locked in One Gear

When a transmission is locked in one gear and cannot be shifted out of that gear, the problem is most likely in the shifting mechanism. Bent or binding gearshift linkage is the most probable cause. Worn shift rails and broken or worn shifter forks or dents can lock the transmission in one gear. Broken gear teeth on the countershaft gear, clutch shaft, or reverse idler can also lock up a transmission.

35.7   PREVENTIVE MAINTENANCE

The only preventive maintenance required on a manual transmission or transaxle is a periodic lubricant level check and drain. The filler plug in the side of the transmission or transaxle case (Fig. 35-1) should be removed and the lubricant level checked

each time the vehicle is lubricated. Fill the transmission or transaxle to the level of the filler plug hole. Transmissions and transaxles use several different lubricants, from thin automatic transmission fluid to heavy gear oil. The manufacturer's recommendations should always be followed.

Some manufacturers do not recommend draining the transmission or transaxle and therefore do not provide a drain plug. For vehicles equipped with a drain plug, the interval between drains is specified in the service manual. Remove the drain plug and the old fluid. Replace the drain plug and refill the transmission or transaxle through the filler plug hole.

35.8   MANUAL TRANSMISSION SERVICE

When troubleshooting procedures indicate a problem inside the transmission or transaxle, it must be removed, disassembled, and inspected for wear and new components must be installed. The following sections give some of the procedures to be followed.

35.9   Transmission Removal

First, remove shift rods from transmission levers. Drain the fluid from the transmission. Disconnect the drive shaft at the rear universal joint. Mark both parts to reassemble in the same position. Carefully pull the drive shaft yoke out of the transmission extension housing. Disconnect the speedometer cable and backup light switch leads. Some models have exhaust systems which will have to be partially

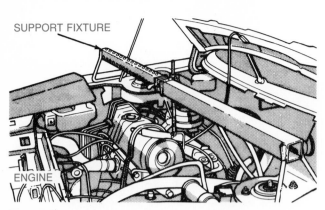

Fig. 35-3 An engine support fixture holds the engine up when the transaxle is removed. (Chrysler Corporation)

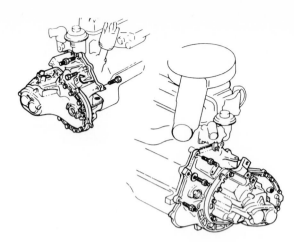

Fig. 35-4 Removing the transaxle-to-engine bolts. (Chevrolet Motor Division, GMC)

removed for clearance. Install an engine support or jack to support the rear of the engine if necessary.

Raise the engine slightly with the support fixture or jack. Disconnect the extension housing from the removable center cross member. Support the transmission with a suitable jack and remove the center cross member. Remove the transmission-to-the-engine bolts. Slide the transmission toward the rear until the clutch shaft clears the clutch disc before lowering the transmission. Lower the transmission and remove it from under the vehicle. Throughly clean the exterior of the transmission.

35.10   Transaxle Removal

In most installations, the transaxle can be un-bolted and removed from the bottom of the car. To remove the transaxle, first disconnect the battery negative cable to prevent any accidental engine cranking. Disconnect the battery ground cable from the transaxle case. If the transaxle has two transaxle strut bracket bolts at the transaxle on the side of the engine compartment, remove them. Disconnect the speedometer cable at the transaxle. For cruise-control cars, remove the transaxle speedometer cable at the cruise-control transducer. Remove the retaining clip and washer from the transaxle shifting linkage at the transaxle case. In order to take the pressure off the engine mounts when the transaxle is removed, install an engine support fixture as shown in Figure 35-3. Attach a fixture hook to the engine lift ring and raise the engine. Remove the transaxle-to-engine bolts (Fig. 35-4).

Unlock the steering column and then raise the car. Remove the drain plug and drain fluid from the transaxle case. Remove the nuts attaching the stabilizer bar to the lower control arm on the driver side. Remove the bolts that attach the retaining plage holding the driver side stabilizer bar to cradle. Loosen the bolts holding the stabilizer bracket on the passenger side of the cradle. If necessary, disconnect and remove the exhaust pipe. Pull the stabilizer bar down on the driver side. Remove the nuts and disconnect the front and rear transaxle mounts at the cradle. Remove the rear center crossmember bolts. Remove the passenger side front cradle attaching bolts. The nuts are reached by pulling back the splash shield next to the frame rail. If there is a top bolt, remove it from the lower front transaxle damper shock absorber.

Remove the left front wheel. Remove the front cradle-to-body bolts on the driver side of the cradle. Remove the rear cradle-to-body bolts. Pull the driver side drive shaft from the transaxle assembly. The passenger side drive shaft may be simply disconnected from the base. When the transaxle assembly is removed, you can swing the passenger side shaft out of the way. Swing the partial cradle to the driver side and wire it securely outboard to the fender well. Remove the flywheel and starter shield bolts. Remove the shields.

Support the transaxle on a floor jack. Make sure all transaxle-to-engine bolts are removed. Slide the transaxle assembly to the left and rear of the car until the mainshaft clears the clutch. Lower the transaxle and remove it from under the vehicle.

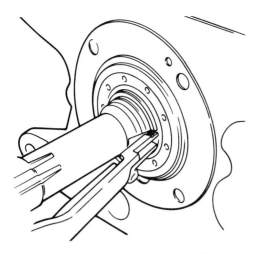

Fig. 35-5 Removing the clutch bearing retainer ring. (Chevrolet Motor Division, GMC)

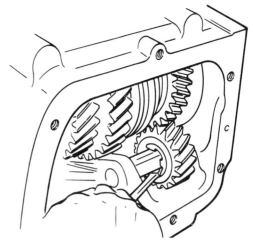

Fig. 35-6 Removing the idler shaft "E" ring. (Chevrolet Motor Division, GMC)

35.11   Disassembly

Disassembly procedures are different for different transmission and transaxles, but the following procedures are typical.

Remove the side cover attaching bolts and side cover assembly. Remove the drive gear bearing retainer and gasket. Remove the drive gear bearing-to-gear stem snap ring. To complete removal, then remove the clutch gear bearing by pulling outward on the clutch gear until a screwdriver or other suitable tool can be inserted between the bearing large snap ring and case (Fig. 35-5). The clutch gear bearing is a slip fit on the gear and into the case bore. (This provides clearance for removal of the clutch gear and mainshaft assembly.) Remove the speedometer driver gear from the extension. Remove the extension-to-case attaching bolts. Remove the reverse idler shaft "E" ring (Fig. 35-6). Remove the drive gear, mainshaft, and extension assembly together through the rear case opening. Remove the drive gear, needle bearings, and synchronizer ring from the mainshaft assembly.

Using snap ring pliers, expand the snap ring in the extension which retains the mainshaft rear bearing (Fig. 35-7) and remove the extension. Drive the countergear woodruff key out the rear of the case (Fig. 35-8). Remove the countergear bearings and thrust washers. Use a long drift or punch through the front bearing case bore and drive the reverse idler shaft and woodruff key through the rear of the case (Fig. 35-9).

The input and output assemblies (Fig. 35-10) are removed from a transaxle in much the same way as that described for a transmission. Some of the disassembly and reassembly procedures involve the differential unit. We will describe these procedures in Chapter 41.

35.12   Cleaning and Inspection

Clean the transmission case thoroughly with a suitable solvent, and allow it to dry. Inspect the case for cracks and stripped threads in the bolt holes. Check the machined mating surfaces for burrs or nicks. The front mating surface should be smooth; if there are any burrs, dress them off with a fine file.

Wash ball bearings with a clean solvent and allow them to dry. Do not spin bearings with air pressure. Spinning unlubricated bearings may cause damage to races and balls. After cleaning, lubricate ball bearings with light grade engine oil. Inspect bearings for roughness by slowly turning the outer race by hand. Inspect all bearing rollers for flat spots or pitting. Inspect all bearing roller spacers for signs of wear or pits. Install new parts as required.

Inspect gear geeth on synchronizer clutch gears and synchronizer rings. If there is evidence of chipping or excessively worn teeth, install new parts at reassembly. Be sure the synchronizer sleeve slides easily on the synchronizer gear. Inspect all gear teeth for chipped or broken teeth and signs of excessive wear. Small nicks or burrs must be sanded off.

Inspect teeth on the clutch shaft gear. If excessively worn, broken or chipped, a new clutch shaft should be installed. If the oil seal contract area on the clutch shaft is pitted, rusted, or scratched, a new shaft is recommended for best seal life.

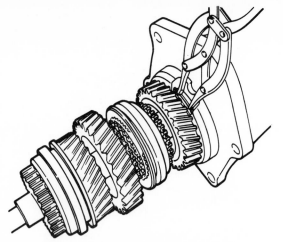

Fig. 35-7 Removing the rear extension housing from mainshaft. (Chevrolet Motor Division, GMC)

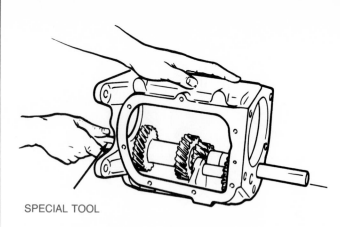

SPECIAL TOOL

Fig. 35-8 Removing the counter gear shaft. (Chevrolet Motor Division, GMC)

Test the interlock sleeve and pin for free movement in the bore of the shift housing. Examine the detent balls for signs of pitting. If lever detents show signs of too much wear, install a new part. Inspect shift forks for wear on the shanks and pads.

Inspect mainshaft gear and bearing mating surfaces. If gear contact surfaces show signs of pitting or are worn too much, install a new mainshaft.

Inspect snap ring grooves for burred edges. Remove the burrs with a fine file or crocus cloth. Inspect synchronizer clutch gear splines on the shaft for burrs. Replace worn parts with new ones as required.

35.13   Reassembly

To reassemble the transmission, use a wooden dowel the same length as the counter gear and load a row of roller bearings and a bearing thrust washer at each end of the countergear. Use heavy grease to hold them in place.

Place the countergear assembly through the case rear opening along with a tanged thrust washer (tang away from gear) at each end and install the countergear shaft and woodruff key from the rear of the case. Be sure the countershaft picks up both thrust washers and that the tangs are aligned with their notches in the case.

Install the reverse idler gear and shaft with its woodruff key from the rear of the case. Do not install the idle shafter "E" ring yet.

Using snap ring pliers, expand the snap ring in the extension and assemble the extension over the rear of the mainshaft and onto the rear bearing. Seat the snap ring in the rear bearing groove. Load the mainshaft pilot bearing into the clutch gear cavity and assemble the third speed synchronizer ring onto the clutch gear clutching surface with its teeth toward the gear.

Guide the clutch gear, pilot bearings, and third speed synchronizer ring assembly over the front of the mainshaft assembly. Do not assemble bearing to gear yet. Be sure the notches in the ring align with the keys in the 2-3 synchronizer assembly.

Place the extension-to-case gasket at the rear of the case, holding it in place with grease and, from the rear of case, assemble the clutch gear, mainshaft, and extension to the case as an assembly. Install the extension-to-case retaining bolts. Install the front bearing outer snap ring to the bearing and position the bearing over the stem of the clutch gear and into the front case bore.

Install the snap ring to the clutch gear stem, and the clutch gear bearing retainer and gasket to the case. The retainer oil return hole should be at the bottom. Install the reverse idler gear retainer "E" ring to the shaft.

Shift the synchronizer sleeves to neutral positions and install the cover, gasket, and fork assembly to the case. Be sure the forks align with their synchronizer sleeve grooves. Install the speedometer driven gear in the extension. Tighten all the bolts to the specified torque. Rotate the clutch gear shaft and shift the transmission to check for free rotation in all gears. Fill the transmission with the required amount of the correct lubricant.

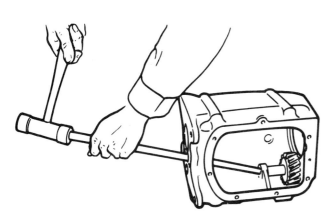

Fig. 35-9 Driving out the reverse idler shaft. (Chevrolet Motor Division, GMC)

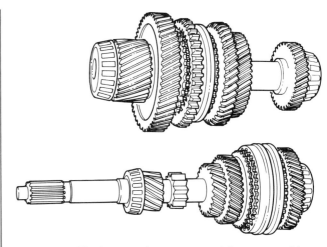

Fig. 35-10 The input and output assemblies removed from a transaxle. (Chevrolet Motor Division, GMC)

35.14 Transmission or Transaxle Installation

Place a small amount of multipurpose lubricant around the inner end of the clutch shaft pilot bushing in the flywheel and on the clutch shaft bearing retainer release bearing sleeve area. Do not lubricate the end of the clutch shaft, clutch disc splines, or clutch release levers.

With the transmission or transaxle on a suitable jack, slide the assembly under the vehicle. Raise the unit into position so that the shaft is lined up with the clutch. On some transaxles, the right side axle shaft may have to be inserted as the transaxle is being raised. Rock the unit back and forth until the shaft enters the clutch disc, then push the unit up against the engine. Do not let the transmission hang on the clutch disc. Install the housing bolts and tighten to specifications with a torque wrench.

Remove the transmission jack and swing the crossmember or cradle into position. On a transaxle, you may have to insert the left axle as you swing the cradle into position. On a transmission, install the driveshaft. Connect the shift linkage, speedometer cable, electrical wires, and clutch cable, if used. Replace the starter, if removed. Tighten all engine mount bolts to specifications, and remove the engine support fixture, if used. Road test the vehicle.

NEW TERMS

Gear clash A condition in which the gears grind during shifting.

Transmission drain plug A plug at the bottom of the transmission used to drain the lubricant.
Transmission filler plug A plug on the side of the transmission used to add transmission lubricant.

CHAPTER REVIEW

1. List the five manual transmission or transaxle problems.
2. What causes hard shifting?
3. What usually causes gear clash?
4. What should be checked if a manual transmission or transaxle is noisy?
5. What is the first thing that should be checked when a transmission or transaxle jumps out of gear?
6. What usually causes a transmission or transaxle to jump out of gear?
7. Explain how to drain the lubricant from a transmission or transaxle.
8. Explain the steps in removing a transmission from a vehicle.
9. Why must an engine be supported when removing a transaxle?
10. Explain how to remove a transaxle from a car.
11. List the steps a mechanic follows in disassembling a transmission or transaxle.

DISCUSSION TOPICS AND ACTIVITIES

1. List common transmission problems presented in the chapter. Explain how to find out the cause of a transmission or transaxle problem.
2. Look up the transmission or transaxle drain interval and the recommended lubricant for the automobile of your choice.

The Automatic Transmission and Transaxle

CHAPTER PREVIEW

Most late model automobiles use an automatic transmission or transaxle (Fig. 36-1), which does the same job as the manually operated clutch and transmission—increasing the engine's turning effort, or torque, to get the automobile moving. The difference is that the engagement and shifting in an automatic transmission or transaxle is done automatically by three mechanisms: torque converter, planetary gearbox, and hydraulic control system.

OBJECTIVES

After studying this chaper, you should be able to do the following:

1. Describe the operation of the torque converter in increasing torque.
2. Explain the operation of the planetary gearbox used in automatic transmissions or transaxles.
3. Describe the operation of planetary holding units such as multiple-disc clutches, bands, and overrunning clutches.
4. Understand the operation of the hydraulic control system.
5. Describe the purpose and operation of the automatic transmission or transaxle cooling system.

36.1   TORQUE CONVERTER

The torque converter (Fig. 36-2), like the manually operated clutch, permits the engine to be coupled and uncoupled from the rest of the drive train. The converter, placed at the front of the transmission where it is attached to the rear of the engine, has three parts (Figs. 36-2 and 36-3). The pump, a round wheel with blades on it, is attached to the engine's flywheel. A similar wheel, the turbine, is mounted to the transmission input shaft. A third, smaller wheel, the stator, is between the pump and turbine (Fig. 36-4).

The pump and turbine are placed very close together and covered by a housing. The small space between these two wheels is filled with automatic transmission fluid. When the engine is running, the pump rotates with the flywheel. Fluid thrown off the blades of the fast-moving pump hits the blades on the turbine with enough force to make the turbine rotate. The input shaft of the transmission, which is splined to the center of the turbine, is also forced to turn. The faster the engine runs, the stronger the flow of oil from the pump to the turbine and the faster the shaft will turn. When the engine slows down to idle speed, the fluid is not thrown off the pump hard enough to make the turbine rotate, and the engine is automatically uncoupled from the power train.

The stator, located between the pump and turbine, allows the torque converter to increase torque. The stator has a series of curved blades or vanes. As oil thrown off the turbine hits the stator blades, they guide it back toward the pump. The pump redirects the oil back toward the turbine. This repeated process increases the engine's turning effort or torque.

The stator provides some directional control to the fluid as it leaves the turbine and enters the pump. The stator is needed, however, only when the pump and turbine are turning at different speeds. It is not needed when the pump and turbine are turning at nearly the same speed because there is very little flow

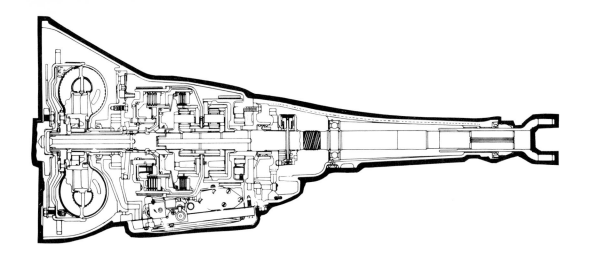

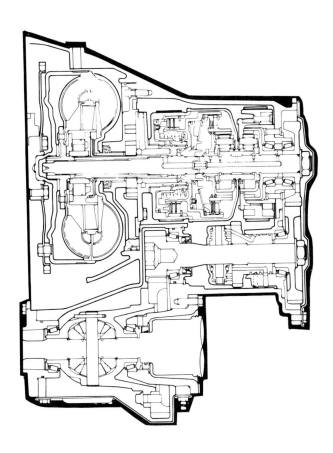

Fig. 36-1 The automatic transmission (top) and automatic transaxle. (Chrysler Corporation)

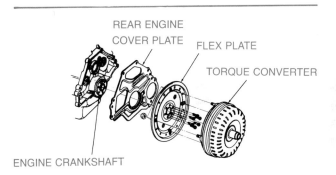

Fig. 36-2 The torque converter is mounted to the flywheel or flex plate. (Ford Motor Company)

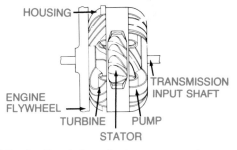

Fig. 36-3 Sectional view of a torque converter.

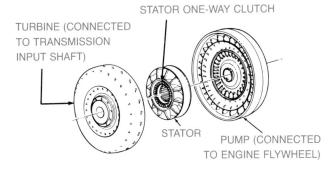

Fig. 36-4 Parts of the torque converter. (Ford Motor Company)

The Automatic Transmission and Transaxle 387

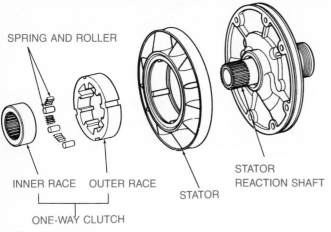

SPRING AND ROLLER

INNER RACE   OUTER RACE   STATOR   STATOR REACTION SHAFT

ONE-WAY CLUTCH

Fig. 36-5 Exploded view of the stator showing one-way clutch. (Ford Motor Company)

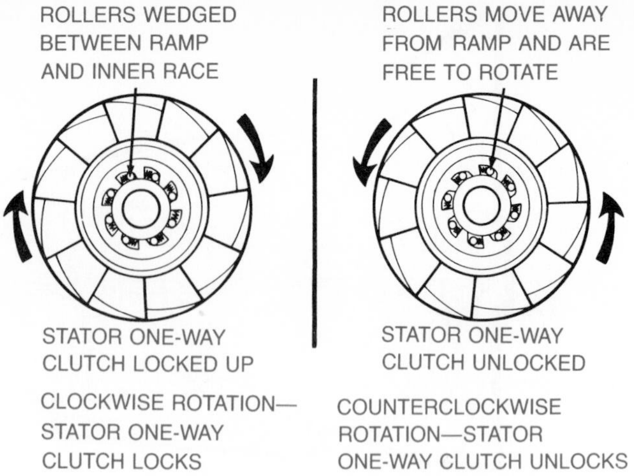

ROLLERS WEDGED BETWEEN RAMP AND INNER RACE

ROLLERS MOVE AWAY FROM RAMP AND ARE FREE TO ROTATE

STATOR ONE-WAY CLUTCH LOCKED UP

STATOR ONE-WAY CLUTCH UNLOCKED

CLOCKWISE ROTATION— STATOR ONE-WAY CLUTCH LOCKS

COUNTERCLOCKWISE ROTATION—STATOR ONE-WAY CLUTCH UNLOCKS

Fig. 36-6 The stator is locked and unlocked by the fluid direction in the torque converter. (Ford Motor Company)

to be redirected. For this reason, the stator is mounted on a reaction shaft at the front of the transmission that does not rotate, that goes into the torque converter. The stator is attached to the reaction shaft through a one-way roller clutch consisting of a number of spring-loaded rollers which allow the stator to turn in one direction but prevent it from turning in the other direction.

The roller clutch (Fig. 36-5) consists of an outer ring or race, an inner ring, a set of rollers, and a set of springs. The inner ring is simply the hub of the clutch. It fits around the transmission input shaft running through the converter. The outer ring, attached to the inner edge of the stator, has grooves which are wide at one end and narrow at the other. These grooves contain the rollers, with the springs placed behind them. When the stator turns clockwise, the outer ring also turns clockwise, pushing the rollers up into the wide end of the grooves so that the stator may rotate freely. But when the stator blades are hit by oil from the pump, pushing the stator in a counterclockwise direction, the rollers are forced into the narrow part of the grooves, locking up the outer ring so that the stator cannot turn.

The stator is locked or unlocked to the reaction shaft by fluid flow conditions (Fig. 36-6). When the vehicle is accelerating from a stop, the fluid leaves the turbine at an angle to strike the stator squarely on the back of its blades. Pushing the stator in this direction locks up the one-way clutch and redirects oil back into the pump.

As the vehicle nears cruising speed, the fluid leaves the turbine at a different angle so that it strikes the front of the stator blades. In this direction the stator clutch permits rotation, so the stator rotates in the same direction as the pump and turbine. Thus, as the turbine speed approaches pump speed, the stator "free wheels" and is carried along with the rotating fluid mass.

36.2   TORQUE CONVERSION

The torque converter increases engine torque a great deal when the difference in speed between the pump and turbine is great. When the difference is slight, there is very little torque increase. This, of course, is exactly what is required, because at low rpm engine torque must be increased to get the vehicle moving.

Torque can be increased in a torque converter because stationary blades on the stator redirect fluid back at the pump to help it turn. If a stream of fluid is directed at a bucket attached to the rim of a wheel (Fig. 36-7), the wheel will turn. The fluid swirls around the curved surface of the bucket and leaves it with almost the same velocity it had when entering. Since the fluid gives up little of its energy to the bucket, there will be only a small push on the bucket.

If a stationary curved vane is installed (Fig. 36-8), fluid coming out of the bucket will enter the stationary curved vane where it will reverse direction and reenter the bucket. The fluid may make many complete trips between the vane and bucket, each time applying force or torque to the bucket. The stationary vane in the torque converter is the stator. The stator redirects fluid at the pump and increases torque. The fluid flow through a torque converter is shown in Figure 36-9.

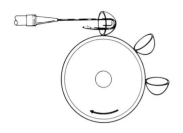

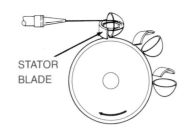

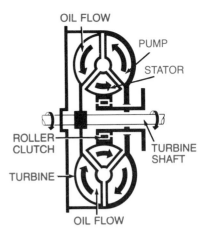

Fig. 36-7 Torque applied to wheel by fluid.

Fig. 36-8 Torque multiplied with stator blades.

Fig. 36-9 Cross section of torque converter showing oil flow. (Pontiac Motor Division, GMC)

36.3 Lock-Up Torque Converter

While the torque converter is an efficient torque multiplier, a certain amount of engine torque is lost to fluid slip in the hydraulic link. To eliminate this inefficiency and improve fuel mileage, the lock-up converter is used on most late model transmissions and transaxles which mechanically link the turbine to the converter cover at various operting speeds, depending on vehicle model and driving conditions. After lock-up, the turbine is driven directly by the converter cover, which is coupled to the engine; the hydraulic link has been eliminated, and the engine is driving the transmission input shaft through a direct mechanical link.

The converter lock-up is accomplished through a centrifugal clutch, which is splined to the turbine through a one-way clutch (Fig. 36-10). As vehicle speed increases, the hydraulically driven turbine and the lock-up clutch splined to it turn with increasing speed. The centrifugal force exerted on the clutch shoes increases as the clutch assembly turns faster and faster. When enough force is present, the shoes will move slowly outward until they contact the inside surface of the converter cover. The face of the shoe is covered with a frictional material that "grips" the cover and mechanically links the cover to the clutch. When vehicle speed drops below a given mph, which is dependent upon vehicle and model operating conditions, turbine speed and centrifugal force will be reduced to a point where return springs will retract the clutch shoes. At this point, the cover is released and the turbine is again hydraulically driven.

The damper assembly is driven through a one-way clutch. With the damper assembly clutch engaged, the driver may release the accelerator pedal slightly, allowing the vehicle to enter a "coast" condition. While the damper one-way clutch remains locked under most conditions, it will release in a "coast" condition. This release is necessary to allow the engine and input shaft to turn at different speeds. The friction shoes cannot release because centrifugal force is holding them against the cover; therefore, the damper one-way clutch has to release to allow the input shaft to overrun engine speed. When the driver accelerates, the damper one-way clutch will again lock the turbine to the clutch and damper assembly.

The damper assembly one-way clutch is incorporated into the lock-up converter to ensure the smoothness of operation associated with an automatic transmission torque converter. Other features built into the lock-up converter to ensure smoothness of operation include dampener springs and variable slip. The dampener springs are built into the centrifugal clutch body to absorb engine vibrations and to cushion engagement of the shoes with the converter cover. Some slip will occur when torque demand, during acceleration, exceeds the holding ability of friction shoes.

36.4 PLANETARY GEARBOX

The planetary gearbox of the automatic transmission contains a set of planetary gears that aid the converter in torque increase (Fig. 36-11). These planetary gears are arranged in a pattern something like the solar system. Thus, the gear at the center is called the sun gear. In mesh with the sun gear are a number

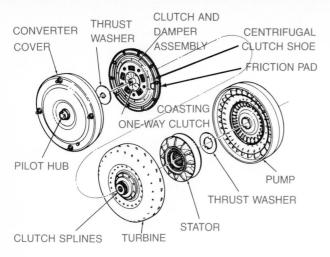

Fig. 36-10 Parts of the lock-up torque converter. (Ford Motor Company)

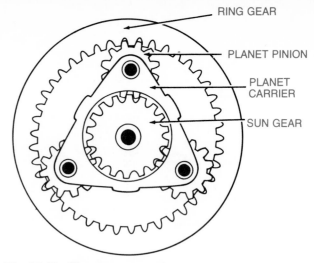

Fig. 36-11 Planetary gear set.

of small planet pinions, held together by a planet carrier. Surrounding the whole unit is a ring gear whose inside teeth are also in mesh with the planets.

36.5 Gear Reduction

A planetary system reduces speed and increases torque by connecting the engine to the ring gear, holding the sun gear stationary, and connecting the carrier to the rear wheels. The motion of the large ring gear causes the planets to move around the stationary sun gear, and the carrier is forced to rotate with the planets. The gears are sized to cause a gear reduction torque increase (Fig. 36-12).

36.6 Reverse

Reverse is also possible in a simple planetary gear set. If the engine is hooked up to drive the sun gear, the planet carrier is held in from turning and the output is taken from the ring gear (Fig. 36-13). The clockwise rotation of the sun gear causes a counterclockwise rotation of the planet pinions. The pinions cannot move around the sun because the carrier is held stationary. The counterclockwise rotation is therefore transferred to the ring gear, the output shaft connected to the rear wheels turns in a reverse direction, and the vehicle can back up.

36.7 Direct Drive and Overdrive

A planetary system can also provide a direct 1:1 drive. If any two members of the planetary system are locked up, the whole system—input and output—

turns as a unit at a 1:1 ratio. On the other hand, if none of the units are held in position, there is nothing for the gears to react against and no power is transferred through the unit. It is in neutral.

Fuel mileage can be increased in a car with an automatic transaxle or transmission if the last gear ratio is an overdrive. Most standard automatic transmissions and transaxles have three forward gear ratios: a first gear reduction, a second gear reduction, and a high gear which is a direct drive. In an automatic overdrive transmission or transaxle a different type of planetary system is used to allow an additional fourth overdrive gear.

In summary, a planetary gear set can provide a gear reduction, a reverse, a 1:1 or direct drive, or an overdrive, and a neutral, all without moving any gears in or out of mesh. Instead, the system changes the gears used for input and output or holds them stationary.

36.8 Complex Planetary Gear Sets

There are two basic types of planetary gear systems in common use. They are both described as complex or compound systems because they use more planetary parts than the simple unit we described previously. These two types of planetary gear arrangments are called the Simpson and Ravenaux designs.

In the Simpson design, common to most automatic transmissions and transaxles without an overdrive, two separate planetary gear systems are combined. As shown in Figure 36-14, there are two separate ring gears, two separate planet carrier sets, and one common sun gear. Both planet sets engage the common sun gear.

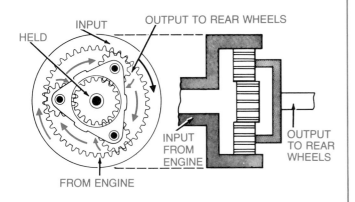

Fig. 36-12 Planetary system in reduction.

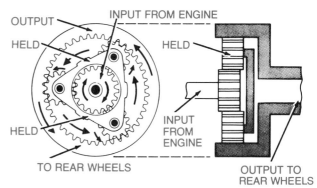

Fig. 36-13 Planetary system in reverse.

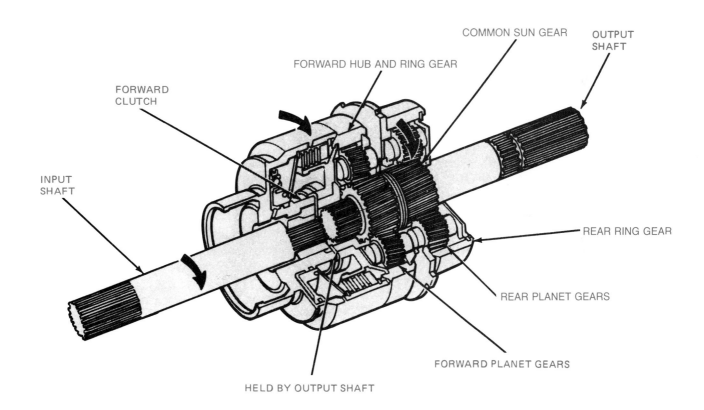

INPUT SHAFT

FORWARD CLUTCH

FORWARD HUB AND RING GEAR

COMMON SUN GEAR

OUTPUT SHAFT

REAR RING GEAR

REAR PLANET GEARS

FORWARD PLANET GEARS

HELD BY OUTPUT SHAFT

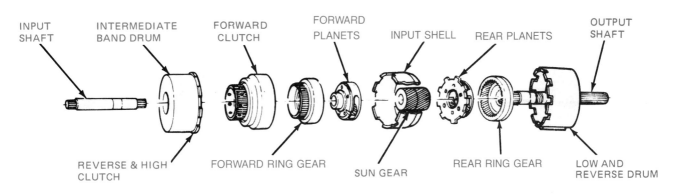

INPUT SHAFT

INTERMEDIATE BAND DRUM

FORWARD CLUTCH

FORWARD PLANETS

INPUT SHELL

REAR PLANETS

OUTPUT SHAFT

REVERSE & HIGH CLUTCH

FORWARD RING GEAR

SUN GEAR

REAR RING GEAR

LOW AND REVERSE DRUM

Fig. 36-14 The Simpson planetary arrangement. (Ford Motor Company)

The Automatic Transmission and Transaxle 391

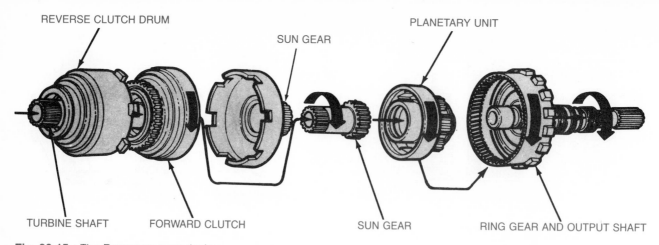

Fig. 36-15 The Ravenaux gear design. (Ford Motor Company)

The Ravenaux gear design is common to automatic transmissions and transaxles using an overdrive. The Ravenaux arrangement (Fig. 36-15) has one planetary carrier that has two sets of planets. One set of planets is long while the other is short. There are two separate sun gears; one in mesh with the short planets and one in mesh with the long planets. A single ring gear is used which is connected to the output shaft. The Ravenaux design will allow for a neutral, first and second reduction, direct drive, overdrive and reverse.

36.9 PLANETARY HOLDING UNITS

In order to shift from one gear to another, various parts of the planetary set have to be held or driven. The components that accomplish this holding and driving are multiple-disc clutches, bands, and overrunning clutches.

36.10 Multiple-Disc Clutches

Most automatic transmission use two or three multiple-disc clutches (Fig. 36-16) to couple and uncouple the two planetary gear sets or to lock up parts of a gear set. Each clutch consists of a number of round clutch discs, some faced with a friction material compatible with hydraulic fluid and others made from steel. These discs are stacked so that each friction disc is sandwiched between two steel discs. Both sets of discs have teeth which are engaged to different components of the planetary set. The multiple-disc clutch provides a great deal of frictional area in a small package.

The clutch assembly is coupled when hydraulic pressure from fluid entering the clutch moves a large

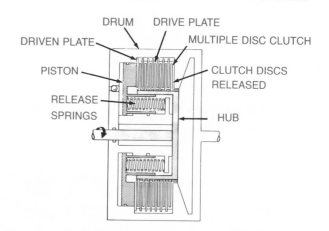

Fig. 36-16 Parts of the multiple disc clutch assembly. (Chevrolet Motor Division, GMC)

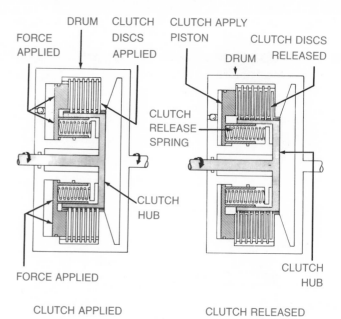

CLUTCH APPLIED   CLUTCH RELEASED

Fig. 36-17 Operation of the multiple disc clutch. (Chevrolet Motor Division, GMC)

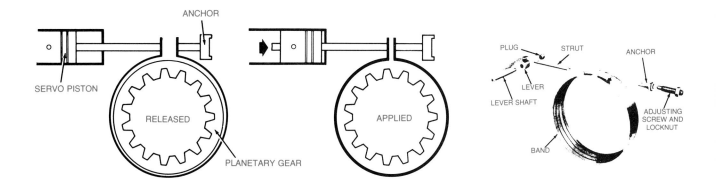

Fig. 36-18 Band and servo components and operation.

piston in the clutch drum which squeezes the discs together. This pressure provides enough contact between the friction and steel plates to lock up the planetary gears so that power can be transmitted through the assembly. When the fluid pressure is released, a return spring releases the piston. The discs are no longer squeezed together, so no power can be transmitted through them. The clutch is unlocked. Clutch apply and release is shown in Figure 36-17.

36.11   Bands

Bands (Fig. 36-18) are another important holding device used in the planetary gearbox. Most automatic transmissions use one or two bands. The unit consists of a band, an anchor strut, and a servo piston assembly.

The band stops rotation of a planetary member. When the band is activated or applied, fluid under pressure is routed to the servo piston. Pressure on the servo piston moves it in its bore. The piston stem attached to the piston also moves and pushes on the band. Since the band is anchored at the other end, this action tightens the band around the drum which is attached to a planetary member. This action stops the rotation of the drum. When the band is disengaged, pressure is removed from the piston, and the return spring pushes the piston back to relieve the tension on the band and free the drum.

36.12   Overrunning Clutch

Most automatic transmissions use one or more one-way clutches in the planetary gearbox to hold planetary members. the one-way clutch is also known as a roller clutch, a sprag clutch, and an overrunning clutch.

The one-way clutch (Fig. 36-19) locks up a planet member when it tries to rotate in one direction and allows it to rotate freely in the opposite direction. The one-way clutch consists of an outer race, an inner race, a set of rollers, and a set of springs. The outer race is usually held to the transmission case, and the inner race is conencted to a planetary member. The operation is the same as that of the stator roller clutch.

The one-way clutch has several advantages for use in an automatic transmission. First, a one-way clutch provides a good deal of holding force in a small place. Second, a one-way clutch is completely self-contained, so there is no need for external controls. Finally, the friction during overruning is very small, so the clutch does not rob much power from the transmission.

36.13   HYDRAULIC FLUID PUMP

The hydraulic pressure that applies the bands and clutches in an automatic transmission is developed by a fluid pump inside the transmission or transaxle.

The most popular front pump in use today is the crescent pump (Fig. 36-20), which consists of an inner gear and a crescent seal, driven by the torque converter housing. Because the two gears are not concentric, a low-pressure area is created as they rotate past the inlet and unmesh. Fluid is pulled in and carried around in the teeth to the outlet. The crescent seals the inlet port from the outlet port. Thus, at the outlet port the fluid has no place to go but out.

The hydraulic fluid moved by the pump or pumps is used for a number of purposes:

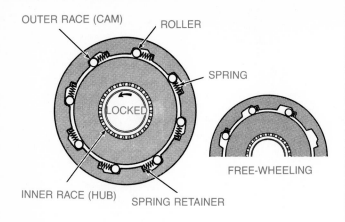

Fig. 36-19 Overrunning clutch in rear of transmission housing. (Chrysler Corporation)

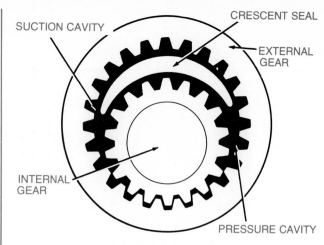

Fig. 36-20 Crescent pump.

1. It is circulated through the transmission or transaxle components for lubrication.

2. It carries heat away from the components and into the radiator heat exchanger.

3. It is pumped into the torque converter where it is used to transmit engine torque.

4. It is used to apply the clutches and bands that put the transmission or transaxle in gear.

36.14 HYDRAULIC CONTROL (VALVE BODY)

The component that controls the way the hydraulic fluid is sent through the transmission to apply the clutches and bands is the hydraulic control system. It senses driving conditions and shifts the transmission to the correct gear. The hydraulic control system consists of a number of small valves, in a part called the valve body, that control the fluid passages leading to the clutches and bands. Which clutch or band is applied depends on which of these valves is moved to allow fluid to pass (Fig. 36-21).

The valves are moved to open and shut the passageways by three systems: manual control linkage; hydraulic pressure from a governor; and hydraulic pressure from a throttle valve or modulator (Fig. 36-22).

36.15 Manual Control Linkage

The manual control linkage is attached to the gear shift quadrant inside the automobile. By moving the gear shift quadrant, the driver selects an operating mode for the transmission. Moving the shift quadrant into position causes the manual control linkage to position a valve in the control system.

If the driver selects low or reverse, the valve sends fluid from the pump directly into the clutches and bands that provide low or reverse. If neutral is selected, the valve blocks the flow into any clutch or band. (The planetary system is in neutral when none of its parts are held stationary.) When the park gear is selected, the shift quadrant causes part of the linkage to engage with a gear on the output shaft. The linkage prevents the gear from turning, which prevents the output shaft from turning, which prevents the automobile from moving.

Up to this point, the driver, through the shift quadrant, has determined manually what gear the transmission will be in. When the linkage is positioned in drive, however, the transmission takes over, shifting up or down automatically to meet driving conditions. That is, the fluid is automatically routed through a series of valves to determine which clutches or bands are applied.

36.16 Governor

Attached to the output shaft at the rear of the transmission or transaxle is the governor, which senses how fast the automobile is going. The governor directs a pressure into the control system to move the valves. When the vehicle is going fast enough, the pressure moves the valves for an upshift. As the vehicle slows down, the governor pressure falls off and the valves move for a down shift (Figs. 36-23 and 36-24).

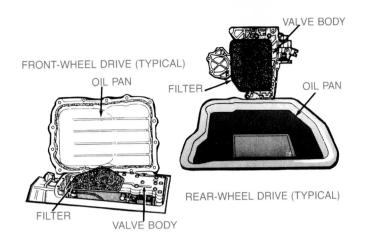

FRONT-WHEEL DRIVE (TYPICAL)

OIL PAN

FILTER

VALVE BODY

VALVE BODY

FILTER

OIL PAN

REAR-WHEEL DRIVE (TYPICAL)

Fig. 36-21 The valve body components determine which band or clutch is applied. (Chrysler Corporation)

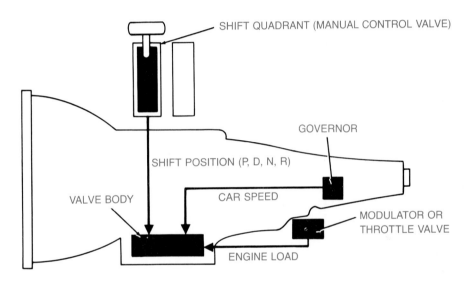

SHIFT QUADRANT (MANUAL CONTROL VALVE)

GOVERNOR

SHIFT POSITION (P, D, N, R)

VALVE BODY

CAR SPEED

MODULATOR OR THROTTLE VALVE

ENGINE LOAD

Fig. 36-22 Hydraulic control system tells transmission when to shift.

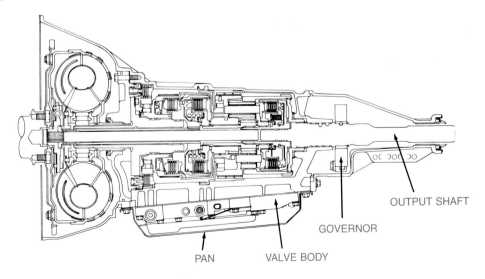

OUTPUT SHAFT

GOVERNOR

PAN

VALVE BODY

Fig. 36-23 The governor mounted on the output shaft senses car speed. (Ford Motor Company)

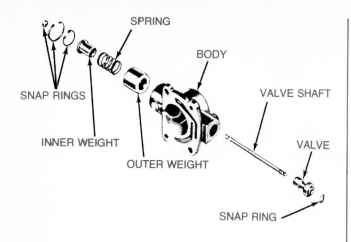

Fig. 36-24 Exploded view of governor assembly. (Chrysler Corporation)

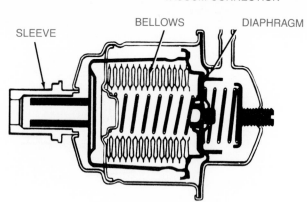

Fig. 36-25 The modulator senses engine load. (Buick Motor Division, GMC)

36.17   Throttle or Modulator Pressure

Throttle or modulator pressure, on the other hand, senses how hard the engine is working. If it is working fairly hard, this system will oppose governor pressure and prevent the transmission or transaxle from upshifting until the vehicle is going faster. For example, if the driver moves away from a stop sign with light accelerator pedal pressure, the transmission may upshift at 20 mph (32 km). If, on the other hand, the driver takes off with the accelerator on the floor, the upshift may not occur until 40 mph (64 km). This delay in shifting helps a hard-working engine get the automobile going.

Some transmission or transaxles sense how hard the engine is working through throttle linkage. In this case, a linkage attached to the throttle or accelerator pedal is pushed down far enough, the linkage moves the throttle valve in the control system. This directs pressure to oppose governor pressure and prevent the transmission or transaxle from upshifting.

Other transmissions and transaxles use a vacuum modulator (Fig. 36-25) to sense how hard the engine is working. The vacuum modulator is a small can mounted to the side of the transmission. A vacuum line from the engine's intake manifold is hooked to the modulator. Intake manifold vacuum works on a diaphragm inside the modulator, which controls a valve in the control system. The amount of vacuum shows how hard the engine is working. Under light throttle conditions, the vacuum is high. Under heavy throttle applications, the vacuum drops. The vacuum signal moves the modulator diaphragm back and forth. When

the engine is working hard, the modulator directs fluid pressure to oppose governor pressure and delays the upshift. When the engine is not working hard, there is less opposition to governor pressure and the upshift occurs earlier.

36.18   AUTOMATIC TRANSMISSION COOLING SYSTEM

The automatic transmission with torque converter presents a cooling problem not present in the manually shifted transmission. Slippage in the torque converter, clutches, and bands generates a tremendous amount of heat. This heat must be removed from the automatic transmission or serious damage might result.

Excessive heat destroys the nonmetallic materials used in friction facings and seals. It has also been determined that transmission fluid fails as a result of being exposed to high temperatures for prolonged periods of time. The fluid fails when so much sludge and varnish have formed that the deposits cannot be removed.

36.19   Water Cooling Systems

The most common method of cooling automatic transmissions is water cooling. The water cooling system uses a heat exchanger in the bottom tank of the engine's radiator to exchange heat from one medium to another—in this case, from the fluid to the cooling water. The heat exchanger is made of a metal with good heat-conducting ability, such as copper.

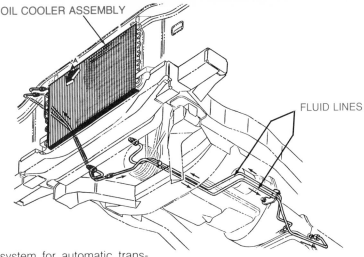

OIL COOLER ASSEMBLY

FLUID LINES

Fig. 36-26 Auxiliary cooling system for automatic transmission. (Chrysler Corporation)

There are many passages in the heat exchanger through which the fluid flows so that it contacts the largest possible metal surface area. The heat is transmitted through the metal to the cooling water. Hot fluid is pumped from the transmission by the front pump through the heat exchanger and then back into the transmission.

36.20 Auxiliary Cooling System

When vehicles are operated in extreme temperatures or under severe operating conditions, the standard cooling system is not enough. Vehicles that spend long periods at idle, such as police vehicles or vehicles used for trailer towing, need more cooling capacity. An auxiliary cooler (Fig. 36-26) is a large heat exchanger that can be mounted next to the vehicle's radiator in the air stream. These heat exchangers may be installed in place of or in addition to the conventional heat exchanger. The auxiliary cooler may be supplied by the vehicle manufacturer as optional equipment on trailer towing packages. It is also supplied by independent manufacturers to be installed as an after-market item.

NEW TERMS

Auxiliary cooling system A special heat exchanger added to the cooling system of an automatic transmission to improve the cooling.
Band A planetary holding unit wrapped around a drum to stop its rotation.

Governor A device on the output shaft of the transmission to sense vehicle speed.
Hydraulic control valves The system of valves that senses driving conditions and automatically shifts the transmission.
Modulator A vacuum canister mounted to the outside of the transmission that senses engine load.
Multiple-disc clutches A clutch that uses several drive and driven discs or plates.
One-way clutch A clutch that holds in one direction but allows movement in another direction.
Overrunning clutch Same as one-way clutch.
Planetary gearbox The system of gears used in an automatic transmission: a sun gear, planet gears, a carrier, and a ring gear.
Planetary carrier The part of a planetary gearbox that supports the planet gears.
Planets The part of the planetary gear system that meshes with the ring and sun gear.
Pump (fluid) The pump used to move fluid throughout the transmission.
Pump (torque converter) One of the main parts of a torque converter connected to the engine.
Ring gear The part of the planetary gear system with internal teeth used to mesh with the planets.
Roller clutch Same as one-way clutch.
Sprag clutch Same as one-way clutch.
Stator One of the main parts of a torque converter used to redirect fluid back at the pump.
Sun gear One of the main parts of a planetary gear system with external teeth used to mesh with the planets.

CHAPTER REVIEW

1. What is the main difference between an automatic and a manually operated transmission or transaxle?

2. What are the three main parts of an automatic transmission or transaxle?

3. List the three main parts of a torque converter.

4. How does the torque converter work to increase torque?

5. Why does the stator have a roller clutch?

6. When is the stator locked up?

7. List the main parts of a planetary gearbox.

8. Describe the operation of the planetary gears when the system is in reduction.

9. Describe the operation of planetary gears when the system is in reverse.

10. How is neutral obtained in a planetary gear set?

11. List the three planetary holding units.

12. Describe the operation of a multiple disc clutch.

13. Describe the operation of a band and servo assembly.

14. How does an overrunning clutch work?

15. What does the fluid pump in the transmission do?

16. What is the job of the hydraulic control valves in an automatic transmission or transaxle?

17. What does the governor do in an automatic transmission or transaxle?

18. What is the job of the modulator?

19. Explain the operation of a liquid cooling system for an automatic transmission.

20. What is the purpose of an auxiliary cooler?

DISCUSSION TOPICS AND ACTIVITIES

1. Use a shop cutaway model of a torque converter to describe how torque is increased.

2. How does a transmission or transaxle shift automatically?

Automatic Transmission and Transaxle Service

There is always a high demand for mechanics who understand and can service automatic transmissions and transaxles. Since the transmission or transaxle affects engine performance, the tune-up mechanic must be able to troubleshoot the vehicle performance problems they cause. The chassis expert must know what noises and vibrations can be caused by the transmission or transaxle. The vehicle's cooling, electric, and vacuum systems are also tied into the transmission or transaxle. No mechanic can afford to be ignorant about automatic transmissions and transaxles.

OBJECTIVES

After studying this chapter, you should be able to do the following:

1. List the steps in finding a problem in an automatic transmission or transaxle.
2. Explain how to check the fluid level in an automatic transmission or transaxle.
3. Describe how to change the fluid in an automatic transmission or transaxle.
4. Explain how bands are adjusted.
5. Describe the adjustment of the control linkages.

37.1 TROUBLESHOOTING

Solving transmission problems begins with thorough knowledge of how a transmission or transaxle works. With this knowledge and a good service man-

ual, the mechanic can isolate and cure automatic transmission problems. There is no substitute for the transmission manufacturer's troubleshooting guide. The mechanic must use the diagnostic procedure outlined by the manufacturer of the transmission or transaxle. The purpose of this unit is to explain the general procedures used in troubleshooting, and to point out the importance of a step-by-step approach.

37.2 Preliminary Checks

When the transmission or transaxle is suspected of malfunctioning, the mechanic must perform a step-by-step procedure to locate the problem. Troubleshooting an automatic transmission or transaxle is a three-phase operation. First, the mechanic must make some preliminary checks to eliminate any obvious problems. Secondly, the vehicle should be road tested. Finally, the mechanic should perform a shop diagnosis. The preliminary checks should include the following five items:

1. *Engine Condition.* A perfecting operating transmission or transaxle will not make the vehicle perform if the engine cannot deliver the power. The mechanic should start the engine to be sure that it starts quickly, runs smoothly, and accelerates without smoking. If there is reason to suspect that the engine is out of tune or in need of service, this should be done before looking for transmission problems.

2. *Fluid Level.* The fluid level is critical to the operation of the automatic transmission. Both the level and condition of the fluid are clues to the general condition of the transmission or transaxle. A low fluid level lets the pump take in air, making the fluid spongy and compressible. Pressure builds up too

BAND AND CLUTCH APPLICATION CHART				
LOW (*Breakaway*)	*LOW* (*Manual*)	*SECOND*	*DIRECT*	*REVERSE*
Rear Clutch	Rear Clutch	Rear Clutch	Rear Clutch	Front Clutch
Overrunning Clutch	Low and Reverse Band	Kickdown Band	Front Clutch	Low and Reverse Band

Fig. 37-1 Band and clutch application chart.

slowly, resulting in delayed shifts and slipping. The slipping causes overheating and rapid wear of clutches and bands. If the fluid level is very low, it will starve the pump. Proper lubrication cannot be maintained, and transmission parts will be damaged.

If the fluid level is too high, other problems occur. The gears in the transmission churn the fluid like an eggbeater, creating foam. The air bubbles in the foam cause slipping and overheating the same as with low fluid level. Even worse, the heat and foam cause the fluid to oxidize.

3. *Fluid Condition.* The condition of the fluid is as important as the level. When the fluid level is checked, the mechanic should closely inspect the fluid on the dip stick. If it is discolored or shows signs of foreign material, the transmission may need major service. If it is very dark and smells burned, frictional material has been overheated. A complete overhaul will probably be necessary to replace the lost frictional material.

Fluid which is milky white indicates that water has entered the transmission. Water may enter the transmission through a broken heat exchanger in the radiator. Rain water may have entered through a raised dip stick sealing cap. Water mixed with transmission fluid swells transmission seals and softens frictional material.

A dipstick that is tacky and will not wipe clean indicates varnish buildup in the transmission. Once varnish starts forming, it builds up in all the valves, servos, and clutches, causing sticking. Sticking valves result in erratic transmission operation. Eventually the varnish formation will clog the filter or screen. Pump pressure will drop and the transmission may fail to operate at all.

4. *Control Linkage.* The manual and throttle control linkage should be checked. Improper transmission or transaxle operation may result from incorrect setting of the linkage. One sign of improper manual control linkage setting is a failure to start unless the shift quadrant lever is moved slightly off Neutral or Park detents. Another sign is creeping when the selector is in Neutral. Improper throttle linkage setting makes the shift feel harsh or slipper. The mechanic should inspect all linkage for damage.

5. *Vacuum Modulator.* The last preliminary check is a test of vacuum modulator operation. To check the vacuum modulator, start the engine and allow it to idle. Pull the vacuum hose off the vacuum modulator canister. The engine speed should change a good deal as the vacuum is lost through the open hose. If engine speed does not change, the vacuum hose should be checked for obstructions and leaks. If the hose is in good shape, a faulty diaphragm in the modulator may be at fault.

37.3   Road Test

If preliminary tests fail to uncover a problem, the vehicle should be road tested. If possible, develop a standard test route so that comparisons can be made between vehicles. The car owner should accompany the mechanic and point out the complaint as it occurs. The test route should include a level section, some hills, and a quiet section for checking noises.

On a road test, the transmission or transaxle should be operated in each range to feel the shifting, check upshift and downshift speeds, and look for evidence of slipping. Slipping in any gear means band or clutch trouble. If only one band or clutch is at fault,

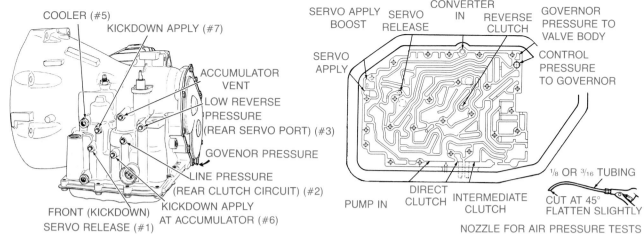

Fig. 37-2 Pressure test plugs for measuring transaxle operating pressures. (Chrysler Corporation)

Fig. 37-3 Transaxle case passages identified for checking with shop air. (Ford Motor Company)

it may be isolated for repair. The technician should note the operating range where the transmission or transaxle slips to determine what is causing the problem by referring to a band and clutch application chart (Fig. 37-1). These charts show what band or clutch is applied to each operating mode. The mechanic will then know which band or clutch to repair.

Much troubleshooting time will be spent on noise diagnosis. Accurate noise diagnosis begins with a systematic check of general noise location. Noises tend to telegraph from the actual source to the various chassis and body components, so air conditioning, alternator, power steering, and fan noises are often mistakenly blamed on the transmission or transaxle. One method of isolating transmission or transaxle from accessory noises is to remove the drive belts from the accessories and drive the vehicle a short distance. If the noise goes away, it was in one of the accessories. Noises that change with speed and road surface most likely come from the tires. Noises that change with speed and direction are probably caused by wheel bearings. Coasting the vehicle in Neutral with the engine shut off will eliminate engine and transmission or transaxle pump noises. Duplicating driving conditions with the vehicle on a hoist will eliminate tire noises. noise.

37.4   Shop Testing

The last phase of trouble shooting involves a shop test, which may involve pressure testing and air checking. Pressure tests are made to determine if fluid pressures in the various circuits are high enough for proper

operation. Several plugs on the outside of the transmission or transaxle case are for pressure gauge hookup (Fig. 37-2).

Connect the pressure gauges to the transmission and either road test the vehicle or test it on a hoist to determine whether pressures are within specifications. The manufacturer's chart shows what each pressure should be so that the problem can be traced to a particular circuit.

Air checking uses air pressure to determine whether units are in proper operating condition or whether their circuits are blocked or leaking. Air checking can be done with the transmission in the vehicle, usually with valve body removed, or with the transmission on the bench. Air checking is not only a valuable aid to diagnosis, but also a check on repairs. Apply shop air to the apply passages for the various clutches and bands and listen for signs of blockage or leakage. The manufacturer's chart (Fig. 37-3) shows where to apply the shop air.

37.5   PREVENTIVE MAINTENANCE

Several periodic preventive maintenance operations should be performed on an automatic transmission to keep it operating in top condition. This section outlines these procedures.

37.6   Fluid Level Check

If the automatic transmission fluid level is too high or too low, there may be a disruption in the normal shifting and a loss of lubrication. The fluid level should be checked at frequent intervals—every second or third gasoline fillup.

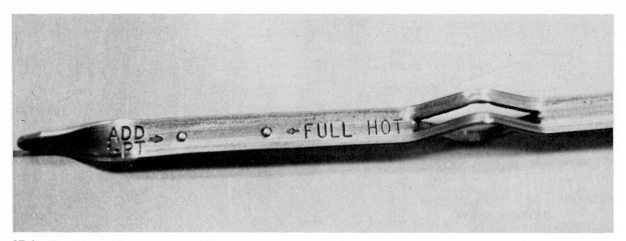

Fig. 37-4 Dipstick markings. (Plymouth/Chrysler Corporation)

When checking the fluid, several precautions should be observed. The engine and transmission or transaxle must be warm. The fluid expands as it warms, so a fluid level check on a cold transmission may show a low level. The transmission or transaxle must be in the correct shift quadrant position for a fluid level check. For some vehicles, transmission fluid level is checked in Park; for others in Drive, and so on. If the level is checked with the transmission or transaxle in the wrong operating range, the level may appear to be too high or too low when it is actually correct. Fluid level in the sump varies in different operating ranges. In some ranges, clutch drums and servos are filled with fluid, causing a low level in the sump. In other ranges, all the fluid is exhausted from servos and clutches, causing a high fluid level. The correct operating range for checking the fluid level is found in the vehicle owner's manual or in a transmission or transaxle shop service manual.

The procedure for checking the fluid level is as follows:

1. Drive the vehicle onto a level floor.
2. Set the emergency brake firmly.
3. Start the engine and let it idle.
4. Move the shift quadrant lever through each of the operating ranges and then position it in the correct mode for checking the fluid level.
5. Remove the transmission dipstick and wipe it clean.
6. Push the dipstick back into position firmly.
7. Remove the dipstick and read the level. Dipsticks (Fig. 37-4) normally have two marks, one for *full* and one for *low* or *add*. The low mark on many dipsticks represents a pint. **There is, however, no standard owner's manual for proper interpretation of the**

marking system for dip sticks. Check the vehicle owner's manual for proper interpretation.
8. Add the proper amount of automatic transmission fluid. **Be sure to use the correct type of fluid.**
9. Replace dipstick.

37.7   Fluid Change

Most manufacturers recommend that automatic transmission or transaxle fluid be changed at regular time or mileage intervals that can be found in the vehicle owner's manual. If recommendations cannot be found, the following intervals could be used. For mild service conditions, that is, driving that does not generate high temperatures, fluid should be changed every 20,000 to 25,000 miles. For severe service, such as heavy traffic with long periods at idle or trailer towing, the interval should be 6,000 to 10,000 miles.

A fluid change involves more than just draining and refilling the sump. Every fluid change should include removing the pan and cleaning or replacing the filter screen. A typical fluid change procedure follows:

1. Jack or hoist vehicle off the ground.
2. Inspect the fluid pan for drain plug. Most late model vehicles DO NOT have a drain plug, so the pan must be removed for a fluid change.
3. If the pan has a drain plug, remove it and allow the fluid to drain. Then remove the pan.
4. On units without a drain plug, remove the pan to drain fluid.
5. Remove the flywheel inspection plate.
6. Rotate the engine and check for drain plug on converter or fluid coupling. Many late model converters do not have plugs and cannot be drained.

Fig. 37-5 Converter drain plug.

7. If the converter can be drained, it will have two plugs, one for a vent and one for a drain. Remove both plugs and drain the converter (Fig. 39-5). Replace the plugs.

8. Remove the filter or filter screen.

9. Clean or replace the filter as specified by the manufacturer.

10. Clean the fluid pan.

11. Install the pan with a new gasket, using a torque wrench to tighten cap screws (Fig. 39-6).

12. Check fluid capacity of the transmission in the owner's manual. If the converter was drained, add only a portion of the fluid to the transmission.

13. Start engine and allow time for warmup.

14. Check fluid level.

15. Add additional fluid as required to bring the unit to the correct level.

37.8 ADJUSTMENTS

Several periodic adjustments may be required on most automatic transmissions. To perform these adjustments correctly, the mechanic must follow carefully the procedures outlined in a transmission service manual. The following adjustments are typical.

1. *Band Adjustment.* An automatic transmission's or transaxle's bands must be properly adjusted for the correct amount of space between drum and frictional material. A correctly adjusted band provides a good positive hold on application, will not drag on release, and provides smooth engagement with correct timing. Older transmissions required frequent band adjustment because of wear on the bands. New frictional materials on late model transmission nearly eliminated the need for this adjustment. When a band began to slip on older transmissions, a band adjust-

ment would usually solve the problem. A slipping band on a late model unit usually indicates a loss of pressure for band application and cannot be cured by an adjustment.

2. *Manual Control Linkage.* The manual control linkage from the shift quadrant to the manual control valve is adjustable. If the linkage is not in correct adjustment, the shift quadrant may not position the manual control valve correctly. Incorrect positioning of the manual valve may cause cross feed, which means that two circuits are pressurized when only one should be. The result is a transmission or transaxle that cannot decide what range to be in. Normally the manual control linkage would not require periodic adjustment, but it may require adjustment if the linkage is disturbed.

3. *Throttle Linkage.* The linkage from the throttle to the automatic transmission or transaxle detent valve or throttle valve is also adjustable. This linkage does not require periodic attention but might require adjustment if it is disturbed. Incorrect adjustment of throttle linkage may cause a number of problems with shift timing. If the transmission shifts early or late, or if it does not downshift, the throttle linkage may be at fault.

37.9 AUTOMATIC TRANSMISSION SERVICE

When troubleshooting indicates an internal transmission or transaxle problem, the unit must be removed, disassembled, inspected for wear, and have new parts installed. Since there are such a large number of transmissions and service procedures are different for each one, no attempt will be made here to detail them. Always locate and follow the appropriate

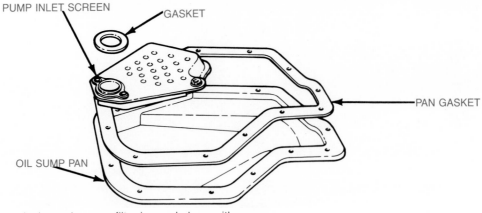

Fig. 37-6 A cleaned or new filter is used along with a new pan gasket. (Ford Motor Company)

service literature when servicing an automatic transmission.

NEW TERMS

Air checking Using shop air to test the operation of clutches and bands.

Band adjustment Setting the proper clearance between the band and its drum by adjusting the band anchor.

Band and clutch application chart A chart showing which bands and clutches are applied in each transmission driving range.

Fluid level The height of the fluid in the pan of the automatic transmission.

Pressure testing Installing pressure gauges in an automatic transmission to measure operating pressure.

Road test Driving the vehicle over a test area to locate a problem.

CHAPTER REVIEW

1. Why should a mechanic who services other automobile components have a working knowledge of automatic transmissions and transaxles?

2. List five preliminary checks for an automatic transmission or transaxle problem.

3. What effect does engine condition have on the transmission or transaxle?

4. What problems can occur if fluid level is too low?

5. What problems can occur if fluid level is too high?

6. What problem is indicated if fluid is very dark and smells burned?

7. What causes milky white fluid?

8. Describe how to check the operation of a vacuum modulator.

9. Explain how to road test a vehicle to find an automatic transmission or transaxle problem.

10. List the two shop tests on a vehicle to find a transmission problem.

11. What is a pressure test?

12. Describe an air check.

13. Explain the steps in checking the fluid level for an automatic transmission or transaxle.

14. Describe the correct procedure for changing the fluid in an automatic transmission or transaxle.

15. List three adjustments required on most automatic transmissions or transaxles.

DISCUSSION TOPICS AND ACTIVITIES

1. Use the proper procedure to check the automatic transmission or transaxle fluid level in the vehicle of your choice. What was the condition of the fluid?

2. Drain the fluid and clean or replace a filter screen on an automatic transmission or transaxle.

3. Visit an automatic transmission repair shop. Report on what you see.

Drive Line Arrangements

CHAPTER PREVIEW

Getting engine torque to the drive wheels is the job of the drive line. On front drive cars the engine usually sits crosswise and has a transaxle. Power flow goes through two drive shafts to the front wheels. Rear-wheel drive cars have the engine mounted lengthwise with a transmission. A single drive shaft connects to the rear axle assembly. Four-wheel drive vehicles have the engine mounted lengthwise, with a transmission and a transfer case. Two drive shafts are used, one from the transfer case to the front wheels, and one from the transmission to the rear axle.

OBJECTIVES

After studying this chapter, you should be able to do the following:

1. Describe the parts and operation of a front-wheel drive arrangement.
2. Explain the purpose and operation of front-wheel drive flexible joints.
3. Describe the parts and operation of a front engine rear-drive arrangement.
4. Identify the parts of the rear-drive universal and slip joints.
5. Describe the parts and operation of a four-wheel drive arrangement.

38.1   FRONT-WHEEL DRIVE

Many late model cars use a drive arrangement called front-wheel drive (Figs. 38-1 and 38-2). The transmission and differential are combined into a trans-axle and mounted directly to the engine. Two drive shafts deliver the power to the front wheels.

Front-wheel drive has several advantages. Combining the transmission and differential into one housing makes the car much lighter, which saves fuel. The lengthwise drive shaft and drive shaft tunnel are eliminated, leaving more passenger space.

38.2   Front-Drive Arrangements

There are two basic front-drive arrangements. The engine may be mounted lengthwise, with the front of the engine toward the front of the vehicle. Because the drive shafts must be directed out to the front wheels, the transaxle is mounted alongside and below the engine. Power flows from the engine to the transaxle through a chain (Fig. 38-1).

The second basic arrangement uses a transverse engine mounting (Fig. 38-2). With this arrangement the engine is mounted sideways in the engine compartment. It is possible with this design to mount the transmission and differential assembly alongside rather than below the engine. This layout has the advantage of lowering the vehicle's center of gravity and making the vehicle more stable during cornering.

38.3   Front-Drive Shafts

The front-wheel drive system uses a drive shaft to deliver power from the transaxle to each of the front wheels (Fig. 38-3). These two drive shafts are sometimes called half-shafts, stub shafts, or axle shafts.

With front-wheel drive, the front wheels are used not only to drive the vehicle, but also to steer it. The

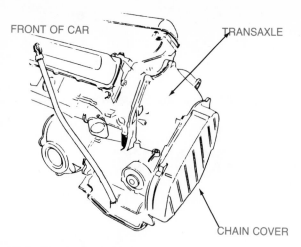

Fig. 38-1 Front-wheel drive arrangement with lengthwise engine mounting. (Buick Motor Division, GMC)

Fig. 38-2 Front-wheel drive arrangement with transverse engine mounting. (Chevrolet Motor Division, GMC)

front wheels are attached to the front suspension system as well. The front wheels move from side to side for steering and up and down during suspension action. The transaxle, though, is mounted rigidly to the engine. The front-drive axles must deliver torque to the front wheels while allowing the required wheel movement.

To allow steering and suspension movement, drive shafts must have two flexible joints. The inboard joint lets the axle shaft move up and down as the front wheel moves up and down during suspension travel. The outboard joint lets the wheel move back and forth for steering. Rubber boots on the joints keep dirt and moisture out and lubricant in.

38.4   REAR-WHEEL DRIVE

Most older and many current larger cars use a drive line arrangement called rear-wheel drive. The engine is mounted lengthwise at the front of the car. The clutch housing and transmission are bolted to the rear of the engine. A long drive shaft delivers the torque to a differential and rear axle assembly at the rear of the car.

The drive shaft's job is made difficutl by the fact that, while the transmission is stationary, the rear axle assembly is mounted on springs. This means that the rear axle assembly can move up and down as the vehicle moves over bumps and holes. The drive line must be able to make changes in both angle and length. A drive shaft may be connected to the rear axle in a straight line when the automobile is on level ground. But as the rear axle moves up or down, the drive shaft must operate at an angle. The drive shaft also must be able to adjust in length, because the distance be-

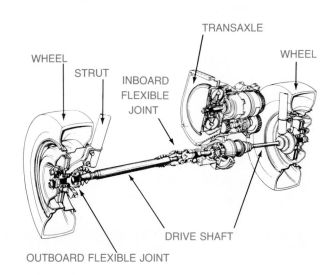

Fig. 38-3 Front-wheel drive shafts. (Chrysler Corporation)

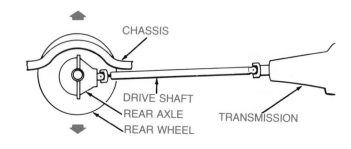

Fig. 38-4 Transmission is stationary while rear wheels move up and down.

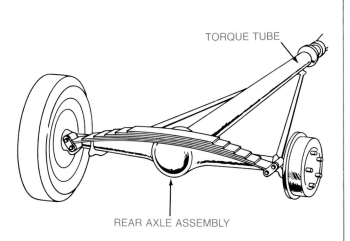

Fig. 38-5   Torque tube drive assembly. (Ford Motor Company)

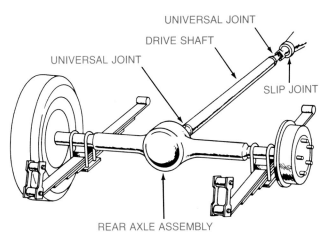

Fig. 38-6   Hotchkiss drive assembly. (Ford Motor Company)

tween the transmission and rear axle assembly changes as the rear axle assembly moves up and down (Fig. 38-4).

38.5   TYPES OF REAR-DRIVE LINES

There are several types of rear-drive line assemblies to handle changes in drive line length and angle.

38.6   Torque Tube Drive

The torque tube drive (Fig. 38-5), the oldest type of drive, is a solid drive shaft enclosed in a large hollow tube called a torque tube. A universal joint, mounted at the transmission end of the drive shaft, allows the entire drive assembly to move up and down to change length. Changes in the length of the drive assembly are achieved by a slip joint.

The disadvantages of this system are that it is extremely heavy and that the drive line and rear axle assembly must be removed to service the transmission.

38.7   Hotchkiss Drive

The disadvantages of the torque tube drive led to the design of the Hotchkiss drive now used in most front-engine, rear-drive automobiles.

The Hotchkiss drive assembly (Fig. 38-6) has an open drive shaft. Universal joints attached to each end of the drive shaft allow it to operate at different angles.

Changes in drive line length are achieved with a slip joint at the transmission end as in the torque tube drive.

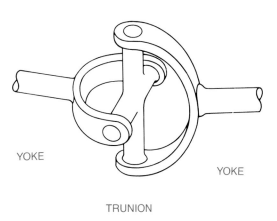

Fig. 38-7   Simple universal joint. (Chevrolet Motor Division, GMC)

In the Hotchkiss drive line, the rear axle housing is usually held in such a position that the drive shaft and drive pinion are not in perfect alignment. Their centerlines are usually at an angle, as we shall see later.

38.8   DRIVE SHAFT

The drive shaft, sometimes called the propeller shaft, is a steel tube that transmits power from the transmission output shaft to the rear axle assembly. To take care of different models, wheelbase, and transmission combinations, drive shafts have different lengths, diameters, and types of splined yokes.

Most drive shafts tend to vibrate because of universal joint action and other factors. To eliminate vibration, cardboard tubes are sometimes

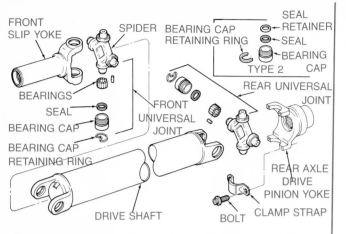

Fig. 38-8 Exploded view of front universal joint. (American Motors Corporation)

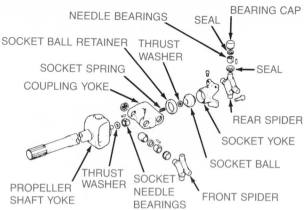

Fig. 38-9 Exploded view of a constant velocity universal joint. (American Motors Corporation)

pressed into the steel tubes. Some drive shafts have rubber biscuits molded on the outside of the smaller diameter steel tube. This assembly is then pressed into the drive shaft tube.

38.9   UNIVERSAL JOINT

The universal joint (Fig. 38-7) consists of two Y-shaped yokes connected by a cross member called a cross or spider. The arms of the cross are called trunions.

In a typical Hotchkiss drive line, the front and rear universal joints are identical in construction and operation (Fig. 38-8). Needle roller bearings support the cross or spider in the yokes. The bearing outer race is a cap deep enough to hold a reserve supply of lubricant. A seal between the cap and cross holds in the lubricant. Unviersal joints make it possible for one shaft to drive another when they are at an angle.

38.10   CONSTANT VELOCITY UNIVERSAL JOINTS

Two universal joints are used in the Hotchkiss drive line. Power flow through the drive line may change direction twice. For example, engine power flowing from the transmission output shaft to the drive shaft may change direction as it flows through the front universal joint. As engine power flows from the drive shaft to the drive pinion, it may again change direction because the axle has moved up or down. When torque is transmitted at an angle through this type of joint, the driving yoke rotates at a constant speed while the driven yoke speeds up and slows down twice per revolution. This changing of speed or velocity of the

driven yoke increases as the angle between the two yoke shafts increases.

When the angles of the universal joints are very large, a constant velocity universal joint is required. A constant velocity universal joint (Fig. 38-9) or double Cardan universal joint uses two unviersal joints closely connected by a centering socket yoke and a center yoke. On some vehicles, the double joint is used at both ends of the drive shaft. On other vehicles, the double joint is used only on the drive end of the drive shaft. In some uses, it is placed in the center of a very long drive shaft.

38.11   SLIP JOINTS

The front yoke of the universal joint, the slip joint, is splined to the external splines of the transmission output shaft as shown in Figure 38.10.

When going over bumps, the rear axle assembly moves up and down on the suspension system, changing the distance between the transmission and the rear axle. The slip joint moves in and out on the transmission shaft to allow this change of distance. This is why the drive shaft is not anchored at the front. The spline of the slip joint fits snugly to the transmission output shaft and is free to move in and out.

The slip joint spline is lubricated by the transmission's lubricant. This lubricant permits the yoke to move in and out easily under all driving conditions.

38.12   FOUR-WHEEL DRIVE

A four-wheel drive arrangement makes it possible for all four wheels to transfer engine torque to the road (Fig. 38-11). Four-wheel drive systems use a

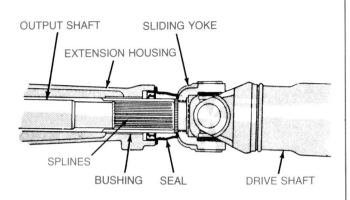

Fig. 38-10 Slip joint. (Chrysler Corporation)

Labels: OUTPUT SHAFT, SLIDING YOKE, EXTENSION HOUSING, SPLINES, BUSHING, SEAL, DRIVE SHAFT

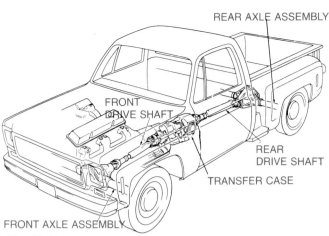

Fig. 38-11 Recirculating roller slip joint. (Ford Motor Company)

Labels: REAR AXLE ASSEMBLY, FRONT DRIVE SHAFT, REAR DRIVE SHAFT, TRANSFER CASE, FRONT AXLE ASSEMBLY

transfer case, a system of gears mounted in a separate housing behind the transmission.

The transfer case provides power to a front drive shaft and front axle. It also provides power to a rear shaft to transmit torque to a rear axle assembly.

There are two general types of transfer cases. One is described as a part-time transfer case system. During normal driving the vehicle uses two-wheel drive. When rough or slippery roads are encountered, the driver engages the gears in the transfer case to deliver power to all four wheels. The other type, the full-time transfer case, provides full time four-wheel drive. Both types of transfer case also provide a gear reduction range lower than the transmission low gear to increase vehicle power in steep conditions.

NEW TERMS

Drive line assembly The parts used to transfer engine power from the transmission to the rear axle assembly.

Drive shaft A large steel tube that transfers engine power from the transmission to the rear axle assembly.

Flexible joints Joints on a front-drive axle which allow the front wheels to turn and move up and down with the suspension.

Full-time transfer case A transfer case that provides four-wheel drive under all road conditions.

Hotchkiss drive A drive line assembly with two or three universal joints and an open drive shaft.

Inboard joint The inside joint on a front-drive axle which allows for front wheel up and down movement.

Outboard joint The outside joint on a front-drive axle which allows the front wheels to turn back and forth.

Part-time transfer case A transfer case that allows the driver to select two- or four-wheel drive by shifting gears in the case.

Transfer case A system of gears in a housing behind the transmission that directs power to a front- and rear-drive axle.

Universal joint The part of the drive line assembly that allows for a change in angle of the drive line as the vehicle goes over bumps.

CHAPTER REVIEW

1. List the three basic types of drive arrangements.
2. What are the two basic types of front-wheel drive arrangements?
3. What is the purpose of the front-wheel drive inboard drive shaft flexible joint?
4. What is the purpose of the front-wheel drive outboard drive shaft flexible joint?
5. What is the purpose of the rear-dirve line assembly?
6. Give one advantage of the torque tube drive.
7. Describe a Hotchkiss drive assembly.
8. List the main parts of a universal joint.
9. What is a constant velocity universal joint?
10. What is the purpose of the four-wheel drive transfer case?

DISCUSSION TOPICS AND ACTIVITIES

1. List the requirements of a drive line. What parts are needed to meet these requirements?
2. Identify the parts of a drive assembly on a shop chassis. Can you explain the operation of all the parts?

Drive Line Service

CHAPTER PREVIEW

Mechanics are often called upon to service drive line components. The drive shaft, especially the universal joints or flexible joints, works under stress which results in wear. In this chapter, we will present troubleshooting, maintenance, and service procedures for rear- and front-wheel drive lines.

OBJECTIVES

After studying this chapter, you should be able to do the following:

1. Troubleshoot a rear- and front-drive line system to determine the source of a problem.
2. Perform the necessary preventive maintenance on a drive line assembly.
3. Disassemble, inspect, and service a rear-drive line assembly.
4. Remove and replace a front-drive shaft.
5. Disassemble, inspect, and service the flexible joints on a front drive shaft.

39.1   TROUBLESHOOTING

Wear on front-wheel drive system drive shafts usually occurs at the inboard or outboard flexible joints. A bad flexible joint will usually result in a noise and vibration problem, which is often worse during turning.

Rear-drive line problems usually show up as a vibration that is especially bad on deceleration or as a noise that occurs when the vehicle begins to move from a stop. Vibrations in the drive line are usually caused by the drive shaft.

One cause of drive shaft vibration is an out-of-balance condition. Undercoating, mud, or any foreign material on one side of the drive shaft can throw it out of balance. A dent in the steel wall of the drive shaft can also make it vibrate. The drive shaft should be inspected visually for these problems.

Drive shaft vibrations may also be due to loose universal joint flange bolts or bent components in the universal joints. These parts should be inspected visually and replaced as necessary.

Other less common causes of drive shaft vibration are too much runout and incorrect drive line angle. Runout or too much wobble of the drive shaft is measured with a dial indicator at both ends of the drive shaft, just forward or behind the balance weight(s). Clean paint and any undercoating from the shaft in those areas.

Attach a dial indicator to a movable support or C-clamp (Fig. 39-1). Mount the dial indicator so the stylus is at a right angle to the shaft. To get an accurate reading, rotate the drive shaft by light downward hand pressure applied at the middle of the shaft. Runout greater than 0.010 inch (0.25mm) is unacceptable. Replace the drive shaft if runout is excessive at the front end.

If runout at the front is acceptable, measure runout at the rear. Attach the dial indicator support to the rear housing pinion boss and use the procedure above. If reading is unacceptable, disconnect the shaft, rotate either the shaft or the rear yoke 180°, and reconnect the shaft. Measure runout at the rear again.

When universal joints operate at an angle, the driven yoke rotation speed will change even though the driving yoke speed is constant. The driven yoke will speed up and slow down twice each revolution. This change in speed depends on the operating angle

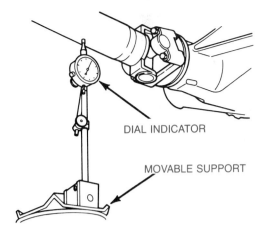

Fig. 39-1 Measuring drive shaft runout with a dial indicator.
(Cadillac Motor Car Division, GMC)

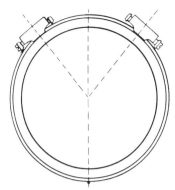

HOSE CLAMP HEADS SPREAD TO
REDUCE WEIGHT IN ONE SPOT

Fig. 39-2 Using hose clamps to balance drive shaft. (Chevrolet Motor Division, GMC)

of the universal joint—the greater the angle, the greater the speed change. The operating angles of the two universal joints on the drive shaft must be controlled to control vibration. A big difference in angles will result in drive line vibration.

Gauges are available for measuring operating angles in the drive line. If the angle is incorrect, shims or spacers for the transmission mount or rear axle mount change the operating angle.

Universal joint wear is most often shown by a squeak, clunk, or knocking noise when the automobile is accelerated. The problem usually shows up just after the transmission has been put into gear, either forward or reverse. The mechanic should drive the vehicle and listen for noises in the drive line area.

39.2 PREVENTIVE MAINTENANCE

Preventive maintenance on the drive line assembly involves cleaning and inspecting the drive shaft and universal joints or flexible joints at regular intervals. Normally the maintenance is done with the vehicle on a hoist during a lubrication service.

For many vehicles, relubrication of the drive shaft universal joints or flexible joints is not recommended. If inspection of the universal or flexible joints shows signs of external leakage or damaged seal or boots, the universal or flexible joints should be replaced.

Some universal joints have a lubrication fitting in the cross. These units may be lubricated during a regular chassis lubrication. If the vehicle is operated under severe conditions and the universal joints do not have lubrication fittings, the universal joints should be disassembled, cleaned, and relubricated every 40,000 miles (64,000 km).

39.3 REAR-WHEEL DRIVE LINE SERVICE

If troubleshooting indicates the drive shaft is out of balance, it must be rebalanced. Electronic balancing equipment does a fast and accurate job. If this equipment is not available, the shaft can be balanced mechanically.

Clean all undercoating and accumulated dirt from the shaft. Raise and support the rear of the automobile at the axle and remove the rear wheels. Operate automobile in gear at approximately 40 mph (64 km) to locate the heavy side of propeller shaft. Use a jackstand as a steady rest and slowly advance a crayon or chalk toward the spinning propeller shaft. At the instant of first contact with the propeller shaft, withdraw the chalk or crayon. This mark indicates the heavy spot of the drive shaft.

Place two worm hose clamps on the drive shaft with heads located 180° from the heavy spot and side clamps as far rear as possible (Fig. 39-2). Operate the vehicle in gear at the vibration speed. If vibration is not reduced, rotate both clamp heads at 90-degree steps around the shaft until vibration is reduced. When the point of lowest vibration is found, rotate both clamp heads an equal distance in opposite directions toward the heavy spot until the vibration is reduced. If the results are not satisfactory, repeat the balance procedure at the front of the drive shaft.

Universal joint service involves disassembling the universal joints and installing a repair kit (Fig. 39.3) consisting of a new cross and bearing assembly.

Remove the drive shaft by unbolting the flange or strap attachment at the rear axle end. Withdraw the drive shaft front yoke from the transmission by

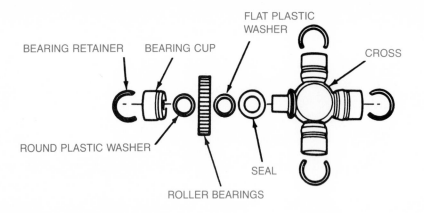

Fig. 39-3 Repair kit for universal joint. (General Motors Corporation)

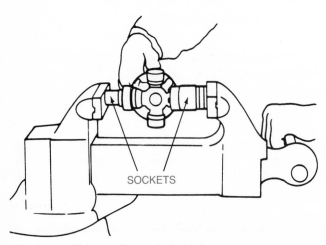

Fig. 39-4 Using a vise and two sockets to remove or install a universal joint kit. (General Motors Corporation)

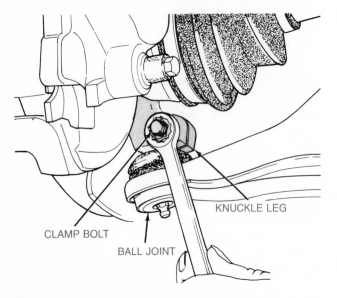

Fig. 39-5 Removing the ball joint to steering knuckle clamp bolt. (Chrysler Corporation)

moving the shaft rearward, passing it under the axle housing. Watch for oil leakage from the transmission output shaft housing.

Before disassembling the universal joint, mark the yoke, cross, and bushings to help reassembly if inspection shows that parts are serviceable. Remove the four bushing retainers from the universal joint cross assembly. Using a socket approximately the same diameter as the bushing, press one bushing and roller assembly out of the yoke by pressing the opposite bushing in (Fig. 39-4). Press out the remaining bushing and roller assembly by pressing on the end of the cross. Remove the cross assembly from the yoke.

Clean all parts in a suitable solvent and allow them to dry. Examine bearing surfaces of the cross. They should be smooth and free from ripples and pits. If bearing surfaces or seal retainers are damaged, replace the cross assembly. Examine rollers in bushings. Rollers that have operated on a worn cross should be replaced. Rollers should be smooth so that they roll freely inside bushings.

Lubricate the bushing and roller assemblies with recommended lubricant. Also fill reservoirs in the ends of the cross. Place the cross in the drive shaft yoke, observing identification marks made at disassembly. Install bushings and roller assemblies in the yoke, matching identifying marks. Use a vise or press to press both bushing assemblies into the yoke while guiding the cross into bushings. Correctly position bushings so retainers can be installed. Position the remaining two bushings assemblies on the cross. Install the retainer strap to hold bushings on the cross during installation of the shaft on the drive pinion flange. Lightly tap outer ends of bushings while rotating the cross to be sure cross and bushings operate freely.

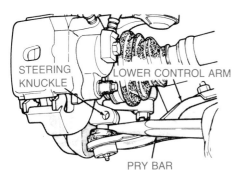

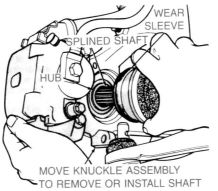

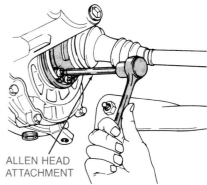

Fig. 39-6 Separating the ball joint from the steering knuckle. (Chrysler Corporation)

Fig. 39-7 Separating the flexible joint from the hub. (Chrysler Corporation)

Fig. 39-8 Removing allen head screws. (Chrysler Corporation)

Constant velocity universal joints are serviced the same as single universal joints. Special tools are often required to remove and replace the centering ball mechanism in the center of the coupling yoke. These universal joints should always be serviced according to the manufacturer's service manual.

39.4 FRONT-WHEEL DRIVE SHAFT SERVICE

If you have determined that an inboard or outboard flexible joint is worn, the drive shaft must be removed. There are different removal procedures for each manufacturer's drive shafts. Be sure to find and follow the specific procedure in the appropriate shop service manual. We will present the general procedures used on most systems in this section.

39.5 Drive Shaft Removal

Remove the front hub cap and pull out the hub nut cotter pin and lock. Loosen hub nut and wheel nuts while vehicle is on floor and brakes applied. Raise the car on a hoist or support it on jack safety stands. Remove the hub nut and the wheel and tire assembly.

Remove the clamp bolt securing the ball joint stud into the steering knuckle (Fig. 39-5). Separate the ball joint stud from the steering knuckle by prying against knuckle leg and control arm. Do not damage the ball joint or the flexible joint boots (Fig. 39-6). Separate the outer flexible joint splined shaft from the

hub by holding the flexible housing while moving the knuckle hub assembly away (Fig. 39-7). The separated outer joint and shaft must be supported during inner joint separation from the transaxle drive flange. Tie the assembly to the control arm while you separate the inboard flexible joint.

Remove the plastic caps (if used) from the Allen head screws which retain the inboard joint by prying under the cap and against the inner joint flange. Using an Allen head socket wrench attachment, remove the Allen head screws which retain the inboard flexible joint to the transaxle (Fig. 39-8). Untie the outer assembly from the control arm. Remove the drive shaft assembly carefully to reduce loss of special lubricant from the inner flexible joint.

On some models of transaxles, the inboard flexible joint is retained by a circlip inside the differential assembly. To remove this style joint, you must first remove a cover from the differential (Fig. 39-9). With the cover removed, you can remove the circlip from inside the differential (Fig. 39-10). The flexible joint can then be separated from the transaxle.

39.6 Servicing the Inboard Flexible Joint

To disassemble an inboard flexible joint, first determine if the unit has a retainer ring on the inside. If it does, remove it. Non-spring loaded inboard joint tripods will slide right out of the housing (Fig. 39-11). There is no retaining ring to prevent their removal. Spring-loaded inboard joints, however, have tabs on

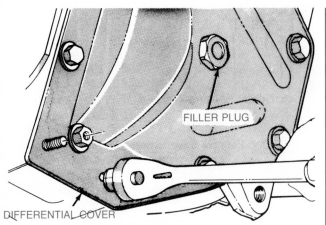

Fig. 39-9 Removing the transaxle cover. (Chrysler Corporation)

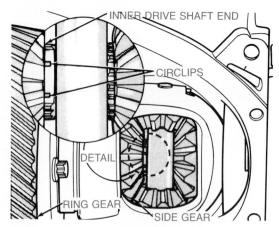

Fig. 39-10 Circlips inside the differential must be removed to separate this style flexible joint from transaxle. (Chrysler Corporation)

the joint cover that prevent the spring from forcing the tripod out of the housing. These tabs must be bent back with a pair of pliers before the tripod can be removed.

Remove the snap ring from the shaft-end groove then remove the tripod with a brass punch. Remove as much grease as possible from the assembly and inspect the joint housing ball raceway and the tripod components for excessive wear and replace if necessary. If the joint contains a spring, also inspect it, the spring cup, and the spherical end of the connecting shaft for excessive wear or damage and replace it if necessary.

To reassemble the inboard tripod joint, first install a new boot. Slide the small end of the boot over the shaft until the small boot end fits in the machined groove on the shaft. Clamp the small boot end by placing the rubber clamp over the boot groove.

Reinstall the tripod on the shaft with the non-chamfered face of the tripod body facing the shaft retainer groove. Install the snap ring in the groove to lock the tripod assembly on the shaft. Using the grease supplied with the boot, grease all the parts of the assembly. Position the housing over the tripod and install the large boot clamp. If there were retaining tabs, bend them back into position.

39.7   Servicing the Outboard Flexible Joint

To disassemble the outboard flexible joint, first, remove the boot clamps on the boot and discard them.

Wipe away all the grease to expose the joint. Support the shaft in a vise with soft jaws, support the outer joint, and using a soft hammer, give a sharp tap to the top of the joint body to dislodge it from the internal circlip installed in a groove at the outer end of the shaft (Fig. 39-12). A wear sleeve is installed on some models of the outer joint housing and provides a wipe surface for the hub bearing seal. If bent or damaged, carefully pry the wear sleeve from the joint machined ledge. Remove the circlip from the shaft groove and discard it.

If outer joint is noisy or badly worn, replace the entire unit. The repair kit will include the boot, clamps, retaining ring (circlip) and lubricant. Check the grease for contamination and all parts for defects. Wash all the parts in solvent and allow them to dry. Inspect the housing ball races for excessive wear and scouring. Check the splined shaft and nut threads for damage. Inspect all balls for pitting, cracks, scouring, and wear. Dulling of the surface of the balls is normal. Inspect the cage for excessive wear on the inside and outside of spherical surfaces. Inspect the inner race (cross) for excessive wear or scouring of ball races. Any of these defects will mean you must replace the assembly as a unit (Fig. 39-12).

To install a new outboard flexible joint assembly, first, slide the small end of the new boot over spacer-ring and shaft and position it in machined groove provided. Insert a new circlip (provided with the kit) in the shaft groove. Do not over expand or twist circlip during assembly. Position the outer joint on the splined end of the shaft, engage the splines, and tap sharply with mallet.

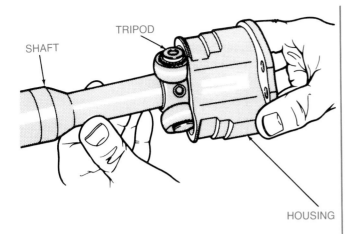

Fig. 39-11 Removing the tripod from the housing. (Chrysler Corporation)

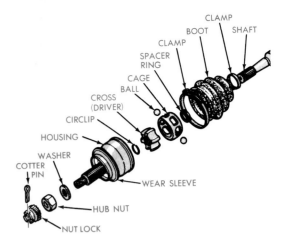

Fig. 39-12 Inspecting the outboard flexible joint. (Chrysler Corporation)

39.8   Drive Shaft Installation

Hold the inner joint assembly at housing while aligning and guiding the inner joint spline into the transaxle. Push the knuckle and hub assembly out and install the splined outer joint shaft in the hub. Reinstall the knuckle assembly on the ball joint stud. Install and tighten the clamp bolt to the specified torque.

If you removed the differential cover to remove circlips, reinstall the circlips. Install the differential cover with a new gasket. Torque the cover bolts to specifications. Fill the differential with the recommended amount and type of lubricant.

The front wheel hub nuts on most models use a lock and cotter pin, which maintain proper wheel bearing preload and prevent the nut from backing off. Install the washer and the new hub nut after cleaning the threads. With brakes applied, tighten the hub nut to specifications with a torque wrench. Install the lock and a new cotter pin. Wrap cotter pin ends tightly around the nut lock. Install the wheel and tire assembly and tighten the wheel nuts to the specified torque. Cover the car and test drive it to check for proper axle shaft operation.

NEW TERMS

Drive shaft out-of-blance   A condition caused by a bent, dirty, or undercoated drive shaft; shows up as a vibration.

Drive shaft runout   A condition in which the drive shaft wobbles as it turns.

Operating angle   The angle of the drive line as it operates.

CHAPTER REVIEW

1. How do rear-drive line problems usually show up?
2. What are the causes of drive shaft out-of balance?
3. Explain how to use a dial indicator to check rear-drive shaft runout.
4. What is the drive shaft operating angle?
5. What is the result of too large an operating angle?
6. How does universal joint wear usually show up?
7. Describe the preventive maintenance required on the drive line.
8. Describe how to balance a drive shaft.
9. Describe how to disassemble, clean, and inspect the parts of a universal joint.
10. Explain how to lubricate and reassemble a universal joint.
11. Explain how to remove a front-drive shaft.
12. How is an inboard flexible joint removed and replaced?
13. How is an outboard flexible joint removed and replaced?
14. What should you look for when inspecting parts of the inboard or outboard flexible joint?
15. Explain how to reinstall a front-drive shaft.

DISCUSS TOPICS AND ACTIVITIES

1. Inspect the drive line on an automobile of your choice. Try to find any of the problems discussed in the chapter.
2. Look up the operating angle for a drive line in a service manual. How could you check this angle?
3. Take apart a shop front-drive shaft. Inspect the parts for wear or damage and reassemble it.

Differential Assembly

CHAPTER PREVIEW

The purpose of the differential assembly is to allow the two drive wheels to turn at different speeds when the car goes around a corner (Fig. 40-1). This is necessary because when cornering, the wheel on the inside of the turn goes through a smaller arc or corner than the wheel on the outside. If the wheels were not allowed to turn at different speeds, they would tend to skip around the corner, and steering would be very difficult.

There are two basic types of differentials. On front-wheel drive cars, the differential is in the same housing as the transmission. The combination of transmission and differential is called a transaxle. On front engine rear-drive cars, the differential is mounted at the rear of the car in a separate housing usually called the rear axle assembly.

OBJECTIVES

After studying this chapter, you should be able to do the following:

1. Describe the components of the differential assembly.
2. Explain the flow of power through the differential.
3. Understand the operation of a limited slip differential.
4. Understand the purpose of the rear axle ratio.
5. Describe the parts and operation of axle shafts and bearings.

40.1   DIFFERENTIAL PARTS

Both the front-drive and rear-drive differential have the same job to do. They also have many of the same parts. The basic difference is the way in which engine torque is delivered to the differential assembly.

A cross-sectional view of a transaxle is shown in Figure 40-2. Power enters the differential from the transmission mainshaft gear. The mainshaft gear is meshed with a large gear in the differential called the ring gear. The ring gear is attached to a housing called the case. The parts in the case are the same as that used on a rear drive differential.

Power enters the rear axle assembly from the drive shaft, connected through the rear universal yoke to a gear called the drive pinion (Fig. 40-3). The drive pinion gear is meshed with the ring gear (Fig. 40-4), which is bolted to the case (Fig. 40-5). This arrangement allows the drive pinion to turn the ring gear.

As the ring gear turns, the case attached to it also turns. A shaft through the case also goes through the middle of two small pinion gears (Fig. 40-6). As the case turns, this shaft turns the small pinion gears, each of which meshes with a side gear. Each side gear is attached to a shaft called an axle, which on a rear-drive system runs through a housing to one of the rear wheels (Fig. 40-7). On a front drive, the side gears are attached to the two drive shafts. The parts of a transaxle differential are shown in Figure 40-8.

40.2   DIFFERENTIAL POWER FLOW

When the automobile is traveling in a straight line, the power flow through the system is fairly sim-

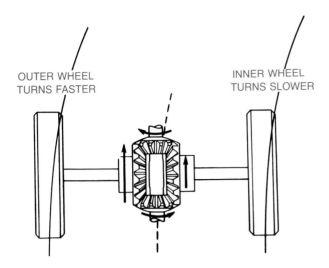

Fig. 40-1 During cornering the inside wheel must turn slower than the outside wheel. (General Motors Corporation)

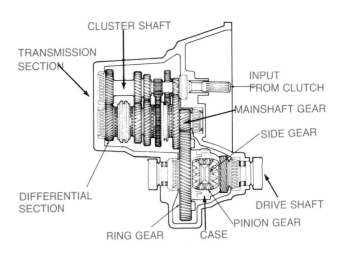

Fig. 40-2 Cross-sectional view of a transaxle. (Ford Motor Company)

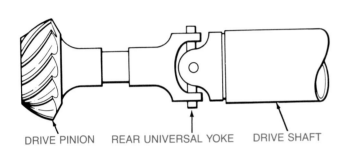

Fig. 40-3 Drive pinion is driven by drive shaft.

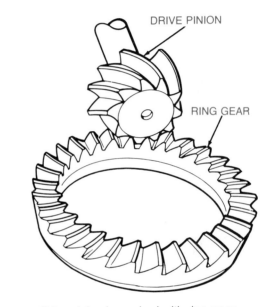

Fig. 40-4 Drive pinion is meshed with ring gear.

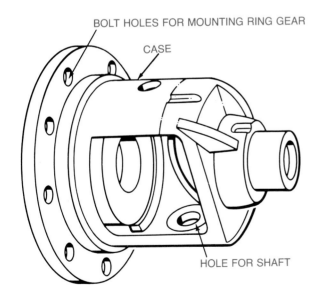

Fig. 40-5 Ring gear is bolted to case.

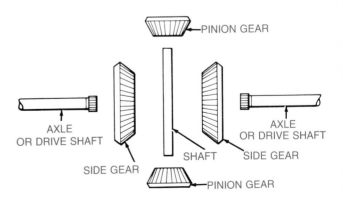

Fig. 40-6 Gears inside carrier.

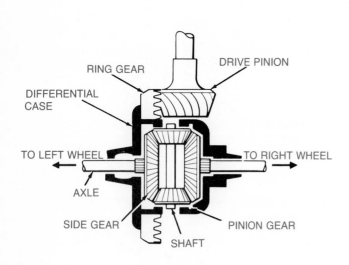

Fig. 40-7 Complete differential assembly.

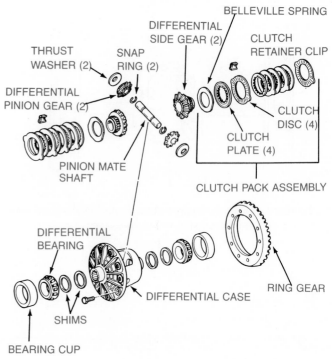

Fig. 40-8 Exploded view of transaxle differential.

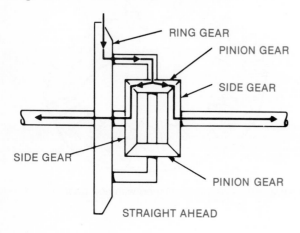

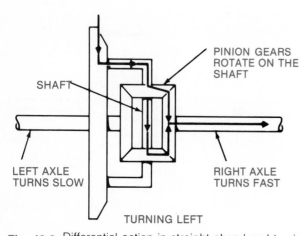

Fig. 40-9 Differential action in straight ahead and turning conditions.

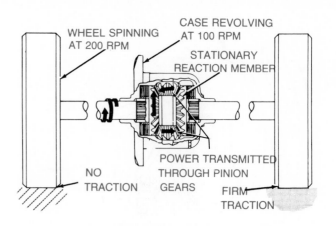

Fig. 40-10 Differential in maximum slip condition. (Chevrolet Motor Division, GMC)

ple. The ring gear turns the case. The case, through its shaft and pinion gears, turns each of the side gears at the same speed. The axles or drive shafts turn the drive wheels, which drive the vehicle.

When the vehicle makes a turn, however, the power flow becomes more complicated. If the automobile is making a left turn, the left drive wheel must go through a sharper corner—or travel through a shorter distance—than the right drive wheel. The ring gear turns the case. Since the left wheel is going through a sharp corner, the left axle is slowed or stopped momentarily. The pinion gears in the case still turn with the case but they also rotate on the case shaft. Thus, they can "walk" around the slowed or stopped left side gear and provide all the power to the right side gear so the right wheel will turn faster than the left wheel (Fig. 40-9).

During a right turn there is more resistance on the right axle, because the right wheel must turn through a sharper corner than the left. The pinions in the case walk around the right side gear and drive the left axle gear.

40.3   LIMITED SLIP DIFFERENTIALS

The standard differential assembly works very well for cornering. It works less well when the automobile wheels are on a slippery surface. When the automobile is driven over snow, ice, sand, or water, the rear wheels may slip or lose traction. The differential is designed to provide all the power to the axle with the least resistance. If, for example, the left wheel should start to slip, there would be less resistance on the left axle. The case pinions would walk around the right side gear because it would have more resistance. All the power would be delivered to the left wheel, making it spin on the slippery surface. The right wheel would not turn, and the automobile would remain stationary.

This problem is eliminated in some differentials by adding a clutch mounted in the case. When one wheel encounters a slippery surface and loses traction, the clutch system is locked up. Power is delivered to the wheel with the better traction. This system still allows a difference in wheel speed for cornering. A differential assembly with a clutch system is called a positraction, nonslip, or limited slip differential.

There are two kinds of limited slip differentials: those with clutch plates (Fig. 40-8) and those with clutch cones. Both units do the same job. Their differential cases have a large internal recess in the area of each side gear to house a clutch pack or a clutch cone.

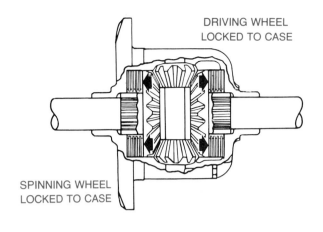

Fig. 40-11   Side force applied to clutch packs. (Chevrolet Motor Division, GMC)

40.4   Differential with Clutch Plates

The clutch pack consists of clutch discs and plates. The clutch discs are splined to the side gear, and the clutch plates are splined to the case. The discs rotate with the side gear and the plates with the differential case. In the other type of limited slip unit, a cone splined to the axle shaft rotates with the side gear only.

A limited slip differential drives the wheel with traction before the other wheel begins to spin. Figure 40-10 shows how a limited slip differential operates when the left wheel is on a slippery surface and the right wheel has good traction. The separating force between pinion gears and side gears pushes the side gears outwards. This outward force squeezes the differential clutch plates between the outer face of the side gear and the inner wall of the case (Fig. 40-11). This application of pressure is called energizing the clutch packs.

Energizing the clutch packs slows the discs to the same speed as the case by holding the left side gear to the case. The results are, first, that increased resistance on the side gears causes the drive torque to apply more force on the clutch packs. Second, when the side gear is forced to turn at the same speed as the case, rapid one-wheel spin cannot occur. Third, and most important, if the case and left side gear are turning at the same speed, the right side gear (wheel with traction) must revolve in the same direction and at the same speed as the differential case. Driving force is applied to the wheel with traction, causing it to rotate.

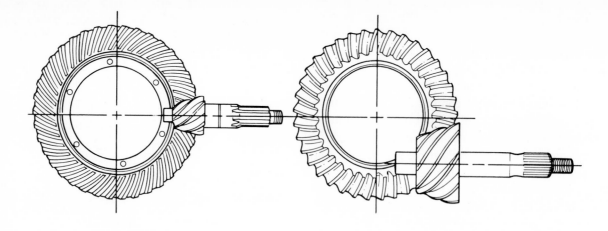

Fig. 40-12 Spiral bevel gears. (Chevrolet Motor Division, GMC)

Fig. 40-13 Hypoid ring and pinion gears. (Ford Motor Company)

40.5 Differential with Clutch Cones

The same action occurs with the cone design. The cones are forced against the case, slowing the case and applying greater force on the differential pinion gears. This forces the other side gear outward, compressing its cone against the case. The cone starts to rotate with the case and, because it is splined to the axle shaft, rotates the axle shaft.

40.6 REAR AXLE RATIO

On a rear-drive differential, the ratio is a ring and pinion gear ratio determined by the number of teeth on the drive pinion and the ring gear. Since the ring gear has more teeth than the drive pinion, the connection causes a further gear reduction torque increase. Most automobile manufacturers offer the buyer several rear axle ratios. A ratio of 3.36 to 1 means that the rear wheels turn once for every 3.36 revolutions of the drive shaft.

For trailer towing and mountain driving, a low ratio is best. This means that the drive shaft should turn several times for each wheel revolution—for example, 4.11 to 1. For economy and a higher top speed, a higher ratio, such as 3.78 to 1, is better. The rear axle ratio can be changed by exchanging the ring and drive pinion for another set with different numbers of teeth.

40.7 HYPOID GEARS

The rear-drive differential transmits power through a 90° angle. When straight bevel and spiral

bevel gears (Fig. 40-12) are used for the ring and pinion gears, as in older vehicles, the drive and driven gear centerlines must meet each other. In order to lower the drive shaft, another type of bevel gear, the hypoid gear (Fig. 40-13), was developed.

The teeth of hypoid gears are curved in a spiral. It is not necessary to match the centerlines of hypoid gears, as the pinion can be set below the centerline of the ring gear. The drive shaft can be lowered so that the tunnel of the car and the entire vehicle can be lowered.

Hypoid gears also allow an end-wise sliding action between the pinion teeth and ring gear teeth along with the rolling action. Because of this sliding action, it is possible to lap the ring and pinion gears. This gives them a more perfect match, smoother action, and quieter operation.

40.8 AXLE SHAFTS AND BEARINGS

On a rear-drive differential, the axles (Fig. 40-14), engaged to the side gears in the differential, drive the rear wheels. Each axle is contained in and protected by a rear axle housing. The gear lubricant flows down the long housing and over the axle where an axle seal prevents leakage. The axles are supported at one end in the carrier. At the wheel end, they are supported by a rear axle bearing, placed between the axle and the housing. The wheel supports the weight of the automobile through the axle and bearing to the housing. The rear axle bearing may be sealed, or it may be lubricated by the oil in the rear axle housing.

Either a ball or a roller bearing assembly supports the axle. The axle usually drives the rear wheel through a flange and stud arrangement. The studs on the flange mount to the wheel with lug nuts. On an-

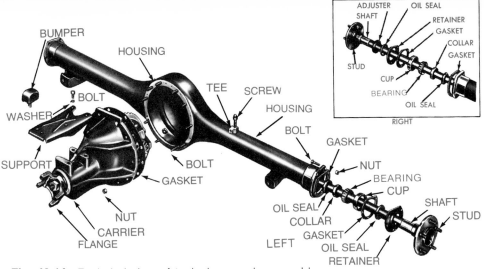

Fig. 40-14 Exploded view of typical rear axle assembly.
(Chrysler Corporation)

other arrangement, the axle has a key or splines that engage a hub to which the wheel is mounted.

NEW TERMS

Axle A shaft that transfers power from the differential to the driving wheels.

Axle gears A gear in the differential carrier that drives the axle.

Differential A system of gears in the rear axle assembly that allows the rear wheels to turn at different speeds when cornering.

Drive pinion A gear in the differential connected to the drive shaft.

Hypoid gears Drive pinion and ring gears whose shape allows them to mesh off center.

Limited slip differential A differential assembly with cone or multiple-disc clutches that directs the power to the wheel with the best traction.

Rear axle assembly A system of gears and axles that transfers power from the drive line assembly to the driving wheels of the automobile.

Rear axle ratio The ratio between the drive pinion and the ring gear in the differential.

Ring gear The gear in the differential that meshes with the drive pinion gear.

CHAPTER REVIEW

1. Describe the purpose of the differential assembly.

2. Why must the rear wheels of an automobile go at different speeds when cornering?
3. Define differential assembly.
4. What are the two main gears in the differential?
5. How are the axles connected into the differential?
6. Describe the differential power flow when the vehicle is going straight.
7. Explain the power flow when the vehicle is cornering.
8. What is a limited slip differential?
9. Why is a limited slip differential necessary?
10. Describe the operation of a limited slip differential with clutch discs.
11. Explain the operation of a limited slip differential with cone clutches.
12. What is a rear axle ratio?
13. Explain what a "low" axle ratio is.
14. What are hypoid gears?
15. What is the advantage of hypoid gears?

DISCUSSION TOPICS AND ACTIVITIES

1. Identify the parts and trace the power flow in a shop differential assembly. How is power flow different when the vehicle is cornering and when it is going in a straight line?
2. Count the teeth on a shop differential and find out the rear axle ratio.
3. Look up the rear axle ratio for the vehicle of your choice. How does this ratio compare to that of the shop unit? Higher? Lower?

CHAPTER 4

Differential Assembly Service

CHAPTER PREVIEW

Differential assembly problems usually show up first as a noise. A mechanic who services these units must be an expert troubleshooter because many other vehicle noises can be confused with rear axle noises. In this chapter, we will present troubleshooting, maintenance, and service procedures for differential assemblies.

OBJECTIVES

After studying this chapter, you should be able to do the following:

1. List the steps in finding a problem in the differential assembly.
2. Explain the preventive maintenance jobs that are done on the differential assembly.
3. Describe the service procedures for the differential assembly.
4. Explain how limited slip differentials are serviced.
5. Describe how rear axle bearings are serviced.

41.1   TROUBLESHOOTING

Any gear driven unit, especially an automotive drive axle where engine torque is increased at a 90° turn in the drive line, produces a certain amount of noise. The mechanic must inspect the vehicle to determine whether the noise signals a problem. Normal operating noise cannot be eliminated by conventional repairs or adjustment.

When troubleshooting differential noise, first get a description of the noise and driving conditions when the noise occurred. Then road test the automobile.

Noises caused by the engine, heater, transmission, tires, wheel bearings, exhaust system, and drive shaft, or the action of wind on the body, grille, travel rack, and air deflectors may be incorrectly diagnosed as differential noises. The automobile must be thoroughly checked and road tested in order to isolate the cause of the problem.

With the automobile stopped and the transmission in neutral, run the engine at different speeds. If there is noise during this test, it is caused by the engine, exhaust system, clutch, transmission, or engine-driven accessories.

Prior to road testing, check tire pressure and differential lubricant level. Some types of tire tread, tread wear, or tread patterns may cause noises. Drive the automobile on different road surfaces. If the noise varies with changes in the road surface, the tires may be the cause.

Noise caused by worn, loose, or damaged wheel bearings may be confused with differential noise. Wheel bearing noise is usually more noticeable when coasting at lower vehicle speeds. Applying the breakes gently will usually change wheel bearing noise. Another test is to turn the vehicle first left, then right. This side loads the bearings, causing the problem bearing to become noisy.

Drive the automobile long enough to bring the differential to operating temperature. Then drive at different speeds and in all transmission gear ranges. Differential noises are usually related to speed rather than engine rpm or transmission gears. Differential noises may be classified into two types: gear noise and bearing noise. Gear noise is identified as a whine or high-pitched resonating sound that is louder at certain speeds.

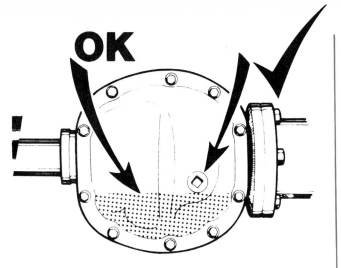

Fig. 41-1 Checking rear axle lubricant level. (American Motors Corporation)

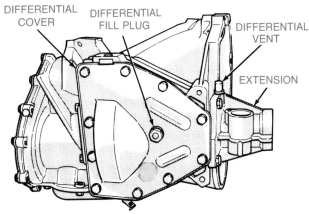

Fig. 41-2 Transaxle differential fill plug. (Chrysler Corporation)

Axle bearing noise is usually constant, and its pitch is directly related to vehicle speed. Since the drive pinion turns faster than the drive gear, the drive pinion bearing noises will be higher pitched than the differential bearing noises. Drive pinion bearings are usually heard at low speeds (20 to 30 mph).

Differential bearing noise is lower in pitch because the bearings turn at the same speed as the wheels when the automobile is driven straight ahead. Differential bearing noise will not change when the vehicle is turned left or right or when the brakes are gently applied.

Rear axle clunk noises may be confused with similar noises caused by a worn universal joint. A clunk from the rear axle may result from too much clearance between the differential side gear and differential pinion or from a loose-fitting differential pinion shaft in the case.

Too much drive gear and drive pinion clearance will also result in a clunk noise. Gear noise can be caused by an incorrect drive gear and drive pinion adjustment. If the drive line clunks on first engaging the transmission, differential side gears in the differential case bores may be loose.

A knocking or clucking noise heard at low speed when coasting may be caused by a loose-fitting differential side gear in the differential case bore. Applying the brakes lightly will usually reduce the sound.

Differential gear noise heard only under certain conditions, such as when spinning a rear wheel during on-the-car wheel balancing or when a rear wheel is spinning on ice, is considered normal. When a noise has been traced to the bearings, the gears do not require replacement unless an inspection shows signs of damage. When noise is caused by the drive pinion and drive gears at low mileage, inspect the bear-

ings during overhaul to see whether they need replacement.

41.2   PREVENTIVE MAINTENANCE

All the gears and axles in the rear axle assembly or manual transaxle are lubricated by a gear oil. This gear lubricant is placed in the housing so that spinning of the gears splashes the oil around for lubrication. The lubricant level is checked periodically by removing the plug and checking to see that enough oil is present (Figs. 41-1 and 41-2).

On older units, the differential is drained by removing the drain plug. The plug is then replaced and lubricant is added to the level of the filler hole.

When the housing does not have a drain plug and lubricant requires changing, a suction gun may be used to remove the contaminated lubricant through the filler hole. New lubricant is then added to the level of the filler hole.

41.3   DIFFERENTIAL SERVICE

Differential service involves disassembling the unit and cleaning the parts. The parts are then inspected for wear. New parts are then installed and necessary adjustments are made. These procedures are explained in the following sections.

41.4   Disassembly

The differential section of a transaxle is normally serviced at the same time as the transmission

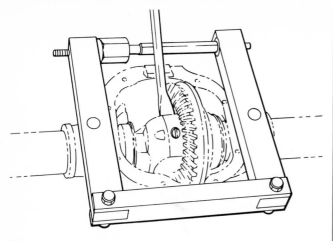

Fig. 41-3 Housing spreader used to remove carrier assembly. (Dodge/Chrysler Corporation)

Fig. 41-4 Case bearing caps must be marked prior to disassembly. (General Motors Corporation)

section is serviced. When the rear drive differential assembly requires service, remove the differential carrier assembly from the rear axle housing. This is done by first removing both rear axles from the rear axle assembly. The axles are often retained by a collar behind the axle flanges which must be removed prior to removing the axles. Next, remove the drive shaft. Drain the fluid from the housing.

On most units the carrier assembly is bolted into the center of the housing. Remove the bolts and lift out the carrier assembly. On some units, the carrier is held by the tension of the housing and bearing caps on the carrier bearing. Use a spreading tool to spring open the housing and remove the carrier assembly after the bolts have been removed (Fig. 41-3). Punch mark case bearing caps (Fig. 41-4).

41.5 Cleaning and Inspection

The carrier assembly can be disassembled according to the manufacturer's service instructions. After disassembly, clean the parts with solvent.

Differential bearings and front and rear pinion bearing cone and cup assemblies should be smooth, with no broken or dented surfaces on rollers or roller contact surfaces. The bearing roller retainer cages must not be distorted or cracked. The ring gear and drive pinion teeth should have a uniform contact pattern: smooth and unbroken surfaces without too much wear. Machined surfaces of the pinion stem (at points of contact with either rear pinion bearing contact journal or rear pinion bearing mounting shim surface) should be smooth. Replace parts which are not in good condition.

41.6 Adjustments

To get the correct meshing of the ring and pinion gears, several adjustments of the differential assembly are necessary. Pinion depth is the position of the drive pinion gear in relation to the ring gear. The pinion may be moved in or out in relation to the ring gear by placing shims between the housing and pinion (Fig. 41-5). Adding or subtracting shims moves the pinion back and forth. Markings on the ring and pinion show that they are a matched set and indicate the proper pinion depth (Fig. 41-6).

The next adjustment is pinion bearing preload. For exactly the proper mesh, the pinion gear must be held to zero end play. Zero end play, in a shaft mounted on two opposed tapered roller bearings, means zero clearance between the cone and rollers and between the rollers and cups in both bearings. If there is any clearance at the rollers, the pinion shaft will walk back and forth as the direction of thrust changes. A walking pinion shaft means that the pinion and ring gear are walking in and out of proper mesh.

To get zero end play, force the bearing cones against the rollers and the rollers against their cups by tightening the pinion shaft nut. As the pinion shaft nut is tightened, the pinion shaft flange, the oil slinger, the front bearing spacer, and the rear bearing cone are forced closer together.

In most rear axles, the bearing spacer is collapsible so that at a specified torque on the pinion nut, the spacer is squeezed to a shorter length. As the spacer gets shorter, the bearing cones are pulled closer together, pressing the bearing rollers against their cups. As the pinion shaft nut is tightened beyond the

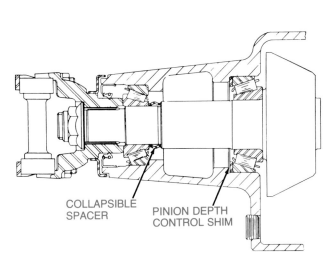

Fig. 41-5 Location of shims behind pinion.
(American Motors Corporation)

COLLAPSIBLE SPACER

PINION DEPTH CONTROL SHIM

Fig. 41-6 Ring and pinion marking. (American Motors Corporation)

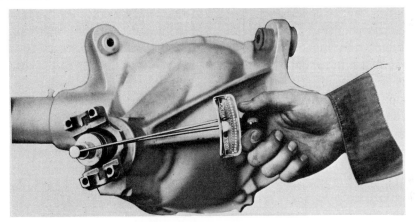

Fig. 41-7 Checking pinion preload. (Pontiac Motor Division, GMC)

Fig. 41-8 Moving ring gear side to side with carrier bearing adjusters. (Chrysler Corporation)

Fig. 41-9 Measuring backlash between ring and pinion. (Chrysler Corporation)

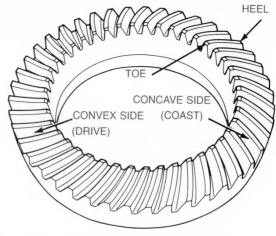

Fig. 41-10 Gear tooth contact chart. (Cadillac Motor Car Division, GMC)

point of zero clearance at the roller bearings, the pinion shaft is stretched. This stretch in the pinion shaft tends to keep the bearing rollers seated under all operating conditions.

Adjust drive pinion preload by tightening the nut on the yoke end of the drive pinion to specifications with a foot-pound or newton-metre torque wrench. Then measure the preload by the amount of torque in inch-pounds required to keep the pinion rotating (Fig. 41-7).

Mount the case assembly into the carrier. The carrier assembly, along with the ring gear, can be positioned from side to side by means of adjusters on each side of the carrier bearings (Fig. 41-8). Leave the bearing caps which mount over the carrier bearings untightened so the adjusters may be used to move the ring gear. Position the ring gear as far into the pinion as possible to remove the play or backlash between the two gears. Position the ring gear away from the pinion to increase the backlash. Measure and adjust backlash to specifications with a dial indicator mounted on the housing and set to measure the backlash on the ring gear (Fig. 41-9). When the backlash is set, tighten the side adjuster and bearing caps to specifications.

Observe the gear tooth contact patterns as a final check to determine if pinion depth and backlash adjustment have brought the ring and pinion into proper mesh. Gear tooth pattern may be observed by coating the ring and pinion gear with a thin film of red or white lead. Rotating the pinion gear through one complete revolution will leave a distinct contact pattern on the ring gear (Fig. 41-10). Charts showing acceptable and unacceptable patterns are provided by the manufacturer. Backlash or pinion depth may have to be readjusted to achieve the correct tooth pattern.

41.7 Reassembly

After a check shows the correct tooth pattern and final adjustments are finished, the differential assembly may be reassembled into the rear axle housing. As the unit is reassembled, coat parts with gear lubricant. Install axle side gears and pinion gears in the carrier. Torque all the bolts to specified limits.

41.8 LIMITED SLIP DIFFERENTIAL SERVICE

Limited slip differentials are serviced and adjusted in the same way as standard units. The multiple-disc clutches or cones require inspection for possible replacement.

To determine the proper operation of a limited slip differential, place the transmission in neutral, raise one wheel, and place a block in front of the other rear wheel. With the tire removed, attach a tool to the axle so that it may be driven with a torque wrench as shown in Figure 41-11. Check specifications for a minimum torque reading to turn the wheel.

41.9 SERVICING REAR AXLE BEARINGS

When troubleshooting locates noise from a rear axle bearing, remove the axle and install a new bearing. Anytime an axle is removed, the axle shaft gaskets and oil seals must be replaced. The axle bearing is pressed on the axle shaft and retained with a retaining collar. Remove the collar by cutting it with a chisel (Fig. 41-12). Then press off the old bearing, install a new bearing, and install a new retaining collar.

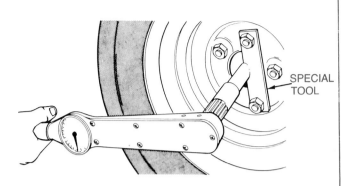

Fig. 41-11   Testing torque on a limited slip differential.
(Ford Motor Company)

Fig. 41-12   Removing bearing retainer. (Chrysler Corporation)

Axle shaft collars or bearings should never be removed with a torch. The use of a torch is unsafe because it sends heat into the axle shaft bearing journal and weakens this area.

NEW TERMS

Backlash   The space or clearance between the teeth of the drive pinion and ring gear.

Gear tooth contact pattern   The area of contact between the drive pinion and ring gear.

Pinion bearing preload   The amount the pinion shaft nut is tightened to preload the pinion bearings.

Pinion depth   The position of the drive pinion in relation to the ring gear.

CHAPTER REVIEW

1. What noises may be confused with rear axle noises?
2. How is a vehicle road tested for rear axle problems?
3. How can the oil be drained from a rear axle housing without a drain plug?

4. Describe how to disassemble a differential.
5. Explain how to clean and inspect differential parts.
6. What is pinion depth?
7. How is pinion depth measured?
8. What is pinion preload?
9. Explain how to measure and adjust pinion preload.
10. What is a collapsible spacer?
11. What is backlash?
12. How is backlash measured?
13. What is a gear tooth contact pattern?
14. Explain how to remove a rear axle bearing.

DISCUSSION TOPICS AND ACTIVITIES

1. Study some worn differential assembly parts found around the shop. Can you identify the wear?
2. Look up the pinion preload, pinion depth, and backlash specifications for the automobile of your choice.
3. Check a limited slip differential for correct operation.

The Automobile Chassis

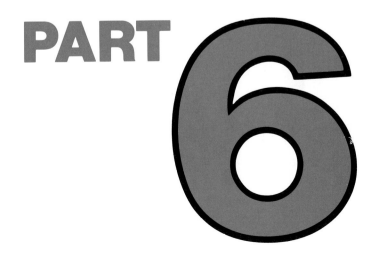

PART **6**

The Suspension System

CHAPTER PREVIEW

The automobile's wheels are mounted to the framework through a system of linkages and springs called the suspension system. The suspension system allows the wheels to bounce up and down on rough roads while the rest of the vehicle remains fairly steady. There are many different suspension designs. The most common are described in this chapter.

OBJECTIVES

After studying this chapter, you should be able to do the following:

1. Identify the parts and describe the operation of the short long arm suspension system.
2. Identify the parts and describe the operation of a MacPherson strut suspension system.
3. Describe the operation of the rigid rear suspension system.
4. Describe the operation of an independent rear suspension system.
5. Understand the operation of a load leveling system.

42.1   INDEPENDENT SUSPENSIONS

In most front suspension systems today, each front wheel is independent of the other (Fig. 42-1). If the left wheel falls into a hole, the right wheel is unaffected. Early automobiles used a rigid system in which the two front wheels were connected on a large axle that ran under the front of the vehicle. If one wheel went over a bump, it would bounce the other wheel through the axle, resulting in a rough ride for the passengers. The independent suspension system solved this problem.

42.2   SHORT LONG ARM SUSPENSION

The most common front independent suspension is called the short long arm. The system gets its name from the linkage or control arms which attach the wheels to the frame (Fig. 42-2). The front wheels are connected to the frame by an upper and a lower control arm which are attached to the frame so they can swivel up and down. The wheels turn on wheel bearings attached to a steering knuckle assembly. The steering knuckle assembly is connected to the control arms through a special joint called a ball joint. The ball joint allows movement in a number of different directions so the assembly can swing around as the wheels are turned left and right. It also permits up-and-down motion as the wheels encounter rough roads.

42.3   Control Arms

The control arms are large steep stampings shaped like the letter A and often called ''A'' arms. The top control arm is shorter than the bottom control arm (Fig. 42-3). If the arms were equal in length, the distance between the two front tires would change as the automobile passed over bumps in the road. This spreading and retracting would drag the tires sideways and result in very rapid tire tread wear. If the upper control arm is made shorter, the arc it swings through is also shorter. This brings the top of the wheel in faster than the bottom control arm. As a result, side scuffing of the tires is greatly reduced.

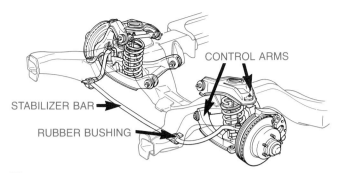

Fig. 42-1 Independent front suspension. (Oldsmobile Division, GMC)

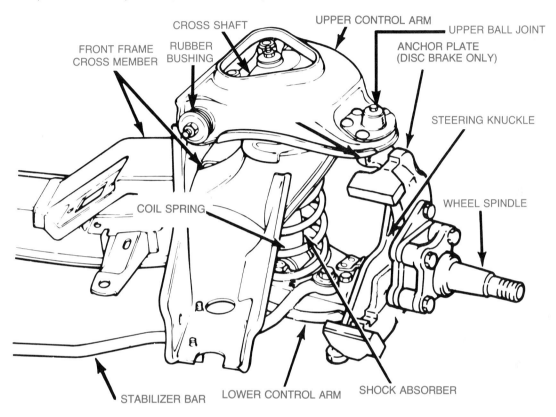

Fig. 42-2 Components of short long arm suspension system. (American Motors Corporation)

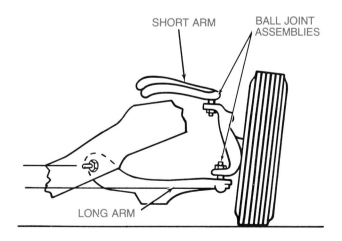

Fig. 42-3 Control arms are different lengths.
(Chevrolet Motor Division, GMC)

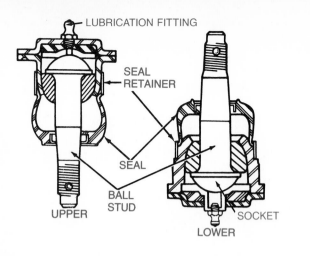

Fig. 42-4 Upper and lower ball joints. (Chevrolet Motor Division, GMC)

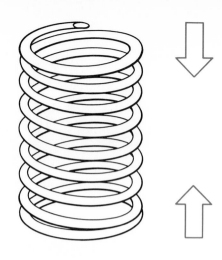

Fig. 42-5 Coil spring.

The inner end of the upper control arm is attached with rubber bushings to a cross shaft which bolts to the frame. Shims between the cross shaft and frame adjust caster and camber to specifications. The outer end of the upper control arm is attached to the steering knuckle with a ball joint.

42.4 Steering Knuckle and Spindle

The wheel spindle is the part of the steering knuckle assembly unit that carries the hub and wheel bearings. The hub assembly supports the drum or brake disc assembly used on most vehicles. The wheel spindle is connected to the vehicle through a steering knuckle and ball joints.

Since the spindle carries the entire wheel load, wheel bearings are used to reduce friction. Their design and placement on the spindle brings the center of the wheel closer to the center of the inner bearing than the outer bearing. The reason for this is to bring the wheel as close as possible to the steering knuckle axis. For this same reason the inner bearing is usually larger than the outer bearing.

42.5 Ball Joints

Ball joints (Fig. 42-4) connect the control arms to the steering knuckle. The upper ball joint is riveted or bolted to the control arm. The lower ball joint is pressed, riveted, or bolted to the control arm. Each ball joint is connected to the steering knuckle through a tapered ball stud held in position with a nut and a cotter pin.

The ball and stud is mounted in a housing shaped like a socket that allows the ball to move freely. The ball is lubricated and either permanently sealed or provided with a lubrication fitting. A seal retainer and rubber seal hold the lubricant in place. Many new ball joints have a phenolic Teflon liner to reduce friction.

42.6 Stabilizer Bar

The stabilizer bar is mounted in rubber cushions and attached to the frame. It is connected to the lower control arms by steel link bolts mounted in rubber bushings at each end of the bolts. The stabilizer bar reduces body sway by resisting independent motion of either side of the front suspension.

42.7 Coil Spring

A large coil spring (Fig. 42-5) connects the frame to either the upper or lower control arm. As the wheel rolls down the road over bumps and holes, the control arms allow the front wheels to go down, and the coil spring is expanded. When the wheels bounce up, the coil spring is compressed (Fig. 42-6). After each bump, the spring bounces or recoils back to its position at rest. If the spring were allowed to bounce too much, the frame and body would also bounce.

42.8 Torsion Bar

Some front suspension arrangements use a round torsion bar instead of a coil spring. The torsion bar is attached to the frame at one end and the control arm at the other (Fig. 42-7). As the control arm moves up or down, the torsion bar twists. When the torsion bar untwists, it returns the control arm to its normal position.

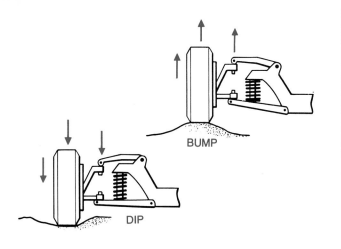

Fig. 42-6 Action of coil spring.

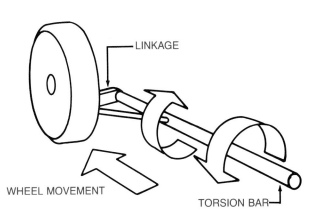

Fig. 42-7 The torsion bar twists and untwists to control wheel movement.

42.9 Shock Absorbers

Shock absorbers (Fig. 42-8) are hydraulic devices that help to control the up-and-down and rolling motion of an automobile body while at the same time controlling wheel and axle movement.

The vehicles' springs support the body, but the shock absorbers control spring movements of the body, wheel, and axle for smooth driving. This is accomplished by changing the movement of the spring (kinetic energy) into heat energy. Therefore, a shock absorber may be considered as a damper to control the energy stored up by the springs under load.

Shock absorbers develop control or resistance by forcing fluid through restricted passages. There are usually four shock absorbers on a car; one located near each wheel. They are called direct-acting because of their direct connection between the car frame (body) and the axle (or wheel mounting member). They are also called double-acting because they control motion in both directions of the suspension travel. Upward movements of the body are called rebound and downward movements are called compression.

A cross-sectional view of a typical shock absorber is shown in Figure 42-8. The upper shock mounting is attached to a piston rod. The piston rod is attached to a piston and rebound valve assembly. A rebound chamber is located above the piston and a compression chamber below the piston. The chambers are full of hydraulic fluid. A compression intake valve is positioned in the bottom of the cylinder and connected, hydraulically, to a reserve chamber also full of hydraulic fluid. The lower mounting is attached to the cylinder tube in which the piston operates.

A schematic of a shock absorber during compression is shown in Figure 42-9. The compression movement of the shock absorber causes the piston to move downward with respect to the cylinder tube, transferring fluid from chamber B (compression chamber) to chamber A (rebound chamber). This is accomplished by fluid moving through the outer piston hole and unseating the piston intake valve. Since all the fluid in chamber B cannot pass into chamber A due to the volume of the piston rod, the fluid equivalent to the rod volume is discharged out of the compression valve into section C of the reserve chamber with a corresponding compression of the air in section D of the reserve chamber.

A schematic of a shock absorber during the rebound stroke is shown in Figure 42-10. A rebound stroke will cause the pressure in chamber B (compression chamber) to fall below that in section C of the reserve chamber. As a result, the compression valve will unseat and allow fluid to flow from the reserve chamber C into the compression chamber B. Section D of the reserve chamber contains air which expands to compensate for the piston rod volume being removed. At the same time, fluid in the rebound chamber A will be transferred into compression chamber B through the inner piston holes and the rebound valve.

As the piston moves, forcing fluid through calibrated orifices, pressure increases with the effective area of the piston, and determines the resistance or control provided by the shock absorber. Low piston velocities create low pressures, whereas high piston velocities with the same orifice result in considerably higher pressures. For example, body lean during a

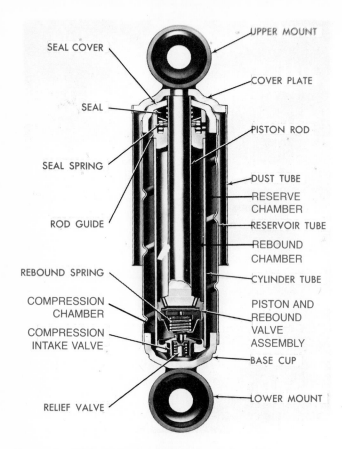

Fig. 42-8 Major components of a shock absorber.
(Monroe Auto Equipment Company)

COMPRESSION FORCE

ROD GUIDE AND SEAL

PISTON ROD

OIL

D

AIR OR GAS FILLED CELL

A

PISTON INTAKE VALVE

BLOW-OFF VALVE

OUTER PISTON HOLES

C

OIL

B

HIGH SPEED ORIFICE

LOW SPEED ORIFICE

BLOW-OFF VALVE

COMPRESSION VALVE

Fig. 42-9 Schematic of a shock absorber during compression. (Chevrolet Motor Division, GMC)

turn will result in low force in a shock absorber due to low piston velocity, while hitting a pot hole at high speeds will generate high resistance forces.

42.10 GAS FILLED SHOCK ABSORBERS

The rapid movement of the fluid between the chambers during the rebound and compression strokes can cause aeration or foaming of the fluid. Foaming is the mixing of free air and the shock fluid. When foaming occurs, the shock develops a lag because the piston is moving through an air pocket which offers no resistance. The foaming results in a decrease of the damping forces, and a loss of spring control. The gas-filled shock absorber was developed to eliminate this foaming.

A sectional view of a gas-filled shock absorber is shown in Figure 42-11. The gas-filled shock absorber uses a piston and oil chamber similar to other shock absorbers. The difference is that instead of a double tube with a reserve chamber, a dividing piston separates the oil chamber from the gas chamber. The oil chamber contains a special hydraulic oil, and the gas chamber contains nitrogen at 25 times atmospheric pressure.

42.11 Non-Drive Wheel Bearings

The non-drive wheels (front wheels with rear-wheel drive and rear wheels with front-wheel drive) are mounted on tapered roller bearings (Figs. 42-12, 42-13, 42-14) so that they roll with a minimum amount of friction. The tire, wheel, and brake drum or brake disc assembly mounts to each front spindle on two tapered roller bearings with a large inner bearing and smaller outer bearing. Bearing cups or races are pressed into a brake drum or brake rotor. Another race, part of the bearing, fits on the spindle. The roller bearings allow the tire, wheel, and brake drum or disc to turn on the spindle. An adjusting nut, lock nut, and cotter pin on the treaded end of the spindle hold the components in operating position.

The roller bearings are lubricated by thick wheel bearing grease packed into the bearings. A grease retainer or seal on the inner end prevents grease from escaping onto the brake assembly. A grease or dust cap on the outer end contains the grease.

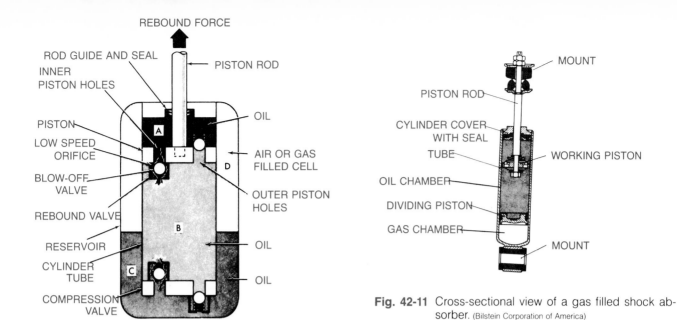

Fig. 42-10 Schematic of a shock absorber during rebound. (Chevrolet Motor Division, GMC)

Fig. 42-11 Cross-sectional view of a gas filled shock absorber. (Bilstein Corporation of America)

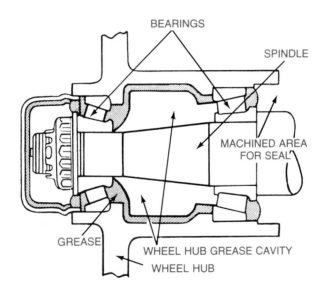

Fig. 42-12 Cross section of wheel bearing assembly mounted on spindle. (Plymouth/Chrysler Corporation)

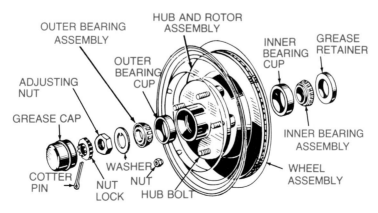

Fig. 42-13 Exploded view of front wheel bearing assembly with disc brakes. (Ford Motor Company)

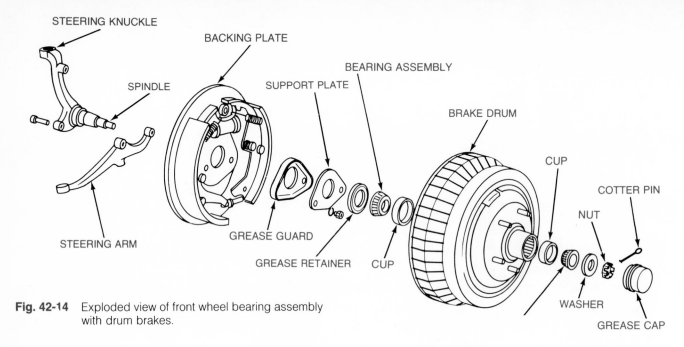

Fig. 42-14 Exploded view of front wheel bearing assembly with drum brakes.

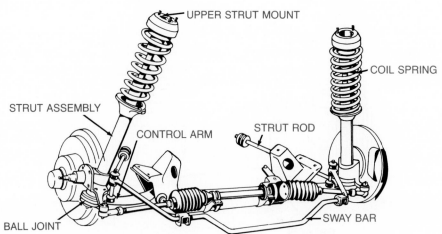

Fig. 42-15 A MacPherson strut suspension system. (Moog Automotive, Inc.)

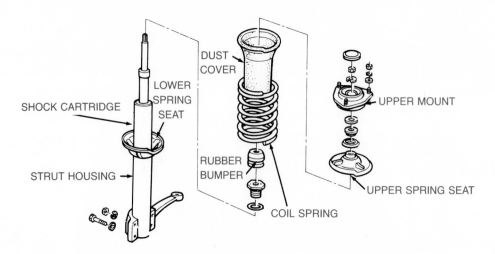

Fig. 42-16 Exploded view of a MacPherson strut assembly. (Nissan Motor Corporation in U.S.A.)

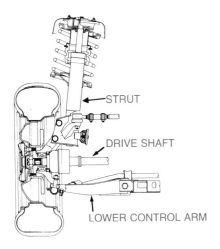

Fig. 42-17 Cross section of MacPherson strut suspension system. (Lancia)

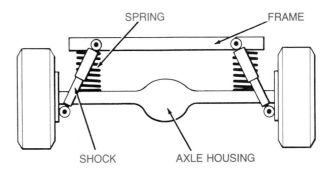

Fig. 42-18 Rigid rear axle for rear wheel drive.

42.12 MacPHERSON STRUT SUSPENSION

The MacPherson strut suspension uses a single lower control arm connected to a long, tubular assembly called a strut (Fig. 42-15), supported by the coil spring at the upper end and by the lower control arm at the bottom. A ball joint is attached to the lower part of the spindle.

An exploded view of the strut assembly is shown in Figure 42-16. The shock absorber is called a cartridge and fits inside the strut housing. A metal dust cover is used on some units to protect the strut cartridge assembly. A coil spring is held in place by a lower spring seat welded to the shock absorber piston rod.

Most MacPherson strut designs use a coil spring. A few cars use a torsion bar connected to the lower control arm. Most front engine, front-drive vehicles use the MacPherson strut design with a large lower control arm, as shown in Figure 42-17.

42.13 RIGID REAR SUSPENSION SYSTEMS

The rear suspension arrangement for most American rear drive automobiles consists of a rigid rear axle assembly mounted to the frame through a spring system (Fig. 42-18). Each side of the rear axle housing is connected to the frame through a spring

and shock absorber. The spring absorbs the wheel and axle movement so that the frame, body, and passengers do not bounce.

Most late model vehicles use coil springs to support each side of the axle housing (Fig. 42-19).

Other rear suspension systems use a leaf spring (Figs. 42-20 and 42-21) composed of strips of spring steel stacked together. The leaf spring is attached at each end to the frame, and the rear axle housing is attached to the middle of the spring. As the rear wheels bounce up and down, the leaf spring flexes.

The spring is made up of leaves of different lengths, with the shortest leaf at the bottom of the spring and the longest, or main leaf, at the top. A bolt, the spring tie bolt, is installed through holes at or near the center of the spring leaves.

Clamps are placed around the spring assembly at several points to distribute the load more evenly over all spring leaves when the vehicle passes over a bump in the road or a hole in the road surface. Without these clamps, so much of the rebound load would be placed on the main leaf that it could be damaged.

The rigid rear axle arrangement has some disadvantages. Both rear wheels are tied together by the axle housing. This means that if the left wheel is bounced, the right wheel will also be bounced. When the entire axle assembly jumps up and down on bumps, a good deal of motion makes its way through the springs to the body, creating a rough ride for the passengers. During fast cornering, there is a second problem. The rigid rear axle makes it difficult to keep both wheels flat on the road for good traction. When the rear wheels lose traction, the driver may lose control and the automobile could spin out.

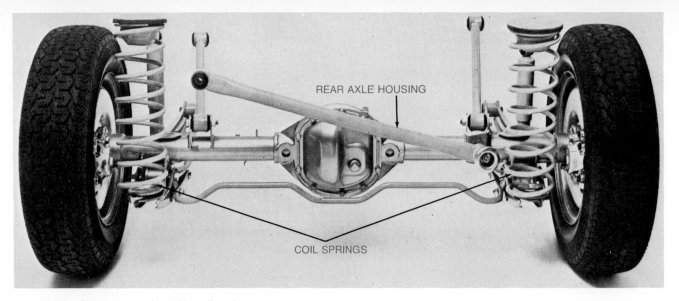

REAR AXLE HOUSING

COIL SPRINGS

Fig. 42-19 Rear suspension with coil springs. (Volvo)

42.14 INDEPENDENT REAR SUSPENSION

Many expensive rear-wheel drive automobiles have an independent rear suspension (Fig. 42-22). When the vehicle has a front engine front drive, the rear wheels are usually suspended independently from a rear crossmember by arms which go to the back or by a trailing arm independent rear suspension (Fig. 42-23).

42.15 LOAD LEVELING SYSTEMS

When a lot of weight is added to the rear trunk of a vehicle or when a trailer is connected to the rear, the rear suspension is compressed. The lowering of the rear affects the operation of both the front and rear suspension, making the vehicle difficult to control.

An air-assist hydraulic shock absorber system is available with trailer towing packages (Fig. 42-24). This system reduces rear-end sag when hauling heavy loads or towing trailers. The system is adjusted by increasing or reducing air pressure through air lines routed from the rear air shocks to an air valve on the rear of the automobile.

Air from a service station air supply is added to a chamber in each of the shock absorbers. The air in the chamber expands the shock absorber, lifting the rear of the vehicle.

An automatic leveling system (Fig. 42-35) is also available as an option on many automobiles. It automatically maintains the correct rear height as weight is added to or removed from the automobile. The system consists of a vacuum-operated compressor, a height control valve, two air cylinders, and connecting lines and fittings.

The compressor mounted in the engine compartment supplies air under pressure to operate the air cylinders. The compressor is operated by engine vacuum and atmospheric pressure.

The height control valve mounted on the frame cross member senses the rear-end height through a link connected to the rear suspension upper arm. The valve works whenever the body lowers or rises from a change in weight.

When added weight lowers the body, the link causes the valve to move to its intake position. This permits air from the compressor to enter the air cylinders and raise the body. When the weight is removed, the body rises and the link reverses the action of the valve. Air is released from the cylinders through an exhaust port in the valve.

A time delay mechanism built into the height control valve prevents the transfer of air to and from the cylinder in normal ride movements. The rubber air cylinders are mounted inside the rear coil springs.

NEW TERMS

Ball joint Ball-shaped bearing used to support suspension system control linkages.

Coil spring A large coil-shaped spring used in the suspension system.

Control arm Linkage that attaches the wheels to the frame.

Independent front suspension A suspension system in which each front wheel is suspended independently of the other.

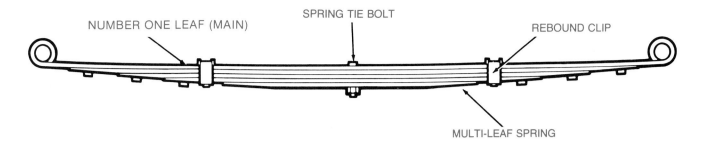

Fig. 42-20 Leaf spring. (American Motors Corporation)

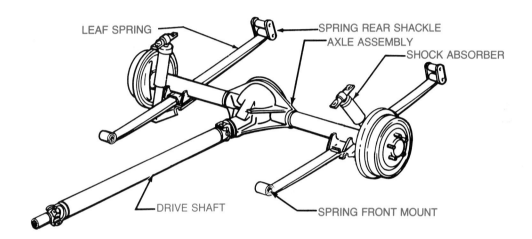

Fig. 42-21 Rear suspension system with leaf spring. (Chevrolet Motor Division, GMC)

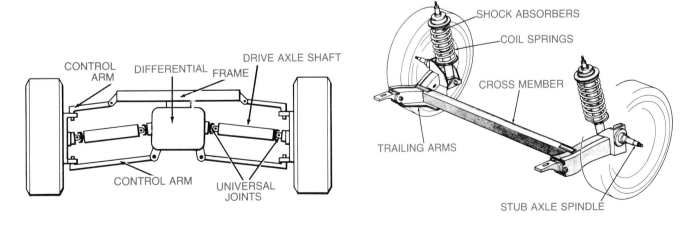

Fig. 42-22 Independent rear suspension.

Fig. 42-23 Trailing arm independent suspension used on a front wheel drive car. (Chrysler Corporation)

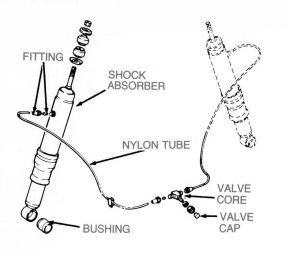

Fig. 42-24 Air shock absorber system. (American Motors Corporation)

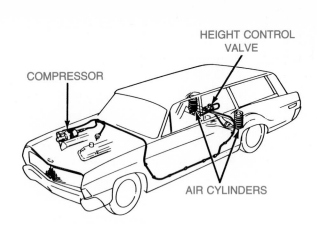

Fig. 42-25 Automatic load leveling system. (Ford Motor Company)

Independent rear suspension A suspension system in which each rear wheel is suspended independently of the other.

Jounce bumper A rubber bumper used to absorb shock during full suspension system movement.

Load leveling system A system used to level a vehicle that is heavily loaded.

MacPherson strut suspension A suspension system that combines the upper control arm, spring, and shock absorber into one strut.

Rigid rear suspension A rear suspension system in which both wheels are attached to a rigid rear axle housing.

Shock absorber A hydraulic device to control spring operation.

Short long arm suspension A suspension system in which a long and a short control arm are used to support the wheel.

Spindle A part of the steering knuckle assembly on which the front wheels are mounted.

Stabilizer bar A bar used to reduce body motion.

Steering knuckle The suspension system component to which the wheels are mounted.

Torsion bar A bar that twists at a controlled rate to act as a spring in a suspension system.

CHAPTER REVIEW

1. What is the purpose of the suspension system?
2. List advantages of an independent front suspension?
3. Why are the control arms on a short long arm suspension system different lengths?
4. What is the spindle used for?
5. What is a ball joint?
6. Where are the ball joints located in the suspension?
7. What is the job of the coil spring?
8. How does a torsion bar work?
9. Explain how shock absorbers work.
10. Describe a MacPherson strut suspension.
11. Why are the front wheels mounted on bearings?
12. Why is a rear suspension system necessary?
13. Describe a rigid rear suspension system.
14. Describe an independent rear suspension system.
15. Explain how a load leveling system works.

DISCUSSION TOPICS AND ACTIVITIES

1. Study the front and rear suspension on an automobile. What type is it? Identify the parts.
2. Look for automobiles with all the different types of suspension systems described in the chapter.

Suspension System Service

The suspension system, especially the front suspension system, is very important to the safety of the automobile's occupants. If a front suspension component fails, the vehicle can be difficult or impossible to control. Suspension components must be inspected frequently and serviced properly to prevent accidents. In this chapter we will present troubleshooting, preventive maintenance, and service procedures for common suspension systems.

OBJECTIVES

After studying this chapter, you should be able to do the following:

1. List the steps in finding a suspension system problem.
2. Describe how to lubricate a ball joint.
3. Describe how to pack front wheel bearings.
4. Explain the procedures for servicing ball joints, springs, and shock absorbers.
5. Remove and replace a MacPherson strut cartridge.

43.1 TROUBLESHOOTING

Suspension system problems may show up in a number of ways. Noise from the suspension during stops and starts or over bumps is a sign of suspension system wear. If the automobile does not go in a straight line unless the driver fights the steering wheel, it has poor directional stability. The vehicle may steer hard or have too much movement or play in the steering wheel. The front wheels may shimmy when the vehicle is driven at highway speed, or it may pull or tend to turn by itself.

All of these are signs of suspension system problems. They may also be due to steering, wheel alignment, or tire problems. Troubleshooting procedures for those areas will be presented in later chapters. When any of these problems show up, the mechanic should inspect each of the suspension components as explained below.

43.2 Ball Joints

To determine ball joint wear, jack up the vehicle to take the coil spring pressure off the ball joint. Place the jack under the bottom control arm (Fig. 43-1) if the spring is mounted to the lower control arm. Place the jack on the frame and use a spring support if the spring is on the top control arm.

Mount a dial indicator to a control arm. Place the plunger tip or stylus against the ball joint housing. Use a pry bar to move the tire up and down. Ball joint play will be shown on the dial indicator (Fig. 43-2). Both upper and lower ball joints should be measured. Play above 0.050 (15mm) to 0.070 (17mm) is excessive, except on some Chrysler models.

Many late model vehicles use ball joints with a visual wear indicator (Fig. 43-3). The base of the nipple into which the grease fitting is threaded sticks out beyond the surface of the ball joint cover on a new, unworn joint. With wear, the seat of the nipple retreats slowly inward.

To inspect for wear, raise the vehicle on a hoist. Support the vehicle by its wheels or frame so the

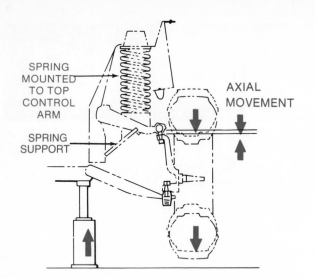

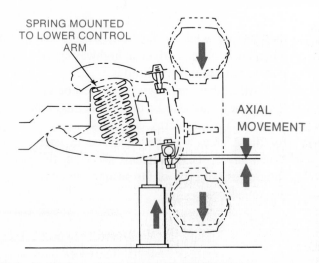

Fig. 43-1 Placing jack for determining ball joint wear.

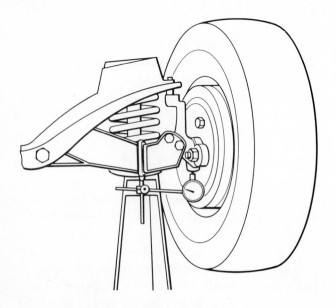

Fig. 43-2 Measuring ball joint wear with dial indicator. (Dodge/Chrysler Corporation)

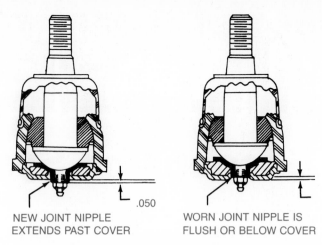

NEW JOINT NIPPLE EXTENDS PAST COVER

WORN JOINT NIPPLE IS FLUSH OR BELOW COVER

Fig. 43-3 Ball joint with visual wear indicator. (Cadillac Motor Car Division, GMC)

lower ball joint is in a loaded condition. Wipe grease fitting and nipple clean and observe the nipple's position in relation to the surface of the ball joint. If the nipple seat is flush or inside the cover surface, replace the ball joint.

43.3   Springs

Coil or leaf springs become fatigued as the vehicle reaches high mileage. As a fatigued spring begins to sag, the front or rear of the automobile starts to droop, affecting wheel alignment and handling. If the vehicle has been driven 50,000 miles or 80 000 kilometres, the springs should be checked by measuring the spring heights.

Place the vehicle on a level surface with an empty trunk and a full tank of gasoline. Take measurements at specific locations on the suspension system (Fig. 43-4) and compare to specifications. If the springs are sagging, they must be replaced.

43.4   Shock Absorbers

Shock absorber failure is a common source of suspension system problems. Shock absorbers become defective for several reasons.

1. *Loss of Fluid.* Oil on the outside of a unit usually indicates leakage from a worn seal or from a small rust hole or rupture in the lower tube. However, oil on the outside of a shock absorber may come from some other source, such as the power steering pump or the transmission. It may also come from spraying the springs or joints with oil and allowing the spray to get on the shock absorbers.

Jeep CJ-7 Renegade, a direct descendant of the original Jeep which appeared almost 40 years ago. (American Motors Corporation)

Above
Jeep Cherokee body construction, showing the large frame members that provide support for the body. (American Motors Corporation)

Left
Jeep Wagoneer LTD, a combination of four-wheel-drive, comfort, and space, in the same vehicle. (American Motors Corporation)

Left
Installing an engine in a Chevrolet Camaro for the International Race of Champions. (Chevrolet Division, General Motors Corporation)

Below
Preparing a Chevrolet Camaro for the International Race of Champions. (Chevrolet Division, General Motors Corporation)

Left
Chevrolet's Astro Van, one of the mini vans that are so popular today. It has rear-wheel drive. (Chevrolet Division, General Motors Corporation)

Below
Interior of the Chevrolet Astro Van. (Chevrolet Division, General Motors Corporation)

Above
Phantom view of the Chevrolet Astro Van. (Chevrolet Division, General Motors Corporation)

Right
Chevrolet Astro Van. Mini vans have lots of space inside, but they look and drive more like a small car.

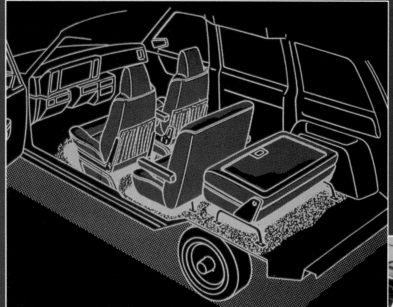

Left
Seating arrangement on a Caravan/Voyager 3-seat, 7-passenger van from Chrysler. (Chrysler Corporation)

Right
Chrysler van assembly line, with robots making spot welds as the bodies move along the line. Not a human in sight. (Chrysler Corporation)

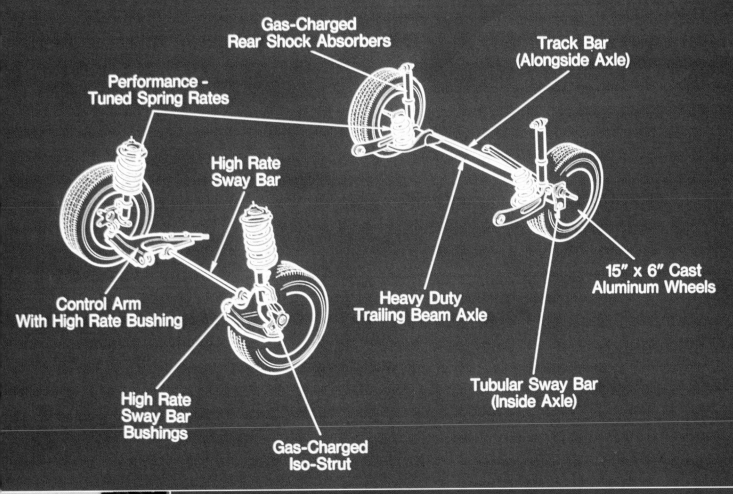

Gas-Charged
Rear Shock Absorbers

Track Bar
(Alongside Axle)

Performance -
Tuned Spring Rates

High Rate
Sway Bar

Control Arm
With High Rate Bushing

Heavy Duty
Trailing Beam Axle

15" x 6" Cast
Aluminum Wheels

High Rate
Sway Bar
Bushings

Gas-Charged
Iso-Strut

Tubular Sway Bar
(Inside Axle)

Chrysler front-wheel-drive suspension, showing their Iso-Strut design. (Chrysler Corporation)

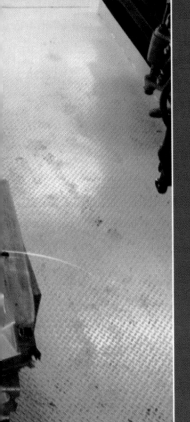

Adjusting alignment-wheel unit on a computerized aligner. Each unit is adjusted and calibrated to the car. (Photo by C.R. King, courtesy Chevron, U.S.A.)

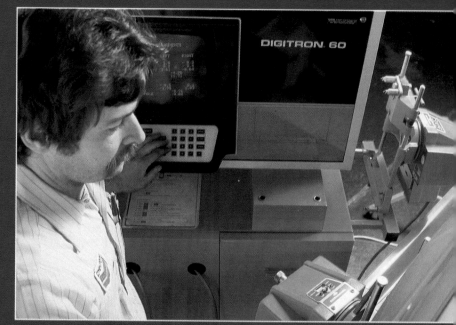

Computerized wheel aligner, showing two wheel units. A four-wheel aligner will have four of these units, and will check or align all four wheels. (Photo by C.R. King, courtesy Chevron, U.S.A.)

Right
Reading the screen on a computerized wheel aligner. The screen gives instructions, and reads out the actual alignment on the car. (Photo by C.R. King, courtesy Chevron, U.S.A.)

Below
Adjusting the alignment on a computerized wheel aligner. (Photo by C.R. King, courtesy Chevron, U.S.A.)

Replacing a strut cartridge. This aligning rack combines a hoist and rack together, so that repairs can be made on the rack without having to move the car to a hoist. (Photo by C.R. King, Courtesy Chevron, U.S.A.)

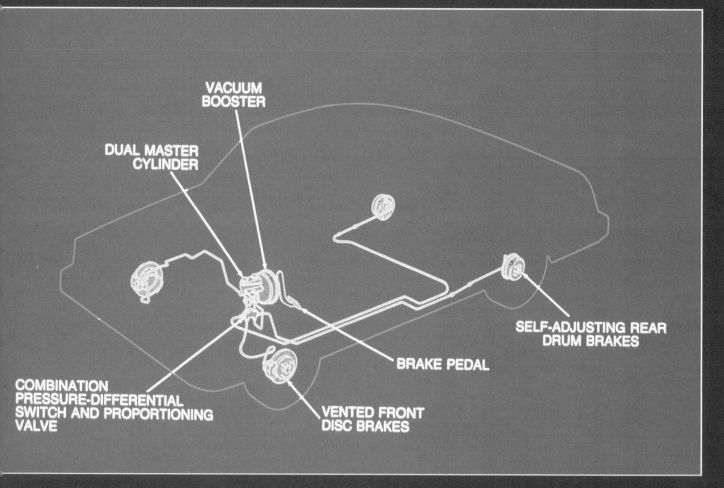

Chrysler power brake system used on Laser and Datona models. (Chrysler Corporation)

VACUUM BOOSTER

DUAL MASTER CYLINDER

SELF-ADJUSTING REAR DRUM BRAKES

BRAKE PEDAL

COMBINATION PRESSURE-DIFFERENTIAL SWITCH AND PROPORTIONING VALVE

VENTED FRONT DISC BRAKES

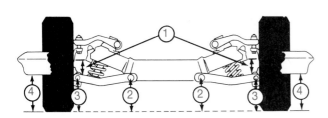

Fig. 43-4 Typical measuring points when troubleshooting springs. (TRW, Inc.)

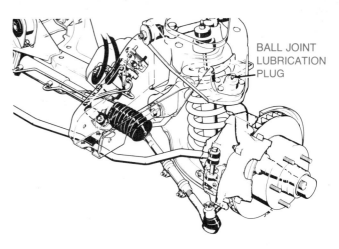

BALL JOINT
LUBRICATION
PLUG

Fig. 43-5 Ball joint lubrication plugs. (American Motors Corporation)

2. *Worn Internal Parts.* Internal parts generally wear only after rather high mileage, but occasionally earlier. After 25,000 miles, there may be 25 to 30 percent control loss. Since the vehicle suspension system also will have lost much of its stiffness, new shock absorbers are usually needed at that mileage.

3. *Broken or Worn Mountings.* Broken or worn mountings often cause very annoying noises that make them easy to find. To determine whether the shock absorbers are defective, drive the vehicle on a smooth pavement or driveway at about 10 mph. Then apply the brakes repeatedly. If this sets up a front-to-rear rocking or pitching, with the front of the car dipping and the rear rising, one or more of the shock absorbers has lost a lot of its control and all the shock absorbers should be checked.

Raise the vehicle on a hoist and examine each shock for signs of leakage and broken mountings or mounting brackets. Disconnect the lower end of each unit and feel its resistance by working it up and down. If there is no resistance, it is worn out. If there is some resistance, compare it to the feel of a new unit for that same vehicle position to judge the loss of control.

43.5   Front Wheel Bearings

Front wheel bearings that are too tight, too loose, or damaged can cause handling problems. Jack up the front of the vehicle so that the front wheels are off the ground. Rotate each front tire by hand. It should spin without any rough sounds. If a wheel turns hard, the bearings may be adjusted too tight. If it is rough sounding, it may be damaged. Check for excessive looseness by holding the top and bottom of the wheel

and rocking it in and out. Too much play here may be due to loose wheel bearings.

43.6   PREVENTIVE MAINTENANCE

There are two common preventive maintenance operations for the front suspension system. The first is a periodic lubrication of the ball joints. The second is a periodic cleaning and lubrication of the wheel bearings.

43.7   Ball Joint Lubrication

The front suspension ball joints on most new automobiles are semipermanently lubricated with a special lubricant at the factory. They should be inspected every six months for damage to the seals, which can result in loss or contamination of lubricant. Clean dirt and lubricant from the outside surface of seals to permit a good inspection. Replace damaged seals or joints immediately to prevent contamination of lubricant or damage to parts. Lubricate ball joints if necessary. A lube plug is provided in the upper and lower ball joint housing.

Remove lube plugs (Fig. 43-5) and temporarily install lube fittings. Use a manual lubrication gun with the recommended lubricant. The manual lubricaton gun delivers lubricant at low pressure (6 to 8 psi or 41 to 44 kPa) to avoid blowing out the ball joint lubricant seals. Guns which deliver lubricant at high pressure could rupture ball joint seals. Apply lubricant slowly. There should be no visual evidence of lubricant escaping past seals. When lubrication is done, remove lube fittings and install lube plugs.

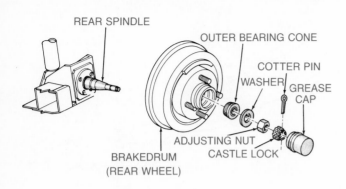

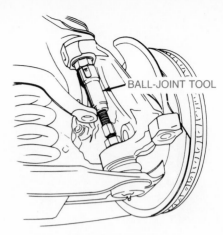

Fig. 43-6 Repacking a non-drive rear wheel bearing. (Chrysler Corporation)

Fig. 43-7 Disconnecting the ball joint from the steering knuckle. (Chevrolet Motor Division, GMC)

43.8   Wheel Bearing Lubrication

Non-drive wheel bearings should be repacked at the recommended intervals or at the time of normal brake service. Lubricant should not be added to the bearings. Raise the vehicle so that the non-drive wheels are free of the floor. Remove the wheel cover, grease cap, cotter pin, nut lock, and bearing adjusting nut. Remove the thrust washer and outer bearing cone. If the vehicle has drum brakes, slide off the wheel hub and drum assemble.

If the vehicle has disc brakes, remove bolts that attach the disc brake caliper assembly to the steering knuckle. Slowly slide the caliper assembly up and away from the brake disc and support the caliper assembly on the steering knuckle arm. Do not let the caliper assembly hang by the brake hose, or the brake hose may be damaged.

Drive out the inner grease seal and remove the inner bearing from the hub. Clean the hub and drum assembly and the bearings in kerosene, mineral spirits, or other similar cleaning fluids. Do not dry the bearings by air spinning. Examine bearing cups for pitting or other damage. If cups or races are damaged, remove them from the hub with a soft steel drift positioned in the slots in the hub. Bearing cup areas in the hub should be smooth. Scored or raised metal could keep the cups from seating against the shoulders in the hub. The bearing cones and rollers should have smooth, unbroken surfaces without any pits. The ends of the rollers and both cone flanges should also be smooth and free from chipping or other damage.

Force the recommended lubricant between bearing cone rollers by hand or repack with a suitable bearing packer. Install the inner cone and a new seal,

with the lip of the seal facing inward. Position the seal flush with the end of the hub. The seal flange may be damaged if a seal driving tool is not used. Clean the spindle and apply a light coating of wheel bearing lubricant over the polished surfaces. Install the wheel, tire, and drum assembly on the spindle. Install the outer bearing cone, thrust washer, and adjusting nut.

Adjust the bearing by tightening the adjustment nut on the spindle (Fig. 43-6) to seat the grease seal and the bearings. Then back it off. Use an inch-pound torque wrench to tighten the nut to specifications. Then back off the nut to a ''just loose'' position.

Tapered roller bearings used on most vehicles have a slightly loose feel when properly adjusted. Tapered roller bearings must never be preloaded. The steady thrust on roller ends which comes from preloading can damage them.

Install the nut lock and/or cotter key. The installation of the grease and hub caps completes the job.

43.9   SUSPENSION SYSTEM SERVICE

Typical suspension service jobs include replacing ball joints, sagging springs, shock absorbers, cartridges, and MacPherson struts.

43.10   Ball Joint and Spring Service

When measurements indicate that ball joints are worn excessively, they must be replaced. Raise the vehicle on a hoist and remove front wheels and brake assemblies to get to the suspension components. Remove the shock absorber and stabilizer bar (if used).

Before the ball joint nuts can be removed, the

Fig. 43-8 New ball joints may be attached with bolts. (Chevrolet Motor Division, GMC)

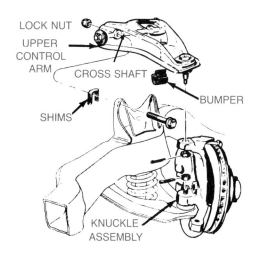

Fig. 43-9 Removing an upper control arm. (Chevrolet Motor Division, GMC)

coil spring must be contained with a spring compressor tool. **Safety Caution: The coil spring between the two control arms is under tremendous pressure. When the control arms are disconnected, the spring could fly out, causing extensive damage or injury.**

With the spring compressed, the ball joint or joints may be removed. The ball joint is held in the steering knuckle assembly by a tapered stud with a nut and cotter key. Remove the cotter key and nut. Since the stud is tapered, it must be pressed out of the steering knuckle with a special tool (Fig. 43-7).

Next remove the ball joint from the control arm. If the ball joints are riveted to the control arm, rivet heads must be ground or chiseled off. Replacement ball joints usually are held with bolts. Remove the worn ball joint and install a new one (Fig. 43-8).

If measurements showed that a spring height was less than specifications, replace the spring. Disconnect the control arm at the ball joint end as explained above, keeping the spring compressed for safety. Remove the old spring and install another. Coil springs should always be replaced in pairs, either in front or rear. This ensures that alignment angles and spring action will be correct.

When ball joints are serviced, inspect the bushings that support the control arms to the frame. Worn or loose bushings must be replaced. After the control arm is disconnected at the ball joint end, remove it by disconnecting if from the frame.

The control arm may be mounted to the frame by pivot bolts or by lock nuts on a cross shaft. Remove these bolts or nuts to remove the control arm (Fig. 43-9).

When the control arm is removed, the bushing assembly can be replaced. The bushing is generally held in the control arm with a press fit. Special tools are available to remove and replace the bushing (Fig. 43-10).

Reassembly of the control arms, spring, and ball joints is about the reverse of disassembly. Mount the control arms to the frame. Mount the spring into position with a compressor in place. Attach the ball joints to the steering knuckle with nuts and cotter keys. Torque all nuts and bolts to specifications. Remove the spring compressor and replace the shock absorber. Replacing the brake and wheel assembly completes the job.

43.11   Shock Absorber Service

When testing indicates that a shock absorber is defective, it must be replaced. Support the vehicle on a jack or hoist by the control arms or rear axle. Carefully observe the position of the original shock absorbers and the location of all mounting parts. Three types of mountings are commonly used (Fig. 43-11).

Be careful not to twist the end off of mounting pins or studs. If the nuts are rusted, apply penetrating oil to the threads and allow a few minutes for the oil to penetrate before removing. If the rust is so bad that penetrating oil will not do the job, use a nut splitter, taking care that no damage is done to the threads on the stud.

Be sure to read and carefully follow the instructions printed on the parts package or on the special instruction sheet which may be supplied with the new unit. Improper installation will cause many problems. Check the mounting parts supplied with the new unit to make sure that all parts needed are on hand.

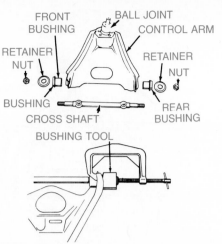

Fig. 43-10 Replacing control arm bushings. (Chevrolet Motor Division, GMC)

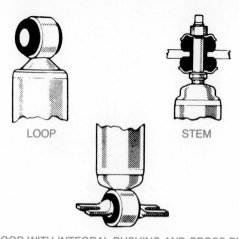

LOOP WITH INTEGRAL BUSHING AND CROSS PIN

Fig. 43-11 Types of shock absorber mountings.

43.12 MacPherson Strut Service

A MacPherson strut may have a problem with a leaking or worn out shock absorber cartridge or a weak coil spring. In either case, the strut must be removed from the car for service. To remove the strut, loosen the wheel lug nuts and raise the car with a jack. Support the car on safety jack stands. Remove the wheel and tire assembly.

If the strut is attached to the lower control arm with a ball joint, remove the brake caliper and tie it up to the frame. Remove the bolts holding the ball joint assembly to the strut. If the strut is bolted to the steering knuckle, remove the cam adjusting bolt, through bolt and brake hose to damper bracket retaining screw. Remove the strut damper to fender shield mounting nut washer assemblies and remove the strut assembly as shown in Figure 43-12.

Install a strut coil spring compressing tool on the spring and compress it enough to get clearance between the spring and retainer (Fig. 43-13). Mark the spring for installation on the same side of the car. **Safety Caution: Do not attempt to disassemble a strut without a strut spring compressing tool as the spring could fly out causing injury.**

The next step is to remove the nut from the end of the strut rod. Some struts have flats on the end of the rod for holding it stationary with a small wrench while turning the nut. If the struts do not have these flats, use an air impact wrench to remove the nut.

Disassemble the spring mount assembly and remove the coil spring. Remove the cartridge hold-

ing nut from the strut tube. A special wrench is usually required to remove this nut. With the nut removed, the cartridge can be lifted out of the tube (Fig. 43-14).

Insert the new cartridge into the tube, install the cartridge retaining nut and torque it to specifications. Compress the coil spring and install it over the strut tube. Install the coil spring retaining assembly and strut rod nut. Torque the nut to specifications.

To install the strut on the car, position the strut into the fender reinforcement and install the retaining nut and washer assemblies. Torque the nuts to specifications. Bolt the ball joint to the strut or install upper and lower through bolts. Line up marks made during disassembly. Torque the bolts to specifications. Install the brake caliper and torque the caliper holding bolts if removed. Install the wheel and tire assembly, and torque the wheel nuts to specifications. Lower the car and road test for proper suspension action.

NEW TERMS

Ball joint play The free space in the ball joint that is measured to determine wear.

Spring height A measurement taken on the suspension to determine whether the springs need replacing.

Visual wear indicator A device on a ball joint used to determine visually whether the ball joint needs replacing.

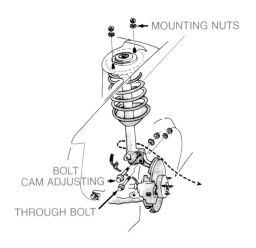

Fig. 43-12 Removing the MacPherson strut assembly. (Chrysler Corporation)

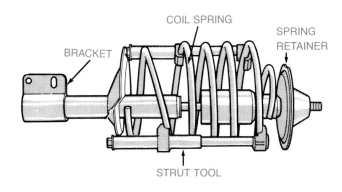

Fig. 43-13 Compressing the coil spring with a strut tool. (Chrysler Corporation)

Wheel bearing packing Removing the old lubricant in a wheel bearing and replacing it with new lubricant.

CHAPTER REVIEW

1. Why is suspension system operation important to safety?

2. List four problems that indicate suspension system trouble.

3. Describe how to check a ball joint with a dial indicator.

4. What is a visual wear indicator?

5. What is spring height?

6. Explain how to check for spring height.

7. List three common reasons for shock absorber failure.

8. Explain how to check for shock absorber operation by driving the automobile.

9. Explain how to check shock absorber operation on a hoist.

10. List two signs of front wheel bearing trouble.

11. Describe how to lubricate semipermanently lubricated ball joints.

12. Explain the procedure for packing and adjusting front wheel bearings.

13. What kind of front wheel bearings are used on most automobiles?

14. Explain how a ball joint and spring is removed and replaced.

15. Describe how to remove and replace a shock absorber.

DISCUSSION TOPICS AND ACTIVITIES

1. Study a collection of used wheel bearings found in the shop. Which ones could be used and which ones should be replaced?

2. Look up the spring height specifications for the automobile of your choice. Measure the spring height and compare it to the specifications. Is the spring in satisfactory condition?

3. Test the shock absorbers on the vehicle of your choice. Do they need replacing?

Steering and Wheel Alignment

CHAPTER PREVIEW

The steering system allows the driver to control the direction of the automobile by means of two major components: the steering gears, which multiply the driver's effort at the steering wheel; and the steering linkage, which connects the gearbox to the front wheels. How well the system works depends on proper alignment of the front wheels for directional control and ease of steering.

OBJECTIVES

After studying this chapter, you should be able to do the following:

1. Explain the operation of the steering gears.
2. Understand the purpose and operation of power steering.
3. Describe the purpose and operation of the steering linkage.
4. Explain the operation of the collapsible steering column.
5. List and describe the different wheel alignment angles.

44.1   STEERING GEARS

The steering wheel is attached to a shaft which runs toward the front of the automobile and enters the steering gearbox. There are two gears in this box, one attached to the steering shaft and the other attached to the linkage hooked to the front wheels.

The steering gears (Figs. 44-1 and 44-2) have two functions: to change the rotary motion of the steering wheel into straight line motion that will move the steering linkage and to provide a gear reduction that will make the automobile easier to steer. A small effort at the steering wheel is multiplied into a larger effort at the steering linkage. The amount of gear reduction is described as the steering ratio. A typical ratio of 18:1 means that in order to turn the front wheels 1 degree the steering wheel has to be rotated 18 degrees. A light sports car with "quick" steering may have a ratio of 12:1, while a large, heavy automobile may have a ratio of 20:1.

44.2   Recirculating Ball Steering Gear

Several types of gears are used in steering gear boxes. Most large automobiles use a worm gear, which looks like a large bolt thread on the end of the steering shaft. Turning the steering wheel turns the worm shaft, which causes a large nut in mesh with the large threads to move up and down the worm. The nut has teeth which mesh with the other gear in the gearbox, the sector gear, so that it also rotates. The sector gear, attached to the Pitman shaft, connected to the steering linkage, completes the gear reduction process that increases the steering wheel's leverage. To reduce friction and steering effort, small ball bearings may be used between the worm and nut. The bearings ride in the threads of the worm and mesh with the nut. This type of steering is called a recirculating ball steering gear (Fig. 44-3).

44.3   Rack and Pinion Steering

Many small automobiles use a rack and pinion steering system (Fig. 44-4), in which the steering

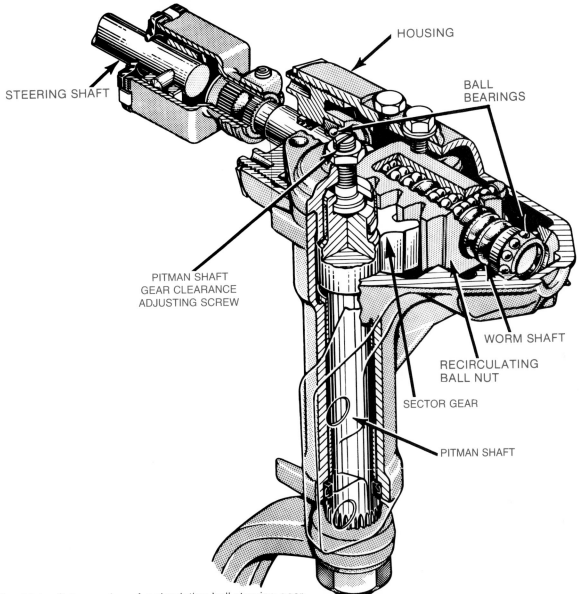

Fig. 44-1 Cutaway view of recirculating ball steering gear.
(Chevrolet Motor Division, GMC)

Labels in Fig. 44-1:
- STEERING SHAFT
- HOUSING
- BALL BEARINGS
- PITMAN SHAFT GEAR CLEARANCE ADJUSTING SCREW
- WORM SHAFT
- RECIRCULATING BALL NUT
- SECTOR GEAR
- PITMAN SHAFT

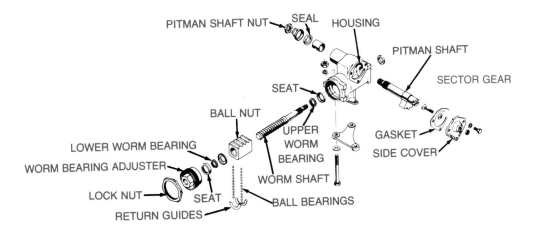

Fig. 44-2 Exploded view of recirculating ball steering gear.
(American Motors Corporation)

Labels in Fig. 44-2:
- PITMAN SHAFT NUT
- SEAL
- HOUSING
- PITMAN SHAFT
- SECTOR GEAR
- SEAT
- BALL NUT
- UPPER WORM BEARING
- GASKET
- SIDE COVER
- LOWER WORM BEARING
- WORM BEARING ADJUSTER
- WORM SHAFT
- LOCK NUT
- SEAT
- BALL BEARINGS
- RETURN GUIDES

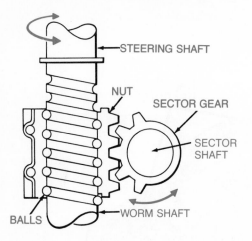

Fig. 44-3 Recirculating ball steering gear.

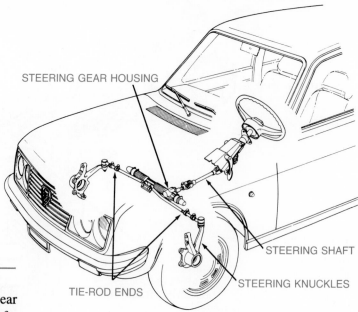

Fig. 44-4 Rack and pinion steering system. (Lancia)

wheel and shaft are connected to a small pinion gear (Fig. 44-5). This gear is in mesh with teeth on top of a long bar, called a rack. Turning the steering wheel turns the pinion gear, which moves the rack back and forth. The rack is attached to the steering linkage that turns the wheels. The main advantage of the rack and pinion system is that it takes up very little space, making it especially suitable for compact vehicles.

44.4 POWER STEERING

Most automobiles use a power-assisted steering system to reduce the steering effort for the driver. The power steering system requires a pump, usually engine driven with a belt, and connected by hydraulic lines to a cylinder or directly to the steering gearbox (Fig. 44-6).

With power assist steering systems, the engagement of the gears is the same as it is for the manual gear, but hydraulic fluid pressure does the work of turning the wheels. Fluid under pressure is supplied by the power assist pump, driven by the engine. Fluid direction is controlled by a valve in the steering gear. When the steering wheel is turned, the power steering pump fluid pressure output is delivered to the steering to turn the wheels.

44.5 VARIABLE RATIO STEERING

Most power steering and some manual units use a variable ratio gear system. Variable ratio steering is made possible by a sector gear that uses a short tooth on either side of a long center tooth. A constant ratio gear has three teeth of equal length (Fig. 44-7).

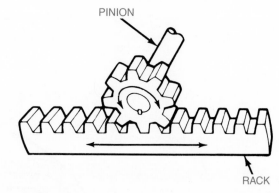

NOTE: ACTUAL GEARS HAVE HELICAL OR CURVED TEETH.

Fig. 44-5 Rack and pinion gears. (Chrysler Corporation)

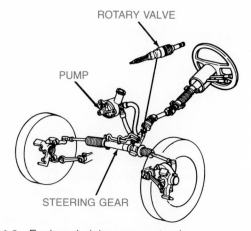

Fig. 44-6 Rack and pinion power steering. (Ford Motor Company)

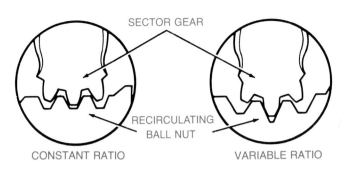

Fig. 44-7 Variable ratio steering. (American Motors Corporation)

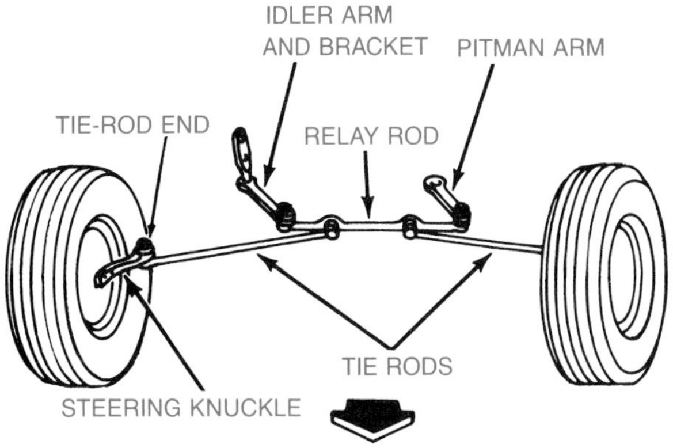

Fig. 44-8 Steering linkage for a recirculating ball steering gear. (American Motors Corporation)

The sector gear works like a series of levers. The sector gear will turn the Pitman arm the same number of degrees with each tooth in the sector. To increase or decrease the ratio, it is only necessary to change the length of the sector gear teeth. Therefore, a low-ratio sector (smaller radius with shorter teeth) causes greater Pitman arm movement than a high-ratio sector with its longer teeth and greater leverage. The variable ratio sector is one long, high-ratio lever at the center, with two lower-ratio levers on each side for left and right turns.

Since only the tip of the long center tooth is in contact with the recirculating ball nut when the front wheels are straight, the first movement of the ball nut in either direction causes a small movement of the sector and Pitman arm. The reason is the high ratio that is caused by the long lever.

44.6   STEERING LINKAGE

With rack and pinion steering systems the rack is connected directly to each of the steering knuckles by tie rods. With recirculating ball steering systems, a series of linkages are necessary to transfer the motion from the steering gear to each of the steering knuckles.

The recirculating ball steering linkage (Fig. 44-8), which connects the steering gearbox Pitman arm to the front wheels, consists of a number of round rods. These rods are connected with a socket arrangement, similar to a ball joint, called a tie-rod end. The tie-rod ends allow the linkage to move back and forth freely so the steering effort will not interfere with the vehicles's up-and-down motion as the wheels go over rough roads. The Pitman arm is attached to a relay rod, which moves when the steering wheel is turned. The relay rod is supported at one end by its connection to the Pitman arm and at the other end by an idler arm mounted to the automobile frame. The idler arm moves back and forth with the relay rod, connected at each end to a tie rod. The tie rods are attached to each wheel's steering knuckle assembly so that movement of the steering wheel through the steering box and linkage results in movements of the front wheels.

As the driver makes a left or right turn, the wheel on the inside of the turn travels through a sharper corner than the one on the outside because of the way the steering linkage is designed.

44.7   STEERING COLUMN

All late model automobiles use a collapsible steering column. In a hard front-end collision, the engine and steering linkage are often forced against the steering gearbox, pushing the shaft into the automobile. At the same time, a driver whose seat belt is not fastened will be thrown against the steering wheel and steering shaft. To prevent serious injury, the steering shaft, and the tube or column which contains it, are made from two pieces that fit together like an extended telescope. During a collision, the column and shaft absorb the energy and the shaft collapses back into the column (Fig. 44-9).

44.8   WHEEL ALIGNMENT

Wheel alignment is the position of the front and rear wheels in relation to the suspension. Proper alignment

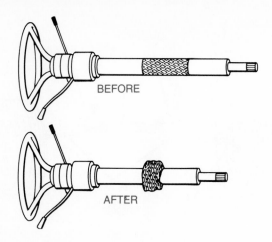

Fig. 44-9 Collapsible steering column.

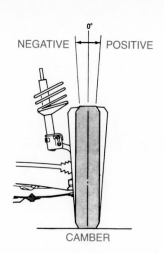

Fig. 44-10 Camber. (Chrysler Corporation)

makes the automobile easy to turn and keeps it stable at high speeds. Incorrect wheel alignment makes a vehicle difficult to steer so that it wanders all over the road. Wheels that are out of alignment also cause very rapid tire wear.

Some alignment factors are designed into the suspension system. Others are designed to be adjusted. The process of measuring and adjusting the wheel positioning or wheel alignment, takes into account camber, caster, steering axis inclination, toe-in, and turning radius.

44.9   Camber

Camber is the tilting of the top of the wheels inward or outward, toward or away from the automobile (Fig. 44-10). If the wheels are tilted outward, they have positive camber. If they are tilted inward, they have negative camber. Properly adjusted wheels have a slightly positive camber to begin with. When the driver and passengers get in the automobile, their weight, through the suspension, straightens out the wheels. The objective is to adjust camber so the wheels will line up straight when the automobile is moving.

Most manufacturers specify a very small camber, usually only two or three degrees from straight up and down. This slight tilt cannot be seen with the naked eye but can be measured with wheel alignment equipment. Camber is usually adjusted with spacers, called shims, that position the top control arm. If camber is not adjusted properly, one edge of the tire will support more load than the other, causing rapid wear on that side.

44.10   Caster

Caster is the backward or forward tilt of the ball joint at the top of the wheel to provide directional control. If the top ball joint is positioned behind the bottom one, the caster is positive. If the top ball joint is positioned to the front of the bottom one, the caster is negative.

When a piece of furniture on casters is pushed, the casters turn on their pivots and line up to guide the furniture in a straight line (Fig. 44-11). Furniture casters line up because of the way they are mounted in their pivots. Each caster's point of contact with the floor is behind the point where the furniture's weight bears so that, when the furniture is pushed, some resistance is created between the floor and the wheel. The weight ahead of the wheel causes it to line up directly behind the direction of the push.

The same principle applies to the wheels of an automobile (Fig. 44-12). If the upper ball joint (on short long arm suspensions) or strut mount (on MacPherson strut units) is moved backward, the automobile has positive caster. The weight of the automobile is supported through the strut mount and ball joint to the wheel and applied ahead of the tire's point of contact with the road. The front wheels tend to stay lined up in a straight line, just like the furniture caster.

Older automobiles depended on positive caster for stability. When wider tires appeared which tended to provide their own stability, manufacturers began to specify less positive caster. It was also discovered that stability could be achieved with another ball joint relationship, leading some manufacturers to choose a

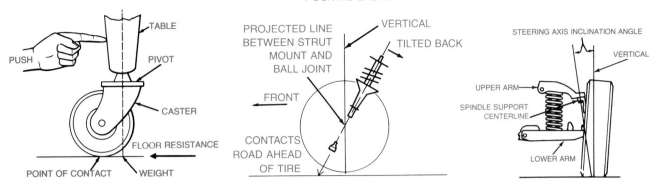

POSITIVE CASTER

TABLE / PIVOT / PUSH / CASTER / FLOOR RESISTANCE / POINT OF CONTACT / WEIGHT

Fig. 44-11 Furniture caster moves wheels in straight line.

PROJECTED LINE BETWEEN STRUT MOUNT AND BALL JOINT / FRONT / CONTACTS ROAD AHEAD OF TIRE / VERTICAL / TILTED BACK

Fig. 44-12 Caster effect on front wheels of automobile. (Chrysler Corporation)

STEERING AXIS INCLINATION ANGLE / VERTICAL / UPPER ARM / SPINDLE SUPPORT CENTERLINE / LOWER ARM

Fig. 44-13 Steering axis inclination. (Moog Automotive, Inc.)

negative caster setting. Negative caster does not provide directional control, but it makes steering easier. If the wheel contact areas are not trailing behind the weight, it is easier to turn the automobile.

Caster is always measured during wheel alignment. Incorrect caster does not cause tire wear, but it can make the automobile wander to the left or the right. The driver must fight the steering wheel to keep the vehicle in a straight line and may also experience hard steering.

44.11 Steering Axis Inclination

Steering axis inclination is the inward slant (at the top) of the steering knuckle from the vertical. This inclination tends to reduce road shock on the steering system by allowing the steering system centerline to intersect the tire centerline near the point where the tire contacts the road. The inward slant or inclination of the steering knuckle tends to keep the wheels straight ahead (Fig. 44-13). The reason is that when the front wheels are straight ahead, the steering knuckle spindles are practically horizontal. As the wheels are turned away from straight ahead, the outer ends of the spindles tend to lower or get closer to the ground. However, because the spindles are fixed in the hub assembly, they cannot get closer to the ground. So the spindles force the steering knuckles to raise the front of the vehicle.

After a turn is completed, and force applied to the steering wheel is released, the weight of the vehicle on the spindles tends to return the front wheels to a straight ahead position. Steering axis inclination is not adjustable.

44.12 Toe-in

The front wheels of a typical automobile at rest are toed in, which means they are a fraction of an inch closer together at their front edges than at their rear edges (Fig. 44-14).

When the vehicle is moving, the wheels should roll perfectly parallel to each other to keep tire wear to a minimum. As the vehicle starts out, the wheels tend to take up slack in the steering system and turn outward. Because of the toe-in, this outward turn positions the wheels in a straight ahead position.

Toe-in is measured during wheel alignment and adjusted by making the steering tie rods longer or shorter. The tie rods have threaded sleeves which make this a relatively easy adjustment. If the toe-in is not set correctly, the tires will wear rapidly as they are scuffed across the pavement.

44.13 Turning Radius

During a turn, the wheel on the inside goes through a sharper corner than the one on the outside. This is usually described as turning radius (Fig. 14-15). The difference, usually only about three degrees, results from the way the steering linkage is designed. Turning radius is checked during wheel alignment. If it is incorrect, it cannot be adjusted. New suspension parts may have to be installed to correct it. A vehicle with incorrect turning radius will drag the wheels around a corner, causing very fast tire wear.

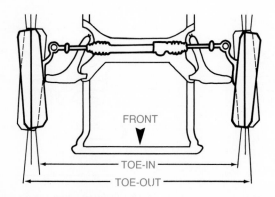

Fig. 44-14   Front wheel toe.

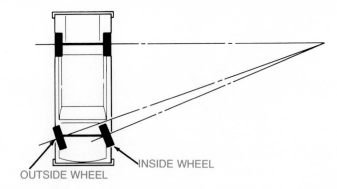

Fig. 44-15   Turning radius.

NEW TERMS

Camber   The inward or outward tilt of the top of a vehicle's tires.

Caster   The backward or forward tilt of the centerline of the ball joints.

Power steering   A steering system that uses hydraulic pressure developed by a pump to decrease driver steering effort.

Rack and pinion steering   A type of steering that uses a toothed rack connected to the wheels and a pinion gear connected to the steering wheel.

Steering axis inclination   An angle formed by the centerline of the ball joints and the vertical centerline.

Steering column   The housing that supports the steering shaft.

Steering gears   Gears in the steering gear box used to turn the front wheels.

Steering gearbox   The housing for the steering gears.

Steering linkage   Linkage that connects the steering gears to the front wheels.

Toe-in   The condition in which the wheels are closer together at the front edge than at the rear edge.

Turning radius   The relative angles of the two front wheels during a turn.

Variable ratio steering   A steering gear that provides a different ratio during different parts of a turn.

Wheel alignment   The position of the front wheels in relation to the suspension.

CHAPTER REVIEW

1. What is the purpose of the steering system?
2. List the two jobs of the steering gears.
3. What is the steering ratio?
4. What are the names of the gears in the steering gearbox?
5. Describe a rack and pinion steering gear.
6. Explain the operation of a power steering unit.
7. What is variable ratio steering?
8. What does the steering linkage do?
9. What is a tie rod end?
10. Describe a collapsible steering column.
11. What is wheel alignment?
12. Define camber.
13. Define caster.
14. Define steering axis inclination.
15. What is toe-in?

DISCUSSION TOPICS AND ACTIVITIES

1. Use a shop cutaway of a steering gearbox to identify parts and explain the flow of power.
2. Turn the front wheels of an automobile on a hoist. Study the operation of the steering linkage. Can you identify the parts?
3. Make a list of all the wheel alignment angles. Describe what they do.

Steering and Wheel Alignment Service

CHAPTER PREVIEW

Steering and wheel alignment problems have become very important to automobile owners and mechanics in recent years. The growing number of highways that allow high-speed driving has made steering and wheel alignment critical to driving comfort and safety. In this chapter we will present the major steering system and wheel alignment service jobs.

OBJECTIVES

After studying this chapter, you should be able to do the following:

1. List the steps in finding the cause of tire wear and wander or pull.
2. List the steps in finding the cause of brake pull and hard steering.
3. Explain the preventive maintenance procedures used on steering systems.
4. Describe the service procedures used on the steering system.
5. Describe the procedure for a wheel alignment.

45.1   TROUBLESHOOTING

The most common signs of steering and wheel alignment problems are too much tire wear, wander or pull, braking pull, and hard steering.

The signs of alignment problems are similar to signs of brake, steering, and suspension problems. The mechanic's first job is to make sure that the problem is not something that can be traced to brakes, steering, suspension, or wheel balance.

Before checking wheel alignment, thoroughly inspect and correct, if necessary, brake and front suspension component condition, tire inflation, and wheel balance. Otherwise, the alignment measurements can be incorrect.

45.2   Tire Wear

Tire wear patterns are clues to wheel misalignment. Using hands and eyes to examine tire treads will tell alot about wheel alignment and the owner's driving habits. Look for these conditions of tire wear: outside shoulder, inside shoulder, both shoulders, center treads, feathered wear, and cupped or dished treads (Fig. 45-1).

If there is too much wear on either the inside or outside shoulder, it is almost certainly caused by incorrect camber. Too much wear on the outer shoulder of the tire usually indicates too much positive camber. When the positive camber is too great, the wheel is tipped outward and too much weight or load is carried by the outside shoulder of the tread. Wear is greatly increased.

Too much wear on the inside shoulder usually points to too much negative camber. When negative camber is too great, the wheel is tipped inward and too much of the weight or load is supported by the tilted-under inside shoulder of the tread. This causes rapid tire wear.

If there is too much wear on both shoulders of properly inflated front tires, the probable cause is sideslip, resulting from speedy cornering. Cornering wear cannot be stopped by an adjustment. Changing the driver's cornering habits is the only answer to this problem.

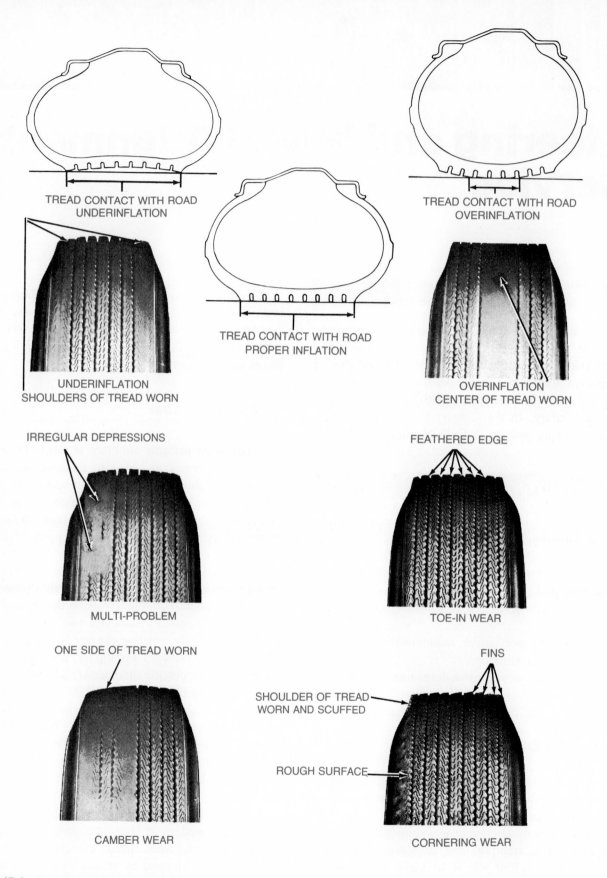

TREAD CONTACT WITH ROAD
UNDERINFLATION

UNDERINFLATION
SHOULDERS OF TREAD WORN

TREAD CONTACT WITH ROAD
PROPER INFLATION

TREAD CONTACT WITH ROAD
OVERINFLATION

OVERINFLATION
CENTER OF TREAD WORN

IRREGULAR DEPRESSIONS

MULTI-PROBLEM

FEATHERED EDGE

TOE-IN WEAR

ONE SIDE OF TREAD WORN

CAMBER WEAR

FINS

SHOULDER OF TREAD
WORN AND SCUFFED

ROUGH SURFACE

CORNERING WEAR

Fig. 45-1 Tire wear and causes. (Pontiac Motor Division, GMC)

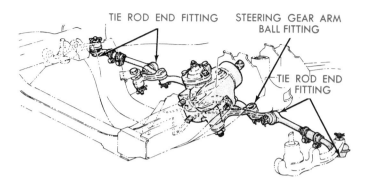

Fig. 45-2 Steering linkage lubrication. (Chrysler Corporation)

If the tire is soft and shows wear at both shoulders, underinflation is the cause. If it is a rear wheel, suspect underinflation rather than cornering wear. Rear wheel camber does not change in a turn. Correcting the tire pressure is usually the way to fix this problem. However, in some cases, the tire may be overloaded. Anytime a correct road contact area cannot be obtained within the recommended inflation pressure limits, the tires may be overloaded.

Too much wear at the center of the tire tread is a sure sign of overinflation.

A feathered wear pattern is a sign of a toe problem. By passing the palm of your hand across the tread of the tire, you can easily detect a cross wear or feathered pattern, even before you are able to see it. One edge of each tread will feel rounded; the other, sharp. If you feel the sharp edge as your hand moves toward the center of the vehicle, the wheel is not toed-in enough. If you feel the sharp edge as you move your hand away from the center of the vehicle, the wheel is toed-in too much.

Irregular or dished depressions can be caused by many problems, often acting together. Worn front suspension components, misalignment, and wheel imbalance are the most common causes.

45.3 Wander or Pull

Wander or pull is the tendency of a vehicle to turn to one side or the other when the driver is trying to move straight ahead. There will always be a tendency to pull on a slanted or crowned road, so the vehicle must be road tested on a stretch of straight, uncrowned highway. If the vehicle does tend to pull from side to side and there is no sign of uneven tire

wear or unequal tire pressure, the cause is probably incorrect camber or unequal caster.

Like caster, steering axis inclination is designed to increase directional stability and return the wheels to the straight ahead position after a turn. If steering axis inclination is not correct, the vehicle may pull or wander.

45.4 Brake Pull

If the vehicle tends to pull or swerve to one side when brakes are applied on an uncrowned road, check the possibility of uneven caster or too much negative caster. First, though, do not overlook the possibility of defective brakes or an underinflated tire.

45.5 Hard Steering

Hard steering may be caused by an inoperative power steering system or a manual system that is out of adjustment or low on lubricant. Hard steering can also be caused by the alignment if the vehicle has excessive positive camber, excessive steering axis inclination, or improper turning radius.

45.6 PREVENTIVE MAINTENANCE

Manual steering systems require periodic attention. The steering gearbox is filled with a lubricant to minimize friction and prevent wear. While regular changes of the lubricant are not required, inspection of the lubricant level is. Remove the filler plug in the gearbox and inspect the level. The lubricant should cover the worm gear. If it is below that level, refill with recommended lubricant.

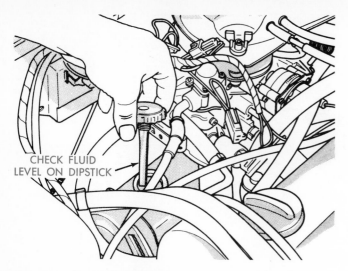

Fig. 45-3 Checking power steering fluid. (Chrysler Corporation)

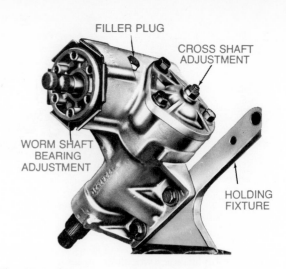

Fig. 45-4 Steering gear adjustments. (Chrysler Corporation)

The tie rod end ball joints (Fig. 45-2) should be inspected at least twice a year or whenever the automobile is serviced for other reasons. Damaged joints or seals should be replaced to prevent leakage or contamination of the grease. They are semipermanently lubricated at the factory with a special grease. In most cases, plugs must be removed and grease fittings installed. When relubricating the steering linkage, use only special long-life chassis grease intended for this purpose.

Power steering systems must be checked periodically for proper reservoir fluid level. A dipstick is often attached to the filler cap (Fig. 45-3) for this purpose. Before removing the reservoir cover, wipe the outside of the case and cover it so dirt cannot fall into the reservoir. Add the proper fluid to bring the level to the required height.

45.7 STEERING SERVICE

The most common manual steering gearbox service is an adjustment (Fig. 45-4) of the worm bearing preload and the sector gear mesh. The worm bearing preload adjustment is controlled by the worm thrust bearing adjuster, which threads into the housing at the upper end of the wormshaft.

The sector shaft adjusting screw, located in the housing cover, raises or lowers the shaft for proper mesh load between the tapered teeth of the sector gear and the tapered teeth of the ball nut. This adjustment can be accurately made only after proper worm bearing preload has been established.

These adjustments are normally made with the gearbox in the vehicle but disconnected from the steering linkage. A torque wrench attached to the

steering shaft nut determines when the adjustment is correct.

Worn or damaged tie-rod ends require replacement. Remove tie-rod ends from the steering knuckle with a puller or wedge. Remove clamps on the rod, screw out old tie-rod ends, and screw in new ones. The toe-in must be adjusted after tie rod replacement.

45.8 WHEEL ALIGNMENT SERVICE

Adjust camber and caster on a short long arm suspension by moving the suspension control arms. The most common system uses shims between the top control arm and the frame (Fig. 45-5). Shims may be added, subtracted, or transferred to change the readings.

Some short long arm systems use an eccentric mount for the control arm (Fig. 45-6). A bolt is loosened and an eccentric turned to change the position of the control arm.

Many MacPherson strut suspensions do not have any adjustments for camber or caster. If measurements show that camber or caster is out of adjustment, the strut or mounting parts are probably bent and will need to be replaced. MacPherson strut systems that are adjustable use a cam bolt to attach the strut assembly to the steering knuckle. To adjust camber, loosen the bolt and turn the cam adjuster (Fig. 45-7). When the adjustment is correct, tighten the bolt to specifications.

Adjust toe-in by turning the tie rod adjusting sleeves or tubes (Fig. 45-8). Lengthening or shortening the tie rods increases toe-in or toe-out.

Camber on the rear wheels has the same effect as on the front. The suspension is designed with a

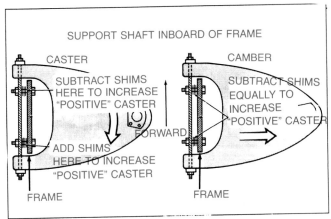

Fig. 45-5 Camber and caster adjustment shims on top control arm. (Chevrolet Motor Division, GMC)

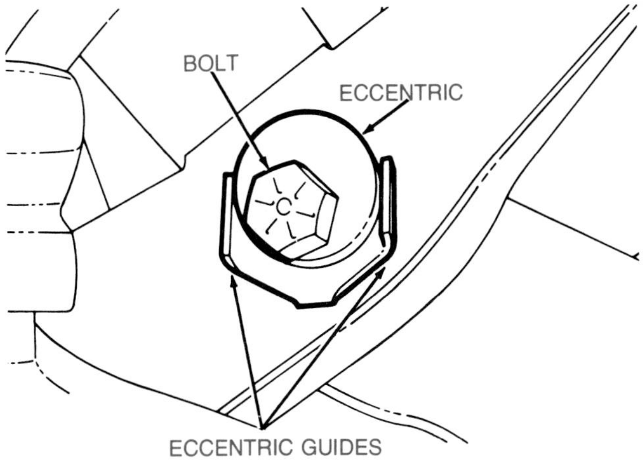

Fig. 45-6 Eccentric used to adjust camber. (American Motors Corporation)

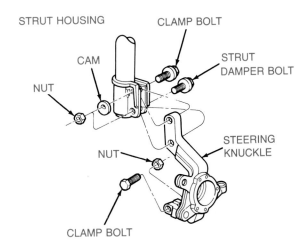

Fig. 45-7 MacPherson strut camber adjustment. (Chrysler Corporation)

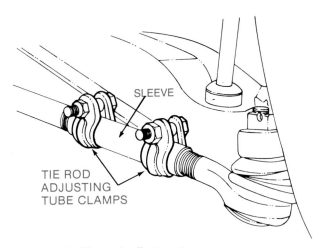

Fig. 45-8 The rod adjustments. (Ford Motor Company)

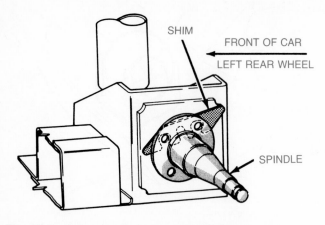

Fig. 45-9 Camber shim on the rear suspension of a front-wheel drive car. (Chrysler Corporation)

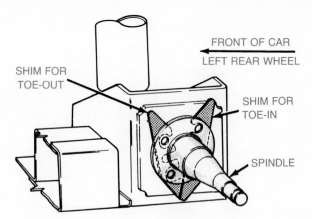

Fig. 45-10 Shims used to set toe on rear suspension of front-wheel drive car. (Chrysler Corporation)

slightly negative camber. This tilts the tops of the wheels in and the bottoms out slightly for improved cornering stability. Camber is adjusted by placing shims between the rear axle mounting plate and brake backing plate. (Fig. 45-9).

Rear wheels are designed with zero to slight toe-in, depending on the vehicle. This provides straight running as driving forces tend to push back the rear spindles. Correct toe is important for increasing tire life. It is also adjusted with shims placed behind the backing plate (Fig. 45-10).

NEW TERMS

Brake pull   A condition in which the vehicle turns each time the brakes are applied.
Sector gear mesh   One of the adjustments of a steering gear.
Wander   A condition in which the vehicle does not follow a straight line.
Worm bearing preload   One of the adjustments of a steering gear.

CHAPTER REVIEW

1. List four of the most common problems of steering and wheel alignment.

2. What can cause tire wear on the outer shoulder?
3. What is the cause of tire wear on the inside shoulder?
4. What is the cause of tire wear on both shoulders?
5. What is the cause of a feathered wear pattern?
6. What can cause vehicle wander or pull?
7. What can cause brake pull?
8. What can cause hard steering?
9. Describe how to check the steering gear lubricant.
10. Explain how to lubricate tie rod ends.
11. Describe how to adjust a steering gearbox.
12. List three wheel alignment angles that are adjustable.
13. How is camber adjusted on a MacPherson strut?
14. How is caster adjusted on a short long arm suspension?
15. How is toe-in adjusted?

DISCUSSION TOPICS AND ACTIVITIES

1. Study the tires on the automobile you drive. Compare the wear pattern with the examples in Figure 45-1. Can you find any evidence of a problem?
2. Check the play in the steering system on the automobile you drive. Compare with the specifications.
3. Look up the wheel alignment specifications for the vehicle you drive.

The Brake System

CHAPTER PREVIEW

Stopping a 3,000-pound automobile moving at highway speed is no easy job. The heart of the brake system is a master cylinder assembly connected to the brake pedal. Pushing on the brake pedal causes the master cylinder to force hydraulic fluid through brake lines out to each of the automobile's four wheels. The hydraulic fluid works the wheel brake assembly on each wheel, which uses friction to stop the wheel from rotating and thus stops the automobile.

OBJECTIVES

After studying this chapter, you should be able to do the following:

1. Understand the operating principles of a brake system.
2. Describe the parts and operation of the master cylinder.
3. Explain the operation and identify the components of a drum brake system.
4. Explain the operation and identify the components of a disc brake system.
5. Describe the operation of brake system accessories such as the warning light, stoplight switch, power brake, and antiskid system.

46.1   FRICTION

Friction is a force that keeps surfaces from sliding upon each other. As a result of friction you are able to walk. The friction between your feet and the floor allows you to step forward.

A force applied to slow up or stop an object in motion is known in the automotive field as braking action. Three factors govern the amount of friction developed in braking action; and a fourth factor of braking action is the result of friction.

The first factor is pressure. When pressure is applied to two frictional surfaces, the surfaces grip each other harder and resist any movement between them.

The second factor is the amount of frictional surface in contact. Two hands will stop a revolving shaft faster than one hand, just as 10 square inches of brake surface works better than 5 square inches.

The third factor is the kind of material that makes up the frictional surface. It takes more force to move some materials over a surface than others, even though the applied pressure is the same. Different materials have different frictional characteristics or coefficients of friction. Mathematically speaking, the force required to slide an object over a surface divided by the weight of the object equals the coefficient of friction.

For instance, it takes about 70 pounds of force to slide a 100-pound block of rubber over a concrete surface, but only about 2 pounds of force for a 100-pound block of ice. If we divide the amount of force by the weight of the load, we find that the coefficient of friction for the rubber block is 0.7 while the coefficient for the ice block 0.02 (Fig. 46-1).

If the coefficient of friction is too high, brakes may grab and cause the wheels to slide. If the coefficient of friction is too low, too much pressure on the brake pedal is required to stop the automobile.

The fourth factor, which is a result of friction, is heat. Friction caused by braking action develops heat,

Fig. 46-1 Rubber and ice blocks have different coefficients of friction.

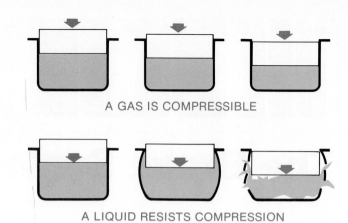

A GAS IS COMPRESSIBLE

A LIQUID RESISTS COMPRESSION

Fig. 46-2 Liquids cannot be compressed.
(Vickers Division, Sperry Rand Corporation)

which results in wear at the contact surfaces. The friction needed to stop a 3,000-pound automobile traveling at 60 mph develops a great amount of heat. In an emergency stop, the temperature of its brakes may rise 450°F (232°C). On a truck, whose weight is greater, the temperature may rise over 1000°F (536°C).

46.2 HYDRAULICS

Brake systems may use the force of mechanical leverage, electricity, air pressure, or hydraulic pressure to apply the brakes. Since automotive brakes use hydraulic pressure, we must examine some principles of hydraulics used in brake systems.

Hydraulic devices like the brake system work because liquids resist compression. A cork pushed into a bottle completely full of water eventually stops moving. If the cork is forced to move further, the bottle breaks (Fig. 46-2). This resistance of fluids to compression allows them to transmit motion and pressure.

If a cylinder contains two pistons separated by a liquid, pushing on piston A will cause movement at piston B (Fig. 46-3). Because piston A starts the movement, it is called the apply piston. Piston B is called the output piston. If the apply piston is moved 8 inches, the output piston will also move 8 inches. This demonstrates that motion may be transmitted by a liquid.

The same principle may be used to transmit motion from one cylinder to another. In Figure 46-4, two cylinders are connected by a pipe. When the apply piston in cylinder A is moved 4 inches, the output piston in cylinder B also moves 4 inches. This principle is used in hydraulic brake systems where a

master cylinder starts a push which is transmitted to each of the vehicle's wheel cylinders.

Pressure may be applied on a confined liquid by applying a force to some area in contact with the fluid. For example, in Figure 46-5, a piston is in contact with the fluid. If 100 pounds (46 kg) of force is applied to a piston with an area of 1-square inch 645 mm2), a pressure of 100 pounds per square inch (690 kPa) is generated. The important thing to understand is that the 100 psi is available everywhere. If a pressure gauge were installed anywhere in the system, it would read 100 psi. This principle, formulated by Pascal in the seventeenth century, is known as Pascal's Law: pressure at any one point in a confined liquid is the same in every direction and applies equal force on equal areas.

46.3 Pressure Equals Force Divided by Area

To find the pressure in a closed system, divide the force applied by the area of the apply piston. In Figure 46-6, a 100-pound force is applied to a piston with a 1-square-inch area. Using the formula, pressure equals Force divided by Area ($P = F/A$), 100 is divided by 1, which equals 100 psi of pressure. If the same force is applied to a piston with a 2-square-inch area, the pressure would be 50 psi.

One of the most important results of Pascal's work was the discovery that fluids may be used to gain leverage. If two cylinders of different diameters are connected (Fig. 46-7) with a fluid trapped between them, a 2-pound force on the piston with the 1-square-inch area develops a pressure in the system of 2 psi ($P = F/A$; $2 = 2/1$). Since this 2 psi is available

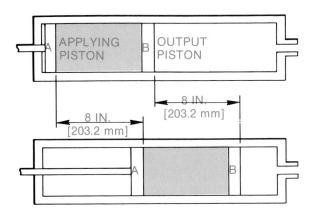

Fig. 46-3 Liquids can transmit motion.
(Chevrolet Motor Division, GMC)

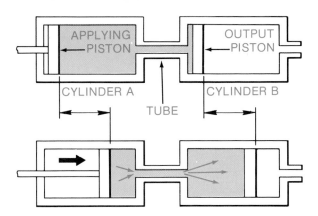

Fig. 46-4 Liquids transmit motion between cylinders.
(Chevrolet Motor Division, GMC)

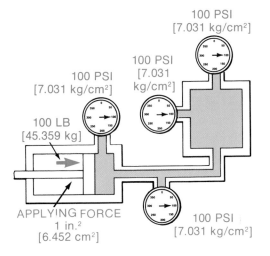

Fig. 46-5 Pressure is transmitted in all directions equally.
(Chevrolet Motor Division, GMC)

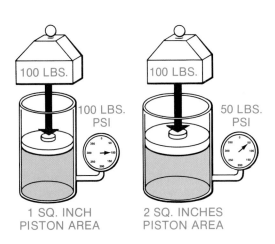

Fig. 46-6 Pressure equals force divided by area.
(General Motors Corporation)

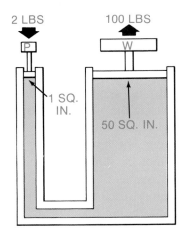

Fig. 46-7 Leverage can be gained hydraulically.
(Vickers Division, Sperry Rand Corporation)

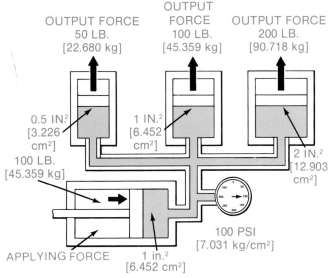

Fig. 46-8 Output force equals pressure times area.
(General Motors Corporation)

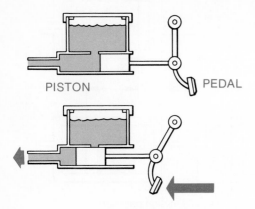

PISTON   PEDAL

Fig. 46-9 Simplified master cylinder operation.

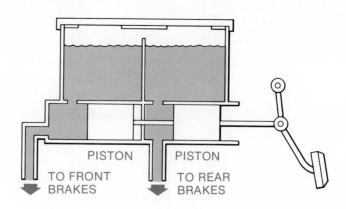

PISTON   PISTON
TO FRONT   TO REAR
BRAKES   BRAKES

Fig. 46-10 Simplified tandem master cylinder.

everywhere in the system, when it is distributed across a piston with a 50-square-inch area, the output force is 100 pounds. In other words, the 2-pound weight on the small piston balances a 50-pound weight on the larger piston.

This principle operating in a hydraulic jack allows a man to lift a 3,000-pound vehicle with his own weight. Leverage is gained, however, at a loss of distance. In order to move the larger piston in Figure 46-7 a single inch, the smaller piston must be moved 50 inches. In using the hydraulic jack, the jack handle must move a greater distance than the vehicle being lifted.

46.4   Output Force Equals Pressure Times Area

The principle of hydraulic leverage may be applied to a system with any number of cylinders. In Figure 46-8, a 4-cylinder system is shown. The apply piston has a 1-square-inch area. A force of 100 pounds on the apply piston develops a pressure in the system of 100 psi. Since each of the output pistons is a different size, there is a different force at each cylinder. The output is calculated by multiplying the pressure in the system by the area of the output piston.

Since the system pressure (Fig. 46-8) is 100 psi, the output force at the 0.5-square-inch area piston is 50 pounds ($100 \times 0.5 = 50$). The output force at the 1-square-inch piston is 100 pounds ($100 \times 1 = 100$). At the 2-square-inch piston, the force is 200 pounds ($100 \times 2 = 200$). The larger the output piston, the larger the output force. A common use of this principle is the hydraulic brake, which uses a small master

cylinder piston to apply pressure to a larger piston at the wheel cylinder, gaining hydraulic leverage.

46.5   MASTER CYLINDER

Pushing on the brake pedal operates the master cylinder in the engine compartment because of linkage connecting the two. The master cylinder is made up of a container for brake fluid and a piston in a cylinder. A hole in the bottom of the brake fluid container allows brake fluid to fill the area in front of the piston. When the brake pedal is pushed, the piston is pushed forward in the cylinder. As the piston covers the hole, the fluid is trapped and forced out a line at the back of the cylinder (Fig. 46-9).

This fluid is then directed through lines to each of the wheel brake assemblies. Since, like all fluids, it resists compression, it can be used to transmit motion. Before hydraulic brakes were invented, mechanical levers and rods worked the wheel brake assemblies. This mechanical linkage was difficult to design and operate, especially its connection to the front wheels, which turn to steer the automobile. Flexible hydraulic lines made this job much easier.

Hydraulic brakes also have disadvantages, however. If the fluid leaks out, the brakes do not work and the automobile cannot be stopped. To provide some protection against complete failure, master cylinders now have two pistons, each with its own fluid reservoir (Fig. 46-10). One piston operates the front brakes; the other operates the rear brakes. If the front system fails, the automobile still has rear brakes, and if the rear system fails, the automobile can be stopped with the front brakes. Some systems use a piston to operate a front brake on one side and a rear brake

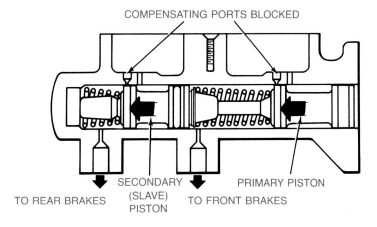

TO REAR BRAKES

SECONDARY (SLAVE) PISTON

TO FRONT BRAKES

PRIMARY PISTON

Fig. 46-11 Master cylinder applied. (Chrysler Corporation)

on the other side. The second piston operates the remaining two brakes. This is called a diagonally split system.

Depressing the brake pedal causes both the primary and the secondary pistons to move forward and exert hydraulic pressure independently in the front and rear brake systems. When the primary piston moves forward, it blocks off the compensating port (Fig. 46-11) and seals the fluid in front of it. As it continues to advance, it transmits fluid pressure to the front wheel brakes as well as to the secondary piston. The secondary piston moves forward and blocks off its compensating port. It seals the fluid in front of it and transmits fluid pressure to the rear wheel brakes.

When the brake pedal is released, the master cylinder's coil springs retract the pistons quickly. However, the caliper seals or brake shoe return springs retract their pistons more slowly. The fluid returns more slowly as a result, and pressure in the master cylinder drops until it is lower than that in the reservoirs. Atmospheric pressure on the reservoir fluid pushes the fluid through the filler ports, past the cups, to equalize pressure in the piston chambers.

Loss of brake fluid through leaks or broken brake lines can be a cause of brake failure. Front wheel braking is lost when the primary system fails (Fig. 46-12). However, initial pedal movement causes the unrestricted primary piston to bottom against the secondary piston. Continued movement of the pedal moves the secondary piston mechanically to displace fluid and transmit pressure to actuate the rear brake system. Similarly, rear wheel braking loss results from failure in the secondary system (Fig. 46-13). Initial pedal movement, in this case, causes the unrestricted secondary piston to bottom against the forward wall of the master cylinder. Movement of the primary pis-

ton displaces fluid and transmits hydraulic pressure to actuate the front brake system.

If the front or rear brakes fail, there will be increased pedal travel as well as increased pedal force, since only a part of the normally available braking surface will be used.

Lower pressure in the failed half of the system will trip a switch and turn on a red warning light. On some systems the light is on only while the driver is pushing on the brake pedal. Other systems keep the light on whenever the ignition switch is on, until the trouble is repaired and the light switch reset.

46.6   DRUM BRAKES

The brake lines connected to the master cylinder route the hydraulic pressure to the four wheel brake assemblies. There are two types of wheel brake assemblies in use: drum brakes and disc brakes.

The drum brake is the older brake system. It is presently used on most smaller automobiles and on the rear wheels of many larger automobiles. The brake drum is a large iron casting shaped like a musical drum. A brake drum, attached by lug bolts to each wheel, turns with the wheel. The rest of the brake system components are designed to stop the drum from turning, thus stopping the wheel.

The drums are stopped by forcing brake shoes against them. Brake shoes are half circles with high-friction brake lining attached that are placed inside the brake drums. When the brake lining contacts the rotating brake drum, the friction between the lining and the drum stops the drum (Fig. 46-14).

The shoes are mounted on a round backing plate

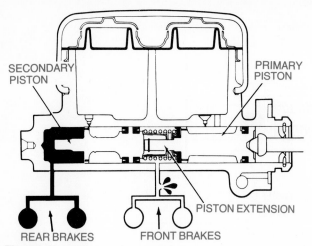

Fig. 46-12 Failure in front brake system. (Chevrolet Motor Division, GMC)

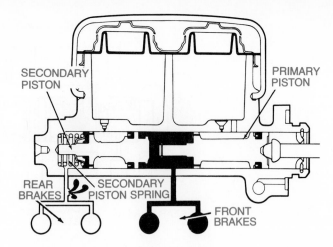

Fig. 46-13 Failure in rear brake system. (Chevrolet Motor Division, GMC)

so they cannot spin with the drum. The rear brake backing plates are mounted to the rear suspension. The front brake backing plates are mounted to a part of the steering knuckle assembly. The brake shoes are held against the backing by several hold-down springs.

When the shoes are pushed against the rotating drum, they try to rotate with the drum, but round anchor pins attached to the top of the backing plates prevent this rotation. The shoes are positioned at the bottom by an adjusting screw, which expands the diameter of the shoe assembly as the brake linings wear.

46.7   Wheel Cylinders

The shoes are pushed out to stop the drum by a hydraulic device called a wheel cylinder (Figs. 46-15 and 46-16). Inside each wheel cylinder are two pistons and a brake line from the master cylinder. When the driver pushes down the brake pedal, hydraulic pressure developed by the master cylinder piston goes into the center of the wheel cylinder, forcing the wheel cylinder pistons outward. Actuating pins mounted in the wheel cylinder pistons transfer this motion to the brake shoes, which are pushed against the brake drums. The friction stops the drum and the wheel attached to it. The automobile stops.

When the driver releases the brake pedal, retracting springs connected to the brake shoes bring the shoes out of contact with the drums and back against the anchor. The pistons in the wheel cylinder are pushed back in. Fluid returns to the master cylinder through the brake lines, and the system is ready to operate again.

46.8   Self-adjusters

For proper brake operation, the correct clearance between the lining and the drum must be maintained. On older automobiles, this adjustment is done manually. A brake adjusting tool is inserted through a slot in the backing plate and turned to bring the shoes closer to the drums.

On newer automobiles, this adjustment is handled automatically by self-adjusters (Fig. 46-17). When the lining wears enough to require adjustment, the adjuster cable lifts the adjuster lever into mesh with the next tooth of the adjuster screw when the brakes are applied in a reverse stop. The automatic adjuster uses movement of the secondary shoes in a reverse brake application to work the adjuster lever. This action repeats on each brake application, until the shoe-to-lining clearance is so small that shoe movement is not enough to make the cable lift the lever to the next tooth.

46.9   Self-energized Brakes

Most modern drum brake systems (See Fig. 46-18) are self-energizing. When the driver presses on the brake pedal and the brake shoes move outward, they contact the drum and tend to rotate with the drum. The primary shoe (usually the front shoe), rotating with the drum, moves away from the anchor pin and applies a rearward force on the adjusting screw. At the same time the other shoe, called the secondary shoe, is rotating around until it contacts the anchor pin.

We can then see that the force applied to the

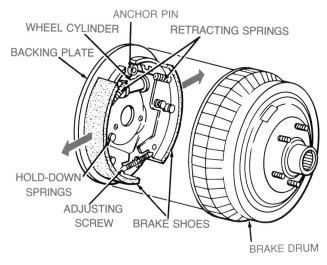

Fig. 46-14 Parts of drum brake system.

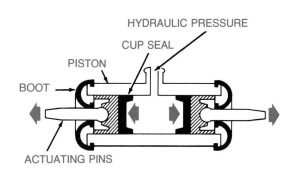

Fig. 46-15 Wheel cylinder operation.

secondary shoe is the sum of the apply force on the primary shoe and the force caused by rotation (friction force) of the primary shoe. This combination of forces is the self-energizing action. The increased force it applies to the brake shoes means less physical effort is required at the brake pedal.

Since greater braking force is applied to the secondary shoe, the secondary shoe lining area is usually larger than the primary shoe lining area.

46.10 DISC BRAKES

Drum brakes are used on the rear of many cars but they have been replaced on the fronts of most cars by disc brakes. Stopping a heavy automobile at high speed generates tremendous heat between the brake shoes and drums. This heat buildup can affect the frictional contact between the drum and shoes so that the brakes fail to work until they cool down. This condition is called brake fade.

Another problem with drum brakes is poor water recovery. When the automobile is operated in wet weather, water can get into the brake shoes, causing the linings to lose their frictional contact. The brakes do not work until they recover or dry out. Disc brakes have better water recovery and resist brake fading.

The disc brake system uses the same master cylinder and brake lines as a drum brake system. The major differences are in the wheel brake assemblies. Instead of a drum, the disc brake system (Fig. 46-19) uses a rotor, a thick, round piece of cast iron attached to the wheel through the lug bolts. The rotor always turns when the wheel turns.

The brake system squeezes two brake pads or shoes against the rotor. When the brake pads, thick pieces of friction material attached to a steel backing, are squeezed against the surface of the rotor, friction stops the rotor from turning. The automobile's wheels, attached to the rotor, also stop.

The brake pads or linings are mounted over the rotor in the caliper assembly, which is mounted on the front steering knuckle assembly of the vehicle. Brake shoes or pads are placed on each side of the rotor so that, when the brakes are applied, the pads are forced into frictional contact with the two sides of the rotor. Hydraulic pressure is transmitted to the brake pads through one or more hydraulic pistons which are part of the caliper assembly. There are two designs of calipers: fixed and floating.

46.11 Fixed Caliper Design

The fixed caliper housing is stationary (Fig. 46-20). One or two hydraulic pistons in each side of the caliper push both pads against the rotor braking surfaces.

The caliper assembly (Fig. 46-21) consists of two caliper housings bolted together. Each half contains either one or two cylinder bores with a piston. A rubber dust boot attached outside seals the cylinder from contamination and rubber piston seals placed in grooves in the cylinder bores provide hydraulic sealing between the pistons and the cylinder bores.

The cylinders are connected hydraulically by passages inside the caliper housings or by an external transfer tube between the two halves of the caliper

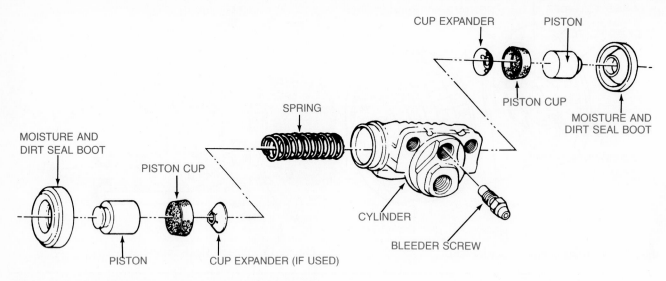

Fig. 46-16 Exploded view of a wheel cylinder assembly. (Chrysler Corporation)

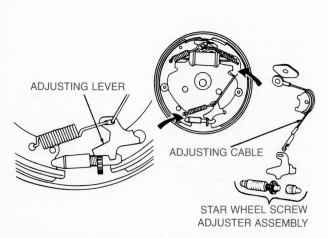

Fig. 46-17 Self-adjuster components. (Chrysler Corporation)

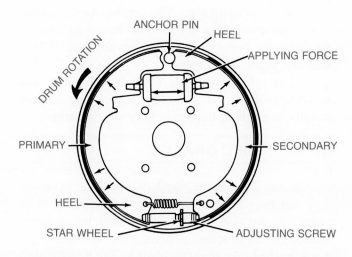

Fig. 46-18 Self-energized brakes. (Chrysler Corporation)

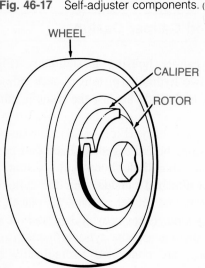

Fig. 46-19 Simplified disc brake system.

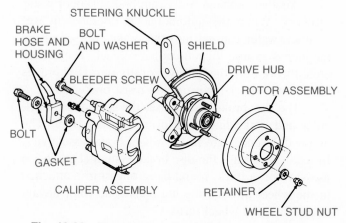

Fig. 46-20 Fixed caliper disc brakes. (Chrysler Corporation)

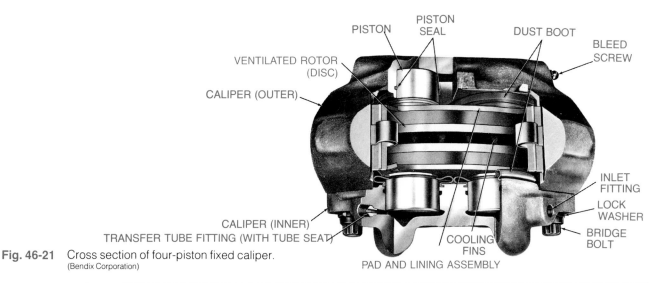

PISTON PISTON SEAL DUST BOOT BLEED SCREW VENTILATED ROTOR (DISC) CALIPER (OUTER) INLET FITTING LOCK WASHER BRIDGE BOLT CALIPER (INNER) TRANSFER TUBE FITTING (WITH TUBE SEAT) COOLING FINS PAD AND LINING ASSEMBLY

Fig. 46-21 Cross section of four-piston fixed caliper.
(Bendix Corporation)

assembly. A bleeder screw and a fluid inlet fitting are provided on each caliper assembly.

When the brake pedal is pushed down, hydraulic pressure from the master cylinder moves the caliper pistons, forcing the linings against both sides of the braking disc or rotor. During brake application, the piston seals are deflected by the hydraulic pressure (Fig. 46-22). When the pressure is released, the seals relax or retract, pulling the pistons back from the shoe and lining assemblies. This seal retraction gives the required running clearance between the pads and the disc. The pistons automatically slide outward from the cylinder bores as the lining wears and move to a new position in relation to the seal to maintain the correct adjustment location at all times.

46.12 Floating Caliper Design

The floating caliper assembly is a simpler design which uses one hydraulic piston (Figs. 46-23 and 46-24). In the floating caliper the inside or inboard shoe is pushed hydraulically into frictional contact with the rotor. The reaction force caused by this contact pulls the outboard shoe into frictional contact. This is possible because the complete caliper assembly is designed to move or "float" a small amount.

As explained previously, when pressure is applied to fluid in a closed system, this pressure is applied equally in all directions. In the floating caliper design hydraulic pressure acts on two surfaces. The first surface is the piston. The second is the bottom of the bore of the caliper housing. Since the area of the piston and the bottom of the caliper bore are equal, equal forces are developed.

Hydraulic force in the caliper bore is transmitted by the piston to the inner brake pad and lining assem-

bly and the inner surface of the rotor. This tends to slide the caliper assembly inboard on the four rubber bushings. The outer lining, which rests on the caliper housing, then applies a force on the outer surface of the rotor so that the two linings brake the automobile. Since equal hydraulic force is applied to the caliper housing and the piston, equal force is applied to the outer and the inner surfaces of the rotor. Since there are equal forces on the pad linings, no flexing or distortion of the rotor occurs, regardless of how hard or how long brakes are applied. Lining wear tends to be equal. As the brake linings wear, the caliper assembly moves inboard and fluid fills the area behind the piston.

As the driver releases the brake pedal, seal retraction immediately releases the piston from the pad. The movement from no application to full application is very slight. As force is removed, the piston and caliper merely relax into the released position and braking effort is removed. Because the lining is in constant contact with the rotor, there is improved brake response, reduced pedal travel, and faster build-up of line pressure. Since the pad is at zero clearance, it also wipes the disc free of any foreign matter.

46.13 HYDRAULIC SYSTEMS FOR DISC AND DRUM COMBINATIONS

While some automobiles use disc brakes on all four wheels, most use disc assemblies on the front and drum brakes on the rear. When both types of brake systems are used, several changes are necessary in the hydraulic system. These include the addition of a metering valve and a proportioning valve (Fig. 46-25).

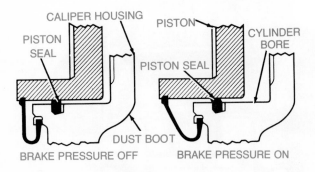

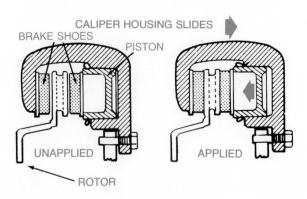

Fig. 46-22 Piston seals retract hydraulic piston. (Raybestos)   Fig. 46-23 Floating caliper design. (Kelsey-Hayes)

46.14   Proportioning Valve

Disc brakes are designed to use higher line pressures on full application than drum brakes. Vehicles equipped with front disc brakes and rear drum brakes have a proportioning valve (Fig. 46-26) in the hydraulic line to the rear (drum) brakes. Its job is to maintain the correct proportion between line pressures to the front and rear brakes for balanced braking.

46.15   Metering Valve

Some vehicles equipped with front disc brakes and rear drum brakes also used a metering valve (Fig. 46-27). This valve, installed in the hydraulic line to the front (disc) brakes, delays pressure buildup to the front brakes until rear brake pressure builds up enough to overcome rear brake shoe return springs. This balances the brake system and lengthens disc brake lining life because it prevents the front disc brakes from carrying all or most of the braking load at low operating line pressures.

46.16   Residual Pressure

On drum brakes, a small amount of residual pressure to the wheel cylinders must be maintained when brakes are not applied. A residual check valve for this purpose is usually placed in the brake master cylinder in a conventional drum brake system. However, residual pressure to a disc brake will cause it to drag, resulting in noisy brakes and premature lining wear. Also, because of the larger pistons in disc brakes, a larger volume of fluid is required for their operation. Therefore the master cylinder section for a disc brake system does not have a residual check valve.

46.17   EMERGENCY AND PARKING BRAKES

All automobiles have an emergency brake system in case the regular brake system fails. It is also used to prevent the vehicle from rolling when it is parked. The system is operated mechanically so that it will continue to work even if there is a complete hydraulic system failure. Emergency brakes usually operate only on the rear wheels. When the parking brake pedal is pushed down, a cable connected to the rear brake shoes pulls them into contact with the drums and prevents drums and wheels from turning (Fig. 46-28).

46.18   STOPLIGHT SWITCH

All automobiles have a stoplight circuit that works a set of rear lights on the vehicle each time the brake pedal is depressed. The stoplight switch assembly (Fig. 46-29) may be installed on the pin of the brake pedal arm so it straddles the master cylinder pushrod. When the brake pedal is depressed, the stoplight switch contacts are pushed against the end of the master cylinder pushrod. This closes the circuit to the stoplights, turning them on. Other systems use a pressure-sensitive switch mounted to the rear of the master cylinder.

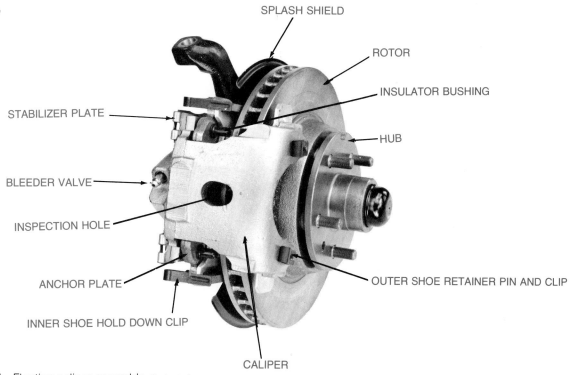

Fig. 46-24   Floating caliper assembly. (Raybestos)

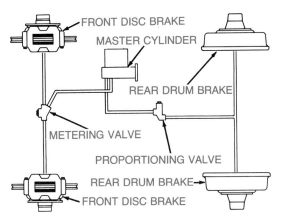

Fig. 46-25   Disc brake hydraulic system. (Kelsey-Hayes)

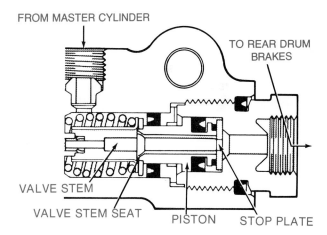

Fig. 46-26   Proportioning valve. (Kelsey-Hayes)

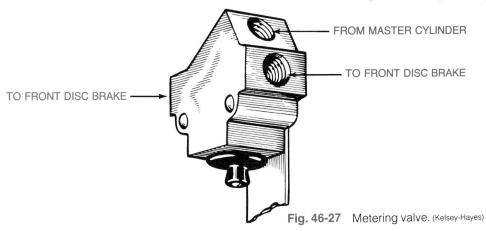

Fig. 46-27   Metering valve. (Kelsey-Hayes)

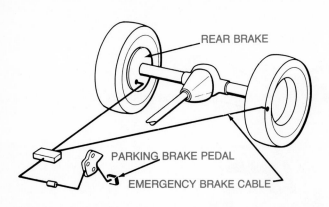

Fig. 46-28 Emergency or parking brake.

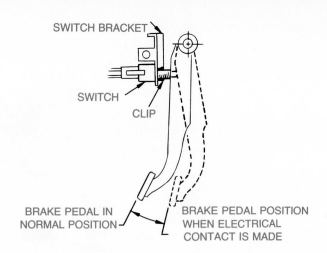

Fig. 46-29 Stoplight switch. (Chevrolet Motor Division, GMC)

46.19   WARNING LIGHT SYSTEM

A brake warning light on the instrument panel is designed to show a brake system failure. The light comes on only after the brakes have been applied. It is controlled by a pressure differential valve which operates when there is a pressure drop in either the front or rear system.

The hydraulic brake lines from the master cylinder output ports are connected to the brake warning light switch. When hydraulic pressure is the same in the front and rear hydraulic systems, the switch piston remains centered (Fig. 46-30) and does not contact the terminal in the switch cylinder bore. If pressure fails in one of the systems, hydraulic pressure moves the piston toward the inoperative side. The shoulder of the piston then contacts the switch terminal to provide a ground for the warning lamp circuit and light the warning lamp (Fig. 46-31).

46.20   POWER BRAKE SYSTEMS

A power brake system is used on many cars to reduce the braking effort required by the driver. There are two general types of power brakes. One type uses intake manifold vacuum acting on a diaphragm to assist the driver in applying effort through the master cylinder. The other type uses hydraulic pressure developed by the power steering pump to operate a hydraulic booster attached to the master cylinder.

The vacuum power assist unit consists of a large canister mounted to the master cylinder (Fig. 46-32). The master cylinder and wheel brake assemblies are the same as on a standard brake system. The linkage from the brake pedal goes through the power assist canister, which contains a large round diaphragm. When the brake pedal is pushed, air is removed from one side of the diaphragm through a vacuum line from the canister to the engine intake manifold. With a vacuum on one side of the diaphragm and atmospheric pressure on the other, the diaphragm moves to help the driver's push on the brakes.

Cars with diesel engines do not have intake manifold vacuum to use as a power source. Some gasoline engines with certain types of emission control equipment have very low intake manifold vacuum. The hydraulic boost type of power brake system was developed for these applications.

The hydraulic booster type of power brakes has three main parts as shown in Figure 46-33. The power steering pump develops pressure which is routed to the hydraulic booster assembly. The master cylinder operates the same as a conventional master cylinder. The hydraulic booster is used to help the driver apply force to the master cylinder pushrod.

The hydraulic power booster unit fits in the same place as a vacuum booster between the brake pedal and the master cylinder. Similarly, its function is to multiply the force of the driver's foot on the pedal. The force of the booster is exerted by the hydraulic (power) piston, and the control is effected in much the same way as with vacuum boosters, by a system of valves operated by brake pedal movement. The supply system for the hydraulic boost has a pump (the power steering pump) and a reservoir (in the power steering pump) for hydraulic fluid.

Power brakes require much less pedal effort to apply. If the system fails, the driver can still apply the brakes, but a great deal of pedal effort is required.

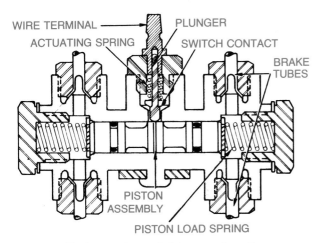

Fig. 46-30 Brake warning switch in normal position.
(American Motors Corporation)

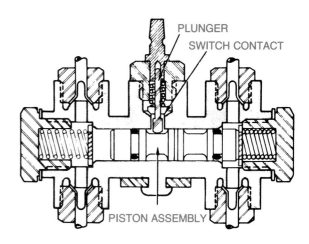

Fig. 46-31 Brake warning switch indicating failure.
(American Motors Corporation)

46.21   ANTISKID BRAKE SYSTEMS

Antiskid or antilock brake systems are designed to prevent the wheels from locking or skidding under heavy braking. Electrically controlled antiskid systems monitor and control the braking action at each wheel to prevent lockup.

Monitoring or sensing devices mounted on each of the controlled braking wheels sense wheel rotation speed. Individual wheel speed is compared to vehicle speed by a small logic control unit. If any wheel locks up and skids, the logic control unit senses the lockup and reduces pressure on that brake, controlling the skid. It then re-applies the hydraulic pressure to maintain the best braking action.

If necessary, the system repeats this cycle about four times a second until either the vehicle speed drops low enough or the brake pedal is released. This gives safe stopping with a single brake application.

The system pumps the brakes for controlled stoppage under slippery or panic conditions. Tests show that under dry road conditions a good antilock system reduces stopping distance as much as 5 percent. Under slippery conditions (ice, snow, oil, or loose gravel) the stopping distance can be shortened by as much as 25 percent.

The main parts of an antiskid system are (1) a wheel rotation counter, a small signal generator attached to each controlled wheel; (2) a logic counter, a small electronic device that computes all wheel signals and decides whether the wheel is skidding or the vehicle has stopped; (3) an actuator, hydraulic valves controlling pressure to the brakes upon signal from the logic controller; and (4) an override system, which assures that if any component of the antiskid system fails, normal braking will be unaffected.

NEW TERMS

Antiskid system   A system designed to prevent the wheels from locking or skidding during heavy braking.

Brake drum   The part of the wheel brake assembly attached to the wheel.

Brake pads   The shoes or friction linings used on disc brake systems.

Brake shoes   The friction linings used on drum brake systems.

Caliper   A housing for the hydraulic components of a disc brake system.

Coefficient of friction   An index of the frictional characteristics of a material.

Disc brakes   A brake system that uses a rotor attached to the wheel and a caliper with brake pads to stop the wheel.

Drum brakes   A brake system that uses a drum attached to the wheel and brake shoes to stop the wheel.

Fixed caliper   A caliper that is mounted stationary.

Floating caliper   A caliper that moves during braking.

Master cylinder   A cylinder connected to the brake pedal whose hydraulic pressure applies the brakes.

Metering valve   A valve that delays pressure build-up to the front brakes.

Parking brake   A mechanically operated brake used for parking or an emergency stop.

Pascal's Law   A principle of hydraulics which states that pressure at any point in a confined liquid is the same in every direction and applies equal force on equal areas.

Power brakes   Brakes that use a vacuum diaphragm to help the driver apply the brakes.

The Brake System   473

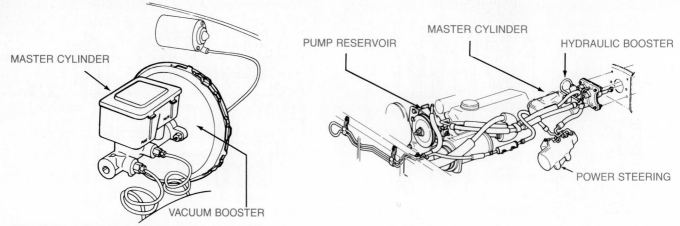

Fig. 46-32 Vacuum-operated power assist brakes. (American Motors Corporation)

Fig. 46-33 Hydraulic type of brake power assist.

Proportioning valve A valve used to maintain the correct proportion of pressure between the front disc and rear drum brakes.

Rotor The part of the disc brake system that turns or rotates with the wheels.

Self-adjusters A cable-operated device used to adjust brake shoes automatically.

Self-energized brakes Brakes that use a wedging action of the brake shoes to help apply the brakes.

Stoplight switch A switch applied by the master cylinder pressure that turns on brake lights.

Warning light A light that warns of a failure in the hydraulic system.

Wheel cylinders Hydraulic cylinders mounted on the wheel brake assemblies that apply the brake shoes.

CHAPTER REVIEW

1. What three factors determine the amount of friction?
2. How can liquids be used to transmit motion?
3. Explain how leverage can be gained using hydraulics.
4. Why does the master cylinder have two pistons?
5. Describe the operation of the master cylinder.
6. Explain the operation of a drum brake assembly.

7. What is the purpose of a wheel cylinder?
8. What is a self-adjuster?
9. Explain how self-energized brakes work.
10. Explain the operation of a disc brake assembly.
11. What is a fixed caliper?
12. What is a floating caliper?
13. Why is a proportioning valve required in some brake systems?
14. What is the purpose of a metering valve?
15. Why is residual pressure not used in disc brakes?
16. Explain how a parking brake works.
17. What is a stoplight switch?
18. Explain the operation of a warning light system.
19. How do power brakes work?
20. What is an antiskid system?

DISCUSSION TOPICS AND ACTIVITIES

1. Use a shop cutaway model to identify the parts and explain the operation of the master cylinder.
2. Compare the operation of a drum and a disc brake system. Which is the better system? Why?
3. Explain why a rolling automobile will stop in a shorter distance than a skidding automobile.

Brake System Service

The brake system is the most important safety system on the automobile. A mechanic must be able to find possible problems in a brake system and service the system so that brakes work correctly. In this chapter, we will present troubleshooting, maintenance, and service procedures for drum and disc brake systems.

OBJECTIVES

After studying this chapter, you should be able to do the following:

1. List the steps in finding a problem in the brake system.
2. Explain the preventive maintenance jobs necessary on a brake system.
3. Explain the procedures for servicing a master cylinder.
4. Explain the procedures for servicing drum brakes.
5. Explain the procedures for servicing disc brakes.

47.1   TROUBLESHOOTING

A number of driver complaints may signal a brake system problem. A low brake pedal, one that takes too much clearance between linings and drums or discs. This usually means worn brake lining.

A brake pedal that goes to the floor under steady pressure or goes to the floor on the first application is a sign of a problem in the hydraulic system. There may be a leak in the system, air in the system, or worn and leaking piston cups in the master cylinder.

The pedal travel required to apply the brakes may get smaller along with a hard pedal. This is often the result of sticking or seized caliper or wheel cylinder pistons. Another possibility is that the master cylinder compensator ports are blocked with dirt. This would prevent fluid from returning to the reservoir. Sticking or seized pistons in the master cylinder bore may also cause this problem.

A spongy brake pedal that feels soft or springy when depressed is most often caused by air in the hydraulic system. A hard pedal that requires too much pedal pressure to stop the vehicle is a sign of brake fade. Brake fade may be caused by a loose or leaking power brake vacuum hose; a brake lining contaminated by grease or brake fluid; incorrect or poor quality brake lining; bent, broken, or distorted brake shoes; or calipers dragging on the anchor plate.

Grabbing brakes work too quickly during brake pedal pressure. This problem may be caused by grease or brake fluid on the brake lining; incorrect brake lining; broken, bent, or cracked brake shoes; or a sticking or seized caliper or wheel cylinder piston.

Dragging brakes that are slow to release after letting up the brake pedal may be caused by sticking or seized caliper or wheel cylinder pistons, blocked ports in the master cylinder, incorrectly adjusted parking brake cables, broken or weak return springs, or malfunctioning automatic adjusters.

A vehicle may pull to one side when the brakes are applied as a result of incorrect front tire pressure or damaged front wheel bearings. Brake system problems may also be the cause: contaminated brake lining, broken or bent brake shoes, and sticking caliper or wheel cylinder pistons.

Brakes that chatter or shudder when applied may have loose components, such as loose wheel bearings

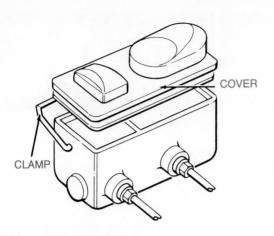

Fig. 47-1 Check master cylinder level by removing clamp and lifting cover. (Dodge/Chrysler Corporation)

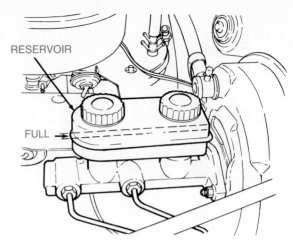

Fig. 47-2 Remove reservoir vent caps to check for fluid level. (Chrysler Corporation)

and loose caliper mounts. Rear drums that are out of round or front rotors that have too much thickness variation or lateral runout may cause chatter or may cause the brake pedal to pulsate up and down during application.

Finally, noisy brakes are a common problem. Brakes may have a squealing, clicking, scraping sound when applied. The most probable causes are bent, broken, distorted brake shoes; worn out brake lining (shoes contacting drum or rotor); foreign material imbedded in the brake lining; broken or loose hold-down or return springs; rough or dry drum brake support plate ledges; and cracked, grooved, or scored rotors or drums.

47.2   PREVENTIVE MAINTENANCE

For proper brake operation, the brake system should be inspected and tested at intervals recommended by the manufacturer. This involves a thorough inspection of the brakes in the shop.

47.3   Pedal Checks

Apply and release foot pressure several times (with the engine running for power brakes) and check for friction and noise. Pedal movement should be smooth with a fast return and no squeaks from pedal or brakes. Apply heavy foot pressure (with the engine running for power brakes) and check for sponginess. Measure the pedal reserve. The pedal should feel firm, not springy. The brake pedal should be over 2 inches (50 mm) from the floor for manual and power brakes.

Check for hydraulic leaks. Hold light foot pressure (with the engine off for power brakes) for 15 seconds and check that there is no pedal movement. Repeat with heavy foot pressure. Repeat the whole check for power brakes with the engine running.

47.4   Master Cylinder and Brake Fluid Inspection

Check that the master cylinder reservoir vent hole(s) in the cap or cover is clean and open. Check that fluid level is within 1/4 inch (6 mm) of reservoir top (both sides for dual units) and that the fluid is clean. Add fluid by removing the clamp and lifting the cover (Fig. 47-1) or unscrewing the reservoir vent caps (Fig. 47-2). Use only the recommended fluid.

Check for external hydraulic leaks. Look for dampness around the body, fittings and head nut, and hydraulic stoplight switch (if used). On manual brakes, flip back the dust boot and look for fluid.

47.5   Hose, Tubing, and Wheel Inspection

Look down under the hood and up with the automobile on a hoist to check hose, tubing, and connections for leaks. Check the backing plates and wheels for signs of brake fluid or grease leaks. Make sure tubing is free from dents or other damage. Check that hose is flexible and free from cracks, cuts, or bulges.

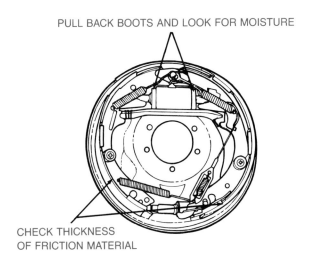

PULL BACK BOOTS AND LOOK FOR MOISTURE

CHECK THICKNESS
OF FRICTION MATERIAL

Fig. 47-3 Inspecting drum type brakes. (Chrysler Corporation)

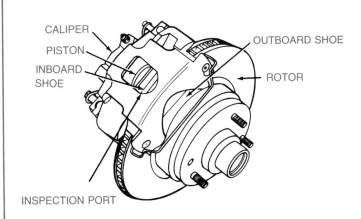

CALIPER
PISTON
INBOARD
SHOE
OUTBOARD SHOE
ROTOR

INSPECTION PORT

Fig. 47-4 Inspecting disc brake lining. (Chrysler Corporation)

47.6 Operational Checks on the Hoist

With the parking brake released, check that all wheels spin freely without drag. With light pressure on the brake pedal, turn wheels by hand. Check that there are no ''free'' and ''tight'' spots on any wheel and that all wheels have the same amount of drag. Apply heavy pressure to the parking brake. The lever or pedal should move no more than 2/3 of full travel. Rear wheels should be locked. Release the parking brake and check that all wheels spin freely without drag.

47.7 Lining Inspection for Wear

Each time the drum brakes are adjusted or at intevals recommended by the automobile manufacturer, pull the right front wheel and drum and inspect the lining for wear (Fig. 47-3). If less than $^1/_{16}$ inch (1.6 mm) of usable lining remains, the brakes should be relined. If the amount of lining left is questionable, pull the remaining drums and inspect these linings.

Inspect disc brake pad linings any time the wheels are removed (tire rotation, etc.). Check both ends of the outboard pad lining by looking in at each end of the caliper, where the highest rate of wear normally occurs. At the same time, check the lining thickness on the inboard shoe to make sure that it has not worn too fast. Look down through the inspection port to view the inboard pad and lining (Fig. 47-4). Whenever the lining is worn to about the thickness of the metal shoe, all shoe and lining assemblies on both brakes should be replaced.

47.8 Brake Mechanism Inspection

At the wheel suspected of causing trouble, or at all wheels if uncertain, visually inspect the brake. Check linings for looseness on shoes, cracks, unusual wear, or foreign material stuck in the lining. Check shoes for cracks, distortion, or broken welds. Make sure all springs are properly installed and free of cracks or distortion. Make sure that shoe hold-down parts—pins, springs, and cups—are properly installed and not damaged.

Check backing plates for distortion or cracks. Make sure that bolts and anchors are tight. Carefully pry each shoe away and check the backing plate pads for grooving or other damage. Make sure pads are properly lubricated.

Inspect wheel cylinder and caliper boots for cuts, cracks, hardening, or other signs of breakdown. Make sure there is no sign of leakage. On self-adjusting brakes, make sure that adjuster parts are properly installed. Check parts for cracks, distortion, or other damage. Check for foreign objects or a build-up of dirt. Brake mechanisms must be reasonably clean in order to operate properly.

47.9 MASTER CYLINDER SERVICE

When troubleshooting procedures show a problem with the master cylinder, it must be serviced. Disconnect the hydraulic lines, remove attaching bolts (or nuts), and remove the master cylinder from

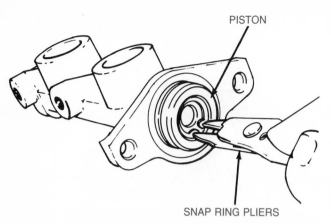

PISTON

SNAP RING PLIERS

Fig. 47-5 Removing the master cylinder snap ring. (Chrysler Corporation)

Fig. 47-6 Honing the master cylinder.

the automobile. On some automobiles the manual pushrod must be disconnected from the brake pedal to permit removal of the master cylinder. Remove the reservoir cover and drain the fluid from both reservoirs. Press the pushrod against the primary piston to compress the spring and remove the piston stop screw. Remove the snap ring (if used) from the inside hub of the cylinder (Fig. 47-5). Then remove primary and secondary piston assemblies. Discard the primary piston assembly. Remove the spring, spring retainer, washer, and cups from the secondary piston.

Clamp the master cylinder in a vise with side outlets up. To remove the outlet port tube seats, thread self-tapping screws into the seats, and pry the screw upward. Thoroughly clean the cylinder and polish the cylinder bore with crocus cloth or a brake hone. If the cylinder is made from alimunum check the shop service manual for reconditioning recommendations. Many aluminum cylinders cannot be honed. Do not use a hone that will result in oversize or a poor finish (Fig. 47-6).

If the cylinder bore is badly pitted, rusted, or scored, replace the cylinder. Check compensating and fluid inlet ports for burrs. Rinse all metal parts to be reused in clean alcohol and place on clean paper. Discard all old parts to be replaced.

Dip all rubber parts in clean brake fluid and place them in a clean pan or on clean paper. Assemble secondary cups and retainer on the secondary piston with cups back to back. From the opposite end of the secondary piston, assemble protector washer, primary cup (flat side next to washer), retainer, and piston return spring. Use an exploded view illustration as a guide to assembly (Fig. 47-7).

Coat the cylinder bore and cups of the second-

ary and primary pistons with clean brake fluid. Guide the secondary piston assembly (spring end first) into the cylinder bore followed by the primary piston assembly. Press against the primary piston to compress the spring approximately 1/4 inch (6 mm) and install the piston stop screw.

Release the piston and tighten the stop screw. If the master cylinder includes a piston-retaining snap ring, rubber seal ring, dust guard, or pushrod, assemble these parts on the master cylinder.

Insert the end of the spring into the recess of the rubber check valve and assemble spring, check valve, and tube seat insert in both outlets. Thread the tube seat plug or tube nuts of the correct thread size into the cylinder to press the tube seat inserts into place.

Remove air from the cylinder by bleeding before installation on the vehicle. Support the cylinder assembly in a vise and fill reservoirs with the correct brake fluid. Make and install two bleed tubes, as shown in Figure 47-8. Press the piston assembly inward slowly with a wooden dowel or pushrod. Allow pistons to return under spring pressure. Repeat until air bubbles no longer appear.

Install the cylinder on the vehicle. Remove the bleed tubes and connect the hydraulic lines. The entire system will require bleeding as explained below.

47.10 BLEEDING THE BRAKE SYSTEM

The brake hydraulic system must be free of air to work properly. If air is mixed with the brake fluid, pedal reserve is lost, since the air in the hydraulic system compresses. The system must be bled each time a hydraulic unit is serviced.

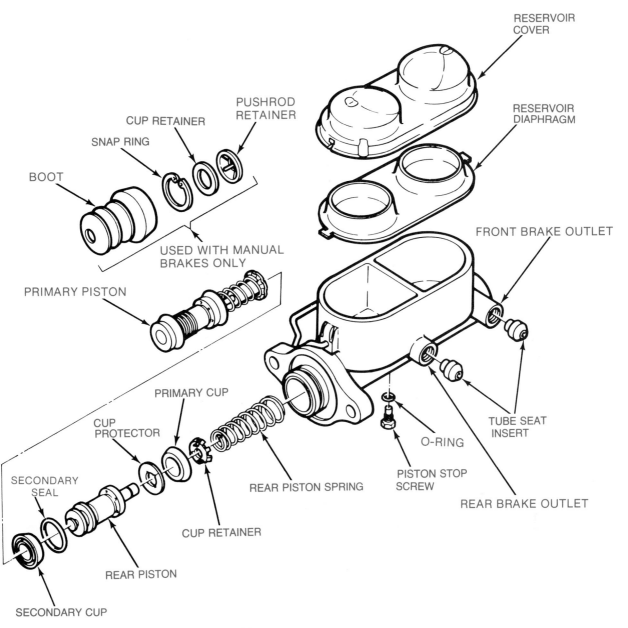

Fig. 47-7 Exploded view of master cylinder assembly. (Bendix Corporation)

Labels in figure:
- RESERVOIR COVER
- RESERVOIR DIAPHRAGM
- PUSHROD RETAINER
- CUP RETAINER
- SNAP RING
- BOOT
- USED WITH MANUAL BRAKES ONLY
- PRIMARY PISTON
- FRONT BRAKE OUTLET
- PRIMARY CUP
- CUP PROTECTOR
- SECONDARY SEAL
- CUP RETAINER
- REAR PISTON SPRING
- PISTON STOP SCREW
- O-RING
- TUBE SEAT INSERT
- REAR BRAKE OUTLET
- REAR PISTON
- SECONDARY CUP

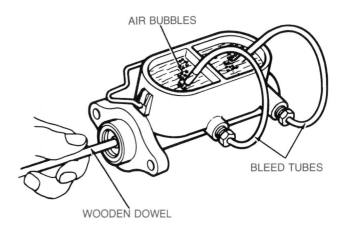

Fig. 47-8 Bleeding master cylinder. (Bendix Corporation)

Labels in figure:
- AIR BUBBLES
- BLEED TUBES
- WOODEN DOWEL

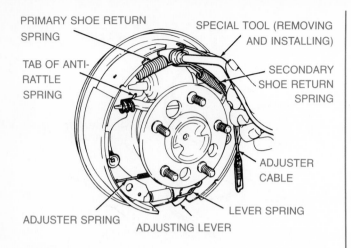

Fig. 47-9 ·Removing shoe return springs. (Chrysler Corporation)

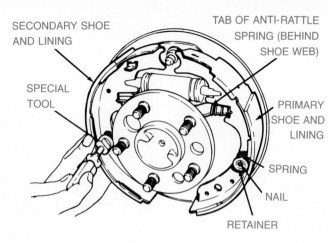

Fig. 47-10 Removing shoe retainers. (Chrysler Corporation)

A bleed screw is provided at each wheel cylinder and each disc brake caliper for removing any air in the hydraulic system. Some master cylinders also have one or two bleed screws. Bleeding the brake system consists of forcing brake fluid and any air in the fluid out of the hydraulic system at one or more of the bleed points.

There are two methods of bleeding the hydraulic system: manual bleeding and pressure bleeding. For either method, a supply of clean hydraulic brake fluid is necessary. Do not reuse brake fluid that has been drained from the hydraulic system. It may be contaminated.

The order in which wheel cylinders are bled does not influence the effectiveness of the bleeding operation. The following order is recommended, however, to reduce the possibility of missing a wheel cylinder; right rear, left rear, right front, and left front.

47.11 Manual Bleeding

On vehicles with power brakes, be sure the engine is off and vacuum is removed from the power brake. Vacuum can be removed by depressing and releasing the brake pedal five or six times.

Fill master cylinder fluid reservoirs with clean brake fluid. Check brake fluid level in reservoirs frequently during the bleeding operation. Keep reservoirs at least half full.

Attach a bleeder drain hose to the right rear wheel cylinder bleed screw. Place the free end of the hose in a glass container partly filled with brake fluid. Have an assistant apply moderate (approximately 50 pounds or 111 N) steady pressure to the brake pedal.

Then open the bleed screw. When fluid coming from the submerged end of the hose is free of air bubbles, close the bleed screw and release the brake pedal.

If the brake pedal goes to the floor without removing all air bubbles, close the bleed screw and release the brake pedal slowly. Repeat the bleeding operation until clean brake fluid, free of air bubbles, flows from the submerged end of the drain hose. Repeat this procedure at left rear, right front, and left front wheel cylinders, in that order, until all air is removed from the hydraulic system. After bleeding is completed, check brake fluid level in master cylinder reservoirs. Fill to within 1/2 inch (13 mm) of the top of the reservoirs. Install the diaphragm and cover.

47.12 Pressure Bleeding

Pressure bleeding equipment is available that allows a single mechanic to bleed a system. The pressure bleeder has a tank filled with brake fluid. Another tank filled with air pressure applies pressure on the fluid through a diaphragm. The fluid is forced under pressure into the brake system.

A pressure bleeder with fittings and adapter for connecting to the master cylinder fluid reservoirs is necessary to pressure bleed the brake hydraulic system. Be sure that enough brake fluid is in the pressure bleeder tank to complete the bleeding operation. The tank should be charged with 20–30 pounds of air pressure (138–207 kPa).

Fill master cylinder reservoirs with clean brake fluid. Attach the pressure bleeder hose to master cylinder reservoirs with a fitting or adapter. Open the

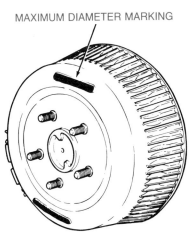

Fig. 47-11 Drum, maximum diameter specifications. (Chrysler Corporation)

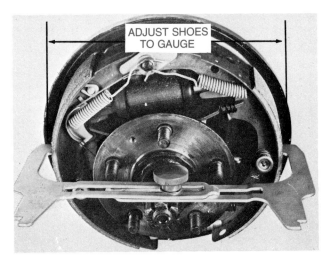

Fig. 47-12 Gauging drum and shoes.

valve in the pressure bleeder hose to pressurize the brake hydraulic system.

Attach a bleeder drain hose to the right rear wheel cylinder bleed screw. Submerge the free end of the hose in a glass container partly filled with brake fluid. Loosen the bleed screw. When fluid coming from the submerged end of the hose is free of air bubbles, close the bleed screw and remove the bleeder hose. Repeat at left rear, right front, and left front wheel cylinders in that order.

If the hydraulic system being bled has a dual system master cylinder with two filler caps, connect the pressure bleeder to the front reservoir to bleed the rear wheels and to the rear reservoir to bleed the front wheels.

47.13 Bleeding Disc Brakes

Vehicles with front disc brakes usually have a metering valve in the hydraulic line to the front disc brakes. With no hydraulic pressure applied, the stem of the metering valve is in the depressed position. When pressure bleeding calipers on vehicles with a metering valve, hold the valve stem in the depressed position. If tape is used to depress the stem, be sure to remove the tape after bleeding is completed. Do not attempt to force the metering valve stem into the valve body. This may damage the valve.

When manually bleeding (with an assistant pushing the brake pedal) calipers on vehicles with a metering valve, the metering valve stem need not be depressed. The hydraulic pressure developed is enough to open the valve.

47.14 SERVICING DRUM BRAKES

Servicing drum brakes involves disassembling the brakes, cleaning and inspecting the parts, resurfacing the brake drums, arcing the shoes, servicing the wheel cylinders and then reassembling and adjusting the brakes. These procedures are presented in the following sections.

47.15 Disassembly

The first step in drum brake disassembly is to remove the tire and wheel assemblies. Remove the drums from each wheel. Front drums are removed by disassembling the front spindle nut and hub assembly. Rear drums are removed by removing locks or axle nuts, depending upon the rear axle used. When removing drums, back off on the adjusting screw or release shoe-adjusting cams or eccentrics to provide enough shoe-to-drum clearance.

Always use wheel cylinder clamps to hold wheel cylinder pistons in place during removal and assembly of brake parts. Before removing brake parts, look at the location of different colored springs and note how springs and other parts are assembled. On brakes with automatic adjusters, observe how adjuster parts are assembled. Always use special brake spring tools for unhooking or attaching brake shoe return springs (Fig. 47-9) to avoid damage to springs and linings.

When removing shoe hold-down springs and pins (Fig. 47-10), hold a finger against the head of the pin at the rear of the backing plate while compressing the spring and turn the retainer washer 90° to the release position. When removing horseshoe or "C"

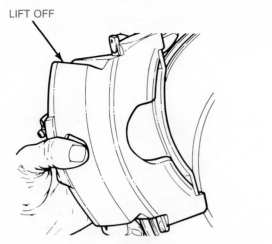

LIFT OFF

Fig. 47-13 Removing the caliper from the rotor. (Ford Motor Company)

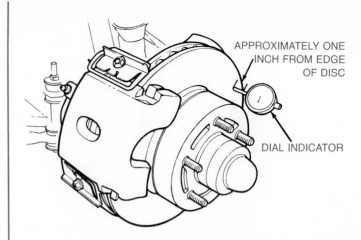

APPROXIMATELY ONE INCH FROM EDGE OF DISC

DIAL INDICATOR

Fig. 47-14 Checking the rotor for runout. (Chrysler Corporation)

washer locks used on emergency brake linkage, use special care to avoid damage to locks. Lay shoes out in pairs at each wheel in the same manner as assembled to the backing plate.

47.16 Cleaning and Inspection

Clean all greasy parts, except the brake lining and brake drums, with mineral spirits or other suitable solvent. Brake fluid may be removed with alcohol. Do not attempt to clean the brake lining. Final cleaning of brake drums should be done with a solution of soap and water.

Pull back wheel cylinder dust boots to inspect for leakage. If there is any sign of leakage, the cylinder should be disassembled and inspected as described later. Polish brake backing plate ledges with fine sandpaper or emory cloth. If there are grooves which may restrict shoe movement after polishing, replace the brake backing plate. Any attempt to remove the grooves by grinding may result in improper shoe-to-drum contact. Inspect the lining wear pattern. If the wear across the width of the lining is uneven, inspect the drums for taper, the shoes for correct positioning, and the backing plate for distortion. Inspect all springs for signs of overheating (discoloration) and fractures. Inspect the self-adjusting cables for kinks, fraying, and wear in the eyelet. Inspect the adjuster screw for freedom of rotation. Inspect the adjuster lever for wear and distortion.

When replacing brake shoes and linings on one wheel, the shoes and linings on the opposite side should also be replaced to maintain proper braking balance. Install new brake shoe return springs and hold-down springs if the old springs have been subjected to overheating or if their strength is questionable. Spring paint discoloration and distorted end coils are signs of an overheated spring.

47.17 Resurfacing Brake Drums

If drums are scored, tapered, heat-checked, or out of round, they must be resurfaced on a brake drum lathe or replaced. Drums cannot be resurfaced beyond the specifications cast on the outside of the drum (Fig. 47-11). A drum that exceeds the specification must be replaced. Oversize drums can cause brake fade, loss of pedal, and brake noise.

Drum diameter is most often measured with a micrometer gauge. Place the brake drum gauge in the drum so the contact points are at the greatest diameter. Move one end of the gauge back and forth until the highest dimension is obtained. Be careful to hold both contact points at the same depth (distance from the outside edge of the drum).

47.18 Arcing Shoes

Brake shoes must be matched to the curvature or arc of the drums. This is especially necessary if the drums have been machined oversize. Manufacturers specify the clearance between the ends of the brake shoes and the drum. The clearance is obtained by grinding the brake shoe lining material on a brake shoe grinder.

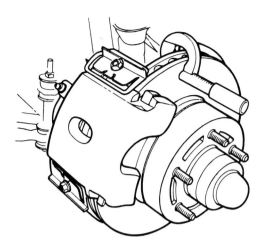

Fig. 47-15 Checking rotor thickness variation. (Chrysler Corporation)

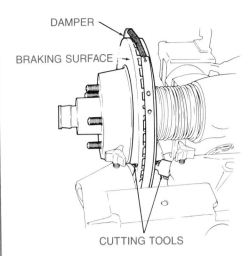

DAMPER

BRAKING SURFACE

CUTTING TOOLS

Fig. 47-16 Machining a rotor. (Chrysler Corporation)

47.19   Servicing Wheel Cylinders

If inspection shows that a wheel cylinder requires service, remove the wheel cylinders from the backing plate. Then remove the boots from the ends of the cylinder. The pistons and cups are forced out of the barrel by the compression spring. Clean all parts in alcohol or clean brake fluid. If the cylinder is scratched or pitted, it may be honed or replaced. Whenever a wheel cylinder is disassembled, replace the cups. Dip all parts in hydraulic brake fluid before assembly.

47.20   Reassembly and Adjustment

Before reassembling parts on the backing plate, lubricate the shoe contact surfaces with brake lubricant. When assembling rear brakes, lubricate the parking brake lever pivot and the part of the lever that contacts the secondary brake shoe. Adjust the brakes as follows. Determine drum diameter with a drum-to-brake shoe clearance gauge (Fig. 47-12). Reverse the gauge and place it on the brake linings. Turn the adjuster screw until the gauge just slides over the brake lining surface. Rotate the gauge around the lining surface to make sure there is enough clearance.

If the wheel cylinders were serviced, the entire system must be bled as described earlier.

47.21   SERVICING DISC BRAKES

If disc brakes require service, raise the vehicle on a hoist. Remove the front wheel covers and wheel and tire assemblies. Remove caliper guide pins, positioners, and antirattle springs. Remove the caliper from the rotor by slowly sliding the caliper assembly out and away from the rotor (Fig. 47-13). Support the caliper firming so as not to damage flexible brake hose. Slide the outboard shoe and lining assembly out of the caliper. Slide the inboard shoe and lining assembly out of the caliper.

47.22   Cleaning and Inspection

Check for piston seal leaks. Look for brake fluid in and around the boot area and inboard lining and check for any ruptures of the piston dust boot. If the boot is damaged or there is fluid leakage, disassemble the caliper assembly and install a new seal, boot, and piston if they are damaged or corroded. Check the mating surfaces on the caliper and clean them with a wire brush if they are corroded or rusty. Inspect braking surfaces of the rotor.

Check the rotor for lateral runout and thickness variation. Lateral runout is the movement of the rotor from side to side (wobble) as it rotates. Excessive lateral rotor face runout results in brake chatter, pedal pumping, too much pedal travel, and vibration during braking. This causes the rotor to strike the brake shoe and lining assemblies and to knock the pistons back into their bores.

To check lateral runout (Fig. 47-14), first tighten the spindle nut until all end play is out of the bearings. Fasten a dial indicator to some part of the suspension so that the point of the stylus contacts the rotor face approximately one inch from the outer edge. Set the dial at zero. Turn the rotor one complete revolution

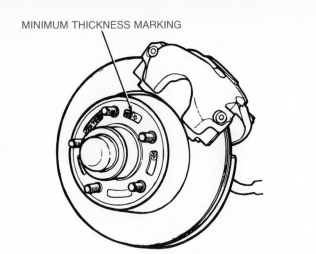

Fig. 47-17 Minimum thickness specification on a rotor. (Chrysler Corporation)

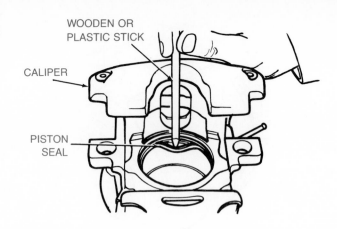

Fig. 47-18 Removing the piston seal. (Chrysler Corporation)

and check the indicator as the rotor moves. Rotor thickness variation beyond the recommended specification causes pedal vibration as well as front-end vibration during brake applications. To check thickness variation, measure the thickness of the rotor at four or more equally spaced points around the braking surface of the rotor. Make all measurements at the same distance from the edge of the rotor (Fig. 47-15).

47.23 Resurfacing Rotors

If the rotor has too much runout, thickness variation, or scoring, it must be replaced or resurfaced. The braking surface can be remachined on a disc rotor lathe by cutting or grinding (Fig. 47-16). Most lathes machine off of each side at the same time. On fixed caliper assemblies the same amount must be machined from each side. A new disc and hub assembly should be installed if refacing the old one brings it below minimum thickness specifications. A minimum thickness specification is typically cast in to the rotor as shown in Figure 47-17. Brake operation may be affected if too much material is removed.

47.24 Servicing Calipers

If a caliper boot or seal shows signs of damage or leaking, it must be overhauled. Drain two-thirds of the brake fluid from the master cylinder reservoir for the front disc brakes (the largest reservoir). Do not drain the reservoir completely. Throw away the fluid that was removed. Wipe all dirt and grease from the brake line fitting at the caliper with a clean shop cloth.

Disconnect the brake hose from the caliper. Cover the open end of the brake hose with tape or a clean shop cloth. Discard the brake hose washer. Remove the caliper and brake pads.

Drain fluid from the caliper. Remove the caliper piston from the piston bore. Remove the dust seal from piston and the piston seal from the piston bore (Fig. 47-18). Use only plastic or wooden tools to remove the piston seal. Metal tools may scratch or score the piston bore or seal grooves. Remove the bleeder screw and the protective plastic cap.

Remove any rust or corrosion from the sliding surfaces of the caliper and caliper anchor plate with a wire brush and crocus cloth. Clean the caliper and caliper piston with alcohol, clean brake fluid, or brake cleaning solvent and allow to air dry.

Inspect the caliper piston for damage and wear. Replace it if it is worn, scored, pitted, or corroded. Inspect the caliper for wear or damage. Replace it if the piston bore, piston seal groove, or dust seal groove is worn, scored, nicked, pitted, or heavily corroded. Light corrosion in the piston bore may be removed with a fiber brush.

Coat the square-cut piston seal with clean brake fluid and install it into the groove in the piston bore. Use fingers to work the seal into the groove (Fig. 47-19). Install the bleeder screw and protective plastic cap, but do not fasten the cap. Seat the bleeder screw. Lubricate the piston with brake fluid and install a new dust boot on the piston. Install the dust boot in the piston groove so that the fold-in boot faces the open end of the piston. Insert the piston in the bore (Fig. 47-20).

Remount the caliper and install caliper and brake lining. Bleed brakes as outlined previously.

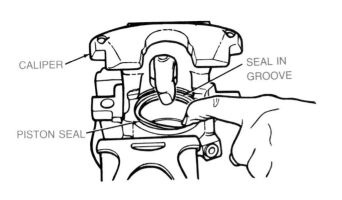

Fig. 47-19 Installing the piston seal in the caliper. (Chrysler Corporation)

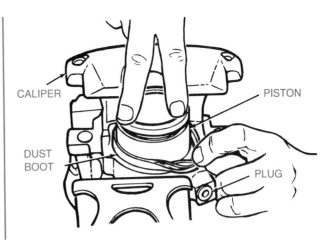

Fig. 47-20 Installing the piston in the caliper. (Chrysler Corporation)

NEW TERMS

Arcing Grinding brake shoe linings to fit the arc of oversize brake drums.

Bleeding Removing air from a hydraulic brake system.

Brake drum gauge A measuring tool with a micrometer scale that determines size and condition of brake drums.

Brake drum lathe Equipment used to machine a drum oversize.

Low brake pedal A brake pedal that travels too far before brakes are applied.

Manual bleeding Brake bleeding that is done by pumping the brake pedal.

Pressure bleeder An air-operated tank used to pressure bleed a brake system.

Pressure bleeding Bleeding a brake system with a pressure bleeder.

Spongy pedal A brake pedal that feels soft or spongy.

CHAPTER REVIEW

1. What can cause a spongy pedal?
2. What could cause grabby brakes?
3. Describe the pedal checks made during preventive maintenance.
4. Explain how to check the fluid level of a master cylinder.
5. How is disc pad lining checked for wear?
6. If a master cylinder is badly pitted or scored, what should a mechanic do?
7. How can air be removed from a master cylinder before it is installed on the vehicle?
8. Why must air be removed from a brake system when it is serviced?
9. Describe a manual bleeding procedure.
10. Explain how to pressure bleed a brake system.
11. If brake drums are scored or out of round, what should the mechanic do?
12. How are brake drums measured?
13. Describe how to check for piston seal leaks in a disc brake caliper.
14. Explain how to check a rotor for lateral runout.
15. If a rotor has too much runout or is scored, what should a mechanic do?

DISCUSSION TOPICS AND ACTIVITIES

1. Following the procedures in this chapter, check the condition of the brakes on the automobile you drive. Do they need replacement?
2. Disassemble a shop master cylinder. Inspect the condition of all parts and then reassemble it.
3. Disassemble a shop drum or disc brake unit. Decide what parts need replacing and then correctly reassemble the unit.

CHAPTER 48

Tires and Wheels

CHAPTER PREVIEW

Tires have two jobs. First, they provide a cushion between the road and the automobile wheels to take up shocks from rough roads. Tires flex, or give, on bumps to reduce the shock to the passengers in the vehicle. Second, the tires provide frictional contact between the wheels and the road for good traction. This allows the power to go through the tires to the road for rapid acceleration, resists the tendency of the vehicle to skid on turns, and allows quick stops when the brakes are applied.

OBJECTIVES

After studying this chapter, you should be able to do the following:

1. Identify the different types of tires used on automobiles.
2. Describe the types of tire construction and design.
3. Explain the different tire size systems in use.
4. Describe the methods used to rate tires.
5. Describe the different types and designs of rims.

48.1 TYPES OF TIRES

Pneumatic, or air-filled, tires either use an inner tube or are tubeless. On tires with an inner tube, both the tube and the tire are mounted on the wheel rim, with the tube inside the tire casing. The inner tube is inflated with air so that the tire casing resists any change of shape. The tubeless tire is mounted on the rim so that air is held between rim and tire casing when the tire is inflated. The amount of air pressure used varies with the size of the vehicle and its equipment.

48.2 TIRE CONSTRUCTION

Most people think of tires as being made from rubber. In fact, a tire is made from several different materials (Fig. 48-1). First, layers of cord, called plies, are formed over a spacing device and rubberized. This unit, which forms the casing for the air, is called the carcass. A steel wire bead, enclosed in an overlap of the carcass fabric, keeps the carcass on the wheel rim. The rubber which forms the tread and sidewall is then vulcanized over the carcass. All tires are constructed of essentially the same parts. They differ, however, in the way the layers of cord are arranged.

48.3 TIRE DESIGNS

Tire designs have changed a great deal over the years. Engineers have found that new tire designs and materials can improve vehicle handling. Just as significant, tire design can be very important in saving fuel.

48.4 Bias Ply

There are three types or designs of tires (Fig. 48-2). In the oldest design, bias ply, the carcass is formed by layers of cords which run at an angle. The criss-crossing pattern allows the cords to expand and contract with relative ease. This flexing of the carcass

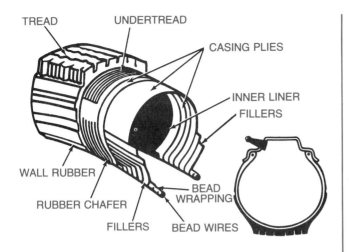

Fig. 48-1 Basic tire construction. (Chevrolet Motor Division, GMC)

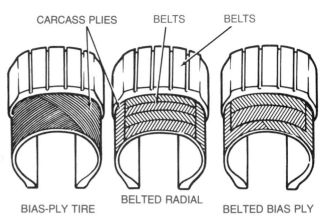

Fig. 48-2 The three tire designs.

gives the conventional bias-ply tire its main advantage —a soft ride for the people in the vehicle. As vehicle speeds increased, a disadvantage became important. Under fast, hard cornering conditions, the bias-ply tire begins to roll under, the sidewall begins to contact the ground, and the tread on the opposite side of the tire begins lifting. When this happens, the driver easily loses control and the automobile spins out. Tire engineers say the tire has an "unstable footprint" (Fig. 48-3) or road contact area.

48.5 Radial Ply

Two different tire designs were developed to get a more stable footprint. In one of these designs, the radial-ply tire, the cords lie at right angles. An additional structural member, called a belt, is added under the tread area of the tire (hence the term, "belted radials"). This combination of radial plies and belts provides a flexible sidewall with a strength and rigidity in the tread area. The result is a stable footprint (Fig. 48-4) and a much safer automobile. An improved footprint makes for easier steering, better traction, and better tire wear. The only problem with radial tires is a harder ride at low speed.

48.6 Belted Bias Ply

The second improved design adds belts to the conventional bias-ply tire. The sidewall of the belted bias-ply tire is softened by adding belts. The result is a footprint better than that of a conventional bias tire. Most experts agree, however, that the radial tire outperforms the belted bias and is also safer.

48.7 CONSTRUCTION MATERIALS

The basic strength of a tire is determined by its internal structure, called a carcass, or casing. The carcass is formed with layers of rubberized metal, or fabric, called plies and belts. Each ply is a layer of rubber with metal or fabric cords embedded in its body. The cords may be made from a variety of materials such as rayon, nylon, polyester, fiberglass, steel, or aramid. The type of material used determines the tires stability and resistance to bruises, fatigue, and heat. The plies are wound at their ends around the beads and bonded into the sides of the tire. Belts are also cords made from rubber reinforced with metal or fabric. The belts do not, however, go all the way down to the bead. The belts fit under the tread area of the tire.

48.8 SIZE AND LOAD RATING

Many tires have metric measurements, such as P195/75R14. The P stands for passenger car, with 195 the section width in millimeters (Fig. 48-5). 75 is the aspect ratio, R for radial construction, and 14 the size of the wheel in inches. The aspect ratio, represented by the number 75, shows the ratio of height to width (Fig. 48-6).

The oldest system of tire size markings uses a letter to indicate the size, followed by the aspect ratio, and then the wheel size, such as H78-14. At one time tires were also rated by the ply system, but now the load range system is used. A tire as strong as a 4-ply tire is now "load range B," although the tire may not actually have 4 plies. C is for six ply strength, and D

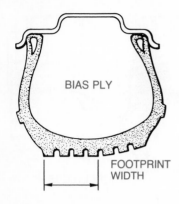

Fig. 48-3 Bias-ply footprint.

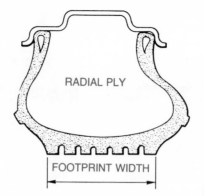

Fig. 48-4 Radial tire footprint.

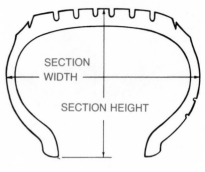

Fig. 48-5 Tire sizes are based on cross section height and width.
(Cadillac Motor Car Division, GMC)

for eight ply.

Some tires are marked only with the size of the section width and wheel, such as 6.95-14.

48.9 TIRE QUALITY GRADING

Premium, first line, 100 level; these terms relate only the price a manufacturer charges for various tires. There is no industry-wide standard use of these terms. Realizing the need for such information, the National Highway Traffic Safety Administration has developed a set of tire grading standards. Tire manufacturers are required by federal law to use a system of tire grading called the Uniform Tire Quality Grading (UTQG). This system grades three tire qualities: tread wear, traction, and resistance to high temperature. The sidewall symbols consist of a number, followed by two letters.

Relative tread wear is indicated by the number. The control number is 100, indicating approximately 30,000 miles of normal driving under test conditions. Thus, a tire rated 080 can be expected to deliver about 20 percent less mileage or 24,000 miles. In the other direction, 160 should wear 60 percent longer or 48,000 miles. Numbers range from 050, (15,000 miles), to 270, (81,000 miles). New tires are no longer required to have the tread wear number, but the letter grading is still in effect.

The first letter, A, B, or C, indicates relative skid resistance on wet pavement. The raing A is best while C is the worst. The second letter, A, B, or C, indicates resistance to overheating at freeway speeds, particularly when slightly overloaded or underin-flated. Again, A is best and C is worst.

For many years, imported radial tires have used a speed rating system. This system is used in the tire size designation. There are three ratings; SR—maximum speed 112 mph, HR—up to 130 mph, and VR—up to 165 mph. The rating is specified in the tire size. For example, the tire may be marked 175SR × 13. This means the tire is 175 mm wide with a speed rating of 112 mph.

48.10 TIRE DOT CODES

Since tires are used in interstate transportation, the Department of Transportation (DOT) specifies that certain be imprinted on each tire. The information required by law is shown in Figure 48-7.

Wheels or rims must have enough strength to carry the weight of the vehicle, transfer driving and braking torque to the tires, and withstand side thrusts over a wide range of speed and road conditions. Modern high speeds require low vehicle centers of gravity. To meet this need, wheels of small diameter manufactured from steel or a light alloy of aluminum and magnesium have been developed.

Most vehicles use steel drop center wheels. The safety rim wheel has raised sections between the rim flanges and the rim well. Inflating of the tire forces the bead over these raised sections. Tire-wheel separation under very hard cornering is prevented by air pressure and these safety humps. Furthermore, in case of a tire failure, the raised sections help hold the tire in position on the wheel until the vehicle can be brought to a safe stop.

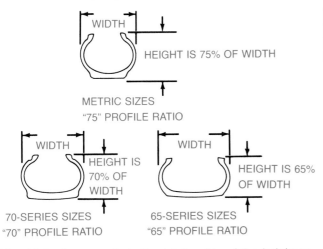

Fig. 48-6 Aspect ratio is the relationship of tire height to width. (American Motors Corporation)

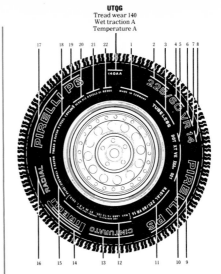

Fig. 48-7 DOT code on a tire. (Pirelli)

1. Country of origin.
2. Cross section of tire in mm.
3. Tube type or tubeless.
4. Aspect ratio (78 is narrow, 60 is wide).
5. Signifies DOT compliance.
6. Speed rated above 130 mph.
7. R for radial construction.
8. Wheel diameter in inches.
9. Tire brand, and line.
10. Who made it, where, when.
11. Cosmetic repeats.
12. Maximum pressure & load.
13. Tire line (Cinturato means belted).
14. Tire brand (trademark).
15. Sidewall construction.
16. Cosmetic repeat.
17. Brand (cosmetic repeat).
18. Tread construction.
19. Tire line.
20. European standards code.
21. Patent number, Italy.
22. Mold identification.

NEW TERMS

Aspect ratio   The ratio of tire height to width.

Belted tire   A tire that is reinforced with a buildup of cord under the tread area.

Bias-ply tire   A tire design in which the layers of cord have a criss crossed pattern.

Cord   The material used to hold the rubber parts of the tire in position.

DOT codes   Construction and manufacturing information required on a tire by the Department of Transportation.

Dropped center rim   A wheel with a lowered center that provides raised flanges to prevent the wheel from getting off the rim during driving.

Load rating   A letter on the sidewall which indicates the amount of load a tire can support.

Load range   A range of tire load ratings at a specific inflation pressure.

Plies   Layers of cord used when the tire is constructed.

Pneumatic tires   Tires that are filled with air.

Quality gradings   A system of tire quality gradings based upon tread wear, traction, and resistance to high temperature.

Radial tire   A tire in which the layers of cord lie at right angles.

Rim   The metal wheel on which the tire is mounted.

Tubeless tire   A tire that has the air sealed between the rim and tire and does not use an inner tube.

CHAPTER REVIEW

1. List the two basic jobs of the tires.
2. List the two basic kinds of tires.
3. What is a tubeless tire?
4. What is a tire bead?
5. What are plies?
6. List the three different tire designs.
7. Describe a bias-ply tire.
8. Describe a radial-ply tire.
9. What is the main advantage of radial-ply tire?
10. What is a belted tire?
11. List four different materials used for cords.
12. List and describe the two basic measurements used to describe a tire.
13. What is a tire aspect ratio?
14. What is the load range used for in a tire?
15. What is the DOT code on a tire?

DISCUSSION TOPICS AND ACTIVITIES

1. What tire design is used on the automobile you drive? What are its advantages and disadvantages?
2. Find the tire size molded into a tire. What does each of the numbers and letters mean?
3. Study a tire cross section. Can you identify all of the parts of a tire?

Tire and Wheel Service

An automobile's performance, ride, and handling qualities are all influenced by tire and wheel condition. The tire and wheel assembly cushions the ride against bad jolts, gives firm support to the vehicle, and provides traction. The tires also provide directional stability and absorb all the stresses of accelerating, braking, and centrifugal forces in turns.

OBJECTIVES

After studying this chapter, you should be able to do the following:

1. List the steps in finding a tire or wheel problem.
2. Describe the preventive maintenance jobs that are done on tires and wheels.
3. Explain how to measure tire and wheel runout.
4. Explain the two kinds of wheel balance.
5. Explain how to repair a tire.

49.1   TROUBLESHOOTING

The most common tire problems involve excessive tread wear, sway, pull, noise, and vibration. The tires often provide clues in diagnosing alignment, steering, and suspension problems, but they can also cause noise, shake, or vibration that may be blamed incorrectly on other parts.

49.2   Excessive Wear

As mentioned previously under wheel alignment, tire wear patterns provide a good deal of information.

An inspection of the tires often shows abnormal wear due to operating conditions or mechanical problems which should be corrected (Fig. 49-1).

For the best results in stability, handling, ride quality, and tire life, tire inflation pressures should not be below specifications. Underinflation results in much faster wear of the shoulders than the center of tread. By holding to specified tire inflation pressure, even wear will take place over the entire tread surface. Overinflation causes faster wear at the center of the tread and increases the possibility of cuts and punctures.

Cracked treads result from exceeding the recommended full rated load, high temperature, and high-speed driving. Excessive positive or negative wheel camber causes the tire to run at an angle on the road so that one side of the tread wears more than the other.

When there is excessive toe-in or toe-out the tires drag instead of rolling true. This causes wear on the edges of the front tires, feathered edges on the outside ribs. The toe-in or toe-out must be adjusted to specifications.

Cupping, scalloping, and bald spotting of tires is caused by driving a vehicle at highway speeds without the recommended tire rotation and with unbalanced wheels. No alignment or balance job can prevent future excessive wear once a front tire gets flat or cupped spots.

Tread wear indicators have been added to tires in the last several years to show when tires are worn to the point of requiring replacement. These indicators molded into the bottom of the tread grooves appear as 1/2-inch (13 mm) wide bands when the tread depth has been reduced to 1/16 inch (1.6 mm) (Fig. 49-2). Tire replacement is necessary when these indicators

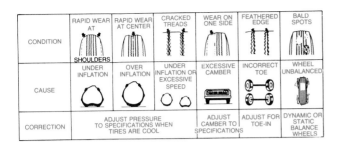

CONDITION	RAPID WEAR AT SHOULDERS	RAPID WEAR AT CENTER	CRACKED TREADS	WEAR ON ONE SIDE	FEATHERED EDGE	BALD SPOTS
CAUSE	UNDER INFLATION	OVER INFLATION	UNDER INFLATION OR EXCESSIVE SPEED	EXCESSIVE CAMBER	INCORRECT TOE	WHEEL UNBALANCED
CORRECTION	ADJUST PRESSURE TO SPECIFICATIONS WHEN TIRES ARE COOL			ADJUST CAMBER TO SPECIFICATIONS	ADJUST FOR TOE-IN	DYNAMIC OR STATIC BALANCE WHEELS

Fig. 49-1 Tire wear patterns. (Dodge/Chrysler Corporation)

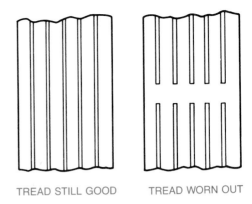

TREAD STILL GOOD   TREAD WORN OUT

Fig. 49-2 Tire tread wear indicator. (American Motors Corporation)

appear in two or more grooves or when all tread is gone in a worn spot.

49.3 Sway

Sway is a condition in which the rear wheels oversteer. The driver must fight the steering wheel, especially in cornering, at high speeds, and in a strong wind. Most overloading is in the rear of the automobile, so the problem of sway starts there most often. When sway is the problem, check for overloading and proper inflation.

49.4 Pull

Underinflation and/or overloading may also cause pull, along with tire noise—especially on curves—when friction increases. Unless uneven tire inflation pressure or overloading can be found, however, pull is nearly always a problem of alignment.

49.5 Noise

Noise usually sounds like a thump with each revolution of the wheel. It can be heard only on smooth blacktop pavement that is free of surface irregularities. Check tire thump by driving the automobile over a smooth blacktop pavement with tires at recommended inflation pressure, then again over the same stretch of road with the tires inflated to 50 psi (345 kPa). Drop the pressure in one tire at a time to normal to identify the tire making noise.

Striking any obstructions or rocks in the road with tires at 50 psi can rupture tire casings. Operate the vehicle with higher than recommended inflation only while testing and never over 50 mph (80 km/h).

Carefully inspect the tire making the noise for bulges, irregular wear, low air pressure, toe and heel wear, and unusual tread design (ribbed tread gives less noise than some all-weather treads; mud and snow treads are very noisy). Checking wheel alignment and rotating tires will usually cure tire noises unless they are caused by tire tread design, heavy irregular tread wear, or tire bulges.

49.6 Vibration

Noise from vibration or shaking can result from imbalance, too much runout of the tires, or, as mentioned previously, drive line misalignment or imbalance. Vibration problems are repaired by testing and correcting tire and wheel runout and balance.

49.7 PREVENTIVE MAINTENANCE

The most important preventive maintenance procedures for tires are maintaining correct inflation pressures, rotating tires, and cleaning tires.

49.8 Tire Inflation

When tire pressure is too low, the automobile is difficult to steer and the front end shimmies. More important, low tires run hotter, increasing the risk of failure. Tires operated for a long time with low pressure show signs of wear on both outside edges. When tires are operated with too much pressure, they are more susceptible to bruises and punctures and the ride is stiff and harsh. Tires operated for a long time while

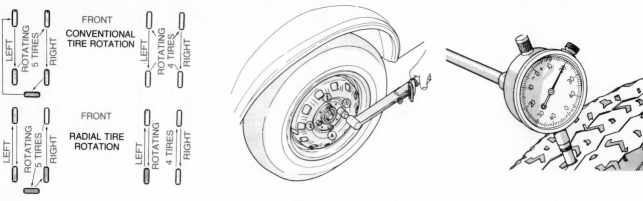

Fig. 49-3 Tire rotation chart. (American Motors Corporation)

Fig. 49-4 Tightening wheel stud nuts in correct order. (Chrysler Corporation)

Fig. 49-5 Measuring tire runout. (Chrysler Corporation and American Motors Corporation)

overinflated show signs of wear on the center. Uneven tire pressure in the two front tires causes the vehicle to pull to one side when the brakes are applied.

For all these reasons, tire pressure must be checked periodically. Use a pocket gauge to measure the pressure in the tires at least every month. Check them in the service station so air can be added if they are low. Do not depend on gauges at service stations. They are frequently misused and out of calibration. Check the service manual for recommended air pressure. Make sure the tires are at operating temperature when you check them, rather than very cold or very hot. When tires get very hot, the pressure inside them increases. Never lower the pressure of a hot tire. It could run even hotter underinflated.

49.9   Tire Rotation

Most service manuals suggest rotating tires at regular intervals to get even tire wear. On some cars, the driving wheels, either front or rear, have the most tire wear. Other cars will wear out the front tires first because of turning corners. Many car makers suggest rotating tires at least every other oil change.

Rotation charts similar to Figure 49-3 are provided in the manufacturer's service manual. Bias-ply tires are normally cross-switches from front to back and side to side. Radial tires are usually moved between front and rear only, so that they keep rotating in the same direction. A radial tire may disintegrate if it is run first in one direction and then in the other. Some tire manufacturers say that cross-switching is permitted if necessary.

Any time tires are removed from the vehicle, the wheel stud nuts must be tightened in the proper order and to the correct amount with a torque wrench (Fig. 49-4). Failure to do this could result in distorted brake drums or rotors.

49.10   Cleaning

A great deal of ordinary road dirt which collects on white sidewall tires may be sponged off with clear water or a mild soap solution. A good whitewall tire cleaner, however, is quicker and better at removing dirt and stains from whitewall tires.

Gasoline, kerosene, or any cleaning fluid containing a solvent made from oil should never be used to clean whitewall tires. Oil in any form is bad on tire rubber and will discolor whitewalls.

49.11   TIRE AND WHEEL SERVICE

Common tire and wheel or rim service procedures include measuring tire and wheel runout, balancing wheels, and repairing leaks.

49.12   Tire and Wheel Runout

Tire and wheel runout is a condition in which the tire or wheel is not concentric. This may be caused by a tire that was not manufactured round or by a bent wheel that wobbles as it rotates. Too much radial and lateral runout of a wheel and tire can cause roughness, tire wear, and steering wheel shaking. To avoid false readings from temporary flat spots in the tires, check the tires as soon as possible after the vehicle has been driven at least ten miles. The amount of runout is

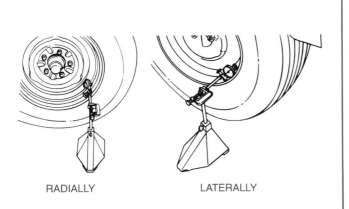

RADIALLY   LATERALLY

Fig. 49-6 Measuring wheel runout. (American Motors Corporation)

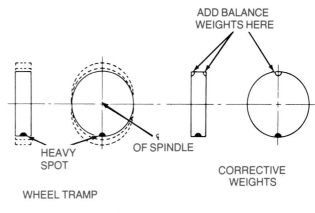

ADD BALANCE WEIGHTS HERE

HEAVY SPOT   OF SPINDLE   CORRECTIVE WEIGHTS

WHEEL TRAMP

Fig. 49-7 Static out-of-balance conditions.

measured with a dial indicator. Make all measurements with the tires inflated to recommended load inflation pressures and front wheel bearings adjusted properly.

Measure tire radial runout in the center of the tread face and lateral runout just above the buffing rib on the tire sidewall (Fig. 49-5). Mark the high points of lateral and radial runout for future use.

When total radial or lateral runout exceeds specified limits, check wheel runout to determine whether the wheel or tire is at fault. Wheel radial runout should be measured just inside of the wheel cover retaining nibs (Fig. 49-6). Wheel lateral runout should be measured on the bead flange just inside of the curved lip. Wheel radial runout should not be more than 0.035 inch (0.89 mm), and lateral runout should not be more than 0.045 inch (1.14 mm). Mark the high points of radial and lateral runout for possible future use.

Where either lateral or radial tire runout is higher than specifications but wheel runout is within specifications, it may be possible to reduce runout by placing the tire on the wheel so that the previously marked high points are 180° apart. In some cases, runout may be corrected only by replacing a tire or wheel.

49.13   Wheel Balance

Wheel balancing is properly distributing the weight around a tire and wheel assembly to counteract centrifugal forces acting upon the heavy areas. There are two kinds of balance, static and dynamic. Static or still balance is the equal distribution of weight

of the wheel and tire assembly about the axis of rotation so that the assembly has no tendency to rotate by itself. Static imbalance causes the pounding action of the front wheels that is called tramp (Fig. 49-7). The speed at which tramp or hop occurs depends on the amount the wheel is out of balance. Usually, the greater the wheel imbalance, the lower the speed at which the tramp or hop occurs.

Dynamic balance means balance in motion. If a wheel and tire assembly is in dynamic balance, it must also be in static balance. However, it does not follow that a wheel and tire assembly which is in static balance is also in dynamic balance. Dynamic or running balance means the wheel is balanced and running smoothly while turning on an axis which runs through the centerline of the wheel and tire perpendicular to the axis of rotation (Fig. 49-8). The requirements for dynamic balance not only include the equal distribution of weight around the axis of rotation, but also equal weight distribution with regard to the center line of the tire and wheel.

A wheel is balanced by determining where the heavy spots are and correcting for these heavy spots with either clamp-on or stick-on wheel weights. There are two general types of wheel balancers. The static wheel balancer (Fig. 49-9) uses the principle of a carpenter's level. The tire and wheel assembly is installed on the balancer while the operator observes a level bubble. The bubble position allows the operator to find and correct for the heavy spot, by adding weights. These types of balancers are often called bubble balancers.

All dynamic wheel balancers balance the wheel by spinning it. When the wheel is in motion, some method is used to sense the vibration caused by un-

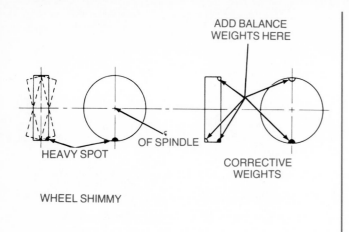

Fig. 49-8 Dynamic out-of-balance conditions.

Fig. 49-9 A static or bubble wheel balancer. (FMC Corporation, Automotive Service Equipment Division)

equal weights around the tire center line. Corrective weights are then added to remove the vibration and balance the tire.

There are two general types of spin balancers. One type, called an on-the-car balancer, uses the car's drive wheel or an electric motor to spin the wheels on the car (Fig. 49-10). Visual or electronic equipment is used to sense the imbalance. The other type is called an off-the-car balancer (Fig. 49-11). The wheel is removed from the car and installed on a spinning unit. Off-the-car balancers are usually faster to use and can sense smaller amounts of imbalance, because they are true dynamic balancers. On the other hand, on-the-car balancers are less expensive.

When using either type of balancer, be sure the rim is clean and all rocks are removed from the tire tread. Remove all the wheel weights from both sides of the rim. Read the instruction booklet for the type of equipment you are using and follow it step-by-step.

49.14   Tire Repair

When a tire loses all or most of its air pressure, it must be removed from the wheel for a complete inspection to determine what damage has occurred. Punctured tires should be removed from the wheel and permanently repaired from the inside.

When a tire is brought in for repairs, the sidewall and tread should be examined for damage or wear. Nails or other sharp objects should be removed and the holes marked with chalk. If a tank is available, the tire and rim should be submerged. Bubbles coming out of the tire will show where the leaks are. Look for leaks particularly around the rim, at the valve, and along the tread. Carefully examine the bead and rim at

any point where leakage is found. If a tank is not available, apply a soapy solution to the tire and look for bubbles.

As you examine the tire, look not only for punctures and other obvious injuries, but signs of swelling or blistering, especially in the shoulder area. Remove the tire from the rim once your inspection is complete. Take care not to damage the bead or liner. Once the tire is off the rim, examine its inside for signs of damage. A ply separation near a puncture or other injury may not be easy to see, for the air will escape through the injury. Probing is the only way to detect separation.

Never repair a puncture in a tire with the following:

1. Ply separation
2. Chafed fabric injuries on tubeless tires
3. Broken or damaged bead wires
4. Flex breaks
5. Loose cords or evidence of having been run flat
6. Tread separation
7. Wear below 1/16 inch (1.6 mm) depth in major grooves
8. Cracks which go into the tire fabric
9. Any open liner cut which shows exposed fabric
10. Sidewall puncture

When a repairable tire problem is discovered, the tire must be taken off the rim. Follow manufacturer's instructions when using tire mounting equipment.

A hot patch kit to repair leaks in tires uses heat to vulcanize the patch to the tire. Scrape and buff the area around the leak and cover with a light coating of cement of the type specified for the patch being used. Carefully remove the backing from the patch and center its base over the injury. Place the clamp over

Fig. 49-10 On-the-car wheel balancer. (Stewart Warner Corporation, Alemite Div.)

Fig. 49-11 A computerized off-the-car dynamic wheel balancer. (Bear)

the patch and tighten. Finger tighten only; do not use a wrench or pliers. Apply heat and allow to cool. When cool, remove the clamp and remount the repaired tire on the rim. Make a final check under water to determine that there are no leaks.

NEW TERMS

Dynamic balance The condition in which a tire and wheel are balanced on an axis which runs through the centerline of the wheel and tire.

Static balance A condition in which tire and wheel are balanced about the axis of rotation.

Tire rotation Changing the position of tires on the automobile to even out the amount of wear.

Tire runout The amount the tire wobbles as it rotates.

Tread wear indicators Molded bars in the tire tread that show up when the tire is worn enough to require replacement.

Wheel balance The proper distribution of weight around a tire and wheel assembly to counteract centrifugal forces acting on heavy areas.

Wheel runout The amount the wheel wobbles as it rotates.

CHAPTER REVIEW

1. What can cause too much tire wear?
2. What is a tire tread indicator?
3. What can cause sway?
4. What can cause pull?
5. Describe how to locate tire noise.
6. What can cause vibration?
7. Explain how to check tire pressure.
8. Why should tires be rotated?
9. How are radial tires rotated?
10. Why should wheel stud nuts be tightened with a torque wrench?
11. Describe how to clean a tire.
12. Explain how to check tire and wheel runout.
13. How can runout be corrected?
14. What is dynamic balance?
15. What is static balance?
16. Describe a tire with a nonrepairable problem.
17. Describe how to hot patch a tire.
18. How can a tire noise problem be located?
19. What can cause tire and wheel vibration?
20. What is tire runout?

DISCUSSION TOPICS AND ACTIVITIES

1. Make a list of tire and wheel problems. Describe how you would find the cause of each problem.
2. Measure the inflation pressure in the tires on the automobile you drive. How do they compare with specifications?
3. Study some old tires found around the shop. Can you find the reason they were removed?

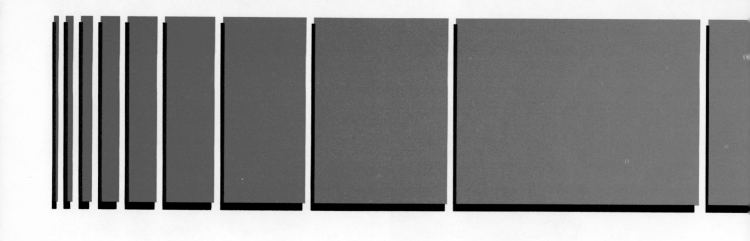
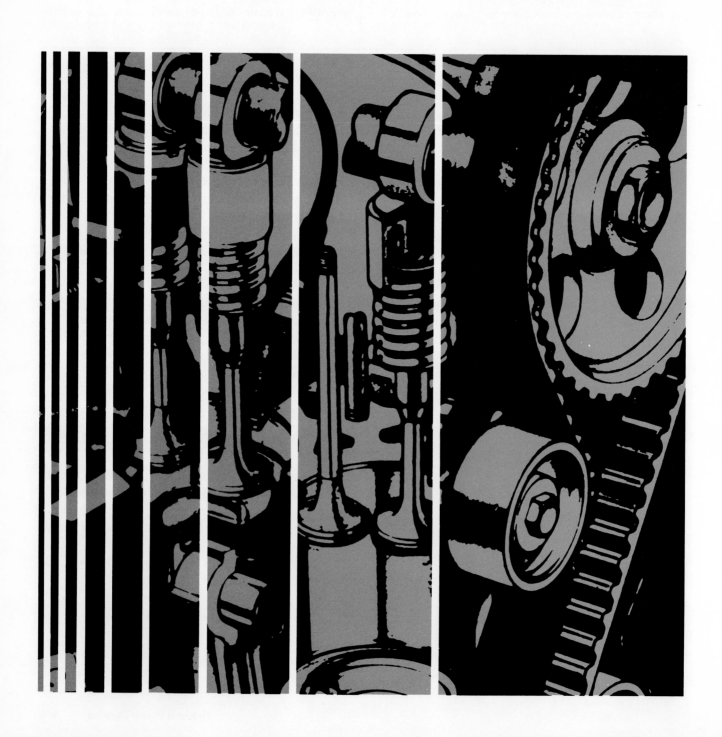

Automobile Heating and Air Conditioning

Heating and Air Conditioning Systems

CHAPTER PREVIEW

Most late model automobiles are equipped with a heater and an air conditioning unit. The purpose of the heater and air conditioner is to improve passenger comfort by controlling the temperature, humidity, and circulation of the air inside the automobile. In this chapter, we will explain how these systems operate.

OBJECTIVES

After studying this chapter, you should be able to do the following:

1. Explain the operation of heating systems and identify their principle parts.
2. Understand how evaporation causes cooling.
3. Describe the operation of the refrigeration cycle.
4. Identify and explain the purpose of the components of the air conditioning system.
5. Describe the service procedures used on air conditioning systems.

50.1   HEATING SYSTEMS

The heating system is designed to heat the air inside the vehicle for cold weather operation. Most heaters use an air mix system in which inside air is heated and then mixed in varying amounts with cooler outside air to get the desired temperature. The system consists of three basic parts: blower and inlet air assembly, heater core and distributor assembly, and heater control assembly.

50.2   Blower and Inlet Air Assembly

The blower and inlet air assembly consists of an electrically controlled fan or blower attached to a system of ducts called the inlet air assembly. The operation of the blower is controlled by a switch on the heater control panel. When it is turned on, the blower and inlet air assembly draws outside air through the outside inlet grill usually located forward of the windshield.

50.3   Heater Core and Distributor Assembly

The heater distributor assembly is a large housing, usually mounted on the engine firewall, which contains the heater core and the doors necessary to control mixing and channeling of the air. The heater core is a heat exchanger that looks like a small radiator (Fig. 50-1). Hot coolant from the automobile's cooling system is directed into the heater core. Two heater hoses, one for inlet and one for outlet, connect the engine to the heater core (Fig. 50-2).

As in any heat exchanger, the hot coolant dissipates heat into the metal of the core, heating air passing through the core. As shown in Figure 50-3, the blower pulls in outside air and directs a part of it over the heater core. This heated air is mixed with cool outside air in the proper amount to regulate the temperature.

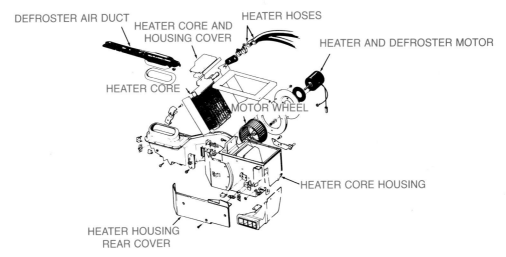

Fig. 50-1 Heater core and housing assembly. (American Motors Corporation)

DEFROSTER AIR DUCT

HEATER CORE AND HOUSING COVER

HEATER HOSES

HEATER AND DEFROSTER MOTOR

HEATER CORE

MOTOR WHEEL

HEATER CORE HOUSING

HEATER HOUSING REAR COVER

50.4 Heater Control Assembly

The heater control assembly mounted on the instrument panel (Fig. 50-4) contains switches and levers to operate the heater. The fan is controlled by an electrical switch. The doors in the distributor assembly are opened or closed by levers connected to cables or vacuum motors. A DEFROST position directs heated air at the windshield to defrost it.

50.5 AIR CONDITIONING SYSTEMS

The air conditioner cools, dehumidifies, cleans, and circulates air. In automotive applications, air conditioner is usually abbreviated A/C. The principles of operation of the automotive A/C are basically the same as those of home air conditioners and refrigerators (Fig. 50-5).

50.6 Cooling by Evaporation

Most refrigeration systems cool by evaporation. Whenever a liquid vaporizes, or turns into a gas, it absorbs a large amount of heat. When your body is overheated, sweat glands release moisture to the surface of your skin. If the air around you is dry enough, that moisture evaporates. As it evaporates, it absorbs heat from your skin and cools you. Sweat in this example acts as a refrigerant.

If you rub alcohol on your skin, it also cools you by evaporation. But it makes you feel colder faster than water does because alcohol is much more volatile: it evaporates much faster than water. The faster the evaporation, the more cooling you experience.

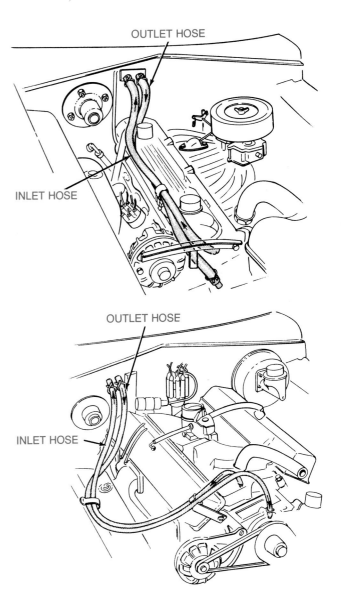

OUTLET HOSE

INLET HOSE

OUTLET HOSE

INLET HOSE

Fig. 50-2 Heater hoses connected to heater core. (Dodge/Chrysler Corporation)

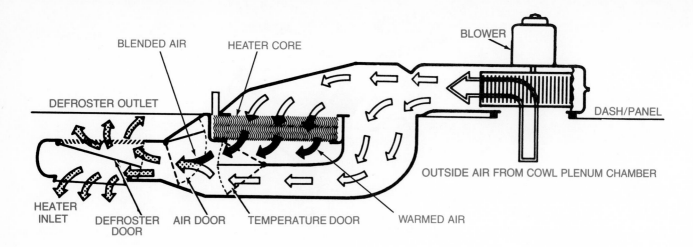

Fig. 50-3 Air flow across heater core. (Chevrolet Motor Division, GMC)

BLENDED AIR

HEATER CORE

BLOWER

DEFROSTER OUTLET

DASH/PANEL

OUTSIDE AIR FROM COWL PLENUM CHAMBER

HEATER INLET

DEFROSTER DOOR

AIR DOOR

TEMPERATURE DOOR

WARMED AIR

50.7 Refrigerants

The substance that carries the heat out of a refrigerator cabinet or an automobile is called a refrigerant. There are many refrigerants known to man. In fact, any liquid that boils at temperatures near the freezing point of water can be used. But a low boiling point is not the only thing that makes a good refrigerant. A refrigerant should also be nonpoisonous and nonexplosive to be safe. Besides that, it should be noncorrosive and mix with oil.

A volatile refrigerant called R-12 is used in automobile air conditioning systems. Refrigerant 12 boils at $-22°F$ ($-30°C$) under atmospheric pressure. In fact, refrigerant 12 can be stored in the liquid state only by subjecting it to high pressure. When the pressure is removed, it evaporates many times faster than alcohol and, of course, absorbs a vast amount of heat. It is this thirst for heat that makes the refrigerant so suitable to use in our air-conditioning systems.

50.8 Conditioning the Air

Many people think that an air conditioner is designed just to cool the air. It controls humidity, cleanliness, and circulation of the air as well. Humidity, the moisture content of the air, is tied in with the temperature of the air. Warm air will hold more moisture than will cold air. When air contains all the moisture it can hold, it is saturated, and the relative humidity is 100 percent. If the air contains only half as much water as it could hold at any given temperature, its relative humidity is 50 percent. Air conditioning controls the relative humidity of the air as well as

its temperature by reducing the moisture content in the air.

50.9 THE REFRIGERATION CYCLE

All air conditioning systems operate on the same basic principle, the refrigeration cycle (Fig. 50-6). Air to be cooled passes through a finned heat exchanger known as the evaporator. The refrigerant boils in the evaporator, absorbing heat as it changes into a vapor. Piping this vapor outside the passenger compartment carries out the heat.

Since heat changed the refrigerant from a liquid to a vapor in the first place, removal of that heat will condense the vapor into a liquid again. Then the liquid refrigerant can return to the evaporator to be used over again.

Actually, the vapor coming out of the evaporator is very cold. Since liquid refrigerant boils at temperatures considerably below the freezing point of water, the vapors are only a little warmer than this. For this reason it is difficult to remove heat from these vapors by "cooling" them in air temperatures that usually range between 60° and 100°F (16-38°C). Heat does not flow from a cold object toward a warmer object. But a pump that compresses the heat-laden vapor into a smaller space also concentrates the heat it contains. In this way, it makes the vapor hotter without adding any heat. Then it can be cooled by warm air.

As the refrigerant leaves the compressor, it is still a vapor although it is now quite hot and ready to give up the heat that it absorbed in the evaporator. To help refrigerant vapor discharge its heat, it is sent through a radiator-like condenser.

A plastic expansion tube, with its mesh screen

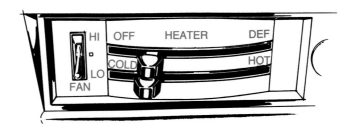

Fig. 50-4 Heater controls. (Chevrolet Motor Division, GMC)

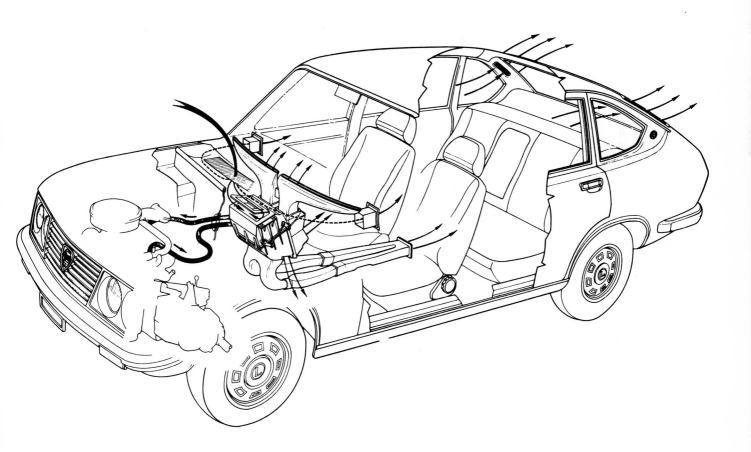

Fig. 50-5 Heating and ventilation flow. (Lancia)

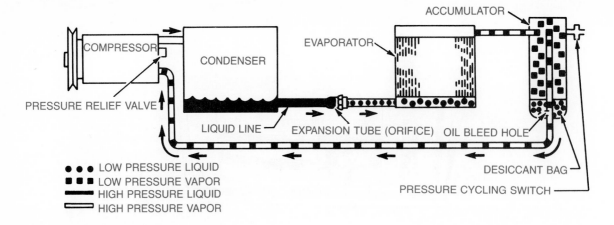

Fig. 50-6 Refrigeration cycle. (Chevrolet Motor Division, GMC)

and orifice, is located in the evaporator inlet pipe at the liquid line connection. It provides a restriction to the high pressure liquid refrigerant in the liquid line, metering the flow of the refrigerant to the evaporator as a low pressure liquid.

The condenser is a very simple device with no moving parts. Its purpose, as the name implies, is to condense high-pressure, high-temperature refrigerant vapor discharged by the compressor into high-pressure liquid refrigerant by exposing it to the considerably cooler metal surfaces of the condenser. Heat travels from the warmer to the cooler substance. As the vapor cools, it condenses into a liquid. It is then routed through a pipe from the condenser back to the evaporator. This completes the closed refrigeration cycle.

50.10 AIR CONDITIONING COMPONENTS

The basic components of an automobile air conditioning system are shown in Figure 50-7. All automotive air conditioning systems use a compressor, condenser, receiver/drier, expansion valve, evaporator and blower.

50.11 Compressor

The compressor (Fig. 50-8) is usually a multi-cylinder, belt-driven pump used to circulate and increase the pressure of the refrigerant in the system. The compressor is driven by a V-belt on the front of the engine. It is activated by a magnetic clutch when the air conditioner is turned on.

50.12 Condenser

The condenser is mounted in front of the radiator where air flowing over the cooling fins will remove heat from the refrigerant. As the refrigerant passes through the condenser, it liquefies or condenses.

50.13 Receiver/Drier

The receiver/drier is a reservoir used to store and dry the precise amount of refrigerant required by the system. The refrigerant level in the receiver/drier must be adequate to provide a steady flow of refrigerant to the expansion valve.

50.14 Expansion Valve

The thermostatic expansion valve is located at the inlet side of the evaporator. It regulates the refrigerant flow to the evaporator. If too much refrigerant goes in, a flooding condition results and the unit will not cool. If too little refrigerant goes in, the system is starved and will not cool. The regulating action of the expansion valve is controlled by the temperature-sensing bulb mounted on the outlet (suction) line of the evaporator.

50.15 Evaporator

The evaporator is an air cooler and dehumidifier. As refrigerant enters the evaporator core, it begins to boil. Air passing over the evaporator gives up its heat to the boiling refrigerant. As the air cools, the moisture in the air condenses on the evaporator core and is drained off as water.

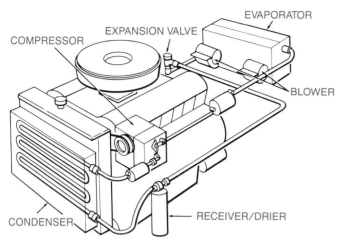

Fig. 50-7 Parts of automotive air conditioner.
(Temp Products)

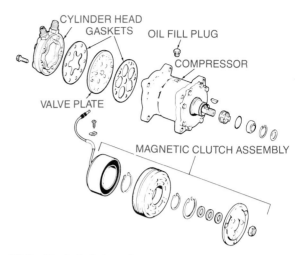

Fig. 50-8 Exploded view of compressor.
(American Motors Corporation)

50.16 Blower

A blower is used to direct the cooled air into the vehicle. The blower is a small fan driven by an electric motor.

50.17 AIR CONDITIONING SERVICE AND REPAIR

Air conditioning service involves troubleshooting to find the cause of the problem and repairing the problem. An air conditioner service set (Fig. 50-9) is the key test instrument used to locate trouble in the refrigeration system. This gauge set, with its manifold, valves, and vacuum pump, provides a means of testing, discharging, evacuating, and charging the system.

A mechanic diagnosing a refrigeration system is concerned with either of two conditions: not enough cooling or no cooling at all. The first condition can be caused by incorrect refrigerant charge level, air in the system, or defective components. Because there is some refrigerant in the system, gauge readings can help narrow down the source of trouble.

Where there is no cooling action at all, the system is probably empty. Since this usually results from a leak, follow the service manual instructions for locating leaks and make the necessary corrections before pressure testing. Leaks are detected with an electronic leak detector (Fig. 50-10).

Always follow the manufacturer's service instructions. Be cautious when connecting the gauge set or handling refrigerant containers. Since escaping refrig-

erant can freeze on contact, wear face and eye protection and also protect your hands when you open the system for tests or servicing. Refrigerant does not damage painted surfaces but will tarnish bright metal, so be careful (Fig. 50-11).

When making leak tests, hold the test hose inlet under the fittings and other test points. Escaping refrigerant vapor drifts downward because it is heavier than air. Vapor can collect in a layer at floor level until it is cleared out by air drafts. Normally, the vapor is not harmful, but refrigerant vapor can change to poisonous gas if exposed to an open flame. Be sure to run the gauge set outlet hose into the shop exhaust system to get rid of discharged refrigerant.

50.18 HEATING SYSTEM SERVICE AND REPAIR

Many cases of poor air conditioner or heater operation are caused by setting the controls in the wrong position. Before assuming that there is something wrong with the air conditioner or heater system, be sure to read the operating instructions in the owner's manual or repair manual.

Lack of airflow in either the heater or air conditioning systems can be caused by a faulty blower motor. Use a test light connected to the battery terminal of the blower and ground to see if the blower motor is receiving electricity. Listen for blower operation at each speed. Use wiring diagrams to locate and check for bad fuses or relays.

The different blower speeds are controlled by a resistor block on many cars (Fig. 50-12). A good repair manual will show the location of the resistor block. It is

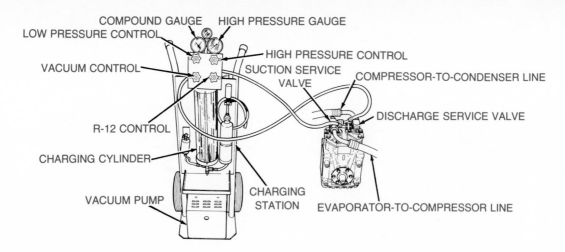

Fig. 50-9 Air conditioning service set. (American Motors Corporation)

usually in the engine compartment on the blower housing. Correct poor connections or replace burned resistors to get proper blower operation. If the blower operates, but airflow is poor, check for leaves or debris in the blower inlet.

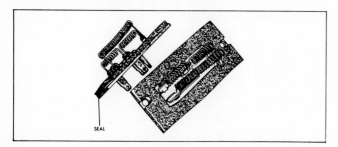

Fig. 50-12 Blower motor resistor block. (Chrysler Corporation)

Blower motors may usually be removed from the housing in the engine compartment (Fig. 50-13). Some cars require cutting a hole in the inner fender to remove

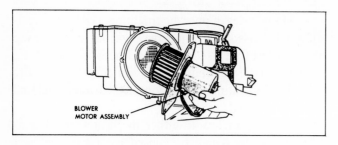

Fig. 50-13 Removing blower motor. (Chrysler Corporation)

the blower. After the repair is completed, a sheet metal patch should be screwed in place over the hole. When replacing a blower, be sure to replace any ground straps. A blower must be grounded or it won't run.

If the blower works but the heater does not put out heat, feel the heater hoses to see if coolant is passing

through the heater. Both inlet and outlet hoses should be hot when the controls are in the on position and the engine is running at normal operating temperature. If the heater core is plugged, it must be flushed out or replaced.

Coolant dripping on the floor inside the car or water vapor coming out of the air outlets usually indicates a leak in the core. Apply pressure to the cooling system with a radiator pressure tester to see if coolant runs out of the heater core inside the car.

Removing a heater core can be as easy as opening a small trapdoor, disconnecting the hoses, and lifting out the core (Fig. 50-14). Or it can involve removing entire instrument panels and consoles. A repair manual will give instructions on how to remove and replace the heater core.

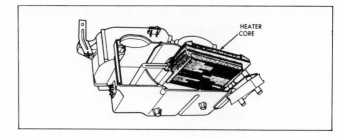

Fig. 50-14 Removing heater core. (Chrysler Corporation)

If the core does not leak, and is not plugged or restricted, lack of heat may be caused by the controls. Use a repair manual to check out the controls such as air doors and water valves. On vacuum operated controls, disconnected or split vacuum hoses can cause poor operation.

Windshield defrosters are usually part of the heater or air conditioning system. The defroster sends warm air to the inside of the windshield to melt snow or frost,

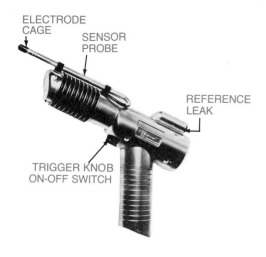

Fig. 50-10 Electronic leak detector. (Pontiac Motor Division, GMC)

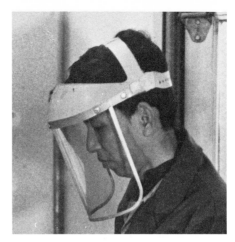

Fig. 50-11 Always wear eye protection when handling refrigerants.

or eliminate fogging. A small door, controlled by a cable or a vacuum diaphragm, controls defroster air. If the heater and air conditioning systems work, but defroster action is poor, check out the defroster door control according to instructions in a good repair manual. Also check for items that may have fallen into the defroster outlets and are plugging the passageways or jamming the door.

NEW TERMS

Air conditioning system A system designed to control the temperature, humidity, and circulation of air inside the automobile.

Blower A fan driven by an electric motor to circulate air.

Compressor A belt-driven pump used to circulate and increase the pressure of refrigerant.

Condenser A device used to condense the high-pressure, high-temperature refrigerant vapor.

Evaporator A finned heat exchanger used to cool the air by evaporation.

Expansion valve A valve used to control the flow of refrigerant to the evaporator.

Heater core A heat exchanger used to warm air in the heater system.

Heating system A system designed to warm the air inside the automobile.

Receiver/drier A reservoir used to store the dry refrigerant.

Refrigerant A substance that carries away heat.

Refrigeration cycle The principles on which the air conditioning systems operate.

CHAPTER REVIEW

1. What is the purpose of the air conditioning system?
2. What is the purpose of the heating system?
3. What does the heater core do?
4. Explain the operation of the heater assembly.
5. Explain how evaporation can cool something.
6. What is a refrigerant?
7. Define *humidity*.
8. What is the refrigeration cycle?
9. What is the purpose of the compressor?
10. What is the condenser used for?
11. What is the purpose of the receiver/drier?
12. What is an expansion valve?
13. What does an evaporator do?
14. What could cause not enough cooling in an air conditioning system?
15. What could cause no cooling at all in an air conditioning system?

DISCUSSION TOPICS AND ACTIVITIES

1. Identify the components of the heating system on the automobile you drive. What does each of the parts do?
2. Identify each of the components of an air conditioning system on your own automobile. Can you explain what each component does?
3. An automobile with an air conditioner has less power and uses more fuel than one without an air conditioner. Why do you think this is so?

Automobile Emission Control

PART 8

Emission Control Systems

CHAPTER PREVIEW

Emission controls are used to control a specific kind of emission from a specific cause. Some of the controls are built into the engine, and some are bolted onto the outside of the engine. In this chapter we describe what emissions are, where they come from, and how they are reduced.

OBJECTIVES

After studying this chapter, you should be able to do the following:

1. Understand the types and causes of air pollution.
2. Explain the system used to control crankcase emissions.
3. Describe the systems used to control evaporative emissions.
4. Explain the operation of systems used to control exhaust emissions inside the engine.
5. Explain the operation of systems used to control exhaust emissions outside the engine.

51.1   AIR POLLUTION

Air pollution is not new. Even before man appeared on earth, organic materials decayed, airborne volcanic ash blew over wide areas, and winds whipped up clouds of dust, sand, pollen and debris. Today, most of the concern centers about a type of air pollution called smog.

The word smog was first used in 1905 to describe the combination of smoke and fog. Today the word is used for air pollution resulting from certain photo-chemical reactions. Photochemical smog is caused when certain hydrocarbons and oxides of nitrogen, both from automobile exhaust and other sources, react in the presence of sunlight, forming a foglike haze.

Air pollution is a major concern because many pollutants, both gases and solid particles, are dangerous to health. In addition, air pollution limits visibility. It attacks many materials by corroding, tarnishing, and discoloring. One of the most widespread effects of polluted air is damage and destruction to vegetation.

51.2   Automobile Pollutants

The automobile is responsible for three major pollutants, called emissions. The first is hydrocarbons, abbreviated HC. Hydrocarbons are composed of many hundreds of combinations of hydrogen (H) and carbon (C) atoms. All petroleum-based fuels, including gasoline, are made up of hydrocarbons.

Almost nothing that is burned ever burns completely. As a result, burning something almost always discharges unburned particles to the air. There are many sources of hydrocarbon pollution, but the major source is the burning of gasoline in the automobile.

Hydrocarbons are a large family of chemicals, most of which are directly harmful only in very large amounts. However, a number of hydrocarbons in small amounts will react in the atmosphere with nitrogen oxides to cause photochemical smog. The reactions which result in smog are very complex. In general, it can be said that a reduction in hydrocarbons results directly in a reduction in smog. For this reason, one of the major ways of controlling automotive pollution is the reduction in hydrocarbon emissions from the engine.

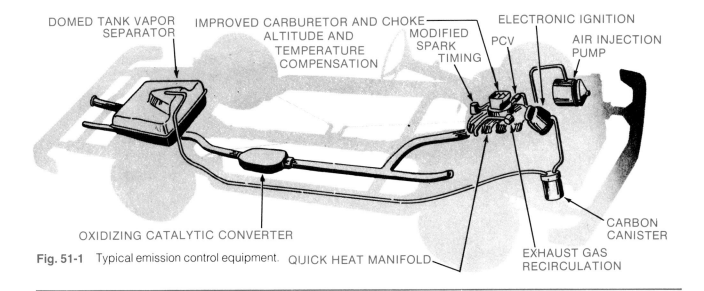

DOMED TANK VAPOR SEPARATOR

IMPROVED CARBURETOR AND CHOKE ALTITUDE AND TEMPERATURE COMPENSATION

MODIFIED SPARK TIMING

ELECTRONIC IGNITION

PCV

AIR INJECTION PUMP

OXIDIZING CATALYTIC CONVERTER

CARBON CANISTER

Fig. 51-1 Typical emission control equipment.

QUICK HEAT MANIFOLD

EXHAUST GAS RECIRCULATION

At the temperatures commonly reached when we burn fuels, nitrogen in the air combines with oxygen to form oxides of nitrogen, abbreviated NOx. Oxides of nitrogen are present in the air wherever fuels are burned, whether or not photochemical smog has been produced.

A third very dangerous pollutant is carbon monoxide, abbreviated CO. The burning of gasoline in the automobile discharges carbon monoxide from the automobile exhaust which stays near the ground. Inside an automobile operating in traffic, the concentrations of carbon monoxide may reach high enough levels to affect the driver and create a safety hazard as well as a health hazard.

51.3   Federal and State Regulations

Realizing the hazards of these pollutants, the federal and state governments have set up pollution controls. These requirements specify the amount of pollution that automobiles may emit. If the vehicle manufacturer cannot meet these requirements, the vehicle cannot be sold. As the regulations have become more strict, the emission control equipment on the automobile has become more complicated (Fig. 51-1). Automobile owners are required to maintain their vehicles so that emission control devices keep down emissions. Automobile mechanics must know both the legal requirements and mechanical systems to service emission controls.

51.4   Sources of Automobile Emissions

There are four sources of pollutants from the automobile (Fig. 51-2). The engine *crankcase,* through its venting system, contributes approximately

20 percent of the pollutants. Evaporative losses from the fuel system account for an additional 20 percent. Exhaust gases contribute the remaining 60 percent of the pollutants. At the present time, federal regulations cover three types of emissions: hydrocarbon (unburned fuel emitted at the carburetor, gas tank, or crankcase vent), carbon monoxide (produced during combustion), and oxides of nitrogen (resulting from extremely high combustion temperatures).

Particulates, consisting of soot or lead, also come from the exhaust. Smoke is mostly particulates, and is covered by local laws.

51.5   CONTROLLING CRANKCASE EMISSIONS

During combustion in a gasoline engine, a highly corrosive gas is produced. Also, for every gallon of gasoline burned, more than a gallon of water is formed. During the last part of the power stroke, some of the unburned fuel and products of combustion leak past the piston rings into the crankcase. This leakage or blow-by is a result of four factors (Fig. 51-3):

1. High combustion chamber pressures
2. Necessary working clearance of piston rings in their grooves
3. Normal ring shifting that sometimes line up clearance gaps of two or more rings
4. Reduction in ring sealing contact area with change in direction of piston travel

Blow-by must be removed before it condenses in the crankcase. In the crankcase it reacts with the oil to form sludge. Sludge speeds up the wear of pistons, rings, valves, and bearings. Since this blow-by also

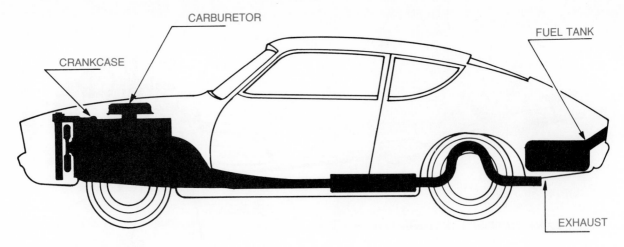

CRANKCASE

CARBURETOR

FUEL TANK

EXHAUST

Fig. 51-2 *Sources of emissions.*

includes unburned fuel, it will dilute the oil if it is not removed. It must be removed in such a way that it will not escape into the air because much of the blow-by is unburned hydrocarbons.

Since the 1960s, engines have been equipped with a positive crankcase ventilation system, abbreviated PCV (Figs. 51-3 and 51-4), to clean up crankcase vapors. Prior to this time, the blow-by vapors were allowed to escape under the vehicle through a tube. The PCV's closed crankcase ventilation pulls blow-by vapors out of the crankcase through a tube and into the intake manifold. The vapors enter the cylinders and are burned with the air-fuel mixture. A small valve, the positive crankcase ventilation or PCV valve (Fig. 51-5), is placed in the tube between the crankcase and intake manifold to control vapor flow. The valve is open most of the time to allow blow-by vapors to enter the intake manifold. During idle, the high intake manifold vacuum closes the valve, reducing the flow of vapors so the carburetor idle mixture will not be diluted with too much air from the crankcase.

The air removed from the crankcase is replaced by clean filtered air, which enters the crankcase through a tube from the air cleaner to the oil filler cap or valve cover. Air is routed through the air cleaner, through the tubes, and into the crankcase through a hole in the oil filler cap. An engine may be so worn that it develops more blow-by than the intake manifold line could handle. In that case the excess vapors could be pushed up the fresh air line and into the air cleaner. They would then be pulled into the intake manifold and burned in the cylinders.

The blowby gases also escape into the air cleaner if intake manifold vacuum is not strong enough to create a vacuum at the PCV valve. This condition exists whenever the engine is driven at wide open throttle. The crankcase gases are then pushed into the air cleaner by the force of their own pressure.

51.6 CONTROLLED EVAPORATIVE EMISSIONS

Approximately 20 percent of overall vehicle emissions consist of gasoline vapors that escape from the fuel tank and the fuel system. These evaporative losses occur not only when the vehicle is operating, but also when it is parked. In fact, most fuel vapors are lost when the vehicle is parked.

Closing the openings in the fuel system that are vented to the atmosphere provides a sealed fuel system. With this system, fuel vapors are trapped and directed to the engine for burning in the normal combustion process. Most current evaporative control systems use canister storage.

51.7 Canister Vapor Storage

The canister vapor storage system is a closed evaporative emission collection system. Gasoline vapors are collected at the fuel system components then routed through lines to a storage container. From here they are routed back to the fuel tank or into the engine. A typical evaporative control system is shown in Figure 51-7.

The fuel tank is equipped with an expansion chamber (Fig. 51-8). This chamber does not fill with fuel when the main tank is filled. It fills slowly to

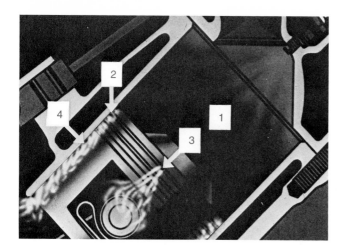

Fig. 51-3 Engine blow-by. (Chevrolet Motor Division, GMC)

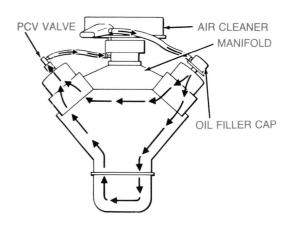

Fig. 51-4 Positive crankcase ventilation.

allow for an air space (expansion) in the main tank. This reserve of air prevents loss of liquid fuel when the tank is full and the automobile is parked on a hot day.

The fuel tank filler cap is sealed; however, it releases vapor at a specific pressure. In case of a malfunction in the system, the pressure release prevents damage to the tank. There is also a vacuum relief valve in the cap that allows fresh air into the tank as fuel is used. This type of filler cap is identified with the words "pressure vacuum." The vapor-liquid separator returns liquid to the fuel tank.

The charcoal canister catches and holds fuel vapors when the engine is not running. As the outside air temperature increases, fuel vapors flow through the liquid separator into the canister. These vapors are collected and held by particles of activated charcoal through absorption. The attaching force is rather weak, which permits the vapor to be easily released by fresh air flowing through the canister (Fig. 51-9).

The typical canister has a staged dual purge or vapor removal feature. Two inlets are provided, one for fuel tank vapor and one for carburetor bowl fuel vapor. A third outlet is connected to intake the manifold vacuum. The fourth is connected to the carburetor ported vacuum.

When the engine is operating, the manifold vacuum causes fresh air to enter through the inlet filter in the canister and purge or remove the stored vapor. When the carburetor ported vacuum increases (increased throttle opening), the secondary purge circuit is opened, and the canister is purged at a much higher rate.

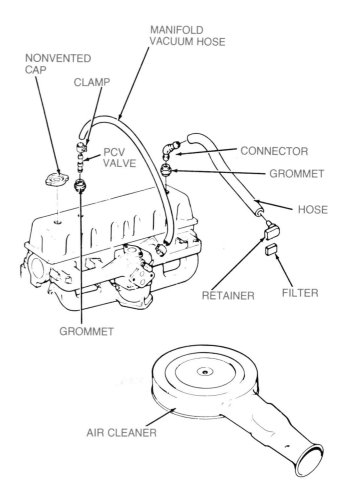

Fig. 51-5 Parts of PCV system. (American Motors Corporation)

Emission Control Systems   511

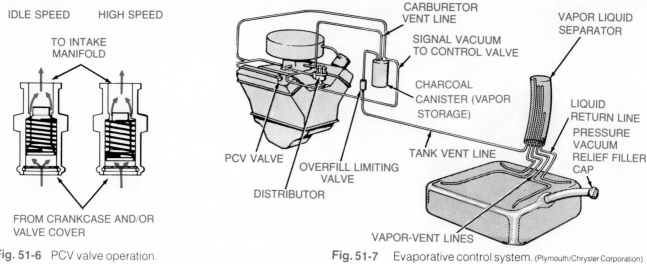

IDLE SPEED   HIGH SPEED

TO INTAKE
MANIFOLD

FROM CRANKCASE AND/OR
VALVE COVER

Fig. 51-6 PCV valve operation.

CARBURETOR
VENT LINE

SIGNAL VACUUM
TO CONTROL VALVE

VAPOR LIQUID
SEPARATOR

CHARCOAL
CANISTER (VAPOR
STORAGE)

LIQUID
RETURN LINE
PRESSURE
VACUUM
RELIEF FILLER
CAP

PCV VALVE

OVERFILL LIMITING
VALVE

DISTRIBUTOR

TANK VENT LINE

VAPOR-VENT LINES

Fig. 51-7 Evaporative control system. (Plymouth/Chrysler Corporation)

51.8   EXHAUST EMISSIONS

The biggest source of automobile pollution is the automobile exhaust, which accounts for 60 percent of hydrocarbons and all the carbon monoxide and oxides of nitrogen. Cleanup and control is most difficult here because of what is called the ''see-saw'' effect. To get rid of carbon monoxide and hydrocarbons, more complete burning of the air-fuel mixture in the cylinder is required. More complete burning usually means more heat during combustion. The more heat during combustion, however, the more oxides of nitrogen is formed. In other words, decreasing one form of pollution increases another form of pollution.

Exhaust emissions are a problem whenever the engine is running. They are especially bad when decelerating or idling. When the driver is decelerating, the drive wheels, through the power train, turn the engine. The engine is turning fast while the throttle valve is closed. The fast-moving pistons try to pull in a full charge of air and fuel. The closed throttle limits the amount of air-fuel mixture drawn into the cylinder. The density of the mixture that does get to the cylinder is greatly reduced. Fuel particles are not packed tightly enough together to ignite easily or burn completely. Unburned and partly burned fuel, therefore, goes out the exhaust.

Engineers reduce exhaust emissions through two different control systems. One makes combustion more complete and thus burns the emissions in the engine. The other treats the exhaust to remove the emissions. Stricter emission standards usually require a vehicle to use both systems.

51.9   EXHAUST CONTROL INSIDE THE ENGINE

There are many different ways to improve combustion in the engine. Redesigning the combustion chamber and cooling system can reduce hydrocarbons by providing more complete vaporization and also by reducing the quench area (Fig. 51-10). The quench area of each cylinder is near the cylinder wall, which is cooler than the center of the cylinder. As the air-fuel mixture enters the chamber, the portion that hits the relatively cool cylinder walls condenses to a certain extent. The ignition flame from the spark plug fails to ignite these condensed vapors near the cylinder walls. By increasing the coolant temperature, the size of the quench area is reduced. The ignition flame can burn more of the fuel and reduce emissions (Fig. 51-10).

The camshaft and intake manifold have also undergone major redesign to increase efficiency. In addition, several external systems have been developed to help reduce exhaust emissions.

51.10   Heated Air Inlet System

Intake air temperature varies widely—from cold on starting to hot during regular operation. The density of the air changes with temperature. Unfortunately, automotive carburetors cannot meter fuel to match density changes and thus maintain a near ideal air/fuel ratio. Since engines operate most of the time with warm or hot air, carburetor jetting is set to give the proper ratio under these conditions. In the cold range the mix is somewhat lean. To compensate, a

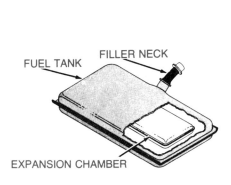

Fig. 51-8 Fuel tank with expansion chamber.

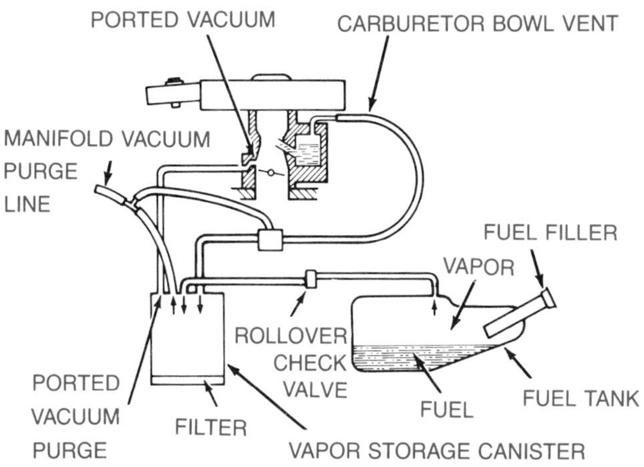

Fig. 51-9 Charcoal vapor storage system. (American Motors Corporation)

method was devised to provide warm air more quickly. Under cold operating conditions, intake air is drawn over an exhaust manifold to warm it prior to mixing with fuel.

To accomplish this, a sensing device in the air cleaner (Fig. 51-11) monitors the temperature of the air entering the carburetor. The device regulates a vacuum motor that operates a valve called the air control valve to select the source of intake air. When the temperature of the air passing over the sensing device is low, as it is on starting, the vacuum motor turns the valve to close the air cleaner inlet and to open the air passage to the "stove." The stove is a sheet metal hood surrounding the exhaust manifold. Air drawn over the exhaust manifold is heated before entering the air cleaner. The operation of the heated air inlet system is shown in Figure 51-12.

51.11 Controlled Timing

Another method used to increase combustion efficiency is to control ignition timing. On cars with engine control computers the computer controls ignition timing. We will see how these systems work in a later section.

The distributor vacuum advance unit may be designed to retard timing at idle speed and while the transmission is passing through lower ranges. The retarded spark increases cylinder temperatures. Advancing the ignition timing on deceleration, when the compression pressures are low, allows more time for complete combustion. A number of controls to regulate timing are used on most ignition systems.

Most ignition timing control systems use one or more spark delay vacuum valves and thermostatic control valves. The purpose of the spark delay vac-

uum valve (Fig. 51-13) is to delay spark advance during rapid acceleration from idle. The spark delay valve also cuts off spark advance immediately upon deceleration. It is installed in the vacuum line between the carburetor and the distributor. The spark delay valve is color-coded to show the amount of built-in restriction for various applications.

A cross section of a spark delay valve is shown in Figure 51-13. It has one or more internal restrictors and an internal umbrella check valve. On mild accelerations, the umbrella check valve remains in the closed position, and the vacuum signal to the distributor load (vacuum) advance mechanism is delayed by the restrictors. After a short delay, the distributor reaches full vacuum advance for normal performance.

During all closed-throttle decelerations and all accelerations, the umbrella check valve opens and allows an unrestricted vacuum signal to reach the load (vacuum) advance mechanism on the distributor. With an unrestricted advance signal, the load advance setting returns to its normal position for that particular speed and load condition. The umbrella check valve operation allows a rapid reduction of spark advance in order to prevent an over-advance on acceleration.

The thermostatic vacuum control valve (Fig. 51-14) is used to regulate vacuum according to engine operating temperature. This valve is mounted in the coolant passage in the cylinder block, cylinder head, or thermostat housing. When the engine coolant is cold, the valve is closed and vacuum cannot pass through the valve. When the engine coolant temperature reaches a specified maximum value, the vacuum valve opens and allows vacuum to pass through to operate the timing system. This valve is also used to control many other types of vacuum operated emission equipment such as the EGR.

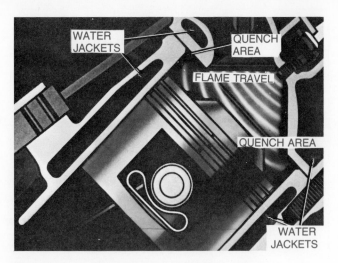

Fig. 51-10 Quench area. (Chevrolet Motor Division, GMC)

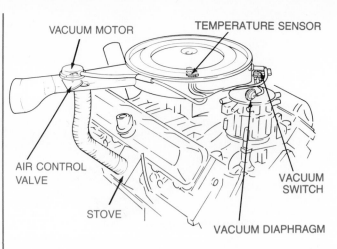

Fig. 51-11 Heated intake air. (Oldsmobile Division, GMC)

51.12   Recirculation (EGR)

The higher temperatures necessary to burn hydrocarbons and carbon monoxide have had the effect of increasing oxides of nitrogen. An exhaust gas recircultion (EGR) system was introduced to control oxides of nitrogen. NO_x can be reduced by adding an inert material, such as exhaust gases, to the air-fuel mixture.

To understand how the system works, it is important to know that NO_x is formed under conditions of high combustion temperatures; thus, the way to reduce NO_x is to reduce the high combustion temperatures.

Since NO_x forms in high temperature combustion, the problem solution is cooler combustion. Unfortunately, lean mixtures which reduce HC and CO increase NO_x. Advanced timing which improves fuel economy also increases NO_x.

The EGR System reduces combustion temperatures by diluting the air-fuel mixture with small amounts (about 6 to 10 percent) of exhaust gases. Since exhaust gases contain no oxygen and will not burn or support combustion, they absorb some of the heat of combustion, lower combustion temperatures, and reduce the formation of NO_x.

The exhaust gas recirculation (EGR) valve is a vacuum operated, poppet-type (Fig. 51-15). The valve fastens to the intake manifold delivery port. The mounting block has two passages; one for exhaust gas into the valve, and one for metered exhaust gas flow out of the valve. The stem operates the poppet valve which seats in the mounting block to close off EGR flow out of the valve. Typical mounting of an EGR valve is shown in Figure 51-16.

Upon cold start, carburetor ported vacuum is applied to a thermostatic controlled vacuum valve. Below the specified temperature the valve blocks vacuum to the EGR valve. Immediately on start, exhaust gases are routed to the inlet passage of the EGR valve. However, the passage is blocked by the spring-loaded poppet valve, so exhaust gas does not recirculate. At the specified temperature, the thermostatic controlled vacuum valve opens, and vacuum applies the EGR valve. Ported vacuum is a low pressure that occurs in the carburetor air horn, above the throttle valve. Ported vacuum only occurs with the engine running and the carburetor throttle open. This is different from manifold vacuum, which occurs below the throttle plate whenever the engine runs, regardless of throttle opening.

At idle, the throttle is closed so there is no ported vacuum. As the throttle cracks open and the opening gets wider, ported vacuum starts as a weak signal (low vacuum), and increases to a stronger signal (higher vacuum). At light throttle and wider openings, ported vacuum is very nearly equal to manifold vacuum. On deceleration, the throttle closes and the ported vacuum signal stops, while the manifold vacuum signal is very strong. At wide open throttle (WOT), both ported and manifold vacuum signals become weak (low vacuum). This design of using a ported vacuum signal provides a method of tailoring vacuum-operated devices (such as the EGR valve), to operate according to throttle opening and engine load. This helps improve driveability.

At mid-throttle (cruise), combustion is more efficient and the formation of NO_x tends to increase due to hotter combustion. Ported vacuum is also stronger, so the EGR valve diaphragm opens the poppet valve more to recirculate a larger percentage of exhaust gases.

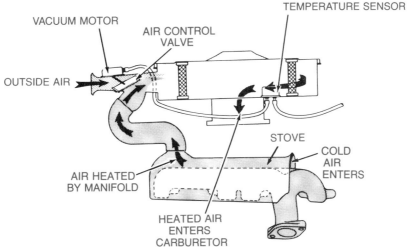

Fig. 51-12 Operation of the heated air inlet system. (Chrysler Corporation)

At WOT, EGR could reduce the maximum power desired. However, at WOT the ported vacuum signal is weak. The diaphragm spring closes the poppet valve to block exhaust gas flow to the airfuel mixture. This minimizes EGR interference with WOT combustion. The operation of the EGR System is shown in Figure 51-17.

51.13 EXHAUST CONTROL OUTSIDE THE ENGINE

Cleaning up emissions after they have left the engine cylinders and entered the exhaust is another approach to emision control. Two common methods of cleaning up exhaust gases after they have left the engine are with the use of an air injection system or a catalytic converter.

51.14 Air Injection System

The air injection system (Fig. 51-18) forces outside air into the exhaust system to reduce HC and CO emissions. The system injects air to the exhaust ports or catalytic converter (described later) or to both places at different times depending on model application and system configuration.

The engine does a good job of burning all of the carburetor air/fuel mixture, and various control systems reduce the engine output of emission levels. However, emission levels in the exhaust manifold are still unacceptable. There is plenty of heat in the exhaust to complete the burning of fuel vapors. But, there is not enough oxygen to support combustion.

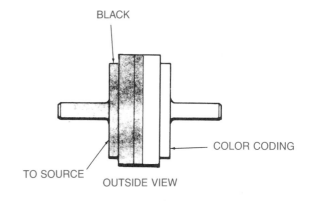

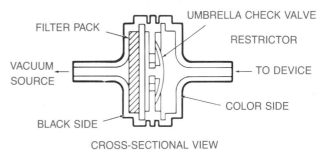

Fig. 51-13 Spark delay vacuum valve. (Ford Motor Company)

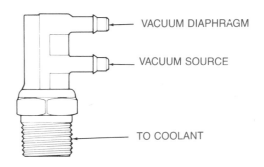

Fig. 51-14 A thermostatic controlled vacuum valve. (Ford Motor Company)

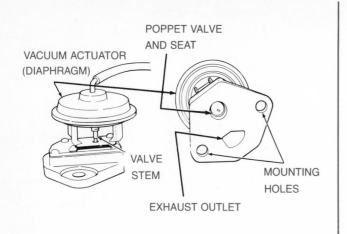

Fig. 51-15 An EGR valve. (Chrysler Corporation)

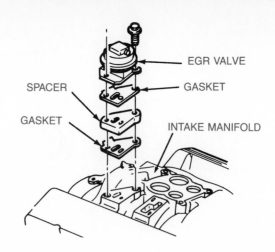

Fig. 51-16 Typical EGR valve mounting. (Chevrolet Motor Division, GMC)

The air injection system provides the oxygen necessary to complete combustion after the mixture has burned in the cylinder. This allows the engine to run with slightly richer air/fuel mixtures for better performance and economy, without hurting emission control. Air injection also starts the oxidation process for the catalytic converter, which improves its efficiency.

Air injection is also used on cars with feedback fuel system carburetors, but the injection point is routed away from the oxygen sensor during feedback operation. This prevents the air flow from influencing the oxygen sensor signals. Some models without feedback also reroute air injection to reduce the presence of oxygen and control NO_x formation.

Most engines use a belt-driven air pump as the source of air injection (Fig. 51-19). The pump is driven by the crankshaft pulley at the front of the engine. Air enters the pump through an inlet. The centrifugal action of the pump pressurizes the air and directs it toward the outlet. Air is injected into the exhaust manifold ports for a short time during engine warmup causing an oxidation of the exhaust gases. After engine warmup, the air flow is switched downstream to a point ahead of the oxidation catalysts. This helps the oxidation catalyst reaction thereby reducing the amounts of carbon monoxide and hydrocarbons emitted from the exhaust.

The switching is accomplished by an air switch/relief valve assembly. The air switch/relief valve consists of a vacuum diaphragm, pressure relief valve, three ports with a control valve, and silencer material in a bypass area (Fig. 51-20). The control valve is spring-loaded by the diaphragm to close the upstream passage port. This position routes air from the pump to the downstream injection point (the converter). With vacuum applied, the diaphragm pulls the control valve to block the downstream port and open the air pump passage to the exhaust ports. The vacuum signal to the valve may be controlled electrically from the engine control computer or with a thermostatic vacuum switch.

A check valve is located in the injection tube assemblies that lead to the exhaust manifold and the catalyst injection points. This valve has a one-way diaphragm which prevents hot exhaust gases from backing up into the hose and pump (Fig. 51-21). This valve will protect the system in the event of pump belt failure, abnormally high exhaust system pressure, or air hose ruptures.

51.15   Catalytic Exhaust System

The catalytic converter (Fig. 51-22) uses a catalyst to remove hydrocarbons, carbon monoxide and oxides of nitrogen from exhaust gas. A catalyst is a substance that speeds up a chemical reaction but is not changed itself in the process. The catalyst is plated on a honeycomb-shaped monolith (Fig. 51-23); or deposited on small beads (Fig. 51-24) in the converter.

There are three basic catalysts used in the converter; platinum, palladium, and rhodium. The presence of platinum or palladium with heat and unburned fuel (HC, CO), adds oxygen to the reaction. This is called oxidizing. The oxidation of HC and CO produces H_2O and CO_2 (water and carbon dioxide).

Most late model cars use a 3-way catalyst for controlling NO_x. These systems require a combination "oxidizing reducing" catalyst. The oxidizing portion

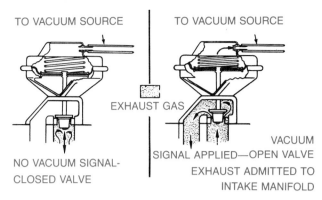

Fig. 51-17 Operation of the EGR valve. (Chevrolet Motor Division, GMC)

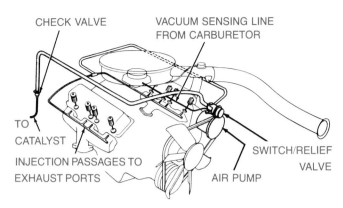

Fig. 51-18 An air injection system. (Chrysler Corporation)

uses platinum or palladium. The reducing portion uses rhodium as a catalyst.

Rhodium in the presence of heat and NO_x removes oxygen from the compounds. This removal is called "reducing" because it reduces the amount of oxygen remaining in the compound. The complete converter assembly lowers HC, CO and NO_x and is called a three-way catalyst. This type of converter requires very precise engine control, such as that provided by electronic feedback carburetor systems.

There are two types of three-way converters in use, but they each treat HC, CO, and NO_x. The smaller one contains a mixture of oxidizing catalyst with reducing catalyst. The other type is larger and contains two elements; one an oxidizing catalyst, the other a three-way catalyst. On this type, air from the air injection system is supplied between the two elements. In most cases, the additional air is used to improve the efficiency of the oxidizing catalyst, by adding oxygen in the presence of very high heat and unburned fuel.

The catalytic converter works along with the air injection system. Upon engine start, air is injected to the exhaust ports. The combination of combustion heat, unburned vapors due to choke-rich mixtures, and fresh air begins the oxidation process in the exhaust port or manifold. The chemical reaction that occurs begins reducing emission levels and raises the temperature of the gases.

When this hot, oxidizing mixture enters the converter, the gases flow through the honeycomb openings. The catalyst increases the reaction and much of the HC and CO is converted to H_2O and CO_2 (water and carbon dioxide). In the three-way converter, the rhodium catalyst also reacts and removes oxygen from the various oxides of nitrogen (NO_x) compounds formed during combustion.

On engines with air injection switching, the switch valve is calibrated to redirect air at specified

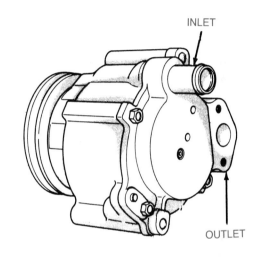

Fig. 51-19 Air pump for the air injection system. (Chrysler Corporation)

TO UPSTREAM INJECTION POINT

PRESSURE RELIEF VALVE

FROM AIR PUMP

TO DOWNSTREAM INJECTION POINT

BYPASS AIR

SILENCER MATERIAL

INTAKE MANIFOLD VACUUM (APPLIED ONLY AT START-UP)

VACUUM CHAMBER

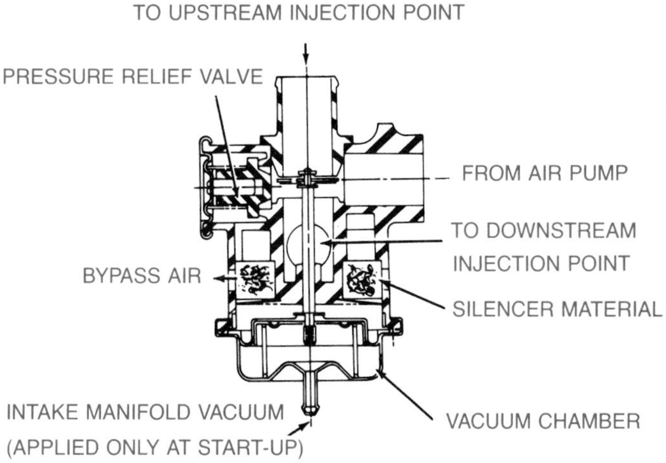

Fig. 51-20 Air switching relief valve assembly. (Chrysler Corporation)

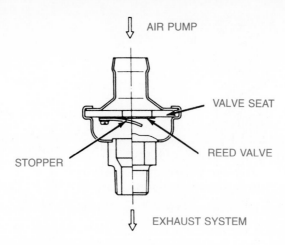

Fig. 51-21 An air injection check valve assembly. (Chrysler Corporation)

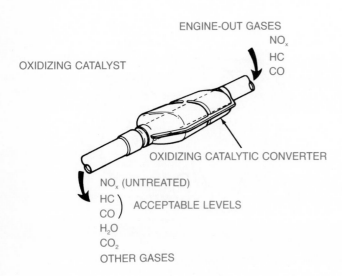

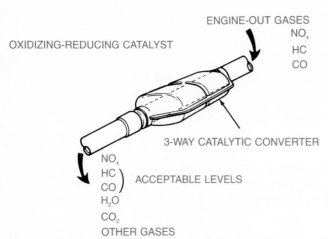

Fig. 51-22 Catalytic converter operation. (Chrysler Corporation)

engine temperature. When this occurs, air is injected into the converter assembly. This heightens the chemical reaction because the converter is very hot. The additional oxygen improves the oxidizing efficiency of the converter.

In all systems the basic catalytic converter operation is the same: HC, CO, and NO_x gases enter the converter; oxidizing catalysts change HC and CO and yield H_2O and CO_2, plus lower levels of HC and CO and the same level of NO_x; oxidizing-reducing catalysts convert HC and CO to H_2O and CO_2, and NO_x to other nitrogen compounds, and yield lower levels of HC and CO, plus H_2O and CO_2. The tailpipe emits these compounds along with soot and various other gases (Fig. 51-25).

Catalytic converters require engine fuel without lead additives. Lead deposits will coat the catalyst and stop the reaction, called lead-fouling. The fuel filler neck restriction prevents entry of leaded fuel to a vehicle marked UNLEADED FUEL ONLY. A federal law also prohibits putting leaded fuel in a no-lead vehicle. If a vehicle fails an emission inspection as a result of a lead-fouling, a new catalytic converter(s) must be installed. The lead cannot be removed.

51.16   Thermal Reactor

Hot exhaust gas many also be routed into a thermal reactor. A thermal reactor (Fig. 51-26) is an elaborate exhaust manifold that absorbs heat from the exhaust gases. Once hot, the reactor oxidizes the un-

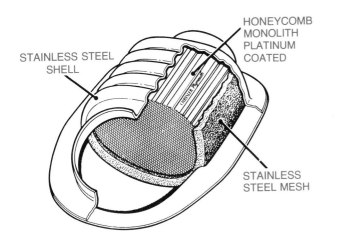

Fig. 51-23 Cross section of converter with honeycomb monolith. (Chrysler Corporation)

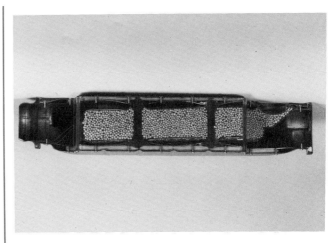

Fig. 51-24 Cutaway view of catalytic converter showing beads. (General Motors Corporation)

burned hydrocarbons and carbon monoxide to form water vapor and carbon dioxide. Some thermal reactors use cooling air to prevent severe overheating.

NEW TERMS

Air injection A system which injects air into the exhaust to burn emissions.

Air pollution Gases and particles that enter the air which are dangerous to our health.

Blow-by Combustion gases that leak past the piston rings into the crankcase.

Canister vapor storage A system in which gasoline vapors are stored in a canister full of charcoal.

Catalytic exhaust system A system that uses a catalyst to change pollution from the exhaust system to harmless compounds.

Computerized engine control A system which controls the engine ignition, fuel, and emission systems with a computer and sets of sensors and actuators.

Controlled timing A system that matches the timing to the emission requirements of the engine.

Crankcase emissions Emissions that result from blow-by in the crankcase.

Crankcase vapor storage An evaporative storage system in which vapors are stored in the crankcase.

Emission control system Any system used to lower automobile emissions to acceptable levels.

Exhaust emissions Emissions that result from the combustion in the engine's cylinders.

Exhaust gas recirculation system (EGR) A system used to reduce oxides of nitrogen (NO_x).

Feedback system A system that senses the engine air-fuel ratio and corrects it to the ideal air-fuel ratio.

Heated inlet air system A system that routes heated air to the carburetor during startup and cold operation.

Oxides of nitrogen Pollutants caused by high temperatures in the combustion chamber.

PCV valve A positive crankcase valve used to control the flow of blow-by gases.

Thermal reactor A system used to burn exhaust emissions in the exhaust manifold.

CHAPTER REVIEW

1. What is the purpose of the emission control system?
2. List the three major pollutants caused by the automobile.
3. List the four sources of automobile emissions.
4. Explain the operation of a positive crankcase ventilation system.
5. What are evaporative emissions?
6. Explain how a canister vapor storage system works.
7. When are exhaust emissions the worst?
8. Describe the operation of a heated air inlet system.
9. How is timing controlled to reduce emissions?

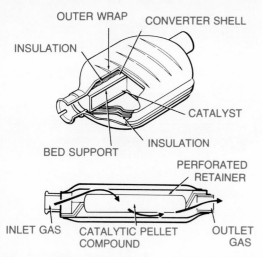

OUTER WRAP   CONVERTER SHELL

INSULATION

CATALYST

INSULATION

BED SUPPORT

PERFORATED
RETAINER

INLET GAS   CATALYTIC PELLET   OUTLET
COMPOUND   GAS

Fig. 51-25 Catalytic converter.

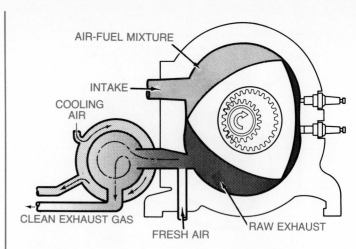

AIR-FUEL MIXTURE

INTAKE

COOLING
AIR

CLEAN EXHAUST GAS

FRESH AIR   RAW EXHAUST

Fig. 51-26 Thermal reactor on rotary engine. (Mazda Motors of America)

10. How are nitric oxides controlled in an engine?

11. What is an air injection system?

12. Explain the operation of a catalytic exhaust system.

13. How are nitric oxides controlled in an engine?

14. What is an air injection system?

15. Explain the operation of a catalytic exhaust system.

DISCUSSION TOPICS AND ACTIVITIES

1. Make a list of the pollutants from an automobile. Explain how they are caused and why they are harmful.

2. Make a list of the types of emission control devices. Explain how they work to remove emissions.

3. Examine the engine in the automobile you drive. How many emission control devices can you find?

Emission System Service

CHAPTER PREVIEW

The troubleshooting, preventative maintenance and servicing of the emission system components are very important to low emission levels. Most manufacturers specify regular intervals for emission component service in order to keep the car operating within government emission standards. The proper servicing of the ignition and fuel system is also very important to maintain low emissions. Whenever you are diagnosing or repairing an emission system always use the appropriate shop service manual and follow the procedures carefully. In this chapter, we will describe the most common types of emissions system servicing.

OBJECTIVES

After studying this chapter, you should be able to do the following:

1. Use an infrared exhaust analyzer to measure exhaust emissions.
2. Explain the procedures used to troubleshoot each of the emission control systems.
3. Use a jumper wire to perform a self-diagnosis test on a computerized engine control system.
4. Perform preventative maintenance on emission control systems.
5. Explain the service procedures typical of most emission systems.

52.1 TROUBLESHOOTING

When troubleshooting an emission system, there are two basic sources of information, one in the shop service manual where you can find specifications and detailed step-by-step diagnosis information. The other is the underhood vehicle emission control information label. This label (Fig. 52-1) provides basic information regarding the type of equipment on the vehicle. Also included on some labels are basic emission control specifications such as curb idle speed, and propane-enriched idle speed. Ignition timing and fast idle speed may also be included on the vehicle emission control label. Because the types of emission control equipment and emission control specifications vary from one vehicle model to another, the labels also vary.

Vehicles sold in California and a few vehicles intended for use in high altitude areas may have some equipment and engine specifications that are different from vehicles sold in the rest of the 49 states. To properly maintain these vehicles, it is absolutely necessary to determine which equipment and specifications are applicable to the vehicle. This information may be obtained from the Vehicle Emission Control Information Label under the hood. A block in the upper center of the label says either "Low Altitude Certification" or "High Altitude Certification." A statement in fine print at the bottom of the label identifies California engines from 49 state engines.

Most emission control systems have many vacuum operated components connected together with vacuum hoses. Correct routing and proper connection of all vacuum hoses are essential to the proper operation of an emission control system. For this reason, a vacuum hose routing diagram is either included on the vehicle emission control label or provided on a separate label under the hood. Many late model cars have a color coded vacuum line diagram which corresponds to colored stripes on the vacuum lines on the car.

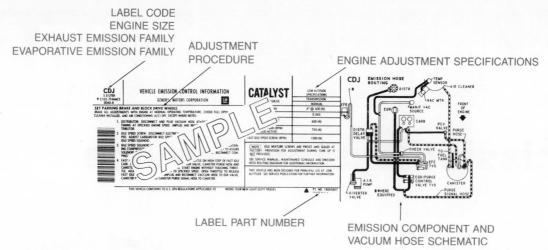

LABEL CODE
ENGINE SIZE
EXHAUST EMISSION FAMILY
EVAPORATIVE EMISSION FAMILY
ADJUSTMENT PROCEDURE

ENGINE ADJUSTMENT SPECIFICATIONS

LABEL PART NUMBER

EMISSION COMPONENT AND VACUUM HOSE SCHEMATIC

Fig. 52-1 Underhood emission control information label.
(Chevrolet Motor Division, GMC)

52.2 Infrared Exhaust Analyzer

The infrared exhaust analyzer is the basic tool used to troubleshoot the emission system (Fig. 52-2). When you test engine exhaust performance, always follow the tester manufacturer's procedures for the make and model of the tester you are using.

With most testers you will attach a tachometer to the vehicle engine. Warm up and calibrate the exhaust emission tester. Select the HI scale range for both the HC and the CO gauges. The button for the HI scale is located below each gauge. When you use the HI scale, you will be reading the upper scale on the gauges. Insert the sampling probe about 12 inches into the exhaust pipe.

Be sure the vehicle's exhaust system is airtight. Air leaking into the system could dilute the exhaust gas and affect the readings. When you test vehicles equipped with dual exhaust, be sure to test each side separately to insure that an exhaust sample from each bank of cylinders has been analyzed. Some cars specify that the probe be inserted at a special tap upstream from the catalytic converter.

Operate the engine at idle and at normal operating temperatures with the transmission in park or neutral and the parking brake on. Accelerate the engine slightly to assure release of the fast-idle cam on the carburetor. After they stabilize, note and record the readings from both the HC and CO gauges. In the sample shown in Figure 52-3, the hydrocarbon gauge shows 600 PPM (parts per million) HC and the carbon monoxide gauge shows 3 percent CO.

Operate the engine at 2500 rpm, and record the readings for both the HC and CO gauges. If the HC gauge reads less than 550 PPM or the CO gauge reads

less than 2.5 percent, switch to the LO gauge scales for easier reading. Disregard 2500 rpm readings on electronic fuel-injected vehicles. Testing of these engines at 2500 rpm must be done on a dynamometer. Stop the engine and depress the tester zero switch button. This will keep the tester ready for use without further warm-up.

After you read emission tester results, compare your readings to manufacturer's specifications if available. The specifications alert you to which readings are considered too high and which ones are too low. Knowing the causes of a reading that is too high will help you to analyze engine performance. When the emission tester readings do not meet the manufacturer's specifications, the vehicle engine must be tuned or emission components replaced.

When you find hydrocarbon readings that exceed specifications, they are usually the result of a misfire that may be caused by any of the following:

Absence of a spark
Timing of a spark
Length of time the plugs fire (poor timing)
Fouled plugs
Broken ignition wire
High spark plug wire resistance
Defective points
Bad vacuum leaks
Leaky exhaust valves; defective guides or lifters
Excessively rich or excessively lean mixtures
Low compression, defective rings, pistons, or
    cylinders

If the carbon monoxide test readings are too high when compared to specifications, they are a result of any restriction in the oxygen or air supply caused by:

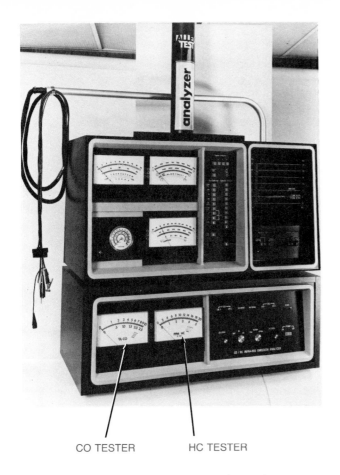

CO TESTER   HC TESTER

Fig. 52-2 An infrared exhaust analyzer is used to measure emissions. (Allen Test)

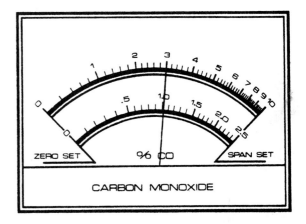

CARBON MONOXIDE

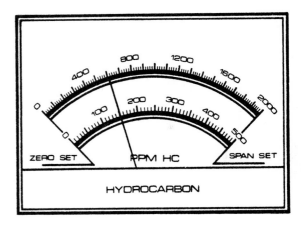

HYDROCARBON

Fig. 52-3 Measuring HC and CO with the exhaust analyzer.

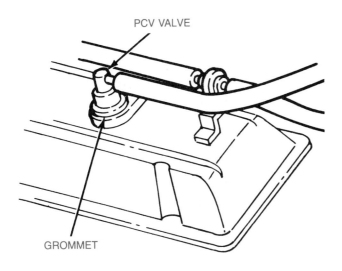

PCV VALVE

GROMMET

Fig. 52-4 The PCV valve is usually located in a rubber grommet on the valve cover. (Chevrolet Motor Division, GMC)

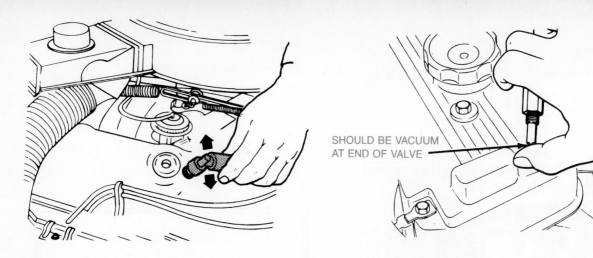

Fig. 52-5 Shaking the valve to check for sticking. (Chrysler Corporation)

SHOULD BE VACUUM AT END OF VALVE

Fig. 52-6 Checking for vacuum at the end of the PCV valve. (Chrysler Corporation)

Restricted or dirty air cleaner

Clogged or dirty air-mix passages in the carburetor

A rich mixture jet adjustment on a carburetor

A stuck or misadjusted choke valve or its mechanism

Restricted or inoperative PCV system

Improper idle speed

If both hydrocarbon and carbon monoxide readings are higher than specifications, they are caused by:

Inoperative PCV system

A heat riser valve stuck open

Air pump malfunction or disconnection

Sticking air cleaner control damper assembly in the thermostatic air cleaner system

Rich idle mixture, leading needles and seats, leaky power valve, wrong float setting, faulty choke action

52.3   Troubleshooting the PCV System

The PCV system should be visually inspected and tested each tune-up. Check both the two-way flow hose and the intake manifold hose for cracks, kinks, and collapsed and loose connections. You should remove the hoses to ensure that they are free from clogs and sludge deposits. Remove the top cover from the carburetor air cleaner and check the PCV filter element for dirt and clogging.

Remove the PCV valve from its mount (usually in the valve cover) by working the valve free from the rubber grommet (Fig. 52-4). Shake the valve. If the valve is free, you should hear a metallic clicking sound

(Fig. 52-5). Be sure to check the grommet to see that it is free from cracks and deterioration.

There are several methods used to test PCV systems. Always refer to the shop service manual for the proper method and specifications recommended for the make, model, and year of the vehicle you are servicing.

Operate the engine at normal curb idle and at normal engine operating temperatures. Remove the PCV valve from the engine rocker cover. You should hear a hissing noise as air passes through the valve. You should also notice an increase in engine rpm. The hissing and the rpm increase indicate that the valve is not plugged. Place you finger over the valve inlet. You should feel a strong vacuum. This also indicates that the valve is not plugged (Fig. 52-6).

Reinstall the PCV valve. Then remove the crankcase inlet air cleaner, inlet hose, or oil filler cap. Hold a parts tag or similar piece of stiff paper loosely at the inlet opening in the valve cover or at the end of the inlet hose. The paper should be pulled in against the opening with some force after about a minute. (It takes about one minute for the engine crankcase pressure to lower.) This indicates that the PCV system is operating properly (Fig. 52-7).

Several types of testers are available that measure the passage of air circulating through the engine crankcase while the engine is operating. Always follow the instructions provided by the manufacturer of the tester.

52.4   Troubleshooting the EGR System

Inspect all EGR vacuum hoses for hardness, cracks, and leaks. Check the hoses for restrictions,

CRANKCASE INLET AIR CLEANER

Fig. 52-7 Checking for crankcase vacuum. (Chrysler Corporation)

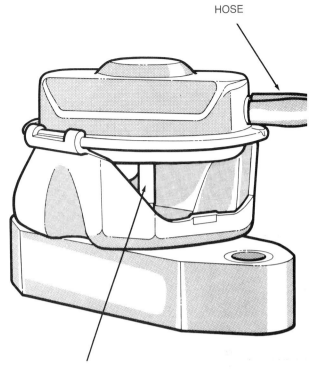

HOSE

VALVE STEM (CHECK FOR UP AND DOWN MOVEMENT)

Fig. 52-8 Checking for EGR valve movement. (Chrysler Corporation)

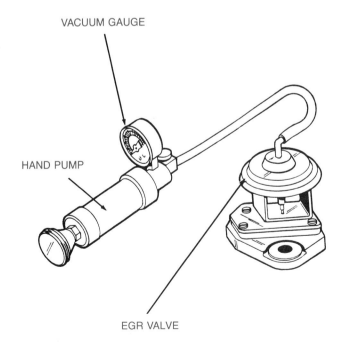

VACUUM GAUGE

HAND PUMP

EGR VALVE

Fig. 52-9 Checking EGR with a hand vacuum pump.

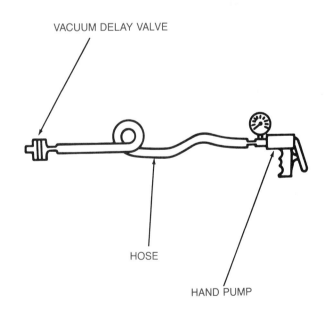

VACUUM DELAY VALVE

HOSE

HAND PUMP

Fig. 52-10 Checking a vacuum delay valve. (Ford Motor Company)

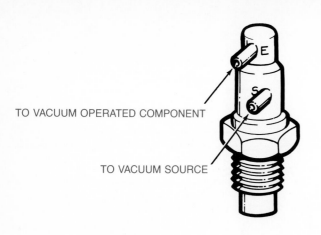

TO VACUUM OPERATED COMPONENT

TO VACUUM SOURCE

Fig. 52-11 Thermostatically controlled vacuum valve. (American Motors Corporation)

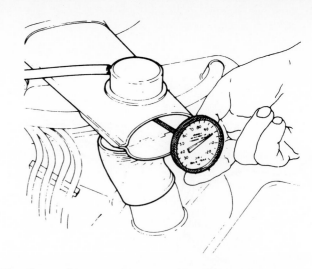

Fig. 52-12 Checking inlet air temperature. (Chrysler Corporation)

faulty connectors, and incorrect routing. Replace any defective hoses and connectors you find. Inspect all hose connections between the carburetor, EGR valve, amplifier, and the coolant valve for proper connection and routing. Look up the vehicle's EGR system in the shop service manual and find out what other vacuum controls are involved.

Start the engine and allow it to warm up at idle in neutral. While you accelerate the engine quickly to approximately 2000 rpm, look at the EGR valve stem to see if it moves (Fig. 52-8). Repeat this procedure a few times to be sure that the EGR valve stem moves or does not move. If the EGR valve stem moves during acceleration, it is operating properly. If there is no movement of the EGR valve stem, the EGR valve should be replaced or serviced, depending on the vehicle manufacturer's recommendations.

Some vehicle manufacturers recommend a different procedure for checking EGR valves, expecially those installations in which the valve stem is not exposed and cannot be seen from outside the engine. For these installations, look in your shop service manual for the EGR valve test procedures and specifications for the proper year, make, and model of the vehicle. Disconnect the vacuum hose from the EGR valve and connect the hand vacuum pump to the valve (Fig. 52-9).

With the engine idling at normal operating temperatures, gradually apply vacuum to the EGR valve. If the EGR valve has an exposed valve stem, the stem should move. Apply 8-10 inches of vacuum (follow vehicle manufacturer's specifications). You should see the engine idle roughen, or engine rpm decrease or stop completely. Some specifications state that engine rpm should drop at least 150 rpm.

If there is no change in the engine or the engine rpm drop is less than 150 rpm, there is a defective valve or a build-up of exhaust deposits in the valve or in the intake manifold EGR passages. The EGR valve should be replaced or serviced, depending on the vehicle manufacturer's recommendations.

52.5 Troubleshooting Timing Controls

Thermostatic vacuum valves and vacuum delay valves should be checked whenever the vehicle has a low performance problem. A hand vacuum pump is used to check a vacuum delay valve.

Connect the hand vacuum pump to the valve with a hose as shown in Figure 52-10. Pump up a vacuum with the hand pump. Valves with one side black or white and the other side colored are good if vacuum can be built-up in one direction, but not the other and if that built-up vacuum can be seen to slowly decrease. Valves with both sides the same color are good if vacuum can be built-up in both directions before visibly decreasing.

Thermostatic vacuum valves (Fig. 52-11) are used in both timing control and EGR systems as well as other vacuum applications. To test a valve, attach a tachometer to the engine. Then connect a vacuum gauge to the hose leading to the vacuum operated component. To do this, disconnect the hose from the valve and insert a tee into the hose.

Look in your technical service manual for the valve temperature specification for the vehicle year, make, and model. Begin the test with a cold engine. Start the engine and look at the vacuum gauge reading. There should be no vacuum reading on a cold engine if the valve is operating properly. Operate the

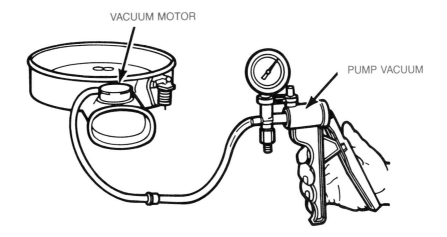

VACUUM MOTOR

PUMP VACUUM

Fig. 52-13 Testing the vacuum motor. (Chrysler Corporation)

engine at 2000 rpm. If the vacuum gauge reading is zero, the valve is okay. If there is any vacuum reading, the valve should be replaced.

Operate the engine at 2000 rpm until the coolant temperature rises about the specified temperature. The vacuum gauge should not indicate the presence of vacuum from the vacuum source. If it does, replace the valve.

52.6 Troubleshooting Heated Intake Air Systems

During every tune-up service, the thermostatic air cleaner vacuum hose and the connector from the heat stove should be checked to make sure that their condition and connections are good. Using a hand mirror, visually inspect the damper valve to see if it is open to outside air (engine warm) or closed to outside air (engine cold). Make this inspection while the engine is operating.

If the vehicle owner complains that the engine stumbles, stalls, and accelerates poorly when the engine is cold, or that the engine pings when it is hot, you will need to check the operation of the entire heated intake air system more accurately.

Start your check with the engine cold and running at idle. The damper assembly door should be in the hot air delivery mode. After the engine warms up, check the air temperature entering at the snorkel or at the sensor with a thermometer (Fig. 52-12). When the air temperature entering the snorkel is 82°F or higher (varies with make and model), the damper assembly's door should be in the down position (cold air delivery mode).

To check the operation of the vacuum motor, apply vacuum with a hand-operated vacuum pump (Fig. 52-13). The damper assembly door should lift off the bottom of the snorkel at not less than 5.5 in. Hg. of vacuum and should be fully in the up position with no more than 8.5 in. Hg. of vacuum. Apply 20 in. Hg. of vacuum to test for leakage. The vacuum motor diaphragm should not bleed down more than 10 in Hg. of vacuum in five minutes.

52.7 Troubleshooting Air Injection

The air injection system should be inspected and tested during every tune-up. Visually inspect the air manifold(s) and hoses for holes, cracks, fractures, kinks, sharp bends, and leaks. Check all connections for tightness.

Start the engine and listen for any hissing or blast of air that would indicate a leak. If you suspect a leak, apply soapy water lightly around the area in question. Any bubbling of the soapy water will pinpoint the leak. Do not get any water near the air pump centrifugal filter, because it might destroy the pump.

Look at the hoses near the check valves for signs that they have been burned. If they are burned, the hot exhaust gases from the engine are backing up past the check valve toward the air pump. The check valve, as well as the hose, should be replaced. Visually inspect the pump drive belt for wear, cracks, and deterioration. Replace it if it is defective.

Start the engine and listen for any excessive belt noise. A squealing belt could be caused by either a loose belt or a seized pump. Stop the engine, remove the belt, and turn the pump pulley by hand. If you cannot turn the pulley, then the belt is slipping, caus-

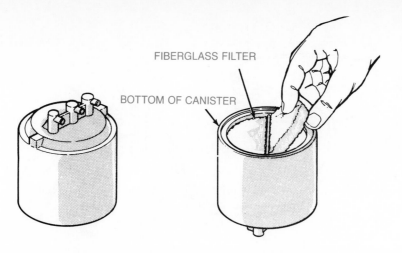

FIBERGLASS FILTER

BOTTOM OF CANISTER

Fig. 52-14 Changing a vapor canister filter. (Chrysler Corporation)

ing the high squeal. The air pump is at fault and needs to be replaced.

Start the engine and listen for excessive noise from the pump. Air pumps are normally noisy. As engine speed increases, the noise of the pump will rise in pitch. The rolling sound made by the pump bearings is okay unless the noise becomes objectionable at certain speeds. A continual knocking sound indicates that the pump rear bearing has failed. The pump will need to be replaced.

A continual hissing sound from the pressure relief valve (located on the pump) at idle indicates a defective valve. The valve will need to be replaced. To check the air pump output, turn off the engine and disconnect the air hose from the diverter valve. Start the engine. Check the air flow from the air pump at the outlet.

Accelerate the engine to approximatley 1500 rpm. The air flow should increase as the engine speed increases. If the air flow does not increase, check for air coming from the diverter valve muffler. The diverter valve should be replaced if air is escaping from the valve at idle speed. If the air pump is not increasing the air flow as described, the pump should be replaced.

To test the diverter valve, start the engine and warm it up to operating temperatures. Disconnect the vacuum sensing line at the diverter valve and check it for vacuum by placing your finger over the end of the line. You should feel a vacuum pull on your finger. If you can feel a vacuum, check the line for kinks, cracks, or loose connections.

Reconnect the vacuum line. Check the diverter valve muffler to be sure that air is not escaping. If air is escaping, there could be a restriction in the hoses

and lines that is causing the pressure relief valve to open. If no restrictions are apparent, replace the diverter valve.

Place your hand by the diverter valve muffler. Open and close the throttle quickly. A blast of air should come out of the muffler for approximately one second. If air does not come out of the diverter valve, the valve is defective and should be replaced.

To test the check valve, visually check for exhaust gases leaking through the check valve. Look for a burned hose; a burned hose would indicate an exhaust leak. Start the engine. With the engine operating, disconnect the air hose from the check valve (work from the air-pump side of the valve).

Operate the engine at 1500 rpm and check for exhaust gas leakage at the valve. If leakage is present, replace the check valve. Turn off the engine and reconnect the hose to the check valve.

52.8   PREVENTIVE MAINTENANCE

Each car manufacturer specifies what emission equipment requires maintenance and at what intervals of mileage or time these components should be maintained. The procedures explained in this section are typical.

52.9   Replacing the Charcoal Canister Filter Element

Replacing the charcoal canister filter element is the most frequent service procedure performed on a vehicle's fuel evaporative emission control system. The

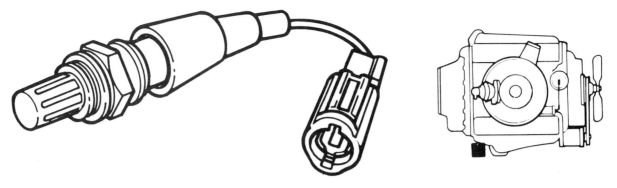

Fig. 52-15 The oxygen sensor is replaced at regular intervals. (Ford Motor Company)

filter element should be replaced at the maintenance interval recommended by the vehicle manufacturer.

To replace the canister filter element, first disconnect the vapor hose(s) from the top of the canister. **Safety Caution: After you disconnect a vapor hose, be sure to plug it to prevent the escape of dangerous fuel vapors.** Loosen the mounting bracket clamp bolt and slide the canister up out of the bracket. On some models, you will have to remove the mounting bracket.

Turn the canister upside down and remove the cover (if used) from the bottom of the canister. Pull the cover down to disengage the holding clips. Pull the filter out from under the retainer bar (Fig. 52-14). Discard the filter element.

If you find raw fuel in the canister, install the new filter element by squeezing it under the retainer bar. Be sure to position it evenly around the engine bottom of the canister with the edges tucked under the canister lip. Snap the bottom cover in place. Reinstall the canister in the mounting bracket. Unplug and reconnect the vapor hoses.

52.10 Replacing the Oxygen Sensor

The oxygen sensor (Fig. 52-15) has a limited service life. The sensor is subject to heat and contamination from exhaust gases. Some cars have a dashboard light which comes on at a specific mileage interval. The light instructs the driver to get the sensor changed.

To change the sensor unplug the electrical connection and use a wrench to unscrew the old sensor. Coat the threads of the new sensor with anti-sieze compound. Install the sensor and tighten it to specifications. Plug in the electrical connection.

52.11 SERVICING THE EMISSION CONTROL SYSTEM

When troubleshooting indicates a problem in the emission control system, the system must be serviced. In most cases, the malfunctioning component is removed and replaced with a new component. The most common service procedures are described in this section.

52.12 Servicing the PCV System

Most vehicle manufacturers recommend that you service the PCV system at every tune-up because of its effect on engine performance. Depending on the results of the PCV parts inspection and PCV system testing, the following service procedures would apply.

PCV hoses (Fig. 52-16) should be replaced whenever they are cracked, kinked, or collapsed. First, loosen the hose clamps (if present) at each end of the PCV hose that is to be cleaned. Disconnect each end of the hose from its fitting and remove the hose from the vehicle. Clean the hose with the correct cleaning solvent. Some manufacturers specify the use of combustion chamber conditioner or a similar solvent. Hoses should not remain in the cleaning solvent for more than half an hour. Allow the hoses to dry.

Most vehicle manufacturers recommend that the PCV valve be replaced if it is not operating properly. In many instances, cleaning a PCV valve is not recommended. To replace the PCV valve, remove the PCV valve from the engine valve cover by working it up and out of its rubber grommet mounting.

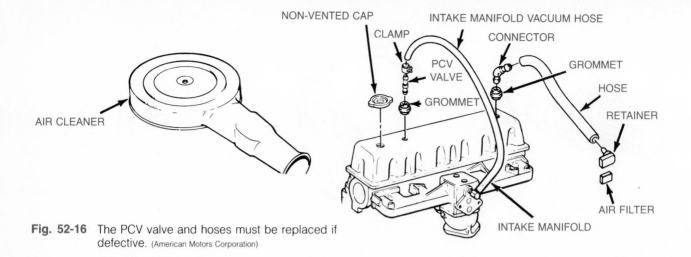

NON-VENTED CAP INTAKE MANIFOLD VACUUM HOSE
CLAMP CONNECTOR
PCV VALVE GROMMET
AIR CLEANER GROMMET HOSE
RETAINER
AIR FILTER
INTAKE MANIFOLD

Fig. 52-16 The PCV valve and hoses must be replaced if defective. (American Motors Corporation)

Loosen the PCV valve hose or the manifold vacuum hose clamp (if present), at the PCV valve end. Remove the valve from the hose. Note the position of the valve in the hose. Look up the correct part number of the PCV valve in the parts catalogue for the vehicle year, make, and model being serviced. It is extremely important that you install the correct valve for the vehicle. Do not try to match the PCV valve visually, because many of them look alike but have different flow rates. Choose a replacement only by part number.

Insert the PCV valve into the PCV hose. Be sure the new PCV valve is positioned correctly, so that the crankcase vapors will move through the valve and into the carburetor or intake manifold. **Safety Caution: Reverse installation of the PCV valve can cause an explosion in the engine.**

Tighten the hose clamp (if present) and install the PCV valve into its mounting grommet on the engine valve cover. Be sure to place the rubber grommet if it is cracked or deteriorated. Retest the PCV system to ensure proper operation.

52.13   Replacing an Air Injection Drive Belt

Replacement of an air pump drive belt requires the same general procedures as the replacement of an alternator belt. To replace the air pump belt, loosen both the belt-adjusting bolt and the air pump mounting bolt. Pivot the air pump toward the crankshaft pulley and work the belt off the pulleys.

Install the new air pump belt around the pulleys and adjust the belt to the belt tension specifications, using a belt tension gauge. Whether the air pump belt needs to be replaced or adjusted, always look up the belt tension specifications for it in the shop service manual.

When you adjust the belt, always pry against the rear cover of the air pump only. Tighten the air pump belt-adjusting bolt and the mounting bolt securely.

52.14   Replacing the EGR Valve

If the EGR valve is not operating properly or is defective, it should be either replaced or cleaned. For specific instructions, refer to the vehicle manufacturer's recommendations in the shop service manual for the vehicle being serviced.

Remove the EGR valve, gasket, and clamp, if present, from their mountings either on the intake manifold or on the carburetor spacer. Inspect the valve for deposits, paying particular attention to the valve poppet and seat area. If there is more than a thin film of deposit buildup, the valve should be cleaned.

Clean the EGR valve seat area with manifold heat control solvent. Allow half an hour for the deposits to soften. Then, using a sharp tool, scrape all the deposit from the poppet and seat. Do not allow the solvent to get on the diaphragm, since it may damage the diaphragm, causing it to fail.

A standard spark plug cleaner can be used to clean the valve and seat. First, blast the valve and seat area for 30 seconds only. Then depress the diaphragm and blast again for 30 seconds. Be sure to get all the abrasive materials out of the valve. Scrape the old gasket material from the EGR valve mounting base and with a new gasket install the EGR valve and tighten the bolts to specifications.

NEW TERMS

Vehicle emission control information label An underhood decal which explains what emission control devices are used on an engine as well as basic emission specifications and vacuum hose routings.

CHAPTER REVIEW

1. What type of information can you find on the underhood emission control information label?
2. Where can you find how to properly connect a vacuum line?
3. Describe how to connect an exhaust analyzer to a car.
4. Explain how to conduct an emissions test with an exhaust system analyzer.
5. List five possible causes for an excessive hydrocarbon reading.
6. List five possible causes for an excessive carbon monoxide reading.
7. List three causes of excessive hydrocarbon and carbon monoxide readings.
8. Explain how to check for proper operation of the PCV system.
9. How can you visually check for proper EGR valve operation?
10. Explain how to use a hand vacuum pump to check an EGR valve.
11. Explain how to test a vacuum delay valve.
12. Explain how to test a heated intake air system for proper operation.
13. Describe how to remove and replace the charcoal canister filter element.
14. Why is it necessary to replace the oxygen sensor periodically?
15. Describe how to remove and replace a PVC valve.

DISCUSSION TOPICS AND ACTIVITIES

1. Connect an exhaust analyzer to an engine. Remove or disarm each of the emission systems one at a time. Measure the amount of increase in emissions.
2. Follow the shop service manual procedure to put a computerized engine control system in self-test. What trouble codes could you find in the system?

Automobile Electronic Control Systems

PART

9

Electronic Fuel Injection Systems

CHAPTER PREVIEW

In the 1970s, fuel injection technology and electronics technology joined in the development of a fuel delivery system called electronic fuel injection (E.F.I.). Electronic fuel injection was the product of efforts to lower emissions and improve fuel mileage.

This system uses fuel spray nozzles mounted in a throttle body, intake manifold, or cylinder head. The nozzles are supplied with fuel under high pressure by a mechanical or electric fuel pump. The nozzles are controlled electronically. The electronic controls insure that the fuel injected at any given moment is precisely the amount the engine needs. Sensing devices on the engine tell the control unit the actual load condition, engine speed, and operating temperature.

OBJECTIVES

After studying this chapter you should be able to do the following:

1. List the three basic types of electronic fuel injection systems in common use.
2. Describe the parts and operation of the airflow-controlled electronic fuel injection system.
3. Explain the operation of the continuous-flow electronic fuel injection system.
4. Explain the difference between individual fuel nozzle and throttle body fuel injection systems.
5. Explain how to troubleshoot an electronic fuel injection system.

53.1   TYPES OF E.F.I. SYSTEMS

There are three basic types of electronic fuel injection systems in common use. These are called air-flow controlled, continuous-flow, and throttle body types. In the following sections we will describe the parts and operation of each of these systems.

53.2   AIRFLOW-CONTROLLED ELECTRONIC FUEL INJECTION

In an airflow-controlled EFI system, a metered amount of fuel is injected into the intake manifold near the intake valves by electronically controlled fuel injectors. An airflow-controlled EFI system has three sub-systems: the fuel flow system, the airflow system, and the electronic control system. The basic parts of these subsystems and their typical location on an automobile are shown in Figure 53-1.

53.3   Fuel Flow System

The purpose of the fuel flow system is to provide the correct amount of fuel to each fuel injector. A typical fuel flow system is shown in Figure 53-2. Fuel is pulled from the fuel tank into the fuel pump which discharges fuel under pressure. As fuel flows through the fuel damper, pulsations in the fuel flow are damped or reduced. The fuel is then cleaned in the fuel filter and continues through the fuel line. It is injected (in a measured amount) into the intake manifold from the fuel injector. Surplus fuel is led through the pressure regulator and returned to the fuel tank.

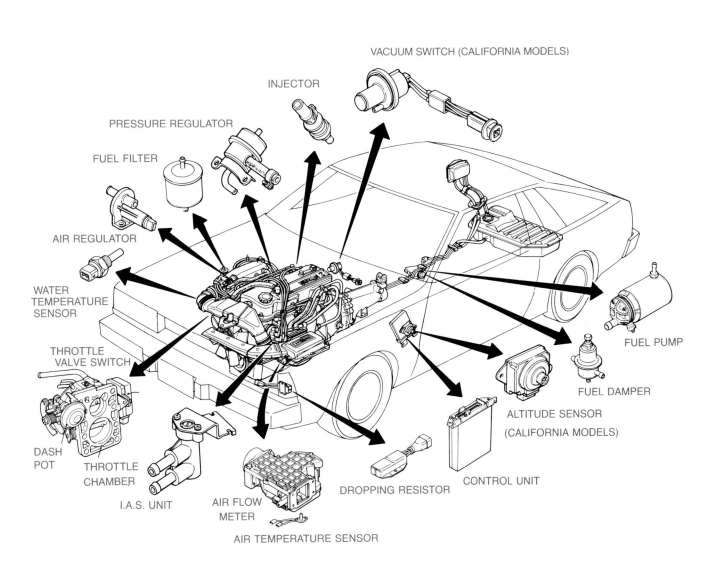

VACUUM SWITCH (CALIFORNIA MODELS)

INJECTOR

PRESSURE REGULATOR

FUEL FILTER

AIR REGULATOR

WATER
TEMPERATURE
SENSOR

THROTTLE
VALVE SWITCH

DASH
POT

THROTTLE
CHAMBER

I.A.S. UNIT

AIR FLOW
METER

AIR TEMPERATURE SENSOR

DROPPING RESISTOR

CONTROL UNIT

ALTITUDE SENSOR

(CALIFORNIA MODELS)

FUEL DAMPER

FUEL PUMP

Fig. 53-1 Parts and location of airflow-controlled EFI. (Nissan
Motor Corporation in U.S.A)

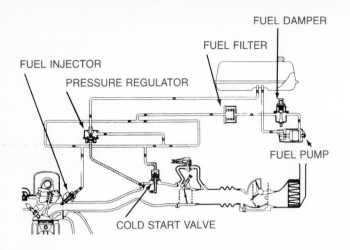

Fig. 53-2 Fuel flow system. (Nissan Motor Corporation in U.S.A.)

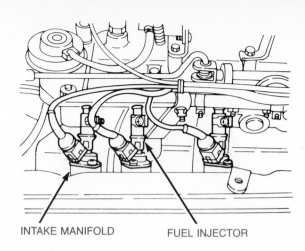

Fig. 53-3 Fuel injectors are mounted in the intake manifold. (Nissan Motor Corporation in U.S.A.)

Filtered fuel flows to each of the fuel injectors—one for each cylinder. The fuel injectors are mounted on the intake manifold for each cylinder (Fig. 53-3). They are supported in a specially shaped, molded rubber mount and are usually clamped, not screwed, into place. Since fuel flows directly to the fuel injectors, fuel pressure is available at the fuel injector at all times.

The fuel injector (Fig. 53-4) contains a small solenoid consisting of a solenoid coil, solenoid plunger, spring, and final filter. The final filter, mounted in the end of the fuel supply line, removes any contaminants from the fuel before it enters the fuel injector. The spring holds the needle valve in a closed position. When current is passed through the solenoid via the electrical connector, the needle valve is pulled from its seat, allowing fuel to be discharged out of the nozzle. The length of time current is allowed to flow is regulated in milliseconds by the electronic control unit described later. The time range is from 1.5 to 10 milliseconds (1/1000 of a second), depending on engine requirements.

Like the carburetion system, the EFI system must provide more fuel to the engine for starting and for the warm-up period. A cold start valve (Fig. 53-5) is used to provide this additional fuel. The cold start valve is actually an additional injector, mounted so that it can spray fuel into the airflow to the cylinders.

The cold start valve is an electromagnetic valve, which electrically is considered a solenoid. It has a spring that presses a movable plunger and seal against the valve seat. This blocks the flow of fuel.

When the plunger and seal are drawn back by the magnetic action of the solenoid coil, the valve seat opens and fuel flows along the sides of the plunger to the swirl nozzle. In the swirl nozzle, a swirling motion is imparted to the fuel, and the fuel leaves the swirl

nozzle in a finely atomized state. The operation of the cold start valve is controlled by the thermo-time switch.

53.4 Airflow System

The purpose of the airflow system (Fig. 53-6) is to provide for the flow of air into the engine. The amount of airflow is measured, and that measurement is used to determine the amount of fuel injected.

Intake air from the air filter is metered through the airflow meter, through the throttle chamber, and into the intake manifold. It then flows through each intake manifold branch into cylinders. Airflow while driving is controlled by the throttle valve located in the throttle chamber. During idling operation, the throttle valve is in its almost closed position, and the air is led through the bypass port mounted on the throttle chamber. In this case, the quantity of suction air is adjusted by means of the idle speed adjusting screw. During warm-up operation, the airflow is bypassed through the air regulator to increase engine rpm.

The main component of the airflow system is the airflow meter (Fig. 53-7). The primary purpose of the airflow meter is to furnish the electronic control unit with a voltage signal concerning the rate of airflow. The airflow is measured as follows.

A baffle plate fitted in the meter and attached to a return spring is mechanically connected to a potentiometer, which converts the baffle plate position into an electric voltage signal sent to the control unit. By using a compensating flap and compensating chamber, a dampening effect is exerted on the baffle plate. This feature reduces the

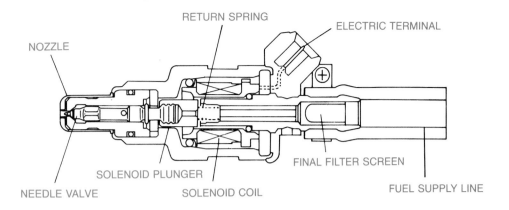

Fig. 53-4 Cross-sectional view of a fuel injector. (Nissan Motor Corporation in U.S.A.)

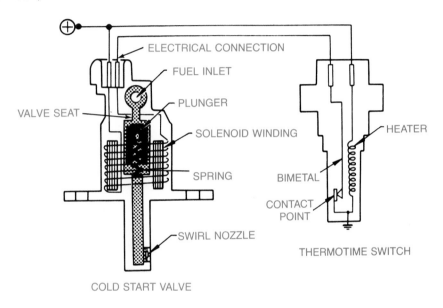

Fig. 53-5 The cold start valve injects fuel for cold starting.
(Nissan Motor Corporation in U.S.A.)

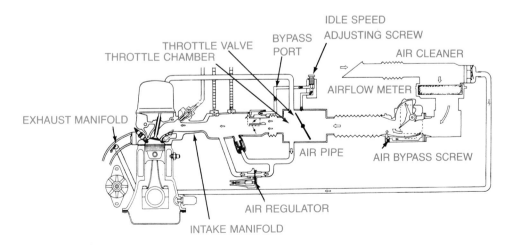

Fig. 53-6 Airflow system. (Nissan Motor Corporation in U.S.A.)

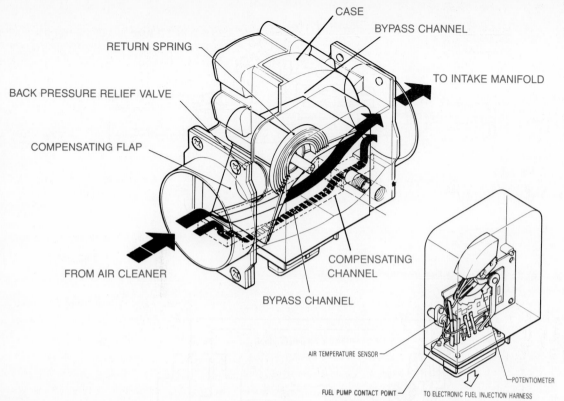

CASE
BYPASS CHANNEL
RETURN SPRING
BACK PRESSURE RELIEF VALVE
TO INTAKE MANIFOLD
COMPENSATING FLAP
FROM AIR CLEANER
COMPENSATING CHANNEL
BYPASS CHANNEL
AIR TEMPERATURE SENSOR
POTENTIOMETER
FUEL PUMP CONTACT POINT
TO ELECTRONIC FUEL INJECTION HARNESS

Fig. 53-7 The airflow meter measures the amount of air entering the engine. (Nissan Motor Corporation in U.S.A.)

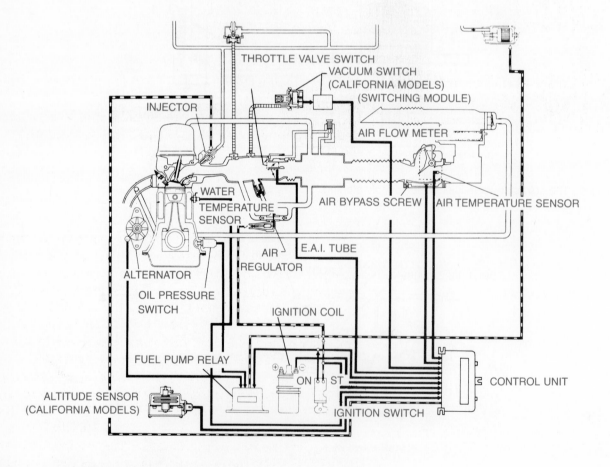

THROTTLE VALVE SWITCH
VACUUM SWITCH (CALIFORNIA MODELS) (SWITCHING MODULE)
INJECTOR
AIR FLOW METER
WATER TEMPERATURE SENSOR
AIR BYPASS SCREW
AIR TEMPERATURE SENSOR
AIR REGULATOR
E.A.I. TUBE
ALTERNATOR
OIL PRESSURE SWITCH
IGNITION COIL
FUEL PUMP RELAY
ON ST
CONTROL UNIT
ALTITUDE SENSOR (CALIFORNIA MODELS)
IGNITION SWITCH

Fig. 53-8 Electrical control system. (Nissan Motor Corporation in U.S.A.)

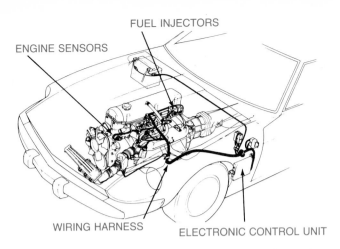

Fig. 53-9 The electronic control unit is connected to engine sensors. (Nissan Motor Corporation in U.S.A.)

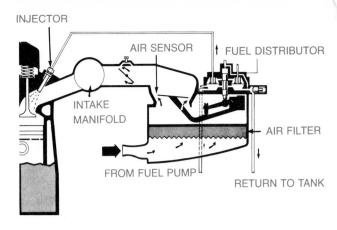

Fig. 53-10 Basic parts of the continuous-flow EFI. (Volkswagen of America, Inc.)

effect of any airflow pulsations and results in smoother operation of the baffle plate. To eliminate any possible damage to the airflow meter from engine backfire, a back-pressure relief valve is built into the baffle plate. A bypass channel is also built into the airflow meter. The bypass channel air is not measured by the airflow meter, but it is used to set the air-fuel mixture at idle. Air flowing into the engine moves the compensating flap. The movement of the flap is converted into an electrical signal by the potentiometer.

53.5 Electronic Control System

The purpose of the electronic control system is to sense engine operating conditions and to regulate the quantity of fuel injected in relation to airflow. A typical wiring diagram for an electronic control system is shown in Figure 53-8.

The fuel flow system delivers a constant fuel pressure to the fuel injectors. The area of the fuel injector nozzle hole is constant. Neither of these factors (fuel pressure and fuel injector nozzle hole area) affect fuel injection quantity. The fuel injector's pulse time regulates fuel injection quantity as it changes. Pulse time is the time in which the fuel injectors are open and providing fuel. It is measured in milliseconds. One millisecond represents one thousandth of a second. The average maximum pulse time for an airflow-sensitive, timed EFI system is about 10 milliseconds. Pulse time is determined from various engine mounted sensors.

An electrical signal from each sensor is sent to the electronic control unit (Fig. 53-9) for processing and response. The pulse time period of the fuel in-

jectors is then determined by the electronic control unit.

Information on the quantity of the air drawn into the engine, the engine's coolant and cylinder head temperatures, the position of the throttle valve, the vehicle starting process, the engine's speed, the start of fuel injection, and the oxygen in the exhaust gas is received by the electronic control unit. It processes this information and transmits signals to the various electrical components of the airflow-sensitive, timed EFI system by means of a multiple-pin plug and wiring harness.

53.6 Continuous-Flow Electronic Fuel-Injection

The continuous-flow EFI system, is different from the airflow-sensitive systems in that fuel is being injected constantly while the engine is running. This system is relatively simple and has fewer parts than any other EFI system in general use. The fuel injectors in this system are not electrically pulsed but are activated by fuel pressure.

The main components of the continuous-flow system are an airflow sensor and a fuel distributor. The basic parts of the system are shown in Figure 53-10.

The air sensor and fuel distributor work together to get the correct amount of fuel to the injectors (Fig. 53-11). The airflow sensor utilizes an air funnel and an airflow sensor plate mounted on a lever which is supported on a pivot. The weight of the lever and airflow sensor plate is balanced by a counterweight. A plunger called the control plunger operates under

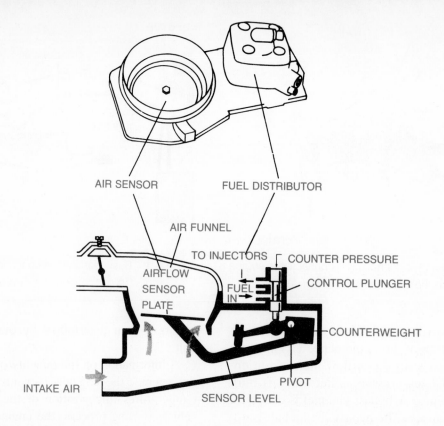

Fig. 53-11 Airflow sensor and fuel distributor. (Volkswagen of America, Inc.)

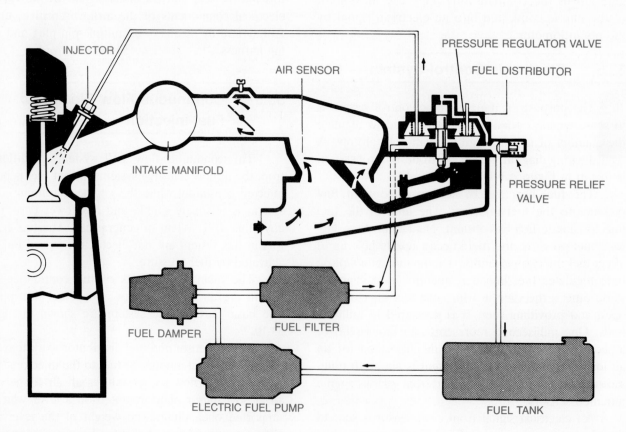

Fig. 53-12 Fuel flow through the continuous-flow system.
(Volkswagen of America, Inc.)

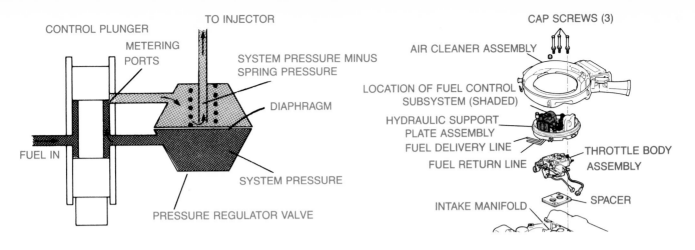

Fig. 53-13 The pressure regulator valve regulates pressure to the injectors. (Volkswagen of America, Inc.)

Fig. 53-14 Throttle body fuel injection. (Chrysler Corporation)

fuel pressure and transmits its force to oppose the force of the airflow on the lever and airflow sensor plate. The intake air flows through the air funnel and lifts the airflow sensor plate until the force of this air and the opposing force of the control plunger are equal.

In this balanced position, which is a volumetric measurement of airflow rate, the control plunger is positioned at a certain point in the fuel distributor, and its horizontal control edge opens the rectangular metering ports by a uniform amount. The fuel which flows through these openings is then fed to the fuel injectors.

The flow of fuel through a continuous-flow EFI system is shown in Figure 53-12. Fuel is drawn from the fuel tank by an electric fuel pump into a fuel damper and through a fuel filter. Filtered fuel enters the fuel distributor and flows through a separate line to each fuel injector. The pressure relief valve limits the pressure to a predetermined value and allows excessive fuel to flow back to the fuel tank through the fuel return line.

The fuel distributor has a separate pressure regulator valve (Fig. 53-13) for each fuel injector. The pressure regulator valve utilizes a diaphragm and valve spring to make certain that fuel will be distributed evenly to each cylinder. The control plunger of the airflow sensor determines the quantity of fuel flow.

As the airflow sensor plate rises, the control plunger opens the fuel feed to the upper side of the pressure regulator valve diaphragm by way of the metering ports. Fuel pressure, plus valve spring pressure on the upper side of the diaphragm, is now greater than the pressure on its lower side. Thus, the diaphragm is pressed downward, causing an increased fuel flow to the fuel injector.

Most continuous-flow systems use a cold start valve or injector similar to those on the airflow-sensitive systems. The system is controlled by the same type of electronic control and engine sensors used on the airflow-sensitive system.

53.7 THROTTLE BODY FUEL INJECTION

Throttle body electronic fuel injection is similar to the other electronic fuel injection systems we have described. An electronic control unit pulses injectors based upon information received from engine sensors. An airflow sensor mounted in the air intake system sends a message to the electronic control unit regarding the amount of air entering the engine. The main difference in this system is that individual injectors are not located in the intake manifold. Instead, one or two injectors are mounted in a housing called the throttle body. The throttle body is mounted in the same position on the intake manifold as the carburetor used to be. A throttle body system is shown in Figure 53-14. Throttle body systems are electronically controlled.

53.8 ELECTRONIC FUEL INJECTION SERVICE

Fuel injection problems cause the same general symptoms as those described for carburetion systems. Troubleshooting an electronic fuel injection system should not be atempted without a detailed troubleshooting procedure provided in the manufacturer's shop service manual. Most EFI systems can be checked

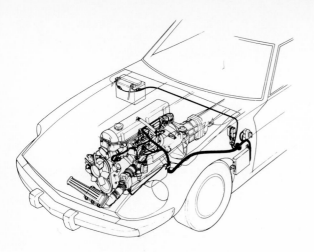

Fig. 53-15 Typical EFI harness and connectors. (Nissan Motor Corporation in U.S.A.)

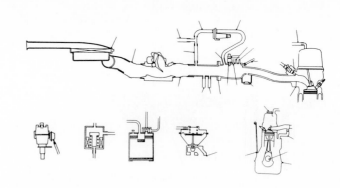

Fig. 53-16 Checking for air leaks on an EFI system. (Nissan Motor Corporation in U.S.A.)

using a voltmeter and ohmmeter along with a pressure gauge.

Safety Caution: The EFI fuel system is under high pressure. Always wear eye protection to avoid fuel being squirted in the eyes. The high pressure in the fuel lines makes opening a fuel line dangerous, even when the engine is stopped. Always check the shop service manual for the correct procedure for bleeding off the pressure before opening any line. Do not reuse fuel hose clamps and always torque them to specifications.

A no-start condition is often caused by a malfunction of the electric fuel pump. If the electric fuel pump does not buzz for a second or two when the ignition is turned on, check the pump fuse. All EFI electric fuel pumps are fused someplace in the vehicle's electrical circuit.

EFI system problems often occur in the connections between the components. Make a quick check of all harnesses and connectors for looseness or corrosion. All the harnesses and connectors should be disconnected and inspected, then reconnected (Fig. 53-15).

Since an EFI system accurately meters the intake airflow through the airflow meter, even a slight air leak causes an improper air-fuel mixture, resulting in faulty engine operation. For this reason, a thorough inspection for air leaks should be made at all the points shown in Figure 53-16.

A common cause of hard starting, poor idle, low power, and engine misfire is a plugged fuel injector or cold start valve (Fig. 53-17). One method of finding a bad injector is a power balance test. If the ignition system is operating correctly, and there is little or no rpm drop when a cylinder is shorted, the problem could be a vacuum leak at the fuel injector seal.

O-rings are a potential source of vacuum leak on any EFI system.

Place your fingers on a good (functioning properly) fuel injector and feel it clicking open and closed. If you do not feel it working, a poor electrical connection may exist at that fuel injector. Switch the fuel injector wires with an adjacent, good fuel injector. If switching the wires causes it to work, the problem is electrical. Check the circuit for corrosion or a poor connection. The EFI fuel system is checked with a pressure gauge. The pressure gauge is installed in the fuel line at a point where the fuel has passed through the fuel filter. Install the correct type of pressure gauge in the correct testing location. **Safety Caution: Use a reinforced fuel line hose that will withstand high pressure and use worm-gear clamps to attach the pressure gauge.**

Make a pressure reading at the idle engine speed recommended by the manufacturer and compare the reading to specifications. When the fuel pressure reading is taken at idle, normal fuel injector pulsation will cause the gauge to fluctuate. Watch the pressure gauge needle carefully, and record the average pressure value. At idle, take the midpoint between the highest and lowest fluctuations (pulsations) of the pressure gauge needle as the pressure reading.

If fuel pressure is not within specifications at idle, the problem may be a clogged fuel filter, a restricted fuel line, or a restricted fuel return line. After taking the idle fuel pressure reading, shut off the engine and watch the pressure gauge. It should hold at 17-20 PSI. If the pressure drops to zero, there is a leak in the EFI system.

Many of the electrical components of the EFI system can be checked with a voltmeter or ohmmeter.

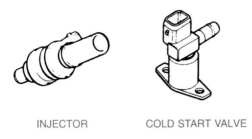

INJECTOR   COLD START VALVE

Fig. 53-17 Faulty injectors or cold start injectors can cause hard starting or poor performance. (Nissan Motor Corporation in U.S.A.)

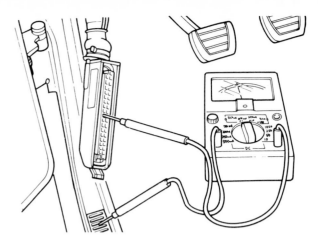

Fig. 53-18 Electrical checks are made at the harness connector. (Nissan Motor Corporation in U.S.A.)

The shop service manual will provide a detailed set of tests and measurements for checking the system. Most of the tests will be made at the EFI electrical harness connector (Figure 53-18).

NEW TERMS

Airflow-controlled electronic fuel injection An electronic fuel injection system that measures the air entering the engine and regulates the amount of fuel injected into the engine based upon that measurement.

Continuous-flow electronic fuel injection An electronic fuel injection system that uses a mechanical fuel distributor to regulate the amount of fuel entering the engine.

Electronic fuel injection A fuel injection system that uses electronically controlled injection nozzles to distribute fuel to the engine's cylinders.

Injector nozzle An electrically controlled device used to spray fuel into the intake manifold in an EFI system.

Throttle body electronic fuel injection An electronic fuel injection system that uses fuel injection nozzles mounted in a throttle body assembly instead of individually mounted injectors.

CHAPTER REVIEW

1. What are the three basic types of electronic fuel injection systems in common use?

2. What are the three subsystems of the airflow-controlled EFI?

3. Where are the fuel injector nozzles mounted on an airflow EFI system?

4. Explain how a fuel injector nozzle works.

5. What is the purpose of the cold start valve?

6. What is the purpose of the airflow meter?

7. What is the purpose of the bypass channel in the airflow meter?

8. What does the electronic control system control?

9. What is the purpose of the sensors?

10. How is the continuous-flow EFI system different from the airflow-controlled system?

11. Where are the injector nozzles located in a throttle body EFI system?

12. Why should eye protection always be worn when servicing an EFI system?

13. Why should you inspect an airflow system for air leaks?

14. How can you check the operation of an injector nozzle?

15. What electrical test instrument is used to check out an EFI system?

DISCUSSION TOPICS AND ACTIVITIES

1. Use a shop service manual to identify the parts on a car with airflow EFI. How many of the parts can you find?

2. Use a shop service manual to identify the parts on a continuous-flow EFI system. Can you locate all the parts?

3. Do you think individual or throttle body mounted injectors make for a more efficient system? Why?

Computerized Engine Control Systems

CHAPTER PREVIEW

The design balance between engine performance, fuel economy, and emission control requires precise coordination of engine systems. This precise control is only possible when an onboard computer is used to control the engine. A computerized control system uses a small microprocessor or computer to control the operation of the ignition fuel and emission systems. Systems are being developed which control transmission shifting, accessory operation, instrumentation and many other vehicle systems. In this chapter we will describe the basic operation and service of a computerized engine control system.

OBJECTIVES

After studying this chapter you should be able to do the following:

1. Describe the function of a computer in an engine control system.
2. Explain the purpose of a sensor in an engine control system.
3. Explain the function of an actuator in an engine control system.
4. Explain the operation of a feedback fuel system in open and closed loop.
5. Describe the self-diagnostic technique used on a computerized engine control system.

54.1   BASIC SYSTEM OPERATION

A computerized engine control system has three main components: (1) a microprocessor or computer, (2) a set of sensors or transducers, (3) a set of switches or actuators.

The main part of the computerized engine control system is the computer (Fig. 54-1). This unit may be called an electronic control unit, a microprocessor, or simply, the computer. Computers are basically switches that control voltage. They do not "think" and they do not make "decisions." When connected into a circuit, they open and close the electrical circuit.

The electronic circuitry inside the computer can be damaged by heat or vibration. To prevent damage to the computer, it is typically mounted in the right hand kick panel in the passenger compartment, or next to the glove box. On some cars, the computer is mounted on the air cleaner to provide an air flow over it for cooling (Fig. 54-2).

The computer is connected to the vehicle electrical system and to the sensors and actuators through its wiring harness. The electrical system provides a voltage to the computer shown as "power" in Figure 54-3. Voltage is the common factor in all electronic units and circuits. Voltage pushes the power in, and voltage pushes the power supply out. The path of voltage flow depends on how the computer connects to the system. Regardless of this, all connections to and from the computer depend on electrical voltage. This includes voltage inputs and voltage outputs.

Voltage comes into the computer (called an input) from sensors or transducers. The sensors are designed to monitor some car or engine function and report back to the computer.

We have added a sensor to our basic block diagram (Fig. 54-4). Typically, at least two wires are connected from the computer to the sensor. A voltage called the reference voltage is sent from the computer to the sensor. The reference voltage is changed by the

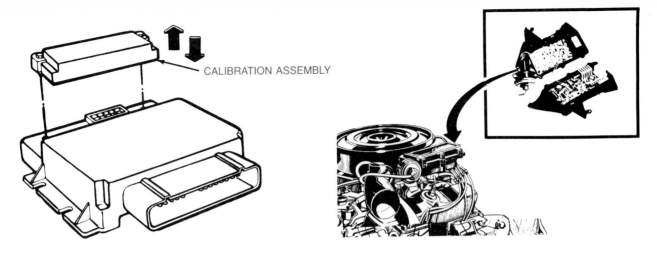

Fig. 54-1 An engine control computer. (Ford Motor Company)

Fig. 54-2 An engine control computer mounted on an air cleaner assembly. (Chrysler Corporation)

sensor to an input voltage which goes back to the computer.

The computer uses or processes the information it receives from the sensors and sends an output voltage to switches or actuators. The actuator is often a solenoid type of switch, which controls some vehicle or engine function. In our block diagram (Fig. 54-5), we have added an actuator. The computer sends a voltage signal called an output to the actuator. The actuator does its job and a return voltage from the actuator to the computer completes the circuit.

54.2 COMPUTERIZED (FEEDBACK) FUEL SYSTEMS

One of the most common uses of the computer is to closely monitor and control the fuel system for maximum economy and lowest possible emissions.

The feedback or closed loop fuel system uses an oxygen sensor located in the exhaust system to sense the amount of oxygen in the exhaust leaving the engine. Using this information, the fuel system changes the air-fuel mixture to the most ideal for low emissions. The feedback or closed loop system is used on both electronic fuel injection and carburetor fuel systems.

The oxygen sensor (Fig. 54-6) is made of a ceramic material called zirconium oxide. The inner and outer surfaces of the ceramic material are coated with platinum. The outer platinum surface is in contact with the exhaust gas, while the inner surface is exposed to the outside air.

The difference in the amount of oxygen contacting the inner and outer surfaces of the sensor creates a pressure which results in a small voltage signal.

If the amount of oxygen in the exhaust system is low, which indicates a rich mixture, the sensor voltage will be high (Fig. 54-7 A). This high voltage is sent to an electronic control unit that will reduce the amount of fuel supplied to the engine. The amount of fuel is reduced until the amount of oxygen in the exhaust system increases, indicating a lean mixture. If the mixture is lean, the oxygen sensor will send a low voltage signal (Fig. 54-7 B) to the electronic control unit. The control unit will increase the quantity of fuel until the sensor voltage increases and then the cycle begins again.

The voltage signal from the oxygen sensor is used in an electronic fuel injection system to regulate the air-fuel mixture. The voltage signal is sent to the EFI electronic control unit. The electronic control unit changes the on/off or pulse time of the injectors to provide a leaner or richer mixture.

Carburetor feedback systems require a mixture control or feedback solenoid on the carburetor (Fig. 54-8). The feedback solenoid (Fig. 54-9) consists of a self-contained fuel control valve at the lower end, and an air bleed control valve at the upper end. Solenoid operation is controlled by the voltage signals from the exhaust gas oxygen sensor.

The solenoid has two positions: on (down) and off (up). The air bleed and fuel control operate simultaneously. With the solenoid on, the air bleed opens and the fuel valve closes (for leaner mixtures). With the solenoid off, the air bleed closes and the fuel valve opens (richer mixtures).

In operation, the solenoid opens and closes the solenoid assembly jet ten times per second. This cycle does not change. Ten times in each second the solenoid ground circuit is completed so voltage is increased to depress the solenoid plunger (close the jet

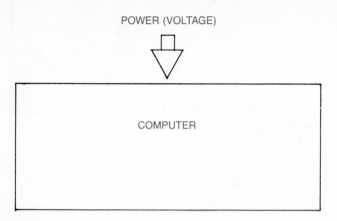

Fig. 54-3 The car's electrical system provides voltage to the computer.

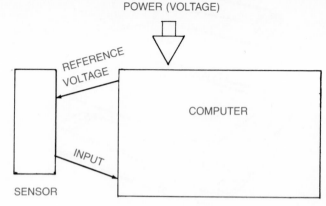

Fig. 54-4 The sensor provides an input signal to the computer.

and open the air bleed), and voltage is decreased to release the solenoid plunger (open the jet and close the air bleed). If voltage control is exactly one half of the time interval for each cycle, then the solenoid will be on and the jet closed for half of each cycle. After ten cycles on and off (or one complete second of time), the jet would have been closed for half or 50% of a second. This percentage of time in which the jet is closed is called "duty cycle." Duty refers to how much worktime or duty the solenoid accomplishes. When control voltage is applied for only half of the time in each second, the duty cycle is 50%.

The total amount of fuel delivered by the main metering primary circuit depends on the duty cycle of the feedback solenoid. If the solenoid control voltage is applied and the jet is closed for only 10% of each second, supplemental fuel flow will be large in volume. This would be a 10% duty cycle.

If the solenoid control voltage is applied and the jet is closed for 90% of each second, supplemental fuel flow will be small in volume. This would be a 90% duty cycle.

Since main jet flow is fixed, the richness or leanness of the main metering circuit primary stage can be varied by controlling the duty cycle of the feedback solenoid. A 0% duty cycle delivers the richest mixture; a 100% duty cycle delivers the leanest mixture.

On General Motors vehicles, the duty cycle can be measured with an ordinary dwell meter, the same type that is used to measure distributor point dwell. Somewhere under the hood on every General Motors car with a computer controlled carburetor there is a green connector hanging out of the wire loom. It is usually near the carburetor, but may be at one side of the engine compartment. The dwell meter must be

in the 6-cylinder position, and properly calibrated to the set line. Connect the red dwell meter lead to the green connector, and the black dwell meter lead to ground. With the engine running, the meter will indicate the amount of dwell on the mixture control solenoid.

If the dwell is varying as the engine idles, it means that the computer is controlling the mixture. Most engines idle at 30 degrees dwell, and the needle should vary a few degrees either side of 30. If the dwell is fixed somewhere near the middle of the scale, the system is in open loop, and the computer is not yet controlling the mixture. When a cold engine is first started, the system remains in open loop for several minutes until the engine and the oxygen sensor warm up to operating temperature.

On some engines the dwell meter is used when adjusting idle mixture. Either the idle mixture needles or an idle-air bleed valve (depending on which is the recommended procedure) are used to change the mixture and thereby change the dwell reading, until it reads 30 degrees. On some carburetors the adjustments are sealed, requiring removal of the carburetor from the engine to make modifications that expose the adjustments.

Any General Motors closed loop carburetor system can be easily checked to see if it is working by richening or leaning the mixture. Move the choke valve toward the closed position to richen the mixture on an idling engine, and the computer will sense a rich mixture at the oxygen sensor. The dwell will then increase as the computer tries to lean the mixture. If you make the mixture rich enough, you can get the dwell to go over 50 degrees.

Removing a vacuum hose to create an air leak

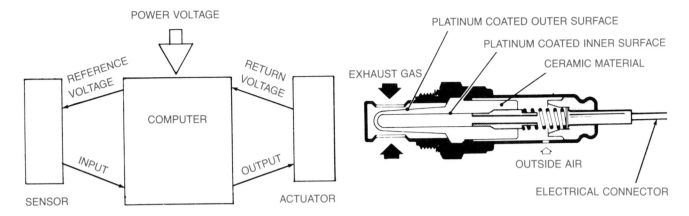

Fig. 54-5 The computer sends an output to the actuator.

Fig. 54-6 Cross-sectional view of an oxygen sensor.
(Volkswagen of America, Inc.)

will test the system also. If the vacuum leak is big enough, the computer will sense the lean mixture at the oxygen sensor and attempt to make the mixture richer. The dwell will move down close to zero. It is important to realize that the computer is working in the opposite direction to what it senses at the oxygen sensor. A rich mixture at the oxygen sensor will result in the computer making the carburetor leaner. If the oxygen sensor picks up a lean mixture, the computer will make the carburetor richer. As there are minute changes at the oxygen sensor, the computer makes minute changes at the carburetor, and the dwell continually varies. The dwell feature is not used on any fuel-injected General Motors cars, including those with throttle body injection. The green connection does not exist on those cars.

54.3 ENGINE CONTROL SYSTEMS

As we said previously, the computer has the capability of handling an ever-increasing number of engine and vehicle operations. The typical engine control system has numerous sensors and actuators. A typical multiple sensor and actuator system is shown in Figure 54-10. This system controls fuel, emission, and ignition timing. As new systems are developed the computer will be assigned more and more control functions for both the engine and the rest of the vehicle.

54.4 COMPUTER CONTROL SERVICE

The advent of the computer to control engine function brought with it a new era in service diag-

nosis. The computer has the capability to perform a self-test. In self-test mode, the computer can make a functional test of itself as well as each of its sensors and actuators.

When performing a self-test diagnosis, it is extremely important that you have and follow the specific shop service manual for the vehicle you are working on. A tester is available for each computer control system. Unlike other engine systems, these tests cannot usually be substituted with simple test instruments. In fact, the incorrect use of jumpers, test lights, or even needle-type voltmeters can create too much current flow in a solid state circuit and damage the computer. You should use only digital voltmeters with at least 10 meg ohm resistance.

Many General Motors cars have a self-diagnosis system. When a problem develops which the self-diagnosis can evaluate, the CHECK ENGINE lamp on the instrument panel will come on and a trouble code will be stored in the computer Trouble Code Memory. The lamp will remain on with the engine running as long as there is a problem. If the problem is intermittent, the CHECK ENGINE lamp will go out, but the trouble code will be stored in the computer trouble code memory.

A 12-terminal connector, located under the dash, is used to check the General Motors Computer Command Control system. Two terminals of this connector (A and B) are used to activate the trouble code system in the computer. The terminals are shown in the underdash connector in Figure 54-11.

Connect a jumper between terminal A and B and turn the ignition to on. This will activate the trouble code system. Since terminal A is a ground, the jumper grounds test terminal B. The CHECK EN-

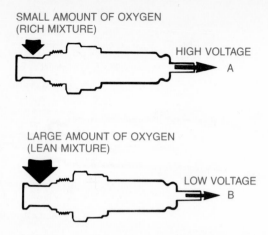

Fig. 54-7 Operation of the oxygen sensor. (Volkswagen of America, Inc.)

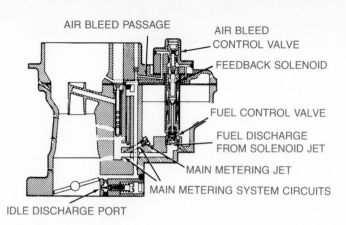

Fig. 54-8 A carburetor with a mixture control solenoid. (Chrysler Corporation)

GINE light will begin to flash a trouble code 12. Code 12 consists of one flash, a short pause, then two flashes. There will be a longer pause and Code 12 will repeat two more times. This check indicates that the self-diagnostic system is working. The cycle will then repeat itself until the engine is started or the ignition is turned off.

If more than one fault is stored in memory, the lowest number code will flash three times followed by the next highest code number, until all faults have been flashed. The faults will then repeat in the same order. Remove the ground from the test terminal before starting the engine.

A trouble code indicates a problem in a given circuit (i.e., trouble code 14 indicates a problem in the coolant sensor, connector, harness, and Electronic Control Module (ECM). A chart like the one in Figure 54-12 is used to explain what each of the trouble codes mean.

The trouble codes stay in the computer memory for 50 starts on most cars. This means that anything that went wrong in the last 50 times the car was started is still in the computer. But the presence of a code in the computer does not mean that there is anything wrong with the car now. The problem that set the code may have happened once and may never happen again. Or the problem may have been corrected by someone. In addition, there may have never been a problem. Someone working on the car may have disconnected something and then connected it again. Such disconnections and reconnections may set a code in the computer.

After reading the codes and writing them down, the code memory should be erased. Do this by cutting off the power to the computer. There are several ways this can be done. Late model cars have a connector near the battery that comes from the positive battery cable. Disconnect this connector for ten seconds and then reconnect it. Or, you may take the computer fuse out of the fuse block for ten seconds. The worst way to erase the memory is by disconnecting the battery ground cable. This will do the job, of course, but will also disturb clock and radio settings as well as any other electronic accessories that lose their programming when the power is cut.

After the codes are erased, ground the test terminal and turn the ignition switch on again. You should get a code 12, which indicates that the engine is dead. Code 12 does not go into the memory. If you get any other codes, your erasing procedure did not work, and you should do it again.

Remove the ground jumper from the test terminal and drive the car for about half an hour. Then check for codes again. If there are any codes other than code 12, you know that the problems are current and should be repaired. If driving the car for half an hour is not convenient, make the next code check after driving for a day or a week. During that time, be sure that no one touches the car under the hood, because you don't want any false codes set.

If codes do reappear, get a manual for your car and follow the code charts to determine what is wrong. We show one code chart for code 13 in Figure 54-12. In the factory shop manuals there are code charts for every code.

54.5 INITIAL TIMING ADJUSTMENT PROCEDURES ON COMPUTER-CONTROLLED ENGINES

On most late-model cars, the same computer that controls the air-fuel mixture also controls ignition tim-

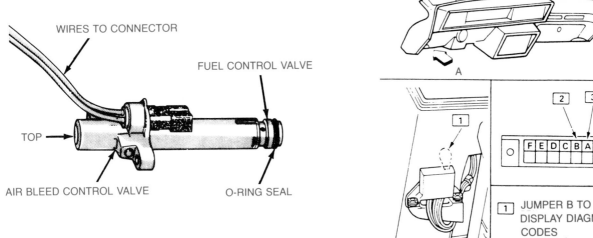

Fig. 54-9 A carburetor feedback or mixture control solenoid. (Chrysler Corporation)

WIRES TO CONNECTOR

FUEL CONTROL VALVE

TOP

AIR BLEED CONTROL VALVE

O-RING SEAL

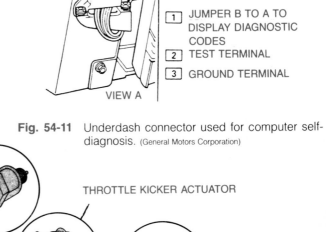

A

1 JUMPER B TO A TO DISPLAY DIAGNOSTIC CODES

2 TEST TERMINAL

3 GROUND TERMINAL

VIEW A

Fig. 54-11 Underdash connector used for computer self-diagnosis. (General Motors Corporation)

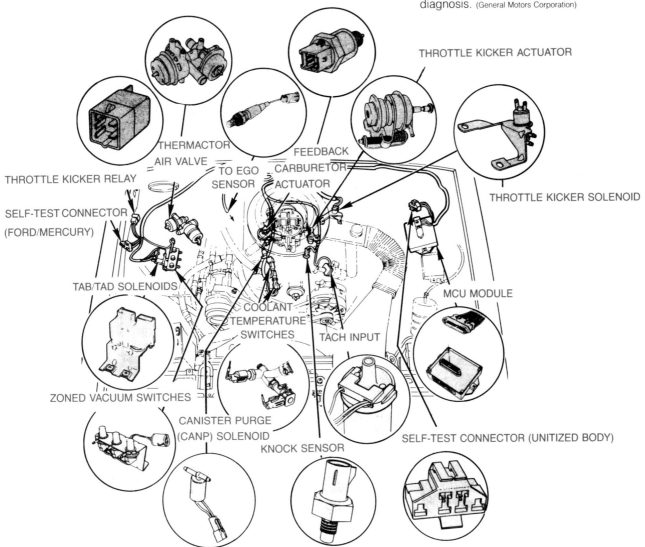

THROTTLE KICKER ACTUATOR

THERMACTOR AIR VALVE

FEEDBACK CARBURETOR ACTUATOR

TO EGO SENSOR

THROTTLE KICKER RELAY

THROTTLE KICKER SOLENOID

SELF-TEST CONNECTOR (FORD/MERCURY)

TAB/TAD SOLENOIDS

COOLANT TEMPERATURE SWITCHES

TACH INPUT

MCU MODULE

ZONED VACUUM SWITCHES

CANISTER PURGE (CANP) SOLENOID

KNOCK SENSOR

SELF-TEST CONNECTOR (UNITIZED BODY)

Fig. 54-10 Electronic engine control system. (Ford Motor Company)

TROUBLE CODE IDENTIFICATION

The "CHECK ENGINE" light will only be "ON" if the malfunction exists under the conditions listed below. If the malfunction clears, the light will go out and a trouble code will be set in the ECM. Code 12 does not store in memory. If the light comes "on" intermittently, but no code is stores, go to the "Driver Comment" section. Any codes stored will be erased if no fault re-occurs within 50 engine starts.

The trouble codes indicate troubles as follows:

TROUBLE CODE 12   No ignition reference Pulses to the ECM. This code is not stored in memory and will only flash while the fault is present.

TROUBLE CODE 13   Oxygen sensor circuit — The engine must run up 1 minute at part throttle, under road load, before this code will set. This code does not set when the coolant temperature is below 70°C and/or the time since engine start has not exceeded 2 minutes.

TROUBLE CODE 14   Shorted coolant sensor circuit — The engine must run up to 2 minutes before this code will set.

TROUBLE CODE 15   Open coolant sensor circuit — The engine must run up to 5 minutes before this code will set.

TROUBLE CODE 21   Idle switch circuit open or WOT switch circuit shorted — The engine must run up to 10 seconds at following two conditions concurrently before this code will set. Idle switch output is in a low voltage state. WOT switch output is in a high voltage state.

TROUBLE CODE 22   Fuel cut solenoid circuit open or grounded — The engine must run under the decelerating condition over 2000 engine rpm before this code will set.

TROUBLE CODE 23   Vacuum control solenoid circuit open or grounded.

TROUBLE CODE 25   Air switching solenoid circuit open or grounded.

TROUBLE CODE 31   No ignition reference pulses to the ECM for 10 seconds at part throttle, under road load. This code will store in memory.

TROUBLE CODE 44   Lean oxygen sensor indication — The engine must run up to 2 minutes at part throttle, under road load, before this code will set. This code does not set when the coolant temperature is below 70°C and/or the air temperature in air cleaner is below 0°C.

TROUBLE CODE 45   Rich System indication — The engine must run up to 2 minutes at part throttle, under road load, before this code will set. This code does not set when the engine exceeds 2500 rpm and/or the coolant temperature is below 70°C and/or the barometric pressure is below 23 in. Hg above 2500 m altitude. (8000 ft.)

TROUBLE CODE 51   Shorted fuel cut solenoid circuit and/or faulty ECM.

TROUBLE CODE 52   Faulty ECM — Problem of RAM in ECM.

TROUBLE CODE 53   Shorted air switching solenoid and/or faulty ECM.

TROUBLE CODE 54   Shorted vacuum control solenoid and/or faulty ECM.

TROUBLE CODE 55   Faulty ECM — Fault of A/D converter in ECM.

Fig. 54-12   Trouble code identification. (Chevrolet Motor Division, GMC)

ing. The computer receives many signals such as engine rpm, engine vacuum, barometric pressure, engine temperature, throttle opening, and others. The kind of signal sent to the computer and the way it is used will vary with the many different systems in use on various cars. But in every car, the object of using the computer is to tailor ignition timing to whatever is needed at any instant. With the old-fashioned centrifugal and vacuum advance systems, any given distributor vacuum and rpm always resulted in the same amount of advance. With the comptuer, advance can vary according to conditions. As engine temperature, rpm, throttle opening, or pressure sensors change their input to the computer, the computer will change the amount of advance.

Because the computer may change the timing at any instant, there must be some way of temporarily taking the computer out of the circuit so that initial timing may be checked or set. Some car makers refer to initial timing as basic, or reference, timing. The procedure varies, even among engines that come from the same car maker. The best way to find out how to do it is to refer to the emission control label in the engine compartment for the timing procedure. If the label is missing, or the information is incomplete, refer to a shop manual. Setting the timing without following the correct procedure may result in an initial timing setting that is several degrees off.

In all cases, the procedure is to either disconnect or make an electrical connection, or disconnect a vacuum hose somewhere on the car. A common procedure is to disconnect the four-wire connector near the distributor. Other cars require making a connection with a jumper at an electrical outlet under the instrument panel. Some cars require adding a ground jumper at a carburetor switch, and disconnecting a hose to the computer. Car makers that formerly used one procedure, may use a different procedure in later years. For example, one engine label warns against disconnecting the four-wire connector near the distributor, and directs you to disconnect a tan wire at the rear of the engine. There are even some engines that sense timing directly off the crankshaft, and inform you on the engine compartment label that the timing is not adjustable.

On those engines where the timing is adjustable, change the timing by loosening the distributor holddown, moving the distributor body and tightening the holddown. In all situations, whatever was done in preparation for checking the timing must be undone after the timing is checked or set. Failure to restore the connections, hoses, etc. will result in total elimination of spark advance.

NEW TERMS

Actuators Engine control components that get command from the computer and adjust some engine function.

Codes A series of numbers of flashes on a tester or dash light used to determine if there is a fault in a computerized system.

Computer A microprocessor unit tht monitors engine functions and makes adjustments according to its programmable memory.

Feedback fuel systems A fuel system that monitors the oxygen in the exhaust gas and uses a computer to adjust the air-fuel mixture accordingly.

Sensor A component of the engine control system that monitors some engine function and sends a signal to the computer.

CHAPTER REVIEW

1. List four areas of vehicle operation that can be controlled by a computer.
2. What are the three main components of a computerized engine control system?
3. What is the purpose of the computer in an engine control system?
4. What is the purpose of a sensor in an engine control system?
5. What is the purpose of an actuator in an engine control system?
6. Where is the computer usually mounted on the vehicle?
7. What is the purpose of a feedback fuel system?
8. What is the purpose of the oxygen sensor?
9. Where is the oxygen sensor usually installed?
10. How does the oxygen sensor work to measure oxygen?
11. What is the purpose of the feedback solenoid?
12. How does the feedback solenoid work to regulate fuel?
13. What is a computer self-test?
14. What is a service code?
15. How can you determine what a service code means?

DISCUSSION TOPICS AND ACTIVITIES

1. Following the procedure in a shop service manual put a computer in self-test. What service codes did the system display?
2. Use a test instrument to read the service codes on a computer-controlled car. What service codes did you find?

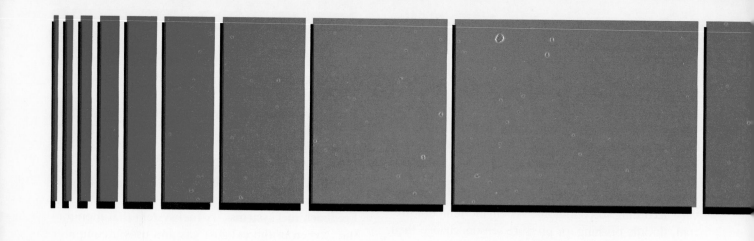

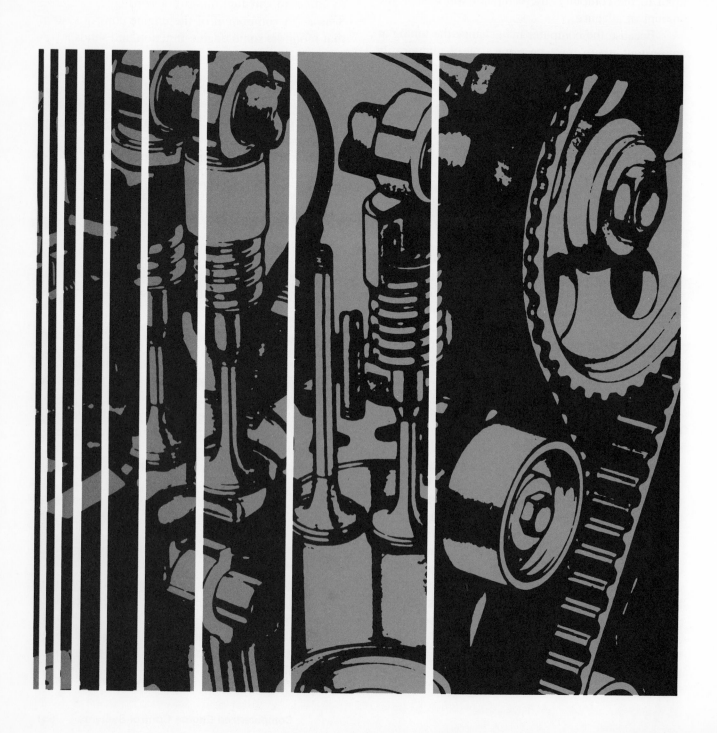

The Automobile of Tomorrow

PART 10

The Future of the Automobile

CHAPTER PREVIEW

The problem of emissions of our present automobile and the prospect of continued oil scarcity have prompted experiments with different types of engines and different kinds of fuels. In this chapter we will describe some engineering changes in the automobile and discuss the possible direction of its future.

OBJECTIVES

After studying this chapter, you should be able to do the following:

1. Explain the operation and advantages of the stratified charge engine.
2. Describe how the automobile may be made more efficient.
3. Describe how the automobile may be made safer.
4. List and describe the different fuels being considered for automobile use.
5. List and describe the operation of the alternate engines being considered for automobile use.

55.1   STRATIFIED CHARGE ENGINE

The need to reduce emissions has been responsible for many changes in automotive design. Much effort is also being spent on basic redesign of the automobile engine to make it pollute less and use less fuel. The major effort in this direction is the stratified charge engine.

There are two ways of lowering carbon monoxide, unburned hydrocarbons, and oxides of nitrogen in the exhaust of internal combustion engines: (1) cleaning up the exhaust by means of a catalyst or other add-on devices, and (2) regulating the combustion of a very lean overall mixture (excess oxygen) to hold down production of the unwanted pollutants. Conventional and rotary engines use the first method. The stratified charge engine uses the second.

The conventional engine operates best with a rather rich air-fuel mixture. If the mixture is made too lean, the engine will begin to misfire because a lean mixture is difficult to ignite with a spark plug.

The stratified charge engine is a four-stroke-cycle gasoline engine with a modified cylinder head and fuel induction system. It is designed to burn a very lean overall mixture. The regulated burning of this lean mixture with much more oxygen enables the stratified charge system to meet the rigid emission standards without the air pump, catalyst, or exhaust gas recirculation required by most other engines.

The stratified charge engine ignites a stratified charge in two chambers, an auxiliary and a main combustion chamber, joined by an opening (Fig. 55-1). The auxiliary combustion chamber, or pre-chamber assembly, uses a single small intake valve. The main combustion chamber uses conventional intake and exhaust valves. All valves are opened by a single overhead camshaft.

On the intake stroke (see Fig. 55-2), a large amount of very lean mixture is drawn through the main intake valve into the main combustion chamber. At the same time, a very small amount of rich mixture is drawn through the auxiliary intake valve into the pre-chamber.

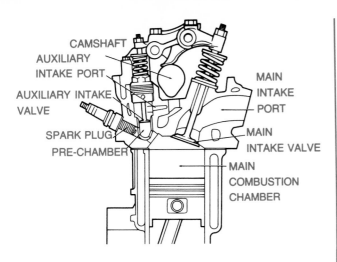

CAMSHAFT
AUXILIARY INTAKE PORT
AUXILIARY INTAKE VALVE
SPARK PLUG
PRE-CHAMBER
MAIN INTAKE PORT
MAIN INTAKE VALVE
MAIN COMBUSTION CHAMBER

Fig. 55-1 Sectional view of stratified charge engine.
(American Honda Motor Company, Inc.)

At the end of the compression stroke, a rich mixture is present in the pre-chamber. A moderate mixture is formed in the main combustion chamber near the pre-chamber outlet. A very lean mixture is in the remainder of the main combustion chamber.

When the spark plug fires, the rich mixture in the pre-chamber easily ignites. The flame from the pre-chamber ignites the moderate mixture. This, in turn, ignites the lean mixture in the main combustion chamber. The formation of carbon monoxide is slowed in this lean mixture.

The stable and slow burning in the main combustion chamber has two desired effects. First, the peak temperature stays low enough to reduce oxides of nitrogen. Second, the average temperature is maintained high enough and long enough to reduce hydrocarbon emissions.

The hot gases exit through the exhaust valve, and oxidation continues in the manifold. For proper intake mixture control under different operating conditions (idle to wide open throttle), the intake air-fuel mixture for each chamber is controlled by three throttle valves in the carburetor. The relatively rich mixture in the auxiliary combustion chamber is ignited by a standard spark plug. Since ignition requirements are similar to those of a conventional engine, no special ignition system is needed. Charge stratification ensures stable and slow combustion under all operating conditions.

The exhaust gas temperature is kept relatively high to warm the intake manifold through heat transfer. This provides quick engine warmup and proper air-fuel mixture distribution. This heat transfer keeps the intake mixture temperatures within the desired operating range.

A number of current engines use a variety of swirl chambers or passages in the combustion chamber to gain more complete combustion. An example of such a swirl chamber is shown in Figure 55-3. The result of this type of combustion chamber is improved fuel economy and lower levels of exhaust emissions.

55.2 MAKING THE PRESENT VEHICLE MORE EFFICIENT

Improving the automobile engine or designing a new engine are not the only ways to conserve our petroleum resources. Engineeers are experimenting with ways of making the vehicle more efficient. Exploring new, lighter materials for vehicle construction and studying more aerodynamic shapes are two important research areas.

55.3 Reducing Weight

It is possible to conserve fuel and minimize pollution by changing vehicle design as well as engine design. One approach is to make the automobile lighter. Smaller, lighter vehicles require much less fuel and, if everything else is equal, pollute less. In general engineers have found that for every 400 pounds they can remove from the car they can increase fuel efficiency by one mile per gallon.

Just making automobiles smaller is less important than reducing their weight. This is possible because of the introduction of lighter metals and nonmetals such as plastic. Many heavy components are being redesigned to make use of lighter materials.

55.4 Improving Aerodynamics

Another key to efficient operation is aerodynamics. Aerodynamics means shaping the vehicle so that it pushes against a minimum of wind as it moves. Overcoming the drag created by air pressure on the front of a vehicle takes a large percentage of the engine's power. Racing vehicles have long been designed to push against the smallest amount of air.

Each automotive manufacturer now conducts drag studies on their automobiles and works on designs which make them more efficient. Automobiles are now equipped with recessed headlights, recessed windshield wipers, and recessed door handles to decrease drag. Air dams and rear spoilers are now used to manage air both over and underneath the car. Concept cars (Fig. 55-4) are used to evaluate new ideas in aerodynamics before they are used on production vehicles.

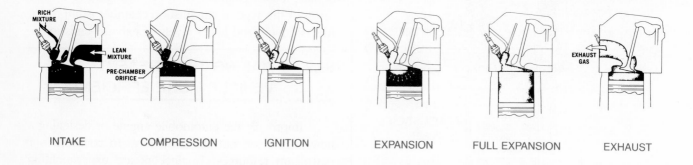

INTAKE   COMPRESSION   IGNITION   EXPANSION   FULL EXPANSION   EXHAUST

Fig. 55-2 Stratified charge engine operation. (American Honda Motor Company, Inc.)

55.5   MAKING THE AUTOMOBILE SAFER

Each year thousands of people are killed or injured in automobile accidents. Reducing the number of accidents has long been a goal of the automobile industry and the government. Programs have been set up to produce safer drivers, safer highways, and safer automobiles.

Accident research and crash-testing programs since the 1940s have resulted in a number of safety devices. Some of these safety devices are seat belts and harness restraint systems, padded interiors, redesigned steering wheels, collapsible steering columns, safety glass, and reinforced passenger compartments (Fig. 55-5).

55.6   Collapsible Bumper

Two recent safety developments are the collapsible bumper and air bags. Collapsible front and rear bumpers are attached to the automobile through energy-absorbing units. If the bumpers hit something, the units telescope to protect passengers from the impact.

The energy-absorbing unit (Fig. 55-6) has two parts: the piston tube and the cylinder tube. The piston tube assembly, filled with a pressurized gas, consists of a bumper bracket, piston tube, orifice, seal piston seal, piston, and stop ring. The cylinder tube assembly, filled with a hydraulic fluid, consists of a frame bracket, cylinder tube, mounting stud, and metering pin.

The piston tube assembly goes into the cylinder tube assembly and the cylinder tube is crimped. The crimp mates with the stop ring to hold the unit together. The groove in the stop ring area is filled with grease to keep out dirt. The gas pressure in the piston tube assembly holds the unit in the extended position. Extension is limited by the stop ring on the outside of the piston tube fitting into the crimp on the cylinder tube. This design provides strength to withstand towing and jacking.

As the energy absorber collapses upon impact, hydraulic fluid in the cylinder tube is forced into the piston tube through the orifice. The metering pin controls the rate at which the fluid passes through the orifice. This controlled passage of fluid provides the absorbing action.

The hydraulic fluid that is forced into the piston tube displaces the floating piston, compressing the gas behind the floating piston. After impact the pressure of the compressed gas behind the piston forces the hydraulic fluid back into the cylinder tube, extending the unit to its original position.

55.7   Air Bag

The air bag (Fig. 55-7) is a safety idea borrowed form the aircraft industry. Large bags mounted in front of the driver and passengers inflate in the event of an accident. The bags absorb impact and prevent people from being thrown forward.

When the front bumper is hit hard enough, a sensor triggers a small explosion in the air tank inflator assembly. A metal container of compressed, nonflammable, nontoxic gas inflates the air bags in a fraction of a second. The main bag in the steering wheel assembly inflates to about the size of two basketballs. The passenger bag in the dashboard area pushes the passenger's legs against the seat so that he or she can-

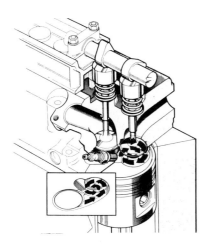

Fig. 55-3 Swirl combustion chamber. (Jaguar Cars Inc.)

Fig. 55-4 A concept car used to evaluate aerodynamics. (Ford Motor Company)

not slide under the bag and into the dash. Gas in the bag is released through its vented surface. The more severe the crash, the greater the pressure on the bag and the faster the gas escapes.

55.8 Experimental Safety Vehicles

Many safety devices were first used on experimental safety vehicles. An experimental safety vehicle is an automobile designed and built to try out safety ideas.

Current experimental safety vehicles are trying out foam-filled steel construction with crushable foam body components. Some vehicles also also have a kind of pedestrian catcher, a soft, trampoline-like device on the hood. The vehicles use antiskid brakes, air bags, and roll bars. A crash recorder similar to that used in aircraft is also being tried. The recorder can provide valuable information about the cause of a crash.

55.9 USING DIFFERENT FUELS

Almost any combustible mixture can be used as a fuel in internal combustion engines. The search for a fuel to replace gasoline was first aimed at reducing emissions. A fuel that burns cleaner and more completely than gasoline could reduce pollution. Lately, the search for other fuels has been carried on because we are running out of oil.

55.10 LPG

Two early alternate fuels were liquefied petroleum gas and natural gas. Liquefied petroleum gases (LPG) such as propane and butane have long been used as a fuel for farm equipment. They have recently been used in automobiles. LPG is stored as a liquid under pressure. It flows as a gas. Conversion units for automobiles have a storage tank in the rear of the vehicle and a mixing valve to mix the LPG with air before metering it into the intake manifold. Some units are designed to operate on either gasoline or LPG.

Liquefied petroleum gas burns very clean. It is more difficult to handle than gasoline, however, and supplies of LPG are limited.

Another very clean fuel is the natural gas used in kitchen ranges and home heaters. One problem with natural gas is that filling tanks take some time. Many fleet operations in which vehicles come to a central yard for service can be adapted to natural gas. Its use as an automotive fuel will probably be limited, however, because reserves of natural gas are as limited as those of oil.

55.11 Alcohol

Another fuel under study is alcohol. Alcohol has long been used in racing vehicles. It is very clean burning and has a high heat content. The problem with alcohol is very low mileage. It takes several more gallons of alcohol than gasoline to go a given distance.

The energy crisis has increased interest in alcohol because it is not refined from oil. Alcohol can be made from a variety of materials. In fact, alcohol can be manufactured from solid municipal waste.

Some engineers are proposing mixing gasoline and alcohol. A blending with 15 percent alcohol improves economy, lowers exhaust temperatures, lowers emissions, and improves performance. Gasohol may be the fuel of the future.

Fig. 55-5 Reinforcing around passenger compartment.
(Chevrolet Motor Division, GMC)

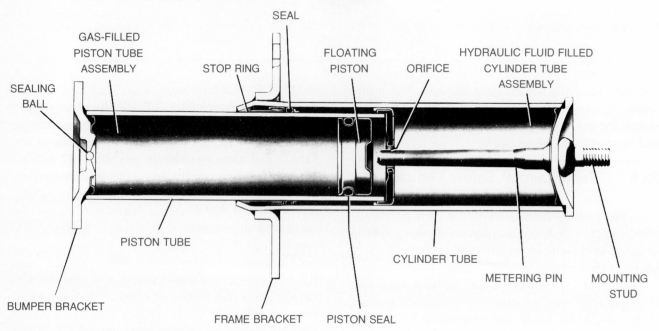

Fig. 55-6 Cutaway of energy-absorbing unit. (Buick Motor Division, GMC)

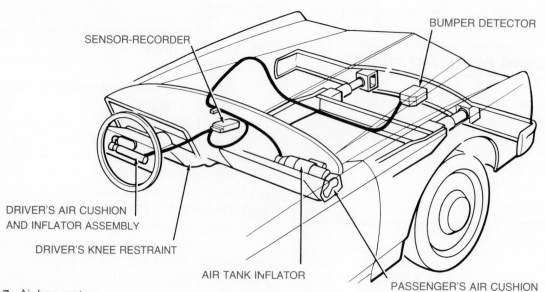

Fig. 55-7 Air bag system.

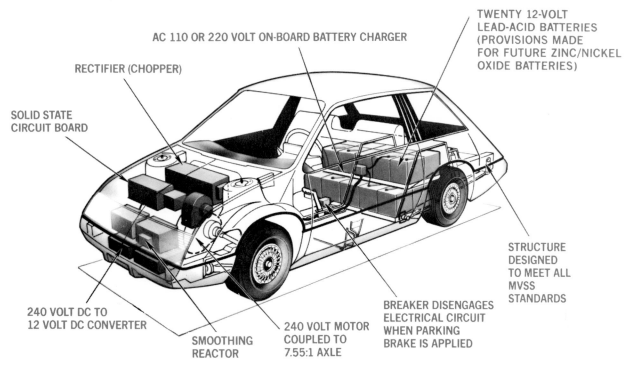

Fig. 55-8 Experimental electric vehicle. (General Motors Corporation)

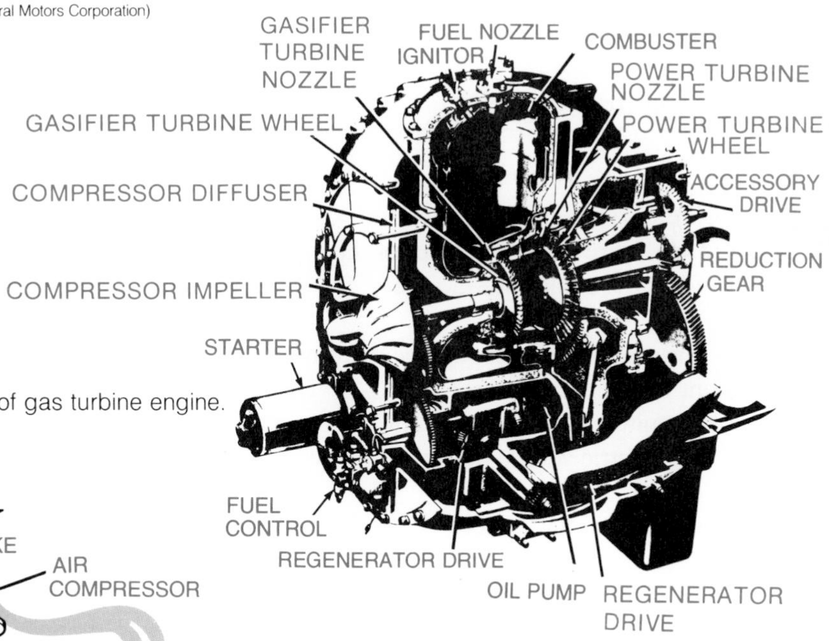

AC 110 OR 220 VOLT ON-BOARD BATTERY CHARGER

RECTIFIER (CHOPPER)

SOLID STATE
CIRCUIT BOARD

TWENTY 12-VOLT
LEAD-ACID BATTERIES
(PROVISIONS MADE
FOR FUTURE ZINC/NICKEL
OXIDE BATTERIES)

STRUCTURE
DESIGNED
TO MEET ALL
MVSS
STANDARDS

240 VOLT DC TO
12 VOLT DC CONVERTER

SMOOTHING
REACTOR

240 VOLT MOTOR
COUPLED TO
7.55:1 AXLE

BREAKER DISENGAGES
ELECTRICAL CIRCUIT
WHEN PARKING
BRAKE IS APPLIED

GASIFIER
TURBINE
NOZZLE

FUEL NOZZLE
IGNITOR

COMBUSTER

POWER TURBINE
NOZZLE

GASIFIER TURBINE WHEEL

POWER TURBINE
WHEEL

COMPRESSOR DIFFUSER

ACCESSORY
DRIVE

REDUCTION
GEAR

COMPRESSOR IMPELLER

STARTER

FUEL
CONTROL

REGENERATOR DRIVE

OIL PUMP

REGENERATOR
DRIVE

Fig. 55-9 Sectional view of gas turbine engine.
(Ford Motor Company)

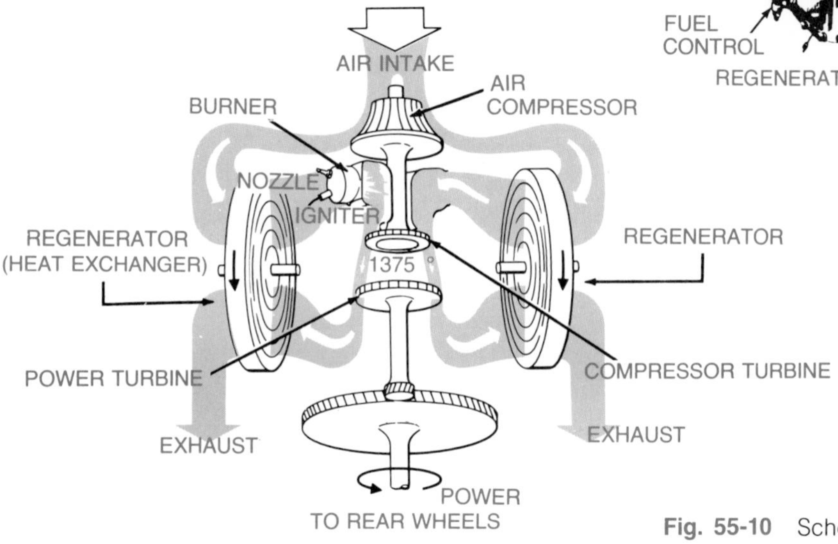

AIR INTAKE

BURNER

AIR
COMPRESSOR

NOZZLE
IGNITER

REGENERATOR
(HEAT EXCHANGER)

1375°

REGENERATOR

POWER TURBINE

COMPRESSOR TURBINE

EXHAUST

EXHAUST

POWER
TO REAR WHEELS

Fig. 55-10 Schematic of gas turbine engine.
(Chrysler Corporation)

Fig. 55-11 Experimental steam vehicle. (Lear Vapordine, Inc.)

55.12   USING DIFFERENT ENGINES

The automobile of the future may be powered by a wholly different type of engine. Operating models of the most promising of these engines have been built and installed in vehicles for testing.

55.13   Electric Vehicle

Automobiles powered by electric motors run by batteries were developed at the same time as gasoline vehicles. They were slow because of high battery weight, and they could not go very far without recharging.

Recently there has been a renewed interest in development of electric vehicles (Fig. 55-8). The electric power required to charge batteries may also be scarce, but an electric vehicle does not directly pollute the air.

A new high-energy battery is needed to make the electric vehicle practical. The battery would have to provide high mileage and high power. The common lead acid battery has too low an energy density. A great many new types of batteries are being tried: sodium-sulphur, zinc-air, lithium-halide, and lithium-chlorine. No practical electric vehicle is likely in the near future, however.

The electric automobile of the future may be powered by a fuel cell. Fuel cells are batteries in which active materials are continuously fed into the cell. Fuel cells are ideal because they have a high efficiency; they can use a wide range of possible fuels; they have no moving parts except pumps and cooling fans; they make very little noise; and they are very reliable with a long life.

55.14   Gas Turbine

The gas turbine engine (Figs. 55-9 and 55-10) is an aircraft engine adapted to automobile use. Air enters the engine through an intake filter and a silencer assembly. It then passes into the impeller. Here, the air is compressed, raising its temperature, and directed outward by the impeller into the diffuser. The diffuser channels direct the compressed air toward the outside of the front half of the regenerator cores. The air passes through the core, absorbing heat from the regenerator. The heated air passes down to the combuster or burner, where air flow reverses. This reversal causes a complex whirling that gives good combustion throughout the range of operating speeds. Fuel is sprayed into the air, and the mixture ignites in the burner.

Hot combustion gases are guided to the first compressor turbine nozzle and wheel. High-velocity gas leaving the wheel is guided through variable nozzle blades that direct it to the power turbine wheel. The exhaust from this second stage is discharged outward through the rear half of the two regenerator cores where some heat is recovered for reuse. The power turbine wheel is connected through a gear system to the vehicle drive train.

There are many advantages to the gas turbine. It has very low emission levels and can operate on very inexpensive fuels. Since all of its components work in a rotary motion, it runs very smooth. It has a high power-to-weight ratio and does not stall.

High cost has been the problem in developing gas turbines for automobiles. Today, however, the gas turbine can compete effectively on a cost-per-horsepower basis with the internal combustion engine. As new and inexpensive materials are developed that can withstand gas temperatures up to 1,800°F, gas turbine engines may be widely used.

55.15   Steam Engine

Water boiled and changed into steam expands about 1,700 times. If this steam is collected in a closed container where it cannot expand, the pressure (and the boiling temperature of the water) will increase. This pressure can be released to do work. In this way heat energy used to boil the water can be converted into mechanical energy. The steam can drive the piston of a steam engine or the blades of a steam turbine. Since most steam engines burn the fuel outside the engine, they are external combustion engines. Wood, coal, oil, or almost anything that will burn can be used as fuel.

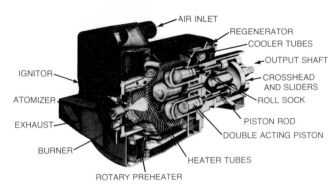

Fig. 55-12 Stirling engine. (Ford Motor Company)

Labels on figure: AIR INLET, REGENERATOR, COOLER TUBES, OUTPUT SHAFT, CROSSHEAD AND SLIDERS, ROLL SOCK, PISTON ROD, DOUBLE ACTING PISTON, HEATER TUBES, ROTARY PREHEATER, BURNER, EXHAUST, ATOMIZER, IGNITOR

A steam-powered vehicle is another example of an old idea rediscovered. Early steam vehicles faded out because they were heavy, complicated, and very slow in starting up. Present-day engineers are trying to overcome these problems. Several manufacturers have steam vehicles in an experimental stage (Fig. 55-11). The advantages of a steam engine are that emission controls would be simpler; it could burn almost any fuel; since it produces maximum torque at zero rpm it can use a cheaper and less complex transmission. The steam engine does not need a cooling system with a radiator, thermostat, fan, fan drive, and water pump.

Development of steam engines for automobies is limited by cost. The steam engine requires an expensive burner assembly, an electronic brain, a steam generator, plus complex sensors and controls. The condenser costs about twice as much as a radiator in a conventional vehicle. The steam car needs a reservoir for the working fluid (water or Freon) in addition to a fuel tank for the burner.

55.16   Stirling Engine

The Stirling engine (Fig. 55-12), named after a Scotsman who conceived the principle in 1816, is among the most promising alternate power plants in terms of emissions, noise control, and fuel economy.

The Stirling is a "hot air" engine, an external combustion engine that increases the pressure of a gas by heating and reduces the pressure by cooling. A gas sealed in the working area above the pistons is heated by an outside power source. The pistons are driven down by the pressure of the hot gas. The gas is then cooled. The cooling reduces the pressure in the working area, pulling the pistons up.

The engine has very low emissions because it is a closed system. Constant burning and large amounts of air available for combustion get rid of HC and CO almost entirely. It has excellent fuel economy and can use almost any fuel. The newer double-acting engine is almost as large and heavy as an ordinary V-8. The single-acting engine was about as heavy and bulky as a diesel of similar output. The Stirling engine is also almost as quiet as an electric motor. Stirling engines are extremely smooth. Because there are no valves or periodic explosions, the engine can be balanced.

Engine parts are expensive because high-temperature materials are needed. Sealing has also been a problem, but this may now be solved. Heat discharge to the radiator was also a problem. The Stirling puts twice the cooling load of a V-8 of similar power into the cooling system.

55.17   INTO THE YEAR 2000

What is the long-term future of the automobile? What will its role be by the year 2000? Accurate predictions are impossible, but trends can be identified.

Future automobiles will be smaller and lighter. They will be capable of more than 50 miles per gallon of fuel. Engines other than the internal combustion engine will certainly be available by the year 2000. They may even overtake the internal combustion engine.

Automotive manufacturers will begin to make better use of inside space with a smaller outside size. Fuels may be made from coal, shale or even vegetable or biological waste. Automobiles will be much safer, and accident rates should be improved. Certainly automobiles will cost more to buy and operate. They should require less maintenance.

By the year 2000 mass transportation should be improved and expanded. But people will still want the personal freedom and mobility that only an automobile can provide. Mass transportation and personal vehicles may blend together. There may be on-the-road, on-the-rail vehicles. In one futuristic proposal, called a dual mode system (Fig. 55-13), a driver would pick up passengers in a sort of bus and drive to a special highway called a guideway. Here the driver would get out while the bus continued with the passengers, guided automatically by the controls built into the guideway.

Personal vehicles could be driven to a rail system and driven onto a small platform called a pallet (Fig. 55-14). A magnetic force between the pallet and the rail would lift the pallet and vehicle up off the rail. Since there would be virtually no friction, the pallet and vehicle could reach a vibration-free speed six times

EXPRESS OPERATION
ON GUIDEWAY UNDER
AUTOMATIC CONTROL

PASSENGER COLLECTION

Fig. 55-13 Dual mode system. (Motor Trend Magazine)

Fig. 55-14 Magnetic pallet system. (Motor Trend Magazine)

as fast as we now travel.

Automobiles of the future might travel on compressed air jets. Friction would be greatly reduced, allowing greater speeds and less vibration.

The automobile of the future is sure to require less driving. It may even be completely automated. The automobile may have a computerized brain that would guide it to a programmed destination while avoiding all obstructions and other vehicles.

NEW TERMS

Aerodynamics Shaping the outside of an automobile so that it uses less energy pushing against the air.

Air bags Bags which are automatically inflated in front of the driver and passenger to cushion the impact in an accident.

Alcohol An alternate fuel not made from petroleum.

Collapsible bumper A bumper attached to an energy-absorbing device that telescopes on impact.

Electric vehicle A vehicle powered by electric motors powered by batteries.

Fuel cell A battery in which the active materials are continuously fed into the cell.

Gas turbine An alternate automobile engine that uses an explosive mixture to drive vaned wheels.

Gasohol A fuel for automobiles made from a mixture of gasoline and alcohol.

Liquefied petroleum gas An alternate fuel for automobile engines that is stored as a gas instead of a liquid; abbreviated LPG.

Natural gas The fuel used for heating and cooking in homes and also used as an alternate automobile fuel.

Steam engine An external combustion engine that uses the energy of steam to push on pistons or turbine blades.

Stirling engine An engine powered by alternately heating and cooling a gas.

Stratified charge engine An engine that uses a lean mixture ignited by a rich mixture from a pre-chamber.

CHAPTER REVIEW

1. List the main problems facing the automobile.
2. What is a stratified charge engine?
3. How does the stratified charge engine work?
4. What is a pre-chamber?
5. How can the present automobile be made more efficient?
6. List five safety devices used on automobiles.
7. Describe how the collapsible bumper works.
8. Explain how an air bag system operates.
9. List three fuels besides gasoline that can be used in automobiles.
10. What is the main problem with an electric vehicle?
11. Describe how a gas turbine works.
12. What are the advantages of a gas turbine?
13. How does a steam engine work?
14. Why is a steam engine called an external combustion engine?
15. What is a Stirling engine and how does it operate?

DISCUSSION TOPICS AND ACTIVITIES

1. List all the safety devices you can find on the automobile you drive.
2. Which alternate engine discussed in the chapter do you think will be in the automobile of the future? Why?
3. What do you think transportation will be like in the year 2000?

Glossary

AC   *See* alternating current.

accelerator   Foot-operated pedal connected to the carburetor throttle.

acrylic   Type of automotive paint.

additive   Material added to an oil or other fluid to change its properties.

air cleaner   Device mounted on the carburetor to clean the intake air.

air-fuel ratio   The ratio of the weight of air to the weight of fuel in the intake mixture.

air gap   *See* gap.

air horn   Part of the carburetor where air enters from the air cleaner.

alignment   Process of lining up of the wheels in the correct direction with respect to the chassis.

alternating current (AC)   Electrical current that rapidly and constantly reverses direction.

alternator   A current-generating device that develops alternating current.

ampere   Unit of measurement for current flow.

ampere-hour rate   Battery rating based on capacity.

antifreeze   Liquid added to the cooling system to prevent freezing.

antismog device   Device added to the engine to reduce emissions.

API   American Petroleum Institute.

armature   Series of coils positioned in a magnetic field, usually in a motor or generator.

axle   Rotating shaft on which a wheel is mounted.

backlash   Clearance or space between two meshing gears.

back pressure   Pressure in the exhaust.

ball bearing   Bearing using steel balls positioned between two races.

battery   Electrochemical source of electricity.

BDC (bottom dead center).   The position of the piston when it is as low as it can go in the cylinders.

bearing   Component used to reduce friction between shafts or pivots.

bell housing   Covering over the clutch or torque converter.

BHP   Brake horsepower.

bore   Diameter of an engine's cylinders.

brake cylinder   Hydraulic cylinder used to activate the brakes.

brake drum   Drum-shaped component attached to the car's wheels.

brake fade   Loss of braking action caused by heat.

brake horsepower   Horsepower measured at the flywheel of an engine.

brake lining   Friction material attached to brake shoes.

brake shoe   Component forced against the brake drum to stop the car.

breaker points   Two-contact switch used to interrupt primary ignition current.

brushes   Sliding contacts used in motors and generators.

calibrate   Adjust an instrument.

caliper   Housing for the hydraulic components of a disc brake system.

cam   *See* camshaft.

cam angle   Number of distributor degrees during which the contact points are closed (also called **dwell**).

camber   Outward tilt of the car's wheels at the top.

camshaft   Shaft with lobes used to open the engine's valves.

carbon monoxide (CO)   Colorless, odorless, poisonous gas produced by incomplete combustion.

carburetor   Device used to mix air and fuel.

caster   Backward or forward tilt of the ball joints.

catalytic converter   A device that uses a catalyst to change pollution from the exhaust system to harmless compounds.

cell   Unit of a battery.

charge   Electrical energy pushed into a battery to restore its activity.

chassis   All the parts of the automobile except the body.

choke   Device used to enrich the fuel mixture to start a cold engine.

circuit   Complete path for electron flow.

clearance   Space between two components.

clutch   Device used to connect and disconnect the engine from the drivetrain.

coil   An electrical device that steps up voltage for ignition.

combustion (internal)   *See* internal combustion.

commutator   Ring of copper bars connected electrically to an armature.

compression   Squeezing a gas to reduce its volume.

compression ratio   Volume of the combustion chamber at top dead center compared to the volume at bottom dead center.

condenser   Device for storing a static electrical charge.

conductor   Material that permits current flow.

connecting rod Part that connects the piston to the crankshaft.

contact points *See* breaker points.

coolant Liquid used in liquid cooling system to carry away heat; usually a mixture of ethylene glycol and water.

crankcase Housing for the crankshaft, usually part of the engine block.

crankshaft Shaft to which the pistons and connecting rods are attached.

current Flow of electricity.

cycle Complete series of events in an engine.

cylinder Circular hole in which the engine's piston strokes up and down.

cylinder block Large housing that includes the crankcase and cylinders.

cylinder head Casting containing the valves and combustion chamber and mounted to the cylinder block.

DC *See* direct current.

detergent Substance added to oil to remove sludge deposits in the engine.

detonation Abnormal combustion caused by excessive pressure in the combustion chamber.

diaphragm A flexible part of the fuel pump.

diesel engine An engine that uses the heat of compression to ignite the air-fuel mixture in the cylinders.

differential Gear mechanism on an axle that allows one wheel to turn more slowly than the other.

diode An electrical check valve.

direct current (DC) Current that flows in one direction continuously.

disc brake Brake that uses a caliper and rotor.

discharge Draining of energy from a battery.

displacement Size of an engine, measured by the volume the pistons displace as they stroke.

distributor Device that distributes the ignition current to the correct cylinder at the correct time.

drive shaft A steel tube or shaft that transfers engine power from the transmission to the rear axle or differential assembly.

dwell *See* cam angle.

dynamometer Machine used to measure horsepower.

electrode Part of a spark plug or distributor cap through which current passes.

electrolyte Mixture of sulphuric acid and water used in a battery.

enamel Type of automotive paint.

energy Ability to do work.

ethyl gasoline Gasoline containing tetra ethyl lead.

exhaust emissions By-products of combustion, discharged through the engine exhaust.

exhaust pipe Pipe connected to muffler to route exhaust gases out from under the car.

feeler gauge Strip of metal used to measure clearance.

F-Head Engine with one valve in the block and one in the head.

field Area in which magnetic lines of force flow.

field coil Coil of wire used to concentrate magnetism.

filter Device used to remove impurities.

float Device used to control the amount of fuel in the carburetor.

flywheel Heavy wheel used to store energy and to keep the crankshaft turning at a smooth, steady rate.

four-cycle engine Engine that delivers power in each cylinder on one stroke out of four.

fuel injection A fuel delivery system that injects fuel directly into the cylinders (diesel) or intake manifold (gasoline).

fuse Electrical protection device.

gasoline Automotive engine fuel.

gasket Soft material placed between two clamped metal surfaces for sealing.

gear ratio Compares revolution of a driving gear to that of the driven gear, normally used to measure multiplication of torque.

generator Device used to create electricity.

heat exchanger Device used to remove heat from one medium to another.

horse power (HP) Power rating system used to compare engines; based on the work accomplished by one horse.

hydocarbon Unburned gasoline, a by-product of incomplete combustion.

hydrometer Tool used to check the state of charge of a battery by measuring the specific gravity of the electroyte.

idle When an engine runs at its slowest pace with the throttle released.

ignition system System used to ignite the air/fuel mixture in the cylinder.

included angle Angle that includes camber and steering axis inclination.

independent suspension Suspension system in which the wheels are not on the same axle.

intake valve Valve that allows air and fuel to enter the engine combustion chamber.

input shaft Transmission shaft to which the engine's power is connected.

insulation Material through which electricity cannot pass.

intake manifold Series of pipes or casting that routes air and fuel into the engine combustion chambers.

internal combustion Rapid burning of air and fuel inside an engine cylinder.

knock Banging noises inside an engine that occur when the air-fuel mixture self-ignites from pressure.

lacquer Type of automotive paint.

L-head Engine with valves located in engine block.

liter A volume equal to 61.027 cubic inches.

manifold System of pipes or passages used to route gas.

master cylinder Hydraulic cylinder used in the brake system and connected to the brake pedal.

millimeter (mm) Metric equivalent of .039370 of an inch.

misfiring Failure of ignition to occur in a cylinder.

modulator Device used in an automatic transmission to sense engine load.

mph Miles per hour.

muffler Canister attached to the exhaust system to reduce noise.

multiple disc clutch Clutch used in an automatic transmission.

nitrous oxides Pollutants caused by high temperatures in the combustion chamber.

octane Measure of a gasoline's resistance to knocking.

odometer Device that measures number of miles traveled.

ohm Unit of measurement for electrical resistance.

oil Fluid made from petroleum, used for lubrication.

oil pan A metal pan covering the bottom of the engine; used to store oil for lubrication.

open circuit Break in an electrical circuit, stopping current flow.

oscilloscope Device used to test the ignition system.

output shaft Shaft that receives the power in the transmission and delivers it to the drive line.

overhead valve engine Engine in which the intake and exhaust valves are located in the cylinder head.

overrunning clutch Clutch used in an automatic transmission that allows rotation in one direction only.

PCV Positive crankcase ventilation.

parking brake Mechanical brake mechanism used when the car is stopped.

Phillips screwdriver Screwdriver with a tip that fits into screws with heads notched in a cross (instead of a slot).

pinion Type of gear wheel.

pinion carrier Housing for pinion gears.

piston Round metal sliding plug attached to the connecting rod.

piston pin Pin that attaches the piston to the connecting rod.

piston ring Expanding sealing rings placed in grooves around the piston.

planetary gears Type of gear assembly used in automatic transmissions.

planet carrier Part of a planetary gear set housing planet gears.

planet gears Small planetary gears that mesh with a sun and ring gear.

polarity Refers to the positive or negative terminal of an electrical circuit.

port Opening in a cylinder head for the passage of intake or exhaust gas.

primary winding Heavy coil of wire in the ignition coil.

propeller shaft *See* drive shaft.

psi Pounds per square inch.

push rod Connecting link between a valve lifter and the rocker arm.

radiator A large heat exchanger which transfers heat from the engine coolant to the atmosphere.

ratchet A driver for a socket wrench that drives in one direction and freewheels or ratchets in the other direction.

reciprocating Back and forth motion.

regulator *See* voltage regulator.

resistor Electrical device used to limit current flow.

ring gear One of the gears in the differential and in a planetary set.

rocker arm Lever used to open the valves of an engine.

rotary engine Engine using an elliptical firing chamber and a triangular shaped rotor; also called a Wankel engine.

rotary valve Rotor in a rotary engine.

rpm Revolutions per minute.

SAE Society of Automotive Engineers.

servo Hydraulic piston used to activate an automatic transmission band.

shock absorber Hydraulic device used to limit suspension oscillation.

solenoid Magnetic remote-controlled switch used in the starting system.

spark Electric current with enough voltage to jump a gap.

spark advance System that causes ignition to occur earlier in the cycle of engine operation.

spark knock *See* knock.

spline Slot cut in a shaft or bore; also, a shaft with splines cut into it.

starter motor The electric motor powered by the battery that cranks the engine to start it.

stator Middle element of a torque converter, a stationary coil of wire in an alternator.

steering axis inclination Angle formed by center line of ball joints and vertical centerline.

steering gear Gears used to change direction of front wheels.

steering column Shaft connecting steering gear with steering wheel.

stroke Distance traveled by the piston in one direction.

sun gear Center gear in a planetary gear set.

sychronizer Device that causes shafts or gears to turn at the same speed.

tachometer Gauge used to measure engine speed.

TDC (top dead center) The position of the piston when it is as high as it can go in the cylinder.

thermostat Heat-controlled valve.

tie rod Connecting linkage in the steering system.

timing chain Chain connecting the camshaft with the crankshaft.

toe-out Exists when car's front wheels point outward.

toe-out on turns Relative angles of the two front wheels when turning.

torque Turning or twisting effort.

torque converter Hydraulic device used to multiply torque.

torque wrench Wrench used to tighten bolts and nuts a specified amount.

torsion bar Rod that twists to provide spring action.

transaxle Combination of transmission and differential assembly.

transmission Device used to multiply an engine's torque.

tune-up Service performed to restore original engine performance, and avoid future breakdowns.

turbine Part of a torque converter connected to the transmission input shaft.

vacuum Absence of air, created when pressure in a certain area falls below atmospheric pressure.

valve Device for opening and closing a port.

valve clearance Space between the valve stem and rocker arm used for expansion.

valve lifter Component that rides on the cam and pushes on the push rod.

valve seat Machined surface for the valve in the cylinder head.

valve spring Spring used to close the valve.

venturi Restricted area inside the carburetor used to create a slight vacuum and draw in fuel.

viscosity Thickness of a fluid.

volatility Tendency of a fluid to evaporate rapidly.

volt Unit of measurement of electrical pressure.

voltage regulator Device for limiting voltage in the electrical system.

voltmeter Device used to measure voltage.

Wankel *See* rotary engine.

watt Unit of electrical pressure.

wheel cylinder Hydraulic cylinders at the wheels, used in braking.

Index

ENGLISH-METRIC CONVERSION

	If You Know	You Can Get	If You Multiply By*
LENGTH	Inches	Millimetres (mm)	25.4
	Millimetres	Inches	0.04
	Inches	Centimetres (cm)	2.54
	Centimetres	Inches	0.4
	Inches	Metres (m)	0.0254
	Metres	Inches	39.37
	Feet	Centimetres	30.5
	Centimetres	Feet	4.8
	Feet	Metres	0.305
	Metres	Feet	3.28
	Miles	Kilometres (km)	1.61
	Kilometre	Miles	0.62
AREA	Inches^2	Millimetres^2 (mm^2)	645.2
	Millimetres^2	Inches^2	0.0016
	Inches^2	Centimetres^2 (cm^2)	6.45
	Centimetres^2	Inches^2	0.16
	Foot^2	Metres^2 (m^2)	0.093
	Metres^2	Foot^2	10.76
CAPACITY-VOLUME	Ounces	Millilitres (ml)	30
	Millilitres	Ounces	0.034
	Pints	Litres (l)	0.47
	Litres	Pints	2.1
	Quarts	Litres	0.95
	Litres	Quarts	1.06
	Gallons	Litres	3.8
	Litres	Gallons	0.26
	Cubic Inches	Litres	0.0164
	Litres	Cubic Inches	61.03
	Cubic Inches	Cubic Centimetres (cc)	16.39
	Cubic Centimetres	Cubic Inches	0.061
WEIGHT (MASS)	Ounces	Grams	28.4
	Grams	Ounces	0.035
	Pounds	Kilograms	0.45
	Kilograms	Pounds	2.2
FORCE	Ounce	Newtons (N)	0.278
	Newtons	Ounces	35.98
	Pound	Newtons	4.448
	Newtons	Pound	0.225
	Newtons	Kilograms (kg)	0.102
	Kilograms	Newtons	9.807
ACCELERATION	Inch/Sec^2	Metre/Sec^2	.0254
	Metre/Sec^2	Inch/Sec^2	39.37
	Foot/Sec^2	Metre/Sec^2 (m/s^2)	0.3048
	Metre/Sec^2	Foot/Sec^2	3.280
TORQUE	Pound-Inch (Inch Pound)	Newton-Metres (N-M)	0.113
	Newton-Metres	Pound-Inch	8.857
	Pound-Foot (Foot-Pound)	Newton-Metres	1.356
	Newton-Metres	Pound-Foot	.737
PRESSURE	Pound/sq. in. (PSI)	Kilopascals (kPa)	6.895
	Kilopascals	Pound/sq. in.	0.145
	Inches of Mercury (Hg)	Kilopascals	3.377
	Kilopascals	Inches of Mercury (Hg)	0.296
FUEL PERFORMANCE	Miles/gal	Kilometres/litre (km/l)	0.425
	Kilometres/litre	Miles/gal	2.352
VELOCITY	Miles/hour	Kilometres/hr (km/h)	1.609
	Kilometres/hour	Miles/hour	0.621
TEMPERATURE	Fahrenheit Degrees	Celsius Degrees	5/9 (F° -32)
	Celsius Degrees	Fahrenheit Degrees	9/5 (C° +32) = F

*Approximate Conversion Factors to be used where precision calculations are *not necessary*